Eighth Joint Conference on Lexical and Computational Semantics (*SEM 2019)

Minneapolis, Minnesota, USA
6-7 June 2019

ISBN: 978-1-5108-8759-6

NAACL HLT 2019

Lexical and Computational Semantics (*SEM)

Proceedings of the Eighth Conference

June 6–7, 2019
Minneapolis

Introduction

Preface by the General Chair and Program Chairs

Welcome to *SEM, the Joint Conference on Lexical and Computational Semantics! Now at its eighth edition, *SEM brings together research on all aspects of semantics, including semantic representations, semantic processing, theoretical semantics, multilingual semantics, and several others. Over the past few years, the increased interest we have witnessed in field of natural language processing has also resulted in an increased interest in semantics, and *SEM has become the main forum to present and discuss the most recent advances in this research area.

We are pleased to present this volume containing the papers accepted at *SEM 2019, co-located with NAACL in Minneapolis, USA, on June 6-7, 2019. Similar to the last edition, *SEM received a high number of submissions, which allowed us to compile a diverse and high-quality program. We received a total of 96 submissions. Out of these, 32 papers were accepted (19 long, 13 short), for an overall acceptance rate of 33%.

Submissions were reviewed in nine different areas:

- Lexical semantics and word representations

- Semantic composition and sentence representations

- Discourse, dialogue and generation

- Machine learning for semantic tasks

- Multilinguality

- Human semantic processing

- Theoretical and formal semantics

- Semantics in NLP applications

- Resources and evaluations

The papers were evaluated by a program committee consisting of 16 area chairs, assisted by a panel of 332 reviewers. Each submission was reviewed by three reviewers, who were furthermore encouraged to discuss any divergence in evaluations. The papers in each area were subsequently ranked by the area chairs. The final selection was made by the program co-chairs after an independent check of all the reviews and discussion with the area chairs. Reviewers' recommendations were also used to shortlist a set of papers nominated for the Best Paper Award.

The final *SEM 2019 program features 16 oral presentations and 16 posters. We are also very excited to have two excellent keynote speakers: Sam Bowman (New York University, joint keynote with SemEval 2019), who will talk about "Task-Independent Sentence Understanding"; and Ellen Riloff (University of Utah), who will discuss her work on "Identifying Affective Events and the Reasons for their Polarity."

We are deeply thankful to all area chairs and reviewers for their help in the selection of the program, for their readiness in engaging in thoughtful discussions about individual papers, and for providing valuable feedback to the authors.

We are grateful to Soujanya Poria for his help in publicizing the conference, and to Kilian Evang for his dedication and thoroughness in turning the program into the proceedings you now have before your eyes. We would also like to thank Priscilla Rasmussen, for all the help she has provided with all our organizational aspects.

We hope you will enjoy the conference, and you will find it inspiring and stimulating!

Ekaterina Shutova and Lun-Wei Ku, Program Co-Chairs
Rada Mihalcea, General Chair

*SEM 2019 Chairs and Reviewers

General Chair:

Rada Mihalcea, University of Michigan, Ann Arbor

Program Chairs:

Ekaterina Shutova, University of Amsterdam
Lun-Wei Ku, Academia Sinica, Taiwan

Publications Chair:

Kilian Evang, University of Düsseldorf

Publicity Chair:

Soujanya Poria, NTU, Singapore

Area Chairs:

Lexical Semantics and Word Representations:
Anna Feldman, Montclair State University
Fabio Massimo Zanzotto, University of Rome Tor Vergata

Semantic Composition and Sentence Representations:
Helen Yannakoudakis, University of Cambridge
Douwe Kiela, Facebook AI Research

Discourse, Dialogue and Generation:
Lea Frermann, Amazon Core AI
Lu Wang, Northeastern University

Machine Learning for Semantic Tasks:
Roi Reichart, Technion – Israel Institute of Technology
Wilker Aziz, University of Amsterdam

Multidisciplinarity and COI:
Preslav Nakov, QCRI

Multilinguality:
Marianna Apidianaki, CNRS

Human Semantic Processing / Psycholinguistics:
Barry Devereux, Queen's University Belfast

Semantics in NLP Applications:
Dan Goldwasser, Purdue University
Saif Mohammad, National Research Council of Canada
Marek Rei, University of Cambridge

Area Chairs (continued):

Resources and Evaluation:
Beata Beigman Klebanov, Educational Testing Service

Theoretical and Formal Semantics:
Mehrnoosh Sadrzadeh, Queen Mary University of London

Reviewers:

Lasha Abzianidze, Heike Adel, Eneko Agirre, Afra Alishahi, Reinald Kim Amplayo, Andrew Anderson, Mikel Artetxe, Ron Artstein, Niranjan Balasubramanian, Francesco Barbieri, Jeremy Barnes, Pierpaolo Basile, Valerio Basile, Roberto Basili, Daniel Beck, Iz Beltagy, Jonathan Berant, Johannes Bjerva, Eduardo Blanco, Danushka Bollegala, Francis Bond, Georgeta Bordea, António Branco, Ellen Breitholz, Ted Briscoe, Susan Windisch Brown, Christopher Bryant, Paul Buitelaar, Heather Burnett, Elena Cabrio, Andrew Caines, Nicoletta Calzolari, Jose Camacho-Collados, Jorge Carrillo-de-Albornoz, Tommaso Caselli, Jackie Chi Kit Cheung, Christos Christodoulopoulos, Grzegorz Chrupała, Philipp Cimiano, Anne Cocos, Trevor Cohen, Paul Cook, Mathias Creutz, Valeria dePaiva, Nina Dethlefs, Luigi Di Caro, Georgiana Dinu, Rotem Dror, Aleksandr Drozd, Xinya Du, Ondřej Dušek, Guy Emerson, Arash Eshghi, Luis Espinosa Anke, Federico Fancellu, Meng Fang, Stefano Faralli, Mariano Felice, Tim Fernando, Mark Finlayson, Stella Frank, Diego Frassinelli, Richard Futrell, Michael Färber, Spandana Gella, Daniela Gerz, Reza Ghaeini, Daniel Gildea, Kevin Gimpel, Hila Gonen, Iryna Gurevych, Udo Hahn, Christian Hardmeier, Daniel Hardt, Bradley Hauer, Luheng He, Kevin Heffernan, Iris Hendrickx, Daniel Hershcovich, Christopher Hidey, Eric Holgate, Phu Mon Htut, Xinyu Hua, Lifu Huang, Julie Hunter, Ignacio Iacobacci, Radu Tudor Ionescu, Sujay Kumar Jauhar, Yangfeng Ji, Elena Karagjosova, Yoshihide Kato, Graham Katz, Ruth Kempson, Casey Kennington, Halil Kilicoglu, Yunsu Kim, Najoung Kim, Roman Klinger, Ekaterina Kochmar, Rik Koncel-Kedziorski, Parisa Kordjamshidi, Valia Kordoni, Yannis Korkontzelos, Sebastian Krause, Gabriella Lapesa, Jey Han Lau, Phong Le, Gianluca Lebani, I-Ta Lee, Els Lefever, Leo Leppänen, Martha Lewis, Chang Li, Junyi Jessy Li, Jing Li, Maoxi Li, Tal Linzen, Yang Liu, Nikola Ljubešić, Wei Lu, Andrea Madotto, Jean Maillard, Prodromos Malakasiotis, Jonathan Mallinson, Alda Mari, Ilia Markov, Héctor Martínez Alonso, Shigeki Matsubara, Tristan Miller, Roser Morante, Alessandro Moschitti, Larry Moss, Marieke Mur, Smaranda Muresan, Reinhard Muskens, Courtney Napoles, Matteo Negri, Yixin Nie, Malvina Nissim, Rodrigo Nogueira, Debora Nozza, Jessica Ouyang, Sebastian Padó, Alexander Panchenko, Gaurav Pandey, Ramakanth Pasunuru, Panupong Pasupat, Viviana Patti, Adam Pease, Gerald Penn, Francisco Pereira, Laura Perez-Beltrachini, Maciej Piasecki, Karl Pichotta, Mohammad Taher Pilehvar, Yuval Pinter, Carl Pollard, Edoardo Maria Ponti, Octavian Popescu, Maja Popović, Christopher Potts, Laurette Pretorius, Matthew Purver, Behrang QasemiZadeh, Alessandro Raganato, Carlos Ramisch, Ari Rappoport, Julia Rayz, Olesya Razuvayevskaya, Martin Riedl, Stephen Roller, Rudolf Rosa, Michael Roth, Subhro Roy, Alla Rozovskaya, Josef Ruppenhofer, Fatiha Sadat, Magnus Sahlgren, Mark Sammons, David Schlangen, Natalie Schluter, Steven Schockaert, Sabine Schulte im Walde, Samira Shaikh, Emily Sheng, Vered Shwartz, Jennifer Sikos, Carina Silberer, Yangqiu Song, Gabriel Stanovsky, Elior Sulem, Stan Szpakowicz, Aarne Talman, Alon Talmor, Niket Tandon, Yi Tay, Patricia Thaine, Jörg Tiedemann, Sara Tonelli, Antonio Toral, Rocco Tripodi, Chen-Tse Tsai, Shyam Upadhyay, Tim Van de Cruys, Esther van den Berg, Lonneke van der Plas, Benjamin Van Durme, Eva Maria Vecchi, Erik Velldal, Marc Verhagen, Yogarshi Vyas, Ekaterina Vylomova, Alex Wang, Wei Wang, Chuan Wang, Bonnie Webber, Zhongyu Wei, Matthijs Westera, Dominikus Wetzel, John Wieting, Adina Williams, Grégoire Winterstein, Guillaume Wisniewski, Michael Wojatzki, Chien-Sheng Wu, Ruochen Xu, Diyi Yang, Hai Ye, Katherine Yu, Frances Yung

Invited Talk: Identifying Affective Events and the Reasons for their Polarity

Ellen Riloff
University of Utah, USA

Abstract: Recognizing affective states is essential for narrative text understanding and for applications such as conversational dialogue, summarization, and sarcasm recognition. Many tools have been developed to recognize explicit expressions of sentiment, but affective states can also be inferred from events. This talk will focus on "affective events", which are generally desirable or undesirable experiences that implicitly suggest an affective state for the experiencer. For example, buying a home is usually desirable and associated with a positive affective state, but being laid off is undesirable and associated with a negative state. First, we will describe a weakly supervised learning method to induce affective events from a text corpus by optimizing for semantic consistency. Second, we aim to characterize affective events based on Human Needs Categories, which often explain people's motivations, goals, and desires. We will present a co-training model for Human Needs categorization that uses an event expression classifier and an event context classifier to learn from both labeled and unlabeled texts.

Bio: Ellen Riloff is a Professor in the School of Computing at the University of Utah. Her primary research area is natural language processing, with an emphasis on information extraction, affective text analysis, semantic class induction, and bootstrapping methods that learn from unannotated texts. Prof. Riloff has served as the General Chair for the EMNLP 2018 conference, Program Co-Chair for the NAACL HLT 2012 and CoNLL 2004 conferences, on the NAACL Executive Board for 2004-2005 and 2017-2018, the Computational Linguistics Editorial Board, and the Transactions of the Association for Computational Linguistics (TACL) Editorial Board. In 2018, Prof. Riloff was named a Fellow of the Association for Computational Linguistics (ACL).

Invited Talk: Task-Independent Sentence Understanding

Sam Bowman
New York University, USA

Abstract: This talk deals with the goal of task-independent language understanding: building machine learning models that can learn to do most of the hard work of language understanding before they see a single example of the language understanding task they're meant to solve, in service of making the best of modern NLP systems both better and more data-efficient. I'll survey the (dramatic!) progress that the NLP research community has made toward this goal in the last year. In particular, I'll dwell on GLUE—an open-ended shared task competition that measures progress toward this goal for sentence understanding tasks—and I'll preview a few recent and forthcoming analysis papers that attempt to offer a bit of perspective on this recent progress.

Bio: Sam Bowman has been on the faculty at NYU since 2016, when he finished his PhD with Chris Manning and Chris Potts at Stanford. At NYU, he is a core member of the new school-level Data Science unit, which focuses on machine learning, and a co-PI of the CILVR machine learning lab. Prof. Bowman's research focuses on data, evaluation techniques, and modeling techniques for sentence understanding in natural language processing, and on applications of machine learning to scientific questions in linguistic syntax and semantics. He is an area chair for *SEM 2018, ICLR 2019, and NAACL 2019; he organized a twenty-three person team at JSALT 2018 and earned a 2015 EMNLP Best Resource Paper Award and a 2017 Google Faculty Research Award.

Table of Contents

Conference Program

Thursday, June 6, 2019

09:00–10:30 *Session 1*

09:15–09:30 *Opening remarks*

09:30–10:30 *Invited Talk by Sam Bowman (New York University): "Task-Independent Sentence Understanding"*

10:30–11:00 *Coffee break*

11:00–12:30 *Session 2: Lexical Semantics*

11:00–11:30 *SURel: A Gold Standard for Incorporating Meaning Shifts into Term Extraction*
Anna Hätty, Dominik Schlechtweg and Sabine Schulte im Walde

11:30–12:00 *Word Usage Similarity Estimation with Sentence Representations and Automatic Substitutes*
Aina Garí Soler, Marianna Apidianaki and Alexandre Allauzen

12:00–12:30 *Beyond Context: A New Perspective for Word Embeddings*
Yichu Zhou and Vivek Srikumar

12:30–14:00 *Lunch break*

14:00–15:30 *Session 3: Sentence Representations*

14:00–14:30 *Composition of Embeddings : Lessons from Statistical Relational Learning*
Damien Sileo, Tim Van de Cruys, Camille Pradel and Philippe Muller

14:30–15:00 *Multi-Label Transfer Learning for Multi-Relational Semantic Similarity*
Li Zhang, Steven Wilson and Rada Mihalcea

15:00–15:30   *Scalable Cross-Lingual Transfer of Neural Sentence Embeddings*
Hanan Aldarmaki and Mona Diab

15:30–16:00   **Coffee break**

16:00–18:00   **Poster session**

16:00–16:50   **Poster booster**

16:50–18:00   **Poster session**

Second-order contexts from lexical substitutes for few-shot learning of word representations
Qianchu Liu, Diana McCarthy and Anna Korhonen

Pre-trained Contextualized Character Embeddings Lead to Major Improvements in Time Normalization: a Detailed Analysis
Dongfang Xu, Egoitz Laparra and Steven Bethard

Bot2Vec: Learning Representations of Chatbots
Jonathan Herzig, Tommy Sandbank, Michal Shmueli-Scheuer and David Konopnicki

Are We Consistently Biased? Multidimensional Analysis of Biases in Distributional Word Vectors
Anne Lauscher and Goran Glavaš

A Semantic Cover Approach for Topic Modeling
Rajagopal Venkatesaramani, Doug Downey, Bradley Malin and Yevgeniy Vorobeychik

MCScript2.0: A Machine Comprehension Corpus Focused on Script Events and Participants
Simon Ostermann, Michael Roth and Manfred Pinkal

Deconstructing multimodality: visual properties and visual context in human semantic processing
Christopher Davis, Luana Bulat, Anita Lilla Verő and Ekaterina Shutova

Friday, June 7, 2019

09:00–10:30 *Session 1*

09:00–10:00 *Invited talk by Ellen Riloff (University of Utah): "Identifying Affective Events and the Reasons for their Polarity"*

10:00–10:30 *Word Embeddings (Also) Encode Human Personality Stereotypes*
Oshin Agarwal, Funda Durupınar, Norman I. Badler and Ani Nenkova

10:30–11:00 *Coffee break*

11:00–12:30 *Session 2: Semantics and Syntax*

11:00–11:30 *Automatic Accuracy Prediction for AMR Parsing*
Juri Opitz and Anette Frank

11:30–12:00 *An Argument-Marker Model for Syntax-Agnostic Proto-Role Labeling*
Juri Opitz and Anette Frank

12:00–12:30 *Probing What Different NLP Tasks Teach Machines about Function Word Comprehension*
Najoung Kim, Roma Patel, Adam Poliak, Patrick Xia, Alex Wang, Tom McCoy, Ian Tenney, Alexis Ross, Tal Linzen, Benjamin Van Durme, Samuel R. Bowman and Ellie Pavlick

12:30–14:00 *Lunch break*

14:00–15:30 *Session 3: Inference*

14:00–14:30 *HELP: A Dataset for Identifying Shortcomings of Neural Models in Monotonicity Reasoning*
Hitomi Yanaka, Koji Mineshima, Daisuke Bekki, Kentaro Inui, Satoshi Sekine, Lasha Abzianidze and Johan Bos

14:30–15:00 *On Adversarial Removal of Hypothesis-only Bias in Natural Language Inference*
Yonatan Belinkov, Adam Poliak, Stuart Shieber, Benjamin Van Durme and Alexander Rush

SURel: A Gold Standard for Incorporating Meaning Shifts into Term Extraction

Anna Hätty[1,2], Dominik Schlechtweg[2], Sabine Schulte im Walde[2]
[1]Robert Bosch GmbH
[2]Institute for Natural Language Proessing (IMS), University of Stuttgart
`anna.haetty@de.bosch.com, {schlecdk, schulte}@ims.uni-stuttgart.de`

Abstract

We introduce SURel, a novel dataset for German with human-annotated meaning shifts between general-language and domain-specific contexts. We show that meaning shifts of term candidates cause errors in term extraction, and demonstrate that the SURel annotation reflects these errors. Furthermore, we illustrate that SURel enables us to assess optimisations of term extraction techniques when incorporating meaning shifts.

1 Introduction

Domain-specific terms often undergo meaning shifts from general-language use to their respective domain-specific language use. For example, the German noun *Schnee* predominantly means 'snow' in its general-language usage, and 'beaten egg whites' in the cooking domain. Terms with these characteristics are referred to as *sub-technical terms* and pose a problem for term extraction: Their hybrid character makes it hard for humans to rank them along with unambiguous terms, and hard for computational models to classify them as terms, because of the strong bias towards their general-language meanings.

In this study, we present SURel (Synchronic **U**sage **R**elatedness), a novel dataset for meaning shifts from general to domain-specific language, based on human annotations on the degrees of semantic relatedness between contexts of term candidates. We illustrate that SURel reflects the error that is commonly made by term extraction measures for sub-technical terms when relying on a general-language reference corpus. In a first experiment, we predict the meaning shift automatically and use SURel for evaluation. We then incorporate the model's prediction as a factor into an established term extraction measure, to correct the error in termhood prediction caused by meaning shifts.

2 Meaning Shifts in Terminology

Sub-Technical Terms Terms are linguistic units that characterize specialized domains (Kageura and Umino, 1996), thus representing opposite extremes of words that are not specific to a domain (Sager, 1990). *Sub-technical terms* (Cowan, 1974; Trimble, 1985; Baker, 1988; Chung and Nation, 2003; Pérez, 2016) occupy intermediary positions on the continuum, because they undergo meaning shifts from general to domain-specific language usage. Baker (1988) distinguishes two types of sub-technical terms with general-language usage: words with a restricted domain-specific meaning (e.g., *effective* means 'take effect' in biology), and words with a complete meaning shift (e.g., *bug* in computer science).

Sub-technical terms are a major problem for term extraction measures which often operate on the word type rather than the word sense level. Pérez (2016) provides empirical evidence that 50% of legal terminology is represented by sub-technical terms. Lay people often do not even notice their terminological character due to their predominant general-language use (Hätty and Schulte im Walde, 2018).

Term Extraction Techniques One of the main strands of term extraction methodologies are *contrastive* techniques, which compare a term candidate in a domain-specific and a general-language corpus (Ahmad et al., 1994; Rayson and Garside, 2000; Drouin, 2003; Kit and Liu, 2008; Bonin et al., 2010; Kochetkova, 2015; Lopes et al., 2016; Mykowiecka et al., 2018, i.a.). For these methods sub-technical terms are problematic, because their meanings are biased towards their general-language use. An illustration is given in Figure 1.

Contrastive term extraction measures are usually designed to identify terms with meaning *stability*, i.e., the meaning in a domain-specific cor-

1

*Proceedings of the Eighth Joint Conference on Lexical and Computational Semantics (*SEM)*, pages 1–8
Minneapolis, June 6–7, 2019. ©2019 Association for Computational Linguistics

pus is the same as the meaning in a general-language corpus. If a term candidate undergoes a meaning shift, either a meaning *reduction* takes place, i.e., only a subset of the general-language meanings occurs in a domain-specific corpus, or we find a complete meaning *change*. Both reduction and change cause errors in the term extraction results, which are stronger for meaning change in comparison to meaning reduction.

It is evident that there are occurrences of senses in the general-language corpus which should not be considered as term meanings (see hatchings).

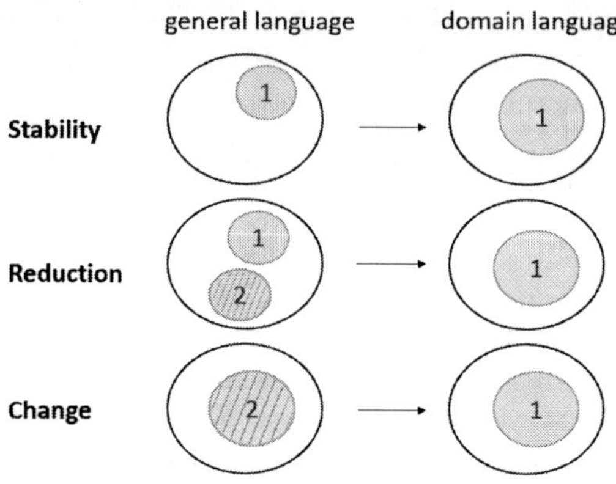

Figure 1: Influence of meaning shifts on a term's sense distributions across languages.

With very few exceptions, sub-technical terms are not explicitly addressed by contrastive measures. Drouin (2004) mentions in his qualitative analysis that some polysemous terms are not found by his extraction system. Menon and Mukundan (2010) and Pérez (2016) do explicitly tackle the extraction of sub-technical terms. Their systems rely on a term candidate's collocation frequencies in a domain and a general reference corpus. But due to the lack of a gold standard, they only perform a qualitative analysis.

This is where our work comes into play: sub-technical terms could be extracted in the same way as terms, if only the corresponding meanings were taken into account when comparing general-language and domain-specific uses. Our novel dataset SURel captures meaning shifts of term candidates and thus serves as a gold standard for the strength of the expected error produced by contrastive term extraction techniques when applied to sub-technical terms.

3 The Dataset: SURel[1]

Dataset Creation SURel was created analogously to DURel (Schlechtweg et al., 2018), a dataset for meaning shifts across time. Our novel dataset comprises a manual annotation of meaning relatedness between uses of target words in a general-language and a domain-specific corpus. The strength of relatedness between uses defines whether the meanings of a word are related or differ, thus indicating if a meaning shift took place.

As general-language corpus (GEN) we subsampled SdeWaC (Faaß and Eckart, 2013), a cleaned version of the web corpus DEWAC (Baroni et al., 2009). As domain-specific corpus (SPEC), we crawled cooking-related texts from several categories (recipes, ingredients, cookware, cooking techniques) from the German cooking recipe websites *kochwiki.de* and *Wikibooks Kochbuch*[2]. The reduced SdeWaC contains $\approx$126 million words, SPEC contains $\approx$1.3 million words.

We selected 22 target words which occurred in both GEN and SPEC, and which we expected to exhibit different degrees of domain-specific meaning shift. For each target word we randomly sampled 20 use pairs (i.e., combinations of two contexts) from GEN, SPEC and across both, a total of 60 use pairs per word and 1,320 use pairs overall. Four native speakers annotated the use pairs on a scale from 1 (unrelated meanings) to 4 (identical meanings), reaching a strong mean pairwise agreement of ρ =0.88. The ranking of the 22 target words by their average strength of relatedness between general-language and domain-specific uses is shown in Figure 2. On the left are target words with highly related meanings in GEN and SPEC; on the right are words with strongly different meanings.[3]

Dataset Analysis In the following, we analyse the meaning relatedness of use pairs within and across GEN and SPEC. Figure 3 shows examples of annotations that nicely correspond to cases of meaning *stability, reduction* and *change*, respectively. The y-axes show how often the use pairs were rated as 1–4. In Figure 3 top left we find *Schnittlauch* 'chive' with strongly related meanings within and across GEN and SPEC, thus indicating meaning stability. Top right, we find

---

[1]The dataset is available at
`www.ims.uni-stuttgart.de/data/surel`.
[2]`de.wikibooks.org/wiki/Kochbuch`
[3]Find an overview of the dataset in the Appendix.

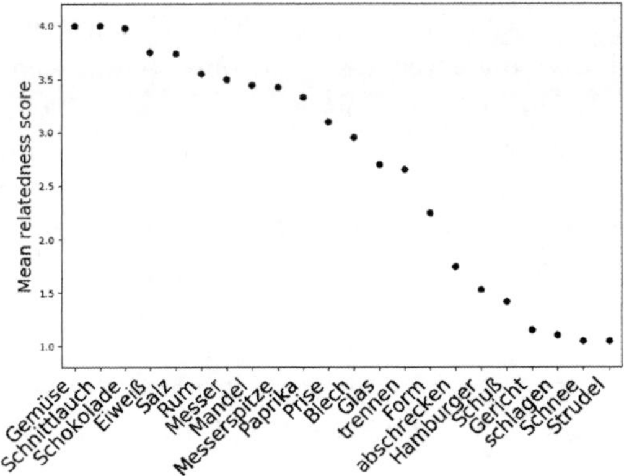

Figure 2: Ranking of target words by average strength of meaning relatedness between GEN and SPEC.

Messer 'knife' with more related meanings in SPEC than in GEN, and even less strongly related meanings across GEN and SPEC, thus indicating meaning reduction. In Figure 3 at the bottom we find *Schnee* 'snow'/'beaten egg whites' with strongly related meanings within GEN and also within SPEC but very different meanings when comparing GEN and SPEC uses, thus indicating a meaning shift. The three examples are taken from the two extremes and a mid position in Figure 2.

4 Incorporating Meaning Shifts into Automatic Term Extraction

After illustrating that the relatedness scores in SURel reflect degrees of meaning shifts from general to domain-specific language usage, the current section demonstrates that (a) a standard measure for automatic term extraction does not capture variants of meaning shifts, and (b) we can utilise SURel to modify existing measures to incorporate meaning shifts into termhood prediction.

A Standard Term Extraction Measure We selected one of the simplest standard contrastive term extraction measures, the *Weirdness Ratio* (WEIRD) (Ahmad et al., 1994), which is still commonly used or adapted (Moreno-Ortiz and Fernández-Cruz, 2015; Cram and Daille, 2016; Roesiger et al., 2016; Hätty et al., 2017, i.a.). It encompasses just the basic ingredients for termhood prediction, a comparison of word frequencies in relation to corpus sizes:

$$\mathrm{WEIRD}(x) = \frac{f_{spec}(x)/s_{spec}}{f_{gen}(x)/s_{gen}},$$

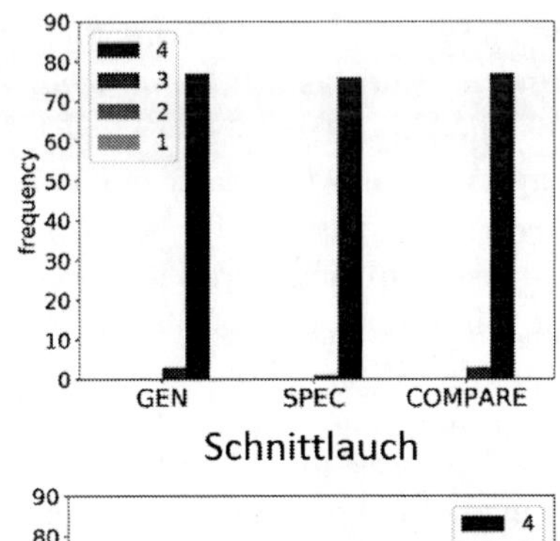

Schnittlauch

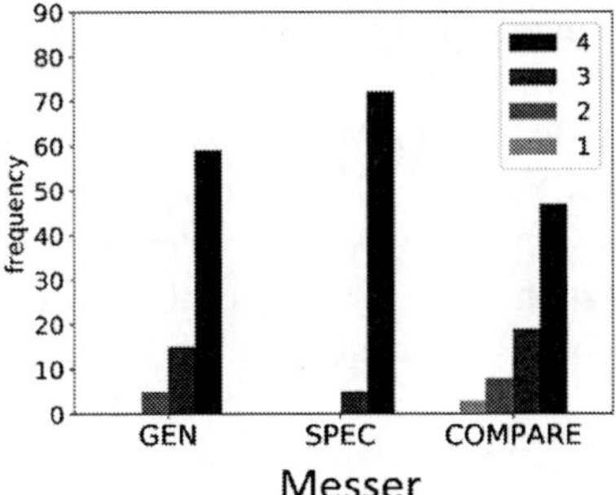

Messer

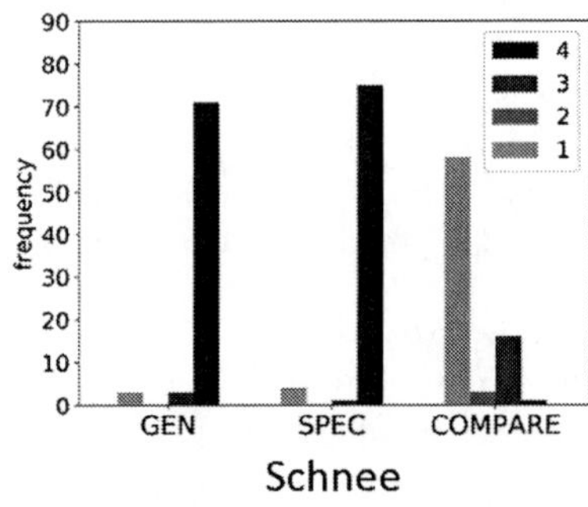

Schnee

Figure 3: Examples indicating meaning stability (top), meaning reduction (centre) and meaning change (bottom). COMPARE denotes cross-corpora relatedness (cf. Schlechtweg et al., 2018).

where f_{spec} and f_{gen} correspond to the frequencies of a term candidate x in a general and a domain-specific corpus, and s_{spec} and s_{gen} are the respective sizes of the corpora.[4]

The left panel in Figure 4 shows the ranking of the SURel target words after computing their WEIRD scores, with decreasing termhood scores for targets from left to right. The figure clearly illustrates that WEIRD ranks the targets words with strongest meaning shifts in SURel lowest, independently of their termhood: targets with high SURel scores are ranked as most terminological by WEIRD and occupy the first ranks (*Messerspitze, Eiweiß, ...*), and targets with low SURel

<hr>

[4]We use versions of our corpora which are limited to content words to be consistent with following experiments.

scores are ranked as the least terminological ones and occupy the last ranks (..., *Form, schlagen*).

To further investigate this bias, we looked up the SURel targets in (a) Wiktionary and Wikipedia, (b) the German dictionary Duden and (c) popular German translation dictionaries (Langenscheidt and PONS). If a word was assigned a cooking or gastronomy tag in any of these resources, we categorised it as a domain term. In this way, ten of our targets[5] were categorised as terms; seven of them are among the ten most non-terminologically ranked targets by WEIRD. This confirms that termhood predictions by WEIRD as a representative of contrastive termhood measures are strongly influenced by terminological meaning shifts.

Although the influence of meaning shifts might not be equally evident in other term extraction measures as in our simple example measure WEIRD, any other measure heavily relying on a general-language word frequency distribution will to some extent be negatively influenced by terminological meaning shifts. Consequently, we need to correct the bias caused by meaning shifts. In the following, we show that we can use SURel to assess factors that potentially reduce the bias.

Correcting the Meaning Shift For automatically predicting meaning shifts we rely on a state-of-the-art model for diachronic meaning change (Hamilton et al., 2016). We learn two separate word2vec SGNS vector spaces for GEN and SPEC. In order to compare the target vectors across spaces the spaces are aligned, i.e., the best rotation of one vector space onto the other is computed. This corresponds to the solution of the orthogonal Procrustes problem (Schönemann, 1966). If G and S are the matrices for the general and the specific vector spaces, then we rotate G by GW where $W = UV^T$, with U and V retrieved from the singular value decomposition $S^T G = U \Sigma V^T$. Following standard practice we then length-normalize and mean-center G and S in a pre-processing step (Artetxe et al., 2017). After the alignment, cosine similarity between the vectors of the same word in both spaces is computed. The cosine score of the two vectors of a word w predicts the strength of meaning change of w between GEN and SPEC, ranging from 0 (complete change) to 1 (stability).[6]

As input for the model, we use POS-tagged versions of our corpora, keeping only content words.

Evaluating the output of the model on the SURel dataset, we reach a Spearman's rank-order correlation coefficient of ρ=0.866 between the model's change predictions and SURel meaning-shift ranks. Inspecting the nearest neighbors (NNs) of our target words in Figure 3 confirms the ability of the model to predict strengths of meaning shifts. For example, the NNs for *Schnee* change completely (from *mud, leaves, foggy* in the GEN space to *egg whites, foamy, beat* in the SPEC space), while for *Schnittlauch* all nearest neighbors in both spaces are cooking-related.

Finally, to correct WEIRD for the meaning-shift error, we incorporate the model's predictions of meaning change into the WEIRD formula, where $\alpha(x)$ corresponds to the model's predicted strength of meaning change for word x:

$$\text{WEIRD}_{MOD}(x) = \frac{f_{spec}(x)/s_{spec}}{(\alpha(x) \cdot f_{gen}(x))/s_{gen}}.$$

The right panel in Figure 4 shows the ranking of the SURel target words based on their WEIRD$_{MOD}$ scores, again with decreasing termhood scores for targets from left to right. The plot clearly shows that WEIRD$_{MOD}$ improves over WEIRD regarding the negative bias for meaning-shifted targets: now shifted target words do not gather in one part of the plot but occur across ranks. While WEIRD only reaches an average precision of 0.45, WEIRD$_{MOD}$ reaches an average precision of 0.59.

In the same way as we incorporated the Hamilton measure of semantic change into WEIRD, we could rely on other contrastive term extraction techniques and incorporate further measures of semantic change. SURel can be utilised to evaluate modifications and thus to optimise termhood prediction techniques regarding the sub-technical terminological meaning shift bias.

5 Extension and Discussion

We presented a gold standard for meaning shifts and how to use it for term extraction. Since our meaning shift prediction method works quite well with the however rather small dataset, we extend the target set and further compute the shifts for all nouns, verbs and adjectives in the cooking corpus with a frequency $\geq$ 50 in both SPEC and GEN. This results in shift values for 1,125 words. In the

---

[5] *Eiweiß, Messerspitze, Paprika, abschrecken, Strudel, Schuß, Schnee, Form, schlagen, Hamburger*

[6] Since *Messerspitze* occurred too few times in GEN, we did not compute a shift value and assumed no shift.

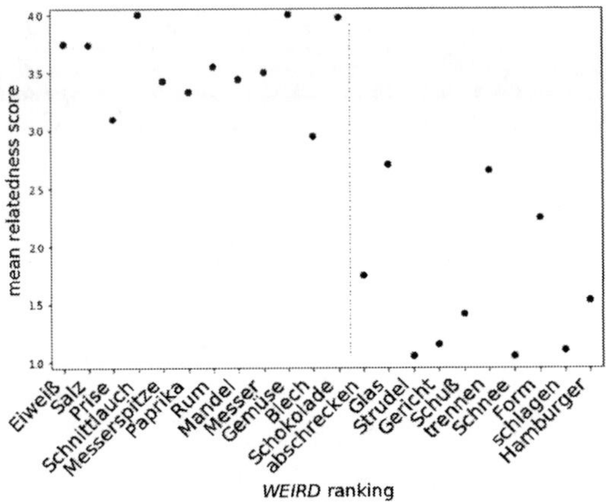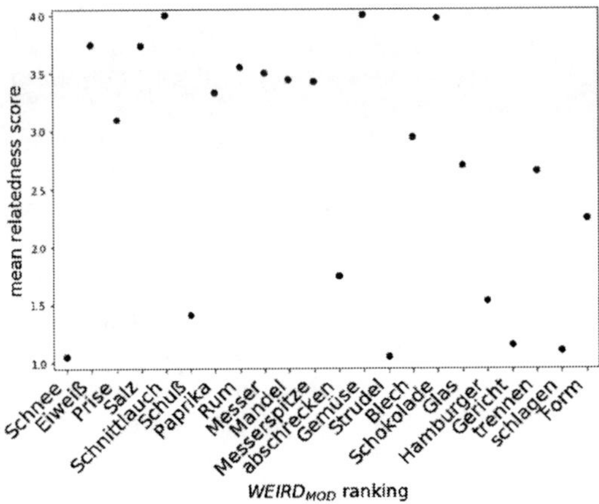

Figure 4: SURel target words ranked by WEIRD (left panel) and WEIRD$_{MOD}$ (right panel), with termhood prediction strength decreasing from left to right; the y-axes show the SURel GEN–SPEC relatedness score.

following, we use the extended dataset for remarks on challenges for term extraction.

First, our dataset contains mostly words with at least some relevance to the cooking domain. The intuition behind this is, that for clearly unterminological words (e.g. *anderes* 'different', *alternativ* 'alternative', *komplett* 'complete', *Ganze* 'whole') there should not be a meaning shift towards the domain. In practice, when applying our method, our system predicts a high degree of meaning shift for those words. Many of those words seem to be highly versatile in GEN and in SPEC. Additionally, especially problematic are words which occur without context in many cases (*Galerie* '[picture] gallery', *Inhaltsverzeichnis* 'table of contents'), or words with repeating similar context (e.g. *Wikipedia*, *Artikel* 'article', *Thema* 'topic' in the reoccurring sentence 'Wikipedia has one article to the topic ...' in the SPEC corpus). For the latter two cases, it is possible to filter the corpus beforehand, but the first case is more difficult.

We achieve some promising results with the following method: We compute a second shift value, but this time shuffle the sentences across the corpora while preserving the target word's context sentence frequencies in each corpus. By that we obtain some kind of ground truth value for the word's context variance. The assumption here is that if a word already has strongly varying contexts throughout the corpora, then the high shift across corpora is most likely a result from that. We finally substract the shuffling value from the shift value. In the resulting ranked list, this method

separates the unterminologic elements to the one end and a lot of terms with meaning shift to the other end: *altbacken* 'dowdy/stale', *gedämpft* 'low voice/steamed', *Schnee*, *Fond* 'fund/stock', *Auflauf* 'crowd/casserole', *Form* 'shape/(baking) mould' together with other cooking-related words like *Spaghetti*, *Pfannkuchen* 'pancake', *Pommes* 'French fries', *Ananas* 'pineapple', where the latter words have a lower original shift value. However, other sub-technical terms like *schlagen* 'beat/whip (cream)', *abschrecken* 'discourage/chill ', *binden* 'tie/thicken (sauce)' are still among the unterminologic elements, most likely because they have rather varying contexts in GEN as well. Nevertheless, for terms with meaning shifts identified with the described method the original shift value could be used to correct a termhood measure.

6 Conclusion

We presented SURel, a German dataset for meaning shift annotations from general to domain-specific language, focusing on the language of cooking. Meaning shifts are relevant for contrastive term extraction systems, because the affected terms are typically biased towards their general-language use and, consequently, might not be recognized as terms. SURel can be used as a gold standard for predicting meaning shifts, and these predictions can be used to optimize term extraction measures. A case study incorporating a state-of-the-art diachronic semantic change measure into a simple term extraction model confirmed this potential of SURel.

References

Khurshid Ahmad, Andrea Davies, Heather Fulford, and Margaret Rogers. 1994. What is a term? The semi-automatic extraction of terms from text. *Translation Studies: An Interdiscipline. Selected Papers from the Translation Studies Congress,Vienna, 1992*, 2:267–278.

Mikel Artetxe, Gorka Labaka, and Eneko Agirre. 2017. Learning bilingual word embeddings with (almost) no bilingual data. In *Proceedings of the 55th Annual Meeting of the Association for Computational Linguistics, Volume 1: Long Papers*, pages 451–462, Vancouver, Canada.

Mona Baker. 1988. Sub-technical vocabulary and the ESP teacher: An analysis of some rhetorical items in medical journal articles. *Reading in a Foreign Language*, 4(2):91–105.

Marco Baroni, Silvia Bernardini, Adriano Ferraresi, and Eros Zanchetta. 2009. The WaCky wide web: A collection of very large linguistically processed web-crawled corpora. *Language Resources and Evaluation*, 43(3):209–226.

Francesca Bonin, Felice Dell'Orletta, Giulia Venturi, and Simonetta Montemagni. 2010. A contrastive approach to multi-word term extraction from domain corpora. In *Proceedings of the 7th International Conference on Language Resources and Evaluation*, pages 19–21, Malta.

Teresa Mihwa Chung and Paul Nation. 2003. Technical vocabulary in specialised texts. *Reading in a Foreign Language*, 15(2):103–116.

J Ronayne Cowan. 1974. Lexical and syntactic research for the design of EFL reading materials. *TESOL Quarterly*, pages 389–399.

Damien Cram and Beatrice Daille. 2016. Terminology extraction with term variant detection. In *Proceedings of ACL-2016 System Demonstrations*, pages 13–18, Berlin, Germany.

Patrick Drouin. 2003. Term extraction using non-technical corpora as a point of leverage. *Terminology. International Journal of Theoretical and Applied Issues in Specialized Communication*, 9(1):99–115.

Patrick Drouin. 2004. Detection of domain specific terminology using corpora comparison. In *Proceedings of the 4th International Conference on Language Resources and Evaluation*, pages 79–82, Lisbon, Portugal.

Gertrud Faaß and Kerstin Eckart. 2013. SdeWaC – A corpus of parsable sentences from the web. In Iryna Gurevych, Chris Biemann, and Torsten Zesch, editors, *Language Processing and Knowledge in the Web*, volume 8105 of *Lecture Notes in Computer Science*, pages 61–68. Springer, Berlin Heidelberg.

William L. Hamilton, Jure Leskovec, and Dan Jurafsky. 2016. Diachronic word embeddings reveal statistical laws of semantic change. In *Proceedings of the 54th Annual Meeting of the Association for Computational Linguistics (Volume 1: Long Papers)*, pages 1489–1501, Berlin, Germany.

Anna Hätty, Michael Dorna, and Sabine Schulte im Walde. 2017. Evaluating the reliability and interaction of recursively used feature classes for terminology extraction. In *Proceedings of the Student Research Workshop at the 15th Conference of the European Chapter of the Association for Computational Linguistics*, pages 113–121, Valencia, Spain.

Anna Hätty and Sabine Schulte im Walde. 2018. A laypeople study on terminology identification across domains and task definitions. In *Proceedings of the 2018 Conference of the North American Chapter of the Association for Computational Linguistics: Human Language Technologies, Volume 2 (Short Papers)*, pages 321–326, New Orleans, Louisiana.

Kyo Kageura and Bin Umino. 1996. Methods of automatic term recognition: A review. *Terminology. International Journal of Theoretical and Applied Issues in Specialized Communication*, 3(2):259–289.

Chunyu Kit and Xiaoyue Liu. 2008. Measuring mono-word termhood by rank difference via corpus comparison. *Terminology. International Journal of Theoretical and Applied Issues in Specialized Communication*, 14(2):204–229.

Natalia A. Kochetkova. 2015. A method for extracting technical terms using the modified weirdness measure. *Automatic Documentation and Mathematical Linguistics*, 49(3):89–95.

Lucelene Lopes, Paulo Fernandes, and Renata Vieira. 2016. Estimating term domain relevance through term frequency, disjoint corpora frequency-tf-dcf. *Knowledge-Based Systems*, 97:237–249.

Sujatha Menon and Jayakaran Mukundan. 2010. Analysing collocational patterns of semi-technical words in science textbooks. *Pertanika Journal of Social Sciences and Humanities*, 18(2):241–258.

Antonio Moreno-Ortiz and Javier Fernández-Cruz. 2015. Identifying polarity in financial texts for sentiment analysis: A corpus-based approach. *Procedia-Social and Behavioral Sciences*, 198:330–338.

Agnieszka Mykowiecka, Małgorzata Marciniak, and Piotr Rychlik. 2018. Recognition of irrelevant phrases in automatically extracted lists of domain terms. *Terminology. International Journal of Theoretical and Applied Issues in Specialized Communication*, 24(1):66–90.

María José Marín Pérez. 2016. Measuring the degree of specialisation of sub-technical legal terms through corpus comparison. *Terminology. International Journal of Theoretical and Applied Issues in Specialized Communication*, 22(1):80–102.

Paul Rayson and Roger Garside. 2000. Comparing corpora using frequency profiling. In *Proceedings of the Workshop on Comparing Corpora*, pages 1–6, Hong Kong.

Ina Roesiger, Julia Bettinger, Johannes Schäfer, Michael Dorna, and Ulrich Heid. 2016. Acquisition of semantic relations between terms: How far can we get with standard NLP tools? In *Proceedings of the 5th International Workshop on Computational Terminology*, pages 41–51, Osaka, Japan.

Juan C. Sager. 1990. *A Practical Course in Terminology Processing*. John Benjamins Publishing, Amsterdam.

Dominik Schlechtweg, Sabine Schulte im Walde, and Stefanie Eckmann. 2018. Diachronic Usage Relatedness (DURel): A framework for the annotation of lexical semantic change. In *Proceedings of the 2018 Conference of the North American Chapter of the Association for Computational Linguistics: Human Language Technologies*, pages 169–174, New Orleans, Louisiana, USA.

Peter H Schönemann. 1966. A generalized solution of the orthogonal Procrustes problem. *Psychometrika*, 31(1):1–10.

Louis Trimble. 1985. *English for Science and Technology. A Discourse Approach*. Cambridge University Press, Cambridge.

Appendix

lexeme	POS	translations	MRS	freq. GEN	freq. SPEC
Strudel	NN	whirlpool, strudel (a pastry)	1.05	232	46
Schnee	NN	snow, beaten egg whites	1.05	2,228	53
schlagen	VV	beat, whip (e.g. cream)	1.10	14,693	309
Gericht	NN	court, dish	1.15	13,263	1,071
Schuß	NN	shot (e.g. gunshot, shot of milk)	1.42	2,153	117
Hamburger	NN	citizen of Hamburg, hamburger	1.53	5,558	46
abschrecken	VV	discourage, chill (with cold water)	1.75	730	170
Form	NN	shape, (baking) mould	2.25	36,639	851
trennen	VV	separate	2.65	5771	170
Glas	NN	glass (e.g. material, drinking glass, jar)	2.70	3,830	863
Blech	NN	iron plate, baking tray	2.95	409	145
Prise	NN	pinch (e.g. of humour, tobacco, salt)	3.10	370	622
Paprika	NN	bell pepper, paprika	3.33	377	453
Messerspitze	NN	point of a knive, pinch (e.g. of salt)	3.43	39	49
Mandel	NN	tonsil, almond	3.45	402	274
Messer	NN	knife	3.50	1,774	925
Rum	NN	rum	3.55	244	181
Salz	NN	salt	3.74	3,087	5,806
Eiweiß	NN	protein, egg white	3.75	1,075	3,037
Schokolade	NN	chocolate	3.98	947	251
Schnittlauch	NN	chives	4.00	156	247
Gemüse	NN	vegetable	4.00	2,696	1,224

Table 1: SURel dataset. MRS (mean relatedness score) denotes the compare rank as described in (Schlechtweg et al., 2018), where high values denote low change. Translations are illustrative for possible meaning shifts, while further senses might exist.

Word Usage Similarity Estimation
with Sentence Representations and Automatic Substitutes

Aina Garí Soler[1], Marianna Apidianaki[1,2] and Alexandre Allauzen[1]

[1]LIMSI, CNRS, Univ. Paris Sud, Université Paris-Saclay, F-91405 Orsay, France
[2]LLF, CNRS, Univ. Paris Diderot
{aina.gari,marianna,allauzen}@limsi.fr

Abstract

Usage similarity estimation addresses the semantic proximity of word instances in different contexts. We apply contextualized (ELMo and BERT) word and sentence embeddings to this task, and propose supervised models that leverage these representations for prediction. Our models are further assisted by lexical substitute annotations automatically assigned to word instances by context2vec, a neural model that relies on a bidirectional LSTM. We perform an extensive comparison of existing word and sentence representations on benchmark datasets addressing both graded and binary similarity. The best performing models outperform previous methods in both settings.

1 Introduction

Traditional word embeddings, like Word2Vec and GloVe, merge different meanings of a word in a single vector representation (Mikolov et al., 2013; Pennington et al., 2014). These pre-trained embeddings are fixed, and stay the same independently of the context of use. Current contextualized sense representations, like ELMo and BERT, go to the other extreme and model meaning as word usage (Peters et al., 2018; Devlin et al., 2018). They provide a dynamic representation of word meaning adapted to every new context of use.

In this work, we perform an extensive comparison of existing static and dynamic embedding-based meaning representation methods on the usage similarity (Usim) task, which involves estimating the semantic proximity of word instances in different contexts (Erk et al., 2009). Usim differs from a classical Semantic Textual Similarity task (Agirre et al., 2016) by the focus on a particular word in the sentence. We evaluate on this task word and context representations obtained using pre-trained uncontextualized word

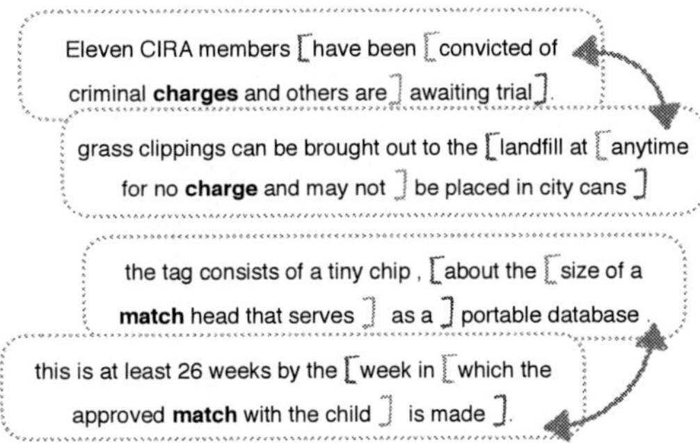

Figure 1: We use contextualized word representations built from the whole sentence or smaller windows around the target word for usage similarity estimation, combined with automatic substitute annotations.

embeddings (GloVe) (Pennington et al., 2014), with and without dimensionality reduction (SIF) (Arora et al., 2017); context representations obtained from a bidirectional LSTM (context2vec) (Melamud et al., 2016); contextualized word embeddings derived from a LSTM bidirectional language model (ELMo) (Peters et al., 2018) and generated by a Transformer (BERT) (Devlin et al., 2018); doc2vec (Le and Mikolov, 2014) and Universal Sentence Encoder representations (Cer et al., 2018). All these embedding-based methods provide direct assessments of usage similarity. The best representations are used as features in supervised models for Usim prediction, trained on similarity judgments.

We combine direct Usim assessments, made by the embedding-based methods, with a substitute-based Usim approach. Building up on previous work that used manually selected in-context substitutes as a proxy for Usim (Erk et al., 2013; McCarthy et al., 2016), we propose to automatize the annotation collection step in order to scale up the method and make it operational on unrestricted text. We exploit annotations assigned to words

*Proceedings of the Eighth Joint Conference on Lexical and Computational Semantics (*SEM), pages 9–21*
Minneapolis, June 6–7, 2019. ©2019 Association for Computational Linguistics

in context by the context2vec lexical substitution model, which relies on word and context representations learned by a bidirectional LSTM from a large corpus (Melamud et al., 2016).

The main contributions of this paper can be summarized as follows:

- we provide a direct comparison of a wide range of word and sentence representation methods on the Usage Similarity (Usim) task and show that current contextualized representations can successfully predict Usim;

- we propose to automatize, and scale up, previous substitute-based Usim prediction methods;

- we propose supervised models for Usim prediction which integrate embedding and lexical substitution features;

- we propose a methodology for collecting new training data for supervised Usim prediction from datasets annotated for related tasks.

We test our models on benchmark datasets containing gold graded and binary word Usim judgments (Erk et al., 2013; Pilehvar and Camacho-Collados, 2019). From the compared embedding-based approaches, the BERT model gives best results on both types of data, providing a straightforward way for word usage similarity calculation. Our supervised model performs on par with BERT on the graded and binary Usim tasks, when using embedding-based representations and clean lexical substitutes.

2   Related Work

Usage similarity is a means for representing word meaning which involves assessing in-context semantic similarity, rather than mapping to word senses from external inventories (Erk et al., 2009, 2013). This methodology followed from the gradual shift from word sense disambiguation models that would select the best sense in context from a dictionary, to models that reason about meaning by solely relying on distributional similarity (Erk and Padó, 2008; Mitchell and Lapata, 2008), or allow multiple sense interpretations (Jurgens, 2014). In Erk et al. (2009), the idea is to model meaning in context in a way that captures different degrees of similarity to a word sense, or between word instances.

Due to its high reliance on context, Usim can be viewed as a semantic textual similarity (STS) (Agirre et al., 2016) task with a focus on a specific word instance. This connection motivated us to apply methods initially proposed for sentence similarity to Usim prediction. More precisely, we build sentence representations using different types of word and sentence embeddings, ranging from the classical word-averaging approach with traditional word embeddings (Pennington et al., 2014), to more recent contextualized word representations (Peters et al., 2018; Devlin et al., 2018). We explore the contribution of each separate method for Usim prediction, and use the best performing ones as features in supervised models. These are trained on sentence pairs labelled with Usim judgments (Erk et al., 2009) to predict the similarity of new word instances.

Previous attempts to automatic Usim prediction involved obtaining vectors encoding a distribution of topics for every target word in context (Lui et al., 2012). In this work, Usim was approximated by the cosine similarity of the resulting topic vectors. We show how contextualized representations, and the supervised model that uses them as features, outperform topic-based methods on the graded Usim task.

We combine the embedding-based direct Usim assessment methods with substitute-based representations obtained using an unsupervised lexical substitution model. McCarthy et al. (2016) showed it is possible to model usage similarity using manual substitute annotations for words in context. In this setting, the set of substitutes proposed for a word instance describe its specific meaning, while similarity of substitute annotations for different instances points to their semantic proximity.[1] We follow up on this work and propose a way to use substitutes for Usim prediction on unrestricted text, bypassing the need for manual annotations. Our method relies on substitute annotations proposed by the context2vec model (Melamud et al., 2016), which uses word and context representations learned by a bidirectional LSTM from a large corpus (UkWac) Baroni et al. (2009).

---

[1]McCarthy et al. use the substitute annotations as features for predicting Usim, clustering instances and estimating the partitionability of words into senses. This offers a way to distinguish between lemmas with distinct senses and others with fuzzy semantics, which would be more challenging in annotation tasks and automatic processing.

<table>
<thead>
<tr><th>Sentences</th><th>Substitutes</th></tr>
</thead>
<tbody>
<tr>
<td>The local **papers** took photographs of the footprint.</td>
<td>GOLD: newspaper, journal
AUTO-LSCNC: press, newspaper, news, report, picture
AUTO-PPDB: newspaper, newsprint</td>
</tr>
<tr>
<td>Now Ari Fleischer, in a pitiful letter to the **paper**, tries to cast Milbank as the one getting his facts wrong.</td>
<td>GOLD: newspaper, publication
AUTO-LSCNC: press, newspaper, news, article, journal, thesis, periodical, manuscript, document
AUTO-PPDB: newspaper</td>
</tr>
<tr>
<td>This is also at the very essence or heart of being a **coach**.</td>
<td>GOLD: trainer, tutor, teacher
AUTO-LSCNC: teacher, counsellor, trainer, tutor, instructor
AUTO-PPDB: trainer, teacher, mentor, coaching</td>
</tr>
<tr>
<td>We hopped back onto the **coach** – now for the boulangerie!</td>
<td>GOLD: coach, bus, carriage
AUTO-LSCNC: bus, car, carriage, transport
AUTO-PPDB: bus, train, wagon, lorry, car, truck, carriage, vehicle</td>
</tr>
</tbody>
</table>

Table 1: Example pairs of highly similar and dissimilar usages from the Usim dataset (Erk et al., 2013) for the nouns *paper* (Usim score = 4.34) and *coach.n* (Usim score = 1.5), with the substitutes assigned by the annotators (GOLD). For comparison, we give the substitutes selected for these instances by the automatic substitution method (context2vec) used in our experiments from two different pools of substitutes (AUTO-LSCNC and PPDB). More details on the automatic substitution configurations are given in Section 4.2.

3 Data

3.1 The LexSub and Usim Datasets

We use the training and test datasets of the SemEval-2007 Lexical Substitution (LexSub) task (McCarthy and Navigli, 2007), which contain instances of target words in sentential context hand-labelled with meaning-preserving substitutes. A subset of the LexSub data (10 instances x 56 lemmas) has additionally been annotated with graded pairwise Usim judgments (Erk et al., 2013). Each sentence pair received a rating (on a scale of 1-5) by multiple annotators, and the average judgment for each pair was retained. McCarthy et al. (2016) derive two additional scores from Usim annotations that denote how easy it is to partition a lemma's usages into sets describing distinct senses: **Uiaa**, the inter-annotator agreement for a given lemma, taken as the average pairwise Spearman's ρ correlation between ranked judgments of the annotators; and **Umid**, the proportion of mid-range judgments over all instances for a lemma and all annotators.

In our experiments, we use 2,466 sentence pairs from the Usim data for training, development and testing of different automatic Usim prediction methods. Our models rely on substitutes automatically assigned to words in context using context2vec (Melamud et al., 2016), and on various word and sentence embedding representa-tions. We also train a model using the gold substitutes, to test how well our models perform when substitute quality is high. Performance of the different models is evaluated by measuring how well they approximate the Usim scores assigned by annotators. Table 1 shows examples of sentence pairs from the Usim dataset (Erk et al., 2013) with the GOLD substitutes and Usim scores assigned by the annotators. The Usim score is high for similar instances, and decreases for instances that describe different meanings. The semantic proximity of two instances is also reflected in the similarity of their substitutes sets. For comparison, we also give in the Table the substitutes selected for these instances by the automatic context2vec substitution method used in our experiments (more details in Section 4.2).

3.2 The Concepts in Context Corpus

Given the small size of the Usim dataset, we extract additional training data for our models from the Concepts in Context (CoInCo) corpus (Kremer et al., 2014), a subset of the MASC corpus (Ide et al., 2008). CoInCo contains manually selected substitutes for all content words in a sentence, but provides no usage similarity scores that could be used for training. We construct our supplementary training data as follows: we gather all instances of a target word in the corpus with at least four substitutes, and keep pairs with (1) no overlap in substitutes, and (2) minimum 75% substitute overlap.[2] We view the first set of pairs as examples of completely different usages of a word (DIFF), and the second set as examples of identical usages (SAME). The two sets are unbalanced in terms of number of instance pairs (19,060 vs. 2,556). We balance them by keeping in DIFF the 2,556 pairs with the highest number of substitutes.

We also annotate the data with substitutes using context2vec (Melamud et al., 2016), as described in Section 4.2. We apply an additional filtering to the sentence pairs extracted from CoInCo, discarding instances of words that are not in the context2vec vocabulary and have no embeddings. We are left with 2,513 pairs in each class (5,026 in total). We use 80% of these pairs (4,020) together with the Usim data to train our supervised Usim models described in Section 4.3.[3]

3.3 The Word-in-Context dataset

The third dataset we use in our experiments is the recently released Word-in-Context (WiC) dataset (Pilehvar and Camacho-Collados, 2019), version 0.1. WiC provides pairs of contextualized target word instances describing the same or different meaning, framing in-context sense identification as a binary classification task. For example, a sentence pair for the noun *stream* is: ['Stream of consciousness' – 'Two streams of development run through American history']. A system is expected to be able to identify that *stream* does not have the same meaning in the two sentences.

WiC sentences were extracted from example usages in WordNet (Fellbaum, 1998), VerbNet (Schuler, 2006), and Wiktionary. Instance pairs were automatically labeled as positive (T) or negative (F) (corresponding to the same/different sense) using information in the lexicographic resources, such as presence in the same or different synsets. Each word is represented by at most three instances in WiC, and repeated sentences are excluded. It is important to note that meanings represented in the WiC dataset are coarser-grained than WordNet senses. This was ensured by excluding WordNet synsets describing highly sim-

ilar meanings (sister senses, and senses belonging to the same supersense). The human-level performance upper-bound on this binary task, as measured on two 100-sentence samples, is 80.5%. Inter-annotator agreement is also high, at 79%. The dataset comes with an official train/dev/test split containing 7,618, 702 and 1,366 sentence pairs, respectively.[4]

4 Methodology

We experiment with two ways of predicting usage similarity: an unsupervised approach which relies on the cosine similarity of different kinds of word and sentence representations, and provides direct Usim assessments; and supervised models that combine embedding similarity with features based on substitute overlap. We present the direct Usim prediction methods in Section 4.1. In Section 4.2, we describe how substitute-based features were extracted, and in Section 4.3, we introduce the supervised Usim models.

4.1 Direct Usage Similarity Prediction

In the unsupervised Usim prediction setting, we apply different types of pre-trained word and sentence embeddings as follows: we compute an embedding for every sentence in the Usim dataset, and calculate the pairwise cosine similarity between the sentences available for a target word. Then, for every embedding type, we measure the correlation between sentence similarities and gold usage similarity judgments in the Usim dataset, using Spearman's ρ correlation coefficient. We experiment with the following embedding types.

GloVe embeddings are uncontextualized word representations which merge all senses of a word in one vector (Pennington et al., 2014). We use 300-dimensional GloVe embeddings pre-trained on Common Crawl (840B tokens).[5] The representation of a sentence is obtained by averaging the GloVe embeddings of the words in the sentence.

SIF (Smooth Inverse Frequency) embeddings are sentence representations built by applying dimensionality reduction to a weighted average of uncontextualized embeddings of words in a sentence

---

[2]Full overlap is rare since annotators propose somewhat different sets of substitutes, even for instances with the same meaning. Full overlap is observed for only 437 of all considered CoInCo pairs (0.3%).

[3]We will make the dataset available at `https://github.com/ainagari`. 20% of the extracted examples were kept aside for development and testing purposes.

[4]The test portion of WiC had not been released at the time of submission. We contacted the authors and ran the evaluation on the official test set, to be able to compare to results reported in their paper (Pilehvar and Camacho-Collados, 2019).

[5]`https://nlp.stanford.edu/projects/glove/`

(Arora et al., 2017). We use SIF in combination with GloVe vectors.

Context2vec embeddings (Melamud et al., 2016). The context2vec model learns embeddings for words and their sentential contexts simultaneously. The resulting representations reflect: a) the similarity between potential fillers of a sentence with a blank slot, and b) the similarity of contexts that can be filled with the same word. We use a context2vec model pre-trained on the UkWaC corpus (Baroni et al., 2009) [6] to compute embeddings for sentences with a blank at the target word's position.

ELMo (Embeddings from Language Models) representations are contextualized word embeddings derived from the internal states of an LSTM bidirectional language model (biLM) (Peters et al., 2018). In our experiments, we use a pre-trained 512-dimensional biLM.[7] Typically, the best linear combination of the layer representations for a word is learned for each end task in a supervised manner. Here, we use out-of-the-box embeddings (without tuning) and experiment with the top layer, and with the average of the three hidden layers. We represent a sentence in two ways: by the contextualized ELMo embedding obtained for the target word, and by the average of ELMo embeddings for all words in a sentence.

BERT (Bidirectional Encoder Representations from Transformers) (Devlin et al., 2018). BERT representations are generated by a 12-layer bidirectional Transformer encoder that jointly conditions on both left and right context in all layers.[8] BERT can be fine-tuned to specific end tasks, or its contextualized word representations can be used directly in applications, similar to ELMo. We try different layer combinations and create sentence representations, in the same way as for ELMo: using either the BERT embedding of the target word, or the average of the BERT embeddings for all words in a sentence.

Universal Sentence Encoder (USE) makes use of a Deep Averaging Network (DAN) encoder trained to create sentence representations by means of multi-task learning (Cer et al., 2018).

USE has been shown to improve performance on different NLP tasks using transfer learning.[9]

doc2vec is an extension of word2vec to the sentence, paragraph or document level (Le and Mikolov, 2014). One of its forms, *dbow* (distributed bag of words), is based on the skip-gram model, where it adds a new feature vector representing a document. We use a dbow model trained on English Wikipedia released by Lau and Baldwin (2016).[10]

We test the above models with representations built from the whole sentence, and using a smaller context window (cw) around the target word. Sentences in the WiC dataset are quite short (7.9 $\pm$ 3.9 words), but the length of sentences in the Usim and CoInCo datasets varies a lot (27.4 $\pm$ 13.2 and 18.8 $\pm$ 10.2, respectively). We want to check whether information surrounding the target word in the sentence is more relevant, and sufficient for Usim estimation. We focus on the words in a context window of $\pm$ 2, 3, 4 or 5 words at each side of a target word. Then, we collect their word embeddings to be averaged (for GloVe, ELMo and BERT), or derive an embedding from this specific window instead of the whole sentence (for USE).

We approximate Usim by measuring the cosine similarity of the resulting context representations. We compare the performance of these direct assessment methods on the Usim dataset and report the results in Section 5.

4.2 Substitute-based Feature Extraction

Following up on McCarthy et al.'s (2016) sense clusterability work, we also experiment with a substitute-based approach for Usim prediction. McCarthy et al. showed that manually selected substitutes for word instances in context can be used as a proxy for Usim. Here, we propose an approach to obtain these annotations automatically that can be applied to the whole vocabulary.

Automatic LexSub We generate rankings of candidate substitutes for words in context using the context2vec method (Melamud et al., 2016). The original method selects and ranks substitutes from the whole vocabulary. To facilitate comparison and evaluation, we use the following pools of candidates: (a) all substitutes that were proposed

---

[6]http://u.cs.biu.ac.il/~nlp/resources/downloads/context2vec/

[7]https://allennlp.org/elmo

[8]This is an important difference with the ELMo architecture which concatenates a left-to-right and right-to-left model.

[9]https://tfhub.dev/google/universal-sentence-encoder/2

[10]https://github.com/jhlau/doc2vec

for a word in the LexSub and CoInCo annotations (we call this substitute pool AUTO-LSCNC); (b) the paraphrases of the word in the Paraphrase Database (PPDB) XXL package (Ganitkevitch et al., 2013; Pavlick et al., 2015) (AUTO-PPDB).[11] In the WiC experiments, where no substitute annotations are available, we only use PPDB paraphrases (AUTO-PPDB). We obtain a context2vec embedding for a sentence by replacing the target word with a blank. AUTO-LSCNC substitutes are high-quality since they were extracted from the manual LexSub and CoInCo annotations. They are semantically similar to the target, and context2vec just needs to rank them according to how well they fit the new context. This is done by measuring the cosine similarity between each substitute's context2vec word embedding and the context embedding obtained for the sentence.

The AUTO-PPDB pool contains paraphrases from PPDB XXL, which were automatically extracted from parallel corpora (Ganitkevitch et al., 2013). Hence, this pool contains noisy paraphrases that should be ranked lower. To this end, we use in this setting the original context2vec scoring formula which also accounts for the similarity between the target word and the substitute:

$$c2v\_score = \frac{cos(s, t) + 1}{2} \times \frac{cos(s, C) + 1}{2} \quad (1)$$

In formula (1), s and t are the word embeddings of a substitute and the target word, and C is the context2vec vector of the context. Following this procedure, context2vec produces a ranking of candidate substitutes for each target word instance in the Usim, CoInCo and WiC datasets, according to their fit in context. Every candidate is assigned a score, with substitutes that are a good fit in a specific context being higher-ranked than others. For every new target word instance, context2vec ranks *all* candidate substitutes available for the target in each pool. Consequently, the automatic annotations produced for different instances of the target include the same set of substitutes, but in different order. This does not allow for the use of measures based on substitute overlap, which were shown to be useful for Usim prediction in McCarthy et al. (2016). In order to use this type of measures, we propose ways to filter the automatically generated rankings, and keep for each instance only substitutes that are a good fit in context.

---

[11]http://paraphrase.org/

Substitute Filtering We test different filters to discard low quality substitutes from the annotations proposed by context2vec for each instance.

- **PPDB 2.0 score**: Given a ranking R of n substitutes $R = [s_1, s_2, ..., s_n]$ proposed by context2vec, we form pairs of substitutes in adjacent positions $\{s_i \leftrightarrow s_{i+1}\}$, and check whether they exist as paraphrase pairs in PPDB. We expect substitutes that are paraphrases of each other to be similarly ranked. If s_i and s_{i+1} are not paraphrases in PPDB, we keep all substitutes up to s_i and use this as a cut-off point, discarding substitutes present from position s_{i+1} onwards in the ranking.

- **GloVe word embeddings**: We measure the cosine similarity (*cosSim*) between GloVe embeddings of adjacent substitutes $\{s_i \leftrightarrow s_{i+1}\}$ in the ranking R obtained for a new instance. We first compare the similarity of the first pair of substitutes ($cosSim(s_1, s_2)$) to a lower bound similarity threshold T. If $cosSim(s_1, s_2)$ exceeds T, we assume that s_1 and s_2 have the same meaning, and use $cosSim(s_1, s_2)$ as a reference similarity value, S, for this instance. The middle point between the two values, $M = (T + S)/2$, is then used as a threshold to determine whether there is a shift in meaning in subsequent pairs. If $cosSim(s_i, s_{i+1}) < M$, for $i > 1$, then only the higher ranked substitute (s_i) is retained and all subsequent substitutes in the ranking are discarded. The intuition behind this calculation is that if $cosSim$ is much lower than the reference S (even if it exceeds T), substitutes possibly have different senses.

- **Context2vec score**: This filter uses the score assigned by context2vec to each substitute, reflecting how good a fit it is in each context. context2vec scores vary a lot across instances, it is thus not straightforward to choose a threshold. We instead refer to the scores assigned to adjacent pairs of substitutes in the ranking produced for each instance, $R = [s_1, s_2, ..., s_n]$. We view the pair with the biggest difference in scores as the cut-off point, considering it reflects a degradation in substitute fit. We retain only substitutes up to this point.

- **Highest-ranked X substitutes**. We also test two simple baselines, which consist in keeping the 5 and 10 highest-ranked substitutes for each instance.

We test the efficiency of each filter on the portion of the LexSub dataset (McCarthy and Navigli, 2007) that was not annotated for Usim. We compare the substitutes retained for each instance after filtering to its gold LexSub susbtitutes using the F1-score, and the proportion of false positives out of all positives. Filtering results are reported in Appendix A. The best filters were GloVe word embeddings ($T = 0.2$) for AUTO-LSCNC, and the PPDB filter for AUTO-PPDB.

Feature Extraction After annotating the Usim sentences with context2vec and filtering, we extract, for each sentence pair (S_1, S_2), a set of features related to the amount of substitute overlap.

- **Common substitutes**. The proportion of shared substitutes between two sentences.

- **GAP score**. The average of the Generalized Average Precision (GAP) score (Kishida, 2005) taken in both directions ($GAP(S_1, S_2)$ and $GAP(S_2, S_1)$). GAP is a measure that compares two rankings considering not only the order of the ranked elements but also their weights. It ranges from 0 to 1, where 0 means that rankings are completely different and 1 indicates perfect agreement. We use the frequency in the manual Usim annotations (i.e. the number of annotators who proposed each substitute) as the weight for gold substitutes, and the context2vec score for automatic substitutes. We use the GAP implementation from Melamud et al. (2015).

- **Substitute cosine similarity**. We form substitute pairs ($S_1 \leftrightarrow S_2$) and calculate the average of their GloVe cosine similarities. This feature shows the semantic similarity of substitutes, even when overlap is low.

4.3 Supervised Usim Prediction

We train linear regression models to predict Usim scores for word instances in different contexts using as features the cosine similarity of the different representations in Section 4.1, and the substitute-based features in 4.2. For training, we use the Usim dataset on its own (cf. Section 3.1), and combined with the additional training examples extracted from CoInCo (cf. Section 3.2).

To be able to evaluate the performance of our models separately for each of the 56 target words in the Usim dataset, we train a separate model for each word in a leave-one-out setting. Each time, we use 2,196 pairs for training, 225 for development and 45 for testing.[12] Each model is evaluated on the sentences corresponding to the left out target word. We report results of these experiments in Section 5. The performance of the model with context2vec substitutes from the two substitute pools is compared to that of the model with gold substitute annotations. We replicate the experiments by adding CoInCo data to the Usim training data.

To test the contribution of each feature, we perform an ablation study on the 225 Usim sentence pairs of the development set, which cover the full spectrum of Usim scores (from 1 to 5). We report results of the feature ablation in Appendix C.

We also build a model for the binary Usim task on the WiC dataset (Pilehvar and Camacho-Collados, 2019), using the official train/dev/test split. We train a logistic regression classifier on the training set, and use the development set to select the best among several feature combinations. We report results of the best performing models on the WiC test set in Section 5. For instances in WiC where no PPDB substitutes are available (133 out of 1,366 in the test set) we back off to a model that only relies on the embedding features.

5 Evaluation

Direct Usim Prediction Correlation results between Usim judgments and the cosine similarity of the embedding representations described in Section 4.1 are found in Table 2. Detailed results for all context window combinations are given in Appendix B. We observe that target word BERT embeddings give best performance in this task. Selecting a context window around (or including) the target word does not always help, on the contrary it can harm the models. Context2vec sentence representations are the next best performing representation, after BERT, but their correlation is much lower. The simple GloVe-based SIF approach for sentence representation, which consists in applying dimensionality reduction to a weighted average of GloVe vectors of the words in a sentence, is much superior to the simple average of GloVe vectors and even better than doc2vec sentence representations, obtaining a correlation comparable to

---

[12]With the exception of 4 lemmas which had 36 pairs, and one which had 44.

Context	Embeddings	Correlation
Full sentence	GloVe	0.142
	SIF	0.274
	c2v	0.290
	USE	0.272
	doc2vec	0.124
	ELMo av	0.254
	BERT av 4	0.289
Target word	ELMo av	0.166
	ELMo top	0.177
	BERT top	0.514
	BERT av 4	**0.518**
cw=2	ELMo top	0.289
cw=3 (incl. target)	GloVe	0.180
	ELMo av	0.280
	BERT av 4	0.395
cw=5 (incl. target)	USE	0.221
	ELMo av	0.266
	ELMo top	0.263
	BERT top	0.309

Table 2: Spearman ρ correlation of different sentence and word embeddings on the Usim dataset using different context window sizes (cw). For BERT and ELMo, *top* refers to the top layer, and *av* refers to the average of layers (3 for ELMo, and the last 4 for BERT).

that of USE.

Graded Usim To evaluate the performance of our supervised models, we measure the correlation of the predictions with human similarity judgments on the Usim dataset using Spearman's ρ. Results reported in Table 3 are the average of the correlations obtained for each target word with gold and automatic substitutes (from the two substitute pools), and for each type of features, substitute-based and embedding-based (cosine similarities from BERT and context2vec). We also report results with the additional CoInCo training data. Unsurprisingly, the best results are obtained by the methods that use the gold substitutes. This is consistent with previous analyses by Erk et al. (2009) who found overlap in manually-proposed substitutes to correlate with Usim judgments. The lower performance of features that rely on automatically selected substitutes (AUTO-LSCNC and AUTO-PPDB) demonstrates the impact of substitute quality on the contribution of this type of features. The addition of CoInCo data does not seem to help the models, as results are slightly lower than in the only Usim setting. This can be due to the fact that CoInCo data contains only extreme cases of similarity (SAME/DIFF) and no in-

termediate ratings. The slight improvement in the combined settings over embedding-based models is not significant in AUTO-LSCNC substitutes, but it is for gold substitutes (p < 0.001). [13]

For comparison to the topic-modelling approach of Lui et al. (2012), we evaluate on the 34 lemmas used in their experiments. They report a correlation calculated over all instances. With the exception of the substitute-only setting with PPDB candidates, all of our Usim models get higher correlation than their model ($\rho = 0.202$), with $\rho = 0.512$ for the combination of AUTO-LSCNC substitutes and embeddings. The average of the per target word correlation in Lui et al. (2012) ($\rho = 0.388$) is still lower than that of our AUTO-LSCNC model in the combined setting ($\rho = 0.500$).

Binary Usim We evaluate the predictions of our binary classifiers by measuring accuracy on the test portion of the WiC dataset. Results for the best configurations for each training set are reported in Table 4. Experiments on the development set showed that target word BERT representations and USE sentence embeddings are the best-suited for WiC. Therefore, 'embedding-based features' here refers to these two representations. Results on the development set can be found in Appendix D. All configurations obtain higher accuracy than the previous best reported result on this dataset (59.4) (Pilehvar and Camacho-Collados, 2019), obtained using DeConf vectors, which are multi-prototype embeddings based on WordNet knowledge (Pilehvar and Collier, 2016). Similar to the graded Usim experiments, adding substitute-based features to embedding features slightly improves the accuracy of the model. Also, combining the CoInCo and WiC data for training does not have a clear impact on results, even in this binary classification setting.

6 Discussion

Results reported for Usim are the average correlation for each target word, but the strength of the correlation varies greatly for different words for all models and settings. For example, in the case of direct Usim prediction with embeddings using BERT target, Spearman's ρ ranges from 0.805 (for the verb *fire*) to -0.111 (for the verb *suffer*). This variation in performance is not surprising,

---

[13] As determined by paired t-tests, after verifying the normality of the differences with the Shapiro-Wilk test

Training set	Features	Gold	c2v AUTO-LSCNC	c2v AUTO-PPDB
Usim	Substitute-based	0.563	0.273	0.148
	Embedding-based	0.494	0.494	0.494
	Combined	**0.626**	0.501	0.493
Usim + CoInCo	Substitute-based	-	0.262	0.129
	Embedding-based	-	0.495	0.495
	Combined	-	0.501	0.491

Table 3: **Graded Usim results**: Spearman's ρ correlation results between supervised model predictions and graded annotations on the Usim test set. The first column reports results obtained using gold substitute annotations for each target word instance. The last two columns give results with automatic substitutes selected among all substitutes proposed for the word in the LexSub and CoInCo datasets (AUTO-LSCNC), or paraphrases in the PPDB XXL package (AUTO-PPDB). The Embedding-based configuration uses cosine similarities from BERT and context2vec.

Training set	Features	Accuracy
WiC	Embedding-based	63.62
	Combined	**64.86**
	DeConf embeddings (Pilehvar and Camacho-Collados, 2019)	59.4
	Random baseline (Pilehvar and Camacho-Collados, 2019)	50.0
WiC + CoInCo	Embedding-based	63.69
	Combined	64.42

Table 4: **Binary Usim results**: Accuracy of models on the WiC test set. The Embedding-based configuration includes cosine similarities of BERT target and USE. The Combined setting uses, in addition, substitute overlap features (AUTO-PPDB).

since annotators themselves found some lemmas harder to annotate than others, as reflected in the Usim inter-annotator agreement measure (Uiaa) (McCarthy et al., 2016). We find that BERT target word embeddings results correlate with Uiaa per target word ($\rho = 0.59, p < 0.05$), showing that the performance of this model depends to a certain extent on the ease of annotation for each lemma. Uiaa also correlates with the standard deviation of average Usim scores by target word ($\rho = 0.66, p < 0.001$). Indeed, average Usim values for the word *suffer* do not exhibit high variance as they only range from 3.6 to 4.9. Within a smaller range of scores, a strong correlation is harder to obtain. The negative correlation between Uiaa and Umid ($-0.46, p < 0.001$) also suggests that words with higher disagreement tend to exhibit a higher proportion of mid-range judgments. We believe that this analysis highlights the difference between usage similarity across target words and encourages a by-lemma approach where the specificities of each lemma are taken into account.

7 Conclusion

We applied a wide range of existing word and context representations to graded and binary usage similarity prediction. We also proposed novel supervised models which use as features the best performing embedding representations, and make high quality predictions especially in the binary setting, outperforming previous approaches. The supervised models include features based on in-context lexical substitutes. We show that automatic substitutions constitute an alternative to manual annotation when combined with the embedding-based features. Nevertheless, if there is no specific reason for using substitutes for measuring Usim, BERT offers a much more straightforward solution to the Usim prediction problem.

In future work, we plan to use automatic Usim predictions for estimating word sense partitionability. We believe such knowledge can be useful to determine the appropriate meaning representation for each lemma.

8 Acknowledgments

We would like to thank the anonymous reviewers for their helpful feedback on this work. We would also like to thank Jose Camacho-Collados for his help with the WiC experiments.

The work has been supported by the French National Research Agency under project ANR-16-CE33-0013.

References

Eneko Agirre, Carmen Banea, Daniel Cer, Mona Diab, Aitor Gonzalez-Agirre, Rada Mihalcea, German Rigau, and Janyce Wiebe. 2016. Semeval-2016 task 1: Semantic textual similarity, monolingual and cross-lingual evaluation. In *Proceedings of the 10th International Workshop on Semantic Evaluation (SemEval-2016)*, pages 497–511, San Diego, California. Association for Computational Linguistics.

Sanjeev Arora, Yingyu Liang, and Tengyu Ma. 2017. A Simple but Tough-to-Beat Baseline for Sentence Embeddings. In *International Conference on Learning Representations (ICLR)*, Toulon, France.

Marco Baroni, Silvia Bernardini, Adriano Ferraresi, and Eros Zanchetta. 2009. The WaCky wide web: a collection of very large linguistically processed web-crawled corpora. *Journal of Language Resources and Evaluation*, 43(3):209–226.

Daniel Cer, Yinfei Yang, Sheng-yi Kong, Nan Hua, Nicole Limtiaco, Rhomni St. John, Noah Constant, Mario Guajardo-Cespedes, Steve Yuan, Chris Tar, Brian Strope, and Ray Kurzweil. 2018. Universal Sentence Encoder for English. In *Proceedings of the 2018 Conference on Empirical Methods in Natural Language Processing: System Demonstrations*, pages 169–174, Brussels, Belgium. Association for Computational Linguistics.

Jacob Devlin, Ming-Wei Chang, Kenton Lee, and Kristina Toutanova. 2018. BERT: Pre-training of Deep Bidirectional Transformers for Language Understanding. *arXiv preprint arXiv:1810.04805*.

Katrin Erk, Diana McCarthy, and Nicholas Gaylord. 2009. Investigations on word senses and word usages. In *Proceedings of the Joint Conference of the 47th Annual Meeting of the ACL and the 4th International Joint Conference on Natural Language Processing of the AFNLP*, pages 10–18, Suntec, Singapore. Association for Computational Linguistics.

Katrin Erk, Diana McCarthy, and Nicholas Gaylord. 2013. Measuring word meaning in context. *Computational Linguistics*, 39:511–554.

Katrin Erk and Sebastian Padó. 2008. A structured vector space model for word meaning in context. In *Proceedings of the 2008 Conference on Empirical Methods in Natural Language Processing*, pages 897–906, Honolulu, Hawaii. Association for Computational Linguistics.

Christiane Fellbaum, editor. 1998. *WordNet: An Electronic Lexical Database*. Language, Speech, and Communication. MIT Press, Cambridge, MA.

Juri Ganitkevitch, Benjamin Van Durme, and Chris Callison-Burch. 2013. PPDB: The Paraphrase Database. In *Proceedings of the 2013 Conference of the North American Chapter of the Association for Computational Linguistics: Human Language Technologies*, pages 758–764, Atlanta, Georgia. Association for Computational Linguistics.

Nancy Ide, Collin Baker, Christiane Fellbaum, Charles Fillmore, and Rebecca Passonneau. 2008. MASC: the Manually Annotated Sub-Corpus of American English. In *Proceedings of the Sixth International Conference on Language Resources and Evaluation (LREC'08)*, Marrakech, Morocco. European Language Resources Association (ELRA).

David Jurgens. 2014. An analysis of ambiguity in word sense annotations. In *Proceedings of the Ninth International Conference on Language Resources and Evaluation (LREC-2014)*, pages 3006–3012, Reykjavik, Iceland. European Language Resources Association (ELRA).

Kazuaki Kishida. 2005. *Property of average precision and its generalization: An examination of evaluation indicator for information retrieval experiments.* Technical Report NII-2005-014E, National Institute of Informatics Tokyo, Japan.

Gerhard Kremer, Katrin Erk, Sebastian Padó, and Stefan Thater. 2014. What substitutes tell us - analysis of an "all-words" lexical substitution corpus. In *Proceedings of the 14th Conference of the European Chapter of the Association for Computational Linguistics*, pages 540–549, Gothenburg, Sweden. Association for Computational Linguistics.

Jey Han Lau and Timothy Baldwin. 2016. An empirical evaluation of doc2vec with practical insights into document embedding generation. In *Proceedings of the 1st Workshop on Representation Learning for NLP*, pages 78–86, Berlin, Germany. Association for Computational Linguistics.

Quoc Le and Tomas Mikolov. 2014. Distributed representations of sentences and documents. In *Proceedings of the 31st International conference on Machine Learning*, pages 1188–1196, Beijing, China.

Marco Lui, Timothy Baldwin, and Diana McCarthy. 2012. Unsupervised estimation of word usage similarity. In *Proceedings of the Australasian Language Technology Association Workshop 2012*, pages 33–41, Dunedin, New Zealand.

Diana McCarthy, Marianna Apidianaki, and Katrin Erk. 2016. Word sense clustering and clusterability. *Computational Linguistics*, 42(2):245–275.

Diana McCarthy and Roberto Navigli. 2007. Semeval-2007 task 10: English lexical substitution task. In *Proceedings of the Fourth International Workshop on Semantic Evaluations (SemEval-2007)*, pages 48–53, Prague, Czech Republic. Association for Computational Linguistics.

Oren Melamud, Jacob Goldberger, and Ido Dagan. 2016. context2vec: Learning Generic Context Embedding with Bidirectional LSTM. In *Proceedings of the 20th SIGNLL Conference on Computational*

Natural Language Learning, pages 51–61, Berlin, Germany. Association for Computational Linguistics.

Oren Melamud, Omer Levy, and Ido Dagan. 2015. A simple word embedding model for lexical substitution. In *Proceedings of the 1st Workshop on Vector Space Modeling for Natural Language Processing*, pages 1–7, Denver, Colorado.

Tomas Mikolov, Kai Chen, Greg Corrado, and Jeffrey Dean. 2013. Efficient estimation of word representations in vector space. In *Proceedings of the International Conference on Learning Representations*, Scottsdale, Arizona.

Jeff Mitchell and Mirella Lapata. 2008. Vector-based models of semantic composition. In *Proceedings of ACL-08: HLT*, pages 236–244, Columbus, Ohio. Association for Computational Linguistics.

Ellie Pavlick, Pushpendre Rastogi, Juri Ganitkevitch, Benjamin Van Durme, and Chris Callison-Burch. 2015. PPDB 2.0: Better paraphrase ranking, fine-grained entailment relations, word embeddings, and style classification . In *Proceedings of the 53rd Annual Meeting of the Association for Computational Linguistics and the 7th International Joint Conference on Natural Language Processing (Volume 2: Short Papers)*, pages 425–430, Beijing, China. Association for Computational Linguistics.

Jeffrey Pennington, Richard Socher, and Christopher Manning. 2014. Glove: Global vectors for word representation. In *Proceedings of the 2014 Conference on Empirical Methods in Natural Language Processing (EMNLP)*, pages 1532–1543, Doha, Qatar. Association for Computational Linguistics.

Matthew Peters, Mark Neumann, Mohit Iyyer, Matt Gardner, Christopher Clark, Kenton Lee, and Luke Zettlemoyer. 2018. Deep contextualized word representations. In *Proceedings of the 2018 Conference of the North American Chapter of the Association for Computational Linguistics: Human Language Technologies, Volume 1 (Long Papers)*, pages 2227–2237, New Orleans, Louisiana. Association for Computational Linguistics.

Mohammad Taher Pilehvar and José Camacho-Collados. 2019. WiC: 10, 000 Example Pairs for Evaluating Context-Sensitive Representations. *Accepted at the 2019 Conference of the North American Chapter of the Association for Computational Linguistics: Human Language Technologies*.

Mohammad Taher Pilehvar and Nigel Collier. 2016. De-conflated semantic representations. In *Proceedings of the 2016 Conference on Empirical Methods in Natural Language Processing*, pages 1680–1690, Austin, Texas. Association for Computational Linguistics.

Karin Kipper Schuler. 2006. *VerbNet: A Broad-Coverage, Comprehensive Verb Lexicon*. Ph.D. thesis, University of Pennsylvania.

A   Filtering experiments

Tables 5 and 6 contain results obtained using the different substitute filters described in Section 4.2. We measure the quality of the substitutes retained in the automatic ranking produced by context2vec after filtering against gold substitute annotations in LexSub data. Here, we only use the portion of LexSub data that does not contain Usim judgments.

We measure filtered substitute quality against the gold standard using the F1-score, and the proportion of false positives (FP) over all positives (TP+FP). Table 5 shows results for annotations assigned by context2vec using the the LexSub/CoInCo pool of substitutes (AUTO-LSCNC). Table 6 shows results for context2vec annotations with the PPDB pool of substitutes (AUTO-PPDB).

Filter	F1	$FP/(TP + FP)$
Highest 10	0.332	0.776
Highest 5	0.375	0.695
PPDB	0.333	0.643
GloVe ($T = 0.1$)	0.371	0.675
GloVe ($T = 0.2$)	0.373	0.661
GloVe ($T = 0.3$)	0.353	0.641
c2v score	0.326	0.671
No filter	0.248	0.848

Table 5: Results of different substitute filtering strategies applied to annotations assigned by context2vec when using the LexSub/CoInCo pool of substitutes (AUTO-LSCNC).

Filter	F1	$FP/(TP + FP)$
Highest 10	0.245	0.838
Highest 5	0.290	0.766
PPDB	0.268	0.731
GloVe ($T = 0.1$)	0.266	0.778
GloVe ($T = 0.2$)	0.268	0.769
GloVe ($T = 0.3$)	0.266	0.750
c2v score	0.250	0.675
No filter	0.142	0.920

Table 6: Results of different substitute filtering strategies applied to annotations assigned by context2vec when using the PPDB pool of substitutes (AUTO-PPDB).

B   Direct Usage Similarity Estimation

Correlations between gold Usim scores for all words and cosine similarities of different embedding types can be found in Tables 7 and 8.

	Embeddings	Correlation
Full sentence embedding	GloVe	0.142
	SIF	0.274
	c2v	0.290
	USE	0.272
	doc2vec	0.124
	ELMo av	0.254
	ELMo top	0.248
	BERT av 4	0.289
Target word embedding	ELMo av	0.166
	ELMo top	0.177
	BERT top	0.514
	BERT av 4	0.518
	BERT concat 4	0.516
	BERT 2nd-to-last	0.486

Table 7: Correlations of sentence and word embeddings on the Usim dataset using different context window sizes (cw). For BERT and ELMo, *top* refers to the top layer, and *av* refers to the average of layers (3 for ELMo, and the last 4 for BERT). *concat 4* refers to the concatenation of the last 4 layers of BERT.

C Feature Ablation on Usim

Results of feature ablation experiments on the Usim development sets are given in Table 9.

D Dev experiments on WiC

Table 10 shows the accuracy of different configurations on the WiC development set.

Context	Embeddings	Correlation
cw=2	ELMo top	0.289
	ELMo av	0.280
	BERT av 4	0.344
	GloVe	0.140
cw=3	ELMo top	0.282
	ELMo av	0.279
	BERT av 4	0.339
	GloVe	0.163
cw=4	ELMo top	0.270
	ELMo av	0.263
	BERT av 4	0.311
	GloVe	0.160
cw=5	ELMo top	0.266
	ELMo av	0.263
	BERT av 4	0.309
	GloVe	0.162
cw=2 (incl. target)	ELMo av	0.284
	ELMo top	0.278
	BERT av 4	0.416
	GloVe	0.159
	USE	0.146
cw=3 (incl. target)	ELMo av	0.280
	ELMo top	0.273
	BERT av 4	0.395
	GloVe	0.180
	USE	0.184
cw=4 (incl. target)	ELMo av	0.267
	ELMo top	0.265
	BERT av 4	0.365
	GloVe	0.176
	USE	0.191
cw=5 (incl. target)	ELMo av	0.266
	ELMo top	0.263
	BERT av 4	0.359
	GloVe	0.175
	USE	0.221

Table 8: Correlations of different sentence and word embeddings on the Usim dataset using different context window sizes (cw).

Ablation	Gold	AUTO-LSCNC	AUTO-PPDB
None	0.729	0.538	0.524
Sub. similarity	0.701	0.537	0.524
Common sub.	0.722	0.538	0.524
GAP	0.730	0.537	0.523
c2v	0.730	0.539	0.523
Bert av 4 target	0.700	0.348	0.283

Table 9: Results of feature ablation experiments for systems trained and tested on the Usim dataset with gold substitutes (*Gold*) as well as automatic substitutes from different pools, Lexsub/CoInCo (AUTO-LSCNC) and PPDB (AUTO-PPDB). Rows indicate the feature that is removed each time. Numbers correspond to the average Spearman ρ correlation on the development set across target words.

Training set	Features	Accuracy
WiC	BERT av 4 last target word	65.24
	c2v	57.69
	ELMo top cw=2	61.11
	USE	63.68
	SIF	60.97
	Only substitutes	55.41
	BERT av 4 target word & USE	**67.95**
	Combined	**66.81**
WiC + CoInCo	BERT av 4 target word	64.96
	c2v	58.12
	ELMo top cw=2	61.11
	USE	63.53
	SIF	59.97
	Only substitutes	56.13
	BERT av 4 target word & USE	**68.66**
	Combined	**66.81**

Table 10: Accuracy of different features and combinations on the WiC development set. On this dataset, the two best types of embeddings, that were chosen for the Embedding-based and Combined configurations, were BERT (target word, average of the last 4 layers) and USE. Both Only-substitutes and Combined use features of automatic substitutes from the PPDB pool, and back off to the Embedding-based model when there were no paraphrases available for the target word in the PPDB.

Beyond Context: A New Perspective for Word Embeddings

Yichu Zhou
School of Computing
University of Utah
`flyaway@cs.utah.edu`

Vivek Srikumar
School of Computing
University of Utah
`svivek@cs.utah.edu`

Abstract

Most word embeddings today are trained by optimizing a language modeling goal of scoring words in their context, modeled as a multiclass classification problem. Despite the successes of this assumption, it is incomplete: in addition to its context, orthographical or morphological aspects of words can offer clues about their meaning. In this paper, we define a new modeling framework for training word embeddings that captures this intuition. Our framework is based on the well-studied problem of multi-label classification and, consequently, exposes several design choices for featurizing words and contexts, loss functions for training and score normalization. Indeed, standard models such as CBOW and FAST-TEXT are specific choices along each of these axes. We show via experiments that by combining feature engineering with embedding learning, our method can outperform CBOW using only 10% of the training data in both the standard word embedding evaluations and also text classification experiments.

1 Introduction

The distributional hypothesis (Firth, 1935; Harris, 1954) has been a cornerstone in NLP. For example, Firth (1935) writes:

> ...the complete meaning of a word is always contextual, and no study of meaning apart from a complete context can be taken seriously.

Operationally, in modern NLP, word embeddings capture this idea and are typically trained using neural language models or word collocations (e.g. Bengio et al., 2003; Collobert and Weston, 2008; Mikolov et al., 2013b; Pennington et al., 2014; Peters et al., 2018; Devlin et al., 2018).

Is word meaning exclusively defined by its context? In this paper, we argue that while the word usage plays a crucial role in defining its meaning (perhaps, centrally so), it is not the only mechanism that endows meaning to words. Indeed, Firth writes in the paragraph before the above quote:

> ...a certain component of the meaning of a word is described when you say what sort of a word it is, that is when you identify it morphologically...

The composition of a word, (i.e., its orthography and morphology) may offer cues about its meaning even if the word is not commonly used, thus allowing us to understand unseen words. For example, we can elide over misspellings of words (e.g., *Bbeijing*) because we observe the similarities in the orthography between words.

By ignoring word-level information, many existing off-the-shelf word embedding approaches suffer from two shortcomings. First, they need a great amount of training data to get high quality word embeddings. Second, even with large amounts of training data, some words (e.g., neologisms, misspellings, technical terms) will not be seen frequently enough to provide statistical support for good embeddings.

In this paper, we are motivated by the observation that both the context of a word and its own internal information contribute to word meaning. To model this in an easy-to-extend manner, we need a new perspective about training word embeddings that not only admits arbitrary word and context features, but also supports conceptual tools to systematically reason about the various model design aspects in terms of familiar modeling techniques.

A common method for training word embeddings is to construct a word prediction problem, and obtain the word embeddings as a side effect. One instantiation of the word prediction task, namely CBOW (Mikolov et al., 2013a), frames it

*Proceedings of the Eighth Joint Conference on Lexical and Computational Semantics (*SEM)*, pages 22–32
Minneapolis, June 6–7, 2019. ©2019 Association for Computational Linguistics

as the multi-class classification problem of predicting a word given a context. We argue that the task is more appropriately framed as multi-label classification — multiple words can fit in the same context. Moreover, since the label set (all words) is massive, word prediction is an instance of *eXtreme* Multi-label Learning (XML) (Balasubramanian and Lebanon, 2012; Bhatia et al., 2015; Bi and Kwok, 2013, inter alia).

Framing word prediction as an XML problem allows us to define a unifying framework for word embeddings. Consequently, we can systematically analyze the problem of training word embeddings using lessons from the XML literature. In particular, we can featurize both inputs and outputs — in our case, contexts and words. Apart from featurization, loss functions and normalization of probability are also design choices available. We show that our approach subsumes several standard word embedding learning methods: specific design choices give us familiar models such as CBOW (Mikolov et al., 2013a) and FAST-TEXT (Bojanowski et al., 2017)[1].

Our experiments study the interplay between the amount of data needed to train embeddings, and the features for words and contexts. We show that, when trained on the same amount of data, using word and context features outperforms the original CBOW and FASTTEXT on both the standard analogy evaluation and a variant where words have introduce typographical errors. Featurizing words and contexts reduces data dependency for training and can achieve similar results as CBOW and FASTTEXT trained on a 10x larger corpus. Finally, we also show that the trained embeddings offer better representations for an text classification evaluation.

In summary, the contributions of this work are: (i) We propose a new family of models for word embeddings that allow both word orthography *and* context to inform its embeddings via user designed features. (ii) We show that our model family generalizes several well-known methods such as CBOW and FASTTEXT. (iii) Our experiments show that exploiting word and context features gives better embeddings using significantly lower amounts of training data. (iv) Our experiments also show that while global normalization is the more appropriate formulation, in practice, the av-

erage number of words in a context is too small for global normalization to prove advantageous.

2 Preliminaries & Notation

In this section, we will briefly look at the tasks of word prediction and extreme multi-label classification with the goal of defining notation.

Word prediction The task of word prediction is commonly used to train word embeddings (e.g. Bengio et al., 2003; Mikolov et al., 2013b). A typical example of this class of models (that includes CBOW and several others) frames the problem as using the context around a word to predict it. The context is defined via a fixed-size window around the word to be predicted.

Suppose y denotes a target word and x represents its context. Then CBOW embeddings are trained by minimizing the log loss:

$$\arg\min_{\theta} \sum_{(x,y)\in\mathcal{D}} -\log P(y|x;\theta) \qquad (1)$$

Here, $\mathcal{D}$ is the set of all training documents and θ are the parameters which defined the probability distribution and are learned. The trained word embeddings are part of the learned parameters.

Extreme Multi-label Learning Suppose we have a classification task with a set of labels $\mathcal{L}$. A multi-label classification problem (e.g. Zhang and Zhou, 2014) is one where inputs can be associated with more than one label. Given an input x, the goal is to predict a subset $\mathcal{Y}$ of the label set. One general strategy to model a multi-label problem is to define a scoring function $f(x, \mathcal{Y}; \theta)$ which uses parameters θ to score sets $\mathcal{Y} \subseteq \mathcal{L}$ as being correct for the input x. We can train such a model by minimizing a loss function ℓ over a training set $\mathcal{D}$:

$$\arg\min_{\theta} \sum_{(x,\mathcal{Y})\in\mathcal{D}} \ell\left(f(x, \mathcal{Y}; \theta)\right) \qquad (2)$$

When the label set $\mathcal{L}$ is large, both training and prediction can become problematic because enumerating all subsets of $\mathcal{L}$ is infeasible. We call such problems eXtreme multi-label learning (XML) problems (e.g. Bhatia et al., 2015).

3 Rethinking Word Embeddings

In this section, we will look at assumptions that underlie the use of word prediction to train word embeddings.

---

[1] In order to have a fair comparison, we always use the CBOW variant of FASTTEXT in this paper.

Words & Features Many embedding methods are built on the assumption that the context defines the meaning of a word, thus accounting for the pervasiveness of the word prediction task to train word embeddings. However, we argue this assumption is incomplete.

The meaning of a word is defined not only by its context, but also the word itself. For example, consider the word *googlize*. Such made-up words may have only limited or no context. Yet, we may be able to infer their meaning (devoid of context) by appealing to our understanding of their parts. In our example, the word is composed of *google* and *-ize*, both of which have their own meanings and the composition (*google* + *-ize*) gives cues as to what *googlize* may mean. A reader may use their understanding of the word *google* and the fact that *-ize* is a common suffix to create verbs to hypothesize the meaning of the word.

The above example illustrates the following principle: *A word is not the smallest meaning unit, but the most common one.* We argue that we should utilize the internal information of words when we train word embeddings.

Some recent work (e.g. Pinter et al., 2017; Kim et al., 2018; Bojanowski et al., 2017; Schick and Schütze, 2018) applies our assumptions implicitly by using character-level information to embed words. While character-based features help capture the internal structure of the word, several other aspects may be helpful, e.g. linguistically motivated prefixes and suffixes, the shape of the word and other possible features. §4.4 describes the various choices we explore.

Word Prediction as XML The second inherent assumption in word prediction is that we can frame the problem of predicting a word that fits a context as a multi-class classification problem. However, in nearly all contexts, more than one word could fit. For example, consider the sentence *The running _______ is chasing after a rabbit.* It can be completed with many words filling the blank, such as *fox, dog, hound.*

Seen this way, word prediction models are better framed as the multi-label classification problem of *using the context to predict all words that could occur in the context.* In the example above, we would use the sentence with the blank to jointly predict all the words such as *fox, dog, hound* that can occupy the blank. Using the notation from §2, the input x to the problem is a context and all

words that could occur in the context form the label set $\mathcal{Y}$ for that input. The label set is a subset of all labels $\mathcal{L}$, i.e., the entire vocabulary. Following this intuition, in the rest of the paper, we will use labels and words interchangeably. Note that since the vocabulary is large, we have an extreme multi-label learning problem at hand.

4 A unifying framework

In this section, we will formalize the intuition illustrated in §3. We will see that this effort reveals several design choices involving normalization, loss functions, label costs, and featurization.

4.1 Modeling Words in Context

Our goal is to frame word prediction as a multi-label classification problem to (i) predict a subset of words for a context, and, (ii) generate embeddings for each word.

Suppose we have a word y in a context x. Let the functions ϕ and ψ denote any feature functions that operate on the word and context respectively. We model the score of the word y given the context x by projecting their feature representations into a common d dimensional space with two matrices V and W. The matrices are the parameters to be learned during training. Using these projections, the scoring function of a pair (x, y) is defined as:

$$S(x, y) = [W\phi(y)]^T [V\psi(x)] \qquad (3)$$

Using the score for a pair (x, y), we can now assign scores to a set of words for a context. In any context, some words are more frequent than others. Suppose we denote the frequency of a label y in a context x as $n_x(y)$. We can then define the score of a set of words $\mathcal{Y}$ as the weighted sum of each word in the set:

$$Score(x, \mathcal{Y}) = \sum_{y \in \mathcal{Y}} n_x(y) S(x, y) \qquad (4)$$

The matrices V and W will be used to compute word embeddings; we will discuss this further in the comparison to CBOW in §5.2.

4.2 Normalization and Loss Functions

As a prelude to defining loss functions for training, we need to decide how to normalize the scoring functions defined above: we have the choice of local or global normalization. With local normalization, we contrast each label in the set of true labels against all other labels individually; with global normalization, we contrast the true label set against other possible *subsets* of labels.

As an illustration, suppose the label set $\mathcal{Y}$ for a context x contains two labels y_1 and y_2. With local normalization, we seek parameters that simultaneously make $S(x, y_1)$ higher than $S(x, y_2)$ *and* $S(x, y_2)$ higher than $S(x, y_1)$. Moreover, local normalization does not prevent a third label y_3 from having a positive score as long as it is less than the scores of the valid labels. As a result, the set of highest scoring labels could be invalid even though all the local constraints are satisfied. To fix this, we can design a globally normalized loss function that demands the score of valid subset $\mathcal{Y}$ to be higher than all other subsets of $\mathcal{L}$.

Irrespective of whether the scores are locally or globally normalized, for the XML problem of word prediction, we can use several loss functions for training. To compare to CBOW and FAST-TEXT, we will focus on log loss here. We refer the interested reader to the supplementary material for details about the global and local hinge loss for the problem.

For a locally normalized log loss, the probability of a pair (x, y) can be defined as:

$$P(y|x) = \frac{e^{S(x,y)}}{\sum\limits_{y' \in \mathcal{L}} e^{S(x,y')}} \qquad (5)$$

The local log loss is defined as the negative log of this probability for a word y that occurs in a context x. Note that each valid word contrasts against all other words in the vocabulary $\mathcal{L}$.

For a globally normalized log loss, the probability of a label $\mathcal{Y}$ for an input x is:

$$P(\mathcal{Y}|x) = \frac{e^{Score(x,\mathcal{Y})}}{\sum\limits_{\overline{\mathcal{Y}} \subseteq \mathcal{L}} e^{Score(x,\overline{\mathcal{Y}})}} \qquad (6)$$

The global log loss is the negative log of this probability for a set $\mathcal{Y}$ of words that are valid in a context x. Note that the valid set $\mathcal{Y}$ contrasts against all other possible subsets of the vocabulary.

4.3 Training

A final consideration for training concerns the fact that frequent words can dominate the loss function unless special care is taken. Sub-sampling of frequent words is commonly used to deal with this problem, where a word y will be retained with probability $g(y)$, which is inversely proportional

to its frequency. In this work, we adopt the strategy of *cost-sensitive classification* which lets directly augment the loss functions. Different labels (i.e., words) are assigned different costs based on their frequency using a cost function $c_x(y)$.

Suppose we have a word y in a context x, whose frequency is $n_x(y)$. We will use the word subsampling probability $g(y)$ above to define the cost for the pair (x, y) as the expected frequency of the pair in the training set. That is,

$$c_x(y) = n_x(y)g(y) \qquad (7)$$

We use the subsampling frequency from word2vec to define $g(y)$ as follows:[2]

$$g(y) = \min\left(1, \left(\sqrt{\frac{n(y)}{\alpha}} + 1\right) \cdot \frac{\alpha}{n(y)}\right) \qquad (8)$$

Here, $n(y)$ is the context-independent frequency of label y in the whole corpus and α is a hyperparameter.

Using these costs, the final form of local log loss can be shown to be:

$$
\begin{aligned}
\ell_{ll}(x, \mathcal{Y}) &= -\sum_{y \in \mathcal{Y}} c_x(y) \log P(y|x) \\
&= -\sum_{y \in \mathcal{Y}} c_x(y) \log \frac{e^{S(x,y)}}{\sum\limits_{y' \in \mathcal{L}} e^{S(x,y')}} \\
&= -\sum_{y \in \mathcal{Y}} c_x(y) S(x, y) + \sum_{y \in \mathcal{Y}} c_x(y) \log \sum_{y' \in \mathcal{L}} e^{S(x,y')}
\end{aligned}
$$
$$(9)$$

For global loss, we can achieve a similar effect by rewriting the weighting term in Eq. 4 with the cost. The global log loss is:

$$
\begin{aligned}
\ell_{gl}(x, \mathcal{Y}) &= -\log P(\mathcal{Y}|x) \\
&= -\log \frac{\prod\limits_{y \in \mathcal{Y}} \exp\left(c_x(y)S(x,y)\right)}{\sum\limits_{\overline{\mathcal{Y}} \subseteq \mathcal{L}} \prod\limits_{y' \in \overline{\mathcal{Y}}} \exp\left(c_x(y')S(x,y')\right)}
\end{aligned}
$$
$$(10)$$

Direcly computing the denominator is expensive. However, we know that:

$$
\begin{aligned}
&\sum_{\overline{\mathcal{Y}} \subseteq \mathcal{L}} \prod_{y' \in \overline{\mathcal{Y}}} \exp\left(c_x(y')S(x,y')\right) \\
&= \exp(0) + \exp\left(c_x(y_1)S(x,y_1)\right) + \exp\left(c_x(y_2)S(x,y_2)\right) + \ldots \\
&\quad + \exp\left(c_x(y_1)S(x,y_1)\right)\exp\left(c_x(y_2)S(x,y_2)\right)\ldots \\
&\quad + \exp\left(c_x(y_1)S(x,y_1)\right)\ldots\exp\left(c_x(y_{|\mathcal{L}|})S(x,y_{|\mathcal{L}|})\right) \\
&= \prod_{y \in \mathcal{L}} \left(\exp\left(c_x(y)S(x,y)\right) + 1\right)
\end{aligned}
$$
$$(11)$$

---

[2]The implementation and the description in the paper are different. We are following the implementation and not the paper. The implementation can be found here:https://code. google.com/archive/p/word2vec/

Then, the global log loss can be rewritten as:

$$\ell_{gl}(x, \mathcal{Y}) = -\sum_{y \in \mathcal{Y}} c_x(y) S(x, y) +$$

$$\sum_{y' \in \mathcal{L}} \log \left(\exp \left(c_x(y') S(x, y') \right) + 1 \right)$$

$$(12)$$

Note that both local and global models are dominated by the $O(|\mathcal{L}|)$ summation, which suggests they have same computational cost.

4.4 Featurizing Words and Contexts

In the scoring function of a pair (x, y), i.e., Eq. 3, we use two feature functions ϕ and ψ to extract features from the label and context respectively. This design choice dictates the information we wish to provide to the model about words and contexts. CBOW and word2vecf uses indicators for the target words, while FASTTEXT uses both the words and their constituent character ngrams. For context, CBOW and FASTTEXT aggregate the same features as the target word, but over the context words. Word2vecf (Levy and Goldberg, 2014) uses dependency information to featurize the context. We generalize these by allowing user or domain dependent features. The output of feature functions ϕ and ψ is a sparse vector and each dimension is a binary value, which indicates the existence of corresponding feature.

Though the ϕ and ψ functions, we can easily incorporate extra information into word embeddings from other resources. For example, we can use hand-crafted gazetteers to indicate whether two words can belong to the same type. If both *Beijing* and *Paris* are in a list of locations, we can identify similarity between the words without any context. Such resources may provide information that we can not learn from the context.

5 Analysis of Modeling Choices

In this section, we discuss the advantages of the framework described in §4 and its connections to CBOW embeddings.

5.1 Word Embeddings

In the framework described in §4, we are not learning the word embeddings, but feature embeddings. Each column of W and V represents the embedding of a certain feature. Given features for a word, we can compute its the embeddings of a word w by computing either $W\phi(w)$ or $V\psi(w)$.

This perspective of feature embeddings presents three advantages.

First, we provide a mechanism for incorporating human knowledge into word embeddings. Feature engineering can be combined with our model naturally. Moreover, using informative features can help produce high quality embeddings even with smaller document collections (e.g., all documents related to a specific project in a company).

Second, because a feature can be shared by different words, each training update for a feature will update all the word embeddings containing this feature. This can lead to better generalization.

Third, it presents an elegant solution for the out-of-vacabulary (OOV) problem. Once we define the feature template, we can extract features of any word, then we can compute the embedding for it. Some recent work (Pinter et al., 2017; Kim et al., 2018; Zhao et al., 2018; Artetxe et al., 2018) address the OOV problem using pre-trained embeddings and mimicking them by training a second model using substrings of a given word. Instead, here we can use arbitrary features and do not need pre-trained embeddings.

5.2 CBOW: A Specific Instance

In this subsection, we will show that CBOW is an instance of our framework. We can rewrite the overall loss on a given dataset D using the local log loss function from Eq. 9 as:

$$\ell_{ll}(D, \theta) = \sum_{(x, \mathcal{Y}) \in D} \sum_{y \in \mathcal{Y}} -c_x(y) \log P(y|x)$$

$$= \sum_{(x, \mathcal{Y}) \in D} \sum_{y \in \mathcal{Y}} -n_x(y) g(y) \log P(y|x)$$

$$(13)$$

As before, $n_x(y)$ is the frequency of label y for the context x, $g(y)$ is the probability of keeping this label y and θ denotes the matrices V and W.

Now, suppose we have a different dataset D' that is constructed from D as follows: for every $(x, \mathcal{Y}) \in D$, for every $y \in \mathcal{Y}$, add $n_x(y)$ copies of (x, y) to the new dataset D'. Now, D' is a *multi-class* classification dataset, where each x is associated with only one label y in a single example. More importantly, D' is exactly the input-output pairing used to train CBOW. With this new dataset representation, we can write the total loss over the dataset D' as:

$$\ell_{\text{CBOW}}(D', \theta) = \sum_{(x, y) \in D'} -\log P(y|x) \qquad (14)$$

In both $\ell_{ll}(D, \theta)$ and $\ell_{\text{CBOW}}(D', \theta)$, $P(y|x)$ is given by Equation 5. If the label features $\phi(y)$ consists only of indicators for the label (i.e., the target word) and the context features $\psi(x)$ is the average of the indicators for the words in the context, then these two loss functions are identical. In other words, CBOW is an instance of our model that minimizes local log loss, and uses these specific features. A similar argument applies for FASTTEXT and word2vecf as well.

There are two important differences: First, CBOW used sub-sampling to reduce the impact of frequent words, while we use costs $c_x(y)$ for this purpose. Second, in CBOW, the matrix V is used as word embeddings. As mentioned above, in fact, both V and W generate word embeddings for a word w as $W\phi(w)$ and $V\psi(w)$. Based on preliminary experiments, we observed that concatenating $W\phi(w)$ and $V\psi(w)$ produces the best embeddings. In this work, we use this concatenation strategy to embed words.

5.3 Local vs. Global Normalization

Given the two normalization methods (§4.2), which one should we pick? In theory, local normalization for word prediction can be problematic as described in §4.2. However, in practice, CBOW, FASTTEXT and word2vecf all use multiclass classification (i.e., local normalization) and work well. This apparent gap between the theory and practice can be explained by the observation that while many words may indeed fit in a given context, the key criterion is the *label density* — that is, the ratio of the number of valid labels ($|\mathcal{Y}|$) to the number of all possible labels ($|\mathcal{L}|$). For the XML problem of word prediction, the label density is small enough that the problem can be approximated as a multiclass problem. In other words, because $|\mathcal{L}|$ is large, the average value of $\frac{|\mathcal{Y}|}{|\mathcal{L}|}$ is small enough that it is close to $\frac{1}{|\mathcal{L}|}$. Unless we have dense labels in specialized document collections, we do not expect globally normalized models to outperform locally normalized ones.

6 Experiments

In this section, we empirically verify that our approach: (i) achieves similar performance as CBOW using the same training set and features, (ii) can outperform CBOW and FASTTEXT with only 10% of the training data if extra features are used, (iii) creates embeddings that generalize bet-ter by evaluating analogies on datasets with misspellings, and, (iv) offers a better feature representation for an extrinsic evaluation of text classification. The overall goal of our experiments is to understand the dependence between dataset size, features, and the quality of embeddings produced.

We conduct our experiments on the training set of the 1 billion language model benchmark corpus (Chelba et al., 2014), consisting of 700M words (with 550K unique words). For all experiments, the embedding size of W and V is 300 and the context window size is set to five words to the left and right of a word. The hyper-parameter α from Eq. 8 is 0.001 (following CBOW's implementation). To compare to CBOW and FAST-TEXT, we use log loss on all our experiments. We optimized the loss using Adam (Kingma and Ba, 2015) and used dropout with keep probability 0.6. Based on preliminary trials, we projected the matrix W onto a unit ball. For efficient learning, we also used the negative sampling approach from word2vec. More experiment setup details are available in supplementary material.

Table 1 summarizes all the feature templates we used. In the table, the feature Gazetteers is a set of lists containing names of entities from Wikipedia, grouped by category. Each list represents an entity type such as cities, organizations, days of the week, etc. If the current word matches one of the words in the list, the corresponding feature is activated. The Quirk feature is a collection of prefixes and suffixes types from Quirk et al. (1987). For example, *un-* is a negative prefix and *-ness* is a noun suffix. For the context feature function ψ, we summed the above features over all the context words.

We implement our model using Pytorch[3]. We train our model on a Nvidia DGX machine using one Tesla (16G video memory) GPU. We train 70 epochs for both local log loss and global log loss. For all experiments, prediction accuracy is used as the evaluation metric.

6.1 Analogy Evaluation

In this subsection, we evaluate our models on these traditional analogy evaluation tests (Mikolov et al., 2013a), in particular the Google and the MSR analogy tests.[4] These evaluations focus on an

---

[3]https://pytorch.org/

[4]Although the Google and Microsoft analogy datasets have been shown to be problematic (Linzen, 2016), they are the most commonly used evaluation datasets.

Features	Description
Word	word itself. e.g. <Beijing>
Prefix and suffix	Prefix and suffix up to length 3. e.g. 0#1#B, 0#2#Be, 0#3#Bei
substring	word substrings from length 3 to 6 e.g. n-grams@Bei, n-grams@eij
Quirk	Known prefix and suffix types from Quirk et al. (1987), e.g. quirk@Conversion
Word shape	word shape of the word. e.g. shape@Xxxx
Gazetteers	Indicators for gazetteer matches e.g. gaz@Locations
MISC	isalpha? isPrintable? isdigit? e.g. special@alpha special@printable
Default	The default feature for every word, functions as a bias feature.

Table 1: Extra feature templates for learning word embeddings. This table uses the word *Beijing* as an example. We use gazetteers from the EDISON package (Sammons et al., 2016).

Model	Features	Google	MSR
CBOW	word	0.398	0.463
Fasttext	subwords	0.424	0.584
local model	word	0.416	0.426
global model	word	0.431	0.410
local model	all	**0.494**	**0.724**
global model	all	**0.480**	**0.692**

Table 2: Comparison between different models trained on 10% corpus using a closed vocabulary. The last two rows use features from Table 1.

analogy question of the form *A:B::C:?*, and the goal is to use word embeddings to find the word that best fills the question slot. Because these results are highly related to the vocabulary used to search for the answers, we divide this evaluation into two different vocabularies: closed and open. Closed vocabulary means it comes directly from the training set; while open vocabulary means it is composed of words coming from the training set and evaluation set. Open vocabulary can ensure there are no OOV words during the evaluation. Our model and FASTTEXT can generate embeddings for OOV words, while CBOW can not. We evaluate CBOW only on the closed vocabulary.

First, we compare our model with CBOW and FASTTEXT trained only on 10% of the corpus with a closed vocabulary (Table 2). Using only

Model	Features	Google	MSR
Fasttext-10%	subwords	0.310	0.507
Fasttext-100%	subwords	**0.490**	0.686
local model	all	0.415	**0.763**
global model	all	0.395	0.719

Table 3: Comparison between our models and FAST-TEXT using open vocabulary. FASTTEXT is trained on 10% and 100% corpus; our models are all trained on 10% corpus with extra features defined in Table 1.

words as features, our model achieves better performance than CBOW on the Google analogy set, and close performance on the MSR set. This difference might be caused by the different optimization algorithms. The global model is close in performance to the local model — this is is expected because the global model is approximated by local model when the density of label is small, and the global model is optimizing for a more stringent goal. With all features, our models (both local and global) outperform both CBOW and FAST-TEXT by a large margin.

Second, we compare our model (trained on 10% of the data) with FASTTEXT using an open vocabulary (Table 3). The first row FASTTEXT is trained on 10% of the data. Our model significantly outperforms it. To understand the impact of the extra features, we compare it with FASTTEXT trained on the entire corpus (second row). On the MSR set, our 10% model with extra feature still outperforms FASTTEXT. We believe the underperformance of our 10% model against the 100% FASTTEXT embeddings on the Google data may be due to the fact that the data contains more complex relations between words, and our feature templates may not be expressive enough.

6.2 Analogies with Typographical Errors

One important advantage of our model is it can dynamically produce embeddings for unseen words using the feature embeddings. To verify its usefulness, we need a set of words that do not have any context in a training corpus, but are still meaningful. Misspelt words are a natural set of such words. Such words usually do not occur in the training set and their meanings are defined by their orthographical similarity to the correct word. Using only word features, CBOW can not deal with OOV words; we only compare against FASTTEXT for this task.

	Google			MSR		
	degree 1	degree 2	degree 3	degree 1	degree 2	degree 3
Fasttext-10%	0.212	0.159	0.035	0.374	0.259	0.073
Fasttext-100%	0.348	0.217	0.036	0.503	0.323	0.080
local model	**0.373**	**0.263**	**0.066**	**0.685**	**0.531**	**0.185**
global model	0.341	0.227	0.054	0.634	0.449	0.134

Table 4: Misspelling evaluation results. Different degrees mean how many words in the quadruple has been changed into a misspelling word. FASTTEXT is trained on 10% and 100% corpus while our model trained on 10% corpus with extra features. CBOW can not generate embeddings for OOV words, which means we can not compare with CBOW on this task.

We create new misspelling datasets by randomly replacing, deleting or inserting one character of each word in MSR and Google analogy datasets. Then we apply the standard analogy test on these misspelling datasets. Table 4 shows the misspelling analogy test results. Different degrees indicate how many words in the analogy quadruple have been changed into a misspelling word. The results show that our model can outperform FASTTEXT in every degree, indicating extra features can capture these similarities between misspelling words and their corrections.

6.3 Extrinsic Task: Dataless Classification

In this subsection, we report the results of an extrinsic evaluation of our trained embeddings. In most extrinsic tasks, embeddings are usually used as a representation of examples which are the inputs of a classifier. As a consequence, the performance on these extrinsic tasks is determined by two factors: the quality of representation and the quality of that classifier. Assigning credit to these two factors for any changes in classifier performance can be difficult.

What we need is a task where performance depends only on the quality of the feature representation. Dataless text classification (Chang et al., 2008) has this characteristic, where the goal is to predict a label for a document without any labeled data. Following Chang et al. (2008), we use the 20 Newsgroup dataset (Lang, 1995) to construct ten binary classification problems. Each label in this dataset is mapped to a short list of words that describe the label, as specified by the original work.

We frame this task as a nearest neighbor task. Each word in the documents and label expansions will be assigned an embedding. We use the average of all the words in the documents and expansions as their embeddings and measure Euclidean

Models	Features	Accuracy
CBOW-10%	word	0.524
CBOW-100%	word	0.569
Fastext-10%	subwords	0.509
Fastext-100%	subwords	0.537
local model	all	**0.593**
global model	all	0.567

Table 5: Dataless task evaluation results. FASTTEXT and CBOW are trained on 100% corpus while our model trained on only 10% corpus.

distance between the labels and a document. For each document, closest label will be chosen as the predicted label.

Table 5 shows the average accuracy of these ten binary classification problem. By using extra features, our model can substantially outperform FASTTEXT and CBOW, even when they were trained on 100% of the corpus.

7 Discussion and Related Work

Word and Label Embeddings Word embeddings are ubiquitous across NLP and word prediction is a common approach to train them. Our modeling unifies this task with multi-label classification. There are other approaches for training word embeddings, such as skipgram (Mikolov et al., 2013b), and Glove (Pennington et al., 2014). A similar formalization of such approaches is a direction for future research.

The idea of embedding labels in a classification task has been previously explored (e.g. Amit et al., 2007; Weston et al., 2011; Srikumar and Manning, 2014). In this paper, we make a formal connection between these lines of work and the word embedding literature.

Feature Engineering The feature functions ϕ and ψ in the scoring function (Eq. 3) provide a systematic way to combine feature engineering and embedding learning. Consequently, the rich history of feature engineering in NLP becomes applicable for constructing word embeddings.

In this work, we use context independent features such as prefix, suffix and word shape. Such character-level features have been used for other NLP tasks (e.g. Sapkota et al., 2015) However, contextual features can also be incorporated into this framework (e.g. Akbik et al., 2018). Furthermore, such contextual features could be informed by traditional feature functions such as POS tags of neighboring words.

eXtreme Multi-label Learning (XML) Embedding-based methods are widely used in extreme multi-label classification (e.g. Bhatia et al., 2015; Balasubramanian and Lebanon, 2012; Bi and Kwok, 2013). However, all these embedding-based methods are not used in word prediction context. In this paper, we point out that essentially, they are the same problem. This paper is the first attempt to combine these two areas; fruitful exchange of ideas between the them may lead both to better predictors and embeddings.

8 Conclusion

In this paper, we argue that assumption that context defines meaning, which is used by most word embedding models is incomplete. Besides the context, the internal information of a word also characterizes its meaning. Using this assumption, we reframe the word prediction task as a multi-label classification problem. This new perspective reveals a family of embedding learning models, which allows different featurizations, loss functions and normalizations. We show that CBOW is one particular instance of our framework, with specific choices for these options. Our experiments demonstrate the value of word and context features for constructing word embeddings.

Acknowledgments

We would like to thank members of the Utah NLP group for several valuable discussions and the anonymous reviewers for their feedback. This work was supported in part by a grant from the US Israel Binational Science Foundation (BSF 2016257) and a hardware gift from NVIDIA Corporation.

References

Alan Akbik, Duncan Blythe, and Roland Vollgraf. 2018. Contextual string embeddings for sequence labeling. In *Proceedings of the 27th International Conference on Computational Linguistics*, pages 1638–1649.

Yonatan Amit, Michael Fink, Nathan Srebro, and Shimon Ullman. 2007. Uncovering shared structures in multiclass classification. In *Proceedings of the 24th international conference on Machine learning*, pages 17–24. ACM.

Mikel Artetxe, Gorka Labaka, Inigo Lopez-Gazpio, and Eneko Agirre. 2018. Uncovering divergent linguistic information in word embeddings with lessons for intrinsic and extrinsic evaluation. In *Proceedings of the 22nd Conference on Computational Natural Language Learning*, pages 282–291.

Krishnakumar Balasubramanian and Guy Lebanon. 2012. The landmark selection method for multiple output prediction. In *Proceedings of the 29th International Coference on International Conference on Machine Learning*, pages 283–290. Omnipress.

Yoshua Bengio, Réjean Ducharme, Pascal Vincent, and Christian Jauvin. 2003. A neural probabilistic language model. *Journal of machine learning research*, 3(Feb):1137–1155.

Kush Bhatia, Himanshu Jain, Purushottam Kar, Manik Varma, and Prateek Jain. 2015. Sparse local embeddings for extreme multi-label classification. In *Advances in neural information processing systems*, pages 730–738.

Wei Bi and James Kwok. 2013. Efficient multi-label classification with many labels. In *International Conference on Machine Learning*, pages 405–413.

Piotr Bojanowski, Edouard Grave, Armand Joulin, and Tomas Mikolov. 2017. Enriching word vectors with subword information. *Transactions of the Association of Computational Linguistics*, 5(1):135–146.

Ming-Wei Chang, Lev Ratinov, Dan Roth, and Vivek Srikumar. 2008. Importance of semantic representation: dataless classification. In *Proceedings of the 23rd national conference on Artificial intelligence-Volume 2*, pages 830–835. AAAI Press.

Ciprian Chelba, Tomas Mikolov, Mike Schuster, Qi Ge, Thorsten Brants, Phillipp Koehn, and Tony Robinson. 2014. One billion word benchmark for measuring progress in statistical language modeling. In *Fifteenth Annual Conference of the International Speech Communication Association*.

Ronan Collobert and Jason Weston. 2008. A unified architecture for natural language processing: Deep neural networks with multitask learning. In *Proceedings of the 25th international conference on Machine learning*, pages 160–167. ACM.

Jacob Devlin, Ming-Wei Chang, Kenton Lee, and Kristina Toutanova. 2018. BERT: Pre-training of deep bidirectional transformers for language understanding. In *Proceedings of the 2019 conference of the North American chapter of the association for computational linguistics: Human language technologies*.

John Rupert Firth. 1935. The technique of semantics. *Transactions of the philological society*, 34(1):36–73.

Zellig S Harris. 1954. Distributional structure. *Word*, 10(2-3):146–162.

Yeachan Kim, Kang-Min Kim, Ji-Min Lee, and SangKeun Lee. 2018. Learning to generate word representations using subword information. In *Proceedings of the 27th International Conference on Computational Linguistics*, pages 2551–2561.

Diederik P. Kingma and Jimmy Ba. 2015. Adam: A method for stochastic optimization. In *3rd International Conference on Learning Representations, ICLR 2015, San Diego, CA, USA, May 7-9, 2015, Conference Track Proceedings*.

Ken Lang. 1995. Newsweeder: Learning to filter netnews. In *Proceedings of the Twelfth International Conference on Machine Learning*, pages 331–339.

Omer Levy and Yoav Goldberg. 2014. Dependency-based word embeddings. In *Proceedings of the 52nd Annual Meeting of the Association for Computational Linguistics (Volume 2: Short Papers)*, volume 2, pages 302–308.

Tal Linzen. 2016. Issues in evaluating semantic spaces using word analogies. In *Proceedings of the 1st Workshop on Evaluating Vector-Space Representations for NLP*, pages 13–18.

Tomas Mikolov, Kai Chen, Greg Corrado, and Jeffrey Dean. 2013a. Efficient estimation of word representations in vector space. In *1st International Conference on Learning Representations, ICLR 2013, Scottsdale, Arizona, USA, May 2-4, 2013, Workshop Track Proceedings*.

Tomas Mikolov, Ilya Sutskever, Kai Chen, Greg S Corrado, and Jeff Dean. 2013b. Distributed representations of words and phrases and their compositionality. In *Advances in neural information processing systems*, pages 3111–3119.

Jeffrey Pennington, Richard Socher, and Christopher Manning. 2014. Glove: Global vectors for word representation. In *Proceedings of the 2014 conference on empirical methods in natural language processing (EMNLP)*, pages 1532–1543.

Matthew Peters, Mark Neumann, Mohit Iyyer, Matt Gardner, Christopher Clark, Kenton Lee, and Luke Zettlemoyer. 2018. Deep contextualized word representations. In *Proceedings of the 2018 Conference of the North American Chapter of the Association for Computational Linguistics: Human Language Technologies, Volume 1 (Long Papers)*, volume 1, pages 2227–2237.

Yuval Pinter, Robert Guthrie, and Jacob Eisenstein. 2017. Mimicking word embeddings using subword rnns. In *Proceedings of the 2017 Conference on Empirical Methods in Natural Language Processing*, pages 102–112.

Randolph Quirk, Sidney Greenbaum, Geoffrey Leech, and Jan Svartvik. 1987. A comprehensive grammar of the english language. *Studies in Second Language Acquisition*, 9(1):109–111.

Mark Sammons, Christos Christodoulopoulos, Parisa Kordjamshidi, Daniel Khashabi, Vivek Srikumar, Paul Vijayakumar, Mazin Bokhari, Xinbo Wu, and Dan Roth. 2016. EDISON: Feature Extraction for NLP, Simplified. In *Proceedings of the Tenth International Conference on Language Resources and Evaluation (LREC 2016)*.

Upendra Sapkota, Steven Bethard, Manuel Montes, and Thamar Solorio. 2015. Not all character n-grams are created equal: A study in authorship attribution. In *Proceedings of the 2015 conference of the North American chapter of the association for computational linguistics: Human language technologies*, pages 93–102.

Timo Schick and Hinrich Schütze. 2018. Learning semantic representations for novel words: Leveraging both form and context. In *Proceedings of the 33rd national conference on Artificial intelligence*.

Vivek Srikumar and Christopher D Manning. 2014. Learning distributed representations for structured output prediction. In *Advances in Neural Information Processing Systems*, pages 3266–3274.

Jason Weston, Samy Bengio, and Nicolas Usunier. 2011. Wsabie: Scaling up to large vocabulary image annotation. In *Twenty-Second International Joint Conference on Artificial Intelligence*.

Min-Ling Zhang and Zhi-Hua Zhou. 2014. A review on multi-label learning algorithms. *IEEE transactions on knowledge and data engineering*, 26(8):1819–1837.

Jinman Zhao, Sidharth Mudgal, and Yingyu Liang. 2018. Generalizing word embeddings using bag of subwords. In *Proceedings of the 2018 Conference on Empirical Methods in Natural Language Processing*, pages 601–606.

A   Local and Global Hinge Loss

We model the score of a word y given the context x by projecting them into a common space with two matrices V and W. The scoring function of pair (x, y) is defined as:

$$S(x, y) = [W\phi(y)]^T [V\psi(x)] \qquad (15)$$

where ϕ and ψ are two feature functions. This scoring function is the same as we saw for log loss in the body of the paper.

A.1 Local Hinge Loss

In this subsection, we will define local hinge loss for word embedding learning under multi-label formulation. Local hinge loss means we want to contrast the target word against all other words in the vocabulary. In our modeling framework, the local hinge loss can be defined as:

$$\ell_{lh}(x,\mathcal{Y}) = \sum_{y\in\mathcal{Y}} \left[c_x(y) \max_{y'\in L} \left[S(x,y') + \Delta(y,y') - S(x,y) \right] \right]$$

(16)

Here, $\Delta(y,y')$ represents the Hamming distance between the ground truth y and any other label y'. That is, it takes the value 1 when $y \neq y'$ and 0 otherwise.

A.2 Global Hinge Loss

For the local hinge loss above, we treat each label associated with the input x as being independent. In contrast, for the global hinge loss, we compare scores for subsets of labels. Given a set of ground truth labels for an example, our goal is to maximize the gap between this set and *all* other subsets of labels.

Let us formalize this intuition. As before, let x denote a context. Let $\mathcal{Y}$ denote its corresponding gold label set. Every set of labels that does not agree with this subset $\mathcal{Y}$ will be penalized. We define the global hinge loss to be:

$$\ell_{gh}(x,\mathcal{Y}) = \max_{\overline{\mathcal{Y}}\subseteq\mathcal{L}} \left[\sum_{y\in\mathcal{Y}} S(x,y) + \Delta(\mathcal{Y},\overline{\mathcal{Y}}) - \sum_{y\in\overline{\mathcal{Y}}} S(x,y) \right]$$

(17)

Here, Δ denotes the cost-sensitive Hamming distance between the true set of labels $\mathcal{Y}$ and any other set of labels $\overline{\mathcal{Y}}$. It can be written as:

$$\Delta(\mathcal{Y},\overline{\mathcal{Y}}) = \sum_{y\in\mathcal{L}} \mathbb{1}[y \in \mathcal{Y}] \oplus \mathbb{1}[y \in \overline{\mathcal{Y}}] c_x(y)$$

where $\mathbb{1}[\cdot]$ is the indicator function and $\oplus$ represents the XOR operation. Essentially, the loss adds up the costs $c_x(y)$ for all labels that are mispredicted, either by mistakenly including a label that is not in the gold set, or by missing one that is in it. The costs $c_x(y)$ are the same as defined in the main body of the paper.

Combining the equations above and re-organizing the summations, we can get the final form of the global hinge loss:

$$\ell_{gh}(x,\mathcal{Y}) = \sum_{y\in\mathcal{Y}} \max\left(c_x(y) - S(x,y), 0\right) + \sum_{y\notin\mathcal{Y}} \max(c_x(y) + S(x,y), 0)$$

(18)

The global hinge loss can be interpreted as a sum of two terms: the first term penalizes labels that should have been predicted, but have scores less than their costs, and the second term penalizes labels that should *not* have been predicted, but have scores that are more than the negative costs.

As in the log loss in the body of the paper, with hinge loss as well, both global and local normalization require $O(|\mathcal{L}|)$ computation.

B Hyper-parameters for experiments

Table 6 shows the hyper-parameters for our experiments.

Hyper-parameters	Setting
10% corpus vocabulary size	155, 525
100% corpus vocabulary size	552, 402
Window size	5
α in subsamping	0.001
embedding dimension	300
minimum word frequency	5
negative sampling size	6
dropout probability	0.6

Table 6: Hyper-parameters in the all experiments.

Composition of Sentence Embeddings:
Lessons from Statistical Relational Learning

Damien Sileo[3,1], Tim Van De Cruys[2], Camille Pradel[1], and Philippe Muller[3]

[1]Synapse Développement, Toulouse, France
[2]IRIT, CNRS, France
[3]IRIT, University of Toulouse, France
damien.sileo@synapse-fr.com

Abstract

Various NLP problems – such as the prediction of sentence similarity, entailment, and discourse relations – are all instances of the same general task: the modeling of semantic relations between a pair of textual elements. A popular model for such problems is to embed sentences into fixed size vectors, and use composition functions (e.g. concatenation or sum) of those vectors as features for the prediction. At the same time, composition of embeddings has been a main focus within the field of Statistical Relational Learning (SRL) whose goal is to predict relations between entities (typically from knowledge base triples). In this article, we show that previous work on relation prediction between texts implicitly uses compositions from baseline SRL models. We show that such compositions are not expressive enough for several tasks (e.g. natural language inference). We build on recent SRL models to address textual relational problems, showing that they are more expressive, and can alleviate issues from simpler compositions. The resulting models significantly improve the state of the art in both transferable sentence representation learning and relation prediction.

1 Introduction

Predicting relations between textual units is a widespread task, essential for discourse analysis, dialog systems, information retrieval, or paraphrase detection. Since relation prediction often requires a form of understanding, it can also be used as a proxy to learn transferable sentence representations. Several tasks that are useful to build sentence representations are derived directly from text structure, without human annotation: sentence order prediction (Logeswaran et al., 2016; Jernite et al., 2017), the prediction of previous and subsequent sentences (Kiros et al., 2015; Jernite et al., 2017), or the prediction of explicit dis-

course markers between sentence pairs (Nie et al., 2017; Jernite et al., 2017). Human labeled relations between sentences can also be used for that purpose, e.g. inferential relations (Conneau et al., 2017). While most work on sentence similarity estimation, entailment detection, answer selection, or discourse relation prediction seemingly uses task-specific models, they all involve predicting whether a relation R holds between two sentences s_1 and s_2. This genericity has been noticed in the literature before (Baudiš et al., 2016) and it has been leveraged for the evaluation of sentence embeddings within the SentEval framework (Conneau et al., 2017).

A straightforward way to predict the probability of (s_1, R, s_2) being true is to represent s_1 and s_2 with d-dimensional embeddings h_1 and h_2, and to compute sentence pair features $f(h_1, h_2)$, where f is a composition function (e.g. concatenation, product, ...). A softmax classifier g_θ can learn to predict R with those features. $g_\theta \circ f$ can be seen as a reasoning based on the content of h_1 and h_2 (Socher et al., 2013).

Our contributions are as follows:

- we review composition functions used in textual relational learning and show that they lack expressiveness (section 2);

- we draw analogies with existing SRL models (section 3) and design new compositions inspired from SRL (section 4);

- we perform extensive experiments to test composition functions and show that some of them can improve the learning of representations and their downstream uses (section 6).

2 Composition functions for relation prediction

We review here popular composition functions used for relation prediction based on sentence em-

*Proceedings of the Eighth Joint Conference on Lexical and Computational Semantics (*SEM), pages 33–43*
Minneapolis, June 6–7, 2019. ©2019 Association for Computational Linguistics

beddings. Ideally, they should simultaneously fulfill the following minimal requirements:

- make use of interactions between representations of sentences to relate;

- allow for the learning of asymmetric relations (e.g. entailment, order);

- be usable with high dimensionalities (parameters θ and f should fit in GPU memory).

Additionally, if the main goal is transferable sentence representation learning, compositions should also incentivize gradually changing sentences to lie on a linear manifold, since transfer usually uses linear models. Another goal can be learning of transferable *relation* representation. Concretely, a sentence encoder and f can be trained on a base task, and $f(h_1, h_2)$ can be used as features for transfer in another task. In that case, the geometry of the sentence embedding space is less relevant, as long as the $f(h_1, h_2)$ space works well for transfer learning. Our evaluation will cover both cases.

A straightforward instantiation of f is concatenation (Hooda & Kosseim, 2017):

$$f_{[,]}(h_1, h_2) = [h_1, h_2] \qquad (1)$$

However, *interactions* between s_1 and s_2 cannot be modeled with $f_{[,]}$ followed by a softmax regression. Indeed, $f_{[,]}(h_1, h_2)\theta$ can be rewritten as a sum of independent contributions from h_1 and h_2, namely $\theta_{[0:d]}h_1 + \theta_{[d:2d]}h_2$. Using a multi-layer perceptron before the softmax would solve this issue, but it also harms sentence representation learning (Conneau et al., 2017; Logeswaran et al., 2018), possibly because the perceptron allows for accurate predictions even if the sentence embeddings lie in a convoluted space. To promote interactions between h_1 and h_2, element-wise product has been used in Baudiš et al. (2016):

$$f_\odot(h_1, h_2) = h_1 \odot h_2 \qquad (2)$$

Absolute difference is another solution for sentence similarity (Mueller & Thyagarajan, 2016), and its element-wise variation may equally be used to compute informative features:

$$f_-(h_1, h_2) = |h_1 - h_2| \qquad (3)$$

The latter two were combined into a popular instantiation, sometimes refered as *heuristic matching* (Tai et al., 2015; Kiros et al., 2015; Mou et al., 2016):

$$f_{\odot-}(h_1, h_2) = [h_1 \odot h_2, |h_2 - h_1|] \qquad (4)$$

Although effective for certain similarity tasks, $f_{\odot-}$ is symmetrical, and should be a poor choice for tasks like entailment prediction or prediction of discourse relations. For instance, if R_e denotes entailment and $(s_1, s_2)=$ ("It just rained", "The ground is wet"), (s_1, R_e, s_2) should hold but not (s_2, R_e, s_1). The $f_{\odot-}$ composition function is nonetheless used to train/evaluate models on entailment (Conneau et al., 2017) or discourse relation prediction (Nie et al., 2017).

Sometimes $[h_1, h_2]$ is concatenated to $f_{\odot-}(h_1, h_2)$ (Ampomah et al., 2016; Conneau et al., 2017). While the resulting composition is asymmetrical, the asymmetrical component involves no interaction as noted previously. We note that this composition is very commonly used. On the SNLI benchmark,[1] 12 out of the 25 listed sentence embedding based models use it, and 7 use a weaker form (e.g. omitting $f_\odot$).

The outer product $\otimes$ has been used instead for asymmetric multiplicative interaction (Jernite et al., 2017):

$$f_\otimes(h_1, h_2) = h_1 \otimes h_2 \text{ where } (h_1 \otimes h_2)_{i,j} = h_{1i}h_{2j} \qquad (5)$$

This formulation is expressive but it forces g_θ to have d^2 parameters per relation, which is prohibitive when there are many relations and d is high.

The problems outlined above are well known in SRL. Thus, existing compositions (except $f_\otimes$) can only model relations superficially for tasks currently used to train state of the art sentence encoders, like NLI or discourse connectives prediction.

3 Statistical Relational Learning models

In this section we introduce the context of statistical relational learning (SRL) and relevant models. Recently, SRL has focused on efficient and expressive relation prediction based on embeddings. A core goal of SRL (Getoor & Taskar, 2007) is to induce whether a relation R holds between two arbitrary entities e_1, e_2. As an example, we would like to assign a score to $(e_1, R, e_2) =$ (Paris, LOCATED_IN, France) that reflects a high probability.

---

[1] `nlp.stanford.edu/projects/snli/`, as of February 2019.

Model	Scoring function	Parameters
Unstructured	$\|e_1 - e_2\|_p$	-
TransE	$\|e_1 + w_r - e_2\|_p$	$w_r \in \mathbb{R}^d$
RESCAL	$e_1^T W_r e_2$	$W_r \in \mathbb{R}^{d^2}$
DistMult	$< e_1, w_r, e_2 >$	$w_r \in \mathbb{R}^d$
ComplEx	$\mathrm{Re} < e_1, w_r, \overline{e_2} >$	$w_r \in \mathbb{C}^d$

Table 1: Selected relational learning models. Unstructured is from (Bordes et al., 2013a), TransE from (Bordes et al., 2013b), RESCAL from (Nickel et al., 2011), DistMult from (Yang et al., 2015) and (Trouillon et al., 2016). Following the latter, $< a, b, c >$ denotes $\sum_k a_k b_k c_k$. $\mathrm{Re}(x)$ is the real part of x, and p is commonly set to 1.

In embedding-based SRL models, entities e_i have vector representations in $\mathbb{R}^d$ and a scoring function reflects truth values of relations. The scoring function should allow for relation-dependent reasoning over the latent space of entities. Scoring functions can have relation-specific parameters, which can be interpreted as relation embeddings. Table 1 presents an overview of a number of state of the art relational models. We can distinguish two families of models: subtractive and multiplicative.

The TransE scoring function is motivated by the idea that translations in latent space can model analogical reasoning and hierarchical relationships. Dense word embeddings trained on tasks related to the distributional hypothesis naturally allow for analogical reasoning with translations without explicit supervision (Mikolov et al., 2013). TransE generalizes the older Unstructured model. We call them subtractive models.

The RESCAL, Distmult, and ComplEx scoring functions can be seen as dot product matching between e_1 and a relation-specific linear transformation of e_2 (Liu et al., 2017). This transformation helps checking whether e_1 matches with some aspects of e_2. RESCAL allows a full linear mapping $W_r e_2$ but has a high complexity, while Distmult is restricted to a component-wise weighting $w_r \odot e_2$. ComplEx has fewer parameters than RESCAL but still allows for the modeling of asymmetrical relations. As shown in Liu et al. (2017), ComplEx boils down to a restriction of RESCAL where W_r is a block diagonal matrix. These blocks are 2-dimensional, antisymmetric and have equal diagonal terms. Using such a form, even and odd indexes of e's dimensions play the roles of real and imaginary numbers respectively. The ComplEx model (Trouillon et al., 2016) and its variations

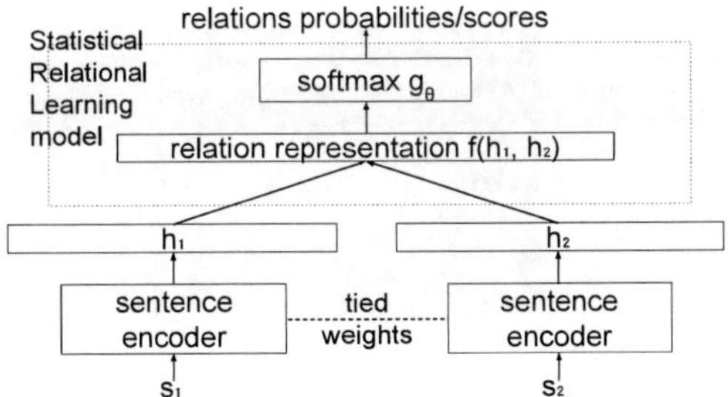

Figure 1: Implicit SRL model in text relation prediction

(Lacroix et al., 2018) yield state of the art performance on knowledge base completion on numerous evaluations.

4 Embeddings composition as SRL models

We claim that several existing models (Conneau et al., 2017; Nie et al., 2017; Baudiš et al., 2016) boil down to SRL models where the sentence embeddings (h_1, h_2) act as entity embeddings (e_1, e_2). This framework is depicted in figure 1. In this article we focus on sentence embeddings, although our framework can straightforwardly be applied to other levels of language granularity (such as words, clauses, or documents).

Some models (Chen et al., 2017b; Seo et al., 2017; Gong et al., 2018; Radford et al., 2018; Devlin et al., 2018) do not rely on explicit sentence encodings to perform relation prediction. They combine information of input sentences at earlier stages, using conditional encoding or cross-attention. There is however no straightforward way to derive transferable sentence representations in this setting, and so these models are out of the scope of this paper. They sometimes make use of composition functions, so our work could still be relevant to them in some respect.

In this section we will make a link between sentence composition functions and SRL scoring functions, and propose new scoring functions drawing inspiration from SRL.

4.1 Linking composition functions and SRL models

The composition function $f_\odot$ from equation 2 followed by a softmax regression yields a score whose analytical form is identical to the Distmult model score described in section 3. Let θ_R denote the softmax weights for relation R. The logit score for the truth of (s_1, R, s_2) is $f(h_1, h_2)\theta_R =$

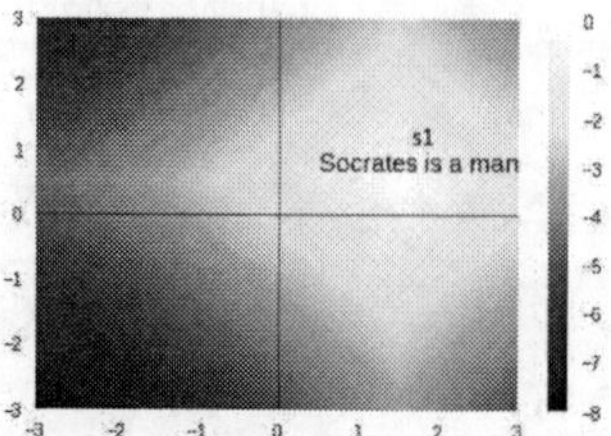

(a) Score map of $(s_1, R_{to\_the\_past}, s_2)$ over possible sentences s_2 using Unstructured composition.

(b) Score map of $(s_1, R_{to\_the\_past}, s_2)$ over possible sentences s_2 using TransE composition.

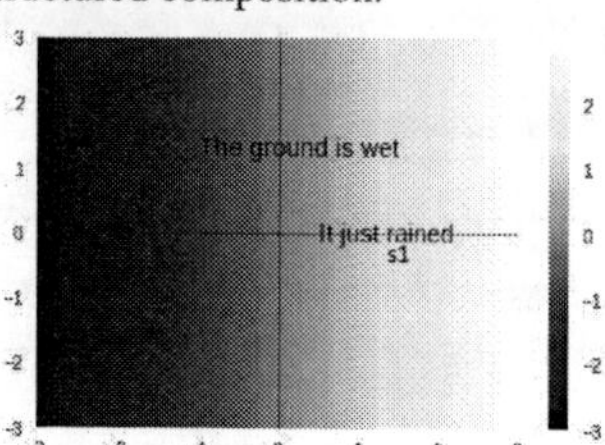

(c) Score map of $(s_1, R_{entailment}, s_2)$ over possible sentences s_2 using DistMult composition.

(d) Score map of $(s_1, R_{entailment}, s_2)$ over possible sentences s_2 using ComplEx composition.

Figure 2: Possible scoring function values according to different composition functions. s_1 and R are fixed and color brightness reflects likelihood of (s_1, R, s_2) for each position of embedding s_2. (b) and (d) are respectively more expressive than (a) and (c).

$(h_1 \odot h_2)\theta_R$ which is equal to the Distmult scoring function $< h_1, \theta_R, h_2 >$ if h_1, h_2 act as entities embeddings and θ_R as the relation weight w_R .

Similarly, the composition f_- from equation 3 followed by a softmax regression can be seen as an element-wise weighted score of Unstructured (both are equal if softmax weights are all unitary).

Thus, $f_{\odot-}$ from 4 (with softmax regression) can be seen as a weighted ensemble of Unstructured and Distmult. These two models are respectively outperformed by TransE and ComplEx on knowledge base link prediction by a large margin (Trouillon et al., 2016; Bordes et al., 2013a). We therefore propose to change the Unstructured and Distmult in $f_{\odot-}$ such that they match their respective state of the art variations in the following sections. We will also show the implications of these refinements.

4.2 Casting TransE as a composition

Simply replacing $|h_2 - h_1|$ with

$$f_t(h_1, h_2) = |h_2 - h_1 + t|, \text{ where } t \in \mathbb{R}^d \quad (6)$$

would make the model analogous to TransE. t is learned and is shared by all relations. A relation-specific translation t_R could be used but it would make f relation-specific. Instead, here, each dimension of $f_t(h_1, h_2)$ can be weighted according to a given relation. Non-zero t makes f_t asymmetrical and also yields features that allow for the checking of an analogy between s_1 and s_2. Sentence embeddings often rely on pre-trained word embeddings which have demonstrated strong capabilities for analogical reasoning. Some analogies, such as *part-whole*, are computable with off-the-shelf word embeddings (Chen et al., 2017a) and should be very informative for natural language inference tasks. As an illustration, let us consider an artificial semantic space (depicted in figures 2a and 2b) where we posit that there is a "to the past" translation t so that $h_1 + t$ is the embedding of a sentence s_1 changed to the past tense. Unstructured is not able to leverage this semantic space to correctly score $(s_1, R_{to\_the\_past}, s_2)$ while TransE is well tailored to provide highest scores for sentences near $h_1 + \hat{t}$ where $\hat{t}$ is an estimation of t that could be learned from examples.

4.3 Casting ComplEx as a composition

Let us partition h dimensions into two equally sized sets $\mathcal{R}$ and $\mathcal{I}$, e.g. even and odd dimension indices of h. We propose a new function $f_\mathbb{C}$ as a way to fit the ComplEx scoring function into a composition function.

$$f_\mathbb{C}(h_1, h_2) = [h_1^\mathcal{R} \odot h_2^\mathcal{R} + h_1^\mathcal{I} \odot h_2^\mathcal{I},$$
$$h_1^\mathcal{R} \odot h_2^\mathcal{I} - h_1^\mathcal{I} \odot h_2^\mathcal{R}] \quad (7)$$

$f_{\mathbb{C}}(h_1, h_2)$ multiplied by softmax weights θ_r is equivalent to the ComplEx scoring function $\mathrm{Re} < h_1, \theta_r, \overline{h_2} >$. The first half of θ_r weights corresponds to the real part of ComplEx relation weights while the last half corresponds to the imaginary part.

$f_{\mathbb{C}}$ is to the ComplEx scoring function what $f_{\odot}$ is to the DistMult scoring function. Intuitively, ComplEx is a minimal way to model interactions between distinct latent dimensions while Distmult only allows for identical dimensions to interact.

Let us consider a new artificial semantic space (shown in figures 2c and 2d) where the first dimension is high when a sentence means that it just rained, and the second dimension is high when the ground is wet. Over this semantic space, Distmult is only able to detect entailment for paraphrases whereas ComplEx is also able to naturally model that ("it just rained", $R_{entailment}$, "the ground is wet") should be high while its converse should not.

We also propose two more general versions of $f_{\mathbb{C}}$:

$$f_{\mathbb{C}^\alpha}(h_1, h_2) = [h_1^{\mathcal{R}} \odot h_2^{\mathcal{R}}, h_1^{\mathcal{I}} \odot h_2^{\mathcal{I}}, \\ h_1^{\mathcal{R}} \odot h_2^{\mathcal{I}} - h_1^{\mathcal{I}} \odot h_2^{\mathcal{R}}] \qquad (8)$$

$$f_{\mathbb{C}^\beta}(h_1, h_2) = [h_1^{\mathcal{R}} \odot h_2^{\mathcal{R}}, h_1^{\mathcal{I}} \odot h_2^{\mathcal{I}}, \\ h_1^{\mathcal{R}} \odot h_2^{\mathcal{I}}, h_1^{\mathcal{I}} \odot h_2^{\mathcal{R}}] \qquad (9)$$

$f_{\mathbb{C}^\alpha}$ can be seen as Distmult concatenated with the asymmetrical part of ComplEx and $f_{\mathbb{C}^\beta}$ can be seen as RESCAL with unconstrained block diagonal relation matrices.

5 On the evaluation of relational models

The SentEval framework (Conneau et al., 2017) provides a general evaluation for transferable sentence representations, with open source evaluation code. One only needs to specify a sentence encoder function, and the framework performs classification tasks or relation prediction tasks using cross-validated logistic regression on embeddings or composed sentence embeddings. Tasks include sentiment analysis, entailment, textual similarity, textual relatedness, and paraphrase detection. These tasks are a rich way to train or evaluate sentence representations since in a triple (s_1, R, s_2), we can see (R, s_2) as a label for s_1 (Baudiš et al., 2016). Unfortunately, the relational tasks hard-code the composition function

from equation 4. From our previous analysis, we believe this composition function favors the use of contextual/lexical similarity rather than high-level reasoning and can penalize representations based on more semantic aspects. This bias could harm research since semantic representation is an important next step for sentence embedding. Training/evaluation datasets are also arguably flawed with respect to relational aspects since several recent studies (Dasgupta et al., 2018; Poliak et al., 2018; Gururangan et al., 2018; Glockner et al., 2018) show that InferSent, despite being state of the art on SentEval evaluation tasks, has poor performance when dealing with asymmetrical tasks and non-additive composition of words. In addition to providing new ways of training sentence encoders, we will also extend the SentEval evaluation framework with a more expressive composition function when dealing with relational transfer tasks, which improves results even when the sentence encoder was not trained with it.

6 Experiments

Our goal is to show that transferable sentence representation learning and relation prediction tasks can be improved when our expressive compositions are used instead of the composition from equation 4. We train our relational model adaptations on two relation prediction base tasks ($\mathcal{T}$), one supervised ($\mathcal{T} = NLI$) and one unsupervised ($\mathcal{T} = Disc$) described below, and evaluate sentence/relation representations on base and transfer tasks using the SentEval framework in order to quantify the generalization capabilities of our models. Since we use minor modifications of InferSent and SentEval, our experiments are easily reproducible.

6.1 Training tasks

Natural language inference ($\mathcal{T} = NLI$)'s goal is to predict whether the relation between two sentences (premise and hypothesis) is *Entailment*, *Contradiction* or *Neutral*. We use the combination of SNLI dataset (Bowman et al., 2015) and MNLI dataset (Williams et al., 2018). We call *AllNLI* the resulting dataset of $1M$ examples. Conneau et al. (2017) claim that NLI data allows universal sentence representation learning. They used the $f_{\odot,-}$ composition function with concatenated sentence representations in order to train their *Infersent* model.

name	N	task	C	representation(s) used
MR	11k	sentiment (movies)	2	h_1
SUBJ	10k	subjectivity/objectivity	2	h_1
MPQA	11k	opinion polarity	2	h_1
TREC	6k	question-type	6	h_1
SICK_s^m	10k	NLI	3	$f_{m,s}(h_1, h_2)$
MRPC_s^m	4k	paraphrase detection	2	$(f_{m,s}(h_1, h_2) + (f_{m,s}(h_2, h_1))/2$
PDTB_s^m	17k	discursive relation	5	$f_{m,s}(h_1, h_2)$
STS14	4.5k	similarity	-	$\cos(h_1, h_2)$

Table 2: Transfer evaluation tasks. N = number of training examples; C = number of classes if applicable. h_1, h_2 are sentence representations, $f_{m,s}$ a composition function from section 4.

We also train on the prediction of discourse connectives between sentences/clauses ($\mathcal{T} = Disc$). Discourse connectives make discourse relations between sentences explicit. In the sentence *I live in Paris but I'm often elsewhere*, the word *but* highlights that there is a contrast between the two clauses it connects. We use Malmi et al.'s (2018) dataset of selected $400k$ instances with 20 discourse connectives (e.g. *however, for example*) with the provided train/dev/test split. This dataset has no other supervision than the list of 20 connectives. Nie et al. (2017) used $f_{\odot,-}$ concatenated with the sum of sentence representations to train their model, *DisSent*, on a similar task and showed that their encoder was general enough to perform well on SentEval tasks. They use a dataset that is, at the time of writing, not publicly available.

6.2 Evaluation tasks

Table 2 provides an overview of different transfer tasks that will be used for evaluation. We added another relation prediction task, the PDTB coarse-grained implicit discourse relation task, to SentEval. This task involves predicting a discursive link between two sentences among {Comparison, Contingency, Entity based coherence, Expansion, Temporal}. We followed the setup of Pitler et al. (2009), without sampling negative examples in training. MRPC, PDTB and SICK will be tested with two composition functions: besides SentEval composition $f_{\odot,-}$, we will use $f_{\mathbb{C}^\beta,-}$ for transfer learning evaluation, since it has the most general multiplicative interaction and it does not penalize models that do not learn a translation. For all tasks except STS14, a cross-validated logistic regression is used on the sentence or relation representation. The evaluation of the STS14 task relies on Pearson or Spearman correlation between cosine similarity and the target. We force the composition function to be symmetrical on the MRPC task since paraphrase detection should be invariant to permutation of input sentences.

6.3 Setup

We want to compare the different instances of f. We follow the setup of Infersent (Conneau et al., 2017): we learn to encode sentences into h with a bi-directional LSTM using element-wise max pooling over time. The dimension size of h is 4096. Word embeddings are fixed GloVe with 300 dimensions, trained on Common Crawl 840B.[2] Optimization is done with SGD and decreasing learning rate until convergence.

The only difference with regard to Infersent is the composition. Sentences are composed with six different compositions for training according to the following template:

$$f_{m,s,1,2}(h_1, h_2) = [f_m(h_1, h_2), f_s(h_1, h_2), h_1, h_2] \tag{10}$$

f_s (subtractive interaction) is in $\{f_-, f_t\}$, f_m (multiplicative interaction) is in $\{f_\odot, f_{\mathbb{C}^\alpha}, f_{\mathbb{C}^\beta}\}$. We do not consider $f_{\mathbb{C}}$ since it yielded inferior results in our early experiments using NLI and SentEval development sets.

$f_{m,s,1,2}(h_1, h_2)$ is fed directly to a softmax regression. Note that Infersent uses a multi-layer perceptron before the softmax, but uses only linear activations, so $f_{\odot,-,1,2}(h_1, h_2)$ is analytically equivalent to Infersent when $\mathcal{T} = NLI$.

6.4 Results

Having run several experiments with different initializations, the standard deviations between them do not seem to be negligible. We decided to take these into account when reporting scores, contrary to previous work (Kiros et al., 2015; Conneau et al., 2017): we average the scores of 6 distinct runs for each task and use standard deviations

---

[2] https://nlp.stanford.edu/projects/glove/

m,s	MR	SUBJ	MPQA	TREC	MRPC$^{\odot}$	PDTB$^{\odot}$	SICK$^{\odot}$	STS14	$\mathcal{T}$	AVG
			Models trained on natural language inference ($\mathcal{T} = NLI$)							
$\odot, -$	81.2	92.7	90.4	89.6	76.1	46.7	86.6	69.5	84.2	79.1
$\alpha, -$	**81.4**	**92.8**	90.5	89.6	75.4	46.6	86.7	69.5	84.3	79.1
$\beta, -$	81.2	92.6	90.5	89.6	76	46.5	86.6	69.5	84.2	79.1
$\odot, t$	81.1	92.7	90.5	**89.7**	**76.5**	46.4	86.5	**70.0**	**84.8**	**79.2**
α, t	81.3	92.6	**90.6**	89.2	76.2	47.2	86.5	**70.0**	84.6	**79.2**
β, t	81.2	92.7	90.4	88.5	75.8	**47.3**	**86.8**	69.8	84.2	79.1

Table 3: SentEval and base task evaluation results for the models trained on natural language inference ($\mathcal{T} = NLI$); AllNLI is used for training. All scores are accuracy percentages, except STS14, which is Pearson correlation percentage. AVG denotes the average of the SentEval scores.

m,s	MR	SUBJ	MPQA	TREC	MRPC$^{\odot}$	PDTB$^{\odot}$	SICK$^{\odot}$	STS14	$\mathcal{T}$	AVG
			Models trained on discourse connective prediction ($\mathcal{T} = Disc$)							
$\odot, -$	**80.4**	92.7	90.2	89.5	74.5	47.3	83.2	57.9	35.7	77
$\alpha, -$	**80.4**	**92.9**	90.2	90.2	75	47.9	83.3	57.8	35.9	77.2
$\beta, -$	80.2	92.8	90.2	88.4	74.9	47.5	82.9	57.7	35.9	76.8
$\odot, t$	80.2	92.8	90.2	**90.4**	74.6	**48.5**	83.4	**58.6**	**36.1**	**77.3**
α, t	80.2	**92.9**	**90.3**	90.3	**75.1**	47.8	83.2	58.3	**36.1**	**77.3**
β, t	80.2	92.8	**90.3**	89.7	74.4	47.9	**83.7**	58.2	35.7	77.2

Table 4: SentEval and base task evaluation results for the models trained on discourse connective prediction ($\mathcal{T} = Disc$). All scores are accuracy percentages, except STS14, which is Pearson correlation percentage. AVG denotes the average of the SentEval scores.

under normality assumption to compute significance. Table 3 shows model scores for $\mathcal{T} = NLI$, while Table 4 shows scores for $\mathcal{T} = Disc$. For comparison, Table 5 shows a number of important models from previous work. Finally, in Table 6, we present results for sentence relation tasks that use an alternative composition function ($f_{\mathbb{C}^\beta, -}$) instead of the standard composition function used in SentEval.

For sentence representation learning, the baseline, $f_{\odot -}$ composition already performs rather well, being on par with the InferSent scores of the original paper, as would be expected. However, macro-averaging all accuracies, it is the second worst performing model. $f_{\mathbb{C}^\alpha, t, 1, 2}$ is the best performing model, and all three best models use the translation ($s = t$). On relational transfer tasks, training with $f_{\mathbb{C}^\alpha, t, 1, 2}$ and using complex $\mathbb{C}^\beta$ for transfer (Table 6) always outperforms the baseline ($f_{\odot, -, 1, 2}$ with $\odot -$ composition in Tables 3 and 4). Averaging accuracies of those transfer tasks, this result is significant for both training tasks at level $p < 0.05$ (using Bonferroni correction accounting for the 5 comparisons). On base tasks and the average of non-relational transfer tasks (MR, MPQA, SUBJ, TREC), our proposed compositions are on average slightly better than $f_{\odot, -, 1, 2}$. Representations learned with our proposed compositions can still be compared with simple cosine similarity: all three methods using the translational composition ($s = t$) very significantly outperform the baseline (significant at level $p < 0.01$ with Bonferroni correction) on STS14 for $\mathcal{T} = NLI$. Thus, we believe $f_{\mathbb{C}^\alpha, t, 1, 2}$ has more robust results and could be a better default choice than $f_{\odot, -, 1, 2}$ as composition for representation learning. [3]

Additionally, using $\mathbb{C}^\beta$ (Table 6) instead of $\odot$ (Tables 3 and 4) for transfer learning in relational transfer tasks (PDTB, MRPC, SICK) yields a significant improvement on average, even when $m = \odot$ was used for training ($p < 0.001$). Therefore, we believe $f_{\mathbb{C}^\beta, -}$ is an interesting composition for inference or evaluation of models regardless of how they were trained.

7 Related work

There are numerous interactions between SRL and NLP. We believe that our framework merges two specific lines of work: relation prediction and modeling textual relational tasks.

Some previous NLP work focused on composition functions for relation prediction between

---

[3]Note that our compositions are also beneficial with regard to convergence speed: on average, each of our proposed compositions needed less epochs to converge than the baseline $f_{\odot, -, 1, 2}$, for both training tasks.

Comparison models								
model	MR	SUBJ	MPQA	TREC	MRPC$^{\odot}$	PDTB$^{\odot}$	SICK$^{\odot}$	STS14	AVG
Infersent	81.1	92.4	90.2	88.2	76.2	46.7-	86.3	70	78.9
SkipT	76.5	93.6	87.1	92.2	73	-	82.3	29	-
BoW	77.2	91.2	87.9	83	72.2	43.9	78.4	54.6	73.6

Table 5: Comparison models from previous work. InferSent represents the original results from Conneau et al. (2017), SkipT is SkipThought from Kiros et al. (2015), and BoW is our re-evaluation of GloVe Bag of Words from Conneau et al. (2017). AVG denotes the average of the SentEval scores..

	$\mathcal{T} = Disc$				$\mathcal{T} = NLI$			
m,s	MRPC$^{\beta}$	PDTB$^{\beta}$	SICK$^{\beta}$	AVG	MRPC$^{\beta}$	PDTB$^{\beta}$	SICK$^{\beta}$	AVG
$\odot, -$	74.8	48.2	83.6	68.9	**76.2**	47.2	86.9	70.1
$\alpha, -$	74.9	**49.3**	83.8	**69.3**	75.9	47.1	86.9	70
$\beta, -$	75	48.8	83.4	69.1	75.8	47	87	69.9
$\odot, t$	74.9	48.7	83.6	69.1	**76.2**	**47.8**	86.8	70.3
α, t	**75.2**	48.6	83.5	69.1	**76.2**	47.6	**87.3**	**70.4**
β, t	74.6	48.9	**83.9**	69.1	**76.2**	**47.8**	87	70.3

Table 6: Results for sentence relation tasks using an alternative composition function ($f_{\mathbb{C}^{\beta}, -}$) during evaluation. AVG denotes the average of the three tasks.

text fragments, even though they ignored SRL and only dealt with word units. Word2vec (Mikolov et al., 2013) has sparked a great interest for this task with word analogies in the latent space. Levy & Goldberg (2014) explored different scoring functions between words, notably for analogies. Hypernymy relations were also studied, by Chang et al. (2018) and Fu et al. (2014). Levy et al. (2015) proposed tailored scoring functions. Even the skipgram model (Mikolov et al., 2013) can be formulated as finding relations between context and target words. We did not empirically explore textual relational learning at the word level, but we believe that it would fit in our framework, and could be tested in future studies. Numerous approaches (Chen et al., 2017b; Seok et al., 2016; Gong et al., 2018; Joshi et al., 2019) were proposed to predict inference relations between sentences, but don't explicitly use sentence embeddings. Instead, they encode sentences jointly, possibly with the help of previously cited word compositions, therefore it would also be interesting to try applying our techniques within their framework.

Some modeling aspects of textual relational learning have been formally investigated by Baudiš et al. (2016). They noticed the genericity of relational problems and explored multi-task and transfer learning on relational tasks. Their work is complementary to ours since their framework unifies tasks while ours unifies composition func-

tions. Subsequent approaches use relational tasks for training and evaluation on specific datasets (Conneau et al., 2017; Nie et al., 2017).

8 Conclusion

We have demonstrated that a number of existing models used for textual relational learning rely on composition functions that are already used in Statistical Relational Learning. By taking into account previous insights from SRL, we proposed new composition functions and evaluated them. These composition functions are all simple to implement and we hope that it will become standard to try them on relational problems. Larger scale data might leverage these more expressive compositions, as well as more compositional, asymmetric, and arguably more realistic datasets (Dasgupta et al., 2018; Gururangan et al., 2018). Finally, our compositions can also be helpful to improve interpretability of embeddings, since they can help measure relation prediction asymmetry. Analogies through translations helped interpreting word embeddings, and perhaps anlyzing our learned t translation could help interpreting sentence embeddings.

References

Isaac K E Ampomah, Seong-bae Park, and Sang-jo Lee. A Sentence-to-Sentence Relation Network for Recognizing Textual Entailment. *World Academy of Science, Engineering and Technology International Journal of Computer and Information Engineering*, 10(12):1955–1958, 2016.

Petr Baudiš, Jan Pichl, Tomáš Vyskočil, and Jan Šedivý. Sentence Pair Scoring: Towards Unified Framework for Text Comprehension. 2016. URL http://arxiv.org/abs/1603.06127.

Antoine Bordes, Xavier Glorot, Jason Weston, and Yoshua Bengio. A Semantic Matching Energy Function for Learning with Multi-relational Data. *Machine Learning*, 2013a. ISSN 0885-6125. doi: 10.1007/s10994-013-5363-6. URL http://arxiv.org/abs/1301.3485.

Antoine Bordes, Nicolas Usunier, Jason Weston, and Oksana Yakhnenko. Translating Embeddings for Modeling Multi-Relational Data. *Advances in NIPS*, 26:2787–2795, 2013b. ISSN 10495258. doi: 10.1007/s13398-014-0173-7.2.

Samuel R Bowman, Gabor Angeli, Christopher Potts, and Christopher D Manning. A large annotated corpus for learning natural language inference. *Proceedings of the 2015 Conference on Empirical Methods in Natural Language Processing, Lisbon, Portugal, 17-21 September 2015*, (September):632–642, 2015. ISSN 9781941643327.

Haw-Shiuan Chang, Ziyun Wang, Luke Vilnis, and Andrew McCallum. Distributional inclusion vector embedding for unsupervised hypernymy detection. In *Proceedings of the 2018 Conference of the North American Chapter of the Association for Computational Linguistics: Human Language Technologies, Volume 1 (Long Papers)*, pp. 485–495, New Orleans, Louisiana, June 2018. Association for Computational Linguistics. doi: 10.18653/v1/N18-1045. URL https://www.aclweb.org/anthology/N18-1045.

Dawn Chen, Joshua C. Peterson, and Tom Griffiths. Evaluating vector-space models of analogy. In *Proceedings of the 39th Annual Meeting of the Cognitive Science Society, CogSci 2017, London, UK, 16-29 July 2017*, 2017a. URL https://mindmodeling.org/cogsci2017/papers/0340/index.html.

Qian Chen, Xiaodan Zhu, Zhen-Hua Ling, Si Wei, Hui Jiang, and Diana Inkpen. Enhanced lstm for natural language inference. In Regina Barzilay and Min-Yen Kan (eds.), *ACL (1)*, pp. 1657–1668. Association for Computational Linguistics, 2017b. ISBN 978-1-945626-75-3. URL http://dblp.uni-trier.de/db/conf/acl/acl2017-1.html#ChenZLWJI17.

Alexis Conneau, Douwe Kiela, Holger Schwenk, Loic Barrault, and Antoine Bordes. Supervised Learning of Universal Sentence Representations from Natural Language Inference Data. *Emnlp*, 2017.

Ishita Dasgupta, Demi Guo, Andreas Stuhlmüller, Samuel J. Gershman, and Noah D. Goodman. Evaluating Compositionality in Sentence Embeddings. (2011), 2018. URL http://arxiv.org/abs/1802.04302.

Jacob Devlin, Ming-Wei Chang, Kenton Lee, and Kristina Toutanova. Bert: Pre-training of deep bidirectional transformers for language understanding. *arXiv preprint arXiv:1810.04805*, 2018.

Ruiji Fu, Jiang Guo, Bing Qin, Wanxiang Che, Haifeng Wang, and Ting Liu. Learning semantic hierarchies via word embeddings. In *Proceedings of the 52nd Annual Meeting of the Association for Computational Linguistics (Volume 1: Long Papers)*, pp. 1199–1209, Baltimore, Maryland, June 2014. Association for Computational Linguistics. doi: 10.3115/v1/P14-1113. URL https://www.aclweb.org/anthology/P14-1113.

Lise Getoor and Ben Taskar. *Introduction to Statistical Relational Learning (Adaptive Computation and Machine Learning)*. The MIT Press, 2007. ISBN 0262072882.

Max Glockner, Vered Shwartz, and Yoav Goldberg. Breaking NLI Systems with Sentences that Require Simple Lexical Inferences. *Proceedings of the 56th Annual Meeting of the Association for Computational Linguistics (Short Papers)*, (3):1–6, 2018. URL http://arxiv.org/abs/1805.02266.

Yichen Gong, Heng Luo, and Jian Zhang. Natural language inference over interaction space. In *International Conference on Learning Representations*, 2018. URL https://openreview.net/forum?id=r1dHXnH6-.

Suchin Gururangan, Swabha Swayamdipta, Omer Levy, Roy Schwartz, Samuel Bowman, and Noah A. Smith. Annotation artifacts in natural language inference data. In *Proceedings of the 2018 Conference of the North American Chapter of the Association for Computational Linguistics: Human Language Technologies, Volume 2 (Short Papers)*, pp. 107–112, New Orleans, Louisiana, June 2018. Association for Computational Linguistics. doi: 10.18653/v1/N18-2017. URL https://www.aclweb.org/anthology/N18-2017.

Sohail Hooda and Leila Kosseim. Argument labeling of explicit discourse relations using lstm neural networks. In *Proceedings of the International Conference Recent Advances in Natural Language Processing, RANLP 2017*, pp. 309–315, Varna, Bulgaria, September 2017. INCOMA Ltd. doi: 10.26615/978-954-452-049-6_042. URL https://doi.org/10.26615/978-954-452-049-6_042.

Yacine Jernite, Samuel R. Bowman, and David Sontag. Discourse-Based Objectives for Fast Unsupervised Sentence Representation Learning. 2017. URL http://arxiv.org/abs/1705.00557.

Mandar Joshi, Eunsol Choi, Omer Levy, Daniel S. Weld, and Luke Zettlemoyer. pair2vec: Compositional word-pair embeddings for cross-sentence inference. In *NAACL*, 2019. URL http://arxiv.org/abs/1810.08854.

Ryan Kiros, Yukun Zhu, Ruslan R Salakhutdinov, Richard Zemel, Raquel Urtasun, Antonio Torralba, and Sanja Fidler. Skip-thought vectors. In *Advances in neural information processing systems*, pp. 3294–3302, 2015.

Timothée Lacroix, Nicolas Usunier, and Guillaume Obozinski. Canonical tensor decomposition for knowledge base completion. In *ICML*, 2018.

Omer Levy and Yoav Goldberg. Linguistic Regularities in Sparse and Explicit Word Representations. *Proceedings of the Eighteenth Conference on Computational Natural Language Learning*, pp. 171–180, 2014. doi: 10.3115/v1/W14-1618. URL http://aclweb.org/anthology/W14-1618.

Omer Levy, Steffen Remus, Chris Biemann, and Ido Dagan. Do Supervised Distributional Methods Really Learn Lexical Inference Relations? *Naacl-2015*, pp. 970–976, 2015. URL http://www.aclweb.org/anthology/N/N15/N15-1098.pdf.

Hanxiao Liu, Yuexin Wu, and Yiming Yang. Analogical Inference for Multi-Relational Embeddings. *Icml*, 2017. ISSN 1938-7228. URL http://arxiv.org/abs/1705.02426.

Lajanugen Logeswaran, Honglak Lee, and Dragomir Radev. Sentence Ordering using Recurrent Neural Networks. pp. 1–15, 2016. URL http://arxiv.org/abs/1611.02654.

Lajanugen Logeswaran, Honglak Lee, and Dragomir R. Radev. Sentence ordering and coherence modeling using recurrent neural networks. In *Proceedings of the Thirty-Second AAAI Conference on Artificial Intelligence, (AAAI-18), the 30th innovative Applications of Artificial Intelligence (IAAI-18), and the 8th AAAI Symposium on Educational Advances in Artificial Intelligence (EAAI-18), New Orleans, Louisiana, USA, February 2-7, 2018*, pp. 5285–5292, 2018. URL https://www.aaai.org/ocs/index.php/AAAI/AAAI18/paper/view/17011.

Eric Malmi, Daniele Pighin, Sebastian Krause, and Mikhail Kozhevnikov. Automatic prediction of discourse connectives. In *Proceedings of the 11th Language Resources and Evaluation Conference*, Miyazaki, Japan, May 2018. European Language Resource Association. URL https://www.aclweb.org/anthology/L18-1260.

Tomas Mikolov, Kai Chen, Greg Corrado, and Jeffrey Dean. Distributed Representations of Words and Phrases and their Compositionality. *Nips*, pp. 1–9, 2013. ISSN 10495258. doi: 10.1162/jmlr.2003.3.4-5.951.

Lili Mou, Rui Men, Ge Li, Yan Xu, Lu Zhang, Rui Yan, and Zhi Jin. Natural language inference by tree-based convolution and heuristic matching. In *Proceedings of the 54th Annual Meeting of the Association for Computational Linguistics (Volume 2: Short Papers)*, pp. 130–136, Berlin, Germany, August 2016. Association for Computational Linguistics. doi: 10.18653/v1/P16-2022. URL https://www.aclweb.org/anthology/P16-2022.

Jonas Mueller and Aditya Thyagarajan. Siamese Recurrent Architectures for Learning Sentence Similarity. In *AAAI*, pp. 2786–2792, 2016.

Maximilian Nickel, Volker Tresp, and Hans-Peter Kriegel. A Three-Way Model for Collective Learning on Multi-Relational Data. *Icml*, pp. 809—-816, 2011.

Allen Nie, Erin D. Bennett, and Noah D. Goodman. DisSent: Sentence Representation Learning from Explicit Discourse Relations. 2017. URL http://arxiv.org/abs/1710.04334.

Emily Pitler, Annie Louis, and Ani Nenkova. Automatic sense prediction for implicit discourse relations in text. *Proceedings of the Joint Conference of the 47th Annual Meeting of the ACL and the 4th International Joint Conference on Natural Language Processing of the AFNLP Volume 2 ACLIJCNLP 09*, 2(August):683–691, 2009. doi: 10.3115/1690219.1690241. URL http://www.aclweb.org/anthology/P/P09/P09-1077.

Adam Poliak, Jason Naradowsky, Aparajita Haldar, Rachel Rudinger, and Benjamin Van Durme. Hypothesis Only Baselines in Natural Language Inference. *Proceedings of the 7th Joint Conference on Lexical and Computational Semantics*, (1):180–191, 2018.

Alec Radford, Karthik Narasimhan, Tim Salimans, and Ilya Sutskever. Improving language understanding by generative pre-training. https://www.cs.ubc.ca/~amuham01/LING530/papers/radford2018improving.pdf, 2018.

Min Joon Seo, Aniruddha Kembhavi, Ali Farhadi, and Hannaneh Hajishirzi. Bidirectional attention flow for machine comprehension. In *5th International Conference on Learning Representations, ICLR 2017, Toulon, France, April 24-26, 2017, Conference Track Proceedings*, 2017. URL https://openreview.net/forum?id=HJ0UKP9ge.

Miran Seok, Hye-Jeong Song, Chan-Young Park, Jong-Dae Kim, and Yu-Seop Kim. Named Entity Recognition using Word Embedding as a Feature 1. *International Journal of Software Engineering and Its Applications*, 10(2):93–104, 2016.

ISSN 1738-9984. doi: 10.14257/ijseia.2016.10.2.08. URL http://dx.doi.org/10.14257/ijseia.2016.10.2.08.

Richard Socher, Danqi Chen, Christopher Manning, Danqi Chen, and Andrew Ng. Reasoning With Neural Tensor Networks for Knowledge Base Completion. In *Neural Information Processing Systems (2003)*, pp. 926–934, 2013. URL https://nlp.stanford.edu/pubs/SocherChenManningNg{_}NIPS2013.pdf.

Kai Sheng Tai, Richard Socher, and Christopher D. Manning. Improved semantic representations from tree-structured long short-term memory networks. In *Proceedings of the 53rd Annual Meeting of the Association for Computational Linguistics and the 7th International Joint Conference on Natural Language Processing of the Asian Federation of Natural Language Processing, ACL 2015, July 26-31, 2015, Beijing, China, Volume 1: Long Papers*, pp. 1556–1566, 2015. URL http://aclweb.org/anthology/P/P15/P15-1150.pdf.

Théo Trouillon, Johannes Welbl, Sebastian Riedel, Éric Gaussier, and Guillaume Bouchard. Complex Embeddings for Simple Link Prediction. In *Proceedings of the 33nd International Conference on Machine Learning*, volume 48, 2016. ISBN 9781510829008. URL http://arxiv.org/abs/1606.06357.

Adina Williams, Nikita Nangia, and Samuel Bowman. A broad-coverage challenge corpus for sentence understanding through inference. In *Proceedings of the 2018 Conference of the North American Chapter of the Association for Computational Linguistics: Human Language Technologies, Volume 1 (Long Papers)*, pp. 1112–1122, New Orleans, Louisiana, June 2018. Association for Computational Linguistics. doi: 10.18653/v1/N18-1101. URL https://www.aclweb.org/anthology/N18-1101.

Min Chul Yang, Do Gil Lee, So Young Park, and Hae Chang Rim. Knowledge-based question answering using the semantic embedding space. *Expert Systems with Applications*, 42(23):9086–9104, 2015. ISSN 09574174. doi: 10.1016/j.eswa.2015.07.009. URL http://dx.doi.org/10.1016/j.eswa.2015.07.009.

Multi-Label Transfer Learning for Multi-Relational Semantic Similarity

Li Zhang and **Steven R. Wilson** and **Rada Mihalcea**
Computer Science and Engineering
University of Michigan
{zharry, steverw, mihalcea}@umich.edu

Abstract

Multi-relational semantic similarity datasets define the semantic relations between two short texts in multiple ways, e.g., similarity, relatedness, and so on. Yet, all the systems to date designed to capture such relations target one relation at a time. We propose a multi-label transfer learning approach based on LSTM to make predictions for several relations simultaneously and aggregate the losses to update the parameters. This multi-label regression approach jointly learns the information provided by the multiple relations, rather than treating them as separate tasks. Not only does this approach outperform the single-task approach and the traditional multi-task learning approach, it also achieves state-of-the-art performance on all but one relation of the Human Activity Phrase dataset.

1 Introduction

Semantic similarity, or relating short texts or sentences[1] in a semantic space – be those phrases, sentences or short paragraphs – is a task that requires systems to determine the degree of equivalence between the underlying semantics of the two sentences. Although relatively easy for humans, this task remains one of the most difficult natural language understanding problems. The task has been receiving significant interest from the research community. For instance, from 2012 to 2017, the International Workshop on Semantic Evaluation (SemEval) has been holding the Semantic Textual Similarity (STS) shared tasks (Agirre et al., 2012, 2013b, 2015, 2016; Cer et al., 2017), dedicated to tackling this problem, with close to 100 team submissions each year.

In some semantic similarity datasets, an example consists of a sentence pair and a single annotated similarity score, while in others, each pair comes with multiple annotations. We refer to the latter as *multi-relational semantic similarity* tasks. The inclusion of multiple annotations per example is motivated by the fact that there can be different relations, namely different types of similarity between two sentences. So far, these relations have been treated as separate tasks, where a model trains and tests on one relation at a time while ignoring the rest. However, we hypothesize that each relation may contain useful information about the others, and training on only one relation inevitably neglects some relevant information. Thus, training jointly on multiple relations may improve performance on one or more relations.

We propose a joint **multi-label** transfer learning setting based on LSTM, and show that it can be an effective solution for the multi-relational semantic similarity tasks. Due to the small size of multi-relational semantic similarity datasets and the recent success of LSTM-based sentence representations (Wieting and Gimpel, 2018; Conneau et al., 2017), the model is pre-trained on a large corpus and transfer learning is applied using fine-tuning. In our setting, the network is jointly trained on multiple relations by outputting multiple predictions (one for each relation) and aggregating the losses during back-propagation. This is different from the traditional multi-task learning setting where the model makes one prediction at a time, switching between the tasks. We treat the multi-task setting and the single-task setting (i.e., where a separate model is learned for each relation) as baselines, and show that the multi-label setting outperforms them in many cases, achieving state-of-the-art performance on all but one relation of the Human Activity Phrase dataset (Wilson and Mihalcea, 2017).

In addition to success on multi-relational semantic similarity tasks, the multi-label transfer learning setting that we propose can easily be

---

[1] In this work, we do not consider word level similarity.

*Proceedings of the Eighth Joint Conference on Lexical and Computational Semantics (*SEM)*, pages 44–50
Minneapolis, June 6–7, 2019. ©2019 Association for Computational Linguistics

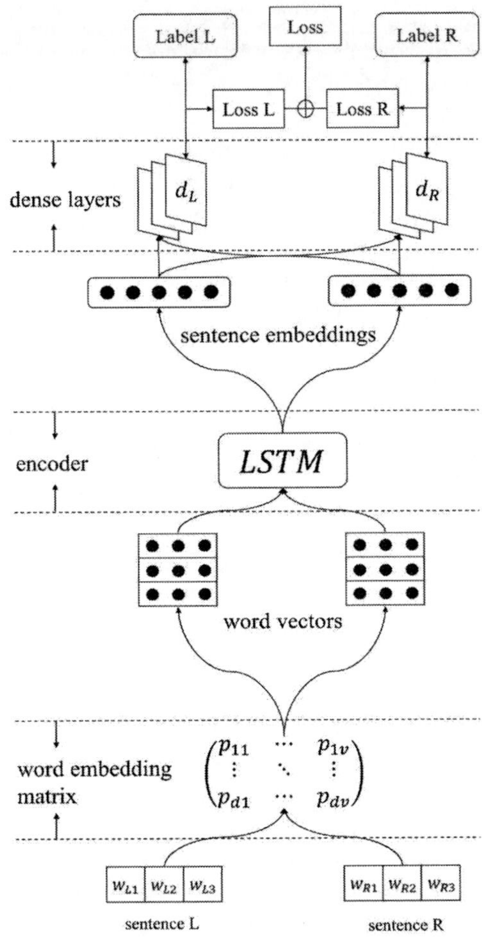

Figure 1: Overview of the multi-label architecture.

paired with other neural network architectures and applied to any dataset with multiple annotations available for each training instance.

2 Multi-Label Transfer Learning

We introduce a multi-label transfer learning setting by modifying the architecture of the LSTM-based sentence encoder, specifically designed for multi-relational semantic similarity tasks.

2.1 Architecture

We employ the "hard-parameter sharing" setting (Caruana, 1998), where some hidden layers are shared across multiple tasks while each task has its own specific output layer. As shown in Figure 1, using an example of a semantic similarity dataset with two relations, sentence L and sentence R in a

pair are first mapped to word vector sequences and then encoded as sentence embeddings. Up to this step, the choice of the word embedding matrix and sentence encoder is flexible, and we outline our choice in the sections to follow. For each relation that has been annotated with a ground-truth label, a dedicated output dense layer takes the two sentence embeddings as input and outputs a probability distribution across the range of possible scores. The output dense layers follow the methods of Tai et al. (2015).

With two such dense output layers, two losses are calculated, one for each relation. The total loss is calculated as the sum of the two losses for back-propagation which updates all parameters in the end-to-end network.

2.2 Model

We use InferSent (Conneau et al., 2017) as the sentence encoder due to its outstanding performances reported on various semantic similarity tasks.

Due to the small sizes of the evaluation datasets, we use the sentence encoder pre-trained on the Stanford Natural Language Inference corpus (Bowman et al., 2015) and Multi-Genre Natural Language Inference corpus (Williams et al., 2018), and transfer to the semantic similarity tasks using fine-tuning. In this process, the output layers for multi-label learning discussed above are stacked on top of the InferSent network, forming an end-to-end model for training and testing on semantic similarity tasks.

2.3 Comparison with Multi-Task Learning

Neither multi-task nor multi-label learning have been used for multi-relational semantic similarity datasets. For these datasets, either multi-task or multi-label learning can be achieved by treating each relation as a "task." The key differences between the two are the relations involved in each forward-backward pass and the timing of the parameter updates.

Consider a training step in the two-relation example in Figure 1:

A **multi-task learning** model would pick a batch of sentences pairs, only consider *Label L*, only calculate *Loss L*, and all parameters except those of dense layer d_R are updated. Then, within the same batch,[2] the model would only consider

---

[2] In general multi-task learning, a new batch is picked after switching tasks. In multi-relational semantic similarity datasets, each task is a relational label, which shares the same

Label R, only calculate *Loss R*, and all parameters except those of dense layer d_L are updated.

A **multi-label learning** model (our model) would pick a batch of sentences pairs, consider both *Label L* and *Label R*, calculate *Loss L* and *Loss R*, aggregate them as the total loss, and update all parameters.

3 Experiments

To show the effectiveness of the multi-label transfer learning setting, we experiment on three semantic similarity datasets with multiple relations annotated, and use one LSTM-based sentence encoder that has been very successful in many downstream tasks.

3.1 Datasets

We study three semantic similarity datasets with multiple relations with texts of different lengths, spanning phrases, sentences, and short paragraphs.

Human Activity Phrase (Wilson and Mihalcea, 2017): a collection of pairs of phrases regarding human activities, annotated with the following four different relations.

- Similarity (SIM): The degree to which the two activity phrases describe the same thing, semantic similarity in a strict sense. Example of high similarity phrases: *to watch a film* and *to see a movie*.

- Relatedness (REL): The degree to which the activities are related to one another, a general semantic association between two phrases. Example of strongly related phrases: *to give a gift* and *to receive a present*.

- Motivational alignment (MA): The degree to which the activities are (typically) done with similar motivations. Example of phrases with potentially similar motivations: *to eat dinner with family members* and *to visit relatives*.

- Perceived actor congruence (PAC): The degree to which the activities are expected to be done by the same type of person. An example of a pair with a high PAC score: *to pack a suitcase* and *to travel to another state*.

The phrases are generated, paired and scored on Amazon Mechanical Turk.[3] The annotated input.

[3] https://www.mturk.com/

scores range from 0 to 4 for SIM, REL and MA, and -2 to 2 for PAC. The evaluation is based on the Spearman's ρ correlation coefficient between the systems' predicted scores and the human annotations. There are 1,000 pairs in the dataset. We also use the supplemental 1,373 pairs from Zhang et al. (2018) in which 1,000 pairs are randomly selected for training and the rest are used for development. We then treat the original 1,000 pairs as a held-out test set so that our results are directly comparable with those previously reported.

SICK (Marelli et al., 2014b,a): the Sentences Involving Compositional Knowledge benchmark, which includes a large number of sentence pairs that are rich in the lexical, syntactic and semantic phenomena. Each pair of sentences is annotated in two dimensions: relatedness and entailment. The relatedness score ranges from 1 to 5, and Pearson's r is used for evaluation; the entailment relation is categorical, consisting of entailment, contradiction, and neutral. There are 4439 pairs in the train split, 495 in the trial split used for development and 4906 in the test split. The sentence pairs are generated from image and video caption datasets before being paired up using some algorithm. Due to the lack of human supervision in the process, some sentence pairs display minimal difference in semantic components, making the SICK tasks simpler than the others we study.

Typed-Similarity (Agirre et al., 2013b): a collection of meta-data describing books, paintings, films, museum objects and archival records taken from Europeana,[4] presented as the pilot track in the SemEval 2013 STS shared task. Typically, the items consist of title, subject, description, and so on, describing a cultural heritage item and, sometimes, a thumbnail of the item itself. For the purpose of measuring semantic similarity, we concatenate all the textual entries such as title, creator, subject and description into a short paragraph that is used as input, although the annotations might be informed of the image aspects of the meta-data. Each pair of items is annotated on eight dimensions of similarity: general similarity, author, people involved, time, location, event or action involved, subject and description. There are 750

[4] http://www.europeana.eu/

pairs in the train split, of which we randomly sample 500 for training and 250 for development, and 721 in the test split. Pearson's r is used for evaluation.

3.2 Baselines

We compare the multi-label setting with two baselines:

- **Single-task**, where each relation is treated as an individual task. For each relation, a model with only one output dense layer is trained and tested, ignoring the annotations of all other relations.

- **Multi-task**, where only one relation is involved during each round of feed-forward and back-propagation.

3.3 Experimental Details

In each experiment, we use stochastic gradient descent and a batch size of 16. We tune the learning rate over $\{0.1, 0.5, 1, 5\}$ and number of epochs over $\{10, 20\}$. For each dataset discussed above, we tune these hyperparameters on the development set. All other hyperparameters maintain their values from the original code.[5] In the single-task setting, the model is trained and tested on each relation, ignoring the annotations of other relations. In the multi-task settings, the model is trained and tested on all the relations in a dataset. In the multi-task setting, relations are presented to the model in the order they are listed in the result tables within each batch.

4 Evaluation

The results are shown in Tables 1, 2 and 3. For every experiment (represented by a cell in the tables), 30 runs with different random seeds are recorded and the average is reported. For each relation (each column in the tables), let the true mean performance of multi-label learning, single-task baseline and multi-task baseline be μ_{MLL}, μ_{single}, μ_{MTL}, respectively. Two one-sided Student's t-tests are conducted to test if multi-label learning outperforms the baselines for that relation. The significance level is chosen to be 0.05. A down-arrow $\downarrow$ indicates that our proposed multi-label learning underperforms a baseline, while an up-arrow $\uparrow$ indicates that our proposed multi-label learning outperforms a baseline.

[5] https://github.com/facebookresearch/InferSent

5 Discussion

5.1 Results

For the Human Activity Phrase dataset, the single-task setting already achieves state-of-the-art performances on SIM, REL and PAC relations, surpassing the previous best results reported by Zhang et al. (2018), which achieved Spearman's correlation coefficient of .710 in SIM, .715 in REL, .690 in MA and .549 in PAC. This approach is based on fine-tuning a bi-directional LSTM with average-pooling pre-trained on translated texts (Wieting and Gimpel, 2018). Using multi-label learning, our model is able to gain a statistically significant improvement in the performance of REL compared to the single-task setting, while maintaining performance for the other relations. The traditional multi-task setting, however, performs significantly worse than the other settings.

For the entailment task on the SICK dataset, our multi-label setting outperforms the single-task baseline and the previous best results of InferSent. These best results consisted of an accuracy of 86.3% achieved using a logistic regression classifier and sentence embeddings generated by pre-trained InferSent as features (Conneau et al., 2017). In the relatedness task, this setting achieved a Pearson's correlation coefficient of .885, which even our our multi-label setting is unable to beat. However, the multi-label setting does have a statistically significant performance gain compared to the single-task setting in the relatedness task, while the traditional multi-task setting underperforms the other settings.

For the Typed-Similarity dataset, the previous best results are achieved using rich feature engineering without the use of sentence embeddings, with a different scoring scheme for each relation (Agirre et al., 2013a). While this method yielded better results than all of the transfer learning approaches we compare, it should be noted that this approach is specific to tackling this dataset, unlike the transfer learning settings that are generalizable to other scenarios. One potential reason for the discrepancy in performance is that some relations such as time, people involved, or events may be easily or sometimes trivially captured by information retrieval techniques such as named entity recognition. Using sentence embeddings and transfer learning for all the relations, though simpler, may face greater challenge in the rela-

	general	author	people	time	location	event	subject	description
MLL	.744	.721	.640	.713	.751	.611	.697	.737
Single	.750↓	.690↑	.619↑	.712	.744↑	.606↑	.694↑	.718↑
MTL	.718↑	.689↑	.611↑	.697↑	.723↑	.579↑	.669↑	.714↑

Table 1: The performance in Pearson's r on the Typed-Similarity dataset, in accordance with the specification of the dataset to allow for direct comparison with previous results. The results of single task and multi-task learning (MTL) are followed by ↑ if it is statically significantly lower than those of multi-label learning (MLL), and they are followed by ↓ otherwise.

	SIM	REL	MA	PAC
MLL	.720	.721	.682	.557
Single	.719	.717↑	.682	.555
MTL	.683↑	.686↑	.651↑	.515↑

Table 2: The performance in Spearman's ρ on the Human Activity Phrase dataset.

	Relatedness	Entailment
MLL	.882	86.7
Single	.874↑	86.4↑
MTL	.871↑	86.2↑

Table 3: The performance in Pearson's r on the SICK dataset, in accordance with the specification of the dataset to allow for direct comparison with previous results.

tions mentioned above. Among the three transfer learning approaches, our multi-label setting is still superior, outperforming the single-task setting in over half of the relations, and outperforming the multi-task setting in all relations.

5.2 Empirical Recommendation

While our results above show that multi-label learning is almost always the most effective way to transfer sentence embeddings in multi-relational semantic similarity tasks, in some situations simply training with one relation might yield better performance (such as the general similarity relation in the Typed-Similarity dataset). This suggests that the choice of multi-label learning or single-task learning can be tuned as a hyperparameter empirically for the optimal performance on a task.

5.3 Other Considerations and Discussions

In the multi-label setting, we calculate the total loss by summing the loss from each dimension. We also explore weighting the loss from each di-mension by factors of 2, 5 and 10, but doing so hurts the performance for all dimensions.

In the multi-task setting, we attempt different ordering of the dimensions when presenting them to the model within a batch of examples, but the difference in performance is not statistically significant. Furthermore, the multi-task setting takes about n times longer to train than the multi-label setting, where n is number of dimensions of annotations.

6   Conclusions

We introduced a multi-label transfer learning setting designed specifically for semantic similarity tasks with multiple relations annotations. By experimenting with a variety of relations in three datasets, we showed that the multi-label setting can outperform single-task and traditional multi-task settings in many cases.

Future work includes exploring the performance of this setting with other sentence encoders, as well as multi-label datasets outside of the domain of semantic similarity. This may include NLP datasets annotated with author information for multiple dimensions, or computer vision datasets with multiple annotations for scenes.

Acknowledgments

This material is based in part upon work supported by the Michigan Institute for Data Science, by the John Templeton Foundation (grant #61156), by the National Science Foundation (grant #1815291), and by DARPA (grant #HR001117S0026-AIDA-FP-045). Any opinions, findings, and conclusions or recommendations expressed in this material are those of the author and do not necessarily reflect the views of the Michigan Institute for Data Science, the John Templeton Foundation, the National Science Foundation, or DARPA.

References

Eneko Agirre, Nikolaos Aletras, Aitor Gonzalez-Agirre, German Rigau, and Mark Stevenson. 2013a. Ubc_uos-typed: Regression for typed-similarity. In *Second Joint Conference on Lexical and Computational Semantics (*SEM), Volume 1: Proceedings of the Main Conference and the Shared Task: Semantic Textual Similarity*, pages 132–137, Atlanta, Georgia, USA. Association for Computational Linguistics.

Eneko Agirre, Carmen Banea, Claire Cardie, Daniel Cer, Mona Diab, Aitor Gonzalez-Agirre, Weiwei Guo, Inigo Lopez-Gazpio, Montse Maritxalar, Rada Mihalcea, German Rigau, Larraitz Uria, and Janyce Wiebe. 2015. Semeval-2015 task 2: Semantic textual similarity, english, spanish and pilot on interpretability. In *Proceedings of the 9th International Workshop on Semantic Evaluation (SemEval 2015)*, pages 252–263, Denver, Colorado. Association for Computational Linguistics.

Eneko Agirre, Carmen Banea, Daniel Cer, Mona Diab, Aitor Gonzalez-Agirre, Rada Mihalcea, German Rigau, and Janyce Wiebe. 2016. Semeval-2016 task 1: Semantic textual similarity, monolingual and cross-lingual evaluation. In *Proceedings of the 10th International Workshop on Semantic Evaluation (SemEval-2016)*, pages 497–511, San Diego, California. Association for Computational Linguistics.

Eneko Agirre, Daniel Cer, Mona Diab, and Aitor Gonzalez-Agirre. 2012. Semeval-2012 task 6: A pilot on semantic textual similarity. In **SEM 2012: The First Joint Conference on Lexical and Computational Semantics – Volume 1: Proceedings of the main conference and the shared task, and Volume 2: Proceedings of the Sixth International Workshop on Semantic Evaluation (SemEval 2012)*, pages 385–393, Montréal, Canada. Association for Computational Linguistics.

Eneko Agirre, Daniel Cer, Mona Diab, Aitor Gonzalez-Agirre, and Weiwei Guo. 2013b. *sem 2013 shared task: Semantic textual similarity. In *Second Joint Conference on Lexical and Computational Semantics (*SEM), Volume 1: Proceedings of the Main Conference and the Shared Task: Semantic Textual Similarity*, pages 32–43, Atlanta, Georgia, USA. Association for Computational Linguistics.

Samuel R. Bowman, Gabor Angeli, Christopher Potts, and Christopher D. Manning. 2015. A large annotated corpus for learning natural language inference. In *Proceedings of the 2015 Conference on Empirical Methods in Natural Language Processing*, pages 632–642, Lisbon, Portugal. Association for Computational Linguistics.

Rich Caruana. 1998. Multitask learning. In *Learning to learn*, pages 95–133. Springer.

Daniel Cer, Mona Diab, Eneko Agirre, Inigo Lopez-Gazpio, and Lucia Specia. 2017. Semeval-2017 task 1: Semantic textual similarity multilingual and crosslingual focused evaluation. In *Proceedings of the 11th International Workshop on Semantic Evaluation (SemEval-2017)*, pages 1–14, Vancouver, Canada. Association for Computational Linguistics.

Alexis Conneau, Douwe Kiela, Holger Schwenk, Loïc Barrault, and Antoine Bordes. 2017. Supervised learning of universal sentence representations from natural language inference data. In *Proceedings of the 2017 Conference on Empirical Methods in Natural Language Processing*, pages 670–680, Copenhagen, Denmark. Association for Computational Linguistics.

Marco Marelli, Luisa Bentivogli, Marco Baroni, Raffaella Bernardi, Stefano Menini, and Roberto Zamparelli. 2014a. Semeval-2014 task 1: Evaluation of compositional distributional semantic models on full sentences through semantic relatedness and textual entailment. In *Proceedings of the 8th International Workshop on Semantic Evaluation (SemEval 2014)*, pages 1–8, Dublin, Ireland. Association for Computational Linguistics.

Marco Marelli, Stefano Menini, Marco Baroni, Luisa Bentivogli, Raffaella Bernardi, and Roberto Zamparelli. 2014b. A sick cure for the evaluation of compositional distributional semantic models. In *Proceedings of the Ninth International Conference on Language Resources and Evaluation (LREC'14)*, pages 216–223, Reykjavik, Iceland. European Language Resources Association (ELRA).

Kai Sheng Tai, Richard Socher, and Christopher D. Manning. 2015. Improved semantic representations from tree-structured long short-term memory networks. In *Proceedings of the 53rd Annual Meeting of the Association for Computational Linguistics and the 7th International Joint Conference on Natural Language Processing (Volume 1: Long Papers)*, pages 1556–1566, Beijing, China. Association for Computational Linguistics.

John Wieting and Kevin Gimpel. 2018. Paranmt-50m: Pushing the limits of paraphrastic sentence embeddings with millions of machine translations. In *Proceedings of the 56th Annual Meeting of the Association for Computational Linguistics (Volume 1: Long Papers)*, pages 451–462, Melbourne, Australia. Association for Computational Linguistics.

Adina Williams, Nikita Nangia, and Samuel Bowman. 2018. A broad-coverage challenge corpus for sentence understanding through inference. In *Proceedings of the 2018 Conference of the North American Chapter of the Association for Computational Linguistics: Human Language Technologies, Volume 1 (Long Papers)*, pages 1112–1122, New Orleans, Louisiana. Association for Computational Linguistics.

Steven Wilson and Rada Mihalcea. 2017. Measuring semantic relations between human activities. In

Proceedings of the Eighth International Joint Conference on Natural Language Processing (Volume 1: Long Papers), pages 664–673, Taipei, Taiwan. Asian Federation of Natural Language Processing.

Li Zhang, Steven R Wilson, and Rada Mihalcea. 2018. Sequential network transfer: Adapting sentence embeddings to human activities and beyond. *arXiv preprint arXiv:1804.07835*.

Scalable Cross-Lingual Transfer of Neural Sentence Embeddings

Hanan Aldarmaki[1] and **Mona Diab**[1,2]
[1]The George Washington University
[2]AWS, Amazon AI
aldarmaki@gwu.edu, diabmona@amazon.com

Abstract

We develop and investigate several cross-lingual alignment approaches for neural sentence embedding models, such as the supervised inference classifier, InferSent, and sequential encoder-decoder models. We evaluate three alignment frameworks applied to these models: joint modeling, representation transfer learning, and sentence mapping, using parallel text to guide the alignment. Our results support representation transfer as a scalable approach for modular cross-lingual alignment of neural sentence embeddings, where we observe better performance compared to joint models in intrinsic and extrinsic evaluations, particularly with smaller sets of parallel data.

1 Introduction

Probabilistic sentence representation models generally fall into two categories: bottom-up compositional models, where sentence embeddings are composed from word embeddings via a linear function like averaging, and top-down compositional models that are trained with a sentence-level objective, typically within a neural architecture. Sequential data like sentences can be modeled using recurrent, recursive, or convolutional networks, which can implicitly learn intermediate sentence representations suitable for each learning task. Depending on the training objective, these intermediate representations sometimes encode enough semantic and syntactic features to be suitable as general-purpose sentence embeddings. For examples, it was shown in Conneau et al. (2017a) that a model trained to maximize inference classification accuracy can yield generic representations that perform well across a wide set of extrinsic classification benchmarks. Other training objectives, like denoising auto-encoders or neural sequence to sequence models (Hill et al.,

2016), can also yield general-purpose representations with different characteristics. While bottom-up models can achieve superior performance in tasks that are independent of syntax, such as topic categorization, neural models often yield representations that encode syntactic and positional features, which results in superior performance in tasks that rely on sentence structure (Aldarmaki and Diab, 2018).

General-purpose sentence embeddings can be used as features in various classification tasks, or to directly assess the similarity of a pair of sentences using the cosine measure. It is often desired to generalize word and sentence embeddings across several languages to facilitate cross-lingual transfer learning (Zhou et al., 2016) and mining of parallel sentences (Guo et al., 2018). For word embeddings, cross-lingual learning can be achieved in various ways (Upadhyay et al., 2016), such as learning directly with a cross-lingual objective (Shi et al., 2015) or post-hoc alignment of monolingual word embeddings using dictionaries (Ammar et al., 2016), parallel corpora (Gouws et al., 2015; Klementiev et al., 2012), or even with no bilingual supervision (Conneau et al., 2017b; Aldarmaki et al., 2018). For bottom-up composition like vector averaging, word-level alignment is sufficient to yield cross-lingual sentence embeddings. For top-down sentence embeddings, the efforts in cross-lingual learning are more limited. Typically, a multi-faceted cross-lingual learning objective is used to align the sentence models while training them, as in Soyer et al. (2014). Cross-lingual sentence embeddings can also be learned via a neural machine translation framework trained jointly for multiple languages (Schwenk and Douze, 2017).

While they indeed yield cross-lingual embeddings, the joint training models in existing literature pose some practical limitations: simultaneous training requires massive computational re-

*Proceedings of the Eighth Joint Conference on Lexical and Computational Semantics (*SEM)*, pages 51–60
Minneapolis, June 6–7, 2019. ©2019 Association for Computational Linguistics

sources, particularly for sequential models like the bi-directional LSTM networks typically used to encode sentences. In addition, the joint framework does not allow post-hoc or modular training, where new languages can be added and aligned to existing pre-trained encoders. More recently, Conneau et al. (2018) proposed an approach for cross-lingual sentence embeddings by aligning encoders of new languages to a pre-trained English encoder using parallel corpora. Such approach promises to be more suitable for modular training of general sentence encoders, although so far it has only been evaluated in natural language inference classification.

In this paper, we develop and evaluate three alignment frameworks: joint modeling, representation transfer learning, and sentence mapping, applied on two modern general-purpose sentence embedding models: the inference-based encoder, InferSent (Conneau et al., 2017a), and the sequential denoising auto-encoder, SDAE (Hill et al., 2016). For most approaches, we rely on parallel sentences as sentence-level dictionaries for cross-lingual supervision. We report the performance on sentence translation retrieval and cross-lingual document classification. Our results support representation transfer as a scalable approach for modular cross-lingual alignment that works well across different neural models and evaluation benchmarks.

2 Related Work

Learning bilingual compositional representations can be achieved by optimizing a bilingual objective on parallel corpora. In Pham et al. (2015), distributed representations for bilingual phrases and sentences are learned using an extended version of the paragraph vector model (Le and Mikolov, 2014) by forcing parallel sentences to share one vector. In Soyer et al. (2014), cross-lingual compositional embeddings are learned by optimizing a joint bilingual objective that aligns parallel source and target representations by minimizing the Euclidean distances between them, and a monolingual objective that maximizes the similarity between similar phrases. The monolingual objective was implemented by maximizing the similarity between random phrases and subphrases within the same sentence. Cross-lingual representations can also be induced implicitly within a machine learning framework that is trained jointly for multiple language pairs. In Schwenk and Douze (2017), encoders and decoders for the given languages are trained jointly using a neural sequence to sequence model (Sutskever et al., 2014) using parallel corpora that are partially aligned; that is, each language within a pair is also part of at least one other parallel corpus. Neural machine translation can also be achieved with a single encoder and decoder that handles several input languages (Johnson et al., 2017), but the latter has not been evaluated as a general-purpose sentence representation model. According to Hill et al. (2016), the quality of the representations induced using a machine translation objective is lower than other neural models trained with different compositional objectives, such as Denoising Auto-Encoders and Skip-Thought (Kiros et al., 2015). Mono-lingual evaluation of sentence representation models can be found in Hill et al. (2016), Aldarmaki and Diab (2018), and Conneau and Kiela (2018). In Aldarmaki and Diab (2016), a modular training objective has been proposed for cross-lingual sentence embedding. However, their application was limited to the specific matrix factorization model they discussed. More recently, Conneau et al. (2018) proposed a modular transfer learning objective and evaluated it on neural sentence encoders using cross-lingual natural language inference classification. Our representation transfer framework is very similar to their approach, although we use a simpler loss function. In addition, we evaluate the framework as a general-purpose sentence encoder and compare it to other frameworks.

3 Approach

We selected two modern general-purpose sentence embedding models, the Inference-based classification model (`InferSent`) described in Conneau et al. (2017a), and the Sequential Denoising Auto-Encoder (`SDAE`) described in Hill et al. (2016). Both are implemented using a bidirectional LSTM network as an encoder followed by a classification or decoding network. We describe three possible cross-lingual alignment frameworks:

Joint cross-lingual modeling: We extend the monolingual objective of each model to multiple languages to be trained simultaneously via direct cross-lingual interactions in the objective function. This is in line with most existing cross-lingual extensions for top-down compositional models

Representation transfer learning: We directly optimize the sentence embeddings of new languages to match their translations in a parallel language (i.e. English). A similar approach was independently developed in Conneau et al. (2018).

Sentence mapping: Following the modular alignment framework for word embeddings (Smith et al., 2017), we fit an orthogonal transformation matrix on monolingual embeddings using a parallel corpus as a dictionary. Sentence mapping has been evaluated for word averaging models in Aldarmaki and Diab (2019).

3.1 Architectures

Most neural sentence embedding models are based on a sequential encoder—typically a bi-directional Long Short-Term Memory (Schuster and Paliwal, 1997)—followed by either a sequential decoder or a classifier. These models can be categorized according to their training objective:

Classification Accuracy: Sentence encoders can be trained by maximizing the accuracy in an extrinsic evaluation task. For example, `InferSent` (Conneau et al., 2017a) is trained on the Stanford Natural Language Inference (SNLI) dataset for inference classification (Bowman et al., 2015sss). This type of model requires labeled training data, which can make it challenging to expand across different languages.

Reconstruction: Using raw monolingual data, sentence encoders can be trained by minimizing the reconstruction loss, where a decoder is trained simultaneously to reconstruct the input sentence from the intermediate representation—e.g. Sequential Auto-Encoder (`SAE`) and Sequential Denoising Auto-Encoder (`SDAE`) (Hill et al., 2016). The latter introduces textual noise on the input sentence to make the embeddings more robust.

Translation: In Neural Machine Translation (NMT), a model is trained to maximizes the accuracy of generating a translation from the intermediate representation of the source sentence. Unlike modern `NMT` systems that rely on attention mechanisms, this model is trained for the purpose of sentence embedding, so only the intermediate representations are used as input to the decoder. This model requires parallel corpora for training.

The three objectives above are illustrated in Figures 1 and 2. We use the single-layer bidirectional LSTM encoder architecture with max-pooling described in Conneau et al. (2017a) for all encoders, and an LSTM decoders for `SDAE` and `NMT`.

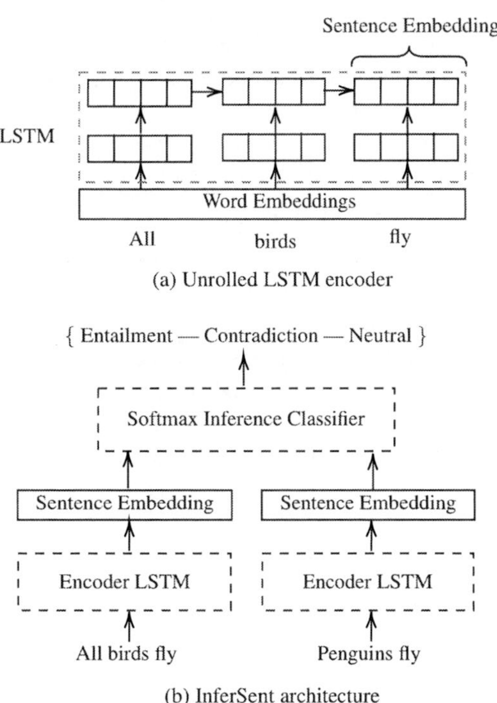

(a) Unrolled LSTM encoder

(b) InferSent architecture

Figure 1: Illustrations of neural sentence embedding architectures based on LSTM encoders. (a) shows an unrolled LSTM encoder with word embeddings. (b) shows InferSent architecture with a softmax classification network on top of the encoder.

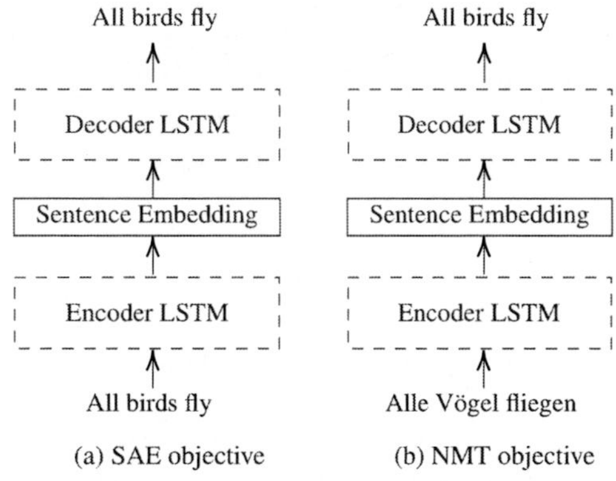

(a) SAE objective

(b) NMT objective

Figure 2: Illustrations of LSTM encoder-decoder architectures for sentence embeddings. (a) Sequential Auto-Encoder objective, where the input and output are the same sentence. (b) Neural Machine Translation objective, where the output is a translation of the input sentence from a parallel corpus.

3.2 Joint Cross-Lingual Modeling

We first discuss our joint cross-lingual neural models based on the above architectures. Note that joint modeling requires modifying the architecture and objective function of each model in a way that includes simultaneous interactions of cross-lingual sentence embeddings. This can be achieved in various ways with any degree of complexity, but we specifically aim to evaluate a direct extension of each loss function without extraneous objectives or constraints.

3.2.1 Joint Cross-Lingual Encoder-Decoder

The Sequential Denoising Auto-Encoder (SDAE) is trained to reconstruct the original input sentence from the intermediate sentence representation, where the input is corrupted with linguistic noise, such as word substitutions and reordering (Hill et al., 2016). This allows the model to robustly learn sentence representations from raw monolingual data. The Neural Machine Translation model, as depicted in Figure 2, has an identical architecture, with the only difference being the language of the input sentence. A cross-lingual extension of SDAE naturally leads to the NMT objective. We combine the SDAE and NMT objectives in a joint architecture, where multiple encoders are trained simultaneously with a single shared decoder. We alternate the input language (and the encoder) in each training batch, and the intermediate sentence embeddings are used as input to the shared decoder. Since the decoder is trained to predict the target sentence from the intermediate sentence representation regardless of input language identity, the encoders are expected to be updated in a way that results in consistent cross-lingual embeddings. Joint multi-lingual NMT has been previously shown to yield cross-lingual representations, as in Schwenk and Douze (2017).

3.3 Joint Cross-Lingual InferSent

Since InferSent is trained with an extrinsic classification objective, bilingual or multilingual optimization requires annotated data in each language. At the time of development, the SNLI dataset was only available in English[1], so we translated the training and evaluation datasets to Spanish and German using Amazon Translate. Note that in practice, machine translation might

---

[1]Other cross-lingual natural language inference corpora are now publicly available (Conneau et al., 2018), but our experiments were conducted before their release.

not be a viable option, especially if we try to extend the model to low-resource languages. Modern NMT systems require millions of parallel sentences to achieve good translation performance. For our purposes, the translated data allow us to assess the performance in different settings.

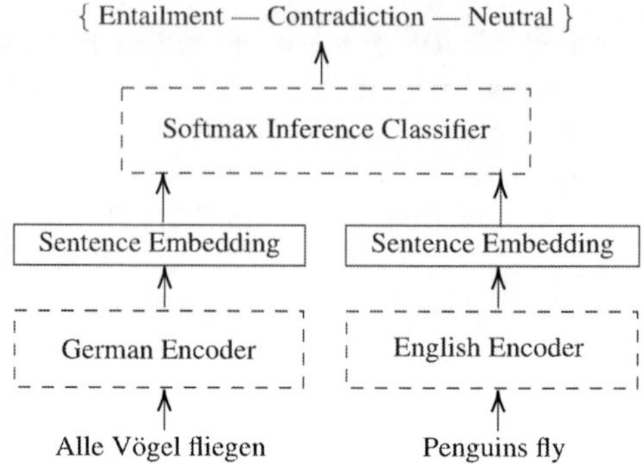

Figure 3: Illustrations of a joint training step, where different languages are used for the premise and hypothesis.

Similar to the joint SDAE/NMT model, we train encoders for all languages simultaneously. Since the input to the classifier consists of an ordered pair of sentences, we randomly pick a language for the premise and a language for the hypothesis in each training batch and use their respective encoders. A single classifier is shared regardless of the input languages. Similar to the monolingual case, the model is trained to maximize the performance in the inference classification task, which is cross-lingual in this case. An illustration of a training example is shown in Figure 3, where the premise is in German and the hypothesis in English.

3.4 Representation Transfer Learning

In the representation transfer framework, we use a monolingual pre-trained model to guide the training of additional encoders without the original supervised training objective. Using a parallel corpus that has source sentences aligned with English translations, we first generate the representations for the English sentences using a pre-trained SDAE or InferSent model. Then, we use these representations as a target to train an encoder for the other language in a supervised manner. The pivot encoder remains unchanged and only the new encoder is updated during training to ensure that independently trained encoders will still be aligned. Several functions can be used to achieve this, such as the L1 or L2 loss to minimize the distances be-

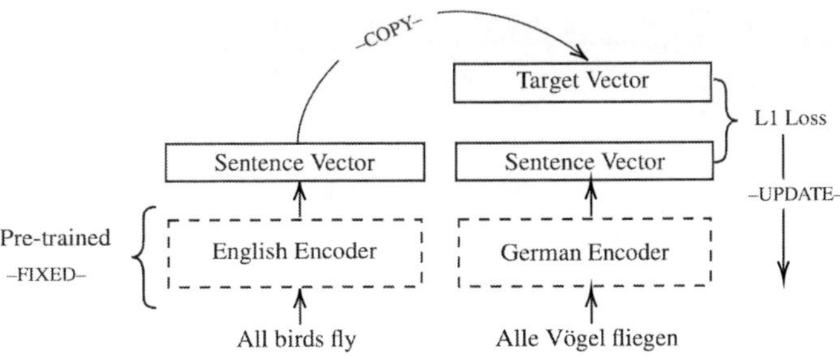

Figure 4: Representation transfer model, with pre-trained English encoder and L1 loss.

tween the source and target representations, or to maximize the cosine of the angle between them. Empirically, we observed no notable difference between these alternatives.[2] The transfer learning approach is illustrated in Figure 4.

3.5 Sentence Mapping

We follow the approach used for word-level transformation, where a dictionary is used to fit an orthogonal transformation matrix from the source to the target vector space (Smith et al., 2017). To extend this to sentences, we use a parallel corpus as a dictionary, and fit a transformation matrix between their sentence embeddings. After training, we apply the learned transformation post-hoc on newly generated sentence embeddings.

4 Evaluation

In a well-aligned cross-lingual vector space, sentences should be clustered with their translations across various languages. As discussed in Schwenk and Douze (2017) this can be measured with sentence translation retrieval: the accuracy of retrieving the correct translation for each source sentence from the target side of a test parallel corpus. This is done using nearest neighbor search with the cosine as a similarity measure. While not exactly an intrinsic evaluation metric, this scheme is the closest measure of alignment quality at the sentence level across all features in the vector space.

We used bottom-up embeddings composed using weighted averaging with smooth inverse frequency (Arora et al., 2017; Aldarmaki and Diab, 2018), which has been shown to work well as monolingual sentence embeddings compared to

other bottom-up approaches. We use skipgram with subword information (Bojanowski et al., 2017) , i.e. `FastText`, for the word embeddings, which are also used as input to the neural models. We applied static dictionary alignment using the approach and dictionaries in Smith et al. (2017), in addition to sentence mapping using the parallel corpora. We trained the monolingual `FastText` word embeddings and SDAE models using the 1 Billion Word benchmark (Chelba et al., 2014) for English, and WMT'12 News Crawl data for Spanish and German (Callison-Burch et al., 2012). We used WMT'12 Common Crawl data for cross-lingual alignment, and WMT'12 test sets for evaluations. We used the augmented SNLI data described in (Dasgupta et al., 2018) and their translations for training the mono-lingual and joint `InferSent` models. For all datasets and languages, the only preprocessing performed was tokenization.

One of our evaluation objective is to assess the minimal bilingual data requirements for each framework, so we split the training parallel corpora into subsets of increasing size from 1,000 to 1 million sentences, where we double the size in each step. We report sentence translation retrieval accuracies in all language directions, using *en* for English, *es* for Spanish, and *de* for German [3].

4.1 Results

The results of the various SDAE models compared with the baselines are shown in Figure 5. With less than 100K parallel sentences, the joint SDAE/NMT model yielded poor performance compared to all models, but with 100K and more

---

[2] We settled on using Adam optimization (Kingma and Ba, 2014) with L1 loss.

[3] This evaluation scheme was recently introduced in Aldarmaki and Diab (2019) with data splits that are now available for download. Note that we used slightly older datasets in our experiments.

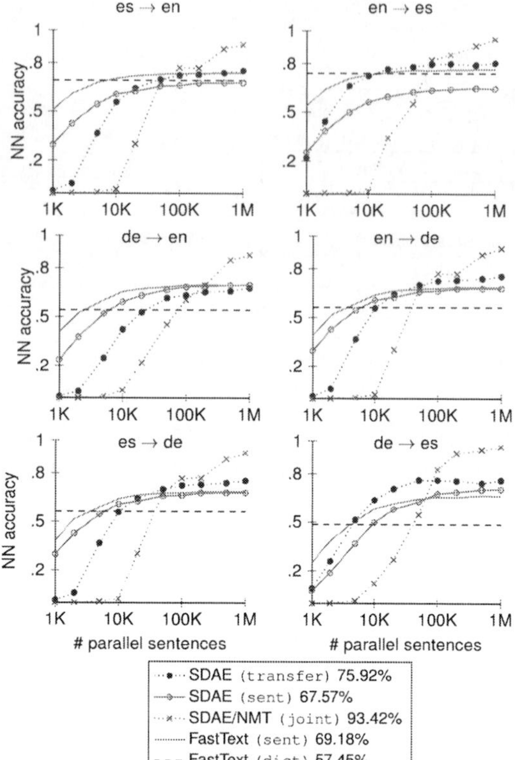

Figure 5: Nearest neighbor translation accuracy as a function of (log) parallel corpus size. (sent) to sentence-level mapping, and (dict) refers to the baseline (using a static dictionary for mapping). The legend shows the average accuracies of each model using 1M parallel sentences.

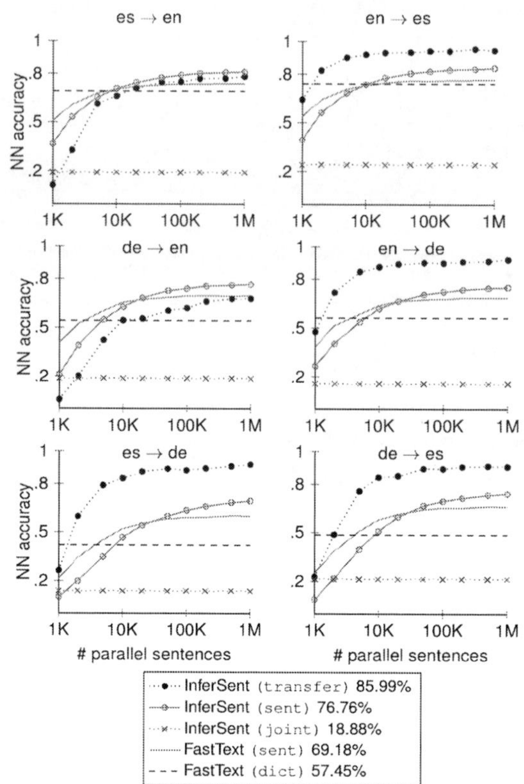

Figure 6: Nearest neighbor translation accuracy as a function of (log) parallel corpus size. (sent) to sentence-level mapping, and (dict) refers to the baseline (using a static dictionary for mapping). The legend shows the average accuracies of each model using 1M parallel sentences.

data, the model quickly exceeded the performance of all others by a large margin. Transfer learning achieved the second best performance, although it lagged behind the joint model with large parallel sets. With small amounts of parallel text, all models outperformed the joint SDAE/NMT, particularly the word based FastText models. Sentence mapping performed on average better than the static dictionary baseline, but FastText sentence mapping was generally better.

Figure 6 shows the results of the InferSent alignment models. Note that the joint InferSent model was trained with supervision using the translated SNLI data instead of the variable-size parallel corpora, so the performance is constant with respect to the number of parallel sentences. The joint model did not learn to align the cross-lingual sentences. Possible explanations of this failure are discussed in section 4.3.

Overall, the transfer learning model worked well for InferSent resulting in high transla-

tion retrieval accuracies even with relatively small amounts of parallel text ($\sim$ 5K sentences). Sentence mapping also performed better than the word-based baselines with additional parallel data ($>$ 20K).

4.2 Overall Evaluation

In this section, we compare the overall performance of different types of models on sentence translation retrieval. We plotted the average cross-lingual accuracy (averaged over all language directions) by the best performing variant of each model in Figure 7. With small amounts of parallel text, around 5K sentences, the best performance was achieved using InferSent transfer model. The model continued to yield the highest performance until it was exceeded by the joint SDAE/NMT model at 500K sentences. The representation transfer models for SDAE exceeded the FastText model at around 20K sentences, and achieved comparable performance to InferSent sentence mapping.

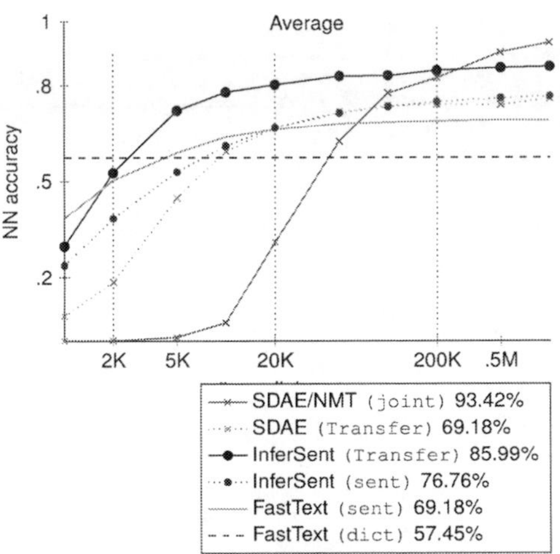

Figure 7: Nearest neighbor translation accuracy as a function of (log) parallel corpus size. The legend shows the average accuracies of each model using 1M parallel sentences.

Language	Monolingual Nearest Neighbors
	Query: Tons of people are gathered around the statue
Spanish	There are **several people sitting around** a table. There are **several people** outside of a building. **There are multiple people** present.
English	The **people** are taking photos of **the statue**. **A group of people** looking at **a statue**. **People are gathered** by the water.
	Query: A vehicle is crossing a river
Spanish	**A sedan** is stuck in the middle of **a river**. People are **crossing a river**. **A taxi cab** is **driving down a path of snow**.
English	A person is near **a river**. People are **crossing a river**. A **Land Rover** is splashing water as it **crosses a river**.

Table 1: Mono-lingual nearest neighbors (or their translations) of a sample of query sentences from SNLI test set using joint `InferSent` encoders. Phrases similar to the query sentences are shown in **bold**.

Language	Cross-lingual Nearest Neighbors
	Query: Tons of people are gathered around the statue
Spanish	Food and wine are on the table that has **many people surrounding** it. **Some people** enjoying their brunch together in the outdoor seating area of a restaurant... The **group of people** are game developers creating a new video game in their office.
English	The **group of people** are flying in the air on their unicorns . A **group of people** are standing around with smiles on their faces... A **group of people** dressed as clowns stroll into the Bigtop Circus holding signs.
	Query: A vehicle is crossing a river
Spanish	People and a baby are **crossing** the street at a crosswalk to get home. The person in the picture is riding **a bike slowing up hill** , pumping the pedals as hard as they can. The man , wearing scuba gear , jumps off the side of **the boat into the ocean** below.
English	A person in a coat with a briefcase **walks down a street** next to the bus lane. A man waterskiing in **a river** with a large wall in the background. A person **waterskiing in a river** with a wall in the background.

Table 2: Cross-lingual nearest neighbors (or their translations) of a sample of query sentences from SNLI test set using joint `InferSent` encoders. Phrases similar to the query sentences are shown in **bold**.

4.3 Analysis of Joint InferSent Performance

The joint `InferSent` model was trained to maximize the cross-lingual classification accuracy on cross-lingual inference data. The cross-lingual inference classification performance was comparable to the monolingual case for each language. The monolingual accuracies were around 83%, 79%, and 79% for English, German, and Spanish, respectively. The cross-lingual accuracy was around 79%. Given this relatively high performance in NLI classification and the poor performance in cross-lingual translation retrieval, we surmise that the 3-way classification objective is not demanding enough to learn general-purpose semantic representations. In addition, high performance in a specific extrinsic evaluation task is not necessarily an indication of general embedding quality.

Tables 1 and 2 show examples of monolingual and cross-lingual nearest neighbors (or their English translations) from the hypotheses in SNLI test sets. The cross-lingual nearest neighbors did share several semantic aspects with the query sentence; subjects or verbs or combinations of these were observed in nearest neighbors. However, the exact translations were not the nearest neighbors in most cases, and the nearest neighbors often included several extraneous pieces of content not present in the query sentence. The mono-lingual nearest neighbors, on the other hand, were more semantically similar to each other, not only in the semantic features that are present, but also in their exclusions of dissimilar details.

We surmise that only a subset of semantic features were learned by the `InferSent` objective given the specific characteristics of the SNLI training sets. In other words, the model was not pushed to preserve the full semantic content since only a small subset of features were useful for entailment relationships. The higher similarity among mono-lingual nearest neighbors is likely an artifact of the underlying word embeddings passing through the same encoder network.

4.4 Extrinsic Evaluation

Relying on a single measure is never sufficient to probe all characteristics of a vector space. Extrinsic evaluation can be another useful tool to measure the effectiveness of various cross-lingual models, although extrinsic tasks typically measure specific and narrow aspects of semantics. Nevertheless, we can still gain some insights about certain characteristics of these models and their applicability. One of the most widely used tasks for cross-lingual evaluation is the Cross-Lingual Document Classification benchmark (CLDC), where a model is trained in one language and tested on another (Schwenk and Li, 2018; Klementiev et al., 2012).

We report the average classification accuracies in CLDC across all language directions (a total of six directions) using the datasets in Schwenk and Li (2018); the multi-layer perceptron was used as a classifier trained for each source language, then tested in the remaining two.

The highest accuracy was achieved using `FastText` vectors, followed by `InferSent` transfer and sentence mapping models. With large enough parallel corpora, the performance of `SDAE/NMT` exceeded the transfer model, but with smaller data, `SDAE` transfer model achieved consistently higher performance.

These results are consistent with the trend of these models in mono-lingual topic categorization (Aldarmaki and Diab, 2018), where word averaging achieved consistently higher performance than all neural models. This indicates that cross-lingual models share the same semantic characteristics as their underlying mono-lingual counterparts. We should underscore that CLDC is a rather coarse categorization task where documents are classified into four categories. Note also that the `FastText` model achieved relatively high performance even when it was aligned with only 1K parallel sentences, a condition in which sentence translation retrieval accuracy was less that 40%. This poor correlation with sentence translation retrieval accuracies indicates that neither evaluation framework is reliable on its own. Our intuition is that sentence translation retrieval is a more com-

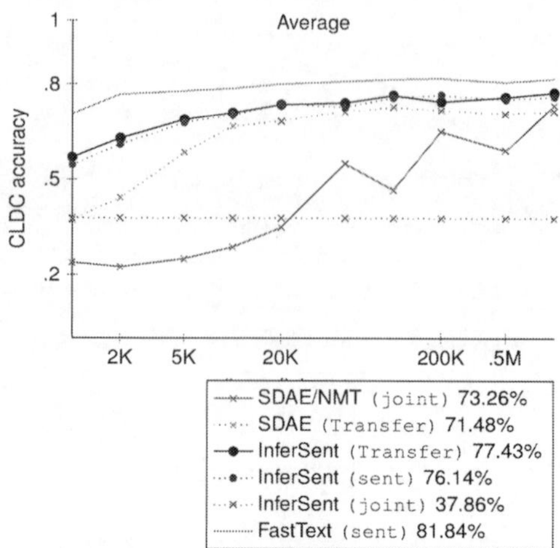

Figure 8: Average cross-lingual document classification accuracy as a function of (log) parallel corpus size. The legend shows the average accuracies of each model using 1M parallel sentences.

prehensive measure since all features in the vector space weigh equally in calculating the cosine similarity; on the other hand, a supervised classifier weighs features according to their correlations with the target classes.

5 Conclusions

We explored different approaches for cross-lingual alignment of top-down sentence embedding models: joint modeling, representation transfer, and sentence mapping. With sufficient amounts of parallel text, joint modeling yielded superior performance in the joint SDAE and NMT model, while joint InferSent failed to yield good alignments. Our results underscore the difficulty of joint modeling itself in addition to its relatively high data and memory requirements. With smaller amounts of parallel text, representation transfer worked reasonably well across all models, whereas sentence mapping was generally worse. Moreover, the transfer and sentence mapping frameworks enable modular training where additional languages can be added without retraining existing models and without labeled training data (as in InferSent), which allows scaling neural models to more languages with less resources. In extrinsic evaluation using cross-lingual document classification, transfer models achieved consistently better performance than joint models. Between the two sentence embedding models we evaluated, InferSent yielded better performance than SDAE and NMT, except in the joint framework.

In practice, joint and transfer learning can be combined in various ways according to data availability and modeling choices. A multi-task framework can be used to optimize both objectives at once. Given the lower data cost of representation transfer models, a joint model can be trained first for a set of resource-rich languages, followed by transfer learning for low-resource languages.

References

Hanan Aldarmaki and Mona Diab. 2016. Learning cross-lingual representations with matrix factorization. In *Proceedings of the Workshop on Multilingual and Cross-lingual Methods in NLP*, pages 1–9.

Hanan Aldarmaki and Mona Diab. 2018. Evaluation of unsupervised compositional representations. *Proceedings of the 27th International Conference on Computational Linguistics*.

Hanan Aldarmaki and Mona Diab. 2019. Context-aware crosslingual mapping. *arXiv preprint arXiv:1903.03243*.

Hanan Aldarmaki, Mahesh Mohan, and Mona Diab. 2018. Unsupervised word mapping using structural similarities in monolingual embeddings. *Transactions of the Association of Computational Linguistics*, 6.

Waleed Ammar, George Mulcaire, Yulia Tsvetkov, Guillaume Lample, Chris Dyer, and Noah A Smith. 2016. Massively multilingual word embeddings. *arXiv preprint arXiv:1602.01925*.

Sanjeev Arora, Yingyu Liang, and Tengyu Ma. 2017. A simple but tough-to-beat baseline for sentence embeddings.

Piotr Bojanowski, Edouard Grave, Armand Joulin, and Tomas Mikolov. 2017. Enriching word vectors with subword information. *Transactions of the Association for Computational Linguistics*, 5:135–146.

Samuel R Bowman, Gabor Angeli, Christopher Potts, and Christopher D Manning. 2015sss. A large annotated corpus for learning natural language inference. *Proceedings of the 2015 Conference on Empirical Methods in Natural Language Processing*.

Chris Callison-Burch, Philipp Koehn, Christof Monz, Matt Post, Radu Soricut, and Lucia Specia. 2012. Findings of the 2012 workshop on statistical machine translation. In *Proceedings of the Seventh Workshop on Statistical Machine Translation*, pages 10–51.

Ciprian Chelba, Tomas Mikolov, Mike Schuster, Qi Ge, Thorsten Brants, Phillipp Koehn, and Tony Robinson. 2014. One billion word benchmark for measuring progress in statistical language modeling. In *Fifteenth Annual Conference of the International Speech Communication Association*.

Alexis Conneau and Douwe Kiela. 2018. Senteval: An evaluation toolkit for universal sentence representations. In *Proceedings of the Eleventh International Conference on Language Resources and Evaluation (LREC-2018)*.

Alexis Conneau, Douwe Kiela, Holger Schwenk, Loïc Barrault, and Antoine Bordes. 2017a. Supervised learning of universal sentence representations from natural language inference data. In *Proceedings of the 2017 Conference on Empirical Methods in Natural Language Processing*, pages 670–680.

Alexis Conneau, Guillaume Lample, Marc'Aurelio Ranzato, Ludovic Denoyer, and Hervé Jégou. 2017b. Word translation without parallel data. *arXiv preprint arXiv:1710.04087*.

Alexis Conneau, Ruty Rinott, Guillaume Lample, Adina Williams, Samuel R. Bowman, Holger Schwenk, and Veselin Stoyanov. 2018. Xnli: Evaluating cross-lingual sentence representations. In *Proceedings of the 2018 Conference on Empirical Methods in Natural Language Processing*. Association for Computational Linguistics.

Ishita Dasgupta, Demi Guo, Andreas Stuhlmüller, Samuel J Gershman, and Noah D Goodman. 2018. Evaluating compositionality in sentence embeddings. *arXiv preprint arXiv:1802.04302*.

Stephan Gouws, Yoshua Bengio, and Greg Corrado. 2015. Bilbowa: Fast bilingual distributed representations without word alignments. In *Proceedings of the 32nd International Conference on Machine Learning (ICML-15)*, pages 748–756.

Mandy Guo, Qinlan Shen, Yinfei Yang, Heming Ge, Daniel Cer, Gustavo Hernandez Abrego, Keith Stevens, Noah Constant, Yun-hsuan Sung, Brian Strope, et al. 2018. Effective parallel corpus mining using bilingual sentence embeddings. In *Proceedings of the Third Conference on Machine Translation: Research Papers*, pages 165–176.

Felix Hill, Kyunghyun Cho, and Anna Korhonen. 2016. Learning distributed representations of sentences from unlabelled data. In *Proceedings of NAACL-HLT*, pages 1367–1377.

Melvin Johnson, Mike Schuster, Quoc V Le, Maxim Krikun, Yonghui Wu, Zhifeng Chen, Nikhil Thorat, Fernanda Viégas, Martin Wattenberg, Greg Corrado, et al. 2017. Google's multilingual neural machine translation system: Enabling zero-shot translation. *Transactions of the Association of Computational Linguistics*, 5(1):339–351.

Diederik P Kingma and Jimmy Ba. 2014. Adam: A method for stochastic optimization. *arXiv preprint arXiv:1412.6980*.

Ryan Kiros, Yukun Zhu, Ruslan R Salakhutdinov, Richard Zemel, Raquel Urtasun, Antonio Torralba, and Sanja Fidler. 2015. Skip-thought vectors. In *Advances in neural information processing systems*, pages 3294–3302.

Alexandre Klementiev, Ivan Titov, and Binod Bhatarai. 2012. Inducing crosslingual distributed representations of words. *Proceedings of COLING 2012*, pages 1459–1474.

Quoc Le and Tomas Mikolov. 2014. Distributed representations of sentences and documents. In *International Conference on Machine Learning*, pages 1188–1196.

Hieu Pham, Thang Luong, and Christopher Manning. 2015. Learning distributed representations for multilingual text sequences. In *Proceedings of the 1st Workshop on Vector Space Modeling for Natural Language Processing*, pages 88–94.

Mike Schuster and Kuldip K Paliwal. 1997. Bidirectional recurrent neural networks. *IEEE Transactions on Signal Processing*, 45(11):2673–2681.

Holger Schwenk and Matthijs Douze. 2017. Learning joint multilingual sentence representations with neural machine translation. In *Proceedings of the 2nd Workshop on Representation Learning for NLP*, pages 157–167.

Holger Schwenk and Xian Li. 2018. A corpus for multilingual document classification in eight languages. In *Proceedings of the Eleventh International Conference on Language Resources and Evaluation (LREC-2018)*.

Tianze Shi, Zhiyuan Liu, Yang Liu, and Maosong Sun. 2015. Learning cross-lingual word embeddings via matrix co-factorization. In *Proceedings of the 53rd Annual Meeting of the Association for Computational Linguistics and the 7th International Joint Conference on Natural Language Processing (Volume 2: Short Papers)*, volume 2, pages 567–572.

Samuel L Smith, David HP Turban, Steven Hamblin, and Nils Y Hammerla. 2017. Offline bilingual word vectors, orthogonal transformations and the inverted softmax. *arXiv preprint arXiv:1702.03859*.

Hubert Soyer, Pontus Stenetorp, and Akiko Aizawa. 2014. Leveraging monolingual data for crosslingual compositional word representations. *arXiv preprint arXiv:1412.6334*.

Ilya Sutskever, Oriol Vinyals, and Quoc V Le. 2014. Sequence to sequence learning with neural networks. In *Advances in neural information processing systems*, pages 3104–3112.

Shyam Upadhyay, Manaal Faruqui, Chris Dyer, and Dan Roth. 2016. Cross-lingual models of word embeddings: An empirical comparison. In *Proceedings of the 54th Annual Meeting of the Association for Computational Linguistics (Volume 1: Long Papers)*, volume 1.

Xinjie Zhou, Xiaojun Wan, and Jianguo Xiao. 2016. Cross-lingual sentiment classification with bilingual document representation learning. In *Proceedings of the 54th Annual Meeting of the Association for Computational Linguistics (Volume 1: Long Papers)*, volume 1, pages 1403–1412.

Second-order contexts from lexical substitutes for few-shot learning of word representations

Qianchu Liu, Diana McCarthy, Anna Korhonen
Language Technology Lab, University of Cambridge
English Faculty Building, 9 West Road, Cambridge CB3 9DA, United Kingdom
ql261@cam.ac.uk, diana@dianamccarthy.co.uk, alk23@cam.ac.uk

Abstract

There is a growing awareness of the need to handle rare and unseen words in word representation modelling. In this paper, we focus on few-shot learning of emerging concepts that fully exploits only a few available contexts. We introduce a substitute-based context representation technique that can be applied on an existing word embedding space. Previous context-based approaches to modelling unseen words only consider bag-of-word first-order contexts, whereas our method aggregates contexts as second-order substitutes that are produced by a sequence-aware sentence completion model. We experimented with three tasks that aim to test the modelling of emerging concepts. We found that these tasks show different emphasis on first and second order contexts, and our substitute-based method achieved superior performance on naturally-occurring contexts from corpora.

1 Introduction

As language vocabulary follows the zipfian distribution, we expect to encounter a large number of rare and unseen words no matter how large the training corpus is. The effective handling of such words is thus crucial for Natural Language Processing (NLP).

Attempts to learn rare and unseen word representations can be categorized into the following three approaches: (1) constructing target word embeddings from the subword components (Pinter et al., 2017; Bojanowski et al., 2017), (2). leveraging definitions or relational structures from external resources such as Wordnet (Bahdanau et al., 2017; Pilehvar and Collier, 2017), and (3) modelling the target word from few available contexts. Our paper falls into the last approach.

We demonstrate improvements in performance by employing an alternative context representation, second-order lexical substitutes, as opposed

to the traditional bag of word context representations. In line with previous research in this area, we evaluate our methodology on three tasks that measure the quality of the induced unseen word representation from contexts (Lazaridou et al., 2017; Herbelot and Baroni, 2017; Khodak et al., 2018). Our results reveal that the three tasks involve different types of contexts which put different emphasis on first or second order contexts. Our second-order substitute-based method achieves the best performance for modelling rare words in natural contexts from corpora. In the tasks in which both first order and second order contexts are important, the ensemble of these two types of contexts yields superior performance. [1]

2 Related work

2.1 First-order context

The most naive way of inducing new word representation from contexts is to simply take the average of context word embeddings that co-occur with the target word in a sentence. With stop words removed, this simple method has proven to be a strong baseline as shown in Lazaridou et al. (2017) and Herbelot and Baroni (2017). A potential improvement from the simple additive baseline model is that we weigh words with ISF (inverse sentence frequency). We follow the definition of ISF in Samardzhiev et al. (2018) and implement it as a baseline model in our study. More recently, Khodak et al. (2018) learn a transformation matrix to reconstruct pre-trained word embeddings, which essentially learns to highlight informative dimensions. Along a different line, Herbelot and Baroni (2017) take a high-risk learning rate and processing strategy for new words but would require the contexts that come at the beginning of the training to be maximally informative. Recent

---

[1]The experiments can be reproduced at https://github.com/qianchu/rare_we.git.

*Proceedings of the Eighth Joint Conference on Lexical and Computational Semantics (*SEM)*, pages 61–67
Minneapolis, June 6–7, 2019. ©2019 Association for Computational Linguistics

work implements a memory-augmented word embedding model (Sun et al., 2018) however our system shows comparable or superior performance on the two intrinsic tasks that they use (Table 1 below and Table 1 of their paper).

2.2 Second-order substitute-based context

An alternative to a bag-of-words representation is a second-order substitute vector generated by a language model for the target word's slot. For example, we can represent the context '*It is a __ move.*' as a substitute vector [big 0.35, good 0.28, bold 0.05, ...] with the numbers indicating fitness weights of each substitute in the context (Melamud et al., 2015; Yatbaz et al., 2012; Melamud et al., 2015). Melamud et al. (2016) later on introduced context2vec which trains both context and word embeddings in a similar setup to CBOW (Mikolov et al., 2013) except that the context is represented with a Bidirectional LSTM rather than as a bag of words. In this way, context2vec captures sequence information in the context, and is able to produce high-quality substitutes for a sentence-completion task, while overcoming the sparseness issues in the previous substitute-based approaches. Kobayashi et al. (2017) fine-tune this context2vec representation to compute entity representations in a discourse for the language modelling task.

A related application of second-order substitutes is word sense induction. Baskaya et al. (2013) represent contexts as second-order substitutes and apply co-occurrence modelling on top of the instance id - substitute pairs. Alagić et al. (2018) propose a similar method to our paper and showed that second-order lexical substitutes and first-order contexts complement each other in word sense induction. Our paper provides alternative evidence for the use of lexical substitutes in the setting of rare word modelling with analysis on the effect from different contexts.

3 Proposed Method

In this paper, we make a simple modification from the previous work by representing the context of an unseen word as the weighted sum of the lexical substitute vectors in a continuous embedding space such as the word2vec space. This can be seen as a post-processing technique applied on an existing embedding space. The substitutes and their fitness scores are generated from context2vec. Compared with the context2vec representation itself, our method isolates the effect of the second-order substitutes and can be applied on top of an existing pre-trained embedding space. For each context, we generate the top N most likely substitutes at the slot of the unseen word by computing the nearest neighbours from the context2vec context representation. [2] We then compute the centroid of these substitutes from our base word embedding space, weighted by each substitute's fitness, cosine similarity, to the context representation. Let $\mathbf{ContextVec}$ [3] be the context representation produced by context2vec, S' be the set of the top 20 substitute target word vectors produced by context2vec, S be the same 20 substitutes that we look up in our base word embedding space, and $f(\mathbf{S_i'})$ be the normalized fitness score of $\mathbf{S_i'}$ as defined in equation 1. The substitute-based context ($\mathbf{SC}$), and thus the unseen word representation for this context, is defined in equation 2. If the unseen word occurs multiple times, we average the unseen word representations across the multiple contexts.

$$f(\mathbf{S_i'}) = \frac{cosine(\mathbf{ContextVec}, \mathbf{S_i'})}{\sum_{j=1}^{20} cosine(\mathbf{ContextVec}, \mathbf{S_j'})} \quad (1)$$

$$\mathbf{SC} = \sum_{i=1}^{20} f(\mathbf{S_i'}) * \mathbf{S_i} \quad (2)$$

To directly compare with the previous studies, we take the word2vec embedding model and the 1.6B Wikipedia training corpus provided by Herbelot and Baroni (2017) for our substitute-based method and for training Context2vec. Model parameters for training Context2vec, as listed in Appendix A, are fine-tuned on the training sets of the intrinsic tasks as there are no development sets.

4 The definitional Nonce dataset (Nonce)

Nonce is introduced in Herbelot and Baroni (2017) as a task that challenges the models to reconstruct target word embeddings from single wikipedia definitions. The quality of the representations is evaluated by measuring how close they are to the original word embeddings trained from the whole

---

[2] From experiments on the training sets of the tasks (Notice that there are no development sets), we found that N=20 is optimal.

[3] Symbols in bold indicate vectors

Methods	Nonce		Chimera		
	MRR	Med. Rank	2 Sent.	4 Sent.	6 Sent.
word2vec (Lazaridou et al., 2017)	0.00007	111012	0.1459	0.2457	0.2498
Additive (Lazaridou et al., 2017)	0.03686	861	0.3376	0.3624	0.4080
Additive ISF	0.04493	531	0.3964	**0.4016**	0.4107
nonce2vec (Herbelot and Baroni, 2017)	0.04907	623	0.3320	0.3668	0.3890
a la carte (Khodak et al., 2018)	**0.07058**	**166**	0.3634	0.3844	0.3941
mem2vec (Sun et al., 2018)	0.05416	518	0.3301	0.3717	0.3897
context2vec(Melamud et al., 2016)	0.04577	536	0.3574	0.3376	0.3692
substitutes	0.05152	1442	0.3946	0.3662	0.4424
substitutes + additive ISF	0.06074	577	**0.4167**	0.3879	**0.4469**

Table 1: Comparison with baselines and the previously-reported state-of-the-art results on the Chimera and Nonce datasets. The Chimera dataset is evaluated with Spearman Rank coefficients. The top half of the table contains first-order context methods and the bottom half has methods using second-order context or ensemble methods using first and second order.

Wikipedia corpora. Following Herbelot and Baroni (2017), we report in the Nonce columns of Table 1 the mean reciprocal rank (MRR) and median rank (Med. Rank) of the gold-vector (trained from the whole Wikipedia) in the ranked list of nearest neighbours from the induced representation in the 300 test cases.

We see strong performance from first-order context representation especially the a la carte method. Manual observations show that definitions are designed to be maximally informative with many synonyms, hypernyms or words semantically related to the target word in the context, and the first-order context models can easily exploit this information. Also, the sequential context around the target word in a definition may not reflect the context in which a target word will be typically used in a corpus. The good performance of first-order context models is therefore to be expected. Furthermore, the Nonce task tests how well the model reconstructs the original embedding but does not probe into the semantic properties or relations captured in the induced word representations. A la carte is thus especially suitable for this task as it has been explicitly trained to match the original embedding. However, we demonstrate in the following experiments that the superior performance from a la carte may not always be transferred to other tasks.

5   The Chimera dataset (Chimera)

In the Chimera dataset, Lazaridou et al. (2017) introduce unseen novel concepts (chimeras), each of which is formed by combining two related nouns

Additive ISF	substitutes
drowning	civet
drown	tapir
drowns	langur
shoos	crocodile
undresses	opossum

Table 2: Nearest neighbours produced by additive ISF and substitutes approaches for the Chimera concept elephant_bison in the context '*but his pleasure soon turns to distress when he sees that a baby ___ is stuck in the mud and drowning .*' (from the Chimeras dataset)

(For example, buffalo and elephant). Each novel concept is accompanied by 2, 4 or 6 natural contexts that originally belong to the related nouns. The model needs to induce representation for these novel concepts from the contexts. The quality of the representations is evaluated by similarity judgment with probe words. Following Herbelot and Baroni (2017) and Lazaridou et al. (2017), we report in the Chimera columns of Table 1 the average Spearman Rank coefficients against human annotations for 110 test cases in each sentence condition .

We observe that the additive ISF model turns out to be the strongest of the first-order context models, outperforming all the other previously-reported results. We see immediate improvement when we represent the context as substitutes in the 6 sentence condition. We see further improvement when combining both additive ISF (first order) and substitutes (second order contexts), which yields the best performance in 2 sentence and 6 sentence conditions. The positive effect of the

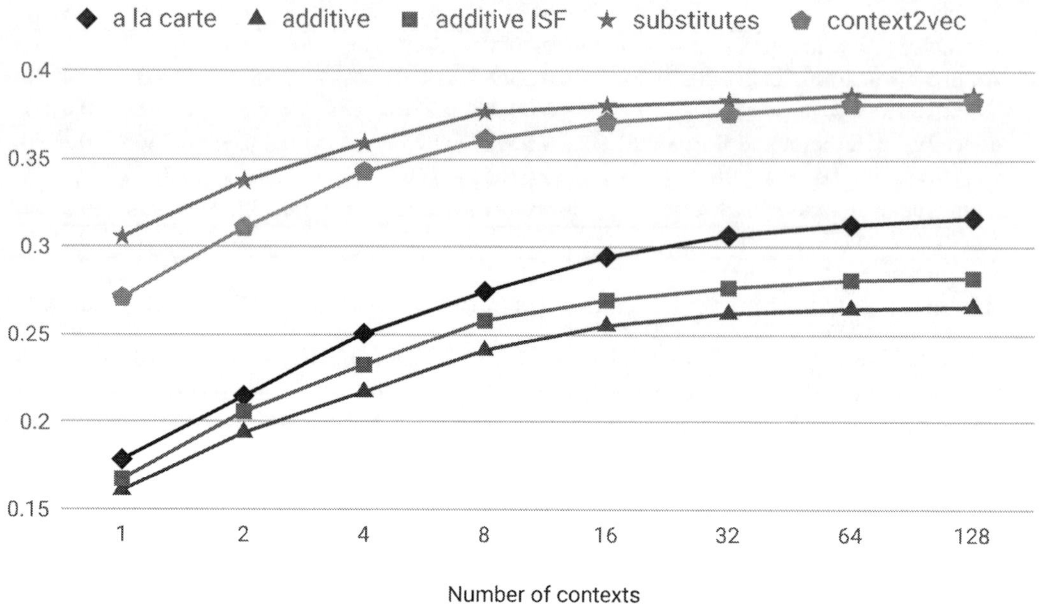

Figure 1: Spearman Rank coefficients averaged across 100 trials on CRW in various context conditions

ensemble method from combining first-order and second-order contexts shows that the two different contexts capture complementary information in this task. This is especially due to the fact that the contexts were controlled for informativeness so as to have different degrees of overlap with feature norms. Therefore at least some, but not all, contexts will have a high bag-of-word overlap with features that are semantically related to the concepts (Lazaridou et al., 2017). These contexts will easily benefit from first-order contexts alone. However, for the other contexts where there is few or even no overlap with feature norms in the context words, it is the contextual sequence, and thus second-order context, that will give the maximum information about the target word. We show such an example with the nearest neighbours of the representations induced by our substitutes model and additive ISF in Table 2. We can see that while the additive ISF representation is easily affected by unrelated words in the sentence, the substitutes approach clearly has at least identified that the target word is likely to be a kind of animal.

6   The Contextual Rare Words dataset (CRW)

The Contextual Rare Words dataset (CRW) was introduced by Khodak et al. (2018). It consists of a subset of 562 word pairs from the original Rare Word (RW) Dataset (Luong et al., 2013). For each pair, the second word is the rare word and is accompanied by 255 contexts. We follow the experiment setup in Khodak et al. (2018) and use their pre-trained vectors on the subcorpus that does not contain any of the rare words from the dataset. This subcorpus is also used to train the context2vec model that generates substitutes. As in Khodak et al. (2018), we randomly choose 2, 4, 6..128 number of contexts as separate conditions for 100 trials, and use these contexts to predict the rare word representations. Cosine similarity is computed between the rare word representation from the given rare word contexts in the trial (2,4..128) and the embedding of the other word in the pair from the pre-trained vectors. The cosine-similarity of each pair is compared against similarity judgments from human annotations. The average Spearman Rank coefficients against human annotations across the trials are reported in Figure 1. Standard deviations are reported in Appendix B.

We see dramatic improvement from the substitutes method over all the other methods including the previous state-of-the-art a la carte in this datasets which come from corpora-based natural contexts of rare words. The result here suggests that, in natural contexts, the sequence information rather than bag of words plays a more important role in predicting a target word's meaning.

We also notice that applying second order information on word2vec space consistently outperforms Context2vec alone which generates the second order substitutes. We suspect that this is because the context representation induced by context2vec is more syntactically-oriented whereas the tasks in our study mainly test semantic relations. We confirm this assumption by following Herbelot and Baroni (2017) to test the target word embeddings produced by context2vec on the MEN dataset (Bruni et al., 2014). We find that context2vec (Spearman $\rho = 0.65$) correlates less with human's semantic relatedness judgment than word2vec (Spearman $\rho = 0.75$) on this dataset. Isolating the second order information from Context2vec and applying it on the word2vec space as an external constraint effectively preserves the semantic relations present in word2vec and at the same time provides a paradigmatic view which finds a both syntactically and semantically appropriate position for the rare word.

7 Conclusion

To conclude, our paper teases apart the effect of second-order context by proposing a simple second-order substitute-based method that can post-process and improve over an existing embedding space. Our substitute-based method achieves the state-of-the-art performance when modelling emerging concepts in natural contexts from corpora. This is not surprising as the substitutes contain rich linguistic constraints from their surrounding contextual sequences to inform the word representation. We plan to investigate whether the second order information is also the key element in the success of the recently-proposed language model embeddings (Peters et al., 2018; Devlin et al., 2018), for example, by testing whether the performance of these contextualized embeddings correlate more with first-order context representation or the second-order substitute context across the different tasks in this study. However, we need further research to find ways to bring type-level and token-level representations of these contextualized embeddings into the same space for these tasks.

Also, as we found that definitions seem to exhibit different properties from natural contexts in corpora, it may be advisable to model definitions and corpora contexts differently. An aspect that we did not cover in this paper is the morphological information from target words. As contexts, definitions and subword information can provide complementary information (Schick and Schütze, 2019), in future work, we plan to leverage subwords, contexts and definitions together in modelling rare or unseen words.

Acknowledgments

We acknowledge Peterhouse College at University of Cambridge for funding Qianchu Liu's PhD research. We also appreciate the helpful discussion and feedback from Dr Ivan Vulić, Dr Nigel H. Collier, Dr Taher Pilehvar and Dr Angeliki Lazaridou. We also would like to thank Dr Aurélie Herbelot for sharing the training corpora and insightful thoughts.

References

Domagoj Alagić, Jan Šnajder, and Sebastian Padó. 2018. Leveraging lexical substitutes for unsupervised word sense induction. In *Thirty-Second AAAI Conference on Artificial Intelligence*.

Dzmitry Bahdanau, Tom Bosc, Stanislaw Jastrzebski, Edward Grefenstette, Pascal Vincent, and Yoshua Bengio. 2017. Learning to compute word embeddings on the fly. *arXiv preprint arXiv:1706.00286*.

Osman Baskaya, Enis Sert, Volkan Cirik, and Deniz Yuret. 2013. Ai-ku: Using substitute vectors and co-occurrence modeling for word sense induction and disambiguation. In *Second Joint Conference on Lexical and Computational Semantics (*SEM), Volume 2: Proceedings of the Seventh International Workshop on Semantic Evaluation (SemEval 2013)*, pages 300–306, Atlanta, Georgia, USA. Association for Computational Linguistics.

Piotr Bojanowski, Edouard Grave, Armand Joulin, and Tomas Mikolov. 2017. Enriching word vectors with subword information. *Transactions of the Association for Computational Linguistics*, 5:135–146.

Elia Bruni, Nam-Khanh Tran, and Marco Baroni. 2014. Multimodal distributional semantics. *Journal of Artificial Intelligence Research*, 49:1–47.

Jacob Devlin, Ming-Wei Chang, Kenton Lee, and Kristina Toutanova. 2018. Bert: Pre-training of deep bidirectional transformers for language understanding. *arXiv preprint arXiv:1810.04805*.

Aurélie Herbelot and Marco Baroni. 2017. High-risk learning: acquiring new word vectors from tiny data. In *Proceedings of the 2017 Conference on Empirical Methods in Natural Language Processing*, pages 304–309. Association for Computational Linguistics.

Mikhail Khodak, Nikunj Saunshi, Yingyu Liang, Tengyu Ma, Brandon Stewart, and Sanjeev Arora. 2018. A la carte embedding: Cheap but effective induction of semantic feature vectors. In *Proceedings of the 56th Annual Meeting of the Association for Computational Linguistics (Volume 1: Long Papers)*, pages 12–22. Association for Computational Linguistics.

Sosuke Kobayashi, Naoaki Okazaki, and Kentaro Inui. 2017. A neural language model for dynamically representing the meanings of unknown words and entities in a discourse. In *Proceedings of the Eighth International Joint Conference on Natural Language Processing (Volume 1: Long Papers)*, pages 473–483. Asian Federation of Natural Language Processing.

Angeliki Lazaridou, Marco Marelli, and Marco Baroni. 2017. Multimodal word meaning induction from minimal exposure to natural text. *Cognitive science*, 41:677–705.

Thang Luong, Richard Socher, and Christopher Manning. 2013. Better word representations with recursive neural networks for morphology. In *Proceedings of the Seventeenth Conference on Computational Natural Language Learning*, pages 104–113. Association for Computational Linguistics.

Oren Melamud, Ido Dagan, and Jacob Goldberger. 2015. Modeling word meaning in context with substitute vectors. In *Proceedings of the 2015 Conference of the North American Chapter of the Association for Computational Linguistics: Human Language Technologies*, pages 472–482. Association for Computational Linguistics.

Oren Melamud, Jacob Goldberger, and Ido Dagan. 2016. context2vec: Learning generic context embedding with bidirectional lstm. In *Proceedings of The 20th SIGNLL Conference on Computational Natural Language Learning*, pages 51–61. Association for Computational Linguistics.

Tomas Mikolov, Kai Chen, Greg Corrado, and Jeffrey Dean. 2013. Efficient estimation of word representations in vector space. *CoRR*, abs/1301.3781.

Matthew Peters, Mark Neumann, Mohit Iyyer, Matt Gardner, Christopher Clark, Kenton Lee, and Luke Zettlemoyer. 2018. Deep contextualized word representations. In *Proceedings of the 2018 Conference of the North American Chapter of the Association for Computational Linguistics: Human Language Technologies, Volume 1 (Long Papers)*, pages 2227–2237. Association for Computational Linguistics.

Mohammad Taher Pilehvar and Nigel Collier. 2017. Inducing embeddings for rare and unseen words by leveraging lexical resources. In *Proceedings of the 15th Conference of the European Chapter of the Association for Computational Linguistics: Volume 2, Short Papers*, pages 388–393. Association for Computational Linguistics.

Yuval Pinter, Robert Guthrie, and Jacob Eisenstein. 2017. Mimicking word embeddings using subword rnns. In *Proceedings of the 2017 Conference on Empirical Methods in Natural Language Processing*, pages 102–112. Association for Computational Linguistics.

Krasen Samardzhiev, Andrew Gargett, and Danushka Bollegala. 2018. Learning neural word salience scores. In *Proceedings of the Seventh Joint Conference on Lexical and Computational Semantics*, pages 33–42. Association for Computational Linguistics.

Timo Schick and Hinrich Schütze. 2019. Learning semantic representations for novel words: Leveraging both form and context. In *Thirty-Third AAAI Conference on Artificial Intelligence*.

Jingyuan Sun, Shaonan Wang, and Chengqing Zong. 2018. Memory, show the way: Memory based few shot word representation learning. In *Proceedings of the 2018 Conference on Empirical Methods in Natural Language Processing*, pages 1435–1444. Association for Computational Linguistics.

Mehmet Ali Yatbaz, Enis Sert, and Deniz Yuret. 2012. Learning syntactic categories using paradigmatic representations of word context. In *Proceedings of the 2012 Joint Conference on Empirical Methods in Natural Language Processing and Computational Natural Language Learning*, pages 940–951. Association for Computational Linguistics.

A Context2vec model parameters for reproducing the experiments in the paper

1. Nonce:

   minimum word freq: 52;
   dimension units 800;
   batchsize: 800;
   learning rate: 0.0001;
   iteration: 12

2. Chimera:

   minimum word freq: 100;
   dimension units 800;

batchsize: 800;
learning rate: 0.0001;
iteration: 14

3. CRW

minimum word freq: 100;
dimension units 800;
batchsize: 600;
learning rate: 0.0005;
iteration: 8

B Standard deviations in the CRW experiment in the main paper

number of contexts	a la carte	additive ISF	additive	substitutes	context2vec
1	0.0274	0.0318	0.0357	0.0281	0.0276
2	0.0272	0.0278	0.0314	0.0229	0.0242
4	0.0184	0.0215	0.0218	0.0168	0.0193
8	0.0158	0.0157	0.0193	0.0108	0.0149
16	0.0114	0.0116	0.0123	0.0082	0.0099
32	0.0070	0.0080	0.0099	0.0054	0.0062
64	0.0051	0.0055	0.0062	0.0035	0.0046
128	0.0032	0.0031	0.0038	0.0022	0.0026

Pre-trained Contextualized Character Embeddings Lead to Major Improvements in Time Normalization: a Detailed Analysis

Dongfang Xu   **Egoitz Laparra**   **Steven Bethard**
School of Information
University of Arizona
Tucson, AZ
`{dongfangxu9,laparra,bethard}@email.arizona.edu`

Abstract

Recent studies have shown that pre-trained contextual word embeddings, which assign the same word different vectors in different contexts, improve performance in many tasks. But while contextual embeddings can also be trained at the character level, the effectiveness of such embeddings has not been studied. We derive character-level contextual embeddings from Flair (Akbik et al., 2018), and apply them to a time normalization task, yielding major performance improvements over the previous state-of-the-art: 51% error reduction in news and 33% in clinical notes. We analyze the sources of these improvements, and find that pre-trained contextual character embeddings are more robust to term variations, infrequent terms, and cross-domain changes. We also quantify the size of context that pre-trained contextual character embeddings take advantage of, and show that such embeddings capture features like part-of-speech and capitalization.

1   Introduction

Pre-trained language models (LMs) such as ELMo (Peters et al., 2018), ULMFiT (Howard and Ruder, 2018), OpenAI GPT (Radford et al., 2018), Flair (Akbik et al., 2018) and Bert (Devlin et al., 2018) have shown great improvements in NLP tasks ranging from sentiment analysis to named entity recognition to question answering. These models are trained on huge collections of unlabeled data and produce contextualized word embeddings, i.e., each word receives a different vector representation in each context, rather than a single common vector representation regardless of context as in word2vec (Mikolov et al., 2013) and GloVe (Pennington et al., 2014).

Research is ongoing to study these models and determine where their benefits are coming from

(Peters et al., 2018; Radford et al., 2018; Khandelwal et al., 2018; Qi et al., 2018; Zhang and Bowman, 2018). The analyses have focused on word-level models, yet character-level models have been shown to outperform word-level models in some NLP tasks, such as text classification (Zhang et al., 2015), named entity recognition (Kuru et al., 2016), and time normalization (Laparra et al., 2018a). Thus, there is a need to study pre-trained contextualized *character* embeddings, to see if they also yield improvements, and if so, to analyze where those benefits are coming from.

All of the pre-trained word-level contextual embedding models include some character or subword components in their architecture. For example, Flair is a forward-backward LM trained over characters using recurrent neural networks (RNNs), that generates pre-trained contextual word embeddings by concatenating the forward LM's hidden state for the word's last character and the backward LM's hidden state for the word's first character. Flair achieves state-of-the-art or competitive results on part-of-speech tagging and named entity tagging (Akbik et al., 2018). Though they do not pre-train a LM, Bohnet et al. (2018) similarly apply a bidirectional long short term memory network (LSTM) layer on all characters of a sentence and generate contextual word embeddings by concatenating the forward and backward LSTM hidden states of the first and last character in each word. Together with other techniques, they achieve state-of-the-art performance on part-of-speech and morphological tagging. However, both Akbik et al. (2018) and Bohnet et al. (2018) discard all other contextual character embeddings, and no analyses of the models are performed at the character-level.

In the current paper, we derive pre-trained contextual character embeddings from Flair's forward-backward LM trained on a 1-billion word corpus of

*Proceedings of the Eighth Joint Conference on Lexical and Computational Semantics (*SEM)*, pages 68–74
Minneapolis, June 6–7, 2019. ©2019 Association for Computational Linguistics

English (Chelba et al., 2014), and observe if these embeddings yield the same large improvements for character-level tasks as yielded by pre-trained contextual word embeddings for word-level tasks. We aim to analyze where improvements come from (e.g., term variations, low frequency words) and what they depend on (e.g., embedding size, context size). We focus on the task of parsing time normalizations (Laparra et al., 2018b) , where large gains of character-level models over word-level models have been observed (Laparra et al., 2018a). This task involves finding and composing pieces of a time expression to infer time intervals, so for example, the expression *3 days ago* could be normalized to the interval *[2019-03-01, 2019-03-02)*.

We first take a state-of-the-art neural network for parsing time normalizations (Laparra et al., 2018a) and replace its randomly initialized character embeddings with pre-trained contextual character embeddings. After showing that this yields major performance improvements, we analyze the improvements to understand why pre-trained contextual character embeddings are so useful. Our contributions are:

- We derive pre-trained contextual character embeddings from Flair (Akbik et al., 2018), apply them to a state-of-the art time normalizer (Laparra et al., 2018a), and obtain major performance improvements over the previous state-of-the-art: 51% error reduction in news and 33% error reduction in clinical notes.
- We demonstrate that pre-trained contextual character embeddings are more robust to term variations, infrequent terms, and cross-domain changes.
- We quantify the amount of context leveraged by pre-trained contextual character embeddings.
- We show that pre-trained contextual character embeddings remove the need for features like part-of-speech and capitalization.

2 Framework

The parsing time normalizations task is based on the Semantically Compositional Annotation of Time Expressions (SCATE) schema (Bethard and Parker, 2016), in which times are annotated as compositional time entities. Laparra et al. (2018a) decomposes the Parsing Time Normalizations task into two subtasks: a) time entity identification using a character-level sequence tagger which detects

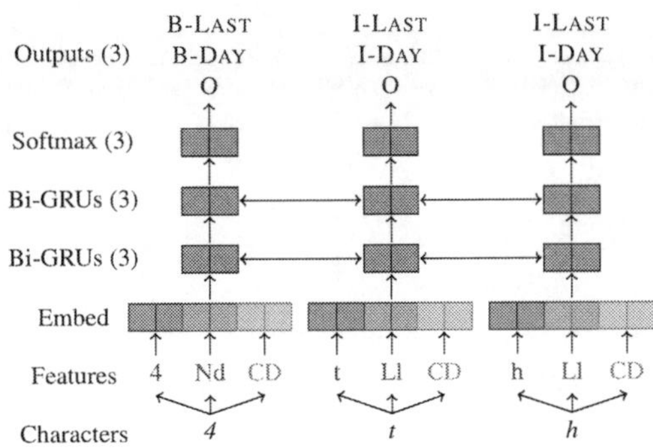

Figure 1: Architecture of Laparra et al. (2018a)'s time identification system. The input is *the 4th of May* (truncated for space). *4th* is a DAY-OF-MONTH, with an implicit LAST over the same span. At the feature layer, *4* is a digit (Nd), *t* and *h* are lowercase letters (Ll), and *4th* has the cardinal number (CD) part-of-speech tag.

the spans of characters that belong to each time expression and labels them with their corresponding time entity; and b) time entity composition using a simple set of rules that links relevant entities together while respecting the entity type constraints imposed by the SCATE schema. These two tasks are run sequentially using the predicted output of the sequence tagger as input to the rule-based time entity composition system. In this paper, We focus on the character-level time entity identifier that is the foundation of Laparra et al. (2018a)'s model.

The sequence tagger is a multi-output RNN with three different input features, shown in Figure 1. Features are mapped through an embedding layer, then fed into stacked bidirectional Gated Recurrent Units (bi-GRUs), and followed by a softmax layer. There are three types of outputs per Laparra et al. (2018a)'s encoding of the SCATE schema, so there is a separate stack of bi-GRUs and a softmax for each output type. We keep the original neural architecture and parameter settings in Laparra et al. (2018a), and experiment with the following embedding layers:

Rand(128): the original setting of Laparra et al. (2018a), where 128-dimensional character embeddings are randomly initialized.

Rand(4096): 4096-dimensional character embeddings are randomly initialized, matching the dimensionality of the Flair forward-backward LM hidden states, i.e., matching the dimensionality of Cont(4096).

Cont(4096): 4096-dimensional pre-trained contextual character embeddings are derived by run-

Model	Domain	Ident.	Parsing	Interv.
Rand(128)-ori	News	61.5	51.2	76.4
Rand(128)	News	59.4	50.5	64.6
Rand(4096)	News	64.8	54.1	68.2
Cont(4096)	News	**80.3**	**66.8**	**81.5**
Rand(128)-ori	Clinical	84.7	57.9	72.1
Rand(128)	Clinical	92.8	65.3	82.1
Rand(4096)	Clinical	93.2	65.3	83.8
Cont(4096)	Clinical	**95.2**	**67.3**	**85.8**

Table 1: Results on Identification (Ident.), Parsing and Interval extraction (Interv.) of time expressions for News and Clinical domain. Rand(128)-ori refers to the original implementation, and Rand(128) and Cont(4096) refer to our re-implementation[1].

ning Flair forward-backward character-level LM Flair's forward and backward character-level language models over the text, and concatenating the hidden states from forward and backward character-level LMs for each character .

We evaluate in the clinical and news domains, the former being more than 9 times larger and the latter having a more diverse set of labels. Three different evaluation metrics are used for parsing time normalization tasks: identification of time entities, which evaluates the predicted span (offsets) and the SCATE type for each entity; parsing of time entities, which evaluates the span, the SCATE type, and properties for each time entity; interval extraction, which interprets parsed annotations as intervals along the timeline and measures the fraction of the correctly parsed intervals. The SemeEval task description paper (Laparra et al., 2018b) has more details on dataset statistics and evaluation metrics.

3 Results

Table 1 shows that the model using pre-trained contextual character embeddings, Cont(4096), outperforms the model of Laparra et al. (2018a) on all three metrics: identification of time entities, parsing, and interval extraction. For identification, our primary focus as we are only modifying the identification portion of Laparra et al. (2018a), Cont(4096) reduces error by 51% (59.4 to 80.3 F_1) on news, and by 33% (92.8 to 95.2 F_1) on clinical notes. For the following experiments, we only use the identification metric to evaluate the performance.

	Domain	Dev	Test
Rand(128)	News	76.5	59.4
Rand(4096)	News	82.7	64.8
Cont(4096)	News	**87.4**	**80.3**
Rand(128)	Clinical	92.9	92.8
Rand(4096)	Clinical	92.6	93.2
Cont(4096)	Clinical	**94.7**	**95.2**

Table 2: Performance (F_1) of time entity identification.

		News		Clinical	
		Dev	Test	Dev	Test
Variation	+var	**+8.4**	**+15.0**	+1.2	+1.3
	-var	+1.6	+8.7	+1.2	**+1.4**
Frequency	≤10	+8.1	+17.6	+2.0	+4.2
	>10	+2.4	+5.0	+1.1	+1.1

Table 3: Effect of term variations and frequency: improvement in F_1 of Cont(4096) over Rand(4096).

4 Where the improvements come from

4.1 Larger character embeddings

Table 2 compares different embedding sizes. Moving from random 128-dimensional to random 4096-dimensional embeddings improves the model: Rand(4096) statistically outperforms[2] Rand(128) on news dev ($p = 0.0001$), news test ($p = 0.0291$), and clinical test ($p = 0.0301$), though it is not statistically different on clinical dev ($p = 0.2524$). Pre-trained contextual embeddings provide additional benefits: Cont(4096) significantly outperforms Rand(4096) on all datasets ($p < 0.001$ in all cases). We conclude that pre-trained contextual character embeddings provide more than just greater model capacity.

4.2 Robustness to variants and frequency

Table 3 shows how pre-trained contextual character embeddings improve performance on both **term variations** and **low frequency words**.

We define **term variations** as time entities that appear in the training data in the following patterns: both upper-case and lower-case, e.g., *DAY*, *Day*, and *day*; abbreviation with and without punctuation, e.g., *AM* and *A.M.*; or same stem, e.g., *Month* and *Months*, *previously* and *previous*. In the dev and test sets, 30.4-35.6% of entities are term variations. The first 2 rows of table 3 show the performance improvements in F_1 of Cont(4096)

---

[1] We upgraded Keras from 1.2 to 2.1 and fixed a code bug that allowed predictions to be made on padding tokens.

[2] We used a paired bootstrap resampling significance test.

	Train	Target	Dev	Test
Rand(128)	Clinical	News	63.4	65.5
Rand(4096)	Clinical	News	62.6	66.9
Cont(4096)	Clinical	News	**68.3**	**78.5**
Rand(128)	News	Clinical	45.3	46.3
Rand(4096)	News	Clinical	43.8	44.3
Cont(4096)	News	Clinical	**57.1**	**59.5**

Table 4: Effect of domain change on performance: (F_1) on News and Clinical datasets.

over Rand(4096) on time entities with (+var) and without (-var) term variations. Cont(4096) is always better than Rand(4096) so all differences are positive, but the improvements in +var are much larger than those of -var in the news domain (+8.4 vs. +1.6 and +15.0 vs. +8.7). In the clinical domain, where 9 times more training data is available, both +var and -var yield similar improvements. We conclude that pre-trained contextual character embeddings are mostly helpful with term variations in low data scenarios.

We define **infrequent terms** as time entities that occur in the training set 10 or fewer times. In the dev and test sets, 73.9-86.9% of terms are infrequent, with about one third of infrequent terms being numerical[3]. The bottom two rows of table 3 show the improvements in F_1 of the Cont(4096) over Rand(4096) on frequent (>10) and infrequent (≤ 10) terms. Cont(4096) is always better than Rand(4096), and in both domains the improvements on low frequency terms are always greater than those on high frequency terms (+8.1 vs. +2.4 in news dev, +17.6 vs. +5.0 in news test, etc.). We conclude that pre-trained contextual character embeddings improve the representations of low frequency words in both low and high data settings.

4.3 Robustness to domain differences

To illustrate the ability of pre-trained contextual character embeddings to handle unseen data, we train the models in one domain and evaluate in the other, as shown in Table 4. We find that Rand(128) and Rand(4096) achieve similar cross-domain performance, e.g., Rand(128) achieves 63.4% of F_1 on news dev and Rand(4096) achieves 62.6% F_1. But Cont(4096) achieves much better cross-domain performance than Rand(128) or Rand(4096): 78.5% vs. 65.5% or 66.9% F_1 on news test, 59.5% vs. 46.3% or 44.3% on clinical test, etc. All these

improvements are significant ($p < 0.001$). We conclude that pre-trained contextual character embeddings generalize better across domains.

4.4 Greater reliance on nearby context

Inspired by Khandelwal et al. (2018)'s analysis of the effective context size of a word-based language model, we present an ablation study to measure performance when contextual information is removed. Specifically, when evaluating models, we retain only the characters in a small window around each time entity in the dev and test sets, and replace all other characters with padding characters.

Figures 2a and 2b evaluate the Cont(4096), Rand(4096) and Rand(128) models across different context window sizes on the news dev and test set, respectively. Rand(128) performs similarly across all context sizes, suggesting that it makes little use of context information. Both Rand(4096) and Cont(4096) depend heavily of context: without any context information (context size 0), they perform worse than Rand(128). Cont(4096) is sensitive to the nearby context, with a $\sim$10 point gain on news dev and $\sim$15 point gain on news test from just the first 10 characters of context, putting it easily above Rand(128). Rand(4096) doesn't exceed the performance of Rand(128) until at least 50 characters of context.

Figures 2c and 2d shows similar trends in the clinical domain, except that the Rand(128) model now shows a small dependence on context, with a $\sim$5 point drop on clinical dev and a $\sim$3 drop on clinical test in the no-context setting. Cont(4096) again makes large improvements in just the first 10 characters, and Rand(4096) now takes close to 100 characters of context to reach the performance of Rand(128). We conclude that pre-trained contextual character embeddings make better use of local context, especially within the first 10 characters.

4.5 Encoding word categories

We perform a feature ablation to see if pre-trained contextual character embeddings capture basic syntax (e.g., part-of-speech) like pre-trained contextual word embeddings do (Peters et al., 2018; Akbik et al., 2018). Table 5 shows that removing both part-of-speech and unicode category features from Cont(4096) does not significantly change performance: news dev ($p = 0.8813$), news test ($p = 0.1672$), clinical dev ($p = 0.5367$), clinical test ($p = 0.8537$). But ablating part-of-speech tags and unicode character categories does decrease per-

---

[3]Numbers are common in time expressions.

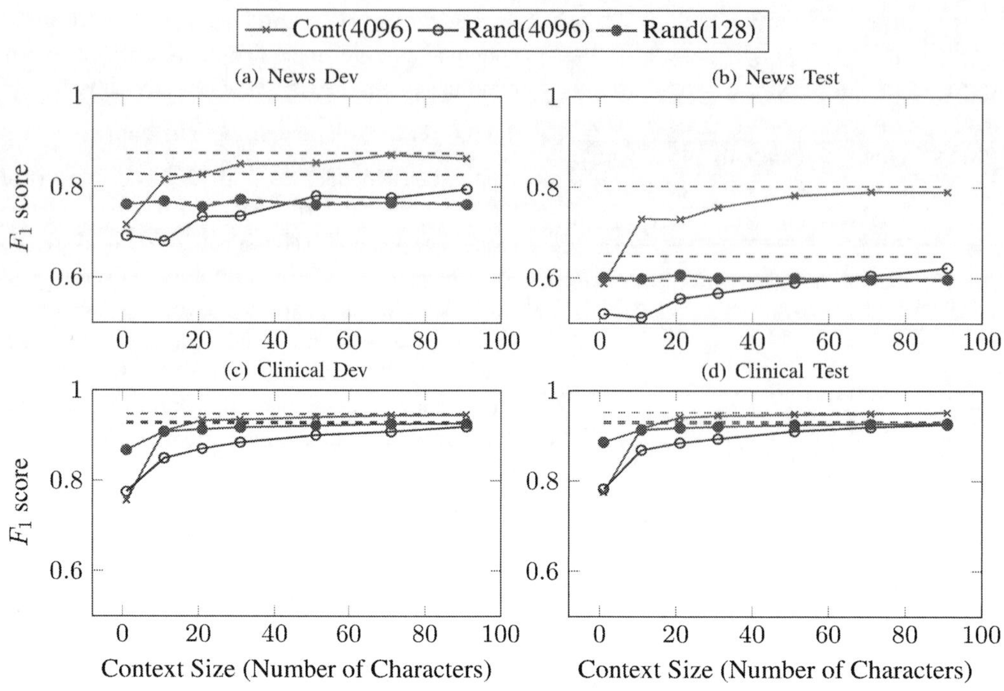

Figure 2: Effect of the context information on the performances for Cont(4096), Rand(4096) and Rand(128) on the dev and test sets. The dashed lines are the performances of models using the original context setting.

| | | News | | Clinical | |
	Set	Dev	Test	Dev	Test
Rand(128)	C	73.6	56.1	91.9	92.1
Rand(128)	CUP	76.5	59.4	92.9	92.8
Rand(4096)	C	80.5	62.4	91.7	92.2
Rand(4096)	CUP	82.7	64.8	92.6	93.2
Cont(4096)	C	87.9	78.1	94.7	95.5
Cont(4096)	CUP	87.4	80.3	94.7	95.2

Table 5: Effect of features on performance: Performance (F_1) with different feature sets, including characters (C), part-of-speech tags (P), and unicode character categories (U).

formance for both Rand(128) and Rand(4096) in all cases. For example, Rand(4096) with all features achieves 82.7 F_1 on news dev, significantly better than the 80.5 F_1 of using only characters ($p = 0.0467$). We conclude that pre-trained contextual character embeddings encode a variety of word category information such as part-of-speech, capitalization, and punctuation.

5   Conclusion

We derive pre-trained character-level contextual embeddings from Flair (Akbik et al., 2018), a word-level embedding model, inject these into a state-of-the-art time normalization system, and achieve major performance improvements: 51% error reduction in news and 33% in clinical notes. Our detailed analysis concludes that pre-trained contextual character embeddings are more robust to term variations, infrequent terms, and cross-domain changes; that they benefit most from the first 10 characters of context; and that they encode part-of-speech, capitalization, and punctuation information.

6   Acknowledgements

We thank the anonymous reviewers for helpful comments on an earlier draft of this paper. This work was supported by National Institutes of Health grants R01GM114355 from the National Institute of General Medical Sciences (NIGMS) and R01LM012918 from the National Library of Medicine (NLM). The computations were done in systems supported by the National Science Foundation under Grant No. 1228509. The content is solely the responsibility of the authors and does not necessarily represent the official views of the National Institutes of Health or National Science Foundation.

References

Alan Akbik, Duncan Blythe, and Roland Vollgraf. 2018. Contextual string embeddings for sequence labeling. In *Proceedings of the 27th International Conference on Computational Linguistics*, pages 1638–1649, Santa Fe, New Mexico, USA. Association for Computational Linguistics.

Steven Bethard and Jonathan Parker. 2016. A semantically compositional annotation scheme for time normalization. In *Proceedings of the Tenth International Conference on Language Resources and Evaluation (LREC 2016)*, Paris, France. European Language Resources Association (ELRA).

Bernd Bohnet, Ryan McDonald, Gonçalo Simões, Daniel Andor, Emily Pitler, and Joshua Maynez. 2018. Morphosyntactic tagging with a meta-bilstm model over context sensitive token encodings. In *Proceedings of the 56th Annual Meeting of the Association for Computational Linguistics (Volume 1: Long Papers)*, pages 2642–2652.

Ciprian Chelba, Tomas Mikolov, Mike Schuster, Qi Ge, Thorsten Brants, Phillipp Koehn, and Tony Robinson. 2014. One billion word benchmark for measuring progress in statistical language modeling. In *Fifteenth Annual Conference of the International Speech Communication Association*.

Jacob Devlin, Ming-Wei Chang, Kenton Lee, and Kristina Toutanova. 2018. Bert: Pre-training of deep bidirectional transformers for language understanding. *arXiv preprint arXiv:1810.04805*.

Jeremy Howard and Sebastian Ruder. 2018. Universal language model fine-tuning for text classification. In *Proceedings of the 56th Annual Meeting of the Association for Computational Linguistics (Volume 1: Long Papers)*, volume 1, pages 328–339.

Urvashi Khandelwal, He He, Peng Qi, and Dan Jurafsky. 2018. Sharp nearby, fuzzy far away: How neural language models use context. In *Proceedings of the 56th Annual Meeting of the Association for Computational Linguistics (Volume 1: Long Papers)*, pages 284–294. Association for Computational Linguistics.

Onur Kuru, Ozan Arkan Can, and Deniz Yuret. 2016. Charner: Character-level named entity recognition. In *Proceedings of COLING 2016, the 26th International Conference on Computational Linguistics: Technical Papers*, pages 911–921.

Egoitz Laparra, Dongfang Xu, and Steven Bethard. 2018a. From characters to time intervals: New paradigms for evaluation and neural parsing of time normalizations. *Transactions of the Association of Computational Linguistics*, 6:343–356.

Egoitz Laparra, Dongfang Xu, Ahmed Elsayed, Steven Bethard, and Martha Palmer. 2018b. Semeval 2018 task 6: Parsing time normalizations. In *Proceedings of The 12th International Workshop on Semantic Evaluation*, pages 88–96.

Tomas Mikolov, Ilya Sutskever, Kai Chen, Greg S Corrado, and Jeff Dean. 2013. Distributed representations of words and phrases and their compositionality. In *Advances in neural information processing systems*, pages 3111–3119.

Jeffrey Pennington, Richard Socher, and Christopher Manning. 2014. Glove: Global vectors for word representation. In *Proceedings of the 2014 conference on empirical methods in natural language processing (EMNLP)*, pages 1532–1543.

Matthew Peters, Mark Neumann, Mohit Iyyer, Matt Gardner, Christopher Clark, Kenton Lee, and Luke Zettlemoyer. 2018. Deep contextualized word representations. In *Proceedings of the 2018 Conference of the North American Chapter of the Association for Computational Linguistics: Human Language Technologies, Volume 1 (Long Papers)*, volume 1, pages 2227–2237.

Ye Qi, Devendra Sachan, Matthieu Felix, Sarguna Padmanabhan, and Graham Neubig. 2018. When and why are pre-trained word embeddings useful for neural machine translation? In *Proceedings of the 2018 Conference of the North American Chapter of the Association for Computational Linguistics: Human Language Technologies, Volume 2 (Short Papers)*, volume 2, pages 529–535.

Alec Radford, Karthik Narasimhan, Tim Salimans, and Ilya Sutskever. 2018. Improving language understanding by generative pre-training. *URL https://s3-us-west-2. amazonaws. com/openai-assets/research-covers/language-unsupervised/language_ understanding_paper. pdf*.

Kelly Zhang and Samuel Bowman. 2018. Language modeling teaches you more than translation does: Lessons learned through auxiliary syntactic task analysis. In *Proceedings of the 2018 EMNLP Workshop BlackboxNLP: Analyzing and Interpreting Neural Networks for NLP*, pages 359–361.

Xiang Zhang, Junbo Zhao, and Yann LeCun. 2015. Character-level convolutional networks for text classification. In C. Cortes, N. D. Lawrence, D. D. Lee, M. Sugiyama, and R. Garnett, editors, *Advances in Neural Information Processing Systems 28*, pages 649–657. Curran Associates, Inc.

A   Appendices

A.1   Examples of the improvement

We analyzed a few examples where Cont(4096) makes correct predictions, but Rand(4096) does not.

Robustness to variants

"…with year-earlier profit of millions…"
In this sentence, the Cont(4096) model labeled *earlier* correctly, while the Rand(4096) model missed it. In the news training set, *earlier* occurs a few times, but none of them have "-" nearby.

Robustness to frequency

"…in the first days after President…"
In this sentence, the Cont(4096) model labeled *first* correctly, while the Rand(4096) model labeled it incorrectly. In the news training set, *first* only occurred once when followed by another time entity, but there were several similar sentences for *second* and *third* in the training set.

Robustness to word order

"…until twenty years after the first astronauts…"
"…comes barely a month after Qantas…"
"…Retaliating 13 days after the deadly…"
In each of the sentences above, the Cont(4096) model labeled *after* correctly, while Rand(4096) labeled it incorrectly. In the training set, there were a few examples where *after* occurred near a time entity, but always before the time entity (e.g., *after ten years, after 22 months, after three days, after a 16-hour flight*) rather than after it as in the examples above. Cont(4096) may have learned a better representation for *after* that allows it to be less dependent on exact word order.

Bot2Vec: Learning Representations of Chatbots

Jonathan Herzig[1]   Tommy Sandbank[*,2]   Michal Shmueli-Scheuer[1]
David Konopnicki[1]   John Richards[1]

[1]IBM Research
[2]Similari

{hjon, shmueli, davidko}.il.ibm.com, tommy@similari.com, ajtr@us.ibm.com

Abstract

Chatbots (i.e., *bots*) are becoming widely used in multiple domains, along with supporting bot programming platforms. These platforms are equipped with novel testing tools aimed at improving the quality of individual chatbots. Doing so requires an understanding of what sort of bots are being built (captured by their underlying conversation graphs) and how well they perform (derived through analysis of conversation logs). In this paper, we propose a new model, BOT2VEC, that embeds bots to a compact representation based on their structure and usage logs. Then, we utilize BOT2VEC representations to improve the quality of two bot analysis tasks. Using conversation data and graphs of over than 90 bots, we show that BOT2VEC representations improve detection performance by more than 16% for both tasks.

1   Introduction

As conversational systems (i.e., chatbots) become more pervasive, careful analysis of their capabilities becomes important. Conversational systems are being used for a variety of support, service, and sales applications that were formerly handled by human agents. Thus, organizations deploying such systems must be able to understand bots behavior to improve their performance. In many cases, such an analysis can be viewed as a classification task whose goal is to check whether a bot or a particular instance of a conversation satisfies some property (e.g., is the conversation successful?). Models for these downstream classification tasks should benefit from conditioning on representations that capture global bot behavior.

For a conversation itself, there exists a natural way to represent it as the concatenation of the human and bot utterances. As for a bot, the question of its representation is more complicated: bots are complex objects that execute logic in order to drive conversations with users. How should they best be represented?

Many commercial companies provide bot programming platforms. These platforms provide tools and services to develop bots, monitor and improve their quality. Due to the increasing popularity of bots, thousands or tens of thousands of bots could be deployed by different companies on each platform[1]. Although bots might have different purposes and different underlying structures, the ability to understand bot behavior at a high level could inspire new tools and services benefitting all bots on the platform. In this work, we explore a commercial platform, and study different bot representations.

Inspired by the success of recently proposed learned embeddings for objects such as graphs (Narayanan et al., 2017), nodes (Grover and Leskovec, 2016), documents (Le and Mikolov, 2014) and words (Mikolov et al., 2013a), we propose a new model, BOT2VEC, that learns bot embeddings, and propose both content and graph based representations. While previous graph embedding representations consider static local structures in the graph (Narayanan et al., 2017; Grover and Leskovec, 2016), our graph representation is based on dynamic conversation paths. As bots are usually represented on bot platforms as some form of directed graph, with conversations represented as traversals on the graph, this approach seems reasonable. It captures the way the bot is actually used, in addition to how it is structured.

In this paper, our goal is to consider various bot embeddings and two different but realistic classification tasks, and test whether some bot representations are more appropriate for these tasks. The first task, at the level of entire bots, aims to detect

---

* Work was done while working at IBM.

[1]https://www.techemergence.com/chatbot-comparison-facebook-microsoft-amazon-google/

*Proceedings of the Eighth Joint Conference on Lexical and Computational Semantics (*SEM)*, pages 75–84
Minneapolis, June 6–7, 2019. ©2019 Association for Computational Linguistics

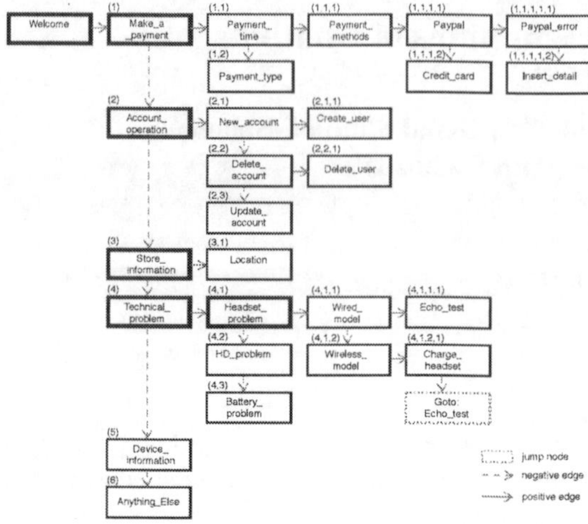

Figure 1: Example of a customer support bot graph.

whether the bot is in production (i.e., in use with real human users) or not. The second task, at the conversation level within each bot, aims to detect problematic conversations with a deployed bot in support of focusing improvement efforts.

The main contributions of this paper are three-fold: (1) this is the first research that leverages information from multiple bots in order to improve bot quality, (2) this is the first research to propose an embedding approach for bots based on their structure and how this structure is exploited during conversations, and (3) we empirically evaluate these representations for two classification tasks using data from more than 90 conversational bots.

We find that our proposed representations lead to more than 16% improvement in classification for our two tasks, with our structure-based representation performing better than our content-based representation. This suggests that the representations explored in this paper are valuable across a range of possible tasks.

2 Bot Overview

Although different programming models can be used to create bots, in practice, most commercial conversational system platforms represent the conversation control flow for bots as graphs. In this paper, we use a bot paradigm based on one of the publicly available commercial platforms, but it is quite general and can be adapted to fit to other bot programming platforms. Our example in Figure 1 shows a part of a customer support bot graph, and we use it to explain how such a graph is used in the context of a conversation.

At every step (i.e., every *turn*) of a conversation with a bot, the human user expresses an utterance and the bot analyzes it, determines how to respond and updates its internal state. This determination is executed by traversing the graph, starting from a special node called the *root* node, and moving along the nodes of the graph according to a given set of rules as described below. Note that this description aims to present and explain key abstractions rather than the implementation details of an actual bot platform.

2.1 Graph Components

Every node in the graph has two internal parts: a user intent, and an optional reply of the bot. Given a user utterance, an intent classifier is used to determine whether the user utterance matches the intent associated with the node. For example, the *Technical_problem* node has been defined to capture cases where users encounter a technical problem with a product, and this is what is being expressed in the utterance at hand (e.g., *"I'm having some issues with my headset"*). In this case, the classifier should be able to classify this utterance as relevant to this intent. In practice, the intent classifier is trained from examples of utterances and their corresponding intents, written by bot programmers.

Every node has two optional outgoing edges: a *positive* edge and a *negative* edge. If a user utterance has been classified positively, the optional node answer is presented to the user, and the execution moves to the node which is the target of the positive edge. When the execution moves along a positive edge, it is possible to obtain additional input from the user, and continue the evaluation using this input. If a user utterance has been classified negatively, the execution moves to the node which is the target of the negative edge. As shown in Figure 1, we represent nodes connected by negative edges along the vertical axis, and nodes connected by positive edges along the horizontal axis.

When there is no positive edge and the classification is positive, the execution stops, and the system waits for the next user utterance. When there is no negative edge and the classification is negative, execution jumps back to the root node to resume evaluation from the start.

In addition to the nodes that we just described, there are special *sink* nodes (in our example, the

Agent: *Hi, I'm Eva a virtual assistant, how may I help you?*
Customer: *I'm having some issues with my headset*
Agent: *Which model are you using?*
Customer: *A wireless one.*
Agent: *Please make sure that they are charged.*
Customer: *Yes they are, and they work well with other devices...*
Agent: *Got you. In this case go and try our echo test.*
Customer: *Well, I'll stop by one of your stores and see a technician.*
Agent: *I'm not trained on that yet, but I'm still learning. You may want to rephrase your question and try again.*
Customer: *What is your closest location?*
Agent: *Check here to see our locations in your city.*

Figure 2: Example of a possible conversation.

Anything_Else node), which are not the source of any edges, and which typically trigger a special default message like *"I'm still in a learning phase, is there anything else I can help you with?"*. As bots support only a limited set of intents, this mechanism is used to let the user know that some intent is beyond the knowledge of the bot, and to initiate a recovery process.

2.2 Graph Execution

A conversation starts by traversing the graph from the root node. The root node is special in that it does not expect a user utterance, and it only has a positive edge. Its optional response, which can be a greeting message for example, is only output once at the beginning of the conversation.

Consequently, a user utterance defines a path in the graph, and each conversation between a human and the bot can be represented as a sequence of paths in the graph. Figure 2 shows an example of such a conversation.

The nodes that are evaluated for the first user utterance in Figure 2 (*"I'm having some issues with my headset"*) are marked in bold in Figure 1. Thus, the path that is created by the analysis of this utterance starts with the root node *Welcome*, then moves to the *Make_a_payment* node, checking whether this utterance expresses the user intention to make a payment. Since it is not, control moves to the *Account_operation* node, and then, in turn, to the *Store_information* node, along the negative edges, until it reaches the *Technical_problem* node. Here, the internal classifier determines that the utterance indeed expresses that the user encountered a technical problem. As a result, the control moves along the positive edge to the *Headset_problem* node. Once the node's reply is presented to the user (*"Which model are you using?"*), the system then waits for the next user utterance. The next user utterance (*"A wireless one."*) leads to the *Wireless_model* node, hence the resulting path for this utterance is a continuation of the previous path.

Note that nodes connected vertically by negative edges represent alternative understandings of an utterance. That is, in our example, an utterance can be identified as *Account_operation*, *Store_information* or *Technical_problem*, etc. Nodes connected by horizontal positive edges represent specializations of the analysis. That is, after the utterance is classified as *Technical_problem*, moving along the positive edge will check whether the utterance expresses a *Headset_problem*, or (moving again vertically along negative edges) a *HD_problem* or, alternatively, a *Battery_problem*.

In addition, special *jump* nodes are nodes that allow the conversation to jump to a designated node. In our example the node below *Charge_headset*, that refers to the *Echo_test* node, is a jump. Such jump nodes are not essential, but simplify the graph by preventing duplication of subgraphs.

2.3 Notations

We define the *depth* of the bot graph as the maximum number of nodes from left to right (ignoring the root node), i.e. nodes connected by positive edges. The depth of a node v is defined as the number of positive edges used to traverse the graph from the root node to v. In our example from Figure 1 the depth of the graph is 5, while the depth of *Headset_problem* is 2. We define the level l as the set of all the nodes whose depth is l. We define the *width* of the graph at level l as the maximum number of nodes connected by negative edges at this level. In our example, the width of level 1 is 6, while the width of level 2 is 3.

To further simplify notations, we consider a grid layout that defines coordinates for the nodes from left to right and from top to bottom. For example, node *Technical_problem* is mapped to (4), which means that it is the 4th node from top to bottom at level 1. The node *Headset_problem* is mapped to (4,1), meaning that it is the 1st node at level 2 of the 4th node at level 1. Similarly, the node *HD_problem* is mapped to coordinate (4,2) and *Wireless_model* is (4,1,2). Note that nodes located deeper in the graph are mapped to a longer list of coordinates. The maximal possible length of a co-ordinate for a node is the depth of the graph.

2.4 Bot Behavior

The graph of a bot determines its behavior, and thus, the structure of the graph captures interesting properties of the bot. For example, there are bots designed to handle simple Q&A conversations, as opposed to bots that handle filling in the details of complex transactions. For Q&A bots, the graph is likely to be of depth 1, with many nodes at this level, representing various alternative questions and answers. For bots handling complex conversations, the graphs are likely to be deeper in order to handle more complicated cases. In general, bots handling narrow use-cases and which are very specific in their dialog capabilities, are likely to have fewer nodes and more jumps to sink nodes. Thus, in order to capture the bot behavior we should consider the different characteristics of its graph, and this is what we would like to capture in our representation.

3 Bot2Vec Framework

3.1 Representation Learning

In this work, we employ a neural network model to learn the BOT2VEC representation. The training input to this model is either a *content-based* representation or a *structure-based* representation of conversations between a human and a bot. Both are described in the following sections. The result of the training is a vector representation for each bot in the dataset.

To learn this BOT2VEC representation, a fully connected network with N hidden layers is used. During training, the input to this network is the representation of a conversation (either content-based or structure-based), and the ground truth is a one-hot vector of the bot that handled this conversation. In other words, given a conversation c, the network predicts which bot handled c using softmax, that is a distribution over the bots. Thus, the output layer vector of the model has the size of the number of bots in the dataset. Once the model is trained, the representation of a bot b is the weights vector $V_{b,}$, where V is the output embedding matrix (the weights matrix connecting the last hidden layer to the output layer).

The motivation for choosing this representation is that the training procedure (using cross-entropy loss) should drive similar bots to simi-lar representations, given that they handle similar conversations. In the context of learning word representations using the Word2Vec skip-gram model (Mikolov et al., 2013b), the output embeddings were found to be of good quality (Press and Wolf, 2017). Hereafter, we denote the content-based model as BOT2VEC-C, and the structure-based model as BOT2VEC-S.

We now describe how a conversation is represented using its textual content and using its bot graph structure which is used as input for the model.

3.2 Content-based Representation

Conversations between users and bots occur in natural language, and as shown in Figure 2, are composed of user utterances and bot responses. The first step for creating our textual representation of a single conversation is to build a vocabulary, which is the union of all terms across all conversations of all the bots in the dataset. We first mask tokens that might reveal the bot's identity, such as bot names, URLs, HTML tags etc. To neglect additional bot specific words (which are probably infrequent), we take the k most popular terms to be the vocabulary.

Now, for a given conversation, we create two vectors with term frequency (TF) entries according to the template just defined, one for the user utterances and one for the bot responses. The conversation is then represented as their concatenation.

3.3 Structure-based Representation

Our goal in this representation is to characterize bot behavior by analyzing its conversations with respect to the structure of the bot graph. This learned representation should capture the characteristics of how bots are being utilized. We would like to capture, for example, which nodes are being visited during a conversation with a user, at which nodes the conversation turns end, etc.

Recall that each conversation can be represented as a sequence of paths on the bot graph (a path for each turn). We now describe how to represent a path as a vector (*bin vector* below), and how to aggregate paths of a single conversation.

Bin vector To be able to compare bots with different bot graph structures, we define a common fixed size *bin vector* to represent paths of different bots.

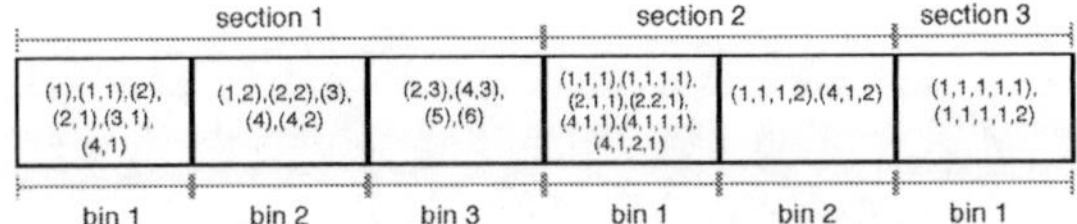

bin 1   bin 2   bin 3   bin 1   bin 2   bin 1

Figure 3: A mapping of a bot graph to the bin vector.

Algorithm 1 Mapping a node to section and bin

	n_l: node depth
	n_w: node width
input	D: graph depth
	$w = w_1, w_2, \ldots, w_D$: graph width at each level
	S: number of sections
	$b = b_1, b_2, \ldots, b_S$: number of bins per section
output	n_s: section index
	n_b: bin index

1: $n_s = \lfloor \frac{(n_l - 1)}{d} \times S + 1 \rfloor$
2: $n_b = \lfloor \frac{(n_w - 1)}{w_l} \times b_{n_s} + 1 \rfloor$
3: **return** n_s, n_b

We create a bin vector such that each node in the bot graph is mapped to a single bin based on its co-ordinates in the graph. Each bin vector is divided into S sections, and each section s is divided into b_s bins (Figure 3). Since the idea is to represent a conversation path in a standardized and compact way across different bots, each level in the bot graph is mapped to a section in the bin vector, and each node in the bot graph is mapped to a bin in the appropriate section (see Algorithm 1). Several levels might be mapped to the same section, and several nodes can be mapped to the same bin (sections do not necessarily have the same number of bins). The number of sections and bins in the bin vector are set based on the depths and widths of all the bot graphs (e.g., the average depth of the graphs and the average width of each level in the graphs). For example, the bin vector in Figure 3 represents the mapping of all nodes for the bot graph in Figure 1. This bin vector has 3 sections. There are 3 bins in section 1, 2 bins in section 2, and 1 bin in section 3.

Utterance modeling We now explain how each utterance is represented using the bin vector. As mentioned above, each user utterance in a conversation is represented by a path in the bot graph, whose nodes can be mapped to sections and bins in the bin vector. In order to capture how every utterance is being analyzed by the bot, we distinguish between different types of nodes in the path:

1. A *success (s)* node is the last node of the path, if it is not a sink node.

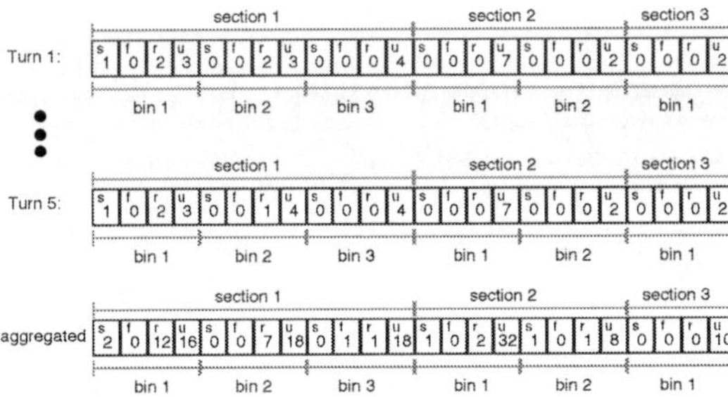

Figure 4: Bin vector representation of turns in a conversation.

2. A *failure (f)* node is the last node of the path, if it is a sink node.

3. All the other nodes that belong to the path are *regular (r)* nodes.

4. Nodes that do not belong to the path are *uninvolved (u)* nodes.

When representing a path, we consider the type of the node it is mapped to, in the corresponding bins in the bin vector: each bin maintains 4 counters, one counter for each type of node mentioned above (*success*, *failure*, *regular* and *uninvolved*). That is, the mapping of the first user utterance *"I'm having some issues with my headset"* to the bin vector is as follows:

- The first node in the bot graph that is visited is *Make_a_payment* (1). This node is mapped to the first bin in section 1 of the bin vector. Thus the *regular* counter is set to 1 for this bin.

- The second node traversed in the bot graph is *Account_operation* (2), which is mapped to the same first bin of section 1 of the bin vector. Hence, the *regular* counter of this bin is set to 2 in the bin vector.

- Similarly, nodes *Store_information* (3) and *Technical_problem* (4) are visited, and that sets the *regular* counter of bin 2 in section 1 to 2.

- Finally, the *Headset_problem* $(4, 1)$ node is visited, and that sets the *success* counter of bin 1 in section 1 to 1, as this is the last node that is being visited for this utterance. Now we can update the *uninvolved* counters of the bins according to the nodes that were not visited during the traversal.

When this path is mapped to the bin vector, we obtain the vector as shown in "Turn 1" of Figure 4.

Conversation modeling As the input to the model is a conversation, we now describe how it is represented. We aggregate the bin vectors of the user utterances paths by summing each counter based on the node types (s, f, r or u) across all the bins in the matching sections. This aggregation captures different patterns of the conversation, such as how many times nodes which are mapped to a bin are visited, how many turns ended successfully in the mapped nodes vs. how many turns failed in these nodes, etc. Figure 4 depicts the detailed vectors for the first and the fifth customer utterance from Figure 2, as well as the aggregated vector obtained for the whole conversation.

4 Classification Tasks

BOT2VEC representations could be used for a variety of bot analytics tasks. In this research, we have examined two such tasks.

Detecting production bots Several companies provide bot development platforms that are used to create and manage conversational bots. Based on analyses of the logs of one commercial platform, we have found that a large percentage of bots are not being used with real users. From the platform provider perspective, understanding bots interaction with actual users could inspire the development of new tools and services that could assist all of bots that use the platform. Thus, it is important to first determine which bots are used in production, rather than in debugging or testing. This is made difficult by the fact that bot testing often involves somewhat realistic simulations of conversations. Thus, in this binary classification task, a bot should be classified as either a production bot or not, given all of its conversations.

Detecting egregious conversations Once in production, bot log analysis forms the basis for continuous improvement. Finding the areas most in need of improvement is complicated by the fact that bots may have thousands of conversations per day, making it hard to find conversations failing from causes such as faulty classification of user intent, bugs in dialog descriptions, and inadequate use of conversational context. Recently, a new analysis (Sandbank et al., 2018), aims at detecting egregious conversations, those in which the bot behaves so badly that a human agent, if available,

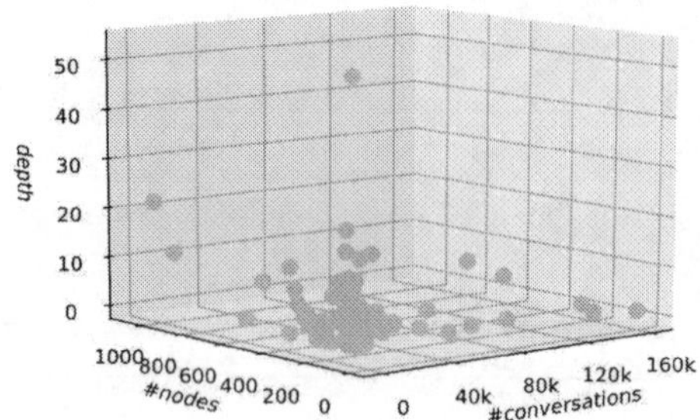

Figure 5: Bots summary: #conversations, #nodes and depth.

would be needed to salvage them. Finding these egregious conversations can help identify where improvement efforts should be focused. In this task, a conversation c should be classified as egregious or not, with the BOT2VEC representation potentially improving performance.

5 Experiments

5.1 Data

We collected two months of data from 92 bots, including their graphs and conversations logs. The bot domains included health, finance, banking, travel, HR, IT support, and more. Figure 5 summarizes the information about number of conversations, number of nodes and graph depth for the bots. In total, we collected 1.3 million conversations, with a minimum of 110 conversations and a maximum of $161,000$ conversations per bot. For 62% of the bots, the number of conversations varied between 1000 to $10,000$. Bot graph depth ranged from 2 to 52 levels with an average depth of 7; the total number of nodes ranged from 11 to 1088 with an average of 160 nodes per bot.

5.2 Experimental Setting

Common bin vector As explained, to capture comparable behavior across bots, we create one common bin vector using the average depth and average width for each level of the bots graphs. Specifically, first, based on the average depth, we define the number of sections to be 7. Then we set the number of bins for each section (based on the average width per level per bot) to 108, 10, 6, 17, 8, 4, and 1, respectively.

Bot2Vec implementation details
Content-based: The content-based model input is comprised of two vectors of size $k = 5000$ each ,

Model	F1-score	% improvement
BOT-STAT	0.519	-
BOT2VEC-C	0.545	5.0
BOT2VEC-S	0.616	18.6

Table 1: Production bots detection - classification results on the test set.

Model	F1-score	% improvement
EGR	0.537	-
bot-STAT	0.597	11.0
BOT2VEC-C	0.617	14.8
BOT2VEC-S	0.626	16.4

Table 2: Egregious conversations - classification results on the test set.

one vector representing the user utterances and the second vector representing the bot responses. The two vectors are concatenated and passed through a fully connected layer with 5000 units. We also calculate the squared difference of the two vectors and an element-wise multiplication of the vectors to capture the interaction between the user and the bot. The three vectors are then concatenated and passed through another two fully connected layers with 1000 and 100 units.

Structure-based: The input is a single vector with the size of 616 (the total number of bins (154) times the 4 counters per bin). This input vector is passed through two fully connected layers with 100 and 20 units.

For both models, the last hidden layer is connected to the output layer (with a size equal to the total number of bots). All hidden layers consists of ReLU activation units, and are regularized using dropout rate of 0.5. The models were optimized using an Adam optimizer with a 0.001 learning rate.

5.3 Task 1 - Production Bots Detection

Ground truth To annotate bots, we randomly sampled 100 conversations from our dataset. The sampled conversations were tagged by two different expert judges. Given a full conversation, each judge tagged the conversation as production or test/debugging. If more than 50% of the conversations were tagged as production, then the bot was tagged as production. In addition, if the bot was annotated as not-production, the experts had to provide a list of reasons for their choice (e.g., repeating users ids, repeating bot response, etc.). We generated true binary labels by considering a bot to be a production bot if both judges agreed. Judges had a Cohen's Kappa coefficient of 0.95 which indicates a high level of agreement. This process generated the production bot class size of 40 (44% of the 92 bots).

Baseline model Inspired by (McIntire et al., 2010; Zhang et al., 2018) we implemented a baseline model denoted BOT-STAT as follows: for each bot we calculated features, such as the number of unique customer sentences, number of conversations, number of unique agent responses, and statistical measures (mean, median, percentile) of the following metrics: number of turns of a conversation, number of tokens in each turn in a conversation, and the time of a turn in a conversation. In total we implemented 17 features.

In our implementation we used an SVM classifier (as we only have 92 samples), measured the F1-score of the production bot class, and evaluated the models using 10-fold cross-validation.

Results Table 1 depicts the classification results for the three models we explored. The BOT2VEC-S model outperformed the other models with a relative improvement of 18.6% over the baseline. The performance of the BOT2VEC-C is slightly better than the baseline which indicates that the information that was captured by the content of the conversations was helpful to detect the usage of the bot. The structure-based representation, however, seems to capture bot variability more effectively, i.e. the coverage of visited nodes, different conversations patterns, etc.

5.4 Task 2 - Egregious Conversations Detection

Ground truth To collect ground truth data, we randomly sampled 12 bots (from the production bots), and for each bot 100 conversations were annotated following the methodology in (Sandbank et al., 2018), namely, given the full conversation, each judge tagged whether the conversation was egregious or not. Judges had a Cohen's Kappa coefficient of 0.93 which indicates a high level of agreement. The size of the egregious class varied between the bots, ranging from 8% to 48% of the conversations. All the conversations were aggregated to one dataset.

Baseline model We implemented the state-of-the-art EGR model, presented in (Sandbank et al., 2018). In addition, our models are an extension of the EGR model, such that for each conversation, its bot representation vector was concatenated to the EGR model's original feature vector.

We measured the F1-score of the egregious class, and evaluated the models using 10-fold cross-validation.

Results Table 2 summarizes the classification results for all models. Specifically, the BOT2VEC-S outperforms all other models with a relative improvement of 16.4%. This suggests that the structure-based representation of the bot encapsulates information which helps the model to distinguish between egregious and non-egregious conversations. Moreover, although the EGR model receives the text of the conversation as input, the content-based representation of the bot also helped to improve the performance of the task.

5.5 Structure-based Analysis

In practice, bots belong to various application domains like *banking*, *IT* and *HR*. Motivated by the semantic similarities between word embeddings (Mikolov et al., 2013b), we further analyzed the structure representation BOT2VEC-S w.r.t bots that belong to the same domain. For the set of production bots, *IT*, *HR*, and the *banking* domains were prominent with 10, 7, and 6 bots respectively, while the other bots belonged to a long tail of domains like *travel*, *medical*, etc. For the prominent domains (that had more than 5 bots), we calculated the average cosine distance between vector representations for pairs of bots that belong to the domain vs. pairs of bots from different domains. We find that the average distance between bots within their domain is 0.614, while the distance between bots from different domains is 0.694. Thus, the representations of bots that belong to the same domain appear to have, as one would expect, a higher level of similarity.

6 Related Work

Despite the popularity of chatbots, research on bot representations and usage analysis is still under explored. Works on chatbot representations are mostly concentrated on neural response generation (Xu et al., 2017; Li et al., 2016; Herzig et al., 2017) and slot filling (Ma and Hovy, 2016; Kurata et al., 2016). In these works, conversation history is used to generate the next bot response. Other works use conversation representations for improving specific tasks useful in dialog, like intent detection (Kato et al., 2017), dia-

log act detection (Kumar et al., 2018), and improving fluency and coherency (Gangadharaiah et al., 2018). Yuwono et al. (2018) learn the quality of chatbot responses by combining word representations of human and chatbot responses using neural approaches. The main difference between these works and ours is that we analyze multiple bots within a service to generate representations useful to each whereas others analyze a single bot at a time. In addition, we show that our representations are beneficial across different tasks. Finally, none of these works consider the structure of the bot as part of the representation.

Learning embeddings for different objects is one of the most explored tasks[2]. As mentioned above, graphs and nodes representations were proposed in (Narayanan et al., 2017; Grover and Leskovec, 2016). Both works considered static local structures in graphs, whereas our graph representation is based on dynamic conversation paths. The work in (Mikolov et al., 2013b) suggested a Word2Vec skip-gram model such that a word is predicted given its context. In our work, we take a similar approach fitted to the more complex structure of bots, and predict a bot id given a representation of a conversation.

Recently, Guo et al. (2018); Pereira and Díaz (2018) presented a chatbot usage analysis over several bots. Guo et al. (2018) compared the performance of various chatbots that participated in the Alexa prize challenge and implemented the same scenario. To do so, the authors used different measures such as conversational depth and breadth, users engagement, coherency, and more. Pereira and Díaz (2018) suggested a list of quality attributes, and analyzed 100 popular chatbots in Facebook Messenger. Our work focuses on learning bot representations targeted towards classification tasks on the level of bots and their conversations.

7 Conclusions

In this paper, we suggest two BOT2VEC models that capture a bot representation based either on the structure of the bot or the content of its conversations. We showed that utilizing these representations improves two platform analysis tasks, both for bot level and conversation level tasks. Future work includes extension of the model to encapsulate both the content and the structure based

---

[2]https://github.com/MaxwellRebo/awesome-2vec

representations combined together using sequential neural networks (such as RNN).

References

Rashmi Gangadharaiah, Balakrishnan Narayanaswamy, and Charles Elkan. 2018. What we need to learn if we want to do and not just talk. In *Proceedings of the 2018 Conference of the North American Chapter of the Association for Computational Linguistics: Human Language Technologies, Volume 3 (Industry Papers)*, pages 25–32. Association for Computational Linguistics.

Aditya Grover and Jure Leskovec. 2016. node2vec: Scalable feature learning for networks. In *Proceedings of the 22nd ACM SIGKDD international conference on Knowledge discovery and data mining*, pages 855–864. ACM.

Fenfei Guo, Angeliki Metallinou, Chandra Khatri, Anirudh Raju, Anu Venkatesh, and Ashwin Ram. 2018. Topic-based evaluation for conversational bots. *CoRR*, abs/1801.03622.

Jonathan Herzig, Michal Shmueli-Scheuer, Tommy Sandbank, and David Konopnicki. 2017. Neural response generation for customer service based on personality traits. In *Proceedings of the 10th International Conference on Natural Language Generation*, pages 252–256. Association for Computational Linguistics.

Tsuneo Kato, Atsushi Nagai, Naoki Noda, Ryosuke Sumitomo, Jianming Wu, and Seiichi Yamamoto. 2017. Utterance intent classification of a spoken dialogue system with efficiently untied recursive autoencoders. In *Proceedings of the 18th Annual SIGdial Meeting on Discourse and Dialogue*, pages 60–64. Association for Computational Linguistics.

Harshit Kumar, Arvind Agarwal, Riddhiman Dasgupta, and Sachindra Joshi. 2018. Dialogue act sequence labeling using hierarchical encoder with CRF. In *AAAI*. AAAI Press.

Gakuto Kurata, Bing Xiang, Bowen Zhou, and Mo Yu. 2016. Leveraging sentence-level information with encoder lstm for semantic slot filling. In *Proceedings of the 2016 Conference on Empirical Methods in Natural Language Processing*, pages 2077–2083. Association for Computational Linguistics.

Quoc Le and Tomas Mikolov. 2014. Distributed representations of sentences and documents. In *Proceedings of the 31st International Conference on International Conference on Machine Learning - Volume 32*, ICML'14, pages II–1188–II–1196. JMLR.org.

Jiwei Li, Michel Galley, Chris Brockett, Georgios Spithourakis, Jianfeng Gao, and Bill Dolan. 2016. A persona-based neural conversation model. In *Proceedings of the 54th Annual Meeting of the Association for Computational Linguistics (Volume 1: Long Papers)*, pages 994–1003. Association for Computational Linguistics.

Xuezhe Ma and Eduard Hovy. 2016. End-to-end sequence labeling via bi-directional lstm-cnns-crf. In *Proceedings of the 54th Annual Meeting of the Association for Computational Linguistics (Volume 1: Long Papers)*, pages 1064–1074. Association for Computational Linguistics.

J. P. McIntire, L. K. McIntire, and P. R. Havig. 2010. Methods for chatbot detection in distributed text-based communications. In *2010 International Symposium on Collaborative Technologies and Systems*.

Tomas Mikolov, Kai Chen, Greg Corrado, and Jeffrey Dean. 2013a. Efficient estimation of word representations in vector space. *arXiv preprint arXiv:1301.3781*.

Tomas Mikolov, Ilya Sutskever, Kai Chen, Greg Corrado, and Jeffrey Dean. 2013b. Distributed representations of words and phrases and their compositionality. *CoRR*, abs/1310.4546.

Annamalai Narayanan, Mahinthan Chandramohan, Rajasekar Venkatesan, Lihui Chen, Yang Liu, and Shantanu Jaiswal. 2017. graph2vec: Learning distributed representations of graphs. *CoRR*, abs/1707.05005.

Juanan Pereira and Oscar Díaz. 2018. A quality analysis of facebook messenger's most popular chatbots. In *Proceedings of the 33rd Annual ACM Symposium on Applied Computing*, SAC '18.

Ofir Press and Lior Wolf. 2017. Using the output embedding to improve language models. In *Proceedings of the 15th Conference of the European Chapter of the Association for Computational Linguistics: Volume 2, Short Papers*, pages 157–163. Association for Computational Linguistics.

Tommy Sandbank, Michal Shmueli-Scheuer, Jonathan Herzig, David Konopnicki, John Richards, and David Piorkowski. 2018. Detecting egregious conversations between customers and virtual agents. In *Proceedings of the 2018 Conference of the North American Chapter of the Association for Computational Linguistics: Human Language Technologies, Volume 1 (Long Papers)*, pages 1802–1811. Association for Computational Linguistics.

Zhen Xu, Bingquan Liu, Baoxun Wang, Chengjie SUN, Xiaolong Wang, Zhuoran Wang, and Chao Qi. 2017. Neural response generation via gan with an approximate embedding layer. In *Proceedings of the 2017 Conference on Empirical Methods in Natural Language Processing*, pages 617–626. Association for Computational Linguistics.

Steven Kester Yuwono, Wu Biao, and Luis Fernando D'Haro. 2018. Automated scoring of chatbot responses in conversational dialogue. In *Proceedings of International Workshop on Spoken Dialog System Technology*.

Saizheng Zhang, Emily Dinan, Jack Urbanek, Arthur
Szlam, Douwe Kiela, and Jason Weston. 2018. Per-
sonalizing dialogue agents: I have a dog, do you
have pets too? *CoRR*, abs/1801.07243.

Are We Consistently Biased?
Multidimensional Analysis of Biases in Distributional Word Vectors

Anne Lauscher and **Goran Glavaš**
Data and Web Science Research Group
University of Mannheim
Mannheim, Germany
{anne, goran}@informatik.uni-mannheim.de

Abstract

Word embeddings have recently been shown to reflect many of the pronounced societal biases (e.g., gender bias or racial bias). Existing studies are, however, limited in scope and do not investigate the consistency of biases across relevant dimensions like embedding models, types of texts, and different languages. In this work, we present a systematic study of biases encoded in distributional word vector spaces: we analyze how consistent the bias effects are across languages, corpora, and embedding models. Furthermore, we analyze the cross-lingual biases encoded in bilingual embedding spaces, indicative of the effects of bias transfer encompassed in cross-lingual transfer of NLP models. Our study yields some unexpected findings, e.g., that biases can be emphasized or downplayed by different embedding models or that user-generated content may be less biased than encyclopedic text. We hope our work catalyzes bias research in NLP and informs the development of bias reduction techniques.

1 Introduction

Recent work demonstrated that word embeddings induced from large text collections encode many human biases (e.g., Bolukbasi et al., 2016; Caliskan et al., 2017). This finding is not particularly surprising given that (1) we are likely project our biases in the text that we produce and (2) these biases in text are bound to be encoded in word vectors due to the distributional nature (Harris, 1954) of the word embedding models (Mikolov et al., 2013a; Pennington et al., 2014; Bojanowski et al., 2017). For illustration, consider the famous analogy-based gender bias example from Bolukbasi et al. (2016): *"Man is to computer programmer as woman is to homemaker"*. This bias will be reflected in the text (i.e., the word *man* will co-occur more often with words like *programmer* or *engineer*, whereas *woman* will more often appear next to *homemaker* or *nurse*),

and will, in turn, be captured by word embeddings built from such biased texts. While biases encoded in word embeddings can be a useful data source for diachronic analyses of societal biases (e.g., Garg et al., 2018), they may cause ethical problems for many downstream applications and NLP models.

In order to measure the extent to which various societal biases are captured by word embeddings, Caliskan et al. (2017) proposed the *Word Embedding Association Test* (WEAT). WEAT measures semantic similarity, computed through word embeddings, between two sets of *target* words (e.g., insects vs. flowers) and two sets of *attribute* words (e.g., pleasant vs. unpleasant words). While they test a number of biases, the analysis is limited in scope to English as the only language, GloVe (Pennington et al., 2014) as the embedding model, and Common Crawl as the type of text. Following the same methodology, McCurdy and Serbetci (2017) extend the analysis to three more languages (German, Dutch, Spanish), but test only for gender bias.

In this work, we present the most comprehensive study of biases captured by distributional word vector to date. We create XWEAT, a collection of multilingual and cross-lingual versions of the WEAT dataset, by translating WEAT to six other languages and offer a comparative analysis of biases over seven diverse languages. Furthermore, we measure the consistency of WEAT biases across different embedding models and types of corpora. What is more, given the recent surge of models for inducing cross-lingual embedding spaces (Mikolov et al., 2013a; Hermann and Blunsom, 2014; Smith et al., 2017; Conneau et al., 2018; Artetxe et al., 2018; Hoshen and Wolf, 2018, *inter alia*) and their ubiquitous application in cross-lingual transfer of NLP models for downstream tasks, we investigate cross-lingual biases encoded in cross-lingual embedding spaces and compare them to bias effects present of corresponding monolingual embeddings.

*Proceedings of the Eighth Joint Conference on Lexical and Computational Semantics (*SEM), pages 85–91*
Minneapolis, June 6–7, 2019. ©2019 Association for Computational Linguistics

Our analysis yields some interesting findings: biases do depend on the embedding model and, quite surprisingly, they seem to be less pronounced in embeddings trained on social media texts. Furthermore, we find that the effects (i.e., amount) of bias in cross-lingual embedding spaces can roughly be predicted from the bias effects of the corresponding monolingual embedding spaces.

2 Data for Measuring Biases

We first introduce the WEAT dataset (Caliskan et al., 2017) and then describe XWEAT, our multilingual and cross-lingual extension of WEAT designed for comparative bias analyses across languages and in cross-lingual embedding spaces.

2.1 WEAT

The Word Embedding Association Test (WEAT) (Caliskan et al., 2017) is an adaptation of the Implicit Association Test (IAT) (Nosek et al., 2002). Whereas IAT measures biases based on response times of human subjects to provided stimuli, WEAT quantifies the biases using semantic similarities between word embeddings of the same stimuli. For each bias test, WEAT specifies four stimuli sets: two sets of *target* words and two sets of *attribute* words. The sets of target words represent stimuli *between* which we want to measure the bias (e.g., for gender biases, one target set could contain male names and the other females names). The *attribute* words, on the other hand, represent stimuli *towards* which the bias should be measured (e.g., one list could contain pleasant stimuli like *health* and *love* and the other negative *war* and *death*). The WEAT dataset defines ten bias tests, each containing two target and two attribute sets.[1] Table 1 enumerates the WEAT tests and provides examples of the respective target and attribute words.

2.2 Multilingual and Cross-Lingual WEAT

We port the WEAT tests to the multilingual and cross-lingual settings by translating the test vocabularies consisting of attribute and target terms from English to six other languages: German (DE), Spanish (ES), Italian (IT), Russian (RU), Croatian (HR), and Turkish (TR). We first automatically translate the vocabularies and then let native speakers of the respective languages (also fluent in English) fix the

incorrect automatic translations (or introduce better fitting ones). Our aim was to translate WEAT vocabularies to languages from diverse language families[2] for which we also had access to native speakers. Whenever the translation of an English term indicated the gender in a target language (e.g., *Freund* vs. *Freundin* in DE), we asked the translator to provide both male and female forms and included both forms in the respective test vocabularies. This helps avoiding artificially amplifying the gender bias stemming from the grammatically masculine or feminine word forms.

The monolingual tests in other languages are created by simply using the corresponding translations of target and attribute sets in those languages. For every two languages, L1 and L2 (e.g., DE and IT), we create two cross-lingual bias tests: we pair (1) target translations in L1 with L2 translations of attributes (e.g., for T2 we combine DE target sets {*Klavier, Cello, Gitarre, . . .*} and {*Gewehr, Schwert, Schleuder, . . .*} with IT attribute sets {*salute, amore, pace, . . .*} and {*abuso, omicidio, tragedia, . . .*}), and vice versa, (2) target translations in L2 with attribute translations in L1 (e.g., for T2, IT target sets {*pianoforte, violoncello, chitarra, . . .*} and {*fucile, spada, fionda, . . .*} with DE attribute sets {*Gesundheit, Liebe, Frieden, . . .*} and {*Missbrauch, Mord, Tragödie, . . .*}). We did not translate or modify proper names from WEAT sets 3–6. In our multilingual and cross-lingual experiments we, however, discard the (translations of) WEAT tests for which we cannot find more than 20% of words from some target or attribute set in the embedding vocabulary of the respective language. This strategy eliminates tests 3–5 and 10 which include proper American names, majority of which can not be found in distributional vocabularies of other languages. The exception to this is test 6, containing frequent English first names (e.g., *Paul, Lisa*), which we do find in distributional vocabularies of other languages as well. In summary, for languages other than EN and for cross-lingual settings, we execute six bias tests (T1, T2, T6–T9).

3 Methodology

We adopt the general bias-testing framework from Caliskan et al. (2017), but we span our study over multiple dimensions: (1) corpora – we analyze the

---

[1] Some of the target and attribute sets are shared across multiple tests.

[2] English and German from the Germanic branch of Indo-European languages, Italian and Spanish from the Romance branch, Russian and Croatian from the Slavic branch, and finally Turkish as a non-Indo-European language.

Test	Target Set #1	Target Set #2	Attribute Set #1	Attribute Set #2
T1	Flowers (e.g., *aster, tulip*)	Insects (e.g., *ant, flea*)	Pleasant (e.g., *health, love*)	Unpleasant (e.g., *abuse*)
T2	Instruments (e.g., *cello, guitar*)	Weapons (e.g., *gun, sword*)	Pleasant	Unpleasant
T3	Euro-American names (e.g., *Adam*)	Afro-American names (e.g., *Jamel*)	Pleasant (e.g., *caress*)	Unpleasant (e.g., *abuse*)
T4	Euro-American names (e.g., *Brad*)	Afro-American names (e.g., *Hakim*)	Pleasant	Unpleasant
T5	Euro-American names	Afro-American names	Pleasant (e.g., *joy*)	Unpleasant (e.g., *agony*)
T6	Male names (e.g., *John*)	Female names (e.g., *Lisa*)	Career (e.g. *management*)	Family (e.g., *children*)
T7	Math (e.g., *algebra, geometry*)	Arts (e.g., *poetry, dance*)	Male (e.g., *brother, son*)	Female (e.g., *woman, sister*)
T8	Science (e.g., *experiment*)	Arts	Male	Female
T9	Physical condition (e.g., *virus*)	Mental condition (e.g., *sad*)	Long-term (e.g., *always*)	Short-term (e.g., *occasional*)
T10	Older names (e.g., *Gertrude*)	Younger names (e.g., *Michelle*)	Pleasant	Unpleasant

Table 1: WEAT bias tests.

consistency of biases across distributional vectors induced from different types of text; (2) embedding models – we compare biases across distributional vectors induced by different embedding models (on the same corpora); and (3) languages – we measure biases for word embeddings of different languages, trained from comparable corpora. Furthermore, unlike Caliskan et al. (2017), we test whether biases depend on the selection of the similarity metric. Finally, given the ubiquitous adoption of cross-lingual embeddings (Ruder et al., 2017; Glavaš et al., 2019), we investigate biases in a variety of bilingual embedding spaces.

Bias-Testing Framework. We first describe the WEAT framework (Caliskan et al., 2017). Let X and Y be two sets of *targets*, and A and B two sets of *attributes* (see §2.1). The tested statistic is the difference between X and Y in average similarity of their terms with terms from A and B:

$$s(X, Y, A, B) = \sum_{x \in X} s(x, A, B) - \sum_{y \in Y} s(y, A, B), \quad (1)$$

with association difference for term t computed as:

$$s(t, A, B) = \frac{1}{|A|} \sum_{a \in A} f(\mathbf{t}, \mathbf{a}) - \frac{1}{|B|} \sum_{b \in B} f(\mathbf{t}, \mathbf{b}), \quad (2)$$

where $\mathbf{t}$ is the distributional vector of term t and f is a similarity or distance metric, fixed to cosine similarity in the original work (Caliskan et al., 2017). The significance of the statistic is validated by comparing the score $s(X, Y, A, B)$ with the scores $s(X_i, Y_i, A, B)$ obtained for different equally sized partitions $\{X_i, Y_i\}_i$ of the set $X \cup Y$. The p-value of this permutation test is then measured as the probability of $s(X_i, Y_i, A, B) > s(X, Y, A, B)$ computed over all permutations $\{X_i, Y_i\}_i$.[3] The effect size, that is, the "amount of bias", is computed as the normalized measure of separation between association distributions:

$$\frac{\mu\left(\{s(x, A, B)\}_{x \in X}\right) - \mu\left(\{s(y, A, B)\}_{y \in Y}\right)}{\sigma\left(\{s(w, A, B)\}_{w \in X \cup Y}\right)}, \quad (3)$$

---

[3]If f is a distance rather than a similarity metric, we measure the probability of $s(X_i, Y_i, A, B) < s(X, Y, A, B)$.

where μ denotes the mean and σ standard deviation.

Dimensions of Bias Analysis. We analyze the bias effects across multiple dimensions. First, we analyze the effect that different embedding models have: we compare biases of distributional spaces induced from English Wikipedia, using CBOW (Mikolov et al., 2013b), GLOVE (Pennington et al., 2014), FASTTEXT (Bojanowski et al., 2017), and DICT2VEC algorithms (Tissier et al., 2017). Secondly, we investigate the effects of biases in different corpora: we compare biases between embeddings trained on the Common Crawl, Wikipedia, and a corpus of tweets. Finally, and (arguably) most interestingly, we test the consistency of biases across seven languages (see §2.2). To this end, we test for biases in seven monolingual FASTTEXT spaces trained on Wikipedia dumps of the respective languages.

Biases in Cross-Lingual Embeddings. Cross-lingual embeddings (CLEs) are widely used in multilingual NLP and cross-lingual transfer of NLP models. Despite the ubiquitous usage of CLEs, the biases they potentially encode have not been analyzed so far. We analyze projection-based CLEs (Glavaš et al., 2019), induced through post-hoc linear projections between monolingual embedding spaces (Mikolov et al., 2013a; Artetxe et al., 2016; Smith et al., 2017). The projection is commonly learned through supervision with few thousand word translation pairs. Most recently, however, a number of models have been proposed that learn the projection without any bilingual signal (Artetxe et al., 2018; Conneau et al., 2018; Hoshen and Wolf, 2018; Alvarez-Melis and Jaakkola, 2018, *inter alia*). Let $\mathbf{X}$ and $\mathbf{Y}$ be, respectively, the distributional spaces of the source (S) and target (T) language and let $D = \{w_S^i, w_T^i\}_i$ be the word translation dictionary. Let $(\mathbf{X}_S, \mathbf{X}_T)$ be the aligned subsets of monolingual embeddings, corresponding to word-aligned pairs from D. We

Metric	T1	T2	T3	T4	T5	T6	T7	T8	T9	T10
Cos	1.7	1.6	-0.1*	-0.2*	-0.2*	1.8	1.3	1.3	1.7	-0.6*
Euc	1.7	1.6	-0.1*	-0.2*	-0.1*	1.8	1.3	1.3	1.7	-0.7*

Table 2: WEAT bias effects (EN FASTTEXT embeddings trained on Wikipedia) for cosine similarity and Euclidean distance. Asterisks indicate bias effects that are insignificant at $\alpha < 0.05$.

then compute the orthogonal matrix $\mathbf{W}$ that minimizes the Euclidean distance between $\mathbf{X_S W}$ and $\mathbf{X_T}$ (Smith et al., 2017): $\mathbf{W} = \mathbf{UV}^\top$, where $\mathbf{U\Sigma V}^\top = SVD(\mathbf{X}_T \mathbf{X}_S{}^\top)$. We create comparable bilingual dictionaries D by translating 5K most frequent EN words to other six languages and induce a bilingual space for all 21 language pairs.

4 Findings

Here, we report and discuss the results of our multi-dimensional analysis. Table 2 shows the effect sizes for WEAT T1–T10 based on Euclidean or cosine similarity between word vector representations trained on the EN Wikipedia using FASTTEXT. We observe the highest bias effects for T6 (Male/Female – Career/Family), T9 (Physical/Mental deseases – Long-term/Short-term), and T1 (Insects/Flowera – Positive/Negative). Importantly, the results show that biases do not depend on the similarity metric. We observe nearly identical effects for cosine similarity and Euclidean distance for all WEAT tests. In the following experiments we thus analyze biases only for cosine similarity.

Word Embedding Models. Table 3 compares biases in embedding spaces induced with different models: CBOW, GLOVE, FASTTEXT, and DICT2VEC. While the first three embedding methods are trained on Wikipedia only, DICT2VEC employs definitions from dictionaries (e.g., Oxford dictionary) as additional resources for identifying strongly related terms.[4] We only report WEAT test results T1, T2, and T7–T9 for DICT2VEC, as the DICT2VEC's vocabulary does not cover most of the proper names from the remaining tests.

Somewhat surprisingly, the bias effects seem to vary greatly across embedding models. While GLOVE embeddings are biased according to all tests,[5] FASTTEXT and especially CBOW exhibit significant biases only for a subset of tests. We

WEAT	CBOW	GLOVE	FASTTEXT	DICT2VEC
T1	1.20	1.41	1.67	1.35
T2	1.38	1.45	1.55	1.66
T3	−0.28*	1.16	−0.09*	–
T4	−0.35*	1.36	−0.17*	–
T5	−0.36*	1.40	−0.18*	–
T6	1.78	1.75	1.83	–
T7	1.28	1.16	1.30	1.48
T8	0.39*	1.28*	1.30	1.30
T9	1.55	1.35	1.72	1.69
T10	0.09*	1.17	−0.61*	–

Table 3: WEAT bias effects for spaces induced (on EN Wikipedia) with different embedding models: CBOW, GLOVE, FASTTEXT, and DICT2VEC methods. Asterisks indicate bias effects that are insignificant at $\alpha < 0.05$.

Corpus	T1	T2	T3	T4	T5	T6	T7	T8	T9	T10
WIKI	1.4	1.5	1.2	1.4	1.4	1.8	1.2	1.3	1.3	1.2
CC	1.5	1.6	1.5	1.6	1.4	1.9	1.1	1.3	1.4	1.3
TWEETS	1.2	1.0	1.1	1.2	1.2	1.2	−0.2*	0.6*	0.7*	0.8*

Table 4: WEAT bias effects for GLOVE embeddings trained on different corpora: Wikipedia (WIKI), Common Crawl (CC), and corpus of tweets (TWEETS). Asterisks indicate bias effects that are insignificant at $\alpha < 0.05$.

hypothesize that the bias effects reflected in the distributional space depend on the preprocessing steps of the embedding model. FASTTEXT, for instance, relies on embedding subword information, in order to avoid issues with representations of out-of-vocabulary and underrepresented terms: additional reliance on morpho-syntactic signal may make FASTTEXT more resilient to biases stemming from distributional signal (i.e., word co-occurrences). The fact that the embedding space induced with DICT2VEC exhibits larger bias effects may seem counterintuitive at first, since the dictionaries used for vector training should be more objective and therefore less biased than encyclopedic text. We believe, however, that the additional dictionary-based training objective only propagates the distributional biases across definitionally related words. Generally, we find these results to be important as they indicate that embedding models may accentuate or diminish biases expressed in text.

Corpora. In Table 4 we compare the biases of embeddings trained with the same model (GLOVE) but on different corpora: Common Crawl (i.e., noisy web content), Wikipedia (i.e., encyclopedic text) and a corpus of tweets (i.e., user-generated content). Expectedly, the biases are slightly more pronounced for embeddings trained on the

---

[4]Two terms A and B are strongly related if B appears in the definition of A and vice versa (Tissier et al., 2017).

[5]This is consistent with the original results obtained by Caliskan et al. (2017).

XW	EN	DE	ES	IT	HR	RU	TR
T1	1.67	1.36	1.47	1.28	1.45	1.28	1.21
T2	1.55	1.25	1.47	1.36	1.10	1.46	0.83
T6	1.83	1.59	1.67	1.72	1.83	1.87	1.85
T7	1.30	0.46*	1.47	1.00	0.72*	0.59*	−0.88
T8	1.30	0.05*	1.16	0.10*	0.13*	0.37*	1.72
T9	1.72	0.82*	1.71	1.57	−0.40*	1.73	1.09*
Avg_{all}	1.56	0.92	1.49	1.17	0.81	1.22	0.88
Avg_{sig}	1.68	1.4	1.54	1.45	1.46	1.54	1.30

Table 5: XWEAT effects across languages (FASTTEXT embeddings trained on Wikipedias). Avg_{all}: average of effects over all tests; Avg_{sig}: average over the subset of tests yielding significant biases for all languages. Asterisks indicate bias effects that are insignificant at $\alpha < 0.05$.

XW	EN	DE	ES	IT	HR	RU	TR
EN	–	1.09*	1.58	1.49	0.72*	1.17*	1.20*
DE	1.53	–	1.50	1.45	0.55*	1.35	1.07*
ES	1.52	0.79*	–	1.38*	0.60*	1.37*	1.09*
IT	1.33*	0.69*	1.27	–	0.53*	0.82*	0.80*
HR	1.47	1.30*	1.29	1.18*	–	1.14*	1.11*
RU	1.47	0.72*	1.35	1.35	0.77*	–	0.80*
TR	1.41	0.90*	1.37*	1.45	0.29*	0.64*	–

Table 6: XWEAT bias effects (aggregated over all six tests) for cross-lingual word embedding spaces. Rows: *targets* language; columns: *attributes* language. Asterisks indicate the inclusion of bias effects sizes in the aggregation that were insignificant at $\alpha < 0.05$.

Common Crawl than for those obtained on encyclopedic texts (Wikipedia). Countering our intuition, the corpus of tweets seems to be consistently less biased (across all tests) than Wikipedia. In fact, the biases covered by tests T7–T10 are not even significantly present in the vectors trained on tweets. This finding is indeed surprising and the phenomenon warrants further investigation.

Multilingual Comparison. Table 5 compares the bias effects across the seven different languages. Whereas many of the biases are significant in all languages, DE, HR, and TR consistently display smaller effect sizes. Intuitively, the amount of bias should be proportional to the size of the corpus.[6] Wikipedias in TR and HR are the two smallest ones – thus they are expected to contain least biased statements. DE Wikipedia, on the other hand, is the second largest and low bias effects here suggest that German texts are indeed less biased than texts in other languages. Additionally, for (X)WEAT T2, which defines a universally accepted bias (Instruments vs. Weapons), TR and HR exhibit the smallest effect sizes, while the highest bias is observed for EN and IT. We measure the highest gender bias, according to (X)WEAT T6, for TR and RU, and the lowest for DE.

Biases in Cross-Lingual Embeddings. We report bias effects for all 21 bilingual embedding spaces in Table 6. For brevity, here we report the bias effects averaged over all six XWEAT tests (we provide results detailing bias effects for each of the tests separately in the supplementary materials). Generally, the bias effects of bilingual spaces are in between the bias effects of the two corresponding monolingual spaces (cf. Table 5): this means that we can roughly predict the amount of bias in a cross-lingual embedding space from the same bias effects of corresponding monolingual spaces. For example, effects in cross-lingual spaces increase over monolingual effects for low-bias languages (HR and TR), and decrease for high-bias languages (EN and ES).

5 Conclusion

In this paper, we have presented the largest study to date on biases encoded in distributional word vector spaces. To this end, we have extended previous analyses based on the WEAT test (Caliskan et al., 2017; McCurdy and Serbetci, 2017) in multiple dimensions: across seven languages, four embedding models, and three different types of text. We find that different models may produce embeddings with very different biases, which stresses the importance of embedding model selection when fair text representations are to be created. Surprisingly, we find that the user-generated texts, such as tweets, may be less biased than redacted content. Furthermore, we have investigated the bias effects in cross-lingual embedding spaces and have shown that they may be predicted from the biases of corresponding monolingual embeddings. We make the XWEAT dataset and the testing code publicly available,[7] hoping to fuel further research on biases encoded in word representations.

Acknowledgments

We thank our six native speakers for manually correcting and improving (i.e., post-editing) the automatic translations of the WEAT dataset.

---

[6]The larger the corpus the larger is the overall number of contexts in which some bias may be expressed.

[7]At: https://github.com/umanlp/XWEAT.

References

David Alvarez-Melis and Tommi Jaakkola. 2018. Gromov-Wasserstein alignment of word embedding spaces. In *Proceedings of EMNLP*, pages 1881–1890.

Mikel Artetxe, Gorka Labaka, and Eneko Agirre. 2016. Learning principled bilingual mappings of word embeddings while preserving monolingual invariance. In *Proceedings of EMNLP*, pages 2289–2294.

Mikel Artetxe, Gorka Labaka, and Eneko Agirre. 2018. A robust self-learning method for fully unsupervised cross-lingual mappings of word embeddings. In *Proceedings of ACL*, pages 789–798.

Piotr Bojanowski, Edouard Grave, Armand Joulin, and Tomas Mikolov. 2017. Enriching word vectors with subword information. *Transactions of the ACL*, 5:135–146.

Tolga Bolukbasi, Kai-Wei Chang, James Zou, Venkatesh Saligrama, and Adam Kalai. 2016. Man is to computer programmer as woman is to homemaker? debiasing word embeddings. In *Proceedings of NIPS*, pages 4356–4364, USA. Curran Associates Inc.

Aylin Caliskan, Joanna J. Bryson, and Arvind Narayanan. 2017. Semantics derived automatically from language corpora contain human-like biases. *Science*, 356(6334):183–186.

Alexis Conneau, Guillaume Lample, Marc'Aurelio Ranzato, Ludovic Denoyer, and Hervé Jégou. 2018. Word translation without parallel data. In *Proceedings of ICLR*.

Nikhil Garg, Londa Schiebinger, Dan Jurafsky, and James Zou. 2018. Word embeddings quantify 100 years of gender and ethnic stereotypes. *Proceedings of the National Academy of Sciences*, 115(16):E3635–E3644.

Goran Glavaš, Robert Litschko, Sebastian Ruder, and Ivan Vulic. 2019. How to (properly) evaluate cross-lingual word embeddings: On strong baselines, comparative analyses, and some misconceptions. *arXiv preprint arXiv:1902.00508*.

Zellig S. Harris. 1954. Distributional structure. *Word*, 10(23):146–162.

Karl Moritz Hermann and Phil Blunsom. 2014. Multilingual models for compositional distributed semantics. In *Proceedings of ACL*, pages 58–68.

Yedid Hoshen and Lior Wolf. 2018. Non-adversarial unsupervised word translation. In *Proceedings of EMNLP*, pages 469–478.

Katherine McCurdy and Oguz Serbetci. 2017. Grammatical gender associations outweigh topical gender bias in crosslinguistic word embeddings. In *Proceedings of WiNLP*.

Tomas Mikolov, Quoc V Le, and Ilya Sutskever. 2013a. Exploiting similarities among languages for machine translation. *CoRR, abs/1309.4168*.

Tomas Mikolov, Ilya Sutskever, Kai Chen, Greg S Corrado, and Jeff Dean. 2013b. Distributed representations of words and phrases and their compositionality. In *Proceesings of NIPS*, pages 3111–3119.

Brian A. Nosek, Anthony G. Greenwald, and Mahzarin R. Banaji. 2002. Harvesting implicit group attitudes and beliefs from a demonstration web site. *Group Dynamics*, 6:101–115.

Jeffrey Pennington, Richard Socher, and Christopher Manning. 2014. Glove: Global vectors for word representation. In *Proceedings of EMNLP*, pages 1532–1543.

Sebastian Ruder, Ivan Vulić, and Anders Søgaard. 2017. A survey of cross-lingual word embedding models. *arXiv preprint arXiv:1706.04902*.

Samuel L. Smith, David H.P. Turban, Steven Hamblin, and Nils Y. Hammerla. 2017. Offline bilingual word vectors, orthogonal transformations and the inverted softmax. In *Proceedings of ICLR*.

Julien Tissier, Christophe Gravier, and Amaury Habrard. 2017. Dict2vec : Learning word embeddings using lexical dictionaries. In *Proceedings of EMNLP*, pages 254–263.

XW1	EN	DE	ES	IT	HR	RU	TR
EN	–	1.28	1.63	1.62	1.59	1.49	1.32
DE	1.55	–	1.28	1.45	1.41	1.03	1.29
ES	1.45	1.25	–	1.28	1.21	1.31	1.09
IT	1.18	1.10	1.28	–	1.29	0.61	1.09
HR	1.57	1.62	1.59	1.62	–	1.62	1.63
RU	1.41	1.12	1.20	1.38	1.46	–	1.29
TR	1.23	1.21	1.06	1.26	1.24	1.04	–

Table 7: XWEAT T1 effect sizes for cross-lingual embedding spaces. Rows denote the target set language, column the attribute set language.

XW2	EN	DE	ES	IT	HR	RU	TR
EN	–	1.35	1.51	1.48	1.60	1.56	1.15
DE	1.37	–	1.25	1.19	1.31	1.47	1.16
ES	1.55	1.50	–	1.53	1.50	1.57	1.22
IT	1.54	1.37	1.28	–	1.47	1.39	1.27
HR	1.19	1.25	0.72	1.09	–	1.26	0.81
RU	1.46	1.26	1.23	1.08	1.13	–	0.71
TR	1.29	1.44	1.21	1.4	1.25	1.57	–

Table 8: XWEAT T2 effect sizes for cross-lingual embedding spaces. Rows denote the target set language, column the attribute set language.

A Additional Results

For completeness, we report detailed results on bias effects for each of the six XWEAT tests and bilingual word embedding spaces for all 21 language pairs. Tables 7 to 12 show bias effects for XWEAT tests T1, T2, and T6–T9.

XW6	EN	DE	ES	IT	HR	RU	TR
EN	–	1.77	1.81	1.88	1.83	1.78	1.89
DE	1.82	–	1.77	1.85	1.84	1.74	1.86
ES	1.71	0.95	–	1.81	1.80	1.61	1.50
IT	1.76	1.58	1.703	–	1.72	1.77	1.76
HR	1.68	1.65	1.66	1.43	–	1.74	1.73
RU	1.86	1.74	1.74	1.82	1.86	–	1.80
TR	1.90	1.66	1.77	1.82	1.77	1.55	–

Table 9: XWEAT T6 effect sizes for cross-lingual embedding spaces. Rows denote the target set language, column the attribute set language.

XW7	EN	DE	ES	IT	HR	RU	TR
EN	–	0.34*	1.36	1.33	0.26*	0.46*	0.49*
DE	1.51	–	1.60	1.42	0.23*	1.33	−0.62*
ES	1.63	0.24*	–	1.26	0.60*	1.29	1.55
IT	1.12	0.65*	1.01	–	0.51*	−0.20*	−1.08
HR	1.46	0.94	0.95	1.27	–	0.62*	0.00*
RU	1.19	−0.51*	1.30	1.09	0.81*	–	−0.79*
TR	1.22	0.07*	0.81*	1.30	−0.23*	−0.48*	–

Table 10: XWEAT T7 effect sizes for cross-lingual embedding spaces. Rows denote the target set language, column the attribute set language.

XW8	EN	DE	ES	IT	HR	RU	TR
EN	–	0.68*	1.49	1.01	−0.38*	−0.06*	0.71*
DE	1.17	–	1.43	1.10	−0.09*	1.06	1.16
ES	1.13	−0.69*	–	0.61*	−0.19*	0.67*	−0.18*
IT	0.75*	−0.76*	0.87	–	−0.18*	−0.52*	0.04*
HR	1.36	0.42*	0.92	0.76*	–	−0.16*	0.90
RU	1.09	−0.84*	0.96	0.99	0.19*	–	1.00
TR	0.93	0.06*	1.49	1.21	−0.47*	−0.43*	–

Table 11: XWEAT T8 effect sizes for cross-lingual embedding spaces. Rows denote the target set language, column the attribute set language.

XW9	EN	DE	ES	IT	HR	RU	TR
EN	–	1.12	1.66	1.61	−0.59*	1.76	1.65
DE	1.74	–	1.68	1.66	−1.39	1.46	1.57
ES	1.64	1.48	–	1.79	−1.34	1.75	1.37
IT	1.62	0.19*	1.47	–	−1.63	1.87	1.74
HR	1.54	1.89	1.87	0.96*	–	1.73	1.59
RU	1.82	1.54	1.64	1.72	−0.84*	–	0.80*
TR	1.88	0.98*	1.88	1.70	−1.80	0.58*	–

Table 12: XWEAT T9 effect sizes for cross-lingual embedding spaces. Rows denote the target set language, column the attribute set language.

A Semantic Cover Approach for Topic Modeling

Rajagopal Venkatesaramani
Computer Science, WUSTL
St. Louis MO 63130
`rajagopal@wustl.edu`

Douglas Downey
EECS, Northwestern University
Evanston IL 60208
`ddowney@eecs.northwestern.edu`

Bradley Malin
Biomedical Informatics, Vanderbilt University
Nashville TN 37209
`b.malin@vanderbilt.edu`

Yevgeniy Vorobeychik
Computer Science, WUSTL
St. Louis MO 63130
`yvorobeychik@wustl.edu`

Abstract

We introduce a novel topic modeling approach based on constructing a semantic set cover for clusters of similar documents. Specifically, our approach first clusters documents using their *Tf-Idf* representation, and then covers each cluster with a set of topic words based on semantic similarity, defined in terms of a word embedding. Computing a topic cover amounts to solving a minimum set cover problem. Our evaluation compares our topic modeling approach to Latent Dirichlet Allocation (LDA) on three metrics: 1) qualitative topic match, measured using evaluations by Amazon Mechanical Turk (MTurk) workers, 2) performance on classification tasks using each topic model as a sparse feature representation, and 3) topic coherence. We find that qualitative judgments significantly favor our approach, the method outperforms LDA on topic coherence, and is comparable to LDA on document classification tasks.

1 Introduction

Topic modeling is one of the core research problems in natural language processing. Approaches to topic modeling range from simple vector comparisons to probabilistic graphical models (Deerwester et al., 1990; Hofmann, 1999; Blei et al., 2003; Mimno and McCallum, 2012). Nevertheless, despite the many approaches proposed over the years, probabilistic topic modeling methods in general, and Latent Dirichlet Allocation (LDA) (Blei et al., 2003) in particular, have become arguably the dominant paradigm. For example, it remains the algorithm of choice in the Amazon's healthcare NLP toolkit (Amazon Web Services, 2018).

However, there have been concerns about the performance of probabilistic models, particularly in the context of datasets comprised of short documents, such as tweets (Davidson et al., 2017;

Yan et al., 2013; Hong and Davison, 2010; Mittos et al., 2018; Steinskog et al., 2017). This is primarily because the sparsity posed by short texts makes it hard for the model to sufficiently account for word co-occurrences, which form the basis of the definition of a topic in the sense of a multinomial distribution over words. Additionally, the language used on Twitter is informal in nature, uses slang and non-dictionary words, and often lacks proper grammatical structure. Moreover, the complexity of the probabilistic topic modeling approaches makes it difficult to interpret the specific choices they make about topics and their constituent words.

In this paper, we propose a novel approach to topic modeling which is conceptually simple and highly interpretable. Our approach is based on two hypotheses about the nature of short texts, such as tweets: first, that such texts can be grouped into relatively few disjoint clusters representing a similar mix of subjects (nominally, we call these clusters topics, recognizing that any such cluster may be comprised of multiple topics), and second, that each such subject mix can be adequately summarized by a small number of concepts (words). Both of these are distinct from LDA, which models a topic as a probability distribution over a large number of words. While LDA models each text as a mixture of multiple topics, we assert that each tweet falls into a single cluster. A more fundamental qualitative distinction of our approach from LDA is that it is deterministic in nature, and admits a much more compact representation of the corpus, since each topic, or cluster, is represented by only a small number of words.

To operationalize our hypotheses, we propose a two-step approach to topic modeling. First, we cluster documents based on their similarity in terms of *Tf-Idf* feature representation. Second, given the clustering, we attempt to find a set of

*Proceedings of the Eighth Joint Conference on Lexical and Computational Semantics (*SEM)*, pages 92–102
Minneapolis, June 6–7, 2019. ©2019 Association for Computational Linguistics

words for each cluster that forms a description of the cluster. Specifically, we use a word embedding, along with a document representation in the same semantic space, to cover each cluster with a small set of topic words that are semantically similar to the documents. More precisely, we say that a word (concept) in a dictionary covers a document if it is among the k most similar words in the semantic embedding space. To cover a collection of documents thereby becomes a minimum set cover problem instance. While the set cover problem is computationally hard, it admits a fast greedy approximation algorithm (Chvatal, 1979), which we utilize to construct the topic descriptions for each document cluster.

Our evaluation combines qualitative and quantitative metrics. We first qualitatively compare our approach to LDA by asking MTurk subjects for their judgments about the quality of respective choices of topics for a random sample of documents from a cluster. We do this through two conceptually different ways, and observe a significant and systematic advantage of our approach over LDA. Quantitatively, we compare our approach and LDA in terms of standard intrinsic topic coherence and performance in text classification. On the intrinsic topic coherence metric, our approach fares significantly better than LDA for 4 out of the 5 datasets we use, and the two are comparable on the fifth dataset. Finally, we consider two classification tasks, spam and hate speech prediction, in which topic modeling is used as a sparse feature representation. In this task, we find that both approaches yield similar performance.

2 Related Work

One of the earlier and more influential topic modeling methods was Latent Semantic Analysis (LSA) (Deerwester et al., 1990) which performs a singular value decomposition on the term-document matrix to discover concepts. Probabilistic Latent Semantic Analysis (pLSA) Hofmann (1999) tackles the limitations of LSA – namely potential negative values in the SVD, and the lack of a proper probability distribution – using a latent variable model, where topics are the latent variables. Arguably the most influential approach to the topic modeling domain is Latent Dirichlet Allocation (Blei et al., 2003). LDA can be thought of as an extension to pLSA, where the priors are Dirichlet distributions. LDA continues

to be widely used in topic modeling, and several derivatives exist – each catering to a specific task, or corpus-structure (Blei et al., 2007; Blei and Lafferty, 2006; Yan et al., 2013).

Concerns about the performance of such probabilistic topic models with short text data (eg. tweets) have been illustrated by Davidson et al. (2017); Yan et al. (2013); Hong and Davison (2010); Mittos et al. (2018); Steinskog et al. (2017). Poor performance is attributed to the sparsity of short text data, which provide insufficient information for an approach like LDA to capture word co-occurrence. Yan et al. (2013) tackle this by explicitly modeling co-occurrence throughout the corpus to enhance topic learning. However, this approach requires $\mathcal{O}(m^2)$ memory (where m is the size of the vocabulary) to maintain all biterms (2-grams) and their frequencies in the corpus, making it inefficient in practice.

Weng et al. (2010) aggregate tweets by the same user into pseudo-documents, yet this approach suffers from a dependence on the availability of user-information, or disproportionate distribution of tweets over users. Hong and Davison (2010) aggregate tweets containing the same word, which improves performance relative to LDA. Combining documents based on single words however induces heavy biases on the topics discovered. In our approach, we include a clustering step that can be thought of as an aggregation method. Documents that are semantically similar are grouped together into a cluster instead of a pseudo document, where similarity is a function of all words in the document.

Rangarajan Sridhar (2015) propose learning a vector space representation of words in a corpus using Word2Vec, similarly to our approach, except without *Tf-Idf* weights, and then fitting a mixture of gaussians on the resulting vectors using standard EM. However, the dimensionality of a Word2Vec representation is typically high (50-300 in practice), where gaussian mixtures are known to perform poorly (Krishnamurthy, 2011). Dimensionality reduction on the Word2Vec space is typically used to alleviate this problem, but it reduces the strength of the representation in the process.

In addition to probabilistic topic modeling, document clustering was successfully used in topic modeling by Aker et al. (2016), who use a supervised framework to train a learning model that predicts similarity scores between comments from news articles. A graph consisting of documents as nodes and similarity-weighted edges is then passed to the Markov Clustering Algorithm (Van Dongen, 2000). A major drawback of this approach is the dependence on availability of ground truth data to begin with.

3 Topic Modeling Using a Semantic Cover

We propose a simple topic modeling framework comprised of two steps. First, we cluster documents based on similarity. Second, we extract a set of topics from each cluster by leveraging a word embedding. The intuition behind the clustering step is that it splits a corpus into qualitatively similar groups of documents. Thus, we expect it to be possible to summarize the subject of each cluster by a small collection of topic words. The second step aims at summarizing each cluster of documents using a small set of topic words. The property we seek in this step is that the topic words chosen are *semantically* representative of the cluster. To achieve this goal, we leverage recent advances in neural word embeddings which empirically demonstrated that such embeddings are semantically meaningful (Mikolov et al., 2013a,b). Semantic similarity between words is roughly captured by cosine similarity in the embedded space. Specifically, we first represent documents in the same embedding space as words, and define the problem of the choice of topic extraction as a set cover problem instance. In the set cover instance, a potential topic word covers a collection of documents if the word is similar to these in the embedding space.

3.1 Document Clustering

Our first step is to partition the set of documents in the corpus into a collection of clusters. For this purpose, we first transform each document into its *Tf-Idf* representation. Depending on the dataset, any standard clustering approach may be used to partition the documents. In our case, we run spectral clustering (Ng et al., 2002) over the documents in their *Tf-Idf* form, where we use cosine similarity between vectors as the similarity metric.

3.2 A Set Cover Approach for Topic Extraction

Having obtained a collection of clusters, we treat them independently, with the goal of extracting a small set of representative topic words for each cluster, which adequately represents the subject of the documents in the cluster. To this end, we first represent words, as well as documents, in a vector space using a word embedding. Aiming for a small set of words is useful both in reducing the effort required for human interpretation, as well as forming a compact representation of a set of documents for quantitative tasks such as document classification.

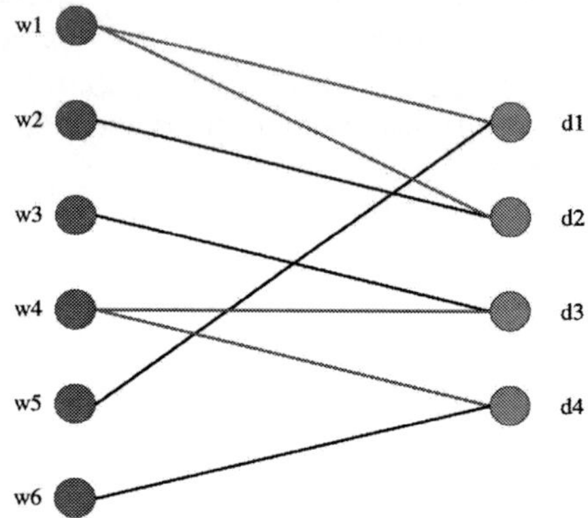

Figure 1: Extracting topic words with *set cover*

Each document (green) in a cluster is connected to its 2 most similar words (blue). The aim is to find the smallest set of words such that the union of the edges originating from them covers all documents in the cluster. In this case, $w1$ and $w2$ form the cover.

Suppose that we have a dictionary W (a collection of words, which is a superset of words that actually occur in the cluster), with each word embedded in a real vector space, i.e., for each $w \in W$, $w \in \mathbb{R}^n$. Moreover, suppose that each document d is represented in the same embedding space. First, we associate each word $w \in W$ with a set of documents, $D(w)$, based on their similarity in the embedding space. Let $s(w, d)$ be a similarity score between a word w and a document d. Given a document d, let $W_k(d)$ be the set of k most similar words to d in terms of $s(w, d)$.

Definition 1 *A word w k-covers a document d if $w \in W_k(d)$.*

Now, the set $D_k(w)$ is the set of all documents d in the cluster k-covered by a word w. Next, we define our topic representation for a cluster C of documents as a set cover.

Definition 2 *A collection of words W_C k-covers a cluster of documents C if $C \subseteq \cup_{w \in W_C} D_k(w)$. A collection of words W_C $(k, 1 - \delta)$-covers a cluster C if $|C \cap (\cup_{w \in W_C} D_k(w))|/|C| \geq 1 - \delta$.*

In words, a collection of words W_C covers a cluster if each document in the cluster is covered by some word $w \in W_C$. If the cover is partial, in the sense that at least a fraction $1 - \delta$ (i.e., most) of the documents are covered, we call it the $1 - \delta$ cover. At this point, it is important to note that in principle the cover W_C *need not include solely words found in the documents in cluster C.*

Having defined what it means for a collection of topical words to cover (exactly or approximately) a document cluster (really, an arbitrary collection of documents), we now observe that our aim is to find a *small* cover—that is, the smallest number of topic words that adequately cover a document cluster. Next, we define this notion precisely.

Definition 3 *Given a k and δ, a minimum $(k, 1 - \delta)$ cover for a document cluster C is a collection W_C^* which is a $1 - \delta$ cover such that $|W_C^*| \le |W_C|$ for any other $(k, 1 - \delta)$ cover W_C of a document cluster C.*

Embedding Words and Documents

To derive a word embedding, we can use one of the standard embedding approaches which has been demonstrated to roughly correspond to semantic relationships among words. We chose Word2Vec for this purpose, although other such embedding approaches can presumably be used in its place. While we used the *Tf-Idf* representation of documents in clustering, this is not well-suited to topic extraction using set cover, since it does not embed documents in the same semantic space as words.

To address this, we represent the documents in a new embedded space by computing a weighted average of Word2Vec (Mikolov et al., 2013a) representations of words occurring in the document, with *Tf-Idf* as the weighting scheme. Using *Tf-Idf* weighting in conjunction with a Word2Vec representation helps alleviate issues that the individual representations face when used independently. Used in isolation, the standard *Tf-Idf* representation only allows us to compute similarities between documents, but not between words - given that words in this case are simply orthonormal one-hot vectors. Using only the Word2Vec representation allows us to compare similarity between words, but does not, by itself, represent documents. As *Tf-Idf* is an information-measure of how important a word is to a document, it is naturally an apt weighting scheme to represent a document as the weighted centroid of the vectors corresponding to the words in the document.

As we describe in the sections to follow, this also allows us to find topic-words for documents that might not necessarily be contained in the documents themselves. To define this representation precisely, suppose that t is the *Tf-Idf* representation of a document over a word dictionary W, and let V be the matrix with columns corresponding to words embedded in real space using Word2Vec. Then the embedded document representation is defined by

$$d = Vt/m,$$

where m is the number of words in the document.

Computing the Minimum Semantic Set Cover

Given the definition of the minimum semantic cover for a cluster of documents, along with an embedding of both words and documents in the same space, we can now extract the topics for each cluster using a greedy algorithm inspired by the $\mathcal{O}(n \log n)$ greedy solution for set-cover (Chvatal, 1979), as follows.

We first convert the documents and words in the embedded space to an unweighted bipartite graph, using our notion of $(k, 1 - \delta)$-cover. Let V_1 be a set of vertices where each vertex corresponds to a word w in the corpus dictionary, W. Let V_2 be a set of vertices, where each vertex corresponds to a document d in the corpus D. We add an edge between a word w and a document d if w $(k, 1 - \delta)$-covers d in the sense of cosine similarity between words and documents, $s(w, d)$, in the embedded space. Thus, the graph $G = \{(V_1 \cup V_2), E\}$. We also have for each document, a cluster assignment from the spectral-clustering step, i.e. $D = \cup_{i=1,\ldots,n} C_i$, where n is the total number of clusters (topics), such that each document belongs to exactly one cluster C_i.

Then, to construct a minimum semantic set cover for a cluster, we proceed as follows. Let the set of topic words, T_i for the ith cluster, C_i be an empty set. Let $V_{2,i} = \{d \in V_2 : d \in C_i\}$, i.e. $V_{2,i}$ is the subset of vertices in V_2 corresponding to documents in the ith cluster. Let $V_{1,i} = \cup_{d \in V_{2,i}} N(d)$, where $N(d)$ represents node neighborhood. In words, $V_{1,i}$ is the subset of corpus words that cover at least one document in cluster C_i, i.e. the set $\cup_{d \in C_i} W_k(d)$.

Let G_i be the subgraph of G induced on $V_{i,1} \cup V_{2,i}$. The greedy algorithm to find the minimum set-cover for a cluster C_i proceeds by picking the node in $V_{1,i}$ that covers the maximum number of documents in $V_{2,i}$. In the case of a tie, we pick all nodes with maximum degree. The words corresponding to the selected vertices are placed in T_i, then the selected nodes, their neighbors in G_i and the edges between them are removed from the graph. We then recompute the degrees of all nodes affected by this removal of edges. This process is repeated until we have covered a desired fraction $(1 - \delta)$ of the cluster. Algorithm 1 details topic-word extraction using set-cover.

Algorithm 1 Greedy Set Cover

1: **for** Cluster C_i **do**
2:     Label Set $T_i \leftarrow \emptyset$
3:     $V_{2,i} = \{v \in V_2 : v \in C_i\}$
4:     $V_{1,i} = \{N(v) \ \forall v \in V_{2,i}\}$
5:     $G_i = $ Subgraph of G induced on $V_{2,i} \cup V_{1,i}$
6:     $k = \delta |V_{2,i}|$
7:     **while** $|V_{2,i}| > k$ **do**
8:         Sort $V_{1,i}$ in descending order of degree
9:         Remove the highest degree node(s), v^* and place in T_i
10:        Remove all neighbors of v^* and corresponding edges from G_i
11:        Recompute degrees for $V_{1,i}$
12:     **end while**
13: **end for**

---

4 Evaluation Methodology

We evaluate our approach in comparison with LDA—the de facto standard in topic modeling—both in qualitative and quantitative terms. Our qualitative evaluation involves human judgments about the appropriateness of topic choices for a subsample of texts. We complement this with two quantitative metrics, one with respect to a standard topic coherence measure, and the second in using topic models for text classification tasks. Throughout, we refer to our approach as *set cover*. Moreover, in our experiments, the Word2Vec vectors are derived by training a skip-gram model on the corpus, with a sliding window of size 4 and the number of dimensions set to 500. Additionally, we compute the minimum 1-cover (i.e. $\delta = 0$), that is, we ensure that all documents in the cluster are covered.

4.1 Qualitative Evaluation

Given the common use of topic modeling in obtaining qualitative insight from text, our first evaluation approach involves human judgments of quality. This evaluation echos other human evaluations of topic modeling, such as by Steinskog et al. (2017) for the topic-intrusion detection task. Also noteworthy is the work by Chang et al. (2009), who demonstrated the poor correlation of the popular perplexity metric (Blei et al., 2003) with human judgments.

For our qualitative evaluation, we set up a series of experiments on Amazon Mechanical Turk (MTurk). For these tasks, we use 4 sets from the health news tweets collected by (Karami et al., 2018) and YouTube comments about 23andMe (we provide specific details in a later section). To ensure fairness to LDA—our chosen baseline—we do this in two different settings based on how we group documents into topically related subsets.

Matched Clusters

In the first setup, we take the document clusters produced by spectral clustering as given, and focus the comparison between LDA and *set cover* on the particular choice of topical words these generate. In this case, we produce a correspondence between a given cluster and an LDA topic by choosing an LDA topic which maximizes the likelihood that the cluster was produced by the topic. More precisely, we assign a cluster C to the topic j which maximizes

$$\sum_{i \in C} P(i|j),$$

where $P(i|j)$ is the LDA-derived likelihood that a document i reflects a topic j. We then generate the collection of topic words for a given cluster using LDA in a standard way. Specifically, we choose the n most probable words in the associated LDA topic, where n is set as the number of topic words produced by the *set cover*.

In the experiment, we assign a random cluster to a subject, who is then presented with the documents in this cluster (or a random subsample of these, if the cluster is too large), the choice of topic words based on LDA, and the choice of topic words based on *set cover*. Additionally, we also ask the subjects for judgments of a collection of n randomly chosen words from the cluster to calibrate the results. We then ask participants to judge how well a topic (i.e., the collection of topic words) describes the given set of documents, and score each result on a 5-point Likert scale, with 1 being very poor and 5 very good.

Independent Clusters

One may naturally object that the above comparison is unfair to LDA insofar as we are choosing the clusters and then retrofitting LDA topics to these. We therefore ran a second set of qualitative experiments in which LDA topics were used to derive clusters of similar documents. Specifically, we clustered all documents based on their associated likelihood given a topic; that is, a document i was assigned to an LDA topic j which maximizes $P(i|j)$. This gives us a collection of document clusters, which we can then present to human subjects for judgment. As before, we used the top most probable n words from an LDA topic as the topic description presented to human subjects. The *set cover* approach, on the other hand, used spectral clustering as before. Since the set of documents presented for judgment is now different for the two approaches, we omitted the random words for calibration. Consequently, while we still presented the subjects with the same 5-point Likert scale as before, this scale is now calibrated differently, as will be made evident in the results section.

4.2 Quantitative Evaluations

To quantitatively compare our algorithms, we use the standard intrinsic topic coherence metric, and two classification tasks to compare the strengths of the sparse representation produced. The topic coherence (Stevens et al., 2012) for a set T of topic words is defined as follows:

$$Coherence(T) = \sum_{(w_i, w_j) \in T} \log \frac{N(w_i, w_j) + \lambda}{N(w_j)},$$

where $N(w)$ is the number of documents that contain the word w and λ is a smoothing factor. We compute average coherence scores over 5 runs, varying cluster sizes between 5 and 25.

Document Classification Accuracy

We set up two classification tasks. The first task is to classify short text messages as Ham or Spam. The second task is to classify tweets as offensive, hate speech or neither. For both, we use topic modeling approaches to arrive at a sparse feature representation of a document. For LDA, the feature vector for a document is comprised of the probabilities that a document was generated by each of the topics. For the *set cover* approach, we construct binary feature vectors that represent the occurrence of topic words in the cluster to which the document is assigned. Given the above feature representations, we use a Linear Support Vector Classifier. For the multi-class problem, we use a One-vs-Rest approach with Linear Support Vector Classifiers for both classification tasks. We maintain a 60%-40% train-test split over the corpus, and average accuracy over 5 runs, varying the number of topics between 5 and 25.

4.3 Data

Our evaluation used several datasets which we describe briefly below.

Twitter - Health News   tweets from more than 15 health news agencies were collected by Karami et al. (2018). The dataset contains separate files for tweets collected from each source. Each source is observed to have had trends in tweets, which implicitly form topic clusters.

YouTube Comments - 23andMe   We collected a sample of 800 YouTube comments from the top 50 YouTube video results for the search term '23andMe'. This dataset is qualitatively different from the Twitter corpus, showing greater variation in document length and significantly more noise.

Twitter - Hate and Offensive Speech   A set of 24802 tweets based on a hate speech lexicon were collected and labelled into 3 categories - *hate speech, offensive speech* and *neither* by Davidson et al. (2017). This dataset is used in one of our two classification tasks.

Ham/Spam Short Messages   5574 short text messages were classified as legitimate (ham) or spam by Almeida et al. (2013). This forms the basis of the second classification task.

5 Results

5.1 Qualitative Evaluations

In the first set of MTurk experiments, where topics from both algorithms were shown in the same task, we asked human judges to score topics from 4 document clusters, collecting 20 responses for each. For instance, the Fox News dataset contains a set of tweets posted in 2015 about the measles outbreak in California, linked to Disney theme parks. The topic words for the measles outbreak cluster identified by the two algorithms are shown in Table 1. Here, we see that LDA picks certain irrelevant terms for the shown cluster sample ('u', 'rare'), while completely missing the term 'measles', which is a key subject of the documents (we note that we remove stop-words during preprocessing using NLTK (Loper and Bird, 2002)). The *set cover* approach, on the other hand, is able to identify highly pertinent words. We refer to this experiment as *Matched Clusters*. This can be thought of as reflecting the propriety of the chosen topic words *conditional* on the clusters of similar documents. The average scores are shown in Table 2.

Cluster Sample	· Disneyland measles outbreak linked to low vaccination rates · More measles cases tied to Disneyland Illinois day care · Amid US measles outbreak few rules on teacher vaccinations · US measles count rises to 121; most linked to Disneyland · Measles cases turn attention to bounty of childhood vaccines · FDA Commissioner says measles outbreak alarming
LDA	study, cancer, say, vaccine, died, disneyland, u, rare, woman, treatment
Set Cover	measles, cases, linked, disney, disneyland, alarming, almost, amid, amidst, bounty

Table 1: Topic Words - Measles Outbreak, 2015

Dataset (Cluster)	Random	LDA	Set Cover
US News (Superfoods)	2.9	3	4.35
Fox News (Disneyland Measles)	1.95	3.05	4.45
US News (Parenting)	1.95	1.6	4.5
YouTube (23andMe, Sale of Info)	2.35	2.7	4.1

Table 2: Average Turker scores for Matched Clusters on a 5-point Likert scale.

Our second set of experiments for clusters chosen independently for the two algorithms was conducted on a significantly larger scale. We uploaded 5 clusters per dataset, and collected 40 responses per cluster, resulting in a total of 2000 data points, 1000 for each algorithm. We refer to this experiment as *Independent Clusters*. Table 3 shows example topic words identified by LDA and Set Cover. The advantages of the clustering step in our approach are evident in this example - the *set cover* cluster contains documents that are more closely related to one another.

More importantly, it is worth noting the choice of the term 'delay' in the *set cover* topic words - while the term does not itself appear in the entire cluster, it is semantically related to documents in the cluster referring to the long wait Maryland residents had to endure to sign up for Obamacare. This is precisely the reason for using a word-embedding such as Word2Vec in our approach - topic words are not restricted to words in the cluster and yet appear to be semantically meaningful. The average judgments from MTurk for these experiments are reported in Table 4.

In both experiments, we can see that *set cover* consistently outperforms LDA, often by a large margin. We also performed a two sided independent samples t-test on the scores. The differences between the means in Table 4 are statistically significant; all but 23andMe for $p < 0.0001$, and the significance for 23andMe is for $p < 0.05$. It is interesting to note that *set cover* performs slightly better in terms of evaluation scores in the *Matched Clusters* study, suggesting that it is judged favorably *particularly* in the context of random calibration and LDA.

Since the clusters are fixed in these experiments, the results reflect the particular advantage of the *set cover* method itself in choosing descriptive words for a collection of similar documents. The *Independent Clusters* study, in contrast, serves more as an evaluation of each approach in an end-to-end fashion, and here, too, the difference is substantial. However, the LDA scores in this case are generally comparable or higher than in the *Matched Clusters* experiments, which suggests that the advantage of *set cover* over LDA may be primarily due to its better choice of topic words, which is its main novelty, rather than the clustering approach.

Cluster Sample	Algorithm (Data set)	Topic Words
· People are having sex after heart bypass surgery, and USN is ON IT: · Most Americans dont know what causes cancer. Do you? WorldCancerDay · Can a fitness tracker help me with my diet as well? USNTechChat · In honor of World Cancer Day, reports on 7 Innovations in Cancer Therapy · How to call a truce & build a healthy relationship with food: · Check out our 2015 BestDiets rankings! Wed love your feedback	LDA (USNews)	surgery cancer know usntech- -chat child say reports lose medical like
· Obamacare Bump: 10 Million Got Insurance, Survey Shows · #AskNBCNews: Obamacare Deadline Day Questions · Obamacare draws last-minute shoppers; site gets nearly 2 million visits · Supreme Court Hears Argument on Charged Obamacare Case · Communty health centers at center of Obamacare · The Longest Wait: Maryland Residents Wait in LIne for Last-Ditch Obamacare	Set Cover (NBC)	obamacare million get new deadline health may questions court delay

Table 3: Topic Words - Independent Clusters

Dataset		LDA	Set Cover
23andMe	Mean	3.94	4.16
	Var	0.95	0.79
NY Times	Mean	2.42	3.515
	Var	1.493	1.039
NBC	Mean	2.315	4.06
	Var	1.265	0.836
Fox	Mean	2.835	3.965
	Var	1.388	1.023
US News	Mean	3.085	3.78
	Var	1.327	1.09

Table 4: Average Turker scores for Independent Clusters on a 5-point Likert scale.

5.2 Quantitative Evaluations

Topic Coherence

The first quantitative comparison between *set cover* and LDA is in terms of the topic coherence metric. For each dataset, we plot topic coherence as a function of the number of topics ranging from 5 to 25 (for the *set cover* approach, the number of topics corresponds to the number of clusters). Figure 2 presents the topic coherence results. In nearly all of these cases (with the few apparent exceptions), *set cover* scores significantly better on this metric than LDA. It is also notable that *set cover* tends to improve as we increase the number of topics, whereas this is typically not the case for LDA (New York Times Health News tweets is an

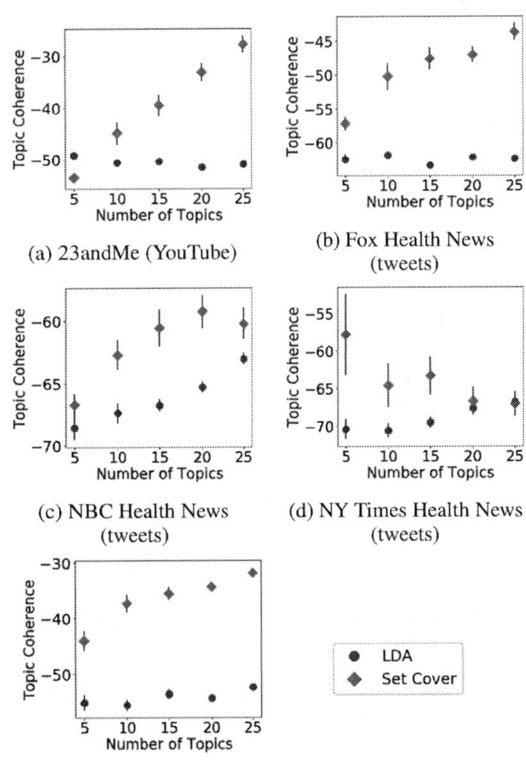

(a) 23andMe (YouTube)

(b) Fox Health News (tweets)

(c) NBC Health News (tweets)

(d) NY Times Health News (tweets)

(e) US News (Health) tweets

Figure 2: Topic Coherence.

exception, where *set cover* scores decrease with the number of topics, while LDA scores increase slightly, so that for a large number of topics the two approaches are indistinguishable).

Classification

The final evaluation uses two objective document classification tasks to compare the effectiveness of *set cover* and LDA in producing a sparse feature representation for such tasks. We present classification accuracy by varying number of topics again from 5 to 25. Figure 3 shows classification results. While LDA appears to be slightly better in the Ham/Spam email classification case, and is occasionally better in the Hate/Offensive speech classification task, the differences are quite small, with both achieving accuracy in the 87-89% range in the former, and 77-78% in the latter.

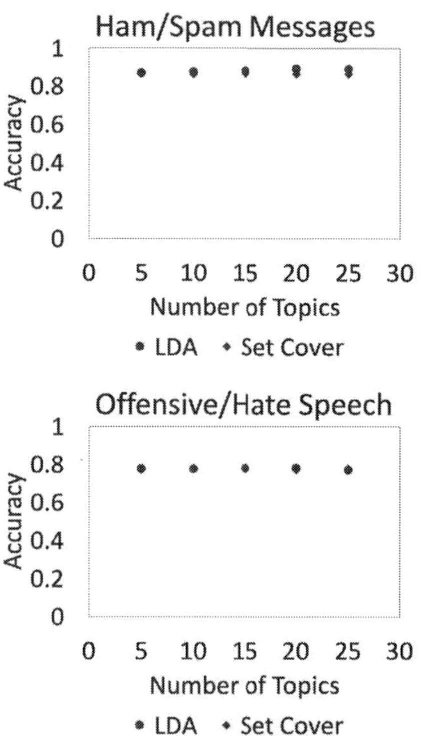

Figure 3: Classification accuracy comparison.

6   Discussion

The reason for LDA's observed inferiority in the qualitative experiments can be traced back to the fact that LDA allows each document to be generated from a mix of topics. However, in most short-text corpora, documents usually pertain to a single topic. Additionally, the number of documents belonging to each topic in a corpora is not (explicitly) captured by LDA.

With the *set cover* approach, the clustering step provides us this information - clusters need not be of uniform size, and such a clustering is easy

to learn. This may explain, for instance, why LDA completely misses the word 'measles' in the Matched Clusters sample shown in Table 1. The number of documents about the measles outbreak in the corpora are relatively few, and treating this set of documents independently of other documents in the corpus makes it easier to identify this theme.

The topic coherence experiments show that the topic words learnt using *set cover* are more likely to co-occur across the corpus as compared to those learnt with LDA, thereby suggesting that *set cover*'s choice of topic words is more meaningful. The results of the classification task are noteworthy, given that our model is far less complex than LDA, and yet produces almost as effective a sparse representation.

7   Conclusion

In this paper, we introduced a conceptually simple and highly interpretable deterministic topic modeling algorithm based on constructing a semantic set cover over clusters of documents in a corpus. Unlike popular probabilistic topic modeling methods, our algorithm performed well on short text data, thereby overcoming the limitations imposed by corpus-sparsity. We demonstrated that our approach significantly outperforms LDA on qualitative scores by human judges as well as the standard topic coherence metric, and that it is comparable to LDA for document classification.

One limitation of our approach is the dependence on a good clustering of documents, in the sense that documents are meaningfully grouped together by the clustering algorithm used, given a dataset. Additionally, we rely on a word embedding, which may not be easy to learn over datasets where terms do not recur in the same contexts frequently. A potential solution to this is to learn the embedding on the union of said dataset with another corpus of similar (thematic and structural) nature, where term co-occurrences are more frequent.

Finally, as future work, we aim to explore set-cover based topic modeling where the covering threshold set as the top-k similar words to a document varies for each topic. Hopefully, this will allow us to capture the notion that some topics are sufficiently captured by a smaller set of words whereas others may need a larger threshold to fully capture their semantics.

References

Ahmet Aker, Emina Kurtic, AR Balamurali, Monica Paramita, Emma Barker, Mark Hepple, and Rob Gaizauskas. 2016. A graph-based approach to topic clustering for online comments to news. In *European Conference on Information Retrieval*, pages 15–29. Springer.

Tiago Almeida, José María Gómez Hidalgo, and Tiago Pasqualini Silva. 2013. Towards sms spam filtering: Results under a new dataset. *International Journal of Information Security Science*, 2(1):1–18.

Amazon Web Services. 2018. Amazon comprehend - developer guide.

David M Blei and John D Lafferty. 2006. Dynamic topic models. In *Proceedings of the 23rd international conference on Machine learning*, pages 113–120. ACM.

David M Blei, John D Lafferty, et al. 2007. A correlated topic model of science. *The Annals of Applied Statistics*, 1(1):17–35.

David M Blei, Andrew Y Ng, and Michael I Jordan. 2003. Latent dirichlet allocation. *Journal of Machine Learning Research*, 3(Jan):993–1022.

Jonathan Chang, Sean Gerrish, Chong Wang, Jordan L Boyd-Graber, and David M Blei. 2009. Reading tea leaves: How humans interpret topic models. In *Advances in Neural Information Processing Systems*, pages 288–296.

Vasek Chvatal. 1979. A greedy heuristic for the set-covering problem. *Mathematics of Operations Research*, 4(3):233–235.

Thomas Davidson, Dana Warmsley, Michael Macy, and Ingmar Weber. 2017. Automated hate speech detection and the problem of offensive language. In *Proceedings of the 11th International AAAI Conference on Web and Social Media*, pages 512–515.

Scott Deerwester, Susan T Dumais, George W Furnas, Thomas K Landauer, and Richard Harshman. 1990. Indexing by latent semantic analysis. *Journal of the American Society for Information Science*, 41(6):391.

Thomas Hofmann. 1999. Probabilistic latent semantic analysis. In *Proceedings of the 15th Conference on Uncertainty in Artificial Intelligence*, pages 289–296.

Liangjie Hong and Brian D Davison. 2010. Empirical study of topic modeling in twitter. In *Proceedings of the 1st Workshop on Social Media Analytics*, pages 80–88. ACM.

Amir Karami, Aryya Gangopadhyay, Bin Zhou, and Hadi Kharrazi. 2018. Fuzzy approach topic discovery in health and medical corpora. *International Journal of Fuzzy Systems*, 20(4):1334–1345.

Akshay Krishnamurthy. 2011. High-dimensional clustering with sparse gaussian mixture models. *Unpublished paper*.

Edward Loper and Steven Bird. 2002. Nltk: The natural language toolkit. In *Proceedings of the ACL-02 Workshop on Effective Tools and Methodologies for Teaching Natural Language Processing and Computational Linguistics - Volume 1*, ETMTNLP '02, pages 63–70, Stroudsburg, PA, USA. Association for Computational Linguistics.

Tomas Mikolov, Ilya Sutskever, Kai Chen, Greg S Corrado, and Jeff Dean. 2013a. Distributed representations of words and phrases and their compositionality. In *Advances in Neural Information Processing Systems*, pages 3111–3119.

Tomas Mikolov, Wen-tau Yih, and Geoffrey Zweig. 2013b. Linguistic regularities in continuous space word representations. In *Proceedings of the 2013 Conference of the North American Chapter of the Association for Computational Linguistics: Human Language Technologies*, pages 746–751. Association for Computational Linguistics.

David Mimno and Andrew McCallum. 2012. Topic models conditioned on arbitrary features with dirichlet-multinomial regression. *arXiv preprint arXiv:1206.3278*.

Alexandros Mittos, Jeremy Blackburn, and Emiliano De Cristofaro. 2018. "23andme confirms: I'm super white" – analyzing twitter discourse on genetic testing. *arXiv preprint arXiv:1801.09946*.

Andrew Y Ng, Michael I Jordan, and Yair Weiss. 2002. On spectral clustering: Analysis and an algorithm. In *Advances in Neural Information Processing Systems*, pages 849–856.

Vivek Kumar Rangarajan Sridhar. 2015. Unsupervised topic modeling for short texts using distributed representations of words. In *Proceedings of the 1st Workshop on Vector Space Modeling for Natural Language Processing*, pages 192–200. Association for Computational Linguistics.

Asbjørn Steinskog, Jonas Therkelsen, and Björn Gambäck. 2017. Twitter topic modeling by tweet aggregation. In *Proceedings of the 21st Nordic Conference on Computational Linguistics*, pages 77–86. Association for Computational Linguistics.

Keith Stevens, Philip Kegelmeyer, David Andrzejewski, and David Buttler. 2012. Exploring topic coherence over many models and many topics. In *Proceedings of the 2012 Joint Conference on Empirical Methods in Natural Language Processing and Computational Natural Language Learning*, pages 952–961. Association for Computational Linguistics.

Stijn Marinus Van Dongen. 2000. *Graph clustering by flow simulation*. Ph.D. thesis, Utrecht University.

Jianshu Weng, Ee-Peng Lim, Jing Jiang, and Qi He. 2010. Twitterrank: finding topic-sensitive influential twitterers. In *Proceedings of the 3rd ACM International Conference on Web Search and Data Mining*, pages 261–270. ACM.

Xiaohui Yan, Jiafeng Guo, Yanyan Lan, and Xueqi Cheng. 2013. A biterm topic model for short texts. In *Proceedings of the 22nd International Conference on World Wide Web*, pages 1445–1456. ACM.

MCScript2.0: A Machine Comprehension Corpus Focused on Script Events and Participants

Simon Ostermann[1]   Michael Roth[1,2]   Manfred Pinkal[1]

[1]Saarland University   [2]Stuttgart University
{simono|pinkal}@coli.uni-saarland.de rothml@ims.uni-stuttgart.de

Abstract

We introduce *MCScript2.0*, a machine comprehension corpus for the end-to-end evaluation of **script** knowledge. MCScript2.0 contains approx. 20,000 questions on approx. 3,500 texts, crowdsourced based on a new collection process that results in challenging questions. Half of the questions cannot be answered from the reading texts, but require the use of commonsense and, in particular, script knowledge. We give a thorough analysis of our corpus and show that while the task is not challenging to humans, existing machine comprehension models fail to perform well on the data, even if they make use of a commonsense knowledge base. The dataset is available at http://www.sfb1102. uni-saarland.de/?page_id=2582

1 Introduction

People have access to a wide range of commonsense knowledge that is naturally acquired during their lifetime. They make frequent use of such knowledge while speaking to each other, which makes communication highly efficient. The conversation in Example 1 illustrates this: For Max, it is natural to assume that Rachel paid during her restaurant visit, even if this fact was not mentioned by Rachel.

(1) Rachel: "Yesterday, I went to this new Argentinian restaurant to have dinner. I enjoyed a tasty steak."
Max: "What did you pay?"

Script knowledge is one of the most important types of commonsense knowledge and subsumes such information (Schank and Abelson, 1977). It is defined as knowledge about everyday situations, also referred to as *scenarios*. It subsumes information about the actions that take place during such situations, and their typical temporal order, referred

to as *events*, as well as the persons and objects that typically play a role in the situation, referred to as *participants*. In the example, script knowledge subsumes the fact that the *paying* event is a part of the *eating in a restaurant* scenario.

Recent years have seen different approaches to learning script knowledge, centered around two strands: Work around narrative chains that are learned from large text collections (Chambers and Jurafsky, 2008, 2009), and the manual induction of script knowledge via crowdsourcing (Regneri et al., 2010; Wanzare et al., 2016). Script knowledge has been represented both symbolically (Jans et al., 2012; Pichotta and Mooney, 2014; Rudinger et al., 2015) and with neural models (Modi and Titov, 2014; Pichotta and Mooney, 2016). Scripts have been evaluated mostly intrinsically (Wanzare et al., 2017; Ostermann et al., 2017). An exception is *MCScript* (Ostermann et al., 2018a), a reading comprehension corpus with a focus on script knowledge, and a predecessor to the data set presented in this work. Previous work has shown, however, that script knowledge is not required for performing well on the data set (Ostermann et al., 2018b). Hence, to date, there exists no evaluation method that allows one to systematically assess the contribution of models of script knowledge to the task of automated text understanding.

Our work closes this gap: We present *MCScript2.0*, a reading **comprehension corpus** focused on script events and participants. It contains more than 3,400 texts about everyday scenarios, together with more than 19,000 multiple-choice questions on these texts. All data were collected via crowdsourcing. About half of the questions require the use of commonsense and script knowledge for finding the correct answer (like the question in Example 1), a notably higher number than in MCScript. We show that in comparison to MCScript, commonsense-based questions in MCScript2.0 are

103

*Proceedings of the Eighth Joint Conference on Lexical and Computational Semantics (*SEM)*, pages 103–117
Minneapolis, June 6–7, 2019. ©2019 Association for Computational Linguistics

T	(...) We put our ingredients together to make sure they were at the right temperature, preheated the oven, and pulled out the proper utensils. We then prepared the batter using eggs and some other materials we purchased and then poured them into a pan. After baking the cake in the oven for the time the recipe told us to, we then double checked to make sure it was done by pushing a knife into the center. We saw some crumbs sticking to the knife when we pulled it out so we knew it was ready to eat !
Q1	*When did they put the pan in the oven and bake it according to the instructions?* After eating the cake. ✗ After mixing the batter. ✓
Q2	*What did they put in the oven?* The cake mix. ✓ Utensils. ✗

Figure 1: Example text fragment from MCScript2.0

also harder to answer, even for a model that makes use of a commonsense database. Thus, we argue that MCScript2.0 is the first resource which makes it possible to evaluate how far models are able to exploit script knowledge for automated text understanding.

Figure 1 shows a text snippet from a text in MCScript2.0, together with two questions with answer alternatives[1]. To find an answer for question 1, information about the temporal order of the steps for baking a cake is required: The cake is put in the oven after mixing the batter, and not after eating it—a piece of information not given in the text, since the event of putting the cake in the oven is not explicitly mentioned. Similarly, one needs script knowledge about which participants are typically involved in which events to know that the cake mix rather than the utensils is put into the oven. Both incorrect answer candidates are distractive: The utensils as well as the action of eating the cake are mentioned in the text, but wrong answers to the question. Our contributions are as follows:

- We present a new collecting method for challenging questions whose answers require commonsense knowledge and in particular script knowledge, as well as a new resource that was created with this method.

[1]More text samples are given in the Supplemental Material.

- We show that the task is simple for humans, but that existing benchmark models, including a top-scoring machine comprehension model that utilizes a resource for commonsense knowledge, struggle on the questions in MCScript2.0; especially on questions that require commonsense knowledge.

- We compare MCScript2.0 to MCScript, the first machine comprehension resource for evaluating models of script knowledge. We show that in comparison to MCScript, the number of questions that require script knowledge is increased by a large margin and that such questions are hard to answer. Consequently, we argue that our dataset provides a more robust basis for future research on text understanding models that use script knowledge.

2 Why another Machine Comprehension Dataset on Script Knowledge?

MCScript (Ostermann et al., 2018a) is the first machine comprehension dataset designed to evaluate script knowledge in an end-to-end machine comprehension application, and to our knowledge the only other existing extrinsic evaluation dataset for script knowledge. Recent research has shown, however, that commonsense knowledge is not required for good performance on the dataset (Ostermann et al., 2018b; Merkhofer et al., 2018).

We argue that this is due to the way in which questions were collected. During the collection process, workers were not shown a text, but only a very short description of the text scenario. As a result, many questions ask about general aspects of the scenario, without referring to actual details. This leads to the problem that there are many questions with standardized answers, i.e. questions that can be answered irrespective of a concrete reading text. Examples 2 and 3 show two such cases, where the correct answer is almost exclusively *in the shower* and *on the stove*, independent of the text or even scenario.

(2) Where did they wash their hair?

(3) Where did they make the scrambled eggs?

Merkhofer et al. (2018) found that such information can essentially be learned from only the training data, using a simple logistic regression classifier and surface features regarding words in the text, question and answer candidates.

Also, many questions require vague inference over general commonsense knowledge rather than script knowledge. Example 4 illustrates this: The simple fact that planting a tree gets easier if you have help is not subsumed by script knowledge about planting a tree, but a more general type of commonsense knowledge.

(4) *Text*: Once you know where to dig , select what type of tree you want. (...) Dig a hole large enough for the tree and roots . Place the tree in the hole and then fill the hole back up with dirt . (...)
Q: Would it have been easier to plant the tree if they had help?
yes ✓
no ✗

We inspected a random sample of 50 questions from the publicly available development set that were misclassified by the logistic model of Merkhofer et al. (2018). We found that for over 90% of the inspected questions, the use of script knowledge would be only marginally relevant.

We present a new data collection method and corpus that results in a larger number of challenging questions that require script knowledge. In particular, we define a revised question collection procedure, which ensures a large proportion of nontrivial commonsense questions.

3 Corpus Creation

Texts, questions, and answer candidates are required for a multiple choice machine comprehension dataset. Our data collection process for texts and answers is based on the MCScript data and the methods developed there, but with several crucial differences. Like Ostermann et al. (2018a), we create the data set via crowdsourcing. The question collection is revised to account for the shortcomings found with MCScript.

Similarly to Ostermann et al. (2018a), we are interested in questions that require inference over script knowledge for finding a correct answer. Creating such questions is challenging: When questions are collected by showing a reading text and asking crowdsourcing workers to write questions, their answer can usually be read off the text. The authors of MCScript thus decided to not show a reading text at all, but only a short summary of the text scenario. This resulted in too general questions, so we decided for a third option: We identi-

fied a number of *target sentences* in the reading text and guided workers to formulate questions about script-related details in these sentences. The target sentences were then hidden from the text, meaning that relevant information would have to be inferred from common sense during the answer collection and also in the task itself. In the following sections, we describe the three data collection steps in detail.

3.1 Text Collection

As a starting point, we reused all texts from MC-Script (2,119 texts on 110 scenarios) for our data set. To increase the topical coverage and diversity of the data set, we added texts for 90 new scenarios to our collection. As for MCScript, we selected topically different and plausible everyday scenarios of varying complexity, which were not too fine-grained (such as *opening a window*). The scenarios were taken from 3 sources: First, we extracted scenarios from several script collections (Wanzare et al., 2016; Regneri et al., 2010; Singh et al., 2002) that are not part of MCScript. Second, we inspected the *spinn3r* blog story corpus (Burton et al., 2009), a large corpus of narrative blog stories and identified additional scenarios in these stories. Third, we added new scenarios that are related to existing ones or that extend them.

We collected 20 texts per new scenario, using the same text collection method as Ostermann et al. (2018a): We asked workers to tell a story about a certain everyday scenario "as if talking to a child". This instruction ensures that the resulting stories are simple in language and clearly structured. Texts collected this way have been found to explicitly mention many script events and participants (Modi et al., 2016; Ostermann et al., 2018a). They are thus ideal to evaluate script-based inference.

3.2 Question Collection

For the question collection, we followed Ostermann et al. (2018a) in telling workers that the data are collected for a reading comprehension task for children, in order to get linguistically simple and explicit questions. However, as mentioned above, we guide workers towards asking questions about target sentences rather than a complete text.

As target sentences, we selected every fourth sentence in a text. In order to avoid selecting target sentences with too much or too little content, we only considered sentences with less than 20 tokens,

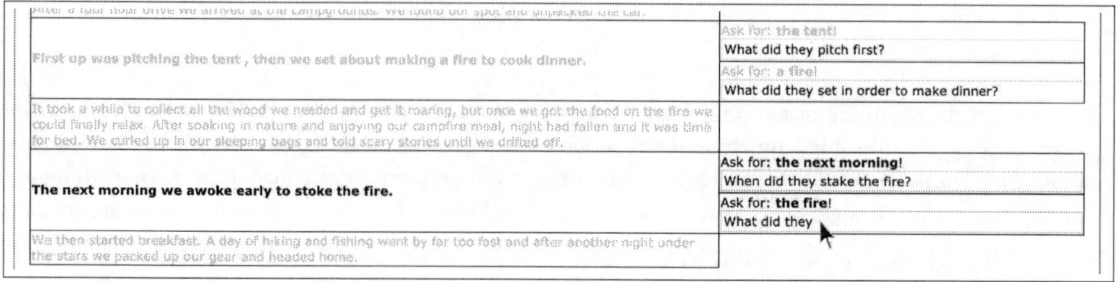

Figure 2: Screenshot of an item in the participant question collection experiment.

but that contained 2 or more noun phrases.[2]

In a series of pilot studies, we then showed the texts with highlighted target sentences to workers and asked them to write questions about these sentences. We however found, that in many cases, the written questions were too general or nonsensical.

We concluded that an even more structured task was required and decided to concentrate on questions of two types: (1) questions that ask about participants, and (2) questions about the temporal event structure of a scenario. Participants are usually instantiated by noun phrases (NPs), while events are described by verb phrases (VPs). We thus used *Stanford CoreNLP* (Manning et al., 2014) to extract both NPs and VPs in the target sentences and split up the experiment into two parts: In the first part, workers were required to write questions that *ask about the given noun phrase*. Figure 2 shows a screenshot of an item from the first part. The first column shows the reading text with the target sentence highlighted. The second columns shows all extracted phrases with a field for one question per phrase.[3] Full details of the experiment instructions are given in the Supplemental Material.

In the second part, we then asked workers to write a temporal question (when, how long, etc.) *using the given verb phrase*. We found that an exact repetition of the NP instructions for the second part ("ask about the given verb phrase") resulted in unnatural questions, so we adapted the instructions. A screenshot of the VP experiment is given in the Supplemental Material.

We showed each text to two workers and asked

them to write one question per VP or NP. Workers were only allowed to work on either the VP or the NP part, since the instructions could easily be confused. In order to exclude yes/no questions, we did not accept inputs starting with an auxiliary or modal verb. Also, all questions needed to contain at least 4 words. We asked workers to use *they* to refer to the protagonist of the story and other types of mentions (e.g. pronouns like *I*, *you*, *we* or the word *narrator*) were not accepted.

3.3 Answer Collection

For collecting answer candidates we hid the target sentences from the texts and showed them with up to 12 questions, to keep the workload at an acceptable level. If there were more questions for a text, we selected 12 questions at random.

Since the target sentences are hidden in the texts, it can be expected that some questions cannot be answered from the text anymore. However, the necessary information for finding an answer might be inferred from script knowledge, so workers were explicitly told that they might need commonsense to find an answer. Some answers can still be read off the text, if other parts of the texts contain the same information as the hidden target sentences. For other questions, neither the text nor script knowledge provides sufficient information for finding an answer.

As for the creation of MCScript, workers first had to conduct a 4-way classification for each question to account for these cases: *text-based* (answer is in the text), *script-based* (answer can be inferred from script knowledge), *unfitting* (question doesn't make sense), *unknown* (answer is not known). Having such class annotations is not only useful for evaluation, but it also sensitizes workers for the fact that they are explicitly allowed to use background knowledge.

In the experiment, workers were also instructed

______

[2]All parameters were selected empirically, by testing different values and analyzing samples of the resulting data.

[3]If the noun phrase was part of a prepositional phrase or a construction of the form "NP *of* NP", we took the whole phrase instead, because it is more natural to ask for the complete phrase. In order to avoid redundancy, we only looked at NPs that had no other NPs as parents. We also excluded noun phrases that referred to the narrator (*I*, *me* etc.).

text-based	script-based	text-or-script	unfitting	unknown
9,357	12,433	2,403	3,240	6,457
total answerable: 24,193			**total not answerable:** 9,397	

Table 1: Distribution of question labels, before validation.

to write both a correct and a plausible incorrect answer for questions labeled as *text-based* of *script-based*. We follow (Ostermann et al., 2018a) and require workers to write an alternative question if the labels *unfitting* or *unknown* are used, in order to level out the workload.

We presented each question to 5 workers, resulting in 5 judgements and up to 5 incorrect and correct answer candidates per question. For the final data set, we considered questions with a majority vote (3 out of 5) on *text-based* or *script-based*. We also included questions without a majority vote, but for which at least 3 workers assigned one of *text-based* or *script-based*. In that case, we assigned the new label *text-or-script* and also accepted the question for the final data set. This seemed reasonable, since at least 3 workers wrote answers for the question, meaning it could still be used in the final data collection. The remaining questions were discarded.

3.4 Answer Candidate Selection

In a last step, we selected one correct and one incorrect answer from all possible candidates per question for the data set. To choose the most plausible correct answer candidate, we adapt the procedure from Ostermann et al. (2018a): We normalize all correct answers (lowercasing, normalizing numbers[4], deleting stopwords[5]) and then merge candidates that are contained in another candidate, and candidate pairs with a Levenshtein (1966) distance of less than 3. The most frequent candidate is then selected as correct answer. If there was no clear majority, we selected a candidate at random.

To select an incorrect answer candidate, we adapt the *adversarial filtering* algorithm from Zellers et al. (2018). Our implementation uses a simple classifier that utilizes shallow surface features. The algorithm selects the incorrect answer candidate from the set of possible candidates that is most difficult for the classifier, i.e. an incorrect answer that is hard to tell apart from the correct

answer (e.g. the incorrect answers in Figure 1: *eating* and *utensils* are also mentioned in the text). By picking incorrect answers with the adversarial filtering method, the dataset becomes robust against surface-oriented methods.

Practically, the algorithm starts with a random assignment, i.e. a random incorrect answer candidate per question. This assignment is refined iteratively, such that the most difficult candidate is selected. In each iteration, the algorithm splits the data into a random training part and a test part. The classifier is trained on the training part and then used to classify *all* possible candidates in the test part. The assignment of answer candidates in the test data is then changed such that the most difficult incorrect answer candidate per question is picked as incorrect answer. After several iterations through the whole dataset, the number of changed answer candidates usually stagnates and the algorithm converges.

For MCScript2.0, we use the logistic classifier mentioned in Section 2, which only uses surface features and is thus well suited for the filtering algorithm. Implementation details and pseudocode are given in the Supplemental Material.

4 Corpus Analysis

4.1 General Statistics

In total, MCScript2.0 comprises 19,821 questions on 3,487 texts, i.e. 5.7 questions on average per text. The average length of texts, questions and answers is 164.4 tokens, 8.2 tokens and 3.4 tokens, respectively.

In the data collection process, we crowdsourced 1,800 new texts, resulting in a total of 3,919 texts for 200 scenarios. On average, there are 1.98 target sentences per text. In the question collection, we gathered 42,132 questions that were then used for the answer collection. For 8,242 questions, there was no clear majority on the question label. Table 1 shows the label distribution on the remaining 33,890 questions. 24,193 of these could be answered, i.e. 71%.

To increase data quality, we conducted a manual validation of the data. Four student assistants re-

---

[4]We used *text2num*, https://github.com/ghewgill/text2num.

[5]*and, or, to, the, a*

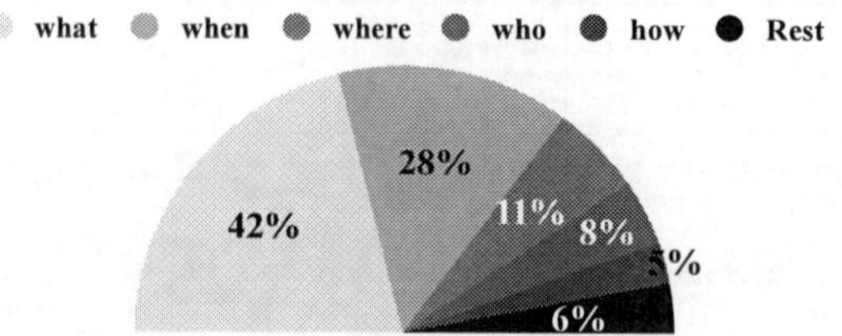

Figure 3: Distribution of question types

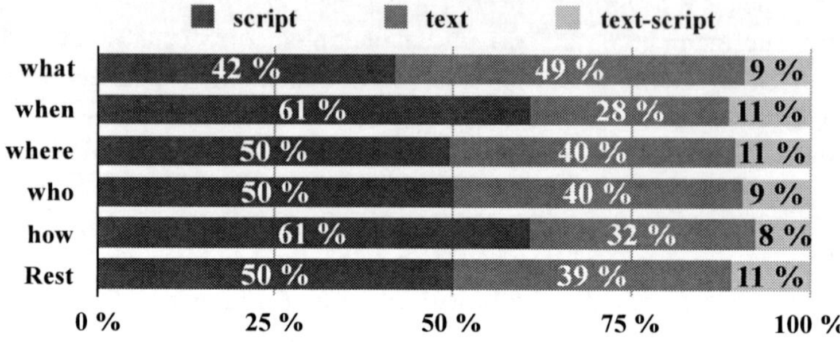

Figure 4: Proportion of labels per question type.

placed erroneous answers and deleted nonsensical questions, question duplicates and incoherent texts.

During validation, 152 texts were found to be incoherent and discarded (along with all questions). Additionally, 3,388 questions were deleted because they were nonsensical or duplicates. 1,620 correct and 2,977 incorrect answers were exchanged, resp., because they were inappropriate. If a question deletion resulted in texts without any questions, or if a text did not have any answerable questions, the text was discarded, too.

After question validation, the final dataset comprises 9,935 questions that are labeled as script-based, 7,908 as text-based, and 1,978 as text-or-script.

4.2 Questions

Figure 3 gives the distribution over question types, which we extracted by looking at the first word in the question. The largest number of questions are *what* questions, most of which ask about participants of a script. *When* questions make up the second largest group, asking for temporal event structure. During the VP question experiment, some workers ignored that we asked for temporal questions only, which resulted in a number of *how* questions.

MCScript2.0 contains 50% questions labeled as script-based, which is a notably larger amount as compared to the approximately 27% of questions in MCScript labeled as script-based. The number of

script-based questions varies between the question types, as can be seen in Figure 4. While *when* and *how* questions require script knowledge for finding an answer in more than 60% of cases, less than half of *what* questions do so. A simple explanation for this could be that *when* or *how* questions typically ask for events, while *what* questions ask for participants. Events are usually referred only once in a text, i.e. with the hiding of the respective event mention, the needed information has to be inferred. Participants in contrast tend to appear more often throughout a story.

Example 5 below illustrates this. Question 1 was originally asked about a sentence in which the plates are set for the dinner guests. The guests still appear in another sentence, so the answer can be inferred from the text. For question 2, in contrast, script knowledge is required for finding an answer: The event of *bringing the items to the table* is not mentioned anymore, so the information that this happens typically after counting plates and silverware needs to be inferred.

(5) **T:** (...) I was told that there would be 13 or 14 guests. First I counted out 14 spoons, then the same number of salad forks, dinner forks, and knives. (...) I set each place with one napkin, one dinner fork, one salad fork, one spoon, and one knife. (...)
Q1: Who are the plate and cup for?
dinner guests ✓   the neighbor ✗
Q2: When did they bring the items over to

the table?

after counting them ✓

after placing them on the table ✗

5 Experiments

We test three benchmark models on MCScript2.0 that were also evaluated on MCScript, so a direct comparison is possible. For the experiments, we split the data into a training set (14,191 questions on 2,500 texts), a development set (2,020 questions on 355 texts) and a test set (3,610 questions on 632 texts). All texts of 5 randomly chosen scenarios were assigned completely to the test set, so a part of the test scenarios are unseen during training.

5.1 Models

Logistic Regression Classifier

As first model, we reimplemented the logistic regression classifier proposed by Merkhofer et al. (2018), which was also used in the adversarial filtering algorithm. The classifier employs 3 types of features: (1) Length features, encoding the length of the text, answer and questions on the word and character level, (2) overlap features, encoding the amount of literal overlap between text, question, and answers, and (3) binary lexical patterns encoding the presence or absence of words or combinations of words in answer, text and question.

Attentive Reader

As second model, we implement an attentive reader (Hermann et al., 2015). We adopt the formulation by Ostermann et al. (2018a) (originally by Chen et al. (2016)). All tokens in text, question and answers are represented with word embeddings. Bidirectional gated recurrent units (GRUs, Cho et al. (2014)) process the text, question and answers and transform them into sequences of contextualized hidden states. The text is represented as a weighted average of the hidden states with a bilinear attention formulation, and another bilinear weight matrix is used to compute a scalar as score for each answer. For a formalization, we refer to Ostermann et al. (2018a) and Chen et al. (2016).

Three-way Attentive Network (TriAN)

As third model, we use a three-way attentive network (Wang et al., 2018), the best-scoring model of the shared task on MCScript[6]. Various types of in-

---

[6]Code available at `https://github.com/intfloat/commonsense-rc`

formation are employed to represent tokens: Word embeddings, part of speech tags, named entity embeddings, and word count/overlap features, similar to the logistic classifier. Three bidirectional LSTM (Hochreiter and Schmidhuber, 1997) modules are used to encode text, question and answers. The resulting hidden representations are reweighted with three attention matrices and then summed into vectors using three self-attention layers.

Additionally, token representations are enhanced with *ConceptNet* (Speer et al., 2017) relations as a form of induced commonsense knowledge. ConceptNet is a large database of commonsense facts, represented as triples of two entities with a predicate. Relevant ConceptNet relations between words in the answer and the text are queried from the database and represented with relation embeddings, which are learned end-to-end during training and appended to the text token representations.

In contrast to Wang et al. (2018), we use the non-ensemble version of TriAN without pretraining on *RACE* (Lai et al., 2017), for better comparability to the other models.

5.2 Human Upper Bound

To assess human performance, 5 student assistants performed the reading comprehension task on 60 texts each. To assess agreement, 20 texts were annotated by all students. The annotators reached averaged pairwise agreement of 96.3% and an average accuracy of 97.4%, which shows that this is a simple task for humans.

5.3 Results

Overall Performance. Table 2 gives details about the performance of the 3 benchmark models on the test set, and on script-based (acc_{scr}) and text-based (acc_{txt}) questions in the test set. As can be seen, the logistic model scores worst, presumably because it has been used for the adversarial filtering algorithm and the data are thus most challenging for this model. TriAN performs best, clearly outperforming the attentive reader. TriAN is apparently superior in its way of text processing, since it employs a richer text representation and exploits attention mechanisms on more levels, which is reflected by a higher accuracy on text-based questions. In contrast, script-based questions seem to be challenging for TriAN. This is interesting, because it shows that ConceptNet alone cannot provide sufficient information for answering the kind of questions that can be found in MCScript2.0.

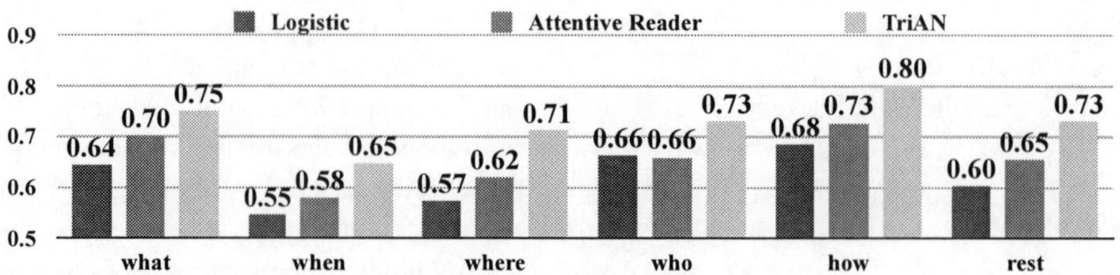

Figure 5: Performance of the models on question types.

	acc	acc_{scr}	acc_{txt}
Logistic Model	0.61	0.56	0.67
Attentive Reader	0.65	0.63	0.68
TriAN	**0.72**	**0.67**	**0.78**
Humans	0.97		

Table 2: Accuracy on test set, and on script/text-based questions (acc_{scr}, acc_{txt}) on **MCScript2.0**. The maximum per column is printed in **bold**.

	acc	acc_{scr}	acc_{txt}
Logistic Model	0.79	0.76	**0.81**
Attentive Reader	0.72	0.75	0.71
TriAN	**0.80**	**0.79**	**0.81**
Humans	0.98		

Table 3: Accuracy on the test set and on script/text-based questions (acc_{scr}, acc_{txt}) on **MCScript**. The maximum per column is printed in **bold**.

Comparison to MCScript. Since the same models were used for MCScript, a comparison of their performance on both datasets is possible. Results on MCScript are given in Table 3.[7] As can be seen, the performance of all three models is worse on MCScript2.0, showing that the dataset is generally more challenging. In contrast to MCScript, script-based questions in MCScript2.0 are clearly harder to answer than text-based questions: All models perform worse on script-based questions as compared to text-based questions. In comparison to MCScript, the performance of TriAN is **12%** lower. This indicates that the new mode of question collection and the answer selection via adversarial filtering resolve some of the difficulties with MCScript.

To assess whether the performance difference to MCScript is due to the 90 new scenarios being more challenging, we additionally evaluated the models on these scenarios only. We found no performance difference on the new vs. old scenarios.

Influence of Adversarial Filtering. To find out how large the influence of the new question collection method and the answer selection via adversarial filtering is, we conducted an additional experiment: We applied the answer selection method of Ostermann et al. (2018a) to our data set to create an alternative version of the data that is not based on adversarial filtering. Correct answers were selected to have the lowest possible overlap with the reading text. Incorrect answers were selected using the majority voting technique described in Section 3.4.

We found that the adversarial filtering accounts for around two thirds of the total accuracy difference of TriAN as compared to MCScript, i.e. one third of the difference can be attributed to the new question collection. This means that both modifications together add to the larger difficulty of MCScript2.0.

Question Types. Figure 5 shows the performance of the models on single question types, as identified in Section 4. It is clear that *when* questions are most challenging for all models. The logistic classifier performs almost at chance level. As far as TriAN is concerned, we found that many cases of errors ask for the typical temporal order of events, as Example 6 illustrates:

(6) **Q:** When did they put the nozzle in their tank?
before filling up with gas. ✓
after filling up with gas. ✗

The event of *put the nozzle in the tank* is not mentioned in the shown version of the text, so it is not possible to read off the text when the event actually took place.

---

[7]For the attentive reader, numbers were taken from (Ostermann et al., 2018b). The other models were retrained (and in the case of the logistic model re-implemented), since no exact numbers on script/text-based questions were published.

How questions are the least difficult questions. This can be explained with the fact that many *how* questions ask for numbers that are mentioned in the text (e.g. *How long did they stay in the sauna?* or *How many slices did they place onto the paper plate?*). The answer to such questions can often be found with a simple text lookup. Another part of how questions asks for the typical duration of an activity. These questions often have similar answers irrespective of the scenario, since most of the narrations in MCScript2.0 span a rather short time period. Such answers can easily be memorized by the models.

Especially for TriAN, *what* and *who* questions seem to be easy. This could be explained with the fact that ConceptNet contains lots of information about entities and their relations to each other, apparently also covering some information about script participants, which seems to be useful for these question types.

6 Related Work

Recent years have seen a number of datasets that evaluate commonsense inference. Like our corpus, most of these data sets choose a machine comprehension setting. The data sets can be roughly classified along their text domain:

News Texts. Two recently published machine comprehension data sets that require commonsense inference are based on news texts. First, *NewsQA* (Trischler et al., 2017) is a dataset of newswire texts from CNN with questions and answers written by crowdsourcing workers. During data collection, full texts were not shown to workers as a basis for question formulation, but only the text's title and a short summary, to avoid literal repetitions and support the generation of non-trivial questions requiring background knowledge. Second, *ReCoRD* (Zhang et al., 2018) contains cloze-style questions on newswire texts that were not crowdsourced, but automatically extracted by pruning a named entity in a larger passage from the text.

Web Texts. Other corpora use web documents. An example is *TriviaQA* (Joshi et al., 2017), a corpus that contains automatically collected question-answer pairs from 14 trivia and quiz-league websites, together with web-crawled evidence documents from *Wikipedia* and *Bing*. While a majority of questions require world knowledge for finding the correct answer, it is mostly factual knowledge. *CommonsenseQA* (Talmor et al., 2018) contains a total of over 9000 multiple-choice questions that were crowdsourced based on knowledge base triples extracted from ConceptNet. Texts were only added post-hoc, by querying a web search engine based on the formulated question, and by adding the retrieved evidence texts to the questions and answers.

Fictional Texts. *NarrativeQA* (Kočiský et al., 2018) is a reading comprehension dataset that largely differs from other corpora by means of text length. Instead of providing short reading texts, models have to process complete books or movie scripts and answer very complex questions.

Because of their domains, the aforementioned data sets evaluate a very broad notion of commonsense, including e.g. physical knowledge (for trivia texts) and knowledge about political facts (for newswire texts). However, none of them explicitly tackle script knowledge.

7 Conclusion

We presented MCScript2.0, a new machine comprehension dataset with a focus on challenging inference questions that require script knowledge or commonsense knowledge for finding the correct answer. Our new question collection procedure results in about half of the questions in MCScript2.0 requiring such inference, which is a much larger amount compared to a previous dataset.

We evaluate several benchmark models on MCScript2.0 and show that even a model that makes use of ConceptNet as a source for commonsense knowledge struggles to answer many question in our corpus. MCScript2.0 forms the basis of a shared task organized at the COIN workshop.[8]

Acknowledgments

We thank our student assistants Leonie Harter, David Meier, Christine Schäfer and Georg Seiler for the help with data validation, and Kathryn Chapman, Srestha Ghosh, Trang Hoang, Ben Posner and Miriam Schulz for help with assessing the human upper bound. We also thank the numerous workers on MTurk for their good work and Carina Silberer and the reviewers for their helpful comments on the paper. This research was funded by the German Research Foundation (DFG) as part of SFB 1102 Information Density and Linguistic Encoding.

---

[8] https://coinnlp.github.io/

References

Kevin Burton, Akshay Java, Ian Soboroff, et al. 2009. The ICWSM 2009 Spinn3r Dataset. In *Third Annual Conference on Weblogs and Social Media (ICWSM 2009)*.

Nathanael Chambers and Dan Jurafsky. 2008. Unsupervised Learning of Narrative Event Chains. In *Proceedings of the 46th Annual Meeting of the Association for Computational Linguistics: Human Language Technologies*, pages 789–797. Association for Computational Linguistics.

Nathanael Chambers and Dan Jurafsky. 2009. Unsupervised Learning of Narrative Schemas and their Participants. In *Proceedings of the Joint Conference of the 47th Annual Meeting of the ACL and the 4th International Joint Conference on Natural Language Processing of the AFNLP*, pages 602–610. Association for Computational Linguistics.

Danqi Chen, Jason Bolton, and Christopher D. Manning. 2016. A Thorough Examination of the CNN/Daily Mail Reading Comprehension Task. In *Proceedings of the 54th Annual Meeting of the Association for Computational Linguistics (Volume 1: Long Papers)*, volume 1, pages 2358–2367.

Kyunghyun Cho, Bart Van Merriënboer, Caglar Gulcehre, Dzmitry Bahdanau, Fethi Bougares, Holger Schwenk, and Yoshua Bengio. 2014. Learning phrase representations using rnn encoder-decoder for statistical machine translation. *arXiv preprint arXiv:1406.1078*.

Karl Moritz Hermann, Tomas Kocisky, Edward Grefenstette, Lasse Espeholt, Will Kay, Mustafa Suleyman, and Phil Blunsom. 2015. Teaching machines to read and comprehend. In *Advances in Neural Information Processing Systems*, pages 1693–1701.

Sepp Hochreiter and Jürgen Schmidhuber. 1997. Long short-term memory. *Neural computation*, 9(8):1735–1780.

Bram Jans, Steven Bethard, Ivan Vulić, and Marie Francine Moens. 2012. Skip N-grams and Ranking Functions for Predicting Script Events. In *Proceedings of the 13th Conference of the European Chapter of the Association for Computational Linguistics*, EACL '12, pages 336–344. Association for Computational Linguistics.

Mandar Joshi, Eunsol Choi, Daniel S. Weld, and Luke Zettlemoyer. 2017. TriviaQA: A Large Scale Distantly Supervised Challenge Dataset for Reading Comprehension. In *Proceedings of the 55th Annual Meeting of the Association for Computational Linguistics*, pages 1601–1611. Association for Computational Linguistics.

Tomáš Kočiský, Jonathan Schwarz, Phil Blunsom, Chris Dyer, Karl Moritz Hermann, Gáabor Melis, and Edward Grefenstette. 2018. The NarrativeQA Reading Comprehension Challenge. *Transactions of the Association of Computational Linguistics*, 6:317–328.

Guokun Lai, Qizhe Xie, Hanxiao Liu, Yiming Yang, and Eduard Hovy. 2017. RACE: Large-scale ReAding Comprehension Dataset From Examinations. In *Proceedings of the 2017 Conference on Empirical Methods in Natural Language Processing*, pages 785–794.

Vladimir I. Levenshtein. 1966. Binary codes capable of correcting deletions, insertions, and reversals. In *Soviet Physics Doklady*, volume 10, pages 707–710.

Christopher D. Manning, Mihai Surdeanu, John Bauer, Jenny Rose Finkel, Steven Bethard, and David McClosky. 2014. The Stanford CoreNLP Natural Language Processing Toolkit. In *ACL (System Demonstrations)*, pages 55–60.

Elizabeth M. Merkhofer, John Henderson, David Bloom, Laura Strickhart, and Guido Zarrella. 2018. MITRE at SemEval-2018 Task 11: Commonsense Reasoning without Commonsense Knowledge. In *Proceedings of the 12th International Workshop on Semantic Evaluations (SemEval-2018)*, pages 1078–1082.

Ashutosh Modi, Tatjana Anikina, Simon Ostermann, and Manfred Pinkal. 2016. InScript: Narrative texts annotated with script information. In *Proceedings of the Tenth International Conference on Language Resources and Evaluation (LREC 2016)*, pages 3485–3493. European Language Resources Association (ELRA).

Ashutosh Modi and Ivan Titov. 2014. Inducing Neural Models of Script Knowledge. In *Proceedings of the Conference on Computational Natural Language Learning (CoNLL)*, pages 49–57.

Simon Ostermann, Ashutosh Modi, Michael Roth, Stefan Thater, and Manfred Pinkal. 2018a. MCScript: A Novel Dataset for Assessing Machine Comprehension Using Script Knowledge. In *Proceedings of the 11th International Conference on Language Resources and Evaluation (LREC 2018)*, pages 3567–3574.

Simon Ostermann, Michael Roth, Ashutosh Modi, Stefan Thater, and Manfred Pinkal. 2018b. SemEval-2018 Task 11: Machine Comprehension using Commonsense Knowledge. In *Proceedings of The 12th International Workshop on Semantic Evaluation*, pages 747–757.

Simon Ostermann, Michael Roth, Stefan Thater, and Manfred Pinkal. 2017. Aligning Script Events with Narrative Texts. *Proceedings of the 6th Joint Conference on Lexical and Computational Semantics (*SEM 2017)*, pages 128–134.

Karl Pichotta and Raymond J. Mooney. 2014. Statistical script learning with multi-argument events. In *Proceedings of the 14th Conference of the European Chapter of the Association for Computational Linguistics (EACL 2014)*, pages 220–229.

Karl Pichotta and Raymond J. Mooney. 2016. Learning Statistical Scripts with LSTM Recurrent Neural Networks. *Proceedings of the 30th AAAI Conference on Artificial Intelligence (AAAI-16)*, pages 2800–2806.

Michaela Regneri, Alexander Koller, and Manfred Pinkal. 2010. Learning Script Knowledge with Web Experiments. In *Proceedings of the 48th Annual Meeting of the Association for Computational Linguistics*, pages 979–988. Association for Computational Linguistics.

Rachel Rudinger, Pushpendre Rastogi, Francis Ferraro, and Benjamin Van Durme. 2015. Script induction as language modeling. *Proceedings of the 2015 Conference on Empirical Methods in Natural Language Processing*, pages 1681–1686.

Roger C. Schank and Robert P. Abelson. 1977. *Scripts, Plans, Goals, and Understanding*. Lawrence Erlbaum Associates.

Push Singh, Thomas Lin, Erik T. Mueller, Grace Lim, Travell Perkins, and Wan Li Zhu. 2002. Open Mind Common Sense: Knowledge Acquisition from the General Public. In *On the move to Meaningful Internet Systems 2002: CoopIS, DOA, and ODBASE*, pages 1223–1237. Springer.

Robyn Speer, Joshua Chin, and Catherine Havasi. 2017. Conceptnet 5.5: An open multilingual graph of general knowledge. In *Proceedings of the Thirty-First AAAI Conference on Artificial Intelligence (AAAI-17)*, pages 4444–4451.

Alon Talmor, Jonathan Herzig, Nicholas Lourie, and Jonathan Berant. 2018. CommonsenseQA: A Question Answering Challenge Targeting Commonsense Knowledge. *arXiv preprint arXiv:1811.00937*.

Adam Trischler, Tong Wang, Xingdi Yuan, Justin Harris, Alessandro Sordoni, Philip Bachman, and Kaheer Suleman. 2017. NewsQA: A Machine Comprehension Dataset. In *Proceedings of the 2nd Workshop on Representation Learning for NLP*, pages 191–200.

Liang Wang, Meng Sun, Wei Zhao, Kewei Shen, and Jingming Liu. 2018. Yuanfudao at SemEval-2018 Task 11: Three-way Attention and Relational Knowledge for Commonsense Machine Comprehension. In *Proceedings of the 12th International Workshop on Semantic Evaluations (SemEval-2018)*, pages 758–762.

Lilian Wanzare, Alessandra Zarcone, Stefan Thater, and Manfred Pinkal. 2016. DeScript: A Crowdsourced Database for the Acquisition of High-quality Script Knowledge. In *Proceedings of the Tenth International Conference on Language Resources and Evaluation (LREC 2016)*, pages 3494–3501. European Language Resources Association (ELRA).

Lilian Wanzare, Alessandra Zarcone, Stefan Thater, and Manfred Pinkal. 2017. Inducing Script Structure from Crowdsourced Event Descriptions via Semi-Supervised Clustering. In *Proceedings of the 2nd Workshop on Linking Models of Lexical, Sentential and Discourse-level Semantics*, pages 1–11. Association for Computational Linguistics.

Rowan Zellers, Yonatan Bisk, Roy Schwartz, and Yejin Choi. 2018. SWAG: A Large-Scale Adversarial Dataset for Grounded Commonsense Inference. In *Proceedings of the 2018 Conference on Empirical Methods in Natural Language Processing*, pages 93–104.

Sheng Zhang, Xiaodong Liu, Jingjing Liu, Jianfeng Gao, Kevin Duh, and Benjamin Van Durme. 2018. ReCoRD: Bridging the Gap between Human and Machine Commonsense Reading Comprehension. *arXiv preprint arXiv:1810.12885*.

A Supplemental Material

A.1 Additional Data Sample

(7) **T:** I am at work . I have a guest sit at the bar . The ordered themselves a beer . I check that he is of age , and that his license is valid . I then go to the beer cooler , and grab a nice cold mug , and fill it up with beer . I place a napkin down and set the beer on top in front of the bar guest . I present him the check and tell him no rush , whenever he is ready . He then places his cash with the receipt . I go to cash him out , offer to be right back with his change , and he responds with , " Keep the change " . I like nights like this .
Q: Why did they receive a nice tip?
the customer was happy with the service ✓
the customer was in a rush ✗
Q: When was the check printed?
after the order ✓
before the order ✗
Q: What did they create at the computer and print?
the check ✓
change ✗

(8) **T:** I wanted to throw a Bachelorette Party for my best friend . She lives in Dallas , but she wants to have her party in New Orleans for a girls weekend . The first thing we did was talk about the theme of the party . We decided on the theme of " Something Blue " . We would have all colors of blue and activities that have titles with the word blue for the whole weekend . She gave me a list of 20 girls . I created an invitation that had blue and included a picture of her . I also included an itinerary of our weekend activities with all of our fun " blue " titles , to set the fun mood . I sealed them before hand writing the addresses and adding a stamp . Next , they were off to the post office , so everyone could be invited to our fun weekend .
Q: What was printed out?
itinerary ✓
invitations to a weddingy ✗
Q: When was each invitation placed into their blue envelope?
Before handwriting addresses ✓
After adding stamps ✗
Q: Where did she place the invitations?
Post office ✓
Dallas ✗

(9) **T:** The restaurant was terrible again and I probably should not have given it another chance . The management at the store level is obviously not paying attention to me so it is time to right to headquarters . I opened the word processing program on my computer and opened a new document . I went all the way to the right side and entered my street address on one line and the city , state and zip code below that . Next I entered the date and then moved all the way to the left and entered the street address of the restaurant headquarters and the city , state and zip code of the headquarters . I started the letter with Dear Sir and on the next lines , proceeded to explain the problems I had been having with this particular location , it 's service and food . I explained that I had tried to resolve it at store level but had been unsuccessful . On the final line , I went all the way to right and entered ' Sincerely ' and hit return a couple times , then added my name below that . I folded it and put it an addressed and stamped envelope , and mailed it to the company headquarters .
Q: What did they print out?
The letter ✓
The receipt from the restaurant ✗
Q: When did they sign above their printed name?
After the letter was printed ✓
After putting the letter in the envelope. ✗
Q: What they did they sign?
The letter ✓
The receipt at the restaurant ✗

A.2 Crowdsourcing Details

All data were collected using Amazon Mechanical Turk[9]. We paid \$0.50 for each item in the text and answer collection experiment. For the question collection experiment, we paid \$0.50 per item, if the text contained 4 or more target sentences,

---
[9]https://www.mturk.com

and \$0.30 per item if fewer target sentences were highlighted.

A.3 Implementation Details

For implementation details and preprocessing of the logistic model and TriAN, we follow (Merkhofer et al., 2018) and (Wang et al., 2018), respectively. NLTK[10] was used as preprocessing tool for the Attentive Reader.

The learning rate was tuned to 0.002 and 0.1 for TriAN and the attentive reader, resp. and the hidden size for both models to 64. As in the original formulation, dropout was set to 0.5 for the attentive reader and to 0.4 for TriAN. Batch size was set to 32 and both models were trained for 50 epochs. The model with the best accuracy on the dev data was used for testing.

A.4 Adversarial Filtering

Data: data set D, a randomly initialized
      assignment S, and a classifier C
Result: $\hat{S}$
repeat
  split the data into test batches of size b,
  such that each batch contains all
  questions for b texts;
  for D_{test} *in batches* **do**
    $D_{train} \longleftarrow D \backslash D_{test}$;
    $\mathcal{D}_{train} \longleftarrow compile(D_{train})$;
    train C on $\mathcal{D}_{train}$;
    for *all instances*
      $< T_i, Q_i, a_i^+, < a_{i,0}^-...a_{i,j}^- > in\ D_{test}$
    do
      use C to classify all incorrect
      answer candidates $a_{i,0}^-...a_{i,j}^-$;
      set $s_{i,j}$ to the index of the answer
      candidate with the highest
      probability of being correct;
    end
  end
until *number of changed assignments*
  stagnates or increases;
Algorithm 1: Adversarial Filtering for MC-Script2.0

Formally, let a dataset be defined as a list of tuples $\langle t_i, q_i, a_i^+, \langle a_{i,0}^-...a_{i,j}^- \rangle \rangle$, where t_i is a reading text, q_i is a question on the text, a_i^+ is the correct answer (as selected via majority vote, s. last Section) and $\langle a_{i,0}^-...a_{i,j}^- \rangle$ is a list of 3 to 5 incorrect answer candidates[11]. The aim of the algorithm is to find an assignment $\hat{S} = \{s_{0,0}...s_{i,j}\}$, where each $s_{i,j}$ is the index of the most difficult answer candidate in $\langle a_{i,0}^-...a_{i,j}^- \rangle$.

A dataset that is *compiled* with the assignment S is a list of instances $< t_i, q_i, a_i^+, a_i^- >$, such that there is only one incorrect answer candidate per question, according to the indices given by S.

Once the algorithm converges, $\hat{S}$ is used to compile the final version of the dataset, $\hat{\mathcal{D}}$, which contains incorrect answer candidates that are most likely to be correct.

For the batch size we tried values in $\{50, 100, 250, 500\}$, but we found that for all values, the performance of the classifier would drop close to chance level after one iteration only. We set $b = 250$, since the performance was closest to chance after convergence with that setting. Also, we defined that the algorithm converges if the number of changed assignments since the last iteration is ≤ 50.

---

[10] https://www.nltk.org

[11] Note that since there are several questions per text, the value of t_i may appear in several instances.

packed and the tent had no holes from the last trip , we put everything into the car and set out on our way. After a four hour drive we arrived at the campgrounds. We found our spot and unpacked the car.	
First up was pitching the tent , then we set about making a fire to cook dinner.	Answer: pitching the tent Question: **When did they pitch the tent?** Answer: making a fire Question: **When did they make a fire?** Answer: to cook dinner Question: **How long did they cook dinner?**
It took a while to collect all the wood we needed and get it roaring, but once we got the food on the fire we could finally relax. After soaking in nature and enjoying our campfire meal, night had fallen and it was time for bed. We curled up in our sleeping bags and told scary stories until we drifted off.	
The next morning we awoke early to stoke the fire.	Answer: **awoke early** Question: **When did they awake early?** Answer: **stoke the fire** Question: **How long did they**
We then started breakfast. A day of hiking and fishing went by far too fast and after another night under the stars we packed up our gear and headed home.	

Instructions

In this experiment, we collect reading comprehension questions for children, based on stories about everyday activities. We want to test if the children understand certain parts of the text, so we are looking for questions about specific phrases in the text.

Your Task:

Please, first read the full text that appears on the left-hand side. Then click the **Continue** button. A number of text fields will appear on the right-hand side, next to a highlighted sentence. Please fill each text field with a question that can be answered with the given phrase, in the context of the highlighted sentence. Then click **Continue**, and the text fields for the second highlighted sentence will appear.

Note that relevant information from the text should be repeated in the question, so that the children have a chance to find an answer. In the example, *What did they make?* would be a bad question, because it is too general, while *What did they light to make dinner?* is specific enough.

Important remarks:

1. Please stick to the following rules, otherwise we reserve the right to reject your work:
   - Do not write yes/no questions. We will check for these questions automatically.
   - Do not write questions that are shorter than 4 words. We will check for these questions automatically.
   - If persons are mentioned by name ("John", "Michael") or function ("the waiter", "the guest"), please refer to them in the same way in the question. If you want to refer to the protagonist (usually "I", "we"), always use "they". Do not use I/you/we. We will check for these pronouns automatically.
   - Please write the questions in grammatical and coherent English. We will manually check a major number of HITs.
2. When you start the experiment, there will be no *Submit* button, but don't worry! You just need to go through the 2 sentences, and the *Submit* button will appear right afterwards. Once you finished one sentence, you can no longer edit your questions.
3. You can access both these instructions and the examples below during the experiment by clicking on one of the two buttons at the top of the experiment page.

Example

We spent a week getting our gear together for our big camping trip. After making sure everything was packed and the tent had no holes from the last trip , we put everything into the car and set out on our way. After a four hour drive we arrived at the campgrounds. We found our spot and unpacked the car.		
First up was pitching the tent , then we set about making a fire to cook dinner.	Ask for **the** tent!	What did they pitch after arriving?
	Ask for **a** fire!	What did they light to make dinner?
It took a while to collect all the wood we needed and get it roaring, but once we got the food on the fire we could finally relax. After soaking in nature and enjoying our campfire meal, night had fallen and it was time for bed. We curled up in our sleeping bags and told scary stories until we drifted off.		
The next morning we awoke early to stoke the fire.	Ask for **the** next morning!	When did they wake up?
	Ask for **the** fire!	What did they stake in the morning?
We then started breakfast. A day of hiking and fishing went by far too fast and after another night under the stars we packed up our gear and headed home.		

Got it. Start the experiment!

Deconstructing multimodality: visual properties and visual context in human semantic processing

Christopher Davis†, Luana Bulat†, Anita Vero†, Ekaterina Shutova‡
† Department of Computer Science & Technology, University of Cambridge, U.K.
{ccd38,luana.bulat,alv34}@cam.ac.uk
‡Institute for Logic, Language and Computation, University of Amsterdam, Netherlands
e.shutova@uva.nl

Abstract

Multimodal semantic models that extend linguistic representations with additional perceptual input have proved successful in a range of natural language processing (NLP) tasks. Recent research has successfully used neural methods to automatically create visual representations for words. However, these works have extracted visual features from complete images, and have not examined how different kinds of visual information impact performance. In contrast, we construct multimodal models that differentiate between internal visual properties of the objects and their external visual context. We evaluate the models on the task of decoding brain activity associated with the meanings of nouns, demonstrating their advantage over those based on complete images.

1 Introduction

Multimodal models combining linguistic and visual information have enjoyed a growing interest in the field of semantics. Recent research has shown that such models outperform purely linguistic models on a range of NLP tasks, including modelling semantic similarity (Silberer and Lapata, 2014), lexical entailment (Kiela et al., 2015), and metaphor identification (Shutova et al., 2016). Despite this success, little is known about the nature of semantic information learned from images and why it is useful. For instance, some concepts may be better characterised by their own (internal) visual properties and others by the (external) visual context, in which they appear. However, existing neural multimodal semantic approaches use entire images to learn visual word representations, without differentiating between these two kinds of visual information. In contrast, we investigate whether differentiating between internal visual properties and external visual context is beneficial compared to learning visual representations

from complete images. We construct three multimodal models combining linguistic and visual information: using (1) *internal* visual features extracted from an object's bounding box, (2) *external* visual features outside the bounding box, i.e. the visual context, and (3) visual features extracted from *complete* images. Figure 1 visualises the different visual information extracted from an image. We use skip-gram (Mikolov et al., 2013) as our linguistic model and extract visual representations from a convolutional neural network (CNN) pretrained on the ImageNet classification task (Fei-Fei, 2010).

We evaluate the models in their ability to decode patterns of brain activity associated with the meanings of nouns, obtained via brain imaging. This choice of task allows us to assess the importance of each type of visual information in human semantic processing. Specifically, we perform two experiments: (1) using the Visual Genome (Krishna et al., 2016) dataset of images where objects are manually annotated with bounding boxes, and (2) using images retrieved from Google Image Search and automatically segmenting them using a Faster R-CNN (FRCNN) model (Ren et al., 2015). We find that all of our multimodal models are able to decode brain activity patterns and that the models relying on internal visual properties are superior to all others.

2 Related Work

Multimodal Semantics Multimodal models are inspired by cognitive science research, suggesting that human semantic knowledge relies on perceptual and sensori-motor experience (Louwerse, 2011). Contemporary approaches use deep CNNs trained on image classification tasks to extract visual representations of words. Kiela and Bottou (2014) extract visual word representations from feature extraction layers in CNNs and con-

*Proceedings of the Eighth Joint Conference on Lexical and Computational Semantics (*SEM)*, pages 118–124
Minneapolis, June 6–7, 2019. ©2019 Association for Computational Linguistics

(a) VIS-WHOLE   (b) VIS-INTERNAL   (c) VIS-EXTERNAL

Figure 1: An example of images processed to extract the internal and external visual features using the bounding box around the concept.

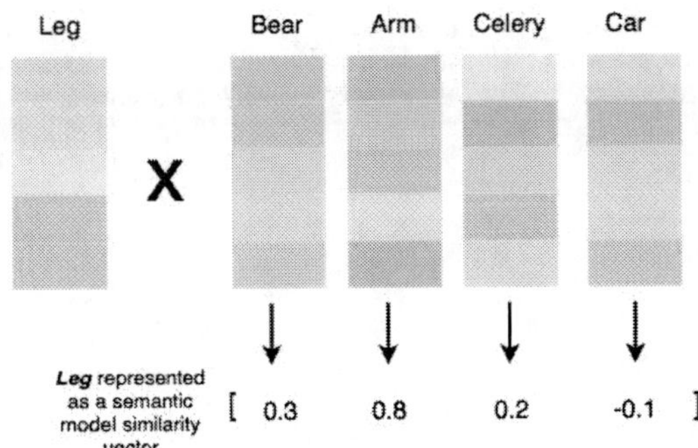

Figure 2: Semantic model similarity encoding. Where the coloured columns represent semantic vectors from the same model (i.e. VIS-INTERNAL). The bottom row represents the similarity codes for the concept "Leg", calculated by computing the Pearson correlation between "Leg" and the other semantic vectors from the dataset.

catenate them with linguistic representations obtained from a skip-gram model. Their results presented empirical improvements over the previous bag-of-visual-words method (Bruni et al., 2012). Other approaches use restricted Boltzmann machines (Srivastava and Salakhutdinov, 2012), recursive neural networks (Socher et al., 2014) and autoencoders (Silberer and Lapata, 2014).

Decoding Brain Activity Research in neuroscience supports the view that concepts are represented as patterns of neural activation and, similarly to distributed semantic representations, are naturally encoded in neural semantic vector space (Haxby et al., 2001; Huth et al., 2012; Anderson et al., 2013). Mitchell et al. (2008) were the first to employ distributional semantic models to predict neural activation in the human brain using data obtained via functional Magentic Resonance Imaging (fMRI). Murphy et al. (2012); Devereux et al. (2010); Pereira et al. (2013) have since successfully tested a wider range of distributional models in this task.

Recent research shows that multimodal models grounded in the visual modality strongly correlate with neural activation patterns associated with word meaning. Anderson et al. (2013) construct semantic models using visual data and show a high correlation to brain activation patterns from fMRI. While Anderson et al. (2015) find that linguistic-only semantic models better predict brain activity associated with linguistic processing, and image-based semantic models better predict similarity within the visual processing portions of the brain. Bulat et al. (2017) compare and evaluate a range of distributional semantic models in their ability to predict brain activity associated with concepts. Two key differences between our work and both Anderson et al. (2013) and Anderson et al. (2015) are 1) we make use of neural-network-based visual features as opposed to SIFT features (Lowe,

2004), and 2) we perform a word-level decoding analysis as opposed to representational similarity analysis (Kriegeskorte et al., 2008).

We aim to further our understanding of the role of vision in semantic processing by evaluating our models on the task of decoding brain activity associated with the meanings of nouns.

3 Data

Visual Data In the first experiment, we used the Visual Genome (Krishna et al., 2016) dataset of images manually-annotated for objects and their bounding boxes. In the second experiment, we trained Faster-RCNN networks on manually annotated images from ImageNet (Deng et al., 2009; Fei-Fei, 2010), and then processed images retrieved from Google Images to construct a dataset of automatically-annotated images. Both Visual Genome and ImageNet were selected as they contain bounding box annotations around objects.

Brain Imaging Data We used a dataset of brain activity patterns associated with the meanings of nouns created by Mitchell et al. (2008) (MITCHELL). The dataset includes 60 concrete nouns from 12 semantic categories, such as *vehicles* or *vegetables*. fMRI images were recorded when participants were presented with line drawings of the objects and the corresponding nouns. We use 50 nouns from the dataset in our experiments, since 10 of the nouns were not covered by the Visual Genome and ImageNet datasets.

Following Mitchell et al. (2008), we select the 500 voxels with the most stable activation pro-

119

Model	P1	P2	P3	P4	P5	P6	P7	P8	P9	Mean
LINGUISTIC	0.90	0.77	0.85	0.86	0.83	0.70	0.84	0.62	0.78	0.79
VIS-INTERNAL	0.90	0.81	0.85	0.82	0.75	0.66	0.79	0.63	0.73	**0.77**
VIS-EXTERNAL	0.82	0.72	0.76	0.81	0.62	0.62	0.73	0.59	0.73	0.71
VIS-WHOLE	0.84	0.69	0.77	0.80	0.63	0.61	0.75	0.60	0.75	0.71
MM-INTERNAL	0.92	0.81	0.86	0.88	0.82	0.69	0.84	0.62	0.79	0.80
MM-EXTERNAL	0.90	0.78	0.85	0.88	0.79	0.70	0.85	0.63	0.82	0.80
MM-WHOLE	0.90	0.76	0.83	0.87	0.79	0.67	0.84	0.63	0.82	0.79
VIS-COMBINED	0.89	0.80	0.82	0.84	0.70	0.66	0.78	0.61	0.77	0.76
MM-COMBINED	0.91	0.80	0.87	0.88	0.80	0.78	0.85	0.63	0.81	**0.81**

Table 1: Average decoding accuracies for the models trained on Visual Genome per participant and the mean over participants. *Vis*=visual, *MM*=multimodal, COMBINED=explicitly differentiates internal and external features.

file across concepts. We perform leave-two-out cross validation and select voxels independently for each of the cross validation folds during training. The stability score for a voxel is measured across six presentations of a word and is approximated as the average pairwise Pearson correlation among activation profiles over the training words in a cross-validation fold. The 500 voxels with the highest stability score are chosen and combined into a vector, used to evaluate how well the multimodal models can decode brain activity patterns.

4 Methods

We construct three visual models using three types of visual information: the internal features of the object, the external context surrounding it, and the whole image. These representations are then combined with linguistic representations to create the multimodal models.

4.1 Learning linguistic representations

We use the skip-gram model with negative sampling (Mikolov et al., 2013) to learn 100-dimensional word embeddings from a lemmatized 2015 copy of Wikipedia (Rimell et al., 2016).

4.2 Learning visual representations

Object detection and segmentation We use the FRCNN unified object detection model (Ren et al., 2015) to automatically detect objects and their bounding boxes in images associated with our nouns. FRCNN combines a region proposal network (RPN) with Fast R-CNN, an object detection network, and minimizes computational cost during training and testing by sharing convolutional layers between the networks. To maximize accuracy, we train an FRCNN network for each semantic class in the MITCHELL dataset, starting from a VGG16 network (Simonyan and Zisserman, 2014) pre-trained on the PASCAL VOC 2007 data set.

The pre-trained model contains many useful lower level features and therefore we expect fine-tuning a pre-trained model to yield optimal results. We train the networks using ImageNet images annotated with bounding boxes. We collected an average of 303 images per concept, with the following nouns lacking annotated images: *foot, arm, eye, igloo, pliers* and *carrot*. Images were split into 10% test, 40% train, and 50% train-validation sets. We trained the networks using approximate joint training. We tuned the step-size to 3000 and used the following default hyperparameter values: learning rate policy: "step"; base learning rate: 0.001; average loss: 100; momentum: 0.9; weight decay: 0.0005; gamma: 0.1. After training, the mean average precision (mAP) score across all semantic classes was 0.73.

Extracting visual features We retrieve 60 images per word using Google Image Search. We then create three sets of images for every word: the INTERNAL image (containing the object denoted by the word), an EXTERNAL image (containing its visual context), and the original WHOLE image. To generate the internal images, we crop and extract each object from within the annotated bounding boxes. To generate external images, we fill in the annotated bounding box area with black pixels, leaving only the visual context (black pixels are used as a simple way to represent no information). All images are re-scaled to 256x256 and the original aspect ratios are maintained, padding any remaining area with black pixels.

We use a Caffe (Jia et al., 2014) implementation of a pre-trained AlexNet model (Krizhevsky et al., 2012) to extract a visual representation for each of the images. We first take an image as input to the network, perform a forward pass, and extract the pre-softmax layer in the network (FC7) as a representation of the image. We use the MMfeat toolkit (Kiela, 2016) to load the AlexNet model and extract visual representations for the INTERNAL, EXTERNAL, WHOLE images corresponding

Model	Mean
LINGUISTIC	0.79
VIS-INTERNAL	**0.80**
VIS-EXTERNAL	0.74
VIS-WHOLE	0.80
MM-INTERNAL	0.81
MM-EXTERNAL	0.81
MM-WHOLE	0.82
VIS-COMBINED	0.79
MM-COMBINED	0.82

Table 2: Average decoding accuracies over the nine participants for the semantic models trained on the automatically annotated images. Naming convention follows Table 1

to the nouns in our data set.

4.3 Multimodal Models

We construct multimodal models by concatenating L2-normalised linguistic and visual representations. This strategy, known as middle fusion, has been shown successful in previous multimodal semantics research (Kiela and Bottou, 2014). We combine the linguistic model with each of our visual models, resulting in the three kinds of multimodal models: INTERNAL, EXTERNAL and WHOLE. Furthermore, we construct two *combined* models: a COMBINED visual-only model concatenating the internal and external models, and a COMBINED multimodal model concatenating the internal, external, and linguistic models.

4.4 Decoding Brain Activity

We evaluate our models in their ability to decode brain activity associated with unseen words, i.e. to predict the correct label associated with their fMRI patterns. We follow the same procedure as Anderson et al. (2016), computing a *semantic model similarity matrix* consisting of semantic model similarity codes for each of the 50 nouns from the Mitchell et al. (2008) dataset. Similarly, we construct a *brain activity similarity matrix* consisting of brain activity similarity codes of the 50 nouns. This process is visualised in Figure 2, where the coloured columns represent semantic model vectors for each word in the dataset, and the bottom row represents the resulting similarity codes for the concept "Leg".

We perform leave-two-out cross validation, selecting the semantic model similarity codes $(\vec{s}_i, \vec{s}_j)$ and brain activity similarity codes $(\vec{a}_i, \vec{a}_j)$ for two nouns. We remove the i-th and j-th elements from each of the similarity codes as these entries correspond to the nouns being tested. Figure 3 visualises an example of the decoding procedure. Decoding is successful if the

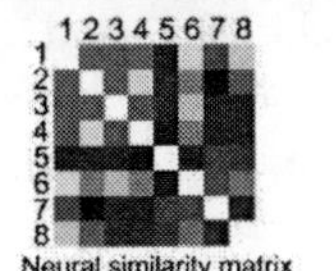
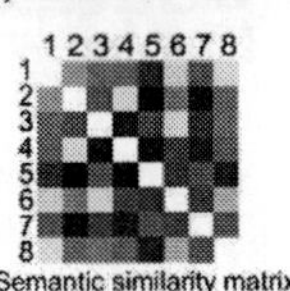
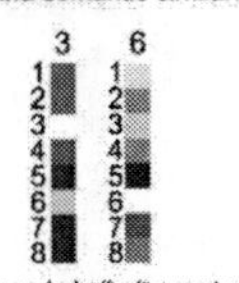
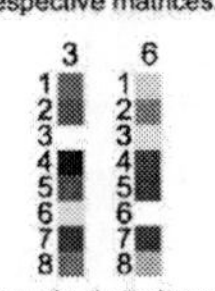
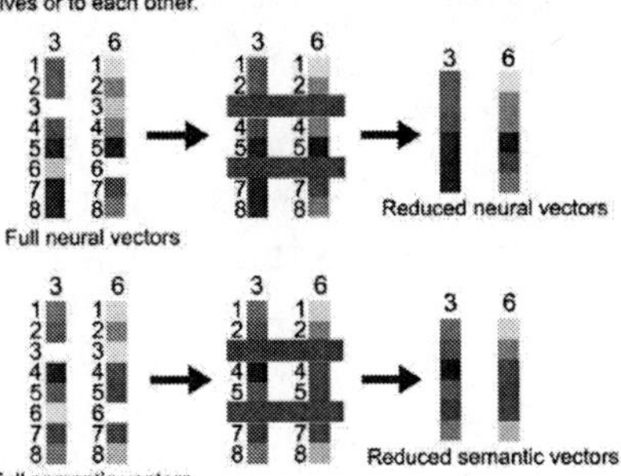
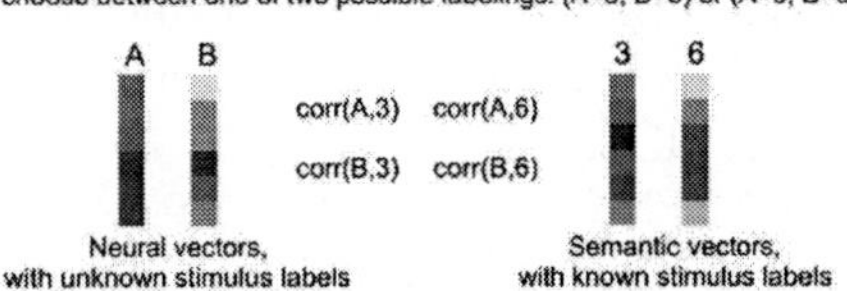

Figure 3: Visualisation of leave-two-out cross validation for semantic model similarity decoding. Visualisation from (Anderson et al., 2016).

sum of Pearson correlations for the correct pairings is greater than the sum of Pearson correlations for the incorrect pairings, resulting in decoding accuracy of 1 for this pair and 0 otherwise. The expected chance-level decoding accuracy is 50% if a model were to match word labels with similarity vectors at random.

5 Experiments

We first experiment with a set of manually-annotated images from Visual Genome and then with images where objects and their bounding boxes have been automatically detected using FR-CNN networks.

5.1 Manually annotated images

Experimental Setup We use 50 nouns from the MITCHELL dataset and assess each model's ability to decode brain activity vectors using leave-two-out cross validation, resulting in 1225 (50 choose 2) cross-validation folds per model.

Results The results, presented in Table 1, demonstrate that all semantic models decode brain activity patterns significantly above chance levels[1]. The INTERNAL visual-only model achieves a mean accuracy of 0.77, significantly[2] outperforming (V={36, 43}, all p<0.015) the EXTERNAL and WHOLE visual-only models, using the paired Wilcoxon signed rank test. The INTERNAL and EXTERNAL multimodal models both achieve a mean accuracy of 0.80, outperforming the WHOLE multimodal model with a mean of 0.79. Finally, the COMBINED multimodal model outperforms the INTERNAL and EXTERNAL multimodal models, and significantly outperforms (V=35, p<0.02) the WHOLE multimodal model with a mean accuracy of 0.81. These results demonstrate that it is beneficial to differentiate between internal and external visual information, but that both are useful for semantic processing, with the internal visual features having the most prominent influence.

We investigated the errors produced during the cross-validation folds, and found the INTERNAL visual-only model outperforms its EXTERNAL and WHOLE counterparts systematically for all but one semantic class: *kitchen utensils*, where the EXTERNAL visual-only model obtains the fewest errors. Overall, these results suggest that internal visual features are superior in this task and correlate strongly with the patterns of human semantic representation.

5.2 Automatically annotated images

Experimental Setup For each of our 50 nouns from the MITCHELL dataset, we retrieve 60 images using Google Image Search. The images are annotated using FRCNNs and then processed to create INTERNAL, EXTERNAL and WHOLE models. We follow the same evaluation procedure as in the previous experiment, performing 1225 (50 choose 2) cross-validation folds.

Results The results, presented in Table 2, demonstrate that all models decode brain activity vectors significantly above chance level. They also show multimodal models constructed with automatic object detection perform on par with representations learned from manually annotated images. Overall, we observe a similar trend, i.e. the INTERNAL visual-only model significantly outperforms (V=43, p<0.015) the EXTERNAL visual-only model (mean accuracies of 0.80 and 0.74).

Our qualitative analysis has shown that the INTERNAL visual model outperforms the others for the following semantic classes, in both experiments: *building*, *furniture* and *insect*. We find the WHOLE visual-only model has fewer class-level errors in this experiment. We believe this is due to the quality of the images; the Visual Genome images contain more objects per image on average, making the external visual context more variable compared to images from Google Images.

Besides corroborating the findings of the previous experiment on the importance of the internal visual features, these results show that high quality visual representations capturing the objects' internal properties and their visual context can be learned through automatic object detection techniques, decreasing the reliance on human annotated datasets (albeit some annotated data is required to train the object detection system) and allowing for a greater scalability of the models.

6 Conclusion

Our results show that multimodal semantic models correlate with human neural semantic representations associated with concrete concepts, and the visual-only model using internal visual features outperforms the other visual-only models in most cases. Similar performance across models using manual and automatically annotated images demonstrates progress in object detection systems, presenting opportunities to expand to other tasks where evaluation datasets may not be covered by manually annotated image datasets.

---

[1]Using permutation testing with 1000 repeats, we found all models perform significantly above chance level. We follow the same shuffling procedure detailed in Anderson et al. (2017) to obtain a null distribution of chance-level decoding accuracies. The p-value of decoding accuracy is the proportion of chance-level accuracies greater than or equal to the observed cross-validated decoding accuracy.

[2]When comparing two models, we used paired Wilcoxon signed rank tests (two-tailed) to tell us whether their mean accuracy scores significantly differ from each other.

References

Andrew J Anderson, Elia Bruni, Ulisse Bordignon, Massimo Poesio, and Marco Baroni. 2013. Of words, eyes and brains: Correlating image-based distributional semantic models with neural representations of concepts. In *EMNLP*, pages 1960–1970.

Andrew J Anderson, Elia Bruni, Alessandro Lopopolo, Massimo Poesio, and Marco Baroni. 2015. Reading visually embodied meaning from the brain: Visually grounded computational models decode visual-object mental imagery induced by written text. *NeuroImage*, 120:309–322.

Andrew J Anderson, Douwe Kiela, Stephen Clark, and Massimo Poesio. 2017. Visually grounded and textual semantic models differentially decode brain activity associated with concrete and abstract nouns. *Transactions of the Association for Computational Linguistics*, 5:17–30.

Andrew J Anderson, Benjamin D Zinszer, and Rajeev DS Raizada. 2016. Representational similarity encoding for fmri: Pattern-based synthesis to predict brain activity using stimulus-model-similarities. *NeuroImage*, 128:44–53.

Elia Bruni, Jasper Uijlings, Marco Baroni, and Nicu Sebe. 2012. Distributional semantics with eyes: Using image analysis to improve computational representations of word meaning. In *Proceedings of the 20th ACM international conference on Multimedia*, pages 1219–1228. ACM.

Luana Bulat, Stephen Clark, and Ekaterina Shutova. 2017. Speaking, seeing, understanding: Correlating semantic models with conceptual representation in the brain. In *Proceedings of the 2017 Conference on Empirical Methods in Natural Language Processing*, pages 1092–1102.

Jia Deng, Wei Dong, Richard Socher, Li-Jia Li, Kai Li, and Li Fei-Fei. 2009. Imagenet: A large-scale hierarchical image database. In *Computer Vision and Pattern Recognition, 2009. CVPR 2009. IEEE Conference on*, pages 248–255. IEEE.

Barry Devereux, Colin Kelly, and Anna Korhonen. 2010. Using fmri activation to conceptual stimuli to evaluate methods for extracting conceptual representations from corpora. In *Proceedings of the NAACL HLT 2010 First Workshop on Computational Neurolinguistics*, pages 70–78. Association for Computational Linguistics.

Li Fei-Fei. 2010. Imagenet: crowdsourcing, benchmarking & other cool things. In *CMU VASC Seminar*.

James V Haxby, M Ida Gobbini, Maura L Furey, Alumit Ishai, Jennifer L Schouten, and Pietro Pietrini. 2001. Distributed and overlapping representations of faces and objects in ventral temporal cortex. *Science*, 293(5539):2425–2430.

Alexander G Huth, Shinji Nishimoto, An T Vu, and Jack L Gallant. 2012. A continuous semantic space describes the representation of thousands of object and action categories across the human brain. *Neuron*, 76(6):1210–1224.

Yangqing Jia, Evan Shelhamer, Jeff Donahue, Sergey Karayev, Jonathan Long, Ross Girshick, Sergio Guadarrama, and Trevor Darrell. 2014. Caffe: Convolutional architecture for fast feature embedding. In *Proceedings of the 22Nd ACM International Conference on Multimedia*, MM '14, pages 675–678, New York, NY, USA. ACM.

Douwe Kiela. 2016. Mmfeat: A toolkit for extracting multi-modal features. In *Proceedings of ACL*.

Douwe Kiela and Leon Bottou. 2014. Learning image embeddings using convolutional neural networks for improved multi-modal semantics. In *EMNLP*, pages 36–45. Citeseer.

Douwe Kiela, Laura Rimell, Ivan Vulic, and Stephen Clark. 2015. Exploiting image generality for lexical entailment detection. In *Proceedings of the 53rd Annual Meeting of the Association for Computational Linguistics (ACL 2015)*, pages 119–124. ACL.

Nikolaus Kriegeskorte, Marieke Mur, and Peter A Bandettini. 2008. Representational similarity analysis-connecting the branches of systems neuroscience. *Frontiers in systems neuroscience*, 2:4.

Ranjay Krishna, Yuke Zhu, Oliver Groth, Justin Johnson, Kenji Hata, Joshua Kravitz, Stephanie Chen, Yannis Kalantidis, Li-Jia Li, David A Shamma, Michael Bernstein, and Li Fei-Fei. 2016. Visual genome: Connecting language and vision using crowdsourced dense image annotations.

Alex Krizhevsky, Ilya Sutskever, and Geoffrey E Hinton. 2012. Imagenet classification with deep convolutional neural networks. In *Advances in neural information processing systems*, pages 1097–1105.

Max M Louwerse. 2011. Symbol interdependency in symbolic and embodied cognition. *Topics in Cognitive Science*, 3(2):273–302.

David G Lowe. 2004. Distinctive image features from scale-invariant keypoints. *International journal of computer vision*, 60(2):91–110.

Tomas Mikolov, Kai Chen, Greg Corrado, and Jeffrey Dean. 2013. Efficient estimation of word representations in vector space. *arXiv preprint arXiv:1301.3781*.

Tom M. Mitchell, Svetlana V. Shinkareva, Andrew Carlson, Kai-Min Chang, Vicente L. Malave, Robert A. Mason, and Marcel Adam Just. 2008. Predicting human brain activity associated with the meanings of nouns. *science*, 320(5880):1191–1195.

Brian Murphy, Partha Talukdar, and Tom Mitchell. 2012. Selecting corpus-semantic models for neurolinguistic decoding. In *Proceedings of the First Joint Conference on Lexical and Computational Semantics-Volume 1: Proceedings of the main conference and the shared task, and Volume 2: Proceedings of the Sixth International Workshop on Semantic Evaluation*, pages 114–123. Association for Computational Linguistics.

Francisco Pereira, Matthew Botvinick, and Greg Detre. 2013. Using wikipedia to learn semantic feature representations of concrete concepts in neuroimaging experiments. *Artificial intelligence*, 194:240–252.

Shaoqing Ren, Kaiming He, Ross Girshick, and Jian Sun. 2015. Faster r-cnn: Towards real-time object detection with region proposal networks. In *Advances in neural information processing systems*, pages 91–99.

Laura Rimell, Jean Maillard, Tamara Polajnar, and Stephen Clark. 2016. Relpron: A relative clause evaluation data set for compositional distributional semantics. *Computational Linguistics*, 42(4):661–701.

Ekaterina Shutova, Douwe Kiela, and Jean Maillard. 2016. Black holes and white rabbits: Metaphor identification with visual features. In *Proc. of the 2016 Conference of the North American Chapter of the Association for Computational Linguistics: Human Language Technologies*, pages 160–170.

Carina Silberer and Mirella Lapata. 2014. Learning grounded meaning representations with autoencoders. In *ACL (1)*, pages 721–732.

Karen Simonyan and Andrew Zisserman. 2014. Very deep convolutional networks for large-scale image recognition. *arXiv preprint arXiv:1409.1556*.

Richard Socher, Andrej Karpathy, Quoc V Le, Christopher D Manning, and Andrew Y Ng. 2014. Grounded compositional semantics for finding and describing images with sentences. *Transactions of the Association for Computational Linguistics*, 2:207–218.

Nitish Srivastava and Ruslan R Salakhutdinov. 2012. Multimodal learning with deep boltzmann machines. In *Advances in neural information processing systems*, pages 2222–2230.

Learning Graph Embeddings from WordNet-based Similarity Measures

**Andrey Kutuzov[1], Mohammad Dorgham[2], Oleksiy Oliynyk[2],
Chris Biemann[2], and Alexander Panchenko[2,3]**

[1]Language Technology Group, University of Oslo, Oslo, Norway
[2]Language Technology Group, University of Hamburg, Hamburg, Germany
[3]Skolkovo Institute of Science and Technology, Moscow, Russia
andreku@ifi.uio.no
{5dorgham,6oliinyk,biemann,panchenko}@informatik.uni-hamburg.de

Abstract

We present *path2vec*, a new approach for learning graph embeddings that relies on structural measures of pairwise node similarities. The model learns representations for nodes in a dense space that approximate a given user-defined graph distance measure, such as e.g. the shortest path distance or distance measures that take information beyond the graph structure into account. Evaluation of the proposed model on semantic similarity and word sense disambiguation tasks, using various WordNet-based similarity measures, show that our approach yields competitive results, outperforming strong graph embedding baselines. The model is computationally efficient, being orders of magnitude faster than the direct computation of graph-based distances.

1 Introduction

Developing applications making use of large graphs, such as networks of roads, social media users, or word senses, often involves the design of a domain-specific graph **node similarity measure** $sim : V \times V \to \mathbb{R}$ defined on a set of nodes V of a graph $G = (V, E)$. For instance, it can represent the shortest distance from home to work, a community of interest in a social network for a user, or a semantically related sense to a given synset in WordNet (Miller, 1995). There exist a wide variety of such measures greatly ranging in their complexity and design from simple deterministic ones, e.g. based on shortest paths in a network (Leacock and Chodorow, 1998) to more complex ones, e.g. based on random walks (Fouss et al., 2007; Pilehvar and Navigli, 2015; Lebichot et al., 2018). Naturally, the majority of such measures rely on walks along edges E of the graph, often resulting in effective, but prohibitively inefficient measures requiring complex and computationally expensive graph traversals. Also, there are measures that in addition take e.g. corpus information into account beyond what is directly given in the graph, see e.g. (Budanitsky and Hirst, 2006). We propose a solution to this problem by decoupling development and use of graph-based measures. Namely, once a node similarity measure is defined, we learn vector representations of nodes that enable efficient computation of this measure. We represent nodes in a graph with dense embeddings that are good in approximating such custom, e.g. application-specific, pairwise node similarity measures. Similarity computations in a vector space are several orders of magnitude faster than computations directly using the graph. Additionally, graph embeddings can be of importance in privacy-sensitive network datasets, since in this setup, explicitly storing edges is not required anymore. The main advantage over other graph embeddings is that our model can learn a custom user-defined application or domain specific similarity measure.

We show the effectiveness of the proposed approach *intrinsically* on a word similarity task, by learning synset vectors of the WordNet graph based on several similarity measures. Our model is not only able to closely *approximate* various measures, but also *to improve* the results of the original measures in terms of (1) correlation with human judgments and (2) computational efficiency, with gains up to 4 orders of magnitude. Our method outperforms other state-of-the-art graph embeddings models.

Besides, we evaluate it *extrinsically* in a WSD task (Navigli, 2009) by replacing the original structural measures with their vectorized counterparts in a graph-based WSD algorithm by Sinha and Mihalcea (2007), reaching comparable performance. Because of being inspired by the *word2vec* architecture, we dub our model '*path2vec*'[1] mean-

---

[1]https://github.com/uhh-lt/path2vec

*Proceedings of the Eighth Joint Conference on Lexical and Computational Semantics (*SEM)*, pages 125–135
Minneapolis, June 6–7, 2019. ©2019 Association for Computational Linguistics

ing it encodes paths (or other similarities) between graph nodes into dense vectors.

Our **first contribution** is an effective and efficient approach to learn graph embeddings based on a user-defined custom similarity measure *sim* on a set of nodes V, e.g. the shortest path distance. The **second contribution** is an application of state-of-the-art graph embeddings to word sense disambiguation task.

2 Related Work

Various methods have been employed in NLP to derive lexical similarity directly from geometrical properties of the WordNet graph, from random walks in (Rao et al., 2008) to kernels in (Ó Séaghdha, 2009). More recently, representation learning on graphs (Bordes et al., 2011) received much attention in various research communities; see (Hamilton et al., 2017a) for a thorough survey on the existing methods. All of them (including ours) are based on the idea of projecting graph nodes into a latent vector space with a much lower dimensionality than the number of nodes.

The method described in this paper falls into the category of 'shallow embeddings', meaning that we do not attempt to embed entire communities or neighborhoods: our aim is to approximate distances or similarities between (single) nodes. Existing approaches to solving this task mostly use either factorization of the graph adjacency matrix (Cao et al., 2015; Ou et al., 2016) or random walks over the graph as in *Deepwalk* (Perozzi et al., 2014) and *node2vec* (Grover and Leskovec, 2016). A completely different approach is taken by Subercaze et al. (2015), who directly embed the WordNet tree graph into Hamming hypercube binary representations. Their model is dubbed 'Fast similarity embedding' (*FSE*) and also optimizes one of our objectives, i.e. to provide a much quicker way of calculating semantic similarities based on WordNet knowledge. However, the *FSE* embeddings are not differentiable, limiting their use in many deep neural architectures, especially if fine-tuning is needed.

TransE (Bordes et al., 2013) interprets entities as vectors in the low-dimensional embeddings space and relations as a translation operation between two entity vectors. For a triplet (head, relation, tail) which holds, the embedding of the tail is close to the embedding of the head plus embedding of the relation. TransH (Wang et al., 2014)

models each relation as a specific hyperplane and projects entity vectors onto the hyperplane. If connection holds then projected vectors of head and tail are connected by a translation vector with low error. As a result, entities have different representations for hyperplanes of different relations where they are involved. *TransR* (Lin et al., 2015) extends *TransE* (Bordes et al., 2013) and *TransH* (Wang et al., 2014), and is based on the idea that an entity may have a few aspects and different relations are focused on them. So the same entities can be close or far from each other depending on the type of the relation. *TransR* projects entity vectors into a relation specific space, and learns embeddings via translation between projected entities.

We quantitatively compare *path2vec* to these methods in Section 5. We did not compare our approach to the *GraphSAGE* embeddings (Hamilton et al., 2017b) and Graph Convolutional Networks (Schlichtkrull et al., 2018), since they make use of input node features, which are absent in our setup.

Also note that unlike retro-fitting and similar techniques (Rothe and Schütze, 2015; Pilehvar and Collier, 2016; Mrkšić et al., 2017), our approach does not use any training corpus or pre-trained input embeddings. The synset representations are trained on the WordNet graph alone.

3 Learning Graph Metric Embeddings

Definition of the Model   The *path2vec* model learns low-dimensional vectors for the graph nodes $\{v_i, v_j\} \in V$ (synsets in the case of Word-Net) such that the dot products between pairs of the respective vectors $(\mathbf{v}_i \cdot \mathbf{v}_j)$ are close to the user-defined similarities between the nodes s_{ij}. This first component of the objective encodes potentially long distances in the graph (the global structure). In addition, the model reinforces direct connections between nodes: We add to the objective similarities $\mathbf{v}_i \cdot \mathbf{v}_n$ and $\mathbf{v}_j \cdot \mathbf{v}_m$ between the nodes v_i and v_j and their respective adjacent nodes $\{v_n : \exists(v_i, v_n) \in E\}$ and $\{v_m : \exists(v_j, v_m) \in E\}$ to preserve local structure of the graph. Therefore, the model preserves both global and local relations between nodes by minimizing the following loss function $\mathcal{L}$:

$$\frac{1}{|B|} \sum_{(v_i, v_j) \in B} \left((\mathbf{v}_i^T \mathbf{v}_j - s_{ij})^2 - \alpha(\mathbf{v}_i^T \mathbf{v}_n + \mathbf{v}_j^T \mathbf{v}_m) \right),$$

where $s_{ij} = sim(v_i, v_j)$ is the value of a 'gold' similarity measure between a pair of nodes v_i and

v_j, $\mathbf{v}_i$ and $\mathbf{v}_j$ are the embeddings of the first and the second node, B is a training batch, α is a regularization coefficient. The second term $(\mathbf{v}_i \cdot \mathbf{v}_n + \mathbf{v}_j \cdot \mathbf{v}_m)$ in the objective function is a regularizer which aids the model to simultaneously maximize the similarity between adjacent nodes (which is maximum by definition) while learning the similarity between the two target nodes.

We use negative sampling to form a training batch B adding n negative samples ($s_{ij} = 0$) for each real ($s_{ij} > 0$) training instance: each real node (synset) pair (v_i, v_j) with 'gold' similarity s_{ij} is accompanied with n 'negative' node pairs (v_i, v_k) and (v_j, v_l) with zero similarities, where v_k and v_l are randomly sampled nodes from V. Embeddings are initialized randomly and trained with the *Adam* optimizer (Kingma and Ba, 2014) with early stopping.[2]

Once the model is trained, the computation of node similarities is approximated with the dot product of the learned node vectors, making the computations efficient: $\hat{s}_{ij} = \mathbf{v}_i \cdot \mathbf{v}_j$.

Relation to Similar Models Our model is similar to the Skip-gram model (Mikolov et al., 2013), where pairs of words (v_i, v_j) from a training corpus are optimized to have their corresponding vectors dot product $\mathbf{v}_i \cdot \tilde{\mathbf{v}}_j$ close to 1, while randomly generated pairs ('negative samples') are optimized to have their dot product close to 0. In the Skip-gram model, the target is to minimize the log likelihood of the conditional probabilities of context words v_j given current words v_i, which is in the case on the negative sampling amounts to minimization of: $\mathcal{L} = -\sum_{(v_i,v_j)\in B_p} \log \sigma(\mathbf{v}_i \cdot \tilde{\mathbf{v}}_j) - \sum_{(v_i,v_j)\in B_n} \log \sigma(-\mathbf{v}_i \cdot \tilde{\mathbf{v}}_j)$, where B_p is the batch of positive training samples, B_n is the batch of the generated negative samples, and σ is the sigmoid function. The model uses local information. However, in *path2vec*, the target values s_{ij} for the dot product are not binary, but can take arbitrary values in the $[0...1]$ range, depending on the path-based measure on the input graph, e.g. the normalized shortest path length in the WordNet between *motor.n.01* and *rocket.n.02* is 0.389.

Further, in our model there is no difference between 'word' and 'context' spaces: we use a single

embedding matrix, with the number of rows equal to the number of nodes and column width set to the desired embedding dimensionality. Finally, unlike the Skip-gram, we do not use any non-linearities.

Another closely related model is Global Vectors (GloVe) (Pennington et al., 2014), which approximates the co-occurrence probabilities in a given corpus. The objective function to be minimized in GloVe model is $\mathcal{L} = \sum_{(v_i,v_j)\in B} f(s_{ij})(\mathbf{v}_i \cdot \tilde{\mathbf{v}}_j - \log s_{ij} + b_i + b_j)^2$, where s_{ij} counts the number of co-occurrence of words v_i and v_j, b_i and b_j are additional biases for each word, and $f(s_{ij})$ is a weighting function to give appropriate weight for rare co-occurrences. Like the Skip-gram, GloVe also uses two embedding matrices, but it relies on global information.

4 Computing Pairwise Similarities

4.1 Selection of the Similarity Measures

Our aim is to produce node embeddings that capture given similarities between nodes in a graph. In our case, the graph is WordNet, and the nodes are its 82,115 noun synsets. We focused on nouns since in WordNet and SimLex999 they are represented better than other parts of speech. Embeddings for synsets of different part of speech can be generated analogously.

The training datasets consist of pairs of noun synsets and their 'ground truth' similarity values. There exist several methods to calculate synset similarities on the WordNet (Budanitsky and Hirst, 2006). We compile four datasets, with different similarity functions: Leacock-Chodorow similarities (*LCH*); Jiang-Conrath similarities calculated over the SemCor corpus (*JCN-S*); Wu-Palmer similarities (*WuP*); and Shortest path similarities (*ShP*). *LCH* similarity (Leacock and Chodorow, 1998) is based on the shortest path between two synsets in the WordNet hypernym/hyponym taxonomy and its maximum depth, while *JCN* similarity (Jiang and Conrath, 1997) uses the lowest common parent of two synsets in the same taxonomy. *JCN* is significantly faster but additionally requires a corpus as a source of probabilistic data about the distributions of synsets ('information content'). We employed the SemCor subset of the Brown corpus, manually annotated with word senses (Kucera and Francis, 1982).

WuP similarities (Wu and Palmer, 1994) are based on the depth of the two nodes in the taxonomy and the depth of their most specific ances-

---

[2] In our experiments, we identified the optimal values of $n = 3$ negative samples, batch size of $|B| = 100$, training for 15 epochs, $\alpha = 0.01$. We report on the influence of the embedding dimensionality parameter d in Section 5. We found it also beneficial to use additionally L_1 weight regularization.

tor node. *ShP* is a simple length of the shortest path between two nodes in the graph. We used the NLTK (Bird et al., 2009) implementations of all the aforementioned similarity functions.

Pairwise similarities for all synset pairs can be pre-computed. For the 82,115 noun synsets in the WordNet, this results in about 3 billion unique synset pairs. Producing these similarities using 10 threads takes about 30 hours on an Intel Xeon E5-2603v4@1.70GHz CPU for *LCH*, and about 5 hours for *JCN-S*. The resulting similarities lists are quite large (45 GB compressed each) and thus difficult to use in applications. But they can be used in *path2vec* to *learn* dense embeddings $\mathbb{R}^d$ for these 82,115 synsets, such that $d \ll 82,115$ and the dot products between the embeddings approximate the 'raw' WordNet similarity functions.

4.2 Pruning the Dissimilar Pairs of Nodes

In principle, one can use all unique synset pairs with their WordNet similarities as the training data. However, this seems impractical. As expected due to the small-world nature of the Word-Net graph (Steyvers and Tenenbaum, 2005), most synsets are not similar at all: with *JCN-S*, the overwhelming majority of pairs feature similarity very close to zero; with *LCH*, most pairs have similarity below 1.0. Thus, we filtered low-similarity pairs out, using similarity threshold of 0.1 for the *JCN-S* and *ShP* datasets, 0.3 for the *WuP* dataset and 1.5 for the *LCH* dataset (due to substantial differences in similarities distributions, as shown in Figure 1). This dramatically reduced the size of the training data (e.g., to less than 1.5 million pairs for the *JCN-S* dataset and to 125 million pairs for the *LCH* dataset), thus making the training much faster and at the same time *improving* the quality of the resulting embeddings (see the description of our evaluation setup below).

With this being the case, we additionally pruned these reduced datasets by keeping only the first 50 most similar 'neighbors' of each synset: the rationale behind this is that some nodes in the WordNet graph are very central and thus have many neighbors with high similarity, but for our procedure only the nearest/most similar ones suffice. This again reduced training time and improved the results, so we hypothesize that such pruning makes the models more generally applicable and more focused on the meaningful relations between synsets. The final sizes of the pruned

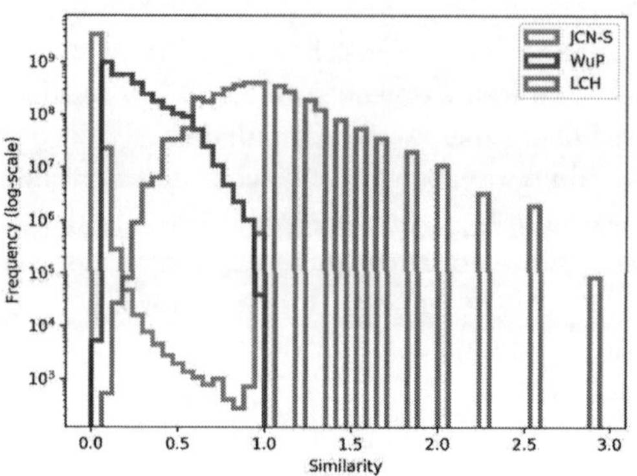

Figure 1: Distribution of similarities between WordNet noun synsets with different distance measures.

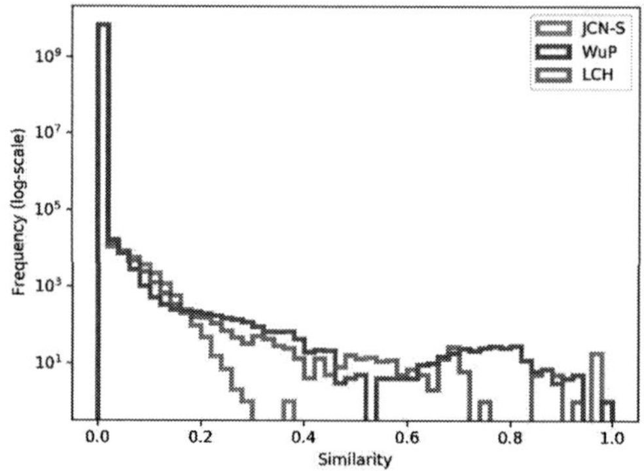

Figure 2: Distributions of pairwise similarities in *path2vec* models trained on different measures.

training datasets are 694,762 pairs for the *JCN-S*, 4,008,446 pairs for the *LCH*, 4,063,293 pairs for the *ShP* and 4,100,599 pairs for the *WuP*[3].

Note also that the *LCH* similarity can take values well above 1.0. After the pruning, we scaled similarities in all datasets to the $[0...1]$ range by unity-based normalization. Also, in some rare cases, NLTK produces *JCN* similarities of infinitely large values (probably due to the absence of particular synsets in SemCor). We clipped these similarities to the value of 1. All the datasets were shuffled prior to training.

---

[3]All the datasets and the trained graph embeddings can be downloaded from https://github.com/uhh-lt/path2vec

5 Experiment 1: Intrinsic Evaluation based on Semantic Similarity

Experimental Setting It is possible to evaluate the models by calculating the rank correlation of their cosine similarities with the corresponding similarities for all the unique pairs from the training dataset, or at least a large part of them. Subercaze et al. (2015) evaluated their approach on *LCH* similarities for all unique noun synset pairs from WordNet Core (about 5 million similarities total); their model achieves Spearman rank correlation of 0.732 on this task. However, this kind of evaluation does not measure the ability of the model to produce meaningful predictions, at least for language data: the overwhelming part of these unique pairs are synsets not related to each other at all. For most tasks, it is useless to 'know' that, e.g., '*ambulance*' and '*general*' are less similar than '*ambulance*' and '*president*'. While the distances between these node pairs are indeed different on the WordNet graph, we find it much more important for the model to be able to robustly tell really similar pairs from the unrelated ones so that they could benefit applications.

As a more balanced and relevant test set, we use noun pairs (666 total) from the SimLex999 semantic similarity dataset (Hill et al., 2015). SimLex999 contains lemmas; as some lemmas may map to several WordNet synsets, for each word pair we choose the synset pair maximizing the WordNet similarity, following (Resnik, 1999). Then, we measure the Spearman rank correlation between these 'gold' scores and the similarities produced by the graph embedding models trained on the WordNet. Further on, we call this evaluation score the 'correlation with WordNet similarities'. This evaluation method directly measures how well the model fits the training objective[4].

We also would like to check whether our models generalize to extrinsic tasks. Thus, we additionally used human-annotated semantic similarities from the same SimLex999. This additional evaluation strategy directly tests the models' correspondence to human judgments independently of WordNet. These correlations were tested in two synset selection setups, important to distinguish:

1.　WordNet-based synset selection (static synsets): this setup uses the same lemma-to-synset mappings, based on maximizing WordNet similarity for each SimLex999 word pair with the corresponding similarity function. It means that all the models are tested on exactly the same set of synset pairs (but the similarities themselves are taken from SimLex999, not from the WordNet).

2.　Model-based synset selection (dynamic synsets): in this setup, lemmas are converted to synsets dynamically as a part of the evaluation workflow. We choose the synsets that maximize word pair similarity *using the vectors from the model itself*, not similarity functions on the WordNet. Then the resulting ranking is evaluated against the original SimLex999 ranking.

The second (dynamic) setup in principle allows the models to find better lemma-to-synset mappings than those provided by the WordNet similarity functions. This setup essentially evaluates two abilities of the model: 1) to find the best pair of synsets for a given pair of lemmas (sort of a disambiguation task), and 2) to produce the similarity score for the chosen synsets. We are not aware of any 'gold' lemma-to-synset mapping for SimLex999, thus we directly evaluate only the second part, but implicitly the first one still influences the resulting scores. Models often choose different synsets. For example, for the word pair '*atom, carbon*', the synset pair maximizing the *JCN-S* similarity calculated on the 'raw' WordNet would be 'atom.n.02 ('*a tiny piece of anything*'), carbon.n.01 ('*an abundant nonmetallic tetravalent element*')' with the similarity 0.11. However, in a *path2vec* model trained on the same gold similarities, the synset pair with the highest similarity 0.14 has a different first element: 'atom.n.01 ('*the smallest component of an element having the chemical properties of the element*')', which seems to be at least as good a decision as the one from the raw WordNet.

Baselines *path2vec* is compared against five baselines (more on them in Section 2): *raw WordNet similarities* by respective measures; *Deepwalk* (Perozzi et al., 2014); *node2vec* (Grover and Leskovec, 2016); *FSE* (Subercaze et al., 2015); and *TransR* (Lin et al., 2015).

DeepWalk, *node2vec*, and *TransR* models were trained on the same WordNet graph. We used all 82,115 noun synsets as vertices and hypernym/hyponym relations between them as edges. Since the *node2vec* C++ implementation accepts

---

[4]Note, however, that it does not mean testing on the training data: for example, 75% of synset pairs from the SimLex999 are **not present** in our pruned *JCN-S* training dataset; for the *LCH* dataset it is 82%. Evaluating these absent pairs only does not substantially change the results.

	Selection of synsets			
Model	JCN-S	LCH	ShP	WuP
WordNet	1.0	1.0	1.0	1.0
TransR	0.568	0.776	0.776	0.725
node2vec	0.726	0.759	0.759	0.787
Deepwalk	0.775	0.868	0.868	0.850
FSE	0.830	0.900	0.900	0.890
path2vec	**0.931**	**0.935**	**0.952**	**0.931**

Table 1: Spearman correlation scores with WordNet similarities on the 666 noun pairs in SimLex999.

	Selection of synsets			
Model	JCN-S	LCH	ShP	WuP
WordNet	0.487	**0.513**	**0.513**	0.474
TransR	0.394	0.395	0.395	0.379
node2vec	0.426	0.434	0.434	0.400
Deepwalk	0.468	0.468	0.468	0.450
FSE	0.490	0.502	0.502	0.483
path2vec	**0.501**	0.470	0.512	**0.491**

Table 2: Spearman correlations with human Sim-Lex999 noun similarities (WordNet synset selection).

an edge list as input, we had to add a self-connection for all nodes (synsets) that lack edges in WordNet. During the training of *DeepWalk* and *node2vec* models, we tested different values for the number of random walks (in the range from 10 to 100), and the vector size (100 to 600). For *DeepWalk*, we additionally experimented with the window size (5 to 100). All other hyperparameters were left at their default values. *FSE* embeddings of the WordNet noun synsets were provided to us by the authors, and consist of 128-bit vectors.

Discussion of Results Table 1 presents the comparison of *path2vec* and the baselines with regards to how well they approximate the WordNet similarity functions output (the raw WordNet similarities always get the perfect correlation in this evaluation setup). All the reported rank correlation value differences in this and other tables are statistically significant based on the standard two-sided p-value. We report the results for the best models for each method, all of them (except *FSE*) using vector size 300 for comparability.

Path2vec outperform other baseline embeddings, achieving high correlation with the raw WordNet similarities. This shows that our simple model can approximate different graph measures. Figure 2 shows the similarities' distributions in the resulting models, reflecting the original measures' distributions in Figure 1.

As expected, vector dimensionality greatly influences the performance of all graph embedding models. As an example, Figure 3 plots the performance of the *path2vec* models trained on *JCN-S* and *WuP* datasets, when using 'dynamic synset selection' evaluation setup (that is, each model can decide for itself how to map SimLex999 lemmas to WordNet synsets). The red horizontal line is the correlation of WordNet similarities with SimLex999 human scores. For the *path2vec* models,

there is a tendency to improve the performance when the vector size is increased, until a plateau is reached beyond 600 dimensions. Note that *Deepwalk*[5] does not benefit much from increased vector size, while *node2vec*[6] yields strangely low scores for 200 dimensions. Interestingly, *path2vec* and *Deepwalk* models consistently *outperform* the raw WordNet (this is also true for *FSE*). This means these embeddings are in some sense 'regularized', leading to better 'disambiguation' of senses behind SimLex999 word pairs and eventually to better similarities ranking.

In Tables 2 and 3, we select the best 300D *path2vec* models from the experiments described above and compare them against the best 300D baseline models and 128D FSE embeddings in static and dynamic evaluation setups. When WordNet-defined lemma-to-synset mappings are used (Table 2), the raw WordNet similarities are non-surprisingly the best, although *FSE* and *path2vec* embeddings achieve nearly the same performance (even slightly better for the *JCN-S* and *WuP* mappings). Following them are the *Deepwalk* models, which in turn outperform *node2vec* and *TransR*. In the dynamic synset selection setup (see Table 3), all the models except *node2vec* and *TransR* are superior to raw WordNet, and the best models are *FSE* and *path2vec ShP/WuP*, significantly outperforming the others. *Path2vec* models trained on *JCN-S* and *LCH* are on par with *Deepwalk* and much better than *node2vec* and *TransR*. We believe it to interesting, considering that it does not use random walks on graphs and is conceptually simpler than *FSE*.

Note that word embedding models trained on text perform *worse* than the WordNet-based em-

---

[5]The reported best *Deepwalk* models were trained with the number of walks 10 and window size 70.

[6]The reported best *node2vec* models were trained with the number of walks 25.

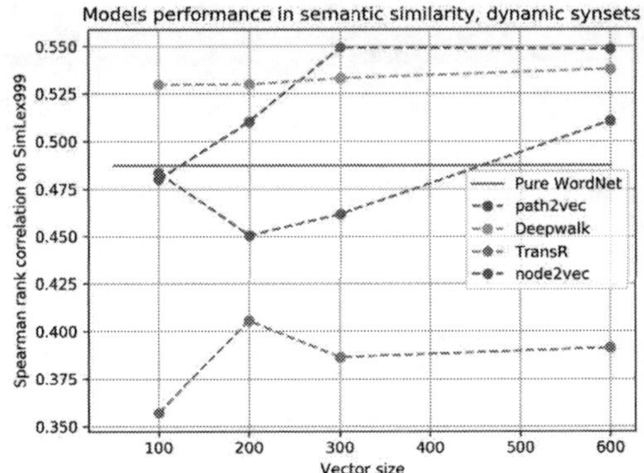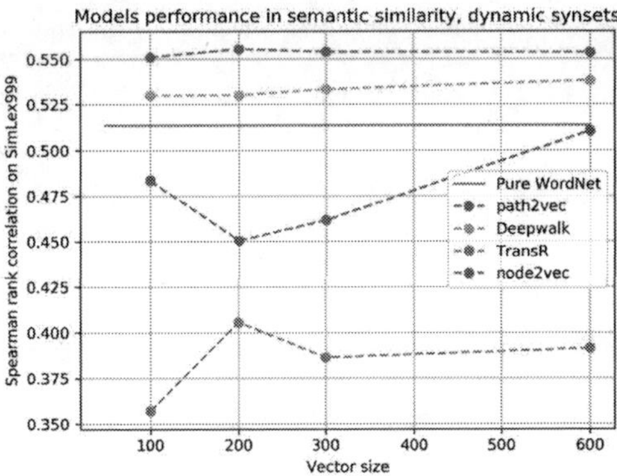

Figure 3: Evaluation on SimLex999 noun pairs, model-based synset selection: *JCN-S* (left) and *WuP* (right).

Model	Correlation
TransR (Lin et al., 2015)	0.386
node2vec (Grover and Leskovec, 2016)	0.462
Deepwalk (Perozzi et al., 2014)	0.533
FSE (Subercaze et al., 2015)	**0.556**
Raw WordNet JCN-S	0.487
Raw WordNet LCH	0.513
Raw WordNet ShP	0.513
Raw WordNet WuP	0.474
path2vec JCN-S	0.533
path2vec LCH	0.532
path2vec ShP	**0.555**
path2vec WuP	**0.555**

Table 3: Spearman correlations with human Sim-Lex999 noun similarities (model synset selection).

beddings (including *path2vec*) on the semantic similarity task. For example, the *word2vec* model of vector size 300 trained on the Google News corpus (Mikolov et al., 2013) achieves Spearman correlation of only 0.449 with SimLex999, when testing only on nouns. The *GloVe* embeddings (Pennington et al., 2014) of the same vector size trained on the Common Crawl corpus achieve 0.404.

6 Experiment 2: Extrinsic Evaluation based on Word Sense Disambiguation

Experimental Setting As an additional extrinsic evaluation, we turned to word sense disambiguation task, reproducing the WSD approach from (Sinha and Mihalcea, 2007). The original algorithm uses WordNet similarities; we tested how using dot products and the learned embeddings instead will influence the WSD performance.

The employed WSD algorithm starts with building a graph where the nodes are the WordNet synsets of the words in the input sentence. The nodes are then connected by edges weighted with the similarity values between the synset pairs (only if the similarity exceeds a threshold, which is a hyperparameter; we set it to 0.95). The final step is selecting the most likely sense for each word based on the weighted in-degree centrality score for each synset (in case of ties, the first synset is chosen). Figure 4 shows a graph generated for the sentence '*More often than not, ringers think of the church as something stuck on the bottom of the belfry*'. Note that we disambiguate nouns only.

Discussion of Results Table 4 presents the WSD micro-F1 scores using raw WordNet similarities, 300D *path2vec*, *Deepwalk* and *node2vec* models, and the 128D *FSE* model. We evaluate on the following all-words English WSD test sets: Senseval-2 (Palmer et al., 2001), Senseval-3 (Mihalcea et al., 2004), and SemEval-15 Task 13 (Raganato et al., 2017). Raw WordNet similarities are still the best, but the *path2vec* models are consistently the second after them (and orders of magnitude faster), outperforming other graph embedding baselines. The largest drop between the original and vector-based measures is for *JCN-S*, which is also the only one which relies not only on graph but also on external information from a corpus, making it more difficult to approximate (see also Figure 2, where this measure distribution seems to be the most difficult to reproduce). Note that both the original graph-based measures and graph embeddings do not outperform the most frequent sense (MFS) baseline, which is in line with the original algorithm (Sinha and Mihalcea, 2007).

Here our aim was not to improve WSD systems

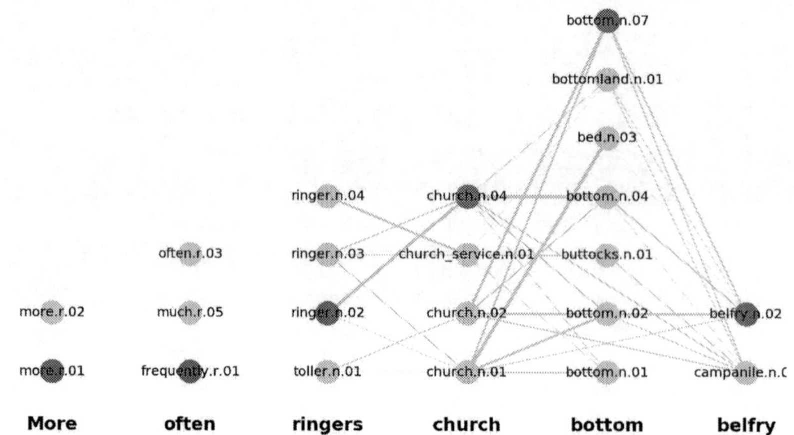

Figure 4: A sentence graph for WSD, where a column lists all the possible synsets of a corresponding word.

Model	Senseval2	Senseval3	SemEval-15
Random sense	0.381	0.312	0.393
Baselines (various graph embeddings)			
TransR	0.540	0.466	0.536
node2vec	0.503	0.467	0.489
Deepwalk	0.528	0.476	0.552
FSE	0.536	0.476	0.523
WordNet (graph-based measures)			
JCN-S	**0.620**	**0.558**	**0.597**
LCH	0.547	0.494	0.550
ShP	0.548	0.495	0.550
WuP	0.547	0.487	0.542
path2vec (vector-based measures)			
JCN-S	0.511	0.463	0.508
LCH	0.527	0.472	0.536
ShP	0.534	**0.489**	**0.563**
WuP	**0.543**	**0.489**	0.545

Table 4: F1 scores on all-words WSD tasks.

but to compare *path2vec* against other graph embedding methods in an extrinsic, task-based evaluation. This is also the reason why we do not compare against many other existing WordNet-based WSD systems: we are interested only in the approaches which learn dense representations of graph nodes, as *path2vec* does.

7   Computational Efficiency Evaluation

Pairwise Similarity Computation   One of the reasons to use *path2vec* embeddings is computational efficiency. Directly employing the WordNet graph to find semantic similarities between synsets is expensive. The dot product computation is much faster as compared to shortest path computation (and other complex walks) on a large

graph. Also, dense low-dimensional vector representations of nodes take much less space than the pairwise similarities between all the nodes.

The time complexity of calculating the shortest path between graph nodes (as in *ShP* or *LCH*) is in the best case linear in the number of nodes and edges (Leacock and Chodorow, 1998). *JCN-S* compares favorably since it is linear in the height of the taxonomy tree (Jiang and Conrath, 1997); however, it still cannot leverage highly-optimized routines and hardware capabilities, which makes the use of vectorized representations so efficient. Calculating Hamming distance between binary strings (as in the *FSE* algorithm) is linear in the sum of string lengths, which are equivalent of vector sizes (Hamming, 1950). At the same time, the complexity of calculating dot product between float vectors (as in *path2vec*) is linear in the vector size by the definition of the dot product and is easily and routinely parallelized.

As an example, let us consider the popular problem of ranking the graph nodes by their similarity to one particular node of interest (finding the 'nearest neighbors'). Table 5 shows the time for computing similarities of one node to all other WordNet noun nodes, using either standard graph similarity functions from NLTK, Hamming distance between 128D binary embeddings, or dot product between a 300D float vector (representing this node) and all rows of a 82115×300 matrix. Using float vectors is 4 orders of magnitude faster than *LCH*, 3 orders faster than *JCN*, and 2 orders faster than Hamming distance.

Construction of the Training Set   Despite its computational efficiency at test time, construct-

Model	Running time
LCH in NLTK	30 sec.
JCN-S in NLTK	6.7 sec.
FSE embeddings	0.713 sec.
path2vec and other float vectors	**0.007** sec.

Table 5: Computation of 82,115 similarities between one noun synset and all other noun synsets in WordNet.

ing a training dataset for *path2vec* (following the workflow described in Section 4) requires calculating pairwise similarities between all possible pairs of graph nodes. This leads to a number of similarity calculations quadratic in the number of nodes, which can be prohibitive in case of very large graphs. However, instead of this, the training datasets for *path2vec* can be constructed much faster by taking the graph structure into account. In essence, this implies finding for each node v the set of other nodes directly connected to it or to its direct graph neighbors (set of second order graph neighbors, V_2). Then, graph similarity is calculated only for the pairs consisting of each v and the nodes in their respective V_2; these pairs constitute the training dataset (the same thresholds and normalization procedures apply).

The amount of pairwise similarity calculations is then linear in the number of nodes times the average number of neighbors in V_2, which is much better. Particularly, in the case of WordNet, each node (synset) has 36 synsets in its V_2 on average, and half of the nodes do not have any neighbors at all. Thus, only 2,935,829 pairwise similarity calculations are needed, 1,000 times less than when calculating similarities between all synset pairs.

Following that, e.g., the training dataset for *JCN-S* can be constructed in 3 minutes, instead of 5 hours, with similar speedups for other graph distance measures. The training datasets constructed in this 'fast' way showed negligible performance decrease compared to the 'full' datasets (0.07...0.03 drop in the semantic similarity experiments, and < 0.03 drop in the WSD experiments). It means that when using *path2vec* in practical tasks, one can construct the training dataset very quickly, preserving embeddings performance.

8   Discussion and Conclusion

We presented *path2vec*, a simple, effective, and efficient model for embedding graph similarity measures. It can be used to learn vector representations of graph nodes, approximating shortest path distances or other node similarity measures of interest. Additionally, if the similarity function is based on the shortest path, this paves the way to a quick and efficient calculation of the shortest distance between two nodes in large graphs.

Our model allow for much more efficient graph distances calculations (3 or 4 orders of magnitude faster depending on a similarity measure). In applications one could replace path-based measures with dot product between *path2vec* embeddings, gaining significant speedup in distance computation between nodes. Thus, our model could be used to speed up various other graph-based algorithms that make use of node distance computations, such as Floyd (1962) algorithm, Dijkstra (1959) algorithm, or algorithms for computing node betweenness centrality (Brandes, 2001).

In this paper, we used our model to learn embeddings of WordNet synsets and showed that in the semantic similarity task, the resulting representations perform better than the state-of-the-art graph embedding approaches based on random walks. Interestingly, the learned embeddings can outperform the original WordNet similarities on which they were trained. *path2vec* was also evaluated on the WSD task (it has not been done before for graph embeddings, to our knowledge), again outperforming other approaches.

However, *path2vec* can be trained on arbitrary graph measures and is not restricted to the shortest path or to only tree-structured graphs. In the future, we plan to explore the possibility of training embeddings able to approximate multiple similarity metrics at once. Another direction of further research is to apply our model to other types of data, such as social networks or graph of roads.

Acknowledgements

This work has been partially supported by Deutsche Forschungsgemeinschaft (DFG) within the JOIN-T (grant BI 1544/4-1 and SP 1999/1-1)) project and the ACQuA project (grant BI 1544/7-1 and HA 5851/2-1), which is part of the Priority Program Robust Argumentation Machines (RATIO) (SPP-1999), and Young Scientist Mobility Grant from the Faculty of Mathematics and Natural Sciences, University of Oslo. We thank three anonymous reviewers for their most useful feedback. Last but not least, we are grateful to Sarah Kohail who helped with computing the first version of the *node2vec* baselines.

References

Steven Bird, Ewan Klein, and Edward Loper. 2009. *Natural language processing with Python: analyzing text with the natural language toolkit*. O'Reilly Media, Inc.

Antoine Bordes, Nicolas Usunier, Alberto Garcia-Duran, Jason Weston, and Oksana Yakhnenko. 2013. Translating embeddings for modeling multi-relational data. In C. J. C. Burges, L. Bottou, M. Welling, Z. Ghahramani, and K. Q. Weinberger, editors, *Advances in Neural Information Processing Systems 26*, pages 2787–2795. Curran Associates, Inc.

Antoine Bordes, Jason Weston, Ronan Collobert, and Yoshua Bengio. 2011. Learning structured embeddings of knowledge bases. In *Twenty-Fifth AAAI Conference on Artificial Intelligence*, pages 301–306, San Francisco, CA, USA. AAAI Press.

Ulrik Brandes. 2001. A faster algorithm for betweenness centrality. *Journal of mathematical sociology*, 25(2):163–177.

Alexander Budanitsky and Graeme Hirst. 2006. Evaluating WordNet-based measures of lexical semantic relatedness. *Computational Linguistics*, 32(1):13–47.

Shaosheng Cao, Wei Lu, and Qiongkai Xu. 2015. Grarep: Learning graph representations with global structural information. In *Proceedings of the 24th ACM International on Conference on Information and Knowledge Management*, pages 891–900. ACM.

Edsger W Dijkstra. 1959. A note on two problems in connexion with graphs. *Numerische mathematik*, 1(1):269–271.

Robert W Floyd. 1962. Algorithm 97: shortest path. *Communications of the ACM*, 5(6):345.

Francois Fouss, Alain Pirotte, Jean-Michel Renders, and Marco Saerens. 2007. Random-walk computation of similarities between nodes of a graph with application to collaborative recommendation. *IEEE Transactions on knowledge and data engineering*, 19(3):355–369.

Aditya Grover and Jure Leskovec. 2016. Node2vec: Scalable feature learning for networks. In *Proceedings of the 22nd ACM SIGKDD international conference on Knowledge discovery and data mining*, pages 855–864. ACM.

William Hamilton, Rex Ying, and Jure Leskovec. 2017a. Representation learning on graphs: Methods and applications. *IEEE Data Engineering Bulletin*, 40(3):52–74.

William Hamilton, Zhitao Ying, and Jure Leskovec. 2017b. Inductive representation learning on large graphs. In *Advances in Neural Information Processing Systems*, pages 1024–1034.

Richard Hamming. 1950. Error detecting and error correcting codes. *Bell System technical journal*, 29(2):147–160.

Felix Hill, Roi Reichart, and Anna Korhonen. 2015. SimLex-999: Evaluating Semantic Models With (Genuine) Similarity Estimation. *Computational Linguistics*, 41(4):665–695.

Jay J. Jiang and David W. Conrath. 1997. Semantic similarity based on corpus statistics and lexical taxonomy. In *Proceedings of the 10th Research on Computational Linguistics International Conference*, pages 19–33, Taipei, Taiwan. The Association for Computational Linguistics and Chinese Language Processing (ACLCLP).

Diederik P. Kingma and Jimmy Ba. 2014. Adam: A method for stochastic optimization. *CoRR*, abs/1412.6980.

Henry Kucera and Nelson Francis. 1982. *Frequency analysis of English usage: Lexicon and grammar*. Boston: Houghton Mifflin.

Claudia Leacock and Martin Chodorow. 1998. Combining local context and WordNet similarity for word sense identification. *WordNet: An electronic lexical database*, 49(2):265–283.

Bertrand Lebichot, Guillaume Guex, Ilkka Kivimäki, and Marco Saerens. 2018. A constrained randomized shortest-paths framework for optimal exploration. *arXiv preprint arXiv:1807.04551*.

Yankai Lin, Zhiyuan Liu, Maosong Sun, Yang Liu, and Xuan Zhu. 2015. Learning entity and relation embeddings for knowledge graph completion. In *Proceedings of the Twenty-Ninth AAAI Conference on Artificial Intelligence*, volume 15, pages 2181–2187, Austin, TX, USA. AAAI Press.

Rada Mihalcea, Timothy Chklovski, and Adam Kilgarriff. 2004. The Senseval-3 English lexical sample task. In *Senseval-3: Third International Workshop on the Evaluation of Systems for the Semantic Analysis of Text*, pages 25–28, Barcelona, Spain. Association for Computational Linguistics.

Tomas Mikolov, Ilya Sutskever, Kai Chen, Greg S. Corrado, and Jeff Dean. 2013. Distributed representations of words and phrases and their compositionality. In *Advances in Neural Information Processing Systems 26*, pages 3111–3119, Lake Tahoe, NV, USA. Curran Associates, Inc.

George A. Miller. 1995. WordNet: A lexical database for English. *Communications of the ACM*, 38(11):39–41.

Nikola Mrkšić, Ivan Vulić, Diarmuid Ó Séaghdha, Ira Leviant, Roi Reichart, Milica Gašić, Anna Korhonen, and Steve Young. 2017. Semantic specialization of distributional word vector spaces using monolingual and cross-lingual constraints. *Transactions of the Association for Computational Linguistics*, 5:309–324.

Roberto Navigli. 2009. Word sense disambiguation: A survey. *ACM Computing Surveys (CSUR)*, 41(2):10.

Diarmuid Ó Séaghdha. 2009. Semantic classification with wordnet kernels. In *Proceedings of Human Language Technologies: The 2009 Annual Conference of the North American Chapter of the Association for Computational Linguistics, Companion Volume: Short Papers*, pages 237–240, Boulder, CO, USA. Association for Computational Linguistics.

Mingdong Ou, Peng Cui, Jian Pei, Ziwei Zhang, and Wenwu Zhu. 2016. Asymmetric transitivity preserving graph embedding. In *Proceedings of the 22nd ACM SIGKDD international conference on Knowledge discovery and data mining*, pages 1105–1114. ACM.

Martha Palmer, Christiane Fellbaum, Scott Cotton, Lauren Delfs, and Hoa Trang Dang. 2001. English tasks: All-words and verb lexical sample. In *Proceedings of SENSEVAL-2 Second International Workshop on Evaluating Word Sense Disambiguation Systems*, pages 21–24, Toulouse, France. Association for Computational Linguistics.

Jeffrey Pennington, Richard Socher, and Christopher D. Manning. 2014. Glove: Global vectors for word representation. In *Proceedings of the 2014 Conference on Empirical Methods in Natural Language Processing (EMNLP)*, pages 1532–1543, Doha, Qatar. Association for Computational Linguistics.

Bryan Perozzi, Rami Al-Rfou, and Steven Skiena. 2014. Deepwalk: Online learning of social representations. In *Proceedings of the 20th ACM SIGKDD international conference on Knowledge discovery and data mining*, pages 701–710, New York, NY, USA. ACM.

Mohammad Taher Pilehvar and Nigel Collier. 2016. De-conflated semantic representations. In *Proceedings of the 2016 Conference on Empirical Methods in Natural Language Processing*, pages 1680–1690, Austin, TX, USA. Association for Computational Linguistics.

Mohammad Taher Pilehvar and Roberto Navigli. 2015. From senses to texts: An all-in-one graph-based approach for measuring semantic similarity. *Artificial Intelligence*, 228:95–128.

Alessandro Raganato, Jose Camacho-Collados, and Roberto Navigli. 2017. Word sense disambiguation: A unified evaluation framework and empirical comparison. In *Proceedings of the 15th Conference of the European Chapter of the Association for Computational Linguistics: Volume 1, Long Papers*, pages 99–110, Valencia, Spain. Association for Computational Linguistics.

Delip Rao, David Yarowsky, and Chris Callison-Burch. 2008. Affinity measures based on the graph Laplacian. In *Coling 2008: Proceedings of the 3rd Textgraphs workshop on Graph-based Algorithms for Natural Language Processing*, pages 41–48, Manchester, UK. Coling 2008 Organizing Committee.

Philip Resnik. 1999. Semantic similarity in a taxonomy: An information-based measure and its application to problems of ambiguity in natural language. *Journal of Artificial Intelligence Research*, 11(1):95–130.

Sascha Rothe and Hinrich Schütze. 2015. Autoextend: Extending word embeddings to embeddings for synsets and lexemes. In *Proceedings of the 53rd Annual Meeting of the Association for Computational Linguistics and the 7th International Joint Conference on Natural Language Processing (Volume 1: Long Papers)*, pages 1793–1803, Beijing, China. Association for Computational Linguistics.

Michael Schlichtkrull, Thomas N. Kipf, Peter Bloem, Rianne van den Berg, Ivan Titov, and Max Welling. 2018. Modeling relational data with graph convolutional networks. In *European Semantic Web Conference*, pages 593–607, Heraklion, Greece. Springer.

Ravi Sinha and Rada Mihalcea. 2007. Unsupervised graph-based word sense disambiguation using measures of word semantic similarity. In *International Conference on Semantic Computing (ICSC)*, pages 363–369, Irvine, CA, USA. IEEE.

Mark Steyvers and Joshua B. Tenenbaum. 2005. The large-scale structure of semantic networks: statistical analyses and a model of semantic growth. *Cognitive science*, 29(1):41–78.

Julien Subercaze, Christophe Gravier, and Frédérique Laforest. 2015. On metric embedding for boosting semantic similarity computations. In *Proceedings of the 53rd Annual Meeting of the Association for Computational Linguistics and the 7th International Joint Conference on Natural Language Processing (Volume 2: Short Papers)*, pages 8–14, Beijing, China. Association for Computational Linguistics.

Zhen Wang, Jianwen Zhang, Jianlin Feng, and Zheng Chen. 2014. Knowledge graph embedding by translating on hyperplanes. In *AAAI Conference on Artificial Intelligence*, pages 1112–1119, Québec City, QC, Canada.

Zhibiao Wu and Martha Palmer. 1994. Verb semantics and lexical selection. In *Proceedings of the 32nd Annual Meeting of the Association for Computational Linguistics*, pages 133–138, Las Cruces, NM, USA. Association for Computational Linguistics.

Neural User Factor Adaptation for Text Classification:
Learning to Generalize Across Author Demographics

Xiaolei Huang and **Michael J. Paul**
Information Science
University of Colorado
Boulder, CO 80309, USA
{xiaolei.huang,mpaul}@colorado.edu

Abstract

Language usage varies across different demographic factors, such as gender, age, and geographic location. However, most existing document classification methods ignore demographic variability. In this study, we examine empirically how text data can vary across four demographic factors: gender, age, country, and region. We propose a multitask neural model to account for demographic variations via adversarial training. In experiments on four English-language social media datasets, we find that classification performance improves when adapting for user factors.

1 Introduction

Different demographic groups can show substantial linguistic variations, especially in online data (Goel et al., 2016; Johannsen et al., 2015). These variations can affect natural language processing models such as sentiment classifiers. For example, researchers found that women were more likely to use the word *weakness* in a positive way, while men were more likely to use the word in a negative expression (Volkova et al., 2013).

Models for text classification, the automatic categorization of documents into categories, typically ignore attributes about the authors of the text. With the growing amount of text generated by users online, whose personal characteristics are highly variable, there has been increased attention to how user demographics are associated with the text they write. Promising recent studies have shown that incorporating demographic factors can improve text classification (Volkova et al., 2013; Hovy, 2015; Yang and Eisenstein, 2017; Li et al., 2018). Lynn et al. (2017) refer to this idea as *user factor adaptation* and proposed to treat this as a domain adaptation problem in which demographic attributes constitute different domains. We extend this line of work in a number of ways:

- We assemble and publish new datasets containing four demographic factors: gender, age, country, and US region. The demographic attributes are carefully inferred from profile information that is separate from the text data.

- We experiment with neural domain adaptation models (Ganin et al., 2016), which may provide better performance than the simpler models used in prior work on user factor adaptation. We also propose a new model using a multitask framework with adversarial training.

- Our approach requires demographic attributes at training time but not at test time: we learn a single representation to be invariant to demographic changes. This approach thus requires fewer resources than prior work.

In this study, we treat adapting across the demographic factors as a domain work problem, in which we consider each demographic factor as a domain. We focus on four different demographic factors (gender, age, country, region) in four English-language social media datasets (Twitter, Amazon reviews, Yelp hotel reviews, and Yelp restaurant reviews), which contain text authored by a diversity of demographic groups.

We first conduct an exploratory analysis of how different demographic variables are associated with documents and document labels (Section 2). We then describe a neural model for the task of document classification that adapts to demographic factors using a multitask learning framework (Section 3). Specifically, the model is trained to predict the values of the demographic attributes from the text in addition to predicting the document label. Experiments on four social media datasets show that user factor adaptation is important for document classification, and that the proposed model works well compared to alternative domain adaptation approaches (Section 4).

*Proceedings of the Eighth Joint Conference on Lexical and Computational Semantics (*SEM)*, pages 136–146
Minneapolis, June 6–7, 2019. ©2019 Association for Computational Linguistics

2 Exploratory Analysis of User Factors

We begin with an empirical analysis of how text is related to various demographic attributes of its authors. We first present a description of the demographic attributes. We then conduct qualitative analyses of demographic variations within the collected data on three cascading levels: document, topic and word. The goal is to get a sense of the extent to which language data varies across different user factors and how these factors might interact with document classification. This will motivate our adaptation methods later and provide concrete examples of the user factors that we have in mind.

2.1 Data

We experiment with four corpora from three social media sources:

- **Twitter:** Tweets were labeled with whether they indicate that the user received an influenza vaccination (i.e., a flu shot) (Huang et al., 2017), used in a recent NLP shared task (Weissenbacher et al., 2018).

- **Amazon:** Music reviews from Amazon labeled with sentiment.

- **Hotel:** Hotel reviews from Yelp labeled with sentiment.

- **Restaurant:** Restaurant reviews from Yelp labeled with sentiment.

The latter three datasets were collected for this study. All documents are given binary labels. For the Amazon and Yelp data, we encode reviews with a score >3 (out of 5) as positive and ≤ 3 as negative. For the Yelp data, we removed reviews that had fewer than ten tokens or a helpfulness/usefulness score of zero.

2.1.1 User Attribute Inference

Previous work on user factor adaptation considered the factors of gender, age, and personality (Lynn et al., 2017). We similarly consider gender and age, and instead of personality, we consider a new factor of geographic location. For location, we consider two granularities as different factors, country and region.

These factors must be extracted from the data. One of our goals is to infer these factors in a way that is completely independent of the text used for classification. This is in contrast with the approach used by Lynn et al. (2017), who inferred the attributes from the text of the users, which could arguably confound the interpretation of the results, as domains are defined using the same information available to the classifier. Thus, we used only information from user profiles to obtain their demographic attributes.

Gender and Age. We inferred user gender and age through the user's profile image using the Microsoft Facial Recognition API.[1] Recent comparisons of different commercial face APIs have found the Microsoft API to be the most accurate (Jung et al., 2018) and least biased (Buolamwini and Gebru, 2018). We filtered out users that are inferred to be younger than 12 years old. If multiple faces are in an image, we used the first result from the API. Gender is encoded with two values, male and female. For simplicity, we also binarized the age values (≤ 30 and >30).

Country and Region. We define two factors based on the location of the user. For the Twitter data, we inferred the location of each user with the Carmen geolocation system (Dredze et al., 2013), which resolves the user's location string in their profile to a structured location. Because this comes from the user profile, it is generally taken to be the "home" location of the user. For Amazon and Yelp, we collected user locations listed in their profiles, then used pattern matching and manual whitelisting to resolve the strings to specific locations (city, state, country). To construct user factors from location data, we first created a binary country variable to indicate if the user's country is the United States (US, the most common country in the data) or not. Among US users, we resolved the location to a region. We follow the US Census Bureau's regional divisions (Bureau, 2012) to categorize the users into four regional categories: Northeast (NE), Midwest (MW), South (S) and West (W). We labeled Washington D.C. as northeast in this study; we excluded other territories of the US, such as Puerto Rico and U.S. Virgin Islands, since these locations do not contain much data and do not map well to the four regions.

Accuracy of Inference Attributes inferred with these tools will not be perfectly accurate. Although such inaccuracies could lead to suboptimal

---

[1] https://azure.microsoft.com/en-us/services/cognitive-services/face/

training, this does not affect our classifier evaluation, since we do not use demographic labels at test time. Nonetheless, we provide a rough estimate of the accuracy of the attributes extracted from faces. We randomly sampled 100 users across our datasets. Two annotators reviewed each image and guessed the gender and age of the user (using our binary categories) based on the profile image. A third annotator chose the final label when the first two disagreed (annotators disagreed on gender in 2% of photos and age in 15% of photos). Our final annotations agreed with the Face API's gender estimates 88% of the time across the four datasets (ranging from 84% to 100%), and age estimates 68% of the time across the four datasets (ranging from 56% to 92%).

2.1.2 Data Summary

We show the data statistics along with the full demographic distributions in the Table 1. While our study does not require a representative sample from the data sources, since our primary goal is to evaluate whether we can adapt models to different demographics, we observe some notable differences between the demographics of our collection and the known demographics of the sources. Namely, the percentage of female users is much higher in our data than among Twitter users (Tien, 2018) and Yelp users (Yelp, 2018) as estimated from surveys. This discrepancy could stem from our process of sampling only users who had profile images available for demographic inference, since not all users provide profile photos, and those who do may skew toward certain demographic groups (Rose et al., 2012).

2.1.3 Privacy Considerations

While our data collection includes only public data, due to the potential sensitivity of user profile information, we stored only data necessary for this study. Therefore, we anonymized the personal information and deleted user images after retrieving the demographic attributes from the Microsoft API. We only include aggregated information in this paper and do not publish any private information associated with individuals including example reviews. The dataset that we share will include our model inferences but not the original image data; instead, the dataset will provide instructions on how the data was collected in enough detail that the approach can be replicated.

2.2 Are User Factors Encoded in Text?

It is known that the user factors we consider are associated with variability in language, including in online content (Hovy, 2015). For example, age affects linguistic style (Wagner, 2012), and language styles are highly associated with the gender of online users (Hovy and Purschke, 2018). Dialectical differences also cause language variation by location; for example, "dese" (these) is more common among social media users from the Southern US than other regions of the US (Goel et al., 2016).

Our goal in this section is to test whether these variations hold in our particular datasets, how strong the effects are, and which of our four factors are most associated with language. We do this in two ways, first by measuring predictability of factors from text, and second by qualitatively examining topic differences across user groups.

2.2.1 User Factor Prediction

We explore how accurately the text documents can predict user demographic factors. We do this by training classifiers to predict each factor. We first downsample without replacement to balance the data for each category. We shuffle and split the data into training (70%) and test (30%) sets. We then build logistic regression classifiers using TF-IDF-weighted 1-, 2-, and 3-grams as features. We use *scikit-learn* (Pedregosa et al., 2011) to implement the classifiers and accuracy scores to measure the predictability. We show the absolute improvements of scores in Table 2.

The results show that user factors are encoded in text well enough to be predicted significantly. Twitter data shows the best predictability towards age, and the two Yelp datasets show strong classification results for both gender and country. We also observe that as the data size increases, the predictability of language usage towards demographic factors also increases. These observations suggest a connection between language style and user demographic factors in large corpora.

2.2.2 Topic Analysis

We additionally examine how the distribution of text content varies across demographic groups. To characterize the content, we represent the text with a topic model. We trained a Latent Dirichlet Allocation (Blei et al., 2003) model with 10 topics using GenSim (Řehůřek and Sojka, 2010) with default parameters. After training the topic model, each document d is associated with a probability

	# Docs	# Users	Gender		Age		Country		Region			
			F	M	≤30	>30	US	¬US	NE	MW	S	W
Twitter	9.8K	9.8K	.575	.425	.572	.428	.772	.228	.104	.120	.145	.631
Amazon	40.4K	34.3K	.333	.667	.245	.755	.900	.100	.097	.096	.132	.675
Hotel	169K	119K	.576	.424	.450	.550	.956	.044	.297	.166	.271	.266
Restaurant	713K	811K	.547	.453	.451	.549	.892	.108	.305	.181	.302	.212

Table 1: Dataset statistics including user demographic distributions for four user factors.

Figure 1: Topic distribution log ratios. A value of 0 means that demographic groups use that topic in equal amounts, while values away from 0 mean that the topic is discussed more by one demographic group than the other group(s) in that factor.

	Gender	Age	Country	Region
Twitter	+9.6	+15.3	+9.0	+3.3
Amazon	+15.2	+12.2	+18.0	+13.0
Hotel	+17.2	+10.9	+25.4	+11.6
Restaurant	+19.0	+13.2	+32.8	+17.5

Table 2: Predictability of user factors from language data. We show the absolute percentage improvements in accuracy over majority-class baselines. For example, the majority-class baselines of accuracy scores are either .500 for the binary prediction or .250 for the region prediction.

distribution over the 10 topics. The model learns a multinomial topic distribution $P(Z|D)$ from a Dirichlet prior, where Z refers to each topic and D refers to each document. For each demographic group, we calculate the average topic distribution across the documents from that group. Then within each factor, we calculate the log-ratio of the topic probabilities for each group. For example, for topic k for the gender factor, we calculate $\log_2 \frac{P(Topic=k|Gender=\text{female})}{P(Topic=k|Gender=\text{male})}$. The sign of the log-ratio indicates which demographic group is more likely to use the topic. We do this for all factors; for region, we simply binarize the four values for the purpose of this visualization (MW + W vs. NE + S). Results are shown in Figure 1.

The topic model was trained without removing stop words, in case stop word usage varies by group. However, because of this, the topics all look very similar and are hard to interpret, so we do not show the topics themselves. What we instead want to show is the degree to which the prevalence of some topics varies across demographic attributes, which are extracted independently from the text used to train the topic models. We see that while most topics are fairly consistent across demographic groups, most datasets have at least a few topics with large differences.

2.3 Are Document Categories Expressed Differently by Different User Groups?

While text content varies across different user groups, it is a separate question whether those variations will affect document classification. For example, if men and women discuss different topics online, but express sentiment in the same way, then those differences will not affect a sentiment classifier. Prior work has shown that the way people express opinions in online social media does vary by gender, age, geographic location, and political orientation (Hinds and Joinson, 2018); thus, there is reason to believe that concepts like sentiment will be expressed differently by different groups. As a final exploratory experiment, we now consider whether the text features that are predictive of document categories (e.g., positive or negative sentiment) also vary with user factors.

To compare how word expressions vary among the demographic factors, we conduct a word-level feature comparison. For each demographic group, we collect only documents that belong to that group and then calculate the n-gram features

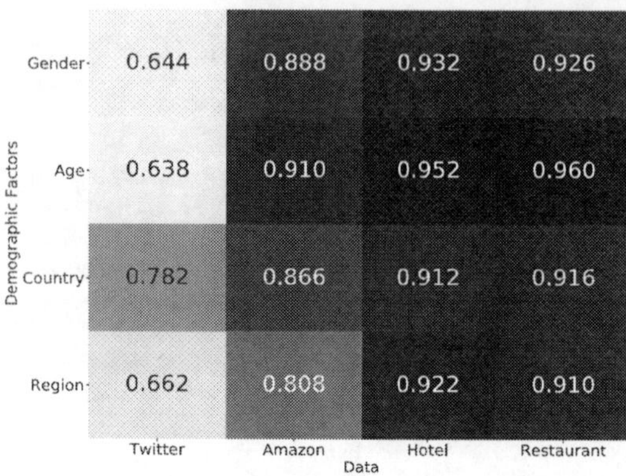

Figure 2: Overlap in most predictive classification features across different demographic groups, calculated for each demographic factor and each dataset. Darker color indicates less variation in word usage across demographic groups.

(same features as in Section 2.2) that are most associated with the document class labels. Using mutual information, we select the top 1,000 features for each attribute. Then within each demographic factor (e.g., gender), we calculate the percentage of top 1,000 features that overlap across the different attribute values in that factor (e.g., male and female). Specifically, if S_0 is the set of top features for one attribute and S_1 is the set of top features for another attribute, the percent overlap is calculated as $|S_0 \cap S_1|/1000$. Results are shown in Figure 2. Lower percentages indicate higher variation in how different groups express the concepts being classified (e.g., sentiment). The Twitter data shows the most variation while the Yelp hotel data shows the least variation.

3 Model

Models for user factor adaptation generally treat this as a problem of *domain adaptation* (Volkova et al., 2013; Lynn et al., 2017). Domain adaptation methods are used to learn models that can be applied to data whose distributions may differ from the training data. Commonly used methods include feature augmentation (Daume III, 2007; Joshi et al., 2013; Huang and Paul, 2018) and structural correspondence learning (Blitzer et al., 2006), while recent approaches rely on domain adversarial training (Ganin et al., 2016; Chen et al., 2016; Liu et al., 2017; Huang et al., 2018). We borrow concepts of domain adaptation to construct a model that is robust to variations across user factors.

In our proposed **Neural User Factor Adaptation (NUFA)** model, we treat each variable of interest (demographic attributes and document class label) as a separate, but jointly modeled, prediction task. The goal is to perform well at predicting document classes, while the demographic attribute tasks are modeled primarily for the purpose of learning characteristics of the demographic groups. Thus, the model aims to learn discriminative features for text classification while learning to be invariant to the linguistic characteristics of the demographic groups. Once trained, this classifier can be applied to test documents without requiring the demographic attributes.

Concretely, we propose the multitask learning framework in Figure 3. The model extracts features from the text for the demographic attribute prediction tasks and the classification task, as well as joint features for all tasks in which features for both demographics and document classes are mapped into the same vector space. Each feature space is constructed with a separate Bidirectional Long Short-Term Memory model (Bi-LSTM) (Hochreiter and Schmidhuber, 1997).

Because language styles vary across groups, as shown in Section 2.2, information from each task could be useful to the other. Thus, our intuition is that while we model the document and demographic predictions as independent tasks, the shared feature space allows the model to transfer knowledge from the demographic tasks to the text classification task and vice versa.

However, we want to keep the feature space such that the features are predictive of document classes in a way that is invariant to demographic shifts. To avoid learning features for the document classifier that are too strongly associated with user factors, we use adversarial training. The result is that the demographic information is encoded primarily in the features used for the demographic classifiers, while learning invariant text features that work *across* different demographic groups for the document classifier.

Domain Sampling and Model Inputs. Our model requires all domains (demographic attributes) to be known during training, but not all attributes are known in our datasets. Instead of explicitly modeling the missing data, we simply sample documents where all user attributes of interest are available. At test time, this limitation does not apply because only the document text is

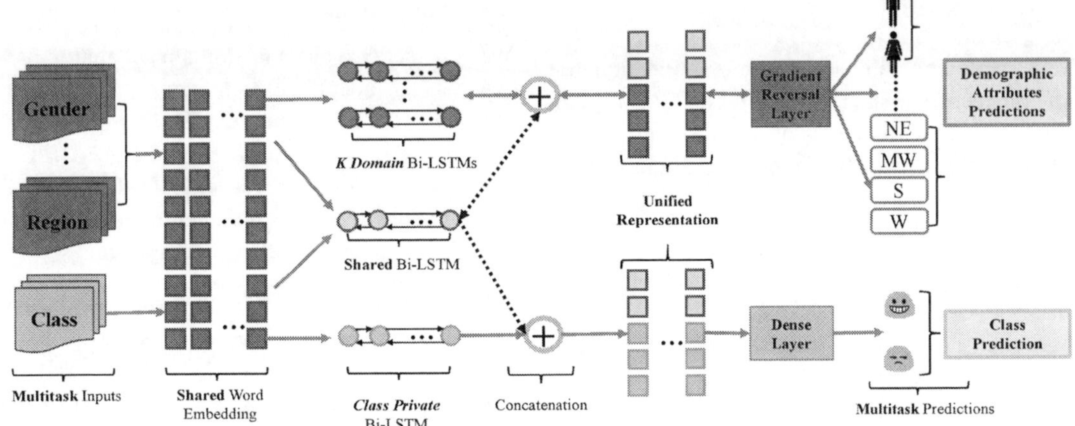

Figure 3: Neural User Factor Adaptation (NUFA) model. NUFA optimizes for two major tasks, demographic prediction (blue blocks and arrows) and text classification (light orange blocks and arrows). During the training phase, documents labeled with demographic information go through the demographic classifier, and documents with class labels go through the document classifier. This helps NUFA learn representations that are useful for classifying documents versus representations that are useful for predicting demographics. At test time, documents are given only to the document classifier, leaving out the demographic classifiers.

required as input to the document classifier.

Shared Embedding Space. We use a common embedding layer for both document and demographic factor predictions. The goal is that the trained embeddings will capture the language variations that are associated with the demographic groups as well as document labels. Parameters are initialized with pre-trained embeddings (Mikolov et al., 2013; Pennington et al., 2014).

K+2 Bi-LSTMs. We combine ideas from two previous works on domain adaptation (Liu et al., 2017; Kim et al., 2017). Kim et al. (2017) proposed $K+1$ Bi-LSTMs, where K is the number of domains, and Liu et al. (2017) proposed to combine shared and independent Bi-LSTMs for each prediction task. In our model, we create one independent Bi-LSTM for each demographic domain (blue), one independent Bi-LSTM for the document classifier (orange), and one shared Bi-LSTM that is used in both the demographic prediction and document classification tasks (yellow). The intuition is to transfer learned information to one and the other through this shared Bi-LSTM while leaving some free spaces for both document label and demographic factors predictions. We then concatenate outputs of the shared LSTM with each task-independent LSTM together. This helps the text classifier capture demographic knowledge.

Demographic Classifier. We adjust the degree to which the demographic classifiers can discriminate between attributes. To find a balance between the invariant knowledge and differences across user demographic factors, we apply domain adversarial training (Ganin et al., 2016) (the blue block indicating the "gradient reversal layer") to each domain prediction task. The predictions use the final concatenated representations, where the prediction is modeled with a softmax function for the region and a binary sigmoid function for the other user demographic factors.

Document Classifier. We feed the concatenated outputs of the document and shared Bi-LSTMs to one layer feed-forward network (the orange block indicating the "dense layer"). Finally, the document classifier outputs a probability via a sigmoid.

Joint Multitask Learning. We use the categorical cross-entropy loss to optimize the $K + 1$ prediction tasks jointly. One question is how to assign importance to the multiple tasks. Because our target is document classification, we assign a cost to the domain prediction loss (L_{domain}). Each prediction task has its own weight, α_k. The final loss function is defined as $L = L_{doc} + \sum_{k=1}^{K} \alpha_k L_{domain,k}$. In summary, the proposed model learns and adapts to user demographic factors through three aspects: shared embeddings, shared Bi-LSTMs, and joint optimization.

4 Experiments

We experiment with document classification on our four corpora using various models. Our goal is to test whether models that adapt to user factors can outperform models that do not, and to understand which components of models can facilitate user factor adaptation.

4.1 Data Processing

We replaced hyperlinks, usernames, and hashtags with generic symbols. Documents were lowercased and tokenized using NLTK (Bird and Loper, 2004). The corpora were randomly split into training (80%), development (10%), and test (10%) sets. We train the models on the training set and find the optimal hyperparameters on the development set. We randomly shuffle the training data at the beginning of each training epoch. The evaluation metric is weighted F1 score.

4.2 Baselines: No Adaptation

We compare to three standard classifiers that do not perform adaptation.

N-gram. We extract TF-IDF-weighted features of 1-, 2-, and 3-grams on the corpora, using the most frequent 15K features with the minimum feature frequency as 2. We trained a logistic regression classifier using the SGDClassifier implementation in scikit-learn (Pedregosa et al., 2011) using a batch size of 256 and 1,000 iterations.

CNN. We used Keras (Chollet et al., 2015) to implement the Convolutional Neural Network (CNN) classifier described in Kim (2014). To keep consistent, we initialize the embedding weight with pre-trained word embeddings (Mikolov et al., 2013; Pennington et al., 2014). We only keep the 15K most frequent words and replace the rest with an "unk" token. Each document was padded to a length of 50. We keep all parameter settings as described in the paper. We fed 50 documents to the model each batch and trained for 20 epochs.

Bi-LSTM. We build a bi-directional Long Short Term Memory (bi-LSTM) (Hochreiter and Schmidhuber, 1997) classifier. The classifier is initialized with the pre-trained word embeddings, and we initialize training with the same parameters used for the NUFA.

4.3 Adaptation Models

We consider two baseline domain adaptation models that can adapt for user factors, a non-neural method and a neural model. We then provide the training details of our proposed model, NUFA. Finally, we consider two variants of NUFA that ablate components of the model, allowing us to evaluate the contribution of each component.

FEDA. Lynn et al. (2017) used a modification of the "frustratingly easy" domain adaptation (FEDA) method (Daume III, 2007) to adapt for user factors. We use a modification of this method where the four user factors and their values are treated as domains. We first extract domain-specific and general representations as TF-IDF-weighted n-gram (1-, 2, 3-grams) features. We extract the top 15K features for each domain and the general feature set. With this method, the feature set is augmented such that each feature has a domain-specific version of the feature for each domain, as well as a general domain-independent version of the feature. The features values are set to the original feature values for the domain-independent features and the domain-specific features that apply to the document, while domain-specific features for documents that do not belong to that domain are set to 0. For example, using gender as a domain, a training document with a female author would be encoded as $[F_{general}, F_{domain,female}, 0]$, while a document with a male author would be encoded as $[F_{general}, 0, F_{domain,male}]$. Different from prior work with FEDA for user-factor adaptation, at test time we only use the general, domain-independent features; the idea is to learn a generalized feature set that is domain invariant. This is the same approach we used in recent work using FEDA to adapt classifiers to temporal variations (Huang and Paul, 2018).

DANN. We consider the domain adversarial training network (Ganin et al., 2016) (DANN) on the user factor adaptation task. We use Keras to implement the same network and deploy the same pre-trained word embeddings as in NUFA. We then set the domain prediction as the demographic factors prediction and keep the document label prediction as the default. We train the model with 20 epochs with a batch size of 64. Finally, we use the model at the epoch when the model achieves the best result on the development set for the final model.

NUFA. We initialize the embedding weights by the pre-trained word embeddings (Mikolov et al., 2013; Pennington et al., 2014) with 200 dimensional vectors. All LSTMs are fixed outputs as 200-dimension vectors. We set the dropout of LSTM training to 0.2 and the flip gradient value to 0.01 during the adversarial training. The dense layer has 128 neurons with ReLU activation function and dropout of 0.2. User factors and document label predictions are optimized jointly using Adam (Kingma and Ba, 2015) with a learning rate of 0.001 and batch size of 64. We train NUFA for up to 20 epochs and select the best model on the development set. For single-factor adaptation (next section), we set α to 0.1; for multi-factor adaptation, we use a heuristic for setting α described in that section. We implemented NUFA in Keras (Chollet et al., 2015).

NUFA–s. To understand the role of the shared Bi-LSTM in our model, we conduct experiments on NUFA without the shared Bi-LSTM. We follow the same experimental steps as NUFA and denote it as NUFA−s (NUFA minus shared Bi-LSTM).

NUFA–a. To understand the role of the adversarial training in our model, we conduct experiments of the NUFA without adversarial training, denoted as NUFA−a (NUFA minus adversarial).

4.4 Results

4.4.1 Single-Factor Adaptation

We first consider user factor adaptation for each of the four factors individually. Table 3 shows the results. Adaptation methods almost always outperform the non-adaptation baselines; the best adaptation model outperforms the best non-adaptation model by 1.5 to 5.5 points. The improvements indicate that adopting the demographic factors might be beneficial for the classifiers. User factor adaptation thus appears to be important for text classification.

Comparing the adaptation methods, our proposed model (NUFA) is best on three of four datasets. On the Hotel dataset, the n-gram model FEDA is always best; this seems to be a dataset where neural methods perform poorly, since even the n-gram baseline with no adaptation often outperformed the various neural models. Whether a neural model is the best choice depends on the

	Twitter	Amazon	Hotel	Rest.
No Adaptation				
N-gram	.866	.793	.857	.866
CNN	.879	.776	.825	.846
Bi-LSTM	.869	.776	.842	.875
Adaptation (Gender)				
FEDA	.814	.809	**.865**	.874
DANN	.864	.832	.813	.855
NUFA−s	.880	*.845*	.857	.869
NUFA−a	.874	.842	.852	.868
NUFA	*.886*	.844	.854	**.881**
Adaptation (Age)				
FEDA	.813	.801	**.865**	.873
DANN	.856	.824	.811	.851
NUFA−s	.872	*.843*	.850	.879
NUFA−a	.882	.841	.852	.878
NUFA	*.885*	.839	.857	*.880*
Adaptation (Country)				
FEDA	.826	.768	**.865**	.877
DANN	.868	.828	.827	.855
NUFA−s	.882	*.844*	.854	*.879*
NUFA−a	.880	.838	.855	.877
NUFA	**.896**	.843	.854	*.879*
Adaptation (Region)				
FEDA	.826	.780	*.864*	.869
DANN	.875	.825	.823	.852
NUFA−s	.874	.833	.854	.878
NUFA−a	.882	.838	.854	.875
NUFA	*.893*	**.848**	.853	*.880*

Table 3: Performance (weighted F1) of no adaptation and single user factor adaptation. For each dataset, the best score within each demographic domain is italicized; the best score overall is bolded.

dataset, but among the neural models, NUFA always outperforms DANN. Finally, the full NUFA model most often outperforms the variants without the shared Bi-LSTM (NUFA−s) and without adversarial training (NUFA−a).

4.4.2 Multi-Factor Adaptation

Finally, we experiment with adapting to all four user factors together. Recall that each domain prediction task in NUFA is weighted by α_k. Initially, we simply used a uniform weighting, $\alpha_k = \alpha/K$, but we find that we can improve performance with non-uniform weighting. Because optimizing the α vector would be expensive, we instead propose a heuristic that weighs the domains based on how much each domain is expected to influence the text. We define $\alpha_k = s_k/(\sum_{k'} s_{k'})$, where s_k

	Twitter	Amazon	Hotel	Rest.
Baseline Adaptation				
FEDA	.806	.778	**.867**	.869
DANN	.880	.828	.830	.858
Proposed Model				
NUFA	.887	.848	.853	.879
NUFA+w	**.901**	**.852**	.855	**.885**

Table 4: Results of adaptation for all four user factors.

is the F1 score of demographic attribute prediction for domain k from Table 2. We denote this method as **NUFA+w**, which refers to this additional weighting process.

Table 4 shows that combining all user factors provides a small gain over single-factor adaptation; the best multi-factor result is higher than the best single-factor result for each dataset. As with single-factor adaptation, FEDA works best for the Hotel datasets, while NUFA+w works best for the other three. Without adding weighting to NUFA, the multi-factor performance is comparable to single-factor performance; thus, task weighting seems to be critical for good performance when combining multiple factors.

5 Related Work

Demographic prediction is a common task in natural language processing. Research has shown that social media text is predictive of demographic variables such as gender (Rao et al., 2010, 2011; Burger et al., 2011; Volkova et al., 2015) and location (Eisenstein et al., 2010; Wing and Baldridge, 2011, 2014). Our work is closely related to these, as our model also predicts demographic variables. However, in our model the goal of demographic prediction is primarily to learn representations that will make the document classifier more robust to demographic variations, rather than the end goal being demographic prediction itself.

Demographic bias has been shown to be encoded in machine learning models. Word embeddings, which are widely used in classification tasks, are prone to learning demographic stereotypes. For example, a study by Bolukbasi et al. (2016) found that the word "programmer" is more similar to "man" than "woman," while "receptionist" is more similar to "woman." To avoid learning biases, researchers have proposed adding demographic constraints (Zhao et al., 2017) or using adversarial training (Elazar and Goldberg, 2018).

While our work is not focused specifically on reducing bias, our goals are related to it in that our models are meant to learn document classifiers that are invariant to author demographics.

6 Conclusion

We have explored the issue of author demographics in relation to document classification, showing that demographics are encoded in language, and the most predictive features for document classification vary by demographics. We showed that various domain adaptation methods can be used to build classifiers that are more robust to demographics, combined in a neural model that outperformed prior approaches. Our datasets, which contain various attributes including those inferred through facial recognition, could be useful in other research (Section 5). We publish our datasets[2] and source code.[3]

7 Acknowledgements

The authors thank the anonymous reviews for their insightful comments and suggestions. The authors thank Zijiao Yang for helping evaluate inference accuracy of the Microsoft Face API. This work was supported in part by the National Science Foundation under award number IIS-1657338.

References

Steven Bird and Edward Loper. 2004. Nltk: the natural language toolkit. In *Proceedings of the ACL 2004 on Interactive poster and demonstration sessions*, page 31. Association for Computational Linguistics.

David M. Blei, Andrew Y. Ng, and Michael I. Jordan. 2003. Latent Dirichlet Allocation. *Journal of Machine Learning Research*, 3:993–1022.

John Blitzer, Ryan McDonald, and Fernando Pereira. 2006. Domain adaptation with structural correspondence learning. In *Proceedings of the 2006 conference on empirical methods in natural language processing*, pages 120–128. Association for Computational Linguistics.

Tolga Bolukbasi, Kai-Wei Chang, James Y Zou, Venkatesh Saligrama, and Adam T Kalai. 2016. Man is to computer programmer as woman is to homemaker? debiasing word embeddings. In *Advances in Neural Information Processing Systems*, pages 4349–4357.

---

[2]`http://cmci.colorado.edu/~mpaul/files/starsem2019_demographics.data.zip`
[3]`https://github.com/xiaoleihuang/NUFA`

Joy Buolamwini and Timnit Gebru. 2018. Gender shades: Intersectional accuracy disparities in commercial gender classification. In *Conference on Fairness, Accountability and Transparency*, pages 77–91.

United States Census Bureau. 2012. 2010 geographic terms and concepts - census divisions and census regions.

John D Burger, John Henderson, George Kim, and Guido Zarrella. 2011. Discriminating gender on Twitter. In *Empirical Methods in Natural Language Processing (EMNLP)*, Stroudsburg, PA, USA.

Xilun Chen, Yu Sun, Ben Athiwaratkun, Claire Cardie, and Kilian Weinberger. 2016. Adversarial deep averaging networks for cross-lingual sentiment classification. *arXiv preprint arXiv:1606.01614*.

François Chollet et al. 2015. Keras. `https://keras.io`.

Hal Daume III. 2007. Frustratingly easy domain adaptation. In *Proceedings of the 45th Annual Meeting of the Association of Computational Linguistics*, pages 256–263.

Mark Dredze, Michael J Paul, Shane Bergsma, and Hieu Tran. 2013. Carmen: A twitter geolocation system with applications to public health. In *AAAI workshop on expanding the boundaries of health informatics using AI (HIAI)*, volume 23, page 45.

Jacob Eisenstein, Brendan O'Connor, Noah A. Smith, and Eric P. Xing. 2010. A latent variable model for geographic lexical variation. In *Empirical Methods in Natural Language Processing (EMNLP)*.

Yanai Elazar and Yoav Goldberg. 2018. Adversarial removal of demographic attributes from text data. In *Proceedings of the 2018 Conference on Empirical Methods in Natural Language Processing*, pages 11–21.

Yaroslav Ganin, Evgeniya Ustinova, Hana Ajakan, Pascal Germain, Hugo Larochelle, François Laviolette, Mario Marchand, and Victor Lempitsky. 2016. Domain-adversarial training of neural networks. *The Journal of Machine Learning Research*, 17(1):2096–2030.

Rahul Goel, Sandeep Soni, Naman Goyal, John Paparrizos, Hanna Wallach, Fernando Diaz, and Jacob Eisenstein. 2016. The social dynamics of language change in online networks. In *International Conference on Social Informatics*, pages 41–57. Springer.

Joanne Hinds and Adam N Joinson. 2018. What demographic attributes do our digital footprints reveal? a systematic review. *PloS one*, 13(11).

Sepp Hochreiter and Jürgen Schmidhuber. 1997. Long short-term memory. *Neural computation*, 9(8):1735–1780.

Dirk Hovy. 2015. Demographic factors improve classification performance. In *Proceedings of the 53rd Annual Meeting of the Association for Computational Linguistics and the 7th International Joint Conference on Natural Language Processing (Volume 1: Long Papers)*, volume 1, pages 752–762.

Dirk Hovy and Christoph Purschke. 2018. Capturing regional variation with distributed place representations and geographic retrofitting. In *Proceedings of the 2018 Conference on Empirical Methods in Natural Language Processing*, pages 4383–4394.

Xiaolei Huang, Lixing Liu, Kate Carey, Joshua Woolley, Stefan Scherer, and Brian Borsari. 2018. Modeling temporality of human intentions by domain adaptation. In *Proceedings of the 2018 Conference on Empirical Methods in Natural Language Processing*, pages 696–701.

Xiaolei Huang and Michael J Paul. 2018. Examining temporality in document classification. In *Proceedings of the 56th Annual Meeting of the Association for Computational Linguistics (Volume 2: Short Papers)*, volume 2, pages 694–699.

Xiaolei Huang, Michael C Smith, Michael J Paul, Dmytro Ryzhkov, Sandra C Quinn, David A Broniatowski, and Mark Dredze. 2017. Examining patterns of influenza vaccination in social media. In *AAAI Joint Workshop on Health Intelligence (W3PHIAI)*, pages 542–546.

Anders Johannsen, Dirk Hovy, and Anders Søgaard. 2015. Cross-lingual syntactic variation over age and gender. In *Proceedings of the Nineteenth Conference on Computational Natural Language Learning*, pages 103–112.

Mahesh Joshi, Mark Dredze, William W Cohen, and Carolyn P Rosé. 2013. Whats in a domain? multidomain learning for multi-attribute data. In *Proceedings of the 2013 Conference of the North American Chapter of the Association for Computational Linguistics: Human Language Technologies*, pages 685–690.

Soon-Gyo Jung, Jisun An, Haewoon Kwak, Joni Salminen, and Bernard Jim Jansen. 2018. Assessing the accuracy of four popular face recognition tools for inferring gender, age, and race. In *Twelfth International AAAI Conference on Web and Social Media*.

Yoon Kim. 2014. Convolutional neural networks for sentence classification. In *Proceedings of the 2014 Conference on Empirical Methods in Natural Language Processing (EMNLP)*, pages 1746–1751.

Young-Bum Kim, Karl Stratos, and Dongchan Kim. 2017. Domain attention with an ensemble of experts. In *Proceedings of the 55th Annual Meeting of the Association for Computational Linguistics (Volume 1: Long Papers)*, volume 1, pages 643–653.

Diederik P Kingma and Jimmy Ba. 2015. Adam: A method for stochastic optimization. In *Proceedings of the 3rd International Conference on Learning Representations (ICLR)*.

Yitong Li, Timothy Baldwin, and Trevor Cohn. 2018. Towards robust and privacy-preserving text representations. In *Proceedings of the 56th Annual Meeting of the Association for Computational Linguistics (Volume 2: Short Papers)*, volume 2, pages 25–30.

Pengfei Liu, Xipeng Qiu, and Xuanjing Huang. 2017. Adversarial multi-task learning for text classification. In *Proceedings of the 55th Annual Meeting of the Association for Computational Linguistics (Volume 1: Long Papers)*, volume 1, pages 1–10.

Veronica Lynn, Youngseo Son, Vivek Kulkarni, Niranjan Balasubramanian, and H Andrew Schwartz. 2017. Human centered nlp with user-factor adaptation. In *Proceedings of the 2017 Conference on Empirical Methods in Natural Language Processing*, pages 1146–1155.

Tomas Mikolov, Ilya Sutskever, Kai Chen, Greg S Corrado, and Jeff Dean. 2013. Distributed representations of words and phrases and their compositionality. In *Advances in neural information processing systems*, pages 3111–3119.

F. Pedregosa, G. Varoquaux, A. Gramfort, V. Michel, B. Thirion, O. Grisel, M. Blondel, P. Prettenhofer, R. Weiss, V. Dubourg, J. Vanderplas, A. Passos, D. Cournapeau, M. Brucher, M. Perrot, and E. Duchesnay. 2011. Scikit-learn: Machine learning in Python. *Journal of Machine Learning Research*, 12:2825–2830.

Jeffrey Pennington, Richard Socher, and Christopher Manning. 2014. Glove: Global vectors for word representation. In *Proceedings of the 2014 conference on empirical methods in natural language processing (EMNLP)*, pages 1532–1543.

Delip Rao, Michael Paul, Clay Fink, David Yarowsky, Timothy Oates, and Glen Coppersmith. 2011. Hierarchical bayesian models for latent attribute detection in social media. In *International Conference on Weblogs and Social Media (ICWSM)*.

Delip Rao, David Yarowsky, Abhishek Shreevats, and Manaswi Gupta. 2010. Classifying latent user attributes in Twitter. In *Workshop on Search and Mining User-generated Contents*.

Radim Řehůřek and Petr Sojka. 2010. Software Framework for Topic Modelling with Large Corpora. In *Proceedings of the LREC 2010 Workshop on New Challenges for NLP Frameworks*, pages 45–50, Valletta, Malta. ELRA. http://is.muni.cz/publication/884893/en.

Jessica Rose, Susan Mackey-Kallis, Len Shyles, Kelly Barry, Danielle Biagini, Colleen Hart, and Lauren Jack. 2012. Face it: The impact of gender on social media images. *Communication Quarterly*, 60(5):588–607.

Shannon Tien. 2018. Top twitter demographics that matter to social media marketers in 2018.

Svitlana Volkova, Yoram Bachrach, Michael Armstrong, and Vijay Sharma. 2015. Inferring latent user properties from texts published in social media. In *AAAI Conference on Artificial Intelligence (AAAI)*, Austin, TX.

Svitlana Volkova, Theresa Wilson, and David Yarowsky. 2013. Exploring demographic language variations to improve multilingual sentiment analysis in social media. In *Proceedings of the 2013 Conference on Empirical Methods in Natural Language Processing*, pages 1815–1827.

Suzanne Evans Wagner. 2012. Age grading in sociolinguistic theory. *Language and Linguistics Compass*, 6(6):371–382.

Davy Weissenbacher, Abeed Sarker, Michael J. Paul, and Graciela Gonzalez-Hernandez. 2018. Overview of the third social media mining for health (smm4h) shared tasks at emnlp 2018. In *Proceedings of the 2018 EMNLP Workshop SMM4H: The 3rd Social Media Mining for Health Applications Workshop and Shared Task*, pages 13–16. Association for Computational Linguistics.

Benjamin Wing and Jason Baldridge. 2014. Hierarchical discriminative classification for text-based geolocation. In *Empirical Methods in Natural Language Processing (EMNLP)*, pages 336–348.

Benjamin P Wing and Jason Baldridge. 2011. Simple supervised document geolocation with geodesic grids. In *Association for Computational Linguistics (ACL)*.

Yi Yang and Jacob Eisenstein. 2017. Overcoming language variation in sentiment analysis with social attention. *Transactions of the Association of Computational Linguistics*, 5(1):295–307.

Yelp. 2018. An introduction to yelp metrics as of september 30, 2018.

Jieyu Zhao, Tianlu Wang, Mark Yatskar, Vicente Ordonez, and Kai-Wei Chang. 2017. Men also like shopping: Reducing gender bias amplification using corpus-level constraints. *arXiv preprint arXiv:1707.09457*.

Abstract Graphs and Abstract Paths
for Knowledge Graph Completion

Vivi Nastase
University of Heidelberg
Heidelberg, Germany
nastase@cl.uni-heidelberg.de

Bhushan Kotnis
NEC Laboratories Europe GmbH
Heidelberg, Germany
bhushan.kotnis@gmail.com

Abstract

Knowledge graphs, which provide numerous facts in a machine-friendly format, are incomplete. Information that we induce from such graphs – e.g. entity embeddings, relation representations or patterns – will be affected by the imbalance in the information captured in the graph – by biasing representations, or causing us to miss potential patterns. To partially compensate for this situation we describe a method for representing knowledge graphs that capture an intensional representation of the original extensional information. This representation is very compact, and it abstracts away from individual links, allowing us to find better path candidates, as shown by the results of link prediction using this information.

1 Introduction

Knowledge graphs have become a very useful framework to organize and store knowledge. Their interconnected nature is not just a natural way to represent facts, but it has potential that the separate storage of facts does not have, such as: (i) we can use it as a relational model of meaning, and derive jointly representations for nodes (entities) and edges (relations); (ii) the structure can be explored to discover systematic patterns that reveal interesting and exploitable regularities, such as paths connecting nodes in direct relations, (iii) discovering and inducing new connections.

Link prediction methods in knowledge graphs (see (Nickel et al., 2016) for an overview) predict additional edges in the graph, based on induced node and edge representations that encode the structure of the graph and thus capture regularities (such as homophily).

Lao and Cohen (2010) introduced a new method that predicts direct links based on paths that connect the source and target nodes. Such paths are not only useful for link prediction (Lao et al.,

2011; Gardner et al., 2014), but also for finding explanations for direct links and help with targeted information extraction to fill in incomplete knowledge repositories (Yin et al., 2018; Zhou and Nastase, 2018).

These approaches rely on the structure of the knowledge graph, which is inherently incomplete. This incompleteness can affect the process in different ways, e.g. it leads to representations for nodes with few connection that are not very informative, it can miss relevant patterns/paths (or derive misleading patterns/paths).

In this paper we investigate whether a higher-level view of a graph – an abstract graph that captures an intensional view of the original extensional graph – can help derive more robust and informative patterns. Such patterns are paths (i.e. sequences of relations) that could be used not only for link prediction, but also for targeted information extraction for completing the graph with external information. This abstract graph will contain only one edge for each relation type, that will connect a node representing the relation's domain (or source) to its range (or target). Additional edges will link the nodes to capture set relations (intersection, subset, superset) information between the different relations' domains and ranges. This step drastically reduces the graph size, making many different graph processing approaches more tractable. We investigate whether in this graph that represents a more general version of the information in the original KG, good patterns/paths are stronger and easier to find, because the aggregated view compensates for individual missing edges throughout the graph. We test the extracted paths through the link prediction task on Freebase (Bollacker et al., 2008) and NELL (Carlson et al., 2010a), using Gardner et al. (2014)'s experimental set-up: pairs of nodes are represented using their connected paths as fea-

*Proceedings of the Eighth Joint Conference on Lexical and Computational Semantics (*SEM)*, pages 147–157
Minneapolis, June 6–7, 2019. ©2019 Association for Computational Linguistics

tures, and a model for predicting the direct relations is learned and tested on training and test sets for 24 relations in Freebase and 10 relations in NELL. Our analysis shows that we find different and much fewer paths than the PRA method does (mostly because the abstract paths do not contain back-and-forth sequences of generalizing or type relations). The paths found in the abstract graphs lead to better performance on NELL than the PRA paths, which could be explained by the fact that NELL's relation inventory was designed to capture interdependencies (Carlson et al., 2010a). On Freebase the results we obtain are lower, but this could be due to a different negative sampling process. Inspection of the paths produced reveal that they seem to capture legitimate dependencies.

2   Related Work

Representing facts in a knowledge graph has multiple advantages: (i) they provide knowledge in an easily accessible and machine-friendly format; (ii) they facilitate various ways of encoding this information and deriving representations for nodes and edges that reflect their connectivity in the graph; (iii) they allow for the discovery of connectivity patterns, and possibly more.

In recent years, projecting the knowledge graph in an n-dimensional vector space, or learning embeddings for predicting missing facts has attracted a lot of interest. Embedding models aim to map entities, relations and triples to vector space such that additional facts can be inferred from known facts using notions of vector similarity. A class of embedding models that aim to factorize the graph are termed as latent factor models. Neural network based models such as ER-MLP (Dong et al., 2014), NTN (Socher et al., 2013), RNNs (Neelakantan et al., 2015; Das et al., 2016) and Graph CNNs (Schlichtkrull et al., 2018) are examples of embedding models while RESCAL (Nickel et al., 2012), DistMult (Yang et al., 2015), TransE (Bordes et al., 2013), ComplEx (Trouillon et al., 2017) are examples of latent factor models.

Lao and Cohen (2010) introduced a novel way to exploit information in knowledge graphs: using weighted extracted paths as features in four different recommendation tasks, which can be modeled as typed proximity queries. The idea of using paths in the graph has then been applied to the task of link prediction (Lao et al., 2011), and extended to incorporate textual information (Gard-

ner et al., 2014). Lao et al. (2011) obtain paths for given node pairs using random walks over the knowledge graph. To be used as features shared by multiple instances, the information about nodes on the paths is removed, transforming the actual paths into "meta-paths".

The paths themselves can be incorporated in different ways in a model – as features (Lao et al., 2011; Gardner et al., 2014), as Horn clauses to provide rules for inference in KGs whether directly or through scores that represent the strength of the path as a direct relation (Neelakantan et al., 2015; Guu et al., 2015), also taking into account information about intermediary nodes (Das et al., 2017; Yin et al., 2018). Gardner and Mitchell (2015) perform link prediction using random walks but do not attempt to connect a source and target node, but rather to characterize the local structure around a (source or target) node using such localized paths. Using these *subgraph features* leads to better results for the knowledge graph completion task.

We focus here on discovering useful and explanatory paths, not on optimizing or further improving the KGC task. Using paths can lead to interpretable models because the paths can help explain the predicted fact. Meng et al. (2015) present a method to automate the induction of meta-paths in large heterogeneous information networks (a.k.a. knowledge graphs) for given node pairs, even if the given node pairs are not connected by a direct relation.

Path information is also found to improve performance since paths help the model learn logical rules. However, mining paths from a large knowledge graph is often computationally expensive since it involves performing a traversal through the graph. To overcome this limitation (Das et al., 2017) proposed deep reinforcement learning and (Chen et al., 2018) proposed RNNS for generating paths. However, many datasets suffer from paths sparsity, lack of enough paths connecting source target pairs, resulting in poor performance for many relations.

Wang et al. (2013) have a different approach – they start with patterns in the form of first-order probabilistic rules, which they then ground in a small subgraph of a large knowledge graph.

The approach we present here combines different elements of these previous approaches in a novel way: we build an abstract graph to find patterns that would be similar to those used by (Wang et al., 2013). To test the quality of these paths we ground them using the original KG and use these grounded paths in a learning framework similar to (Gardner et al., 2014).

3 Abstract Graphs and Abstract Paths

Knowledge graphs are incomplete in an imbalanced way. Figures 1a-1b show how much the relation and node frequencies for Freebase 15k and NELL vary, and the fact that numerous nodes and edges have very low frequency (each data point corresponds to a node/relation, and the value is the degree of the node/frequency of the relation respectively). Freebase and NELL have a helpful characteristic: they have strongly typed relations, i.e. the source and target of a relation have a very specific type. NELL for example, has relations such as like *ActorStarredinMovie*, *StateHasLake*, and Freebase has */film/film/rating*, */book/literary_series/author*, whose arguments have type *Person, Movie, State*, etc.

Previous work has shown that using node type information – provided in Freebase through the domain and range types for each relation – can help optimize computation for link prediction by filtering the entity matrix for each relation based on the relation's domain and range types (Chang et al., 2014), improve prediction by adding a factor in the loss function that accounts for the type of the entities involved in a relation (Kotnis and Nastase, 2017), or improve predictions based on paths in the graph by using the types of intermediary entities (Yin et al., 2018).

Entity types and the type of the domain and range of a relation have been proven to be useful for improving link prediction models. We investigate here the hypothesis that by relying on the fact that such strong constraints on the arguments of relations in Freebase exist, we can build an intensional graph of the knowledge repository that is smaller and thus easier to analyze than the full KG. We also hypothesize that at this abstract level we can induce better patterns/paths that are indicative of direct relations, because individual missing relation instances will not obfuscate useful patterns. We verify whether these patterns are good by testing their usefulness for link prediction. Finding qualitative patterns would have additional benefits, as they could be used to explain direct relation, and

fill in the KG through targeted information extraction (Zhou and Nastase, 2018).

3.1 Abstract graphs

A knowledge graph (KG) is an extensional representation of a relation schema, where each instance of a relation type r corresponds to an edge connecting two nodes, a source s and a target t, usually represented as a triple: $< s, r, t >$. We replace this representation with an intesional representation, where we have only one edge for each relation type, and draw additional edges to capture set relations (intersection, subset, superset) between the (original graph's) relations' domain and ranges. These edges are weighed with the size of the overlap between the sets. Formally:

for a knowledge graph
$$\mathcal{KG} = (\mathcal{V}, \mathcal{E}, \mathcal{R})$$
with:
vertices $\mathcal{V} = \{v_1, ..., v_n\}$,
relation types $\mathcal{R} = \{r_1, ..., r_k\}$
relation instances (i.e. edges)
$\mathcal{E} = \{(v_i, r_x, v_j) | v_i, v_j \in \mathcal{V}; r_x \in \mathcal{R}\}$,

we build the abstract graph
$$\mathcal{KG}_A = (\mathcal{V}_A, \mathcal{E}_A, \mathcal{R}_A)$$
with:
vertices $\mathcal{V}_A = \{V_{1,s}, V_{1,t}, V_{2,s}, V_{2,t}, ..., V_{k,s}, V_{k,t}\}$, where:
the source node of relation r_i in the abstract graph is the *set of source nodes* (the domain) of relation r_i in $\mathcal{KG}$:
$V_{i,s} = \{v_x | (v_x, r_i, *) \in \mathcal{E}\}$
the target node of relation r_i in the abstract graph is *the set of target nodes* (the range) of r_i in $\mathcal{KG}$:
$V_{i,t} = \{v_x | (*, r_i, v_x) \in E\}$
relation types $\mathcal{R}_A = \mathcal{R} \cup \mathcal{R}_{set}$ where:
$\mathcal{R}$ is the set of relation types of $\mathcal{KG}$,
$\mathcal{R}_{set} = \{intersection, subset, superset\}$[1].
weighted edges
$$\mathcal{E}_A = \{(V_{i,s}, r_i, V_{i,t}, 1) | r_i \in \mathcal{R}, V_{i,s}, V_{i,t} \in \mathcal{V}_A\}$$
$$\cup \{(V_{i,x}, r, V_{j,y}, w) | r \in \mathcal{R}_{set}, V_{i,x}, V_{j,y} \in \mathcal{V}_A$$
$$w = overlap(V_{i,x}, V_{j,y}))\}$$

where the weight of a set relation between $\mathcal{KG}_A$'s nodes quantifies the overlap between the two sets:
$$overlap(V_{i,x}, V_{j,y}) = \frac{|V_{i,x} \cap V_{j,y}|}{|V_{i,x}|}$$

---

[1] There is no *equal* relation because if two sets are equal there will be only one node to represent them.

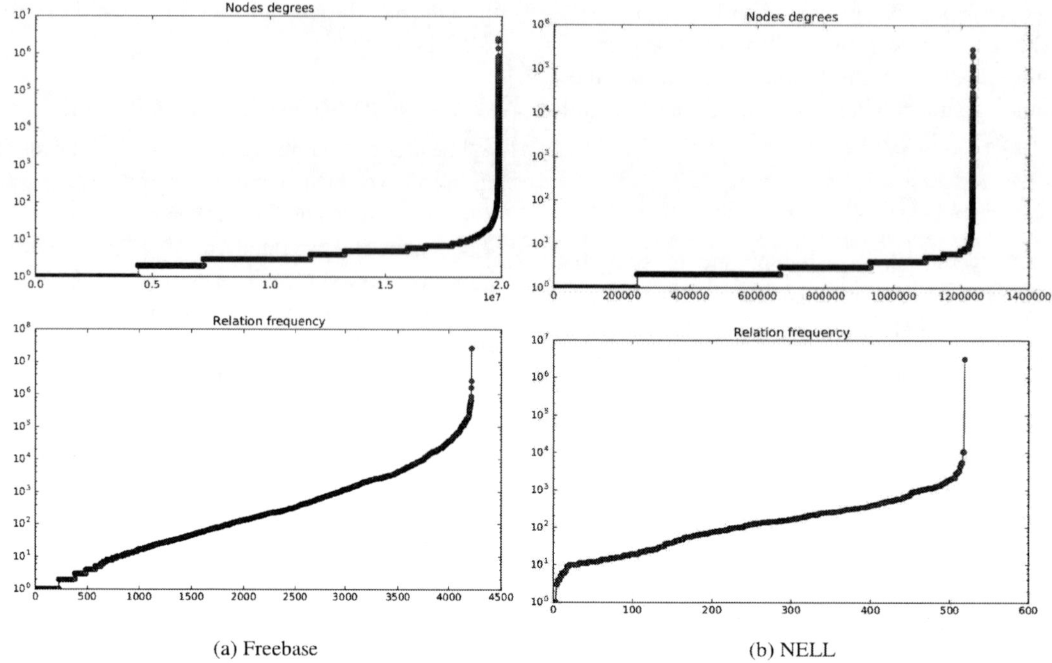

Figure 1: Knowledge graphs statistics on a logarithmic scale: relation and nodes frequencies for Freebase and NELL (the version used by (Gardner et al., 2014) and in this paper). Every data point is the degree of a node (top plots), or frequency of a relation (bottom plots). The data points are ordered monotonically, the x axis is just an index.

Building such a graph makes sense only for knowledge repositories that have strongly typed relations – like Freebase and NELL – but we do not require knowledge of the types of the relations' domains and ranges. Such information is not fine-grained enough: for example, the relation *capital* has a type *City* as a domain, but capital cities are a very small subset of the set of all cities. Using an "atomic" node to represent the domain/range of a relation would not allow us to make finer grained connections and distinctions between the domains and ranges of the existing relations.

Figure 2 shows a subset of the abstract graph built from the Freebase dataset. The blue edges are set relations – intersection, superset, subset – between the domains and ranges of a subset of the relations in the dataset. The black edges correspond to the actual relations in the dataset.

3.2 Abstract paths

The Path Ranking Algorithm formalism originally proposed by (Lao and Cohen, 2010) performs two main steps to represent of a pair of nodes in a graph: (i) feature selection – adding paths that connect the node pair; (ii) feature computation –

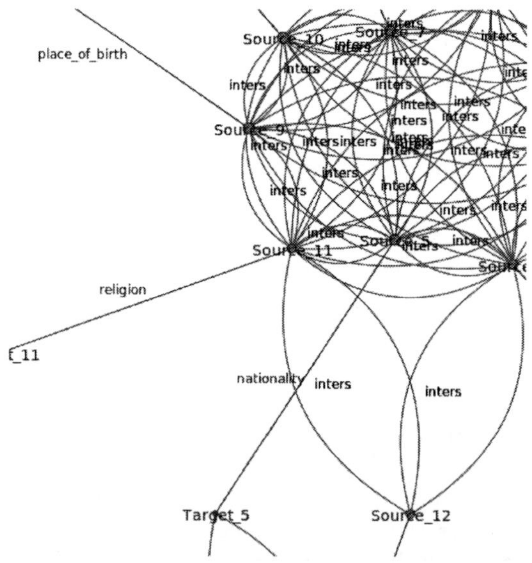

Figure 2: An abstract graph built on a subset of the Freebase dataset. The blue edges are set relations between the domains and ranges of the included relations, the black edges are the actual relations from the dataset.

KB variation	Freebase				NELL			
	Original graph		Abstract graph		Original graph		Abstract graph	
	# nodes	# edges	# nodes	# edges	# nodes	# edges	# nodes	# edges
KB	20M	67M	4086	22,946	1.2M	3.4M	587	2746
KB + SVO	30M	97M	35,905	1.7M	20M	71M	68,149	512,503
KB + Vector SVO	30M	97M	4112	23,257	1.3M	4.3M	613	3383
KB + Clustered SVO	30M	125M	4138	24,098	1.3M	3.9M	639	3818

Table 1: Graph statistics on the datasets used by (Gardner et al., 2014), and their abstract versions

associating a value for each added path.

Obtaining paths from a large graph is a computationally intensive problem, particularly in graphs that have numerous nodes with high degrees. Figure 1a shows that about 60% of Freebase nodes have degree higher than 10, which leads to an exponential growth in the number of paths starting in a node. Algorithms that harness path information often mine paths either by performing costly random walks (Guu et al., 2015), traversals (Gardner et al., 2014; Neelakantan et al., 2015; Das et al., 2016) or by constructing paths through generative models (Das et al., 2017; Ding et al., 2018). Here, we adopt a different approach, by abstracting the graph first, then finding paths in this graph through traversal algorithms.

For a relation r_i, we start at its domain (source) node $V_{i,s}$ and search for a path to its range (target) node $V_{i,t}$ using breadth first search. We constrain this path to contain at most k "proper" relations[2], and we do not allow consecutive set relations, thus forcing the algorithm to move from one "proper" relation to another through a set relation that connects the range of one with the domain of the next. An abstract path, just like a meta-path extracted by previous work, is a sequence of relation types: $\pi_j = < r_{j,1}, r_{j,2}, ... r_{j,m} >$, some of which are "proper" relations, some are set relations.

Because of the more general view of the graph, we lose information about individual paths (i.e. instances of a path in the original graph). Because of this, the paths we extract are hypothetical, but will have associated a confidence score based on the frequency of occurrence of relations in the original KG, and the strength of the connection of the range of one relation on the path with the domain of the next one. The weight of an abstract path π_j is computed as:

$$w(\pi_j) = \prod_{i=1}^{m} w(r_{j,i})$$

---

[2]In our experiments we used $k = 5$

where the weight $w(r_{j,i})$ of an individual relation is defined based on whether $r_{i,j}$ is a "proper" relation or a set relation as:

$$w(r_{j,i}) = \begin{cases} \frac{|\{<*, r_{j,i}, *> \in \mathcal{E}\}|}{|\mathcal{E}|} & \text{if } r_{j,i} \in \mathcal{R} \\ overlap(r_{j,i}) & \text{if } r_{j,i} \in \mathcal{R}_{set} \end{cases}$$

We use this weight to rank abstract relations for potential filtering, and to compute the weight of its grounding for specific node pairs.

3.3 Grounded paths

The abstract paths are hypothetical paths that could connect the source s and target t of a $< s, r, t >$ tuple. They can be used in different ways, e.g. (i) as features in a link prediction system (e.g. (Gardner et al., 2014)), (ii) to fill in larger portions of the graph by producing, rather than finding, groundings of the path for specific instances.

In the work presented here we test the abstract paths through the link prediction task, so we will try to ground abstract paths for relation instances in the training and test data. After finding the set of abstract paths $\{\pi_{i,r}\}$ associated with a relation r, for a given instance of the relation $r - < s, r, t > -$ we can (try to) ground the paths as follows: (i) we first eliminate set relations from the abstract paths: at this point set relations between relation types domain and ranges are not useful (they were necessary only for the connectivity and search process in the abstract graph). Set relations have no counterpart in the extensional graph, as at this level nodes themselves make the connection between successive relations (ii) starting at the source node, we follow again a breadth first traversal, constraining at each step the type of relation to follow based on the "cleaned up" abstract path.

We compute the weight of a grounded path $gp = < v_0, r_{x_1}, v_1, ..., v_{l-1}, r_{x_l}, v_l >$ (where $v_0 = s$ and $v_l = t$) as a combination of the weight of the corresponding abstract path $\pi = < r_1, ..., r_m >$ ($r_{x_i} \in \pi$) and specific information for the current node pair (s, t):

$$w(\pi) = \prod_{i=1}^{l} w(v_{i-1}, r_i, v_i)$$

where the weights of the relations on the grounded path reflect the specificity of the relation to its source node:

$$w(v_{i-1}, r_i, v_i) = \begin{cases} \frac{1}{|\{<v_{i-1}, r_i, *> \in E\}|} & \text{if } r_i \in gp \\ 1 & \text{if } r_i \in \mathcal{R}_{set} \end{cases}$$

4 Experiments

Because we want to compare the abstract paths found using the abstract graph with paths found using PRA, we use the experimental set-up of (Gardner et al., 2014), where we replace the feature selection and feature computation steps with the approach presented here. A big difference will be caused by the negative sampling, which also makes the results not directly comparable. The issues are explained in the **negative sampling** paragraph below. The data thus obtained is used for training a linear regression model (similarly to (Gardner et al., 2014)), and tested on the provided test sets and evaluated using mean average precision (MAP).

4.1 Data

We build abstract graphs and paths from the Freebase and NELL data described in (Gardner et al., 2014). We then use the extracted paths for link prediction.

The graphs built by Gardner et al. (2014) cover several variations, where the KGs were enhanced with $< subject, verb, object >$ triples extracted from dependency parses of ClueWeb documents. Table 1 shows the statistics for each original and abstract graph. The generated abstract graph is several degrees of magnitude smaller compared to the original KG. The abstract graph approach we present here does not fit well the combination of the knowledge base (Freebase or NELL) with unstructured SVO triples, because we rely on strongly typed relations to build node sets. The SVO triples bring in numerous low frequency relations, that without additional processing are not beneficial. The results presented by Gardner et al. (2014) show that this configuration very rarely (and never overall) leads to better results than the other graph variations. The numerous relation types brought in by the SVO triples also lead to high computation time for the abstract graph: its shortcoming is the computation of set relations between the different relations' domains and ranges,

KG	Avg. no. inst	min	max
NELL train	650.7	81	1468
NELL test	163.2	21	367
Freebase train	122.9	10	600
Freebase test	41.6	4	200

Table 2: Statistics on the size of the training and test sets

which grows quadratically with the number of relation types. We will skip this graph variation in the rest of the experiments presented here.

Gardner et al. (2014) use these graphs to generate paths for augmenting the representation of node pairs, for link prediction, for a subset of 24 relation types from Freebase's inventory, and 10 relations from NELL. Each relation has a training and test set, whose numbers vary quite a bit, as shown through the statistics in Table 2.

Negative sampling The number of negative instances used in (Gardner et al., 2014) is not clearly stated. Both the number and methods of generating the negative samples can impact the results (Kotnis and Nastase, 2018). We use (up to) 200 negative samples for each positive pair: for a pair (s, t) in the provided training or test sets for each relation r, we make 100 negative samples by corrupting the source s, and 100 negative samples by corrupting the target t. The corrupted s' and t' are chosen from r's domain $V_{r,s}$ and range $V_{r,t}$ respectively, such that these corrupted triples are not part of the training, test or graph. If 100 instances do not exist, we extract as many as possible.

$$Neg(s, r, t) = \{(s', r, t)|s' \in V_{r,s}, (s', r, t) \notin \mathcal{E}\}$$
$$\cup \{(s, r, t')|t' \in V_{r,t}, (s, r, t') \notin \mathcal{E}\}$$

Because the relations are strongly typed, producing negative instances by corrupting the source/target nodes from the relation's domain and range leads to difficult negative instances. Instances with source and target nodes that don't match the argument types of the direct relation we want to predict can be filtered out before the link prediction.

Representing instances For each of these 24 Freebase and 10 NELL relations we mine paths in the abstract graph using depth first traversal. An example of abstract path found for the NELL rela-

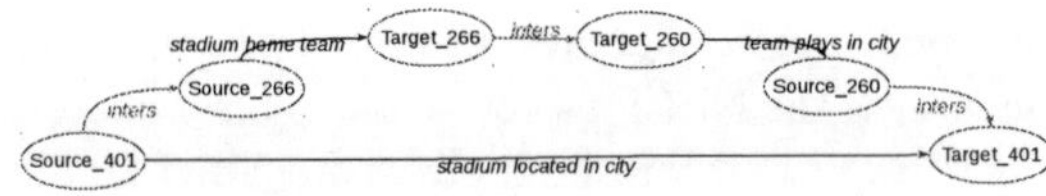

Figure 3: An abstract path for relation *StadiumLocatedInCity* from NELL

tion *StadiumLocatedInCity* is shown in figure 3.

Each of the 24 Freebase and 10 NELL relations has a set of training and test examples. After building abstract paths, for each instance $< s, r, t >$ in these datasets we will ground the corresponding abstract paths as described in Section 3.3. For each relation type the set of features representing the corresponding data will be twice the number of abstract paths. We produce two features for each abstract path: one that is the weight of this path, and one that is the weight of its grounding for a given relation instance. If a relation instance does not have a grounding for an abstract path, the values of these features will be 0.

4.2 Results and discussion

The overall results of the experiments are presented in Table 3, and the relation-level results are in Tables 4 for NELL, and 5 for Freebase.

graph	Freebase		NELL	
	MAP_G	MAP_{KG_A}	MAP_G	MAP_{KG_A}
KB	0.278	0.186	0.193	0.246
KBCl	0.326	0.233	0.276	0.411
KBVec	0.350	0.223	0.301	0.306

Table 3: Results on the three graph variations of Freebase and NELL as reported by (Gardner et al., 2014) (G) and using abstract graphs (KG_A).

Overall, the results indicate that enhancing Freebase and NELL with additional facts from textual sources leads to better results, particularly when these additional facts ($<$ $subject, verb, object >$ triples) are processed and clustered using low dimensional dense representations (Gardner et al.; Gardner et al. (2014; 2013) use embeddings obtained by running PCA on the matrix of SVO triples).

Freebase has 4200+ relation types, and NELL 500+. More than 500 relation types in Freebase have less than 10 instances, wheres NELL does not have this issue (see Figures 1a and 1b). Because we test the approach for knowledge graph completion using classification based on the patterns as features, having features that appear too

Relation	PRA best	KB	KB Cl	KB Vec
ActorStarredInMovie	**0.037**	0	0	0
AthletePlaysForTeam	**0.589**	0.145	0.089	0.136
CityLocatedInCountry	**0.347**	0.078	0.071	0.057
JournalistWritesForPub.	0.319	0.317	**0.515**	0.436
RiverFlowsThroughCity	0.076	0.027	**0.146**	0.058
SportsTeamPos.ForSport	0.217	0	**0.615**	0
StadiumLocatedInCity	0.321	0.316	**0.414**	0.110
StateHasLake	0.000	0	**0.688**	0.681
TeamPlaysInLeague	**0.947**	0.910	0.916	0.917
WriterWroteBook	0.202	**0.661**	0.659	0.661

Table 4: Relation results for the NELL KB. The second column is the best result for each relation reported by (Gardner et al., 2014).

few times will not help the system find a robust model. For the purpose of the presented experiments we filter the Freebase abstract graph to use only relation types that have at least 10 instances (Table 1 shows the statistics for this configuration).

It is not surprising that overall the results for NELL are higher – NELL has been designed on the principle of coupled learning, where connections between different relations are the basis of the resource and its continuous growth (Carlson et al., 2010b). It also has more training data for each relation (see table in Section 4.1). There is no consistent trend – for some relations using the paths extracted with this approach leads to better results, for others it does not (although, as we frequently mentioned, the fact that we used different negative sampling methods, the results are not directly comparable).

A more complete picture emerges when we look at the paths found, and compare them with the paths obtained with the PRA approach[3]. For all Freebase KG configurations, Gardner et al. (2014) have 1000 paths for most relations (approx. 6 of the relations have between 230 and 973). For NELL the number varies more, between 58 and 5509, 6 of the relations have more than 1000 metapaths. With the abstract graphs the numbers are much lower. For Freebase we find between 1 and 258 abstract paths, most of the relations (21) having fewer than 30 abstract paths for all KG configurations. For NELL we find between 1 and 157 paths, 5 of the relations having more than 100 ab-

---

[3]We used the archive shared by Matt Gardner `https://github.com/matt-gardner/pra`, in particular the translated paths for each relation.

Relation	PRA best	KB	KB Cl	KB Vec
/amusement/parks/park_rides	0.013	**0.503**	0.503	0.503
/arch./arch./ struc._designed	**0.376**	0	0	0
/astronomy/constel./contains	0.017	**0.503**	0.503	0.503
/autom./auto._class/examples	0.006	0	0	0
/autom./model/auto._class	**0.768**	0.009	0.009	0.009
/aviation/airline/hubs	**0.336**	0.279	0.279	0.330
/book/literary_series/author	**0.830**	0.461	0.461	0.461
/comp./sw_genre/sw._in_genre	0.001	**0.002**	0.002	0.002
/edu./field_of_study/ journals_in_this_disc.	0.003	**0.005**	0.005	0.005
/film/film/rating	**0.914**	0.087	0.096	0.136
/geo./island/body_of_water	**0.602**	0.286	0.286	0.286
/geo./lake/basin_countries	**0.437**	0.083	0.075	0.112
/geo./lake/cities	0.177	0.003	**0.442**	0.442
/geo./river/cities	0.066	0	**0.127**	0.127
/ice_h./h._player/h._position	**0.364**	0.007	0.007	0.007
/loc./adm._division/ country	**0.991**	0.189	0.199	0.199
/medicine/disease/symptoms	0.078	0.035	**0.088**	0.060
/medicine/drug/drug_class	0.169	0	**0.212**	0.002
/people/ethnicity/lang._spoken	**0.226**	0.128	0.135	0.115
/spaceflight/astronaut/miss.	**0.848**	0.272	0.272	0.272
/transp./bridge/body_of_water_spanned	**0.727**	0.190	0.384	0.384
/tv/tv_prog._cr./prog._created	0.181	**0.646**	0.646	0.646
/vis._art/art_period_movement/ assoc._artists	0.046	0.318	**0.340**	0.340
/vis._art/vis._artist/assoc._per._or_mov.	0.295	0.474	0.509	**0.516**

Table 5: Statistics of the number of instances in the training and testing sets for the relations analyzed, and the number of paths extracted for each set (in parentheses the number of abstract paths for each graph).

stract paths. The overlap between the sets of paths discovered with the two methods is very small: for Freebase the average overlap with respect to PRA is around 0.004 (for the different graph configurations), and with respect to the abstract paths around 0.2; for NELL around 0.003 relative to PRA and 0.27 relative to the abstract paths.

We note that overall, the system found more paths than what could be grounded for the given training instances for both Freebase and NELL. Another general observation is that relations for which we found the most patterns (*AthletePlaysForTeam* and *StateHasLake* for NELL, */medicine/disease/symptoms* and */film/film/rating* for Freebase) do not necessarily perform the best.

NELL The results for each relation in terms of average precision are presented in Table 4. We include the best result on PRA (on any variation of the graph), as reported by (Gardner et al., 2014), although since we used different negative

instances the results are not directly comparable. Several of the NELL target relations have interesting patterns in the abstract graph, in particular StadiumLocatedInCity, TeamPlaysInLeague. In several cases, the algorithm has discovered "parallel" relations. For the relation *WriterWroteBook*, the most useful feature is the relation *AgentCreated*, which connects many of the source-target pairs in the *WriterWroteBook* relation. We found a similar situation with the relation *JournalistWritesForPublication*, which has *WorksFor* paralleling it in the graph.

Looking at specific relations, the paths extracted from the abstract graph are more focused. An example of this is the relation *StadiumLocatedInCity*. Numerous paths detected by PRA seem irrelevant, as illustrated by the following (highest frequency) paths:

$$generalizations \rightarrow generalizations^{-1}$$
$$generalizations \rightarrow generalizations^{-1}$$
$$\rightarrow generalizations \rightarrow generalizations^{-1}$$
$$generalizations \rightarrow generalizations^{-1}$$
$$\rightarrow CityHotels$$
$$generalizations \rightarrow generalizations^{-1}$$
$$\rightarrow StadiumLocatedInCity$$
$$generalizations \rightarrow generalizations^{-1}$$
$$\rightarrow BuildingLocatedInCity$$

The paths found in the abstract graph, as the example in Figure 3 shows, seem to capture more informative relation interdependencies.

Our system does not always find high quality patterns. It also finds surprising and most probably idiosyncratic patterns. In particular, for the *StateHasLake* relation, from the paths found, some very unexpected ones had groundings for the given training data:

$$Agric.Prod.GrowingInStateOrProv.^{-1}$$
$$\rightarrow Agric.Prod.GrowingInStateOrProv.$$
$$\rightarrow StateHasLake$$

$$MaleMovedToStateOrProv.^{-1}$$
$$\rightarrow MaleMovedToStateOrProv.$$
$$\rightarrow StateHasLake$$

While the first rule could be justified (having lakes may favour the growing of certain types of agricultural products), the second one seems completely accidental. With a stronger filtering method based on the computed path scores we could eliminate some of these false patterns.

Paths extracted using PRA
$/type/object/type \rightarrow /type/object/type^{-1} \rightarrow /film/content\_rating/film^{-1}$
$/film/performance/film^{-1} \rightarrow /type/object/type \rightarrow /type/object/type^{-1}$ $\rightarrow /film/performance/film \rightarrow /film/film/rating$
$/type/object/type \rightarrow /type/object/type^{-1} \rightarrow /film/film/rating$
$/film/performance/film^{-1} \rightarrow /type/object/type \rightarrow /type/object/type^{-1}$ $\rightarrow /film/performance/film \rightarrow /film/content\_rating/film^{-1}$
$/film/film\_genre/films\_in\_this\_genre^{-1} \rightarrow /film/film/genre^{-1} \rightarrow /film/film/rating$
$/film/film/genre \rightarrow /film/film/genre^{-1} \rightarrow /film/film/rating$
$/film/film/language \rightarrow /film/film/language^{-1} \rightarrow /film/film/rating$
Paths extracted using abstract graphs
$/film/film/edited\_by \rightarrow /film/editor/film \rightarrow /film/film/rating$
$/film/film/directed\_by \rightarrow /film/producer/film \rightarrow /film/film/rating$
$/film/film/cinematography \rightarrow /film/cinematographer/film \rightarrow /film/film/rating$
$/film/film/costume\_design\_by \rightarrow /film/film/costumer\_designer\_costume\_design\_for\_film$ $\rightarrow /film/film/rating$
$/film/film/music \rightarrow /film/music/contributor\_film \rightarrow /film/film/rating$
$/film/film/film\_production\_design\_by \rightarrow /film/film\_prod.\_designer/films\_prod.\_designed$ $\rightarrow /film/film/rating$

Table 6: Sample relations extracted using PRA and abstract graphs, respectively

Freebase The fine-grained results for Freebase, in terms of average precision, are presented in Table 5. We make the same observation as for NELL – for several relations, the paths obtained from the abstract graph are different and more focused than the PRA ones. For the relation */film/film/rating* for which the PRA approach gives very high results with the abstract graph has lower scores, some of the highest scoring paths found by the PRA are presented in Table 6. For comparison we also include the highest rated paths obtained using the abstract graph. While some of these paths were also found by the PRA, they are much lower in the list of extracted paths. The highest weighted paths found in the abstract graph connect specific properties of films with their rating.

An archive containing the abstract graphs, the abstract paths, the train/test data, negative samples and the groundings of the abstract paths for these relations for the variations of Freebase and NELL presented here is available from the University of Heidelberg[4].

5 Conclusions

We proposed and evaluated a method for obtaining paths from large knowledge graphs by compressing them into their intensional versions. We relied on the fact that these graphs have strongly typed relations, such that their domain and ranges consist of homogeneous sets that have overlaps only with the domains and ranges of a small number of other relations. This compression step leads to a smaller graph to work with, where we found paths that seem to capture qualitative patterns in the data. The results on link prediction on Freebase and NELL show the advantage of using such paths for some of the relations, but the task does not showcase the full potential of this representation. Further work will explore the potential of such patterns as explanatory links between directly connected nodes, or as a source of additional patterns for filling in the knowledge graphs not only with missing links, but also missing nodes, either by predicting intermediate nodes or by using the paths as patterns for targeted information extraction.

---

[4] `https://www.cl.uni-heidelberg.de/ english/research/downloads/resource_ pages/AbstractGraphs/AbstractGraphs. shtml`

References

Kurt Bollacker, Colin Evans, Praveen Paritosh, Tim Sturge, and Jamie Taylor. 2008. Freebase: A collaboratively created graph database for structuring human knowledge. In *Proceedings of the 2008 ACM SIGMOD International Conference on Management of Data*, SIGMOD '08, pages 1247–1250, New York, NY, USA. ACM.

Antoine Bordes, Nicolas Usunier, Alberto Garcia-Duran, Jason Weston, and Oksana Yakhnenko. 2013. Translating embeddings for modeling multi-relational data. In C. J. C. Burges, L. Bottou, M. Welling, Z. Ghahramani, and K. Q. Weinberger, editors, *Advances in Neural Information Processing Systems 26*, pages 2787–2795. Curran Associates, Inc.

Andrew Carlson, Justin Betteridge, Bryan Kisiel, Burr Settles, Estevam R. Hruschka, and Tom M. Mitchell. 2010a. Toward an architecture for never-ending language learning. In *AAAI*.

Andrew Carlson, Justin Betteridge, Richard C. Wang, Estevam R. Hruschka, Jr., and Tom M. Mitchell. 2010b. Coupled semi-supervised learning for information extraction. In *Proceedings of the Third ACM International Conference on Web Search and Data Mining*, WSDM '10, pages 101–110, New York, NY, USA. ACM.

Kai-Wei Chang, Wen-tau Yih, Bishan Yang, and Christopher Meek. 2014. Typed tensor decomposition of knowledge bases for relation extraction. In *Proceedings of the 2014 Conference on Empirical Methods in Natural Language Processing (EMNLP)*, pages 1568–1579. Association for Computational Linguistics.

Wenhu Chen, Wenhan Xiong, Xifeng Yan, and William Wang. 2018. Variational knowledge graph reasoning. *arXiv preprint arXiv:1803.06581*.

Rajarshi Das, Shehzaad Dhuliawala, Manzil Zaheer, Luke Vilnis, Ishan Durugkar, Akshay Krishnamurthy, Alex Smola, and Andrew McCallum. 2017. Go for a walk and arrive at the answer: Reasoning over paths in knowledge bases using reinforcement learning. *arXiv preprint arXiv:1711.05851*.

Rajarshi Das, Arvind Neelakantan, David Belanger, and Andrew McCallum. 2016. Chains of reasoning over entities, relations, and text using recurrent neural networks. *arXiv preprint arXiv:1607.01426*.

Boyang Ding, Quan Wang, Bin Wang, and Li Guo. 2018. Improving knowledge graph embedding using simple constraints. *arXiv preprint arXiv:1805.02408*.

Xin Dong, Evgeniy Gabrilovich, Geremy Heitz, Wilko Horn, Ni Lao, Kevin Murphy, Thomas Strohmann, Shaohua Sun, and Wei Zhang. 2014. Knowledge vault: a web-scale approach to probabilistic knowledge fusion. In *KDD*.

Matt Gardner and Tom Mitchell. 2015. Efficient and expressive knowledge base completion using subgraph feature extraction. In *Proceedings of the 2015 Conference on Empirical Methods in Natural Language Processing*, pages 1488–1498. Association for Computational Linguistics.

Matt Gardner, Partha Talukdar, Jayant Krishnamurthy, and Tom Mitchell. 2014. Incorporating vector space similarity in random walk inference over knowledge bases. In *Proceedings of the 2014 Conference on Empirical Methods in Natural Language Processing (EMNLP)*, pages 397–406, Doha, Qatar. Association for Computational Linguistics.

Matt Gardner, Partha Pratim Talukdar, Bryan Kisiel, and Tom Mitchell. 2013. Improving learning and inference in a large knowledge-base using latent syntactic cues. In *Proceedings of the 2013 Conference on Empirical Methods in Natural Language Processing*, pages 833–838, Seattle, Washington, USA. Association for Computational Linguistics.

Kelvin Guu, John Miller, and Percy Liang. 2015. Traversing knowledge graphs in vector space. In *Proceedings of the 2015 Conference on Empirical Methods in Natural Language Processing*, pages 318–327. Association for Computational Linguistics.

Bhushan Kotnis and Vivi Nastase. 2017. Learning knowledge graph embeddings with type regularizer. In *Proceedings of the Knowledge Capture Conference*, K-CAP 2017, pages 19:1–19:4. ACM.

Bhushan Kotnis and Vivi Nastase. 2018. Analysis of the impact of negative sampling on link prediction in knowledge graphs. In *Workshop on Knowledge Base Construction, Reasoning and Mining (KB-COM)*.

Ni Lao and William W. Cohen. 2010. Relational retrieval using a combination of path-constrained random walks. *Mach. Learn.*, 81(1):53–67.

Ni Lao, Tom Mitchell, and William W. Cohen. 2011. Random walk inference and learning in a large scale knowledge base. In *Proceedings of the Conference on Empirical Methods in Natural Language Processing*, EMNLP '11, pages 529–539, Stroudsburg, PA, USA. Association for Computational Linguistics.

Changping Meng, Reynold Cheng, Silviu Maniu, Pierre Senellart, and Wangda Zhang. 2015. Discovering meta-paths in large heterogeneous information networks. In *Proceedings of the 24th International Conference on World Wide Web*, WWW '15, pages 754–764.

Arvind Neelakantan, Benjamin Roth, and Andrew McCallum. 2015. Compositional vector space models for knowledge base completion. In *Proceedings of the 53rd Annual Meeting of the Association for Computational Linguistics and the 7th International*

Joint Conference on Natural Language Processing (Volume 1: Long Papers), pages 156–166. Association for Computational Linguistics.

Maximilian Nickel, Lorenzo Rosasco, and Tomaso Poggio. 2016. Holographic embeddings of knowledge graphs. In *Proceedings of the Thirtieth AAAI Conference on Artificial Intelligence*, AAAI'16, pages 1955–1961. AAAI Press.

Maximilian Nickel, Volker Tresp, and Hans-Peter Kriegel. 2012. Factorizing yago: Scalable machine learning for linked data. In *Proceedings of the 21st International Conference on World Wide Web*, WWW '12, pages 271–280, New York, NY, USA. ACM.

Michael Schlichtkrull, Thomas N Kipf, Peter Bloem, Rianne van den Berg, Ivan Titov, and Max Welling. 2018. Modeling relational data with graph convolutional networks. In *European Semantic Web Conference*, pages 593–607. Springer.

Richard Socher, Danqi Chen, Christopher D Manning, and Andrew Ng. 2013. Reasoning with neural tensor networks for knowledge base completion. In C. J. C. Burges, L. Bottou, M. Welling, Z. Ghahramani, and K. Q. Weinberger, editors, *Advances in Neural Information Processing Systems 26*, pages 926–934. Curran Associates, Inc.

Théo Trouillon, Christopher R Dance, Johannes Welbl, Sebastian Riedel, Éric Gaussier, and Guillaume Bouchard. 2017. Knowledge graph completion via complex tensor factorization. arXiv preprint arXiv:1702.06879.

William Yang Wang, Kathryn Mazaitis, and William W. Cohen. 2013. Programming with personalized Pagerank: A locally groundable first-order probabilistic logic. In *Proceedings of the 22Nd CIKM*, pages 2129–2138, New York, NY, USA. ACM.

Bishan Yang, Wen-tau Yih, Xiaodong He, Jianfeng Gao, and Li Deng. 2015. Embedding entities and relations for learning and inference in knowledge bases. In *Proceedings of the 2015 International Conference on Representation Learning*.

Wenpeng Yin, Yadollah Yaghoobzadeh, and Hinrich Schütze. 2018. Recurrent one-hop predictions for reasoning over knowledge graphs. In *Proceedings of the 27th ACL*, pages 2369–2378. Association for Computational Linguistics.

Mengfei Zhou and Vivi Nastase. 2018. Using patterns in knowledge graphs for targeted information extraction. In *Workshop on Knowledge Base Construction, Reasoning and Mining (KBCOM)*.

A Corpus of Negations and their Underlying Positive Interpretations

Zahra Sarabi, Erin Killian, Eduardo Blanco and Alexis Palmer
University of North Texas
`zahrasarabi@my.unt.edu, erinkillian@my.unt.edu,`
`eduardo.blanco@unt.edu, alexis.palmer@unt.edu`

Abstract

Negation often conveys implicit positive meaning. In this paper, we present a corpus of negations and their underlying positive interpretations. We work with negations from Simple Wikipedia, automatically generate potential positive interpretations, and then collect manual annotations that effectively rewrite the negation in positive terms. This procedure yields positive interpretations for approximately 77% of negations, and the final corpus includes over 5,700 negations and over 5,900 positive interpretations. We also present baseline results using seq2seq neural models.

1 Introduction

Negation is present in every human language. It is in the first place a phenomenon of semantical opposition. As such, negation relates an expression e to another expression with a meaning that is in some way opposed to the meaning of e (Horn and Wansing, 2015). Sentences containing negation are generally (a) less informative than affirmative ones (e.g., *Milan is not the capital of Italy* vs. *Rome is the capital of Italy*), (b) morphosyntactically more marked—all languages have negative markers while only a few have affirmative markers, and (c) psychologically more complex and harder to process (Horn and Wansing, 2015).

Negation often conveys implicit positive meanings (Rooth, 1992). This meaning ranges from implicatures to entailments, and we refer to it as *positive interpretations*. Consider the following text from Simple Wikipedia:[1] *An abjad is an alphabet in which all its letters are consonants. Though vowels can be added in some abjads, they are not needed to write a word correctly. Some examples of abjads are the Arabic alphabet and the*

1	Mr. Smith apologized for <u>not</u> getting involved.
	Mr. Smith apologized for staying passive.
2	I <u>never</u> heard of this guy before they started doing these commercials on television and radio.
	I heard of this guy after they started doing these commercials on on television and radio.
3	In Hinduism, beef is <u>not</u> allowed to be eaten.
	In Hinduism, chicken is allowed to be eaten.
	In other religions, beef is allowed to be eaten.

Table 1: Three sentences containing a negation and their positive interpretations (italics).

Hebrew alphabet. Humans intuitively understand that the negation (second sentence) implies the following positive interpretation: *Though vowels can be added in some abjads, only consonants are needed to write a word correctly*. Table 1 shows three sentences containing negation and their underlying positive interpretations. Positive interpretations do not have any negation cues (e.g., *not*, *never*) and Example 3 shows that some negations may have more than one underlying positive interpretation depending on the context.

Revealing the underlying positive interpretation of negation is challenging. First, we need to identify which tokens are intended to be negated (e.g., *getting involved* and *before* in Examples 1 and 2 from Table 1). Second, we need to rewrite those tokens to generate an actual positive interpretation (e.g., *getting involved*: *staying passive*).

This paper presents a corpus of negations and their underlying positive interpretations.[2] The main contributions are: (a) deterministic procedure to generate potential positive interpretations from negations, (b) corpus of negations and their positive interpretations manually annotated, (c) detailed analysis including which subtrees in the dependency tree are more likely to be rewritten and qualitative analysis of positive interpreta-

---

[1] `https://simple.wikipedia.org/wiki/`
`Abjad`

[2] Available at: `https://zahrasarabi.com`

*Proceedings of the Eighth Joint Conference on Lexical and Computational Semantics (*SEM)*, pages 158–167
Minneapolis, June 6–7, 2019. ©2019 Association for Computational Linguistics

tions. Additionally, we establish baseline results with sequence-to-sequence neural models.

2 Background and Definitions

Negation is well-understood in grammars and the valid ways to express negation are documented (Quirk et al., 2000; van der Wouden, 1997). In this paper, we focus on verbal negations, i.e., when the negation mark—usually an adverb such as *never* and *not*—is grammatically associated with a verb.
Positive Interpretations. In philosophy and linguistics, it is accepted that negation conveys positive meaning (Horn, 1989). This positive meaning ranges from implicatures, i.e., what is suggested in an utterance even though neither expressed nor strictly implied (Blackburn, 2008), to entailments. Other terms used in the literature include implied meanings (Mitkov, 2005), implied alternatives (Rooth, 1985) and semantically similar (Agirre et al., 2013). We do not strictly fit into any of this terminology, we reveal positive interpretations as intuitively done by humans when reading text. Note that a *positive* interpretation is a statement that does not contain negation, not a statement that conveys positive sentiment. For example, *The seller didn't ship the right parts* implicitly conveys *The seller shipped the wrong parts*, which has negative sentiment.
Potential Positive Interpretations. Given a sentence containing negation, we use the term *potential positive interpretation* to refer to positive interpretations that are automatically generated by replacing selected tokens with a placeholder. If the placeholder can be rewritten so that the result is an affirmative statement that is true given the original sentence, *potential* positive interpretations become *actual* positive interpretations.
Negation and natural language understanding. Generating positive interpretations from negation has several potential applications.

First, while neural machine translation is in general superior to phrase-based methods, that is not the case when translating negation (Bentivogli et al., 2016). Since our positive interpretations effectively rewrite negation-containing sentences to remove the negation, we argue that they have the potential to help machine translation.

Second, current benchmarks for natural language inference (Bowman et al., 2015), do not include challenging examples with negation. As a result, state-of-the-art approaches (Chen et al., 2017) trained on these benchmarks are unable to solve text-hypothesis pairs that contain negation. Indeed, we tested the aforecited systems with 100 text-hypothesis pairs from our corpus (text: sentence with negation, hypothesis: positive interpretation with correctness score of 4; see examples in Table 7), and discovered that 48 of them are predicted *contradiction*, 30 *neutral* and only 22 *entaioment* (the correct prediction is entailment for all of them). While relatively small, we argue that the corpus presented here is a step towards language understanding when negation is present.

3 Previous Work

From a theoretical perspective, it is accepted that negation has scope and focus, and that the focus yields positive interpretations (Horn, 1989; Rooth, 1992). Scope is "the part of the meaning that is negated" and focus "the part of the scope that is most prominently or explicitly negated" (Huddleston and Pullum, 2002).

Scope of negation detection has received a lot of attention (Özgür and Radev, 2009; Packard et al., 2014), mostly using two corpora: BioScope (Szarvas et al., 2008), and CD-SCO (Morante and Daelemans, 2012). F-scores are 0.96 for negation cue detection, and 0.89 for negation cue and scope detection (Velldal et al., 2012; Li et al., 2010).

Identifying the focus of negation is generally more challenging than the scope. The challenge lies on determining which tokens within the scope are *intended* to be negated. The largest corpus to date is PB-FOC, which was released as part of the *SEM-2012 Shared Task (Morante and Blanco, 2012). PB-FOC annotates the semantic role most likely to be the focus in the 3,993 negation in PropBank (Palmer et al., 2005). Anand and Martell (2012) refine PB-FOC and argue that 27.4% of negations with a focus annotated in PB-FOC do not actually have a focus. Sarabi and Blanco (2016) present a complementary approach grounded on syntactic dependencies. All of these efforts identify the tokens that are the focus of negation. We build upon them and generate actual positive interpretations from negation.

4 Corpus Creation

This section details our data collection and annotation effort. We follow 5 steps. First, we describe the source corpus. Second, we ouline the procedure to select negations so that the annota-

			#	%
# negations	1 negation		69,365	93.3%
	≥2 negations		4,981	7.7%
# tokens	≤5		683	0.9%
	>5 & ≤25		50,070	67.3%
	>25		23,593	31.7%

Table 2: Basic counts for sentences containing negation in Simple Wikipedia.

			#	%
Negation Types	Verbal	root	24,125	32.4%
		not_root	31,386	42.2%
	Nominal		11,003	14.8%
	Adjectival		2,325	3.1%
	Other		5,507	7.4%
	All		74,346	100.0%

Table 3: Distribution of negation type in Simple Wikipedia.

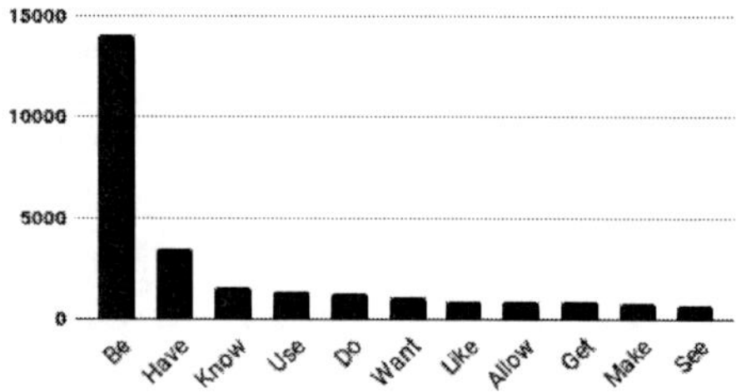

Figure 1: The most frequent negated verb lemmas in Simple Wikipedia.

tion effort is feasible. Third, we discuss the steps to automatically generate potential positive interpretations. Fourth, we detail the annotation effort to rewrite placeholders in the potential positive interpretations to generate actual positive interpretations. Fifth, we present the final validation strategy to ensure quality of the final corpus.

4.1 Selecting the Source Corpus: Simple Wikipedia

We chose to work with Simple Wikipedia texts.[3] Simple Wikipedia is a version of Wikipedia that is written in basic English. Compared to regular Wikipedia, articles in Simple Wikipedia use simpler words, shorter sentences, and simple grammar. These characteristics help us to reduce the overhead of dealing with complex sentences and leads to a more realistic learning task. We process Simple Wikipedia with spaCy (Honnibal and Johnson, 2015) to obtain part-of-speech tags and dependency trees. Inspired by Fancellu et al.

(2016), we identify sentences containing negation using the following cues: *n't, not, never, no, nothing, nobody, none, nowhere*. Note that this method selects negations that would be discarded if we relied only on dependency type *neg*.

Table 2 shows basic counts for sentences containing at least one negation in Simple Wikipedia. 93% of them contain only one negation, and 67% have medium length (between 6 to 25 tokens). Table 3 categorizes the Simple Wikipedia negations based on their type. We identify negation types using the part-of-speech tag of the syntactic head of the negation cue, i.e., the syntactic parent or governor of the negation cue. More than 70% of the negations in Simple Wikipedia are verbal negations, and the verb is the root of the dependency tree in 44% of them. Finally, Figure 1 shows the most frequent verbal negations in Simple Wikipedia. We observe that many verbs and in particular the verb *to be* are very frequent, and there is a long tail of (relatively) infrequent verbs.

4.2 Selecting Negations

Working with all negation types in Simple Wikipedia is out of the scope of this paper. After doing pilot annotations and manual examination, we decided to limit the negation types grounded on the counts presented in Section 4.1. Table 4 summarizes the filters and the number of negations that remain after running each filter. We apply sequentially five filters (Filters 1–5) on negations and four filters (Filters 6–9) on sentences. Filter 1 discards non-verbal negations (recall that 74.6% of negations are verbal, Table 3). Filter 2 discards those verbal negations which are not the root of the dependency tree. Filter 3 discards infrequent verbal negations, more specifically, those whose verbs occurred less than five times. Filter 4 caps the number of verbal negations per verb to 200 negations to increase verb coverage (recall that some verbs are negated very frequently, Figure 1). Filter 5 discards verbal negations with part-of-speech tag *interjection* (less than 1%, e.g., *They said "no" to his offer*). Filter 6 discards sentences whose length is not greater than five tokens and less than 26 tokens (recall that most sentences containing negation satisfy this filter: 67.3%, Table 2). Filter 7 discards sentences with more than one verbal negation (93% of sentences containing negation only contain one, Table 2). Filter 8 discards negated sentences in question form (i.e., the first

[3]Version 2018-03-01; available at `https://dumps.wikimedia.org/simplewiki/`

	Filters	#	%
Initial #	-	74,346	100.0
Negations	F1: non_verbal	58,756	79.0
	F2: not_root	27,370	36.8
	F3: infrequent	18,618	25.0
	F4: limit_freq	16,185	21.7
	F5: intj	16,136	21.1
Sentences	F6: limit_len	13,859	19.1
	F7: multi_negs	10,614	14.8
	F8: questions	10,476	14.6
	F9: other	7,469	10.1

Table 4: Initial number of negations in Simple Wikipedia, and how many remain after each filter.

# pot. positive interpretations	#	%
1	1,132	15.53
2	3,723	51.07
3	2,004	27.49
4	437	5.99
5	29	0.39
6	3	0.04
All	7,469	100.00

Table 5: Distribution of negations by number of potential positive interpretations generated.

token has any of the following part-of-speech tags: WDT, WP, WRB). Filter 9 discards sentences that include any of the following tokens: *because, until, but, if, except*. The final dataset consists of 7,469 negations, which are approximately 10% of negations in Simple Wikipedia.

4.3 Generating Potential Positive Interpretations

We convert each negation into its positive counterpart in four steps following the rules by Huddleston and Pullum (2002): remove the negation cue, remove auxiliaries, fix third-person singular and past tense, and rewrite negatively-oriented polarity-sensitive items. These steps can be implemented using straightforward regular expressions. For example, the positive counterpart of *The seller did not ship the right part*, is *The seller shipped the right parts*. Then, we automatically generate all plausible positive interpretations of the negation by traversing the dependency tree and selecting all direct dependents of the negated verb. We filter out subtrees whose syntactic dependency is *aux, auxpass, punct* (auxiliary, passive auxiliary and punctuation). We also exclude the verb. These exceptions were defined after manual examination of several examples. Finally, we replace the selected subtrees with a placeholder.

Table 5 shows the number of negations depending on how many positive interpretations are generated. We generate two or more potential positive interpretations for over 84% of negations.

4.4 Rewriting Placeholders

In order to rewrite placeholders in potential positive interpretations and collect actual positive interpretations, we implement an annotation inter-face using Amazon Mechanical Turk Sandbox.[4] This rewriting process was done in-house by one linguistics student. A second annotator validated the rewrites independently (Section 4.5).

Each negation along with its context and all its potential positive interpretations are grouped into a Human Intelligence Task (HIT) for annotation purposes. Each HIT presents a set of instructions to the annotator along with examples. Potential positive interpretations are presented in consecutive rows, and each token in a cell. The placeholders generated in Section 4.3 are presented as blank cells and the annotator fills the blanks (or, in other words, the annotator rewrites placeholders) based on the context around the negation or world knowledge. A sample HIT along with the answers collected is shown in Figure 2.

In the rest of the paper, we use *unknown* answer to refer to placeholders for which the annotator cannot find a rewriting. We divide *unknown* answers into *invalid* and *not specified*, and ask the annotator to distinguish between them. *Invalid* is used to refer to placeholders that cannot be rewritten. *Not specified* describes placeholders that hypothetically can be rewritten but the answer is unknown given the context. We also provide an extra empty box at the bottom of the interface for additional positive interpretations. If the annotator cannot find any answers for the rewrites, she can write a positive interpretation from scratch.

4.5 Validating Positive Interpretations

In order to validate the rewrites of placeholders and resulting positive interpretations (Section 4.4), a second annotator validates them. We create a similar interface to the one in Figure 2, but this time we only show the negation in context (*Text* in Figure 2), and one positive interpretation at a time (i.e., potential positive interpretation for which the

---

[4]`https://requester.mturk.com/developer/sandbox`

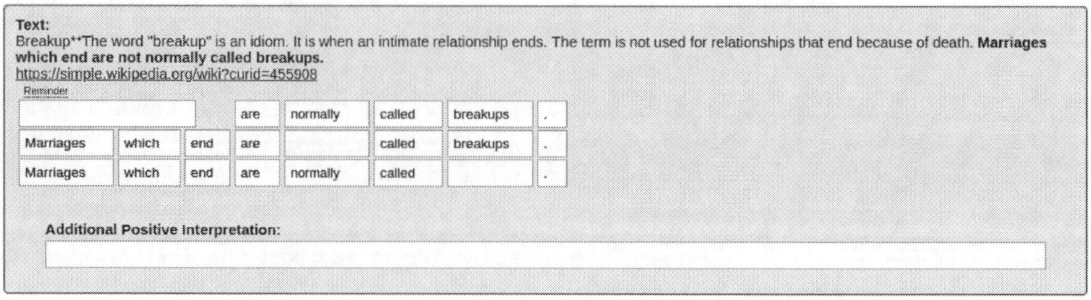

Figure 2: Sample negation along with its context and automatically-generated potential positive interpretations. The annotation process reveals three positive interpretations: "*Relationships* that end are normaly called breakups," "Marriages which end are *rarely* called breakups," and "Marriages which end are normaly called *divorce*."

placeholder was rewritten). The annotator determines correctness and novelty as follows.

Correctness measures whether a positive interpretation is true given the negation in context. It is measured using the following scale:

1. After reading the *text*, it is clear that the positive interpretation is false.
2. After reading the *text*, the positive interpretation is probably false, but I am not sure.
3. After reading the *text*, the positive interpretation is probably true, but I am not sure.
4. After reading the *text*, it is clear that the positive interpretation is true.

Novelty measures whether the meaning conveyed by a positive interpretation is already explicitly stated in the *text*, and it is measured using the following numeric scale:

1. The positive interpretation is stated explicitly in the *text* with the very same words. I could copy and paste chunks from *text* and get the positive interpretation.
2. The positive interpretation is not stated in the *text* with the same words. The positive interpretation and the *text* have synonyms in common, but I could not get the positive interpretation simply copying and pasting from *text*.
3. The positive interpretation is not stated in the *text* with the same words. Additionally, there are few synonyms in common between the positive interpretation and *text*.

5   Corpus Analysis

The procedure described in Section 4 generates 15,875 potential positive interpretations from 7,469 negations. Out of all potential positive interpretations, we rewrite 3,831 with an actual answer and annotate 12,044 with an unknown answer

| | Known | | Unknown | | | | Total |
| | | | not spec. | | invalid | | |
	#	%	#	%	#	%	
prep	953	29	2089	63	262	8	3305
dobj	763	30	1652	65	121	5	2537
advmod	700	50	629	45	68	5	1398
nsubj	511	11	3860	83	295	6	4667
nsubjpass	212	14	1267	82	62	4	1542
ccomp	207	34	357	58	52	8	617
xcomp	168	38	248	57	21	5	438
advcl	131	18	534	73	63	9	729
agent	60	29	142	68	5	2	208
Other	128	27	250	53	99	20	477

Table 6: Corpus analysis. For each dependency type (left column), we show the number of potential positive interpretations generated with known and unknown rewrites (and *not specified* and *invalid* rewrites).

(11,030 *not specified* and 1,014 *invalid*). We also rewrite a new positive interpretation from scratch for 2,158 negations for which we cannot find any actual rewrites. Overall, we rewrite 5,989 positive interpretations for 5,770 unique negations. In other words, the procedure in Section 4 yields a positive interpretation for 77% of negations.

Table 6 shows the distribution of *known* vs *unknown* rewrites per dependency type, where *dependency type* refers to the dependency type from the selected subtree of the verb to the verb itself. Out of all dependency types, *advmod* and *xcomp* (adverbial modifier and open clausal complement respectively) have the highest ratios of known rewrites, and *nsubj* (nominal subject) has the most unknown answers. In other words, the easiest placeholders to rewrite are those whose syntactic function is adverbial modifier or open clausal complement, and the most challenging are those whose syntactic function is nominal subject.

To understand high-level characteristics of negations and their positive interpretations beyond

Category	Subcat.	Examples	%
Quantities	specific	Members of Congress cannot serve for more than *three out of any six years.*	3%
	abstract	*Many* do not use their real names, as Everett does.	22%
Times	actual	*Since 2012,* this channel never goes off the air during the day.	4%
	abstract	Rabbits should not be bred *too early* though.	11%
Objects	-	It does not need *sunlight* to grow and can stay in the same pot for many years.	9%
Adjectives	-	Crops did not grow *as well* when they were close together.	27%
Proper nouns	-	*Cosworth* does not currently provide engines to any American open wheel racing series.	2%
Others	-	*The mass number* is not shown on the periodic table.	22%

Table 7: Categories and subcategories discovered in a sample of 100 negations and all their positive interpretations.

dependency types, we explore a random sample of 100 negations and all their positive interpretations. We discover six major categories (quantities, times, objects, adjectives, proper nouns and others) and 4 subcategories (Table 7):

- The first category is *quantities* and includes both *specific* and *abstract* quantities. An example of abstract quantity is <u>Many</u> *do not use their real names, as Everett does* and its corresponding positive interpretation <u>Few</u> *use their real names, as Everett does.* A fourth of positive interpretations in the sample were obtained after rewriting quantities.
- The second category is *time* and includes both *actual* and *abstract* times. An example of actual time is <u>Since 2012,</u> *this channel never goes off the air during the day* and its positive interpretation <u>Before 2012,</u> *this channel went off the air during the day.* 15% of positive interpretations in the sample were obtained rewriting temporal expressions.
- The third category is *objects* and refers to positive interpretations obtained by rewriting verbal objects. An example is *It does not need <u>sunlight</u> to grow* and its positive interpretation *It needs <u>water</u> to grow.* 9% of positive interpretations in the sample were obtained after rewriting the verbal objects.
- The fourth category is *adjectives* and refers to positive interpretations obtained by rewriting adjectives. An example is *Crops did not grow <u>as well</u> when they were close together* and its positive interpretation *Crops grew <u>poorly</u> when they were close together.* 27% of positive interpretations in the sample were obtained after rewriting adjectives.
- The fifth category is *proper nouns.* An example is <u>Cosworth</u> *does not currently provide engines to any American open wheel racing series* and its positive interpretation <u>IndyCar Series</u> *currently provide engines to American open wheel racing series.* 2% of positive interpretation in the sample were obtained after rewriting proper nouns.

5.1 Annotation Quality

To assess the quality of the rewrites and positive interpretations, we ask a second annotator to validate them based on two criteria: correctness and novelty (Section 4.5). Recall that correctness ranges from 1 (minimum) to 4 (maximum) and novelty from 1 (minimum) to 3 (maximum). We assess novelty only if positive interpretations are correct (correctness scores 3 or 4). Figure 3 reports the validation results. Out of all positive interpretations obtained during the annotation process, 90% are either correct (77%) or probably correct (13%) (correctness scores 4 and 3), and 95% of them are either very novel (52%) or novel (43%). This validation scores mean not only that positive interpretations are sound given the original negation (correctness score), but also that they are not explicitly stated in the context and thus reveal implicit meaning (novelty score).

5.2 Annotation Examples

Table 8 presents three negations, all potential positive interpretations, and manual annotations along with the correctnes and novelty scores.

Example (1) is a simple negated clause. The procedure described in Section 4.3 generates four potential positive interpretations, and three of them were rewritten. Given *Phosgene usually does not cause its worst effects right away* and its context, the following positive interpretations are deemed correct (correctness = 4) with different degrees of novelty (2, 3 and 1 respectively): *Phosgene rarely causes its worst effects right away* (Interpretation 1.2), *Phosgene usually causes mild effects right away* (Interpretation 1.3), and *Phosgene usually causes its worst effects 12 hours after a person breathes it in* (Interpretation 1.4). Note that

1	Context: Phosgene can be a liquid or a gas. As a gas, it is heavier than air, so it can stay near the ground (where people can breathe it in for long periods of time). It smells like freshly cut grass or moldy hay. Along with being a choking agent, phosgene is also a blood agent. This means it keeps oxygen from getting into the body's cells. Without oxygen, a person's cells will die, and the person will suffocate. *Phosgene usually does not cause its worst effects right away.* The worst symptoms do not happen until 12 hours after a person breathed in phosgene. The person usually dies within 24 to 48 hours.		
	Sentence containing negation: Phosgene usually does not cause its worst effects right away.		
		Correctness	Novelty
	- Interpretation 1.1: [NS] usually causes its worst effects right away.	-	-
	- Interpretation 1.2: Phosgene *rarely* causes its worst effects right away.	4	2
	- Interpretation 1.3: Phosgene usually causes *mild effects* right away.	4	3
	- Interpretation 1.4: Phosgene usually causes its worst effects *12 hours after a person breathes it in.*	4	1
2	Context: Hungary uses Central European Time (CET) which is 1 hour ahead of Coordinated Universal Time (UTC+1). *Hungary has not observed summer time since 1916.*		
	Sentence containing negation: Hungary has not observed summer time since 1916.		
		Correctness	Novelty
	- Interpretation 2.1: [NS] has observed summer time since 1916.	-	-
	- Interpretation 2.2: Hungary has observed *Central European Time* since 1916.	4	1
	- Interpretation 2.3: Hungary has observed summer time *prior to 1916.*	4	2
3	Sentence containing negation: This does not stop him from finding ways to try to get more money.		
		Correctness	Novelty
	- Interpretation 3.1: This stops [NS] from finding ways to try to get more money.	-	-
	- Interpretation 3.2: This stops him [NS].	-	-
	- Addtl. Interpretation: He's always trying to get more money despite being rich.	4	3

Table 8: Sentences containing negation (and context if relevant to obtain positive interpretations), all automatically-generated positive interpretations, positive interpretations manually annotated (italics indicate placeholder rewritings), and validation scores (correctness and novelty).

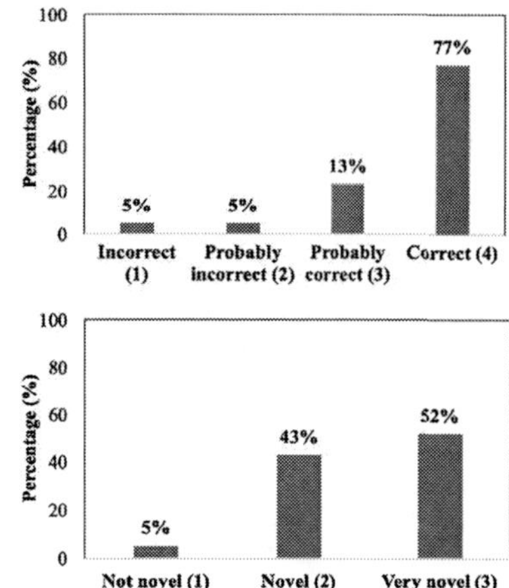

Figure 3: Distribution of correctness (top) and novelty (bottom) scores in our corpus.

Interpretation 1.1 is most likely correct, but context does not provide clues about which chemicals cause their worst effects right away and thus it is annotated *not specified* (NS).

Example (2) has three potential positive interpretations, and we rewrite two of them. Note that Intepretation 2.2, *Hungary has observed Central European Time since 1916*, is correct but not novel because it is explicitly stated in the context. Interpretation 2.3 is correct but received novelty score of 2 because it only replaces *since* with *prior to*.

Example (3) shows an example in which rewriting placeholders is not successful. The additional interpretation, however, reveals that *He* has the intention of getting more money. Context, which is not shown in Table 8, support the correctness and validation scores (e.g., *He* is wealthy).

6 Experiments

The task of generating positive interpretations from a sentence containing negation can be approached with sequence-to-sequence (seq2seq) models (input: sentence containing negation, output: positive interpretation). In this section, we present baseline results with existing seq2seq models. Specifically, we experiment with a basic seq2seq model (Cho et al., 2014), two seq2seq models with attention (Luong et al., 2015; Bahdanau et al., 2014), and Google's neural machine translation (NMT) system (Wu et al., 2016), which is also seq2seq model with attention and arguably the most complex. We acknowledge that these systems are usually trained with orders of magnitude more examples, and comparing them when trained with our fairly small corpus may be unfair because they were designed for other tasks. Our goal is not to obtain the best results possible, but rather provide baseline results for our task and corpus.

Models	Short Sentences			Long Sentences		
	BLEU	Gram.	Corr.	BLEU	Gram.	Corr.
seq2seq (basic) (Cho et al., 2014)	10.31	23%	5%	2.13	6%	1%
seq2seq + attention (Bahdanau et al., 2014)	20.51	65%	22%	9.20	41%	12%
seq2seq + attention (Luong et al., 2015)	28.08	**68%**	**30%**	14.53	51%	19%
seq2seq + Google's NMT attention (Wu et al., 2016)	12.54	42%	15%	4.40	12%	3%

Table 9: Results (BLEU-4, grammaticality and correctness) obtained with the test set.

The 3,831 negations become source sentences and the correct positive interpretations become target sentences. We randomly select 100 short sentences (up to 12 tokens) and 100 long sentences (over 12 tokens) for testing, 200 sentences for development, and the remainder for training. All positive interpretations collected from a negation are assigned to the testing, development or training splits in order to ensure a more realistic scenario.

Evaluation and Results. We use three metrics to evaluate the models: BLEU-4, correctness and grammaticality. BLEU-4 is automated, convenient and useful for development purposes. While larger BLEU-4 scores generally indicate better correctness and grammaticality scores, we do not observe a linear correlation (Table 9). Correctness is measured manually with the scale presented in Section 4.5. Finally, grammaticality is measured manually using the following numeric scale:

1. The sentence is not grammatical at all, e.g., it does not contain a verb.
2. The sentence is mostly ungrammatical, e.g., it contains a verb but the word order is wrong.
3. The sentence has a few grammatical issues, e.g., the subject-verb agreement is wrong, missing punctuation.
4. The sentence is grammatically correct (regardless of its correctness).

Table 9 shows the results. In general terms, results are better for short sentences than long ones. This is not surprising given the small size of our corpus. The basic seq2seq model performs poorly: it barely generates any correct positive interpretaions, and most are ungrammatical. Adding attention performs better. The best results are with the system by Luong et al. (2017): 30% of the short positive interpretations generated are correct, and 68% grammatical. We believe Google's NMT performs the worst because of the small corpus.

We also conduct a manual analysis of the correct positive interpretations generated by the best system. Following with the categories described in Section 5 and Table 7, 37% of them belong to the *adjectives* category, 27% to *abstract quanti-*

ties, 17% to *objects*, and 10% to *abstract time*.

7 Conclusions

We have presented a corpus of negations and their positive interpretations. Positive interpretations do not contain negations, range from implicatures to entailments, and are intuitively understood by nonexperts when reading the negations. We work with verbal negations selected from Simple Wikipedia, automatically generate potential positive interpretation by replacing subtrees with placeholders, and manually collect rewrites for the placeholders in order to obtain actual positive interpretations. This strategy yields positive interpretations for 77% of negations, and manual validation step ensures both correctnes and novelty.

Neural machine translation struggles with negation, and natural language inference benchmarks do not account for the intricacies of negation (Section 2). While small, we believe the corpus presented here is a step towards enabling natural language understanding when negation is present.

Acknowledgments

This material is based upon work supported by the National Science Foundation under Grants Nos. 1734730, 1832267 and 1845757. Any opinions, findings, and conclusions or recommendations expressed in this material are those of the authors and do not necessarily reflect the views of the National Science Foundation. The Titan Xp used for this research was donated by the NVIDIA Corporation.

References

Eneko Agirre, Daniel Cer, Mona Diab, Aitor Gonzalez-Agirre, and Weiwei Guo. 2013. *sem 2013 shared task: Semantic textual similarity. In *Second Joint Conference on Lexical and Computational Semantics (*SEM), Volume 1: Proceedings of the Main Conference and the Shared Task: Semantic Textual Similarity*. Association for Computational Linguistics, Atlanta, Georgia, USA, pages 32–43. http://www.aclweb.org/anthology/S13-1004.

Pranav Anand and Craig Martell. 2012. Annotating the focus of negation in terms of questions under discussion. In *Proceedings of the Workshop on Extra-Propositional Aspects of Meaning in Computational Linguistics*. Association for Computational Linguistics, Stroudsburg, PA, USA, ExProM '12, pages 65–69. `http://dl.acm.org/citation.cfm?id=2392701.2392709`.

Dzmitry Bahdanau, Kyunghyun Cho, and Yoshua Bengio. 2014. Neural machine translation by jointly learning to align and translate. *arXiv e-prints* abs/1409.0473. `https://arxiv.org/abs/1409.0473`.

Luisa Bentivogli, Arianna Bisazza, Mauro Cettolo, and Marcello Federico. 2016. Neural versus phrase-based machine translation quality: a case study. In *Proceedings of the 2016 Conference on Empirical Methods in Natural Language Processing*. Association for Computational Linguistics, pages 257–267. `https://doi.org/10.18653/v1/D16-1025`.

Simon Blackburn. 2008. *The Oxford Dictionary of Philosophy*. Oxford University Press. `//www.oxfordreference.com/10.1093/acref/9780199541430.001.0001/acref-9780199541430`.

Samuel R. Bowman, Gabor Angeli, Christopher Potts, and Christopher D. Manning. 2015. A large annotated corpus for learning natural language inference. In *Proceedings of the 2015 Conference on Empirical Methods in Natural Language Processing*. Association for Computational Linguistics, pages 632–642. `https://doi.org/10.18653/v1/D15-1075`.

Qian Chen, Xiaodan Zhu, Zhen-Hua Ling, Si Wei, Hui Jiang, and Diana Inkpen. 2017. Recurrent neural network-based sentence encoder with gated attention for natural language inference. In *Proceedings of the 2nd Workshop on Evaluating Vector Space Representations for NLP*. Association for Computational Linguistics, Copenhagen, Denmark, pages 36–40. `http://www.aclweb.org/anthology/W17-5307`.

Kyunghyun Cho, Bart van Merriënboer, Ça?lar Gülçehre, Dzmitry Bahdanau, Fethi Bougares, Holger Schwenk, and Yoshua Bengio. 2014. Learning phrase representations using rnn encoder–decoder for statistical machine translation. In *Proceedings of the 2014 Conference on Empirical Methods in Natural Language Processing (EMNLP)*. Association for Computational Linguistics, Doha, Qatar, pages 1724–1734. `http://www.aclweb.org/anthology/D14-1179`.

Federico Fancellu, Adam Lopez, and Bonnie Webber. 2016. Neural networks for negation scope detection. In *Proceedings of the 54th Annual Meeting of the Association for Computational Linguistics (Volume 1: Long Papers)*. Association

for Computational Linguistics, Berlin, Germany, pages 495–504. `http://www.aclweb.org/anthology/P16-1047`.

Matthew Honnibal and Mark Johnson. 2015. An improved non-monotonic transition system for dependency parsing. In *Proceedings of the 2015 Conference on Empirical Methods in Natural Language Processing*. Association for Computational Linguistics, Lisbon, Portugal, pages 1373–1378. `https://aclweb.org/anthology/D/D15/D15-1162`.

Laurence R. Horn. 1989. *A natural history of negation*. Chicago University Press, Chicago.

Laurence R. Horn and Heinrich Wansing. 2015. Negation. In Edward N. Zalta, editor, *The Stanford Encyclopedia of Philosophy*. Summer 2015 edition.

Rodney D. Huddleston and Geoffrey K. Pullum. 2002. *The Cambridge Grammar of the English Language*. Cambridge University Press.

Junhui Li, Guodong Zhou, Hongling Wang, and Qiaoming Zhu. 2010. Learning the Scope of Negation via Shallow Semantic Parsing. In *Proceedings of the 23rd International Conference on Computational Linguistics (Coling 2010)*. Coling 2010 Organizing Committee, Beijing, China, pages 671–679. `http://www.aclweb.org/anthology-new/C/C10/C10-1076.bib`.

Minh-Thang Luong, Eugene Brevdo, and Rui Zhao. 2017. Neural machine translation (seq2seq) tutorial. *https://github.com/tensorflow/nmt* .

Thang Luong, Hieu Pham, and Christopher D. Manning. 2015. Effective approaches to attention-based neural machine translation. In *Proceedings of the 2015 Conference on Empirical Methods in Natural Language Processing*. Association for Computational Linguistics, pages 1412–1421. `https://doi.org/10.18653/v1/D15-1166`.

Ruslan Mitkov. 2005. *The Oxford handbook of computational linguistics*. Oxford University Press.

R. Morante and W. Daelemans. 2012. Annotating modality and negation for a machine reading evaluation. In *CLEF 2012 Evaluation Labs and Workshop Online Working Notes*.

Roser Morante and Eduardo Blanco. 2012. *sem 2012 shared task: Resolving the scope and focus of negation. In *Proceedings of the First Joint Conference on Lexical and Computational Semantics - Volume 1: Proceedings of the Main Conference and the Shared Task, and Volume 2: Proceedings of the Sixth International Workshop on Semantic Evaluation*. Association for Computational Linguistics, Stroudsburg, PA, USA, SemEval '12, pages 265–274. `http://dl.acm.org/citation.cfm?id=2387636.2387679`.

Arzucan Özgür and Dragomir R. Radev. 2009. Detecting Speculations and their Scopes in Scientific Text. In *Proceedings of the 2009 Conference on Empirical Methods in Natural Language Processing*. Association for Computational Linguistics, Singapore, pages 1398–1407. `http://www.aclweb.org/anthology-new/D/D09/D09-1145.bib`.

Woodley Packard, Emily M. Bender, Jonathon Read, Stephan Oepen, and Rebecca Dridan. 2014. Simple negation scope resolution through deep parsing: A semantic solution to a semantic problem. In *Proceedings of the 52nd Annual Meeting of the Association for Computational Linguistics (Volume 1: Long Papers)*. Association for Computational Linguistics, Baltimore, Maryland, pages 69–78. `http://www.aclweb.org/anthology/P14-1007`.

Martha Palmer, Daniel Gildea, and Paul Kingsbury. 2005. The Proposition Bank: An Annotated Corpus of Semantic Roles. *Computational Linguistics* 31(1):71–106.

Randolph Quirk, Sidney Greenbaum, and Geoffrey Leech. 2000. *A comprehensive grammar of the English language*. Longman, London.

Mats Rooth. 1985. *Association with focus*. Ph.D. thesis.

Mats Rooth. 1992. A theory of focus interpretation. *Natural language semantics* 1(1):75–116.

Zahra Sarabi and Eduardo Blanco. 2016. Understanding negation in positive terms using syntactic dependencies. In *Proceedings of the 2016 Conference on Empirical Methods in Natural Language Processing*. Association for Computational Linguistics, Austin, Texas, pages 1108–1118. `https://aclweb.org/anthology/D16-1119`.

György Szarvas, Veronika Vincze, Richárd Farkas, and János Csirik. 2008. The BioScope corpus: annotation for negation, uncertainty and their scopein biomedical texts. In *Proceedings of BioNLP 2008*. ACL, Columbus, Ohio, USA, pages 38–45.

Ton van der Wouden. 1997. *Negative contexts: collocation, polarity, and multiple negation*. Routledge, London.

Erik Velldal, Lilja Ovrelid, Jonathon Read, and Stephan Oepen. 2012. Speculation and negation: Rules, rankers, and the role of syntax. *Comput. Linguist.* 38(2):369–410. `https://doi.org/10.1162/COLI_a_00126`.

Yonghui Wu, Mike Schuster, Zhifeng Chen, Quoc V. Le, Mohammad Norouzi, Wolfgang Macherey, Maxim Krikun, Yuan Cao, Qin Gao, Klaus Macherey, Jeff Klingner, Apurva Shah, Melvin Johnson, Xiaobing Liu, Lukasz Kaiser, Stephan Gouws, Yoshikiyo Kato, Taku Kudo, Hideto Kazawa, Keith Stevens, George Kurian, Nishant Patil, Wei Wang, Cliff Young, Jason Smith, Jason Riesa, Alex Rudnick, Oriol Vinyals, Gregory S. Corrado, Macduff Hughes, and Jeffrey Dean. 2016. Google's neural machine translation system: Bridging the gap between human and machine translation. *CoRR* abs/1609.08144.

Enthymemetic Conditionals: Topoi as a guide for acceptability

Eimear Maguire

Laboratoire Linguistique Formelle (UMR 7110), Université de Paris

`eimear.maguire@etu.univ-paris-diderot.fr`

Abstract

To model conditionals in a way that reflects their acceptability, we must include some means of making judgements about whether antecedent and consequent are meaningfully related or not. Enthymemes are non-logical arguments which do not hold up by themselves, but are acceptable through their relation to a topos, an already-known general principle or pattern for reasoning. This paper uses enthymemes and topoi as a way to model the world-knowledge behind these judgements. In doing so, it provides a reformalisation (in TTR) of enthymemes and topoi as networks rather than functions, and information state update rules for conditionals.

1 Introduction

The content of the antecedent and consequent of a conditional, not just their truth or falsity, makes a difference to whether we find the conditional acceptable or not, generally rejecting those that seem disconnected (Douven, 2008). If we are to model conditionals in a way that reflects their acceptability, we must include some means of making those judgements. Enthymemes are non-logical arguments which do not hold up by themselves, but are acceptable through their relation to a topos, an already-known general principle or pattern for reasoning. Arguments and justifications in interaction tend to be underpinned by general principles and rules of thumb, rather than being truly 'logical'. For models of dialogue to be adequate then, these non-logical arguments need to be handled – namely, as proposed by Breitholtz (2014a), through incorporating enthymemes and topoi into the dialogue model. Apart from the evidence from their own acceptability conditions, which correlate strongly with judgements of high conditional probability, conditional structures are also associated with 'that kind of thinking', being used as plain-language explanations of particular topoi (e.g. "if something is a bird, then it flies" in Breitholtz, 2014b), or used as materials on reasoning in any number of experiments (e.g. Pijnacker et al., 2009). If we are going to explicitly recognise the use of such 'rule' type objects in discourse, then conditionals are one place where they show up, at least sometimes.

This paper has two aims. First, to propose a formalisation of enthymemes and topoi that is geared towards relating them to more complex rule-based world knowledge, including a distinction between knowledge about causality, non-causality, and ambiguity about causality. Second, to account for the acceptability (or not) of conditionals by proposing an enthymeme-like structure as associated with *if*-conditionals, such that topoi can enhance their content and are used in judging whether a given conditional is acceptable or not. The acceptability of conditionals is linked to perceived relationships between the antecedent and consequent cases: with enthymemes and topoi, whose presence in the model is independently justified, we can incorporate this non-arbitrarily into the dialogue state.

The rest of this section will provide some background. Section 2 is focused on enthymemes, topoi, and specification of the alternative formalism, while Section 3 uses this in a proposal of update rules associated with conditionals. Lastly, Section 4 provides a conclusion. This paper draws on work on enthymemes and topoi elsewhere in Breitholtz (2014a,b) etc., and will likewise use Type Theory with Records (Cooper, 2012, hereafter referred to by the acronym TTR) for formalisation.

1.1 Enthymemes and Topoi

Enthymemes are incomplete non-logical arguments that get treated as complete ones. They are

*Proceedings of the Eighth Joint Conference on Lexical and Computational Semantics (*SEM)*, pages 168–177
Minneapolis, June 6–7, 2019. ©2019 Association for Computational Linguistics

incomplete in that to be accepted, they must be identified as a specific instance of a more general pattern that is already in the agent's resources – a topos. Topoi encode world knowledge that comes as a 'rule of thumb', such as characteristics typical of groups, and a speaker may hold contradictory topoi as equally valid in different scenarios, with no clash experienced unless both are used at the same time. Speakers make enthymemetic arguments by linking what on the surface might technically be non-sequiturs, but are easily identified as an argument using accepted principles. For example, a speaker might say "Let's go left here, it's a shortcut". This argument invokes the assumption that shorter routes are better, and that therefore the left turn being a shortcut is a good reason to take it – but they might equally say "it's longer", invoking an assumption that a longer route is preferable.

Topoi have been proposed to be a resource available to speakers, and consequently a means to address non-monotonic reasoning (Breitholtz, 2014b), the treatment of non-logical rules as expressing necessity, and contradictory claims being equally assertable, as in the route-taking example above (Breitholtz, 2014a).

To these ends, they have been formalised in TTR for use in dialogue (Breitholtz and Cooper, 2011), as functions from records to record types, as in this example (Breitholtz, 2014a):

(1)   a.   *Topos:*
$$\lambda r : \begin{bmatrix} x & : Ind \\ c_{bird} & : \mathrm{bird}(x) \end{bmatrix} \left(\begin{bmatrix} c_{fly} & : \mathrm{fly}(r.x) \end{bmatrix} \right)$$

      b.   *Enthymeme:*
$$\lambda r : \begin{bmatrix} x = \mathrm{Tweety} & : Ind \\ c_{bird} & : \mathrm{bird}(x) \end{bmatrix} \left(\begin{bmatrix} c_{fly} & : \mathrm{fly}(\mathrm{Tweety}) \end{bmatrix} \right)$$

Both are of type *Rec* → *RecType*, and the fields of the specified record types match, but fields of the enthymeme have been restricted to specific values. A function to a record type does not by itself indicate what happens once we have access to that type. For these functions to be useful, they are additionally governed by a theory of action, which will license various actions that can be performed with the type, e.g. judging that the original situation is additionally of that type, judging that there exists some situation of the type described, or creating something of that type (Cooper, in prep).

1.2 Conditionals

The assumption that conditionals express a proposition is fundamental to most linguistic work on the topic, both that which follows the commonly accepted restrictor theory of conditional semantics based on the work of Lewis (1975), Kratzer (1986) and Heim (1982), and that which does not (e.g. Gillies (2010)).

By conditionals being 'propositional', we mean that adding an *if*-clause to some indicative clause does not fundamentally change the kind of semantic object it is: for indicative clause "I'm going home", just as the conjunction "I'm going home *and I'm watching a film*" still expresses a proposition, so does "*If this doesn't get interesting soon, I'm going home*".

As mentioned at the beginning, the acceptability of conditionals correlates strongly with their conditional probability: the more likely the consequent is in the antecedent-case, the more acceptable the conditional tends to be be. Stalnaker (1970) proposed that the probability of a conditional and the conditional probability of the consequent on the antecedent are one and the same, in what is usually referred to as *the Equation*. That is, the overall probability $P(if\ this\ doesn't\ get\ interesting\ then\ I'm\ going\ home)$ is the same as the conditional probability $P(I'm\ going\ home|This\ doesn't\ get\ interesting)$. A subsequent proof by Lewis (1976) found that there is no single proposition based on the antecedent and consequent such that its probability will consistently match the conditional probability. Therefore one could have a propositional theory of conditionals, or validate the Equation – but not both.

However, conditional probability seems so important to the meaning of conditionals that in the view of some non-linguists, (e.g. Edgington, 1995; Bennett, 2003) conditionals should properly be considered be probabilistic, directly expressing the conditional probability of the consequent on the antecedent, P(*cons*|*ant*). Subsequent empirical work overwhelmingly supports the intuition behind the original Equation, and shows that conditional probability does indeed tend to correlate with acceptability (e.g. Evans et al., 2003; Oaksford and Chater, 2003). Conditional probability thus needs to be taken seriously, whether one believes it is the core content of a conditional or not: indeed, figuring out how propositional theories can accommodate its relationship to acceptability is an important issue (e.g. Douven and Verbrugge, 2013). Conditional probability is also not the only factor in acceptability: it is further moderated by whether there appears to be a connection between antecedent and consequent (Skovgaard-Olsen et al., 2016). To make these judgements, we need to know about the relationships between the antecedent and consequent states.

As a note, this paper remains technically agnostic about whether the propositional or probabilistic analysis is correct: your mileage may vary on whether the update rules in Section 3 should also add a proposition associated with *if p, q* to the agent's knowledge base, were they to be more comprehensively specified. The underlying acceptability issue, and the potential use of topoi in the metrics underlying those acceptability judgements, means that this does not impact on the core of the proposals here.

1.3 TTR: a brief overview

Since it will be used later, this section provides a very brief introduction to TTR.

A central idea in TTR is the judgement of objects as being of some type. If a is judged to be of type T, this is written as $a : T$. Several of these judgements, or requirements for judgements, can be collected in structured objects as records and record types. In a record type, fields consist of a label and type, while fields in a record consist of a label and a value. For a record r to be of a record type RT, it must have fields with the labels specified in RT, and the values in those fields in r must be the types specified by the equivalently labelled fields in RT. For example, the records in (2) and (3) are both of the record type (4), provided that x is of type T_1. The type of a field need not be stand-alone either: it may also be constructed from a predicate and arguments, like the field d in (5).

$$(2) \quad \begin{bmatrix} a = x \end{bmatrix} \qquad (4) \quad \begin{bmatrix} a : T_1 \end{bmatrix} \qquad (6) \quad \begin{bmatrix} a : T_1 \\ b : T_2 \end{bmatrix}$$

$$(3) \quad \begin{bmatrix} a = x \\ b = y \\ c = z \end{bmatrix} \qquad (5) \quad \begin{bmatrix} a : T_1 \\ d : p(a) \end{bmatrix} \qquad (7) \quad \begin{bmatrix} a : T_1 \\ c : T_3 \end{bmatrix}$$

There also exist sub- and super-type relations between types. One record type is a subtype of another if it is a more specified version of it. This means that it has at least the same fields as the supertype, whose types are the same type or subtypes of the equivalent fields in the supertype. For example, (6) and (7) are different types, but are both subtypes of the more general (4). A record of type (6) is not necessarily of type (7), but will be of type (4). Depending on whether $x : T_1$, $y : T_2$ and $z : T_3$, the record in (3) will be of all three types.

2 Enthymemes, Topoi and Other Knowledge

Given that their presence in an agent's resources has already been motivated, topoi are a natural way to account for the required knowledge about some 'dependence' between antecedent and consequent. Enthymemes and topoi are snippets of reasoning, rather than complex networks, but they should also be related explicitly to other rule-like world knowledge, which includes the possibility of multiple relationships between more than two cases, and knowledge of explicitly causal relations. If we are going to use topoi to express the kind of knowledge that also forms such networks (i.e. informative about causality or related probabilities), then they should be in the same form as that knowledge: the alternative, to keep rule-like topoi apart from knowledge about rule-based(ish) systems, is counter-intuitive.

Bayesian networks (a combination of directed acyclic graphs and probability distributions) are a common way to encode causal relations. They have two components, the first of which is a directed acyclic graph, with the various variables as nodes, and directed edges describing any direct relationships. Graphs and networks are a useful way to describe relationships, and express a more complex set of relationships than a linear chain of functions. The graph structure is in accordance with constraints about what direct parenthood in the graph can mean – that the parent is part of the minimal set of preceding nodes whose value determines the probability distribution of the child.

The second component to a Bayesian Network is a set of probability functions for determining the values of variables given the values of their parents – their conditional probabilities. Associated probabilities are also a natural means of modelling learning, by adjusting the confidence in a given rule on the basis of evidence and experience, allow us to make explicit the level of confidence in a judgement beyond a binary. For unreliable rules, a high (but below 1) probability can be used to express that they are likely to be correct in a given case, but not certain.

2.1 Graphical Topoi

The proposal is as follows. Topoi and enthymemes are of the same type as any other 'relational' knowledge, by which I mean knowledge about causal and correlational relations. This knowledge can be encoded as a graph: topoi and enthymemes as usually discussed are minimal examples, containing only two nodes. The direction(s) of the links between connected nodes, along with additional constraints, indicate either causal or non-causal relations via directed or bi-directed links respectively.

Where there is a bi-directional link somewhere in a path between two nodes, their relationship is confirmed as non-causal. Where there is an absence of any path between two nodes, the relationship may be treated as potential independence, while where there are links in one direction only, the relationship may be treated as potential causality. However, neither the potential independence or causality is locked in: there should be a distinction between merely lacking information, and having confirmation about an absence. Certainty about independence or causality is expressed via constraints explicitly preventing the creation of any path that would violate them.

The choice of bi-directed rather than undirected edges to express non-causality is motivated by a desire for the difference in belief from potentially causal to non-causal to be something that changes easily (i.e. with the addition of information, not replacement of one thing with another of a different type), and for creation of a 'casual' (not a typo) middle-ground, where only one direction is of relevance and there is no strong commitment either way. It can be treated as potentially causal, being the only direction of interest, but whether this is the whole story between the two is not specified.

All this is meant to allow for a more complex set of relationships than expressed in your average topos which, as stated earlier, is a minimal case with just two nodes. The original example can be thought of as follows, graphs with only two nodes:

(8) a. *Topos:*

$$\left(\begin{bmatrix} x & : Ind \\ c_{bird} & : \mathrm{bird}(x) \end{bmatrix}_1\right) \xrightarrow{0.95} \left(\begin{bmatrix} c_{fly} : \mathrm{fly}(1.x) \end{bmatrix}_2\right)$$

  b. *Enthymeme:*

$$\left(\begin{bmatrix} x = \text{Tweety} : Ind \\ c_{bird} : \mathrm{bird}(\text{Tweety}) \end{bmatrix}_1\right) \xrightarrow{0.95} \left(\begin{bmatrix} c_{fly} : \mathrm{fly}(\text{Tweety}) \end{bmatrix}_2\right)$$

Once x is filled (as 'Tweety'), this should be reflected in any other nodes where the same variable appears. The confidence rating of 0.95 has been somewhat arbitrarily set here for topoi to imply high confidence without certainty. Generally, the confidence rating associated with a link in a known network should be subject to change on the basis of experience, increasing or decreasing as their predictions are borne out or subverted. Topoi as 'rules of thumb' are particularly robust to contradictory evidence, with the same agent in different contexts accepting and using topoi that lead to opposite conclusions: see, for example, notions *opposites attract* vs. *birds of a feather flock together*. Integration of ordinary learning with the potential for entrenched 'against all evidence' beliefs is a larger topic that is not addressed here, but will be necessary in future work.

Enthymemes are distinguished from other arguments by the fact they don't hold up by themselves, but are instead accepted on the basis of identification with a topos – this doesn't include arguments that are accepted despite being unsupported. However, the terms enthymeme and topos will continue to be used here: this is partly for convenience, but also because once the context indicates that an enthymemetic argument is being made (such as a recognisable suggestion+motivation pattern like "Let's go left here, it's a shortcut"), an unsupported 'enthymeme', once accepted, can be used to establish a potential new topos (Breitholtz, 2015).

2.2 Graphical Topoi in TTR

This subsection provides a treatment in TTR of the above proposal. The variable at each node is a $RecType$, representing a situation, with the probability of a $RecType$ being across whether it is true or false (for type T, whether $\exists a : T$). Let $RecType_i$ be a $RecType$ associated with an index, and $ProbInfo$ be a constraint on some probability. The supertype of enthymemes and topoi, rather than a function $Rec{\rightarrow}RecType$, is the type *Network*:

(9) *Network* $=_{def}$

$$\begin{bmatrix} \text{nodes} : \left\{ RecType_i \right\} \\ \text{links} : \left\{ \langle RecType_i, RecType_i \rangle \right\} \\ \text{probs} : \left\{ ProbInfo \right\} \\ c_{index} : \forall \langle x'_j, y_p \rangle, \in \text{links}, x'_j \sqsubseteq_r x_i \in \text{nodes}, i = j, \\ \qquad \forall \langle z_q, x''_k \rangle \in \text{links}, x''_k \sqsubseteq_r x_i \in \text{nodes}, i = k. \\ c_{links} : \forall \langle x'_i, y'_p \rangle \in \text{links}, \exists x_i, y_p \in \text{nodes}, x'_i \sqsubseteq_r x_i, y'_p \sqsubseteq_r y_p \end{bmatrix}$$

The *nodes* field is the set of nodes in the graph, while the *links* field is the set of directed edges between them, each 'link' being an ordered pair. Let $\sqsubseteq_r$ indicate a subtype relation where subtyping is through restriction of one or more fields i.e. not through the specification of extra fields. The first constraint c_{index} enforces co-indexing, that if subtypes of a node are included in members of *links*, they all share the same index. The second constraint c_{links} specifies that any members of *links* are between (potentially restricted subtypes of) members of *nodes*. For ease of reading and the sake of space, the constraints will not be repeated in further examples. In a link $\langle x_i, x_j \rangle$, the specification of member x_i may use j to indicate some $r : x_j$, and vice versa, e.g. where a is some field in x_i and b is some field in x_j, in x_i we can specify that $a = j.b$.

Causality, non-causal correlation and independence are interpreted on the basis of the members of *links*. Where a path is a sequence of indices $\langle 1, \dots, k \rangle$ such that for each $i, i + 1$ there is $\langle x_i, x_{i+1} \rangle \in links$, the node indexed i is a predecessor of the node indexed j (shorthand: *predecessor*$(i, j, links)$) if there is a path from i to j, given the contents of *links*. In this way the set *links* can be checked for evidence that two nodes are in a non-causal relation (if there is a bi-directional *predecessor* relation somewhere in a path between the two, e.g. if $\langle x_i, x_j \rangle, \langle x_j, x_i \rangle \in links$), are potentially independent (there is no *predecessor* relation at all between the two), or in a potentially causal relation (one is a *predecessor* of the other, but not the other way around). We can distinguish direct and indirect causality by whether a minimal path with a direct link $\langle x_i, x_j \rangle$ is possible or not. As a rule, when we talk about causality, we will mean direct causality.

For $n : Network$ containing nodes x_i and x_j, independence and causality can be expressed in updated n' as follows, where $a \wedge b$ indicates the merge of two records, a record containing all fields from both, and $a \boxed{\wedge} b$ indicates their asymmetric merge (see Cooper and Ginzburg, 2015), where in event of a field appearing in both records, the field from b is the one found in the merge, effectively overwriting the field of a.

(10) *Independence of i and j:*
$$n' = n \wedge$$
$$\begin{bmatrix} c_{ind_{ij}} : \neg predecessor(i, j, links) \\ \qquad \wedge \neg predecessor(j, i, links) \end{bmatrix}$$

(11) *Direct causality from i to j:*
$$n' = n \wedge$$
$$\begin{bmatrix} c_{cause_{ij}} : \langle i, j \rangle \in links \\ \qquad \wedge \neg predecessor(j, i, links) \end{bmatrix}$$

(12) *Indirect causality from i to j:*
$$n' = n \wedge$$
$$\begin{bmatrix} c_{indcaus_{ij}} : predecessor(j, i, links) \\ \qquad \wedge \neg predecessor(j, i, links) \end{bmatrix}$$

The original example can now be rewritten as (13):

(13) *Topos:*
$$\begin{bmatrix} \text{nodes} = \\ \left\{ \begin{bmatrix} x : \text{Ind} \\ c_{bird} : \text{bird(x)} \end{bmatrix}_1, \begin{bmatrix} x : \text{Ind} \\ c_{fly} : \text{fly(x)} \end{bmatrix}_2 \right\} : \left\{ RecType_i \right\} \\ \text{links} = \\ \left\{ \left\langle \begin{bmatrix} x : \text{Ind} \\ c_{bird} : \text{bird(x)} \end{bmatrix}_1, \begin{bmatrix} \mathbf{x} = 1.\mathbf{x} : \text{Ind} \\ c_{fly} : \text{fly(x)} \end{bmatrix}_2 \right\rangle \right\} : \left\{ \langle RecType_i, RecType_i \rangle \right\} \\ \text{probs} = \\ \left\{ P \left(\begin{bmatrix} \mathbf{x} = \mathbf{r}.\mathbf{x} : \text{Ind} \\ c_{fly} : \text{fly(x)} \end{bmatrix}_2 \ \middle|\ r : \begin{bmatrix} x : \text{Ind} \\ c_{bird} : \text{bird(x)} \end{bmatrix}_1 \right) = 0.95 \right\} : \left\{ \text{ProbInfo} \right\} \end{bmatrix}$$

(14) *Enthymeme:* as above, but all variants indexed with 1 are replaced with
$$\begin{bmatrix} \mathbf{x} = \mathbf{Tweety} : \text{Ind} \\ c_{bird} : \text{bird(x)} \end{bmatrix}_1$$

An *Enth* is defined as a *Network* containing a node that has at least one field restricted to a specific object, removing its generality. A *Topos* is a *Network* in which no fields are restricted to a specific object.

An enthymeme e may be identified with a topos t if its nodes and links have equivalents in t, that is if for every node $x_i \in e.nodes, \exists y_p \in t.nodes$ such that $x_i \sqsubseteq y_p$ and for any links $\langle x'_i, x'_j \rangle \in e.links, \exists \langle y'_p, y'_q \rangle \in t.links$ such that $x'_i \sqsubseteq y'_p$ and $x'_j \sqsubseteq y'_q$. This may be by a clear match for the topos fields, but may also include the types of fields in the enthymeme as subtypes of fields in the topos[1].

3 Conditionals and Reasoning

Having reformalised topoi and enthymemes as an object intended for more general correlational and causal knowledge, i.e. like a Bayesian network[2] we turn back to conditionals.

---

[1] as in the example "Give a coin to the porter, he carried the bags all the way here" from (Breitholtz, 2014b), where carrying someone else's bags is recognised as a subtype of work, and the enthymemetic argument is on the basis of a topos like *work should be rewarded*

[2] though not strictly: the graph of a Bayesian network should be acyclic, while these do allow for cycles

Firstly, and as mentioned at the beginning, expressing this kind of relational knowledge is (both intuitively and according to empirical evidence) strongly associated with conditionals, and existence of a dependence relation and high conditional probability usually determine their acceptability. Van Rooij and Schulz (2019) suggest a way to combine these two features into a single measure, the relative difference the state of the parent in a relation makes to the likelihood of the child. Pleasingly, with some independence assumptions this measure works not only for the 'causal' direction typically expressed by conditionals (*if there's fire, there's smoke*), but for the reverse as expressed by evidential conditionals (*if there's smoke, there's fire*). However, for it to do so, the direction of the relationship still has to be recognised even when the 'usual' roles of antecedent as parent and consequent as child have flipped. This kind of structural knowledge is topoic.

Secondly, and while it feels almost trivial to point out, we use conditionals to tell each other new things, e.g. the speaker explaining their experiences with "if you done anything wrong well you get, you get the cane and anything else" (BNC, *H5G 78*). When we are informed of something through the use of a conditional, we don't necessarily know beforehand that they lie in such a relation: otherwise they would only be useful to draw attention to connections we haven't made, not to tell each other things that are entirely new. Indeed, Skovgaard-Olsen et al. (2016) found evidence that when faced with a conditional, people assume that there is a positive connection between antecedent and consequent unless they have reason to believe otherwise. It is not so much that an acceptable conditional has to be backed up by pre-existing knowledge about the relation between the antecedent and consequent cases, but at the very least it should not *clash* with any.

Breitholtz (2014a) mentions how an enthymemetic argument can be recognised on the basis of the current conversational game/expected rules (with the specific example of knowledge that a suggestion may be followed by the speaker providing a motivation), or by an explicit lexical cue. With the above in mind, I will suggest that use of an *if*-conditional is one such linguistic cue.

3.1 Enthymemetic Conditionals

The overall suggestion is as follows. *If*-conditionals are associated with the making of enthymeme-like arguments. Note that I say "enthymeme-*like* arguments", not "enthymemetic arguments". Enthymemes depend on identification with a previously-known topos, while conditionals can be used to teach new relations, rather than just make statements that rely on existing knowledge to make sense. Although they are structured like the characterisation of enthymemes and topoi above, they are not all strictly speaking 'enthymemetic'. The content of a conditional can be checked against the topoi in the agent's resources. Given a match with a topos, an enhanced version can be added to the agent's knowledge.

Even without a guiding topos, conditionals allow us to express or learn information via an assumption that there is a positive connection between antecedent and consequent – provided we do not already know that the two are independent, or that the consequent shouldn't follow from the antecedent. If no supporting topos is found, a more minimal version can be added without the benefit of any extra details a topos might have provided.

The direction of antecedent as parent is 'default' in the sense that it should be preferred if distinct topoi in both directions are available, and is the direction assumed in case neither a supporting topos nor a conflicting one is found. The topoi in an agent's resources may conflict with each other, and by necessity one of them was learned first: despite this, a conditional does not lead to formation of an acceptable enthymeme when such a clashing topos is already present. If there only exists a potential match for the nodes in a topos that specifies there is definitely no link, or is a conflicting link, then the conditional should be rejected.

The processes of comparing a potential enthymeme with a topos and of updating structured knowledge on the basis of a conditional can be thought of algorithmically as follows:

(15) *Match between an enthymeme and topos:*
Search known topoi for topos with a node matching the first enthymeme node
If none: no match, `false`.
If found: check topos for nodes matching each further node in enthymeme.
If any failure: resume searching topoi.

If found: check each edge in enthymeme has an equivalent in topos.

If any failure: resume searching topoi.

If found: check any constraints in enthymeme have an equivalent in topos.

If found: match, `true`.

If any failure: resume searching topoi.

(16) *Enhancing an enthymeme with a topos:*
Make new copy of topos.

For each node in topos with an equivalent in enthymeme, add any further specification.

For any node in topos with no equivalent node in enthymeme, but with elements also found in a node that was further specified, update accordingly.

(17) *Updating with a conditional:*
Check for conflicting topos.

If found, `reject`.

If not found, check for topos matching *ant→cons* equivalent link.

If found, `enhance` *ant→cons* and `add`.

If not found, check for topos matching *ant←cons* equivalent link.

If found, `enhance` *ant←cons* and `add`.

If not found, `add` *ant→cons*.

Below are illustrations of what should be understood from the evidential conditional "If the glass fell, the cat pushed it", given knowledge of a topos equivalent to *if someone pushes something, the thing falls.*

(18) *Ant. content:* (19) *Cons. content:*

$$\begin{bmatrix} x = \mathrm{obj}_3 \\ c_{glass} = \mathrm{glass(obj}_3) \\ c_{fall} = \mathrm{fall(obj}_3) \end{bmatrix} \qquad \begin{bmatrix} x = \mathrm{obj}_4 \\ y = \mathrm{obj}_3 \\ c_{cat} = \mathrm{cat(obj}_4) \\ c_{push} = \mathrm{push(obj}_4, \mathrm{obj}_3) \end{bmatrix}$$

(20) *Topos:*

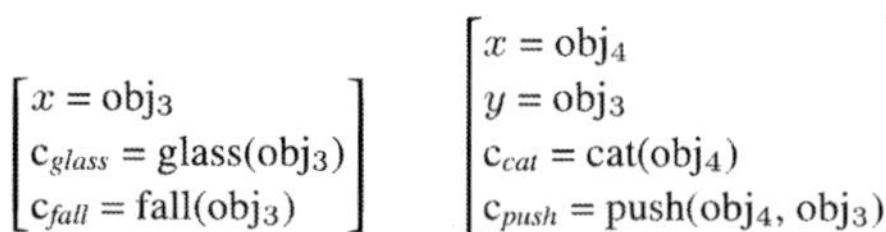

(21) *Enhanced enthymeme:*

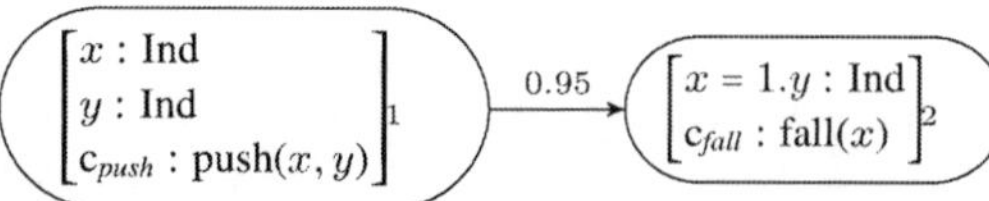

The following subsections describe dialogue state update rules associated with conditionals, characterised in TTR.

3.2 Enthymemetic Conditionals in TTR

To begin with, the type of an information state is minimally given as (22), broadly following the decisions for the place of enthymemes and topoi in Breitholtz (2014a) etc.

(22) *InfoState* $=_{def}$

$$\begin{bmatrix} \mathrm{priv} & : \begin{bmatrix} \mathrm{Topoi} & : \{\mathrm{Topos}\} \end{bmatrix} \\ \mathrm{shrd} & : \begin{bmatrix} \mathrm{enths} & : \{\mathrm{Enth}\} \\ \mathrm{Topoi} & : \{\mathrm{Topos}\} \\ \mathrm{Moves} & : \mathrm{list(LocProp)} \end{bmatrix} \end{bmatrix}$$

(23) *Update rule* $=_{def}$

$$\begin{bmatrix} \mathrm{pre} & : \mathrm{InfoState} \\ \mathrm{effects} & : \mathrm{Infostate} \end{bmatrix}$$

The information state has two parts: the agent's private resources, and their representation of the shared context. The *private* resources include a set of general topoi which they can use as resources. A public *Topoi* field tracks which topoi have been introduced onto the dialogue gameboard. The general form for update rules is given in (23): *pre* describes the preconditions for states to which the rule can be applied, and *effects* the changes.

Next we will add a few useful functions on the basis of some of the content of Section 2.1: a means to describe whether there is a successful match between an enthymeme and a topos, and a means to reference the result of an enthymeme that has been enriched by the content of a topos.

(24) *enthMatch*(e : Enth, t : Topos) : Bool,
true iff all of the following hold

(i) All e's nodes are subtypes of t's nodes:
$\forall x_i \in e.nodes, \exists y_p \in t.nodes$
such that $x_i \sqsubseteq y_p$,

(ii) All e's links are subtypes of t's links:
$\forall \langle x_i', x_j' \rangle \in e.links, \exists \langle y_p', y_q' \rangle \in t.links$
such that $x_i' \sqsubseteq y_p'$ and $x_j' \sqsubseteq y_q'$,

(iii) For any constraints on links in e, the same constraints hold for equivalent links in t:
$\forall c_{ind_{ij}} \in e, \exists c_{ind_{pq}} \in t$ or $c_{ind_{qp}} \in t$,
$x_i \in e.nodes, y_p \in t.nodes, x_i \sqsubseteq y_p$ and
$x_j \in e.nodes, y_q \in t.nodes, x_j \sqsubseteq y_q$.
Likewise for all $c_{cause_{ij}} \in e$, there is an equivalent $c_{cause_{pq}} \in t$.

(25) *enhanceEnth*(e : Enth, t : Topos) : Enth,
e' such that e' is an asymmetric merge of t and e,

where the sets in *nodes*, *links* and *probs* undergo asymmetric union such that for any nodes $x_i \in e.nodes, y_p \in t.nodes$, $x_i \sqsubseteq y_p$, the corresponding node $z_u \in e'.nodes = y_p \boxed{\wedge} x_i$.

Likewise for any subtypes x_i' and y_p', $x_i' \sqsubseteq y_p'$ in members of $e.links$, $t.links$, $e.probs$ and $t.probs$.

That is, the asymmetric aspect of the merge is at the level of the indexed nodes, not the fields containing them.

The update rules for each case are given in the subsections below. There are three rules given: where there is a supporting topos in the 'default' direction, where there is not but there is a supporting topos in the reverse direction, and where there is neither support nor a clash.

3.2.1 Recognising a supporting topos

First are the update rules for when the agent has a topos linking the two parts of the conditional: The update in case of a supporting topos in the $ant{\rightarrow}cons$ direction is given in (26):

(26) *default direction, $ant{\rightarrow}cons$:*

$$\begin{bmatrix} \text{pre}: \begin{bmatrix} \text{priv}: \begin{bmatrix} \text{Topoi} & : \{\text{Topos}\} \\ t & : \text{Topos} \\ c_{member} & : t \in \text{Topoi} \\ c_{def} & : enthMatch(x:X,t) \end{bmatrix} \\ \text{shrd}: \begin{bmatrix} \text{Moves[0]} = \text{Assert(if(a, b))} & : \text{LocProp} \end{bmatrix} \end{bmatrix} \\ \text{effects}: \begin{bmatrix} \text{shrd}: \\ \begin{bmatrix} enths = \text{pre.shrd.enths} \\ \qquad \cup\, enhanceEnth(x:X,t) : \{\text{Enth}\} \\ \text{Topoi} = \text{pre.shrd.Topoi} \cup \text{pre.priv}.t : \{\text{Topos}\} \end{bmatrix} \end{bmatrix} \end{bmatrix}$$

where X is the type

$$\begin{bmatrix} nodes = \{\text{a.sit-type}_1, \text{b.sit-type}_2\} : RecType_i \\ links = \{\langle\text{a.sit-type}_1, \text{b.sit-type}_2\rangle\} : \langle RecType_i, RecType_i\rangle \\ probs = \{\text{P(b.sit-type}_2 \,|\, \text{r}: \text{a.sit-type}_1) = 0.95\} : \text{ProbInfo} \end{bmatrix}$$

This rule may be applied following assertion of a conditional, where an agent knows a topos t that matches an enthymeme based on the content of the conditional, with a link from antecedent to consequent. In this case, the agent may add such an enthymeme enhanced with the topos to their *enths*, and add the underlying topos to the set of currently active topoi in the conversation.

Where such an option does not exist, a topos with only a link from consequent to antecedent can be used, as described in (27). The enthymeme added to *enths* in this case will contain a link only in the $ant{\leftarrow}cons$ direction.

(27) *alternative direction, $ant{\leftarrow}cons$:*

$$\begin{bmatrix} \text{pre}: \begin{bmatrix} \text{shrd}: \begin{bmatrix} \text{Moves[0]} = \text{Assert(if(a, b))} & : \text{LocProp} \end{bmatrix} \\ \text{priv}: \begin{bmatrix} \text{Topoi} & : \{\text{Topos}\} \\ t & : \text{Topos} \\ c_{member} & : t \in \text{Topoi} \\ c_{no\text{-}def} & : \nexists t', t' \in Topoi \wedge enthMatch(x:X,t') \\ c_{alt} & : enthMatch(y:Y,t) \end{bmatrix} \end{bmatrix} \\ \text{effects}: \begin{bmatrix} \text{shrd}: \begin{bmatrix} enths = \text{pre.shrd.enths} \\ \qquad \cup\, enhanceEnth(y:Y,t) : \{\text{Enth}\} \\ \text{Topoi} = \text{pre.shrd.Topoi} \cup \text{pre.priv}.t : \{\text{Topos}\} \end{bmatrix} \end{bmatrix} \end{bmatrix}$$

where X is as defined in (26), and Y is the type

$$\begin{bmatrix} nodes = \{\text{a.sit-type}_1, \text{b.sit-type}_2\} : RecType_i \\ links = \{\langle\text{b.sit-type}_2, \text{a.sit-type}_1\rangle\} : \langle RecType_i, RecType_i\rangle \\ probs = \{\text{P(a.sit-type}_1 \,|\, \text{r}: \text{b.sit-type}_2) = 0.95\} : \{\text{ProbInfo}\} \end{bmatrix}$$

Relative to (26), the update rule for this case has a constraint in its preconditions that there are no topoi with a link in the $ant{\rightarrow}cons$ direction, and the enthymeme is instead enhanced by a topos that does support the alternative order.

3.2.2 New information

The last rule describes the case where the agent's known topoi have neither evidence about a link between the antecedent or consequent, the definite absence of one, or a conflicting one. In this case, an 'enthymeme' with a link in the $ant{\rightarrow}cons$ direction may be added to *enths* solely on the basis of the conditional content. No additional topos is added to the list of active topoi – the process for generalising an acceptable enthymeme to a reusable topos is not addressed here.

The shorthand for presence of a clashing topos is given in (28) as *enthClash*. An enthymeme clashes with a topos where the equivalent parent nodes lead to mutually exclusive child nodes, i.e. child nodes where a true type cannot be formed from their meet.

(28) *enthClash$(e : \text{Enth}, t : \text{Topos}) : \text{Bool}$,*
  true iff
  $\exists x_i, y_j \in e.nodes,\, p_i, q_j \in b.nodes,\, x_i \sqsubseteq p_i,$
  $\exists \langle x_i', y_j'\rangle \in e.links,\, x_i' \sqsubseteq x_i, y_j' \sqsubseteq y_j,$

$$\exists \langle p_i', q_j' \rangle \in t.links,\ p_i' \sqsubseteq p_i,\ q_j' \sqsubseteq q_j,$$
$$\text{and } \neg T, \text{ where } T = y_j' \wedge q_j'$$

(29) *neither support nor opposing knowledge:*

$$\begin{bmatrix} \text{pre} : \begin{bmatrix} \text{shrd} : \begin{bmatrix} \text{Moves}[0] = \text{Assert(if(a, b))} : \text{LocProp} \end{bmatrix} \\ \text{priv} : \begin{bmatrix} \text{Topoi} : \{\text{Topos}\} \\ c_{no\text{-}clash} : \not\exists t, t \in Topoi \wedge enthClash(x : X, t) \\ c_{no\text{-}def} : \not\exists t, t \in Topoi \wedge enthMatch(x : X, t) \\ c_{no\text{-}alt} : \not\exists t, t \in Topoi \wedge enthMatch(y : Y, t) \\ c_{no\text{-}ind} : \not\exists t, t \in Topoi \wedge enthMatch(z : Z, t) \end{bmatrix} \end{bmatrix} \\ \text{effects} : \begin{bmatrix} \text{shrd} : \begin{bmatrix} \text{enths} = \text{pre.shrd.enths} \cup x : X \end{bmatrix} \end{bmatrix} \end{bmatrix}$$

where X, Y are as in (26), (27), and Z is the type

$$\begin{bmatrix} \text{nodes} = \{a.\text{sit-type}_1, b.\text{sit-type}_2\} : RecType_i \\ \text{links} = \varnothing : \{\langle RecType_i, RecType_i \rangle\} \\ \text{probs} = \varnothing : \{ProbInfo\} \\ c_{ind_{12}} : \neg predecessor(1, 2, \text{links}) \\ \qquad\qquad \wedge \neg predecessor(2, 1, \text{links}) \end{bmatrix}$$

Relative to the previous two update rules, the preconditions in this rule specify that there is no known topos that supports an enthymeme with a link between the antecedent and consequent in either direction, which has an explicit constraint enforcing independence between the two, or which otherwise clashes with the possible conditional enthymeme.

4 Conclusion

The acceptability of a conditional is often determined by the conditional probability of the consequent on the antecedent, and recognition of some meaningful link between the two. However, both intuitively and according to experimental evidence, positive acceptability judgements can still be made without fore-knowledge of such a connection. This paper presented two proposals on the basis that the knowledge enabling these judgements is topoic, integrating these factors into the representation of the dialogue state and agent resources. First, a formalisation of enthymemes and topoi as graphs was presented, on the grounds that they should be in the same form as other knowledge about causal and correlational relationships. Second, update rules for conditionals using topoi and enthymemes were presented, drawing on topoi to recognise the presence and direction of a 'meaningful' connection between antecedent and consequent, and making an assumption of one in the absence of any evidence.

There are several avenues for further work. Most work focuses on declarative conditionals, the most common form by far. However, conditional clauses are also used to form conditionalised questions and directives. The proposals here should be related to these forms, whether because to an extent they apply in those cases too, or because this topoic association is exclusive to declarative conditionals. This paper has also said nothing about more standard propositional aspects of conditionals. The proposals here about structural knowledge associated with conditionals should be integrated with this more standard fare.

Acknowledgements

Thanks to Jonathan Ginzburg for helpful discussion of and feedback on this work, and to the reviewers  for useful comments which have (I hope) made this paper clearer. This project has received funding from the European Union's Horizon 2020 research and innovation programme under the Marie Skłodowska-Curie grant agreement No 665850.

References

Jonathan Bennett. 2003. A Philosophical Guide to Conditionals. Oxford University Press.

Ellen Breitholtz. 2014a. Enthymemes in Dialogue: A micro-rhetorical approach. Ph.D. thesis, University of Gothenburg.

Ellen Breitholtz. 2014b. Reasoning with topoi – towards a rhetorical approach to non-monotonicity. In Proceedings of the 50th anniversary convention of the AISB, 1st–4th April.

Ellen Breitholtz. 2015. Are widows always wicked? learning concepts through enthymematic reasoning. In Proceedings of the TYTLES workshop on Type Theory and Lexical Semantics, Barcelona.

Ellen Breitholtz and Robin Cooper. 2011. Enthymemes as rhetorical resources. In Proceedings of the 15th Workshop on the Semantics and Pragmatics of Dialogue (SemDial 2011), pages 149–157.

Robin Cooper. Type theory and language: From perception to linguistic communication. In prep.

Robin Cooper. 2012. Type theory and semantics in flux. In Ruth Kempson, Tim Fernando, and Nicholas Asher, editors, Philosophy of Linguistics, Handbook of the Philosophy of Science, pages 271 – 323. North-Holland, Amsterdam.

Robin Cooper and Jonathan Ginzburg. 2015. TTR for natural language semantics. In Chris Fox and Shalom Lappin, editors, Handbook of Contemporary Semantic Theory, 2 edition, pages 375–407. Blackwell, Oxford.

Igor Douven. 2008. The evidential support theory of conditionals. Synthese, 164(1):19–44.

Igor Douven and Sara Verbrugge. 2013. The probabilities of conditionals revisited. Cognitive Science, 37(4):711–730.

Dorothy Edgington. 1995. On conditionals. Mind, 104(414):235–329.

Jonathan St. B. T. Evans, Simon J. Handley, and David E. Over. 2003. Conditionals and conditional probability. Journal of Experimental Psychology: Learning, Memory, and Cognition, 29(2):321–335.

Anthony S Gillies. 2010. Iffiness. Semantics and Pragmatics, 3:1–42.

Irene Heim. 1982. The Semantics of Definite and Indefinite Noun Phrases. Ph.D. thesis, MIT.

Angelika Kratzer. 1986. Conditionals. Chicago Linguistics Society, 22(2):1–15.

David Kellogg Lewis. 1975. Adverbs of quantification. In Edward L. Keenan, editor, Formal Semantics of Natural Language, pages 3–15. Cambridge University Press.

David Kellogg Lewis. 1976. Probabilities of conditionals and conditional probabilities. The Philosophical Review, 85(3):297–315.

Mike Oaksford and Nick Chater. 2003. Conditional probability and the cognitive science of conditional reasoning. Mind and Language, 18(4):359–379.

Judith Pijnacker, Bart Geurts, Michiel van Lambalgen, Cornelis C. Kan, Jan K. Buitelaar, and Peter Hagoort. 2009. Defeasible reasoning in high-functioning adults with autism: Evidence for impaired exception-handling. Neuropsychologia, 47(3):644–651.

Robert van Rooij and Katrin Schulz. 2019. Conditionals, causality and conditional probability. Journal of Logic, Language and Information, 28(1):55–71.

Niels Skovgaard-Olsen, Henrik Singmann, and Karl Christoph Klauer. 2016. The relevance effect and conditionals. Cognition, 150:26–36.

Robert Stalnaker. 1970. Probability and conditionals. Philosophy of Science, 37(1):64–80.

Acquiring Structured Temporal Representation via Crowdsourcing: A Feasibility Study

Yuchen Zhang
Brandeis University
`yuchenz@brandeis.edu`

Nianwen Xue
Brandeis University
`xuen@brandeis.edu`

Abstract

Temporal Dependency Trees are a structured temporal representation that represents temporal relations among time expressions and events in a text as a dependency tree structure. Compared to traditional pair-wise temporal relation representations, temporal dependency trees facilitate efficient annotations, higher inter-annotator agreement, and efficient computations. However, annotations on temporal dependency trees so far have only been done by expert annotators, which is costly and time-consuming. In this paper, we introduce a method to crowdsource temporal dependency tree annotations, and show that this representation is intuitive and can be collected with high accuracy and agreement through crowdsourcing. We produce a corpus of temporal dependency trees, and present a baseline temporal dependency parser, trained and evaluated on this new corpus.

1 Introduction

Temporal relation extraction is an important NLP task for a range of downstream applications, such as question answering, summarization, and storyline generation. This task has attracted a significant amount of research interest (Pustejovsky et al., 2003a; Verhagen et al., 2007, 2010; Uz-Zaman et al., 2012; Bethard et al., 2016, 2017; Dligach et al., 2017; Leeuwenberg and Moens, 2017; Ning et al., 2017, 2018a,b; Zhang and Xue, 2018a,b). One practical challenge in temporal relation extraction is to represent the temporal relations in a text in a way that is feasible for manual annotation and producing training data for machine learning models. Given a text of n events and time expressions, there are $\binom{n}{2}$ possible relations if the temporal relation between all pairs of events and time expressions is annotated. This quickly becomes infeasible even for a text of modest length. One way to address this problem is to represent the temporal relations in a text as a Temporal Dependency Tree (TDT) structure (Zhang and Xue, 2018b). TDT models all time expressions and events in a text as "nodes" in a dependency tree, and temporal relations between each time/event and its parent time/event as "edges" in the tree. Figure 1 gives an example text and its TDT. Each (parent, child) pair in Figure 1 is annotated with a temporal relation. The number of temporal relations that need to be annotated in a text is therefore linear to the number of events and time expressions in a text, making the annotation task feasible. At the same time, additional temporal relations can be inferred as needed based on the TDT structure. For example, in Figure 1 since "1918" *includes* the "born" event and "1929" *includes* the "won" event, it can be inferred that the "born" event occurred *before* the "won" event.

By providing annotators with detailed guidelines and training them in multiple iterations, Zhang and Xue (2018b) have shown that the TDT representation can be annotated with high inter-annotator agreement. Zhang and Xue (2018a) further show that a neural ranking model can be successfully trained on the corpus. However, this "traditional" approach to annotation is time-consuming and expensive. The question we want to answer in this paper is whether TDT can be performed with crowdsourcing, a method that has gained popularity as a means to acquire linguistically annotated data quickly and cost-effectively for NLP research.

Crowdsourcing has been used to annotate data for a wide range of NLP tasks that include question answering, word similarity, text entailment, word sense disambiguation, machine translation, information extraction, summarization, and semantic role labeling (Snow et al., 2008; Finin et al., 2010; Zaidan and Callison-Burch, 2011; Lloret et al., 2013; Rajpurkar et al., 2018). The

178

*Proceedings of the Eighth Joint Conference on Lexical and Computational Semantics (*SEM)*, pages 178–185
Minneapolis, June 6–7, 2019. ©2019 Association for Computational Linguistics

key to acquiring high quality data via crowd-sourcing is to make sure that the tasks are intuitive or can be decomposed into intuitive subtasks. In this paper, we show that it is possible to acquire high quality temporal dependency structures through crowdsourcing, and that a temporal dependency parser can be successfully trained on crowdsourced TDTs.

The rest of the paper is organized as follows. We first explain in detail how we set up this dependency tree crowdsourcing annotation task (§2). In (§3) we present experimental results that show that if temporal dependency structures are broken into smaller subtasks, high inter-annotator agreement can be achieved. In (§4), we show that crowdsource data can be used to successfully train temporal dependency parsers, including an attention-based neural model (§4). We discuss related work (§5) and conclude with future work (§6).

The main contributions of this paper are: (1) we introduce an effective approach to crowdsource structured temporal annotations, a relatively complex annotation task; (2) we build an English temporal dependency tree corpus through crowdsourcing that we plan to make publicly available; and (3) we experiment with automatic temporal dependency parsers on this new corpus and report competitive results.

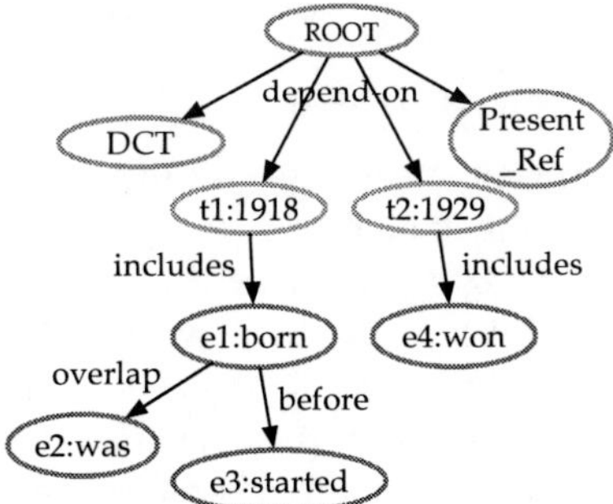

Figure 1: Example text and its temporal dependency tree. The nodes in blue are meta nodes (e.g., document creation time "DCT", present reference time "Present_Ref", etc.), the nodes in orange are time expressions, and the nodes in green are events.

2   Crowdsourcing Tasks Setup

2.1   Data Setup

Our TDT annotations are performed on top of the TimeBank corpus (Pustejovsky et al., 2003b), with time expressions and events already extracted. Following (Zhang and Xue, 2018b), we focus only on events that are matrix verbs (i.e. main verbs) in a sentence. In order to extract matrix verbs, we use the gold constituent trees for the part of TimeBank that overlaps with the Penn Treebank, and parse the rest of TimeBank with the Berkeley Neural Parser (Kitaev and Klein, 2018). All time expressions in TimeBank are kept.

To facilitate quality control in crowdsourcing and agreement evaluation, we distinguish two subsets of the TimeBank dataset: (1) TB-small is a small subset of 10 short Wall Street Journal news documents with 59 matrix verbs. (2) TB-dense consists of the same 36 documents as in the TimeBank-Dense corpus (Cassidy et al., 2014). It contains 654 matrix verbs. TB-small and TB-dense are annotated by both crowd workers and experts.

2.2   Annotation Tasks

We set up two annotation tasks. The first is full temporal dependency tree annotation, where crowd workers need to annotate both the dependency tree structure and the temporal relations between each parent and child. The second is relation-only annotation, where crowd workers are given the gold temporal dependency trees and their job is just to label the temporal relation for each parent-child pair.

2.3   Crowdsourcing Design

For the full temporal dependency tree annotation, in order to simplify the questions/instructions to crowd workers, we split the task of annotating a full dependency tree into (1) finding the "parent" for each individual event, and then (2) deciding the temporal relation between the "parent" and the event. A crowd worker is given a text with a highlighted target event and a list of candidate parent time expressions and events. The job of the crowd worker is to select one parent from the given list of candidates, and label the temporal relation between the parent and the target event. For relation-only annotation, a crowd worker is presented a text with the target event and its parent highlighted. The job of the worker is to decide the temporal

179

relation between the two. See Appendix A for example crowdsourcing instructions and questions.

Following standard crowdsourcing quality control, we perform a qualifying test on both annotation tasks. Any crowd worker who wants to work on these tasks needs to complete annotations on TB-small and reach at least 70% accuracy against the expert gold annotation. We also perform a surviving test on the relation-only annotation task. Crowd workers have to maintain at least a cumulative accuracy of 70% for their annotation. Workers with a lower accuracy will get blocked from the task and all of their annotations will be discarded. Every annotation is completed by at least 3 annotators and the majority vote is the final annotation.

3   Annotation Experiments

Crowdsourcing annotations on the full TimeBank corpus was performed. We report Inter-Annotator Agreement (IAA) scores in Table 1.

	UAA	LOA	LAA
Crowd v.s. Expert	.82	.83	.53
Crowd IAA	.81	.85	.52

Table 1: Inter-Annotator Agreement scores between crowdsourced and expert annotations, and IAAs among crowd worker annotations.

First, crowdsourced majority annotations on TB-dense are evaluated against expert annotations, representing the quality of the crowdsourced data. For this comparison, the standard dependency parsing evaluation metrics (Kübler et al., 2009) are used as our IAA scores: structure-only annotation subtask is evaluated with the Unlabeled Attachment Agreement (UAA) score, relation-only annotation subtask is evaluated with the Label Only Agreement (LOA) score, and full pipeline annotation is evaluated with the Labeled Attachment Agreement (LAA) score.

Second, crowd worker annotations are compared against each other, indicating the difficulty, consistency, and confidence of the crowdsourced data. Since crowd workers annotate isolated events/times instead of full dependency structures, the standard dependency parsing metrics are not applicable for this comparison[1]. Therefore, we adopt the Worker Agreements With Aggregate (WAWA) metric (Ning et al., 2018a) as our IAA

scores. WAWA indicates the average number of crowd worker responses agreed with the aggregate answer (i.e. majority aggregation for each annotation instance), representing the agreements among crowd workers and how consistent their annotations are with each other.

As shown in the table, high accuracies and agreements are achieved for both the subtasks of structure annotation and relation-only annotation (above 80%).

Statistics on our corpus and other similar TimeBank-based temporal relation corpora are presented in Table 2. As the number of temporal relations is linear to the number of events and time expressions in a text, fewer temporal relations need to be annotated in our corpus. In comparison, the recently crowdsourced temporal structure corpus MATRES (Ning et al. (2018a), see Section 5 for more details) only annotates verb events in a document while TB-dense annotates a larger number of time expressions and events in a much smaller number of documents. Our corpus retains the full set of TimeBank time expressions and covers comparable number of events as MATRES. We pay $0.01 for each individual annotation and the entire TimeBank TDT annotation cost about $300 in total.

	Docs	Timex	Events	Rels
TimeBank	183	1,414	7,935	6,418
TB-Dense	36	289	1,729	12,715
MATRES	275	-	1,790	13,577
This work	183	1,414	2,691	4,105

Table 2: Documents, timex, events, and temporal relation statistics in various temporal corpora.

4   System Experiments

We experiment with a state-of-the-art attention-based neural temporal dependency parser (Zhang and Xue, 2018a)[2] on our newly annotated data. Our training data consists of two parts. The first part is the crowdsourced temporal dependency annotations over the TimeBank documents (excluding documents that are in the dev and test sets in the TimeBank-Dense corpus[3]). The second part is our expert-annotated TDTs on the TimeBank-Dense training set documents. The parser is tuned

---

[1]And for the same reason, Cohen's kappa and Fleiss' kappa scores are not applicable here either.

[2]`https://github.com/yuchenz/tdp_ranking`

[3]Standard TimeBank-Dense train/dev/test split can be found in Cassidy et al. (2014).

and evaluated on our expert TDT annotations on the TimeBank-Dense dev and test sets, respectively. This neural model represents words with bi-LSTM vectors and uses an attention-based mechanism to represent multi-word time expressions and events.

We also experiment with two baseline parsers from Zhang and Xue (2018a): (1) a simple baseline that takes an event's immediate previous time expression or event as its parent and assigns the majority "overlap" as the temporal relation between them; and (2) a logistic regression model that represents time expressions and events with their time/event type features, lexical features, and distance features. Table 3 shows the performance of these systems on our data.

Model	Structure-only F		Structure + Relation F	
	dev	test	dev	test
Simple Baseline	.43	.42	.15	.18
LogReg Baseline	.64	.70	.26	.29
Neural Model	**.75**	**.79**	**.53**	**.60**

Table 3: Parsing results of the simple baseline, logistic regression baseline, and the neural temporal dependency model.

Improved performance over the simple baseline with both the LogReg system and the Neural system show that temporal dependency information can be learned from this crowdsourced corpus. Comparisons between the LogReg baseline and the Neural model show that the Neural model adapts better to new data sets than the LogReg model with manually-crafted language-specific features.

5 Related Work

Although crowdsourcing is widely used in other NLP tasks, there have been only a few temporal relation annotation tasks via crowdsourcing. The first attempt on crowdsourcing temporal relation annotations is described in Snow et al. (2008). They selected a restricted subset of verb events from TimeBank and performed strict before/after temporal relation annotation through crowdsourcing. They reported high agreements showing that simple temporal relations are crowdsourceable. Ng and Kan (2012) adopts the TimeML representation from the TimeBank, and crowdsourced temporal annotations on news articles crawled from news websites. Their experiments show that the large crowdsourced data improved classifier performance significantly. However, both of these works focused on pair-wise temporal relations and didn't experiment with crowdsourcing more complex temporal structures. Vempala and Blanco (2018) uses a crowdsourcing approach to collect temporal and spatial knowledge. However, they first automatically generated such knowledge and then used crowdsourcing to either validate or discard these automatically generated information, and crowdsourcing was not utilized to do annotation from scratch.

Ning et al. (2018a) proposed a "multi-axis" representation of temporal relations in a text, and published the MATRES corpus by annotating "multi-axis" temporal structures on top of the TempEval-3 data through crowdsourcing. In this representation, events are annotated on different "axes" according to their eventuality types, and for events on the same axis, pair-wise temporal relations are annotated. Their annotation task is broken down to two smaller subtasks too. In the first subtask, crowd workers annotate whether an event is on a given axis. In the second subtask, crowd workers annotate the temporal relations between pairs of events on the same axis. The main differences between their work and ours are as follows. First, they only model events, excluding time expressions which are important temporal components in text too. Second, our temporal dependency tree representation is very different from their multi-axis temporal representation, which requires different crowdsourcing task designs. In their first subtask, crowd workers need to distinguish different eventuality types, while our annotation experiments show that crowd workers can also consistently recognize "parents" as defined in Zhang and Xue (2018b) for given events.

6 Conclusion and Future Work

In this paper, we introduce a crowdsourcing approach for acquiring annotations on a relatively complex NLP concept – temporal dependency structures. We build the first English temporal dependency tree corpus through high quality crowdsourcing. Our system experiments show that competitive temporal dependency parsers can be trained on our newly collected data. In future work, we plan to crowdsource more TDT data across different domains.

References

Steven Bethard, Guergana Savova, Wei-Te Chen, Leon Derczynski, James Pustejovsky, and Marc Verhagen. 2016. Semeval-2016 task 12: Clinical tempeval. In *Proceedings of the 10th International Workshop on Semantic Evaluation (SemEval-2016)*, pages 1052–1062.

Steven Bethard, Guergana Savova, Martha Palmer, and James Pustejovsky. 2017. Semeval-2017 task 12: Clinical tempeval. In *Proceedings of the 11th International Workshop on Semantic Evaluation (SemEval-2017)*, pages 565–572.

Taylor Cassidy, Bill McDowell, Nathanael Chambers, and Steven Bethard. 2014. An annotation framework for dense event ordering. In *Proceedings of the 52nd Annual Meeting of the Association for Computational Linguistics (Volume 2: Short Papers)*, volume 2, pages 501–506.

Dmitriy Dligach, Timothy Miller, Chen Lin, Steven Bethard, and Guergana Savova. 2017. Neural temporal relation extraction. In *Proceedings of the 15th Conference of the European Chapter of the Association for Computational Linguistics: Volume 2, Short Papers*, volume 2, pages 746–751.

Tim Finin, Will Murnane, Anand Karandikar, Nicholas Keller, Justin Martineau, and Mark Dredze. 2010. Annotating named entities in twitter data with crowdsourcing. In *Proceedings of the NAACL HLT 2010 Workshop on Creating Speech and Language Data with Amazon's Mechanical Turk*, pages 80–88. Association for Computational Linguistics.

Nikita Kitaev and Dan Klein. 2018. Constituency parsing with a self-attentive encoder. In *Proceedings of the 56th Annual Meeting of the Association for Computational Linguistics (Volume 1: Long Papers)*, Melbourne, Australia. Association for Computational Linguistics.

Sandra Kübler, Ryan McDonald, and Joakim Nivre. 2009. Dependency parsing. *Synthesis Lectures on Human Language Technologies*, 1(1):1–127.

Tuur Leeuwenberg and Marie-Francine Moens. 2017. Structured learning for temporal relation extraction from clinical records. In *Proceedings of the 15th Conference of the European Chapter of the Association for Computational Linguistics*, pages 1150–1158.

Elena Lloret, Laura Plaza, and Ahmet Aker. 2013. Analyzing the capabilities of crowdsourcing services for text summarization. *Language resources and evaluation*, 47(2):337–369.

Jun-Ping Ng and Min-Yen Kan. 2012. Improved temporal relation classification using dependency parses and selective crowdsourced annotations. *Proceedings of COLING 2012*, pages 2109–2124.

Qiang Ning, Zhili Feng, and Dan Roth. 2017. A structured learning approach to temporal relation extraction. In *Proceedings of the 2017 Conference on Empirical Methods in Natural Language Processing*, pages 1027–1037.

Qiang Ning, Hao Wu, and Dan Roth. 2018a. A multi-axis annotation scheme for event temporal relations. *arXiv preprint arXiv:1804.07828*.

Qiang Ning, Zhongzhi Yu, Chuchu Fan, and Dan Roth. 2018b. Exploiting partially annotated data in temporal relation extraction. In *Proceedings of the Seventh Joint Conference on Lexical and Computational Semantics*, pages 148–153.

James Pustejovsky, José M Castano, Robert Ingria, Roser Sauri, Robert J Gaizauskas, Andrea Setzer, Graham Katz, and Dragomir R Radev. 2003a. Timeml: Robust specification of event and temporal expressions in text. *New directions in question answering*, 3:28–34.

James Pustejovsky, Patrick Hanks, Roser Sauri, Andrew See, Robert Gaizauskas, Andrea Setzer, Dragomir Radev, Beth Sundheim, David Day, Lisa Ferro, et al. 2003b. The timebank corpus. In *Corpus linguistics*, volume 2003, page 40. Lancaster, UK.

Pranav Rajpurkar, Robin Jia, and Percy Liang. 2018. Know what you don't know: Unanswerable questions for squad. *arXiv preprint arXiv:1806.03822*.

Rion Snow, Brendan O'Connor, Daniel Jurafsky, and Andrew Y Ng. 2008. Cheap and fast—but is it good?: evaluating non-expert annotations for natural language tasks. In *Proceedings of the conference on empirical methods in natural language processing*, pages 254–263. Association for Computational Linguistics.

Naushad UzZaman, Hector Llorens, James Allen, Leon Derczynski, Marc Verhagen, and James Pustejovsky. 2012. Tempeval-3: Evaluating events, time expressions, and temporal relations. *arXiv preprint arXiv:1206.5333*.

Alakananda Vempala and Eduardo Blanco. 2018. Annotating temporally-anchored spatial knowledge by leveraging syntactic dependencies. In *Proceedings of the Eleventh International Conference on Language Resources and Evaluation (LREC-2018)*.

Marc Verhagen, Robert Gaizauskas, Frank Schilder, Mark Hepple, Graham Katz, and James Pustejovsky. 2007. Semeval-2007 task 15: Tempeval temporal relation identification. In *Proceedings of the 4th International Workshop on Semantic Evaluations*, pages 75–80. Association for Computational Linguistics.

Marc Verhagen, Roser Sauri, Tommaso Caselli, and James Pustejovsky. 2010. Semeval-2010 task 13: Tempeval-2. In *Proceedings of the 5th international workshop on semantic evaluation*, pages 57–62. Association for Computational Linguistics.

Omar F Zaidan and Chris Callison-Burch. 2011. Crowdsourcing translation: Professional quality from non-professionals. In *Proceedings of the 49th Annual Meeting of the Association for Computational Linguistics: Human Language Technologies-Volume 1*, pages 1220–1229. Association for Computational Linguistics.

Yuchen Zhang and Nianwen Xue. 2018a. Neural ranking models for temporal dependency structure parsing. In *Proceedings of the 2018 Conference on Empirical Methods in Natural Language Processing*, pages 3339–3349.

Yuchen Zhang and Nianwen Xue. 2018b. Structured interpretation of temporal relations. In *Proceedings of 11th edition of the Language Resources and Evaluation Conference (LREC-2018)*, Miyazaki, Japan.

A Appendix: Example Crowdsourcing Instructions and Questions

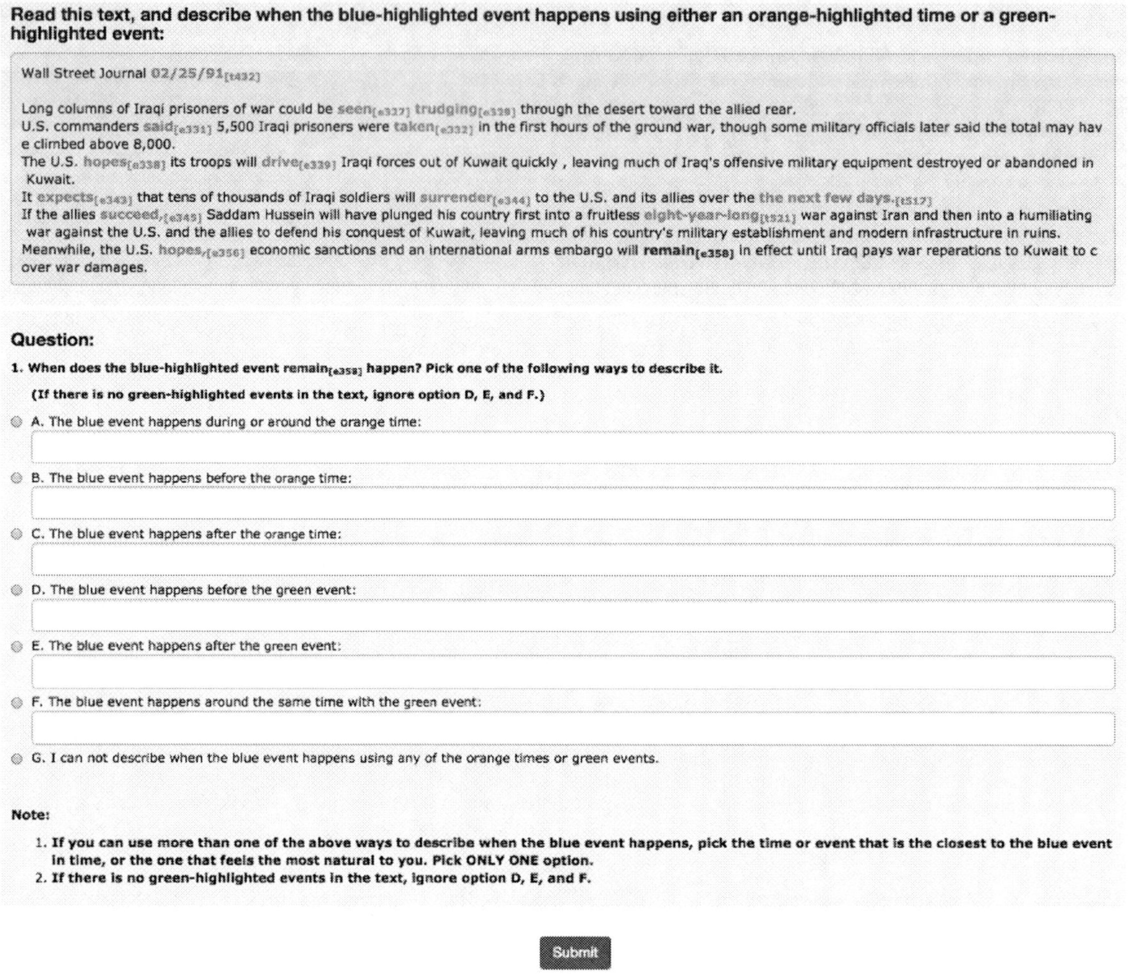

Read this text, and describe when the blue-highlighted event happens using either an orange-highlighted time or a green-highlighted event:

Wall Street Journal 02/25/91$_{[t432]}$

Long columns of Iraqi prisoners of war could be seen$_{[e327]}$ trudging$_{[e328]}$ through the desert toward the allied rear.
U.S. commanders said$_{[e331]}$ 5,500 Iraqi prisoners were taken$_{[e332]}$ in the first hours of the ground war, though some military officials later said the total may hav e climbed above 8,000.
The U.S. hopes$_{[e338]}$ its troops will drive$_{[e339]}$ Iraqi forces out of Kuwait quickly , leaving much of Iraq's offensive military equipment destroyed or abandoned in Kuwait.
It expects$_{[e343]}$ that tens of thousands of Iraqi soldiers will surrender$_{[e344]}$ to the U.S. and its allies over the the next few days.$_{[t517]}$
If the allies succeed,$_{[e345]}$ Saddam Hussein will have plunged his country first into a fruitless eight-year-long$_{[t521]}$ war against Iran and then into a humiliating war against the U.S. and the allies to defend his conquest of Kuwait, leaving much of his country's military establishment and modern infrastructure in ruins.
Meanwhile, the U.S. hopes,$_{[e356]}$ economic sanctions and an international arms embargo will **remain$_{[e358]}$** in effect until Iraq pays war reparations to Kuwait to c over war damages.

Question:

1. When does the blue-highlighted event remain$_{[e358]}$ happen? Pick one of the following ways to describe it.

(If there is no green-highlighted events in the text, ignore option D, E, and F.)

- A. The blue event happens during or around the orange time:
- B. The blue event happens before the orange time:
- C. The blue event happens after the orange time:
- D. The blue event happens before the green event:
- E. The blue event happens after the green event:
- F. The blue event happens around the same time with the green event:
- G. I can not describe when the blue event happens using any of the orange times or green events.

Note:

1. **If you can use more than one of the above ways to describe when the blue event happens, pick the time or event that is the closest to the blue event in time, or the one that feels the most natural to you. Pick ONLY ONE option.**
2. **If there is no green-highlighted events in the text, ignore option D, E, and F.**

Submit

Figure 2: Example crowdsourcing instructions and questions for full structure and relation annotation.

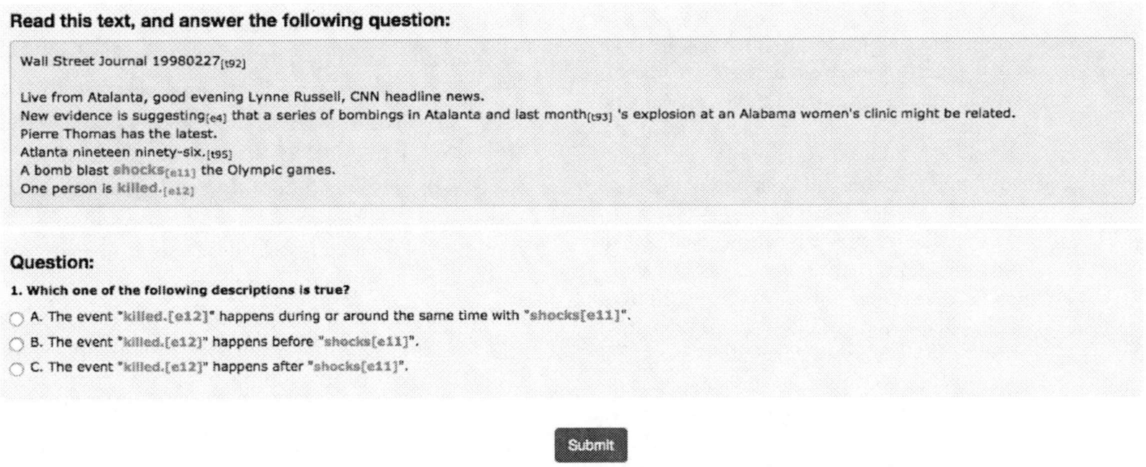

Figure 3: Example crowdsourcing instructions and questions for relation only annotation.

Exploration of Noise Strategies in Semi-supervised Named Entity Classification

Pooja Lakshmi Narayan
University of Arizona
poojal@email.arizona.edu

Ajay Nagesh[*]
DiDi AI Labs
ajaynagesh@didiglobal.com

Mihai Surdeanu
University of Arizona
msurdeanu@email.arizona.edu

Abstract

Noise is inherent in real world datasets and modeling noise is critical during training as it is effective in regularization. Recently, novel semi-supervised deep learning techniques have demonstrated tremendous potential when learning with very limited labeled training data in image processing tasks. A critical aspect of these semi-supervised learning techniques is augmenting the input or the network with noise to be able to learn robust models. While modeling noise is relatively straightforward in continuous domains such as image classification, it is not immediately apparent how noise can be modeled in discrete domains such as language. Our work aims to address this gap by exploring different noise strategies for the semi-supervised named entity classification task, including statistical methods such as adding Gaussian noise to input embeddings, and linguistically-inspired ones such as dropping words and replacing words with their synonyms. We compare their performance on two benchmark datasets (OntoNotes and CoNLL) for named entity classification. Our results indicate that noise strategies that are linguistically informed perform at least as well as statistical approaches, while being simpler and requiring minimal tuning.

1 Introduction

Modeling noise is a fundamental aspect of machine learning systems. The real world where these systems are deployed are certainly exposed to noisy data. Furthermore, noise is used as an effective regularizer during the training of neural networks (*e.g.*, dropout (Srivastava et al., 2014)). Correct prediction in the presence of noisy input demonstrates robustness of learning systems. A simple analogy to illustrate this is, during image classification, the addition of limited random Gaussian noise to an image can be barely perceived by our visual system and does not drastically change the label a human assigns to an image (Raj, 2018). With the emphasis on compliance and recent advances in adversarial techniques, modeling noise has assumed renewed importance (Goodfellow et al., 2014).

Noise is an important factor in recent state-of-the-art semi-supervised learning systems for image classification (Tarvainen and Valpola, 2017; Rasmus et al., 2015; Miyato et al., 2018). In image processing modeling random noise is relatively straightforward as it is a continuous domain. For instance, adding a small amount random Gaussian jitter can be considered as noisy input. So are other image transformations such as translation, rotation, removing color and so on. However, a discrete domain such as language is not easily amenable to noise augmentation. While one can certainly add random Gaussian noise to embeddings of words (continuous vector representation such as *word2vec* rather than one-hot encoding), the intuition behind such perturbation is not apparent. Algorithms which require explicit modeling of noise require careful thinking in the language domain and is challenging (Clark et al., 2018; Nagesh and Surdeanu, 2018a).

To the best of our knowledge, previous work in the area of modeling noise in natural language processing (NLP) applications has been limited. Clark et al. (2018) acknowledge the difficulty of modeling noise for language and incorporate a simple word dropout in their experiments. So does the work by Nagesh and Surdeanu (2018a). Nagesh and Surdeanu (2018b) add a standard Gaussian perturbation with a fixed variance to the pretrained word vectors to simulate noise. Belinkov and Bisk (2017) is perhaps one of the most comprehensive works that explore various noise strategies with a different end goal in mind. Their work

---

[*] work done during AN's post-doc at Univ. of Arizona

*Proceedings of the Eighth Joint Conference on Lexical and Computational Semantics (*SEM)*, pages 186–191
Minneapolis, June 6–7, 2019. ©2019 Association for Computational Linguistics

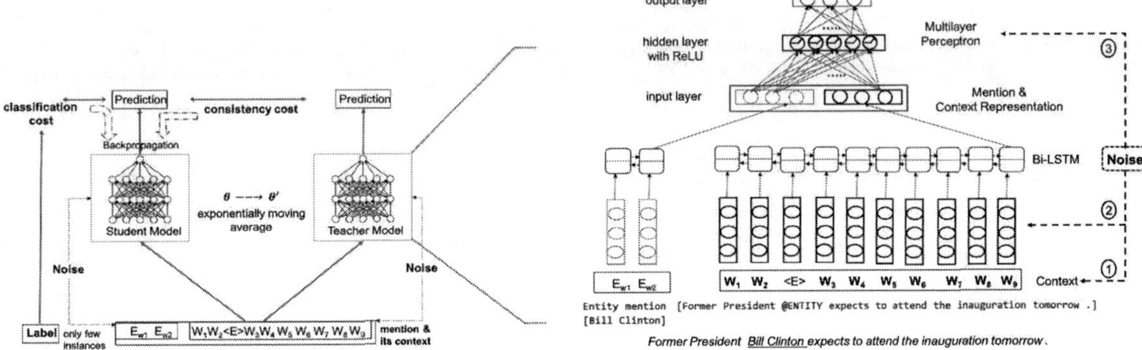

Figure 1: Mean Teacher framework for the named entity classification task (left). E_{wi} are words in the entity mention, W_i are words in the context with entity mention replaced by $<E>$ token. *cost = (classification_cost) + λ(consistency_cost)*. Unlabeled examples have only consistency cost. Backprop only through student model, teacher model parameters are averaged. The architecture of the student or teacher model (right). Noise can be added to parts in boldface. *predictions = softmax(output_layer)*

explores the degree of robustness of various neural network approaches to different types of noise on a machine translation task.

In this paper, we discuss several noise strategies for the semi-supervised named entity classification task. Some of these, such as word-dropout and synonym-replace, are linguistic and are discrete in nature while others such as Gaussian perturbation to word embeddings are statistical. We show that linguistic noise, while being simple, perform as well as statistical noise. A combination of linguistic and network dropout provides the best performance.

2 Semi-supervised Deep Learning

Semi-supervised learning (SSL) is one of the cornerstones in machine learning (ML) (Zhu, 2005). This is especially true in the case of natural language processing (NLP), as obtaining labeled training data is a costly and tedious process for most of the data-hungry deep learning models.

There has been a flurry of recent work in SSL in the image processing community (Tarvainen and Valpola, 2017; Rasmus et al., 2015). Some of these recent works have achieved impressive performance on hard perceptive tasks. However, repurposing these works to NLP is not a straight forward exercise. As stated earlier, many of these approaches require noise (along with an optional input augmentation step such as rotation) to change the percept slightly, to achieve robust performance. However, augmenting data with noise for NLP tasks is not very clear, as the input domain

consists of discrete tokens rather than continuous inputs such as images.

In our previous work (Nagesh and Surdeanu, 2018a), we evaluated three different semi-supervised learning paradigms, namely, bootstrapping-based approaches (Gupta and Manning, 2015), ladder networks (Rasmus et al., 2015) and mean-teacher (Tarvainen and Valpola, 2017) for the semi-supervised named entity classification (NEC) task. The mean-teacher (MT) approach produced the best performance. However, our exploration of noise was limited in the previous study and hence is the focus of the current paper.

The MT framework belongs to the general class of teacher-student networks that learns in the semi-supervised setting *i.e.*, limited supervision and a large amount of unlabeled data and is illustrated in the left part of Figure 1. It consists of two models, termed *student* and *teacher* which are structurally identical but differ in the way their parameters are updated. While the student is updated using regular back-propagation, the parameters of the teacher are a weighted average of the student parameters across different epochs. Further, the cost function is a linear combination of supervision cost (from the limited number amount of supervision) and consistency cost (agreement between the representation from the teacher and student models measured as the L^2 norm difference between them). The motivation of using consistency in the cost function and averaging the parameters in the teacher is to reduce confirmation bias in the teacher when its own predictions are used as pseudo-labels during the training process (akin to averaged perceptron). This provides a strong proxy for the student to rely on in the absence of labeled training data (Tarvainen and Valpola, 2017).

The specific model we employ for semi-supervised named entity classification (NEC) task along with a canonical input data point is depicted in the right part of Figure 1. The input consists of an entity mention and the sentence it appears in, as the context. The goal is to predict the label of the entity. In the semi-supervised setting only a few labeled data points are provided, the rest of the data is unlabeled. We initialize the words in the example with pre-trained word embeddings and run a bi-directional LSTM on both the entity mention and its context. We concatenate the final LSTM state of both the mention and the context representations and run a multi-layer perceptron with one hidden layer to produce the output layer.

A key aspect of the MT framework is the augmentation of the input and/or the network with noise as shown in the right part of Figure 1. We explain this in detail in the next section.

3 Exploration of Noise Strategies

A critical component in the algorithm is the addition of noise to the models. Noise can be added mainly in three key places to the model presented in the previous section as depicted in Figure 1 (parts in boldface). We add a similar but distinct noise to both the teacher and the student models. (1) *Input noise* – In the form of linguistically motivated noise such as *word dropout*, or *replacing words* with their synonyms (more details below). (2) *Statistical noise* – In the form of standard Gaussian perturbations to pre-trained word embeddings. (3) *Network noise* – Dropout in the intermediate layers of the student and teacher networks.

The idea of adding noise is to regularize the model parameters and help learn robust models in the scenario of very limited labeled training data using the teacher and student models via the consistency cost. Consequently, the MT framework can also be perceived as a consistency regularization technique.

The input noise is applied to the context of an entity mention. The noise was added to a fixed number of words in a context. We explored different types of *input noise*: (1) *Word-dropout*

- dropping words randomly in the input context (2) *Synonym-replace* - replace a randomly chosen word in the context by its synonym from WordNet (3) *Word-dropout-idf* - drop the most informative word in the context, as determined by the inverse document frequency (IDF) of context words computed offline. (4) *Synonym-replace-idf* - replace the words in the context according to their IDF (as described above).

For the *statistical noise*, we perturbed the pre-trained word embeddings with standard Gaussian noise with a fixed standard deviation. We varied the amount of standard deviation and the number of words to which this type of noise is added. As we demonstrate in the experiments, this requires careful tuning. Further, adding Gaussian noise is a computationally intensive process as we need to perform this operation in every minibatch during the training process.

We implemented network noise with dropout with fixed probability in both the context representation and the hidden layer in the multi-layer perceptron.

Finally, we combined network noise with input noise. Empirically, we show that this combination yields the best possible performance for the task addressed.

4 Experiments

Task and datasets: The task investigated in this work is named entity classification (NEC), defined as identifying the correct type of an entity mention in a given context, e.g., classifying *"Bill Clinton"* in the sentence *"Former President Bill Clinton expects to attend the inauguration tomorrow."* as a person name. We define the context as the complete sentence in which the entity mention appears. We use standard benchmark datasets, namely, CoNLL-2003 shared task dataset (Tjong Kim Sang and De Meulder, 2003) and Ontonotes-2013 (Pradhan et al., 2013). Our setting is semi-supervised NEC, so we randomly select a very small percentage of the training dataset (40 datapoints *i.e.* 0.18% of CoNLL and 440 datapoints *i.e.* 0.56% of Ontonotes as labeled data, and artificially remove the labels of the remaining datapoints to simulate the semi-supervised setting. Our task is to predict the correct labels of the unlabeled datapoints. CoNLL had 4 label categories while Ontonotes has 11. We measure the accuracy as the percentage of the datapoints which have

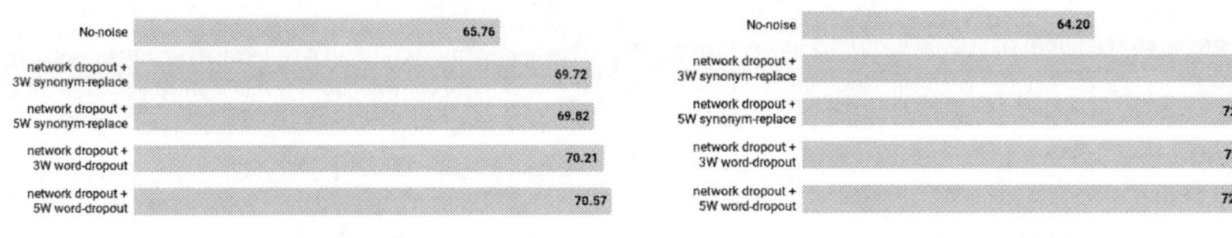

Figure 2: Performance upon combining noise strategies, CoNLL (left) and Ontonotes (right). Best performance: *network dropout + 5W word-dropout - 70.57% (CoNLL)*, *network dropout + 3W synonym-replace - 72.78%* (Ontonotes)

		CoNLL	Ontonotes
No noise		65.76 ($\pm$2.06)	64.20 ($\pm$2.27)
Word-dropout	1 W	67.70 ($\pm$2.97)	67.46 ($\pm$3.53)
	2 W	68.15 ($\pm$3.15)	68.19 ($\pm$3.35)
	3 W	**68.54** ($\pm$3.38)	68.42 ($\pm$3.94)
Synonym-replace	1 W	67.56 ($\pm$3.04)	67.70 ($\pm$3.20)
	2 W	67.95 ($\pm$3.17)	68.40 ($\pm$3.62)
	3 W	68.35 ($\pm$3.07)	**68.46** ($\pm$4.06)
Word-droput-idf	1 W	67.59 ($\pm$3.03)	67.38 ($\pm$3.29)
	2 W	68.11 ($\pm$3.17)	68.14 ($\pm$3.63)
	3 W	68.49 ($\pm$3.27)	68.30 ($\pm$3.77)
Synonym-replace-idf	1 W	67.51 ($\pm$3.02)	67.24 ($\pm$3.55)
	2 W	67.79 ($\pm$3.15)	68.23 ($\pm$3.42)
	3 W	68.26 ($\pm$3.05)	67.95 ($\pm$3.96)
Gaussian (stdev=4)	all W	62.98 ($\pm$2.66)	64.89 ($\pm$5.12)
Network Dropout		**68.40** ($\pm$3.11)	**71.77** ($\pm$2.18)

Table 1: Overall accuracies comparing all noise strategies on CoNLL and Ontonotes datasets. *No noise* is the baseline. X W $\Rightarrow X$ words perturbed by noise. Accuracy is % of correctly classified datapoints. $(\pm y) \Rightarrow$ variance of 5 runs.

	CoNLL	Ontonotes
1 W	69.70 ($\pm$2.93)	68.75 ($\pm$3.02)
5 W	68.48 ($\pm$2.65)	68.22 ($\pm$3.45)
10 W	66.55 ($\pm$4.20)	67.32 ($\pm$3.42)
stdev=0.05	68.51 ($\pm$3.13)	68.42 ($\pm$4.15)
stdev=1	66.94 ($\pm$2.59)	66.79 ($\pm$3.67)
stdev=2	65.43 ($\pm$2.68)	65.90 ($\pm$4.35)
stdev=4	62.98 ($\pm$2.66)	64.94 ($\pm$5.91)
stdev=8	62.49 ($\pm$2.76)	64.02 ($\pm$4.92)
stdev=16	62.87 ($\pm$3.08)	64.85 ($\pm$6.25)

Table 2: Tuning Gaussian noise - #words & stdev

been predicted with the correct labels.

Experimental settings: We use the entity boundaries for all datapoints during training but only use labels for a small portion of the data as indicated above. We demonstrate an input to our model in the bottom-right of Figure 1. To reduce computational overhead, we filtered out entity mentions which were greater than length 5 from the Ontonotes dataset (4 respectively for CoNLL), and contexts which were greater than length 59 or smaller than length 5 (40 and 3 respectively for CoNLL). Following Nagesh and Surdeanu (2018a), we intialized the pre-trained word-embeddings from Levy and Goldberg (2014) (300d). We ran a 100d bi-directional LSTM on both the entity and context representations, concatenated their outputs and fed them to a 300d multi-layer perceptron with ReLU activations. For network dropout we used $p = 0.2$. This is similar to dropout regularization used in deep neural networks but since the dropout layer drops neurons randomly in teacher and student, this acts as noise

in the MT framework. We tried a few variations of this model such as augmenting the LSTM with position embeddings, attention and replacing the LSTM with an average model, but did not observe a considerable improvement in performance.

Results: We present our main results in Table 1. An important note is that the results are the accuracy of classification over 21,373 and 78,492 datapoints in CoNLL and Ontonotes respectively, using only a tiny sliver of the labels in these datasets as supervision. Increasing the number of labeled examples as supervision has the expected effect of improvement in performance. However it is often difficult to obtain sufficient number of examples in the real world. The datapoints for supervision are chosen randomly having equal representation in all classes. The analysis of amount of supervision and its effect on accuracy is reported in Nagesh and Surdeanu (2018a). We report the average (along with their variance) of 5 randomized runs in each noise setting. Our baseline is the *no noise* setting, where the input to the student and teacher models are not augmented by noise.

From Table 1, we observe that adding noise is necessary for good performance, as we see that the various noise strategies consistently improve performance over the baseline on both the datasets. Network noise is a crucial factor for good performance. Input noise which are linguistically motivated, such as *word-dropout* and *synonym-replace* perform as well as the statistical noise. More specifically, *word-dropout* of 3 words and *synonym-replace* of 3 words, are the highest performing non-network noise strategies on CoNLL and Ontonotes respectively. *Synonym-replace* is an interesting strategy as we believe it makes the input more interpretable. In the sense that, the word embedding of a synonym word is closer to the actual word in the vector space. As opposed to gaussian embedding noise, which is a random delta noise added to the embedding to perturb it and we are not sure of its orientation in the high dimensional space. Adding *Gaussian* noise to all words results in performance poorer than or close to baseline. [1] Furthermore, *Gaussian* noise requires fine-tuning over the value of stdev and the number of words on which these should be applied which makes this computationally expensive approach (Table 2). The performance on *-*-*idf* runs suggest that random word selection is as good or better. This is ideal, since it is simpler and independent of the data distribution. Finally, *network noise* in combination with linguistic input noise provides the best possible performance, as seen in Figure 2. One possible explanation for this could be that ensembling two high performance systems is akin to combining two good signals achieving better overall results.

5 Conclusion and Future Work

The modeling of noise in discrete domains such as language has received limited focus so far, in the language processing community. In this work we explore several noise strategies for the semi-supervised named entity classification task using the mean teacher framework, where noise augmentation is a crucial factor. We show that linguistic noise such as word-dropout and synonym-replace perform as well as statistical noise, while being simpler and easier to tune. A combination of linguistic and network dropout provides the best performance. As part of future work, we wish to explore noise augmentation in other language processing tasks such as fine-grained entity typing.

---

[1] In Table 1, for *Gaussian* noise, stdev value is chosen randomly as 4. If we have the luxury to tune this parameter then Table 2 noise, gives the best performance at stdev 0.05.

References

Yonatan Belinkov and Yonatan Bisk. 2017. Synthetic and natural noise both break neural machine translation. *CoRR*, abs/1711.02173.

Kevin Clark, Thang Luong, Christopher D. Manning, and Quoc V. Le. 2018. Semi-supervised sequence modeling with cross-view training.

Ian J Goodfellow, Jonathon Shlens, and Christian Szegedy. 2014. Explaining and harnessing adversarial examples. *arXiv preprint arXiv:1412.6572*.

Sonal Gupta and Christopher D. Manning. 2015. Distributed representations of words to guide bootstrapped entity classifiers. In *Proceedings of the Conference of the North American Chapter of the Association for Computational Linguistics*.

Omer Levy and Yoav Goldberg. 2014. Dependency-based word embeddings. In *Proceedings of the 52nd Annual Meeting of the Association for Computational Linguistics (Volume 2: Short Papers)*, Baltimore, Maryland. Association for Computational Linguistics.

T. Miyato, S. Maeda, S. Ishii, and M. Koyama. 2018. Virtual adversarial training: A regularization method for supervised and semi-supervised learning. *IEEE Transactions on Pattern Analysis and Machine Intelligence*, pages 1–1.

Ajay Nagesh and Mihai Surdeanu. 2018a. An exploration of three lightly-supervised representation learning approaches for named entity classification. In *COLING*.

Ajay Nagesh and Mihai Surdeanu. 2018b. Keep your bearings: Lightly-supervised information extraction with ladder networks that avoids semantic drift. In *NAACL HLT 2018*.

Sameer Pradhan, Alessandro Moschitti, Nianwen Xue, Hwee Tou Ng, Anders Bjrkelund, Olga Uryupina, Yuchen Zhang, and Zhi Zhong. 2013. Towards robust linguistic analysis using ontonotes. In *Proceedings of the Seventeenth Conference on Computational Natural Language Learning*, pages 143–152, Sofia, Bulgaria. Association for Computational Linguistics.

Bharath Raj. 2018. Data augmentation - how to use deep learning when you have limited data - part 2. https://bit.ly/2IvKw11. Accessed: 2018-12-10.

Antti Rasmus, Harri Valpola, Mikko Honkala, Mathias Berglund, and Tapani Raiko. 2015. Semi-supervised learning with ladder network. *CoRR*, abs/1507.02672.

Nitish Srivastava, Geoffrey Hinton, Alex Krizhevsky, Ilya Sutskever, and Ruslan Salakhutdinov. 2014. Dropout: A simple way to prevent neural networks from overfitting. *Journal of Machine Learning Research*, 15:1929–1958.

Antti Tarvainen and Harri Valpola. 2017. Weight-averaged consistency targets improve semi-supervised deep learning results. *CoRR*, abs/1703.01780.

Erik F. Tjong Kim Sang and Fien De Meulder. 2003. Introduction to the CoNLL-2003 shared task: Language-independent named entity recognition. In *Proceedings of CoNLL-2003*, pages 142–147. Edmonton, Canada.

Xiaojin Zhu. 2005. Semi-supervised learning literature survey. Technical Report 1530, Computer Sciences, University of Wisconsin-Madison.

Improving Generalization in Coreference Resolution via Adversarial Training

Sanjay Subramanian
University of Pennsylvania
sanjayssub34@gmail.com

Dan Roth
University of Pennsylvania
danroth@seas.upenn.edu

Abstract

In order for coreference resolution systems to be useful in practice, they must be able to generalize to new text. In this work, we demonstrate that the performance of the state-of-the-art system decreases when the names of PER and GPE named entities in the CoNLL dataset are changed to names that do not occur in the training set. We use the technique of adversarial gradient-based training to retrain the state-of-the-art system and demonstrate that the retrained system achieves higher performance on the CoNLL dataset (both with and without the change of named entities) and the GAP dataset.

1 Introduction

Through the use of neural networks, performance on the task of coreference resolution has increased significantly over the last few years. Still, neural systems trained on the standard coreference dataset have issues with generalization, as shown by (Moosavi and Strube, 2018).

One way to improve the understanding of how a system overfits a dataset is to study the change in the system's performance when the dataset is modified slightly in a focused and relevant manner. We take this approach by modifying the test set so that each PER and GPE (person and geopolitical entity) named entity is different from those seen in training. In other words, we ensure that there is no leakage of PER and GPE named entities from the training set into the test set. We demonstrate that the performance of the (Lee et al., 2018) system, which is the current state-of-the-art, decreases when the named entities are replaced. An example of a replacement that causes the system to make an error is given in Table 1.

Motivated by these issues of generalization, this paper aims to improve the training process of neu-

Original: But **Dirk Van Dongen** , president of the **National Association of Wholesaler - Distributors** , said that last month 's rise " is n't as bad an omen " as the 0.9 % figure suggests . " If you examine the data carefully , the increase is concentrated in energy and motor vehicle prices , rather than being a broad - based advance in the prices of consumer and industrial goods , " he explained .
Replacement: Replace *Dick Van Dongen* with *Vendemiaire Van Korewdit.*

Table 1: An excerpt from the CoNLL test set. The coreference between the two highlighted mentions is correctly predicted by the (Lee et al., 2018) system, but after the specified replacement, the system incorrectly resolves "he" to a different name occurring outside this excerpt.

ral coreference systems. Various regularization techniques have been proposed for improving the generalization capability of neural networks, including dropout (Srivastava et al., 2014) and adversarial training (Goodfellow et al., 2015; Miyato et al., 2017). The model of (Lee et al., 2018), like most neural approaches, uses dropout. In this work, we apply the adversarial fast-gradient-sign-method (FGSM) described by (Miyato et al., 2017) to the model of (Lee et al., 2018), and show that this technique improves the model's generalization even when applied on top of dropout.

The CoNLL-2012 Shared Task dataset (Pradhan et al., 2012) has been the standard dataset used for both training and evaluating English coreference systems since the dataset was introduced. The dataset includes seven genres that span multiple writing styles and multiple nationalities. We demonstrate that the system of (Lee et al., 2018) retrained with adversarial training achieves state-of-the-art performance on the original CoNLL-2012 dataset (Pradhan et al., 2012) as well as the CoNLL-2012 dataset with changed named entities. Furthermore, the system trained with the adversarial method ex-

*Proceedings of the Eighth Joint Conference on Lexical and Computational Semantics (*SEM)*, pages 192–197
Minneapolis, June 6–7, 2019. ©2019 Association for Computational Linguistics

hibits state-of-the-art performance on the GAP
dataset (Webster et al., 2018), a recently released
dataset focusing on resolving pronouns to people's names in excerpts from Wikipedia. The
code and other relevant files for this project
can be found via https://cogcomp.org/
page/publication_view/871.

2 Related Work

(Moosavi and Strube, 2017, 2018) also study generalization of neural coreference resolvers. However, they focus on transfer and indicate that the
ranking of coreference resolvers (trained on the
CoNLL training set) induced by their performance
on the CoNLL test set is not preserved when the
systems are evaluated on a different dataset. They
use the Wikicoref dataset (Ghaddar and Langlais,
2016), which is limited in that it consists of only
30 documents. They then show that the addition
of features representing linguistic information improves the performance of a coreference resolver
on the out-of-domain dataset.

The adversarial fast-gradient-sign-method
(FGSM) was first introduced by (Goodfellow
et al., 2015) and was applied to sentence classification tasks through word embeddings by (Miyato
et al., 2017). Gradient-based adversarial attacks
have since been used to train models for various
NLP tasks, such as relation extraction (Wu et al.,
2017) and joint entity and relation extraction
(Bekoulis et al., 2018).

Our replacements of named entities can also
be viewed as a way of generating adversarial examples for coreference systems; it is related to
the earlier method proposed in (Khashabi et al.,
2016) in the context of question answering and to
(Alzantot et al., 2018), which provides a way of
generating adversarial examples for simple classification tasks.

3 Adversarial Training for Coreference

In coreference resolution, the goal is to find and
cluster phrases that refer to entities. We use
the word "span" to mean a series of consecutive
words. A span that refers to an entity is called a
mention. If two mentions i and j refer to the same
entity and mention i occurs before mention j in
the text, we say that mention i is an antecedent of
mention j. For a given mention i, the candidate
antecedents of i are the mentions that occur before
i in the text. In Figure 1, each line segment repre-

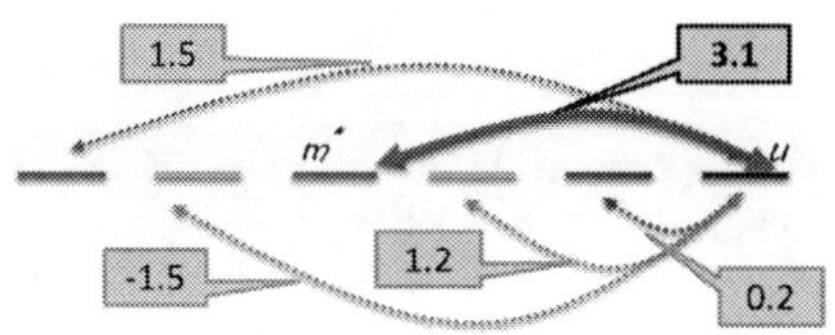

Figure 1: For each mention, the model computes scores
for each of the candidate antecedent mentions and
chooses the candidate with the highest score to be the
predicted antecedent. This image was created by the
authors of (Chang et al., 2013).

sents a mention and the arrows are directed from
one mention to its possible antecedents.

We now review the model architecture of (Lee
et al., 2018) and describe how we apply the fast-
gradient-sign-method (FGSM) of (Miyato et al.,
2017) to the model. Using GloVe (Pennington
et al., 2014) and ELMo (Peters et al., 2018) embeddings of each word and using learned character
embeddings, the model computes contextualized
representations $\{x_1, x_2, ..., x_n\}$ of each word x_i
in the input document using a bidirectional LSTM
(Hochreiter and Schmidhuber, 1997). For candidate span i, which consists of the words at indices
$start_i, start_i + 1, ..., end_i$, the model constructs
a span representation g_i by concatenating x_{start_i},
x_{end_i}, $\frac{1}{\sum_{j=start_i}^{end_i} \beta_j} \sum_{j=start_i}^{end_i} \beta_j x_j$, and $\phi(end_i -
start_i)$, where the β_j's are learned scalar values
and $\phi(\cdot)$ is a learned embedding representing the
width of the span (Lee et al., 2017). The span
representations are then used as inputs to feedforward networks that compute mention scores for
each span and that compute antecedent scores for
pairs of spans. In Figure 1, the number associated with each arrow is the antecedent score for
the associated pair of mentions. The coreference
score for the pair of spans (i, j) is the sum of the
mention score for span i, the mention score for
span j, and the antecedent score for (i, j). For
each span i, the antecedent span predicted by the
model is the span j that maximizes the antecedent
score for (i, j). Let $g = \{g_i\}_{i=1}^N$ denote the set
of the representations of all N candidate spans.
Let $\mathcal{L}(g)$ denote the original model's loss function. (Note that the model's predictions and the
loss depend on the input text only through the
span representations.) For each $i \in \{1, ..., N\}$, let
$g_i^{adv}(g) = \nabla_{g_i} \mathcal{L}\left(\{g_i\}_{i=1}^N\right)$ denote the gradient
of the loss with respect to the span embeddings.

Then the adversarial loss with the FGSM is

$$\mathcal{L}_{adv}(\{\mathbf{g}_i\}_{i=1}^N) = \mathcal{L}\left(\left\{\mathbf{g}_i + \epsilon \frac{\mathbf{g}_i^{adv}(\mathbf{g})}{\|\mathbf{g}_i^{adv}(\mathbf{g})\|}\right\}_{i=1}^N\right).$$

The total loss used in training is

$$\mathcal{L}_{total}(\mathbf{g}) = \alpha\mathcal{L}(\mathbf{g}) + (1 - \alpha)\mathcal{L}_{adv}(\mathbf{g}).$$

In our experiments, we find that $\alpha = 0.6$ and $\epsilon = 1$ work well. A key difference between our method and that employed by (Miyato et al., 2017) is that the latter applies the adversarial perturbation to the input embeddings, whereas we apply it to the span representations, which are an intermediate layer of the model. We found in our experiments that applying the FGSM to the character embeddings in the initial layer was not as effective as applying the method to the span representations as described above. Another difference between our method and that of (Miyato et al., 2017) is that we do not normalize the span embeddings before applying the adversarial perturbations.

4   No Leakage of Named Entities

Named entities are an important subset of the entities a coreference system is tasked with discovering. (Agarwal et al., 2018) provide the percentages of clusters in the CoNLL dataset represented by the PER, ORG, GPE, and DATE named entity types – 15%, 11%, 11%, and 4%, respectively. It is important for generalization that systems perform well with names that are different from those seen in training. We found that in the CoNLL dataset, roughly 34% of the PER and GPE named entities that are the head of a mention of some gold cluster in the test set are also the head of a mention of a gold cluster in the train set. Therefore, there is considerable overlap, or leakage, between the names in the train and test sets. In this section, we describe a method for evaluating on the CoNLL test set without leaked name entities.

We focus on PER and GPE named entities because they are two of the three most common entity types and because in general when replacing a PER or GPE name with another name, it is easy to not change the true coreference structure of the document. In particular, changing the name of an organization while ensuring that it is compatible with nominals in the cluster is nontrivial without a finer semantic typing. By contrast, we describe below how we control for gender and location type

when replacing PER and GPE names, respectively. We also ensure that the capitalization of the first letter in the replacement name is the same as in the original text. Finally, we note that the diversity of PER and GPE entities exceeds that of other named entity types; this increases the importance of generalization to new names and, at the same time, enables us to find matching names to use as replacements. Table 2 provides examples of text in the original CoNLL-2012 dataset and the corresponding text after our modifications.

4.1   Replacing PER entities

For replacing PER entities, we utilize the publicly available list of last names from the 1990 U.S. Census and a gazetteer of first names that has the proportion of people with this name who are males. The gazetteer was collected in an unsupervised fashion from Wikipedia. We denote the list of last names by $\mathcal{L}$, the list of male first names (i.e. first names with male proportion greater than or equal to 0.5 in the gazetteer) by $\mathcal{M}$, and the list of female first names (i.e. first names with male proportion less than or equal to 0.5 in the gazetteer) by $\mathcal{F}$. We remove all names occurring in training from $\mathcal{L}$, $\mathcal{M}$, and $\mathcal{F}$. We use the spaCy dependency parser (Honnibal and Johnson, 2015) to find the heads of each mention. We say that a mention is a person-mention if the head of the mention is a PER named entity, and we say that the name of the person-mention is the PER named entity that is its head. We use the dependency parser and the gold NER to identify all of the person-mentions. For each gold cluster containing a person-mention, we find the longest name among the names of all of the person-mentions in the cluster. If the longest name of a cluster has only one token, we assume that the name is a last name, and we replace the name with a name chosen uniformly at random from the remaining last names in $\mathcal{L}$. Otherwise, if the longest name has multiple tokens, we say that the cluster is male if the cluster contains no female pronouns ("she", "her", "hers") and one of the following is true: the first token does not appear in $\mathcal{M}$ or $\mathcal{F}$, if the token appears in $\mathcal{M}$, or the cluster contains a male pronoun ("he", "him", "his"). We say that the cluster is female if it is not male. Then we (1) replace the last token with a name chosen uniformly at random from the remaining last names in $\mathcal{L}$, and (2) replace the first token with a name chosen uniformly at random from the remaining

Original	No Leakage
We asked **Judy Muller** if she would like to do the story of a fascinating man . She took a deep breath and said , okay .	We asked **Sallie Kousonsavath** if she would like to do the story of a fascinating man . She took a deep breath and said , okay .
The last thing President **Clinton** did today before heading to the Mideast is go to church – appropriate , perhaps , given the enormity of the task he and his national security team face in the days ahead .	The last thing President **Golia** did today before heading to the Mideast is go to church – appropriate , perhaps , given the enormity of the task he and his national security team face in the days ahead .
In theory at least , tight supplies next spring could leave the wheat futures market susceptible to a supply - demand squeeze , said Daniel Basse , a futures analyst with AgResource Co. in **Chicago** .	In theory at least , tight supplies next spring could leave the wheat futures market susceptible to a supply - demand squeeze , said Daniel Basse , a futures analyst with AgResource Co. in **Machete** .

Table 2: Excerpts from the CoNLL-2012 test set and their versions after we have replaced PER and GPE names to avoid name leakage.

first names in $\mathcal{M}$ if the cluster is male or from the remaining first names $\mathcal{F}$ if the cluster is female. Note that our sampling from each of $\mathcal{L}$, $\mathcal{M}$, and $\mathcal{F}$ is without replacement, so no last name is used as a replacement more than once, no male first name is used more than once, and no female first name is used more than once.

4.2 Replacing GPE entities

Our approach to replacing GPE entity names is very similar to that used for PER names. We use the GeoNames[1] database of geopolitical names. In addition to providing a list of GPE names, this database also categorizes the names by the type of entity to which they refer (e.g. city, state, county, etc.). The data includes the names and categories of more than $11,000,000$ locations in the world. We restrict our attention to GPE entities that satisfy the following requirements: (1) they occur in the GeoNames database and (2) they are not countries. We say that a mention is a GPE-mention if its head (as given by the dependency parser) is a GPE named entity satisfying these three requirements. (Again, we use the gold NER to identify GPE names in the CoNLL text.) We remove all GPE names occurring in the training set from the list of replacement GPE names for each location category. Then for each cluster containing a GPE-mention, we find the GeoNames category for the mention's GPE name and replace the name with a randomly chosen name from the same category. As with PER names, we sample names from each category without replacement, so each GPE name is used for replacement at most once.

5 Experiments

We trained the (Lee et al., 2018) model architecture with the adversarial approach on the CoNLL training set for 355000 iterations (the same number of iterations for which the original model was trained) with the same training hyperparameters used by original model. For comparing with the (Lee et al., 2017) and (Lee et al., 2018) systems, we use the pretrained models released by the authors.[2]

The datasets used for evaluation are the CoNLL and GAP datasets.

5.1 CoNLL Dataset

Table 3 shows the performance on the CoNLL test set, as measured by CoNLL F1, of the (Lee et al., 2018) system with and without our adversarial training approach. The replacement of PER and GPE entities decreased the performance of the original system by more than 1 F1.

5.2 GAP Dataset

The GAP dataset (Webster et al., 2018) focuses on resolving pronouns to named people in excerpts from Wikipedia. The dataset, which is gender-balanced, consists of examples in which

---

[1] http://www.geonames.org/

[2] Available at `https://lil.cs.washington.edu/coref/final.tgz` and `http://lsz-gpu-01.cs.washington.edu/resources/coref/c2f_final.tgz`

	Original	**No Leakage**
(Lee et al., 2018)	72.96	71.86
+Adv. Training	**73.23**	**<u>72.36</u>**

Table 3: Results (CoNLL F1) on the CoNLL Test Set. "Original" refers to the original test set, and "No Leakage" refers to the test set modified with the replacement of named entities described in Section 4. For each dataset, highest score for each dataset is **bolded** and is <u>underlined</u> if the difference between it and the other model's score is statistically significant ($p < 0.20$ per a stratified approximate randomization test similar to that of (Noreen, 1989)).

	M	**F**	**O**
(Lee et al., 2017)	68.7	60.0	64.5
(Lee et al., 2018)	75.8	70.6	73.3
+Adv. Training	**77.3**	**72.1**	**<u>74.7</u>**

Table 4: Results (F1 metric defined by (Webster et al., 2018)) on the GAP Test Set. **M** refers to male pronouns, **F** refers to female pronouns, and **O** refers to the full evaluation data. For each category, highest score is **bolded** and underlined if difference between it and next-highest score is statistically significant ($p < 0.05$ per the McNemar test (McNemar, 1947)).

the system must determine whether a given pronoun refers to one, both, or neither of two given names. Thus, the task can be viewed a binary classification task in which the input is a (pronoun, name) pair and the output is True if the pair is coreferent and False otherwise. Performance is evaluated using the F1 score in this binary classification setup. Table 4 shows the performance on the GAP test set of the (Lee et al., 2017)[3] and (Lee et al., 2018) systems as well as the system trained with our adversarial method. The adversarially trained system performs significantly better over the entire dataset in comparison to the previous systems, and the difference is consistent between genders. In particular, we observe that the bias (i.e. ratio of female to male F1 score) is roughly the same (0.93) for the (Lee et al., 2018) system with and without adversarial training and that this bias is better (i.e. the ratio is closer to 1) than that exhibited by the (Lee et al., 2017) system (0.87).

---

[3]The results that we report for the (Lee et al., 2017) system differ slightly from those reported in Table 10 of (Webster et al., 2018) due to a difference in the parser and potentially small differences in the algorithm for converting the system's output to the binary predictions necessary for the GAP scorer.

6 Conclusion

We show that the performance of the (Lee et al., 2018) system decreases when the names of PER and GPE entities are changed in the CoNLL test set so that no names from the training set leak to the test set. We then retrain the same system using an application of the fast-gradient-sign-method (FGSM) of adversarial training, showing that the retrained system consistently performs better on the original CoNLL test set, the CoNLL test set with No Leakage, and the GAP test set. Our new model is a new state-of-the-art for all these data sets.

Acknowledgements

We thank Sihao Chen for providing a gazetteer of first names collected from Wikipedia with scores for their gender likelihood, and the anonymous reviewers for their comments. This work was supported in part by contract HR0011-18-2-0052 with the US Defense Advanced Research Projects Agency (DARPA). The views expressed are those of the authors and do not reflect the official policy or position of the Department of Defense or the U.S. Government.

References

Oshin Agarwal, Sanjay Subramanian, Ani Nenkova, and Dan Roth. 2018. Named person coreference in english news. *arXiv preprint arXiv:1810.11476*.

Moustafa Alzantot, Yash Sharma, Ahmed Elgohary, Bo-Jhang Ho, Mani Srivastava, and Kai-Wei Chang. 2018. Generating natural language adversarial examples. In *Proceedings of the 2018 Conference on Empirical Methods in Natural Language Processing*, pages 2890–2896.

Giannis Bekoulis, Johannes Deleu, Thomas Demeester, and Chris Develder. 2018. Adversarial training for multi-context joint entity and relation extraction. In *Proceedings of the 2018 Conference on Empirical Methods in Natural Language Processing*, pages 2830–2836.

Kai-Wei Chang, Rajhans Samdani, and Dan Roth. 2013. A constrained latent variable model for coreference resolution. In *EMNLP*.

Abbas Ghaddar and Philippe Langlais. 2016. Wikicoref: An english coreference-annotated corpus of wikipedia articles. In *LREC*.

Ian Goodfellow, Jonathon Shlens, and Christian Szegedy. 2015. Explaining and harnessing adversarial examples. In *International Conference on Learning Representations*.

Sepp Hochreiter and Jürgen Schmidhuber. 1997. Long short-term memory. *Neural computation*, 9(8):1735–1780.

Matthew Honnibal and Mark Johnson. 2015. An improved non-monotonic transition system for dependency parsing. In *Proceedings of the 2015 Conference on Empirical Methods in Natural Language Processing*, pages 1373–1378.

Daniel Khashabi, Tushar Khot, Ashish Sabharwal, Peter Clark, Oren Etzioni, and Dan Roth. 2016. Question answering via integer programming over semistructured knowledge. In *Proc. of the International Joint Conference on Artificial Intelligence (IJCAI)*.

Kenton Lee, Luheng He, Mike Lewis, and Luke Zettlemoyer. 2017. End-to-end neural coreference resolution. In *Proceedings of the 2017 Conference on Empirical Methods in Natural Language Processing*, pages 188–197.

Kenton Lee, Luheng He, and Luke Zettlemoyer. 2018. Higher-order coreference resolution with coarse-to-fine inference. In *Proceedings of the 2018 Conference of the North American Chapter of the Association for Computational Linguistics: Human Language Technologies, Volume 2 (Short Papers)*, pages 687–692.

Quinn McNemar. 1947. Note on the sampling error of the difference between correlated proportions or percentages. *Psychometrika*, 12(2):153–157.

Takeru Miyato, Andrew M. Dai, and Ian Goodfellow. 2017. Adversarial training methods for semi-supervised text classification. *ICLR*.

Nafise Sadat Moosavi and Michael Strube. 2017. Lexical features in coreference resolution: To be used with caution. In *Proceedings of the 55th Annual Meeting of the Association for Computational Linguistics (Volume 2: Short Papers)*, pages 14–19.

Nafise Sadat Moosavi and Michael Strube. 2018. Using linguistic features to improve the generalization capability of neural coreference resolvers. In *Proceedings of the 2018 Conference on Empirical Methods in Natural Language Processing*, pages 193–203.

Eric W Noreen. 1989. *Computer-intensive methods for testing hypotheses*. Wiley New York.

Jeffrey Pennington, Richard Socher, and Christopher Manning. 2014. Glove: Global vectors for word representation. In *Proceedings of the 2014 conference on empirical methods in natural language processing (EMNLP)*, pages 1532–1543.

Matthew Peters, Mark Neumann, Mohit Iyyer, Matt Gardner, Christopher Clark, Kenton Lee, and Luke Zettlemoyer. 2018. Deep contextualized word representations. In *Proceedings of the 2018 Conference of the North American Chapter of the Association for Computational Linguistics: Human Language Technologies, Volume 1 (Long Papers)*, pages 2227–2237.

Sameer Pradhan, Alessandro Moschitti, Nianwen Xue, Olga Uryupina, and Yuchen Zhang. 2012. Conll-2012 shared task: Modeling multilingual unrestricted coreference in ontonotes. In *Joint Conference on EMNLP and CoNLL-Shared Task*, pages 1–40. Association for Computational Linguistics.

Nitish Srivastava, Geoffrey Hinton, Alex Krizhevsky, Ilya Sutskever, and Ruslan Salakhutdinov. 2014. Dropout: a simple way to prevent neural networks from overfitting. *The Journal of Machine Learning Research*, 15(1):1929–1958.

Kellie Webster, Marta Recasens, Vera Axelrod, and Jason Baldridge. 2018. Mind the gap: A balanced corpus of gendered ambiguou. In *Transactions of the ACL*, page to appear.

Yi Wu, David Bamman, and Stuart Russell. 2017. Adversarial training for relation extraction. In *Proceedings of the 2017 Conference on Empirical Methods in Natural Language Processing*, pages 1778–1783.

Improving Human Needs Categorization of Events with Semantic Classification

Haibo Ding[*], **Ellen Riloff**[†], **Zhe Feng**[*]

[*]Bosch Research and Technology Center, Sunnyvale, CA 94085, USA

[†]School of Computing, University of Utah, Salt Lake City, UT 84112, USA

`{haibo.ding,zhe.feng2}@us.bosch.com, riloff@cs.utah.edu`

Abstract

Human Needs categories have been used to characterize the reason why an affective event is positive or negative. For example, *"I got the flu"* and *"I got fired"* are both negative (undesirable) events, but getting the flu is a Health problem while getting fired is a Financial problem. Previous work created learning models to assign events to Human Needs categories based on their words and contexts. In this paper, we introduce an intermediate step that assigns words to relevant semantic concepts. We create lightly supervised models that learn to label words with respect to 10 semantic concepts associated with Human Needs categories, and incorporate these labels as features for event categorization. Our results show that recognizing relevant semantic concepts improves both the recall and precision of Human Needs categorization for events.

1 Introduction

Affective events have a positive or negative impact on the people who experience the event. For example, being hired for a job is typically a beneficial (positive) event, but being fired is usually a detrimental (negative) event. Recognizing affective events is critical to understand people's motivations, goals, desires, and empathy in narrative stories and conversations. Previous research has proposed several methods to recognize affective events and their polarity (e.g., (Deng et al., 2013; Vu et al., 2014; Reed et al., 2017; Ding and Riloff, 2016)). To achieve a deeper level of understanding, Ding and Riloff (2018a) further classified affective events into categories associated with theories of Human Needs (Maslow et al., 1970; Max-Neef et al., 1991) in psychology: *Physiological*, *Health*, *Leisure*, *Social*, *Finance*, and *Cognition*, to characterize the reason for the event's affective polarity. For example, breaking your arm is a negative event because it violates a need to maintain one's *Health*, but fighting with your spouse is negative because it violates a need for good *Social* relations with friends and family.

Human Needs categories naturally align with several broad conceptual classes, and we hypothesized that learning to recognize relevant semantic concepts would lead to more effective Human Needs categorization. For example, the *Physiological* need corresponds to basic functions such as breathing, sleeping, eating, and drinking. Learning to recognize FOOD/DRINK concepts should help identify events that belong to this category. Broadly, semantic concepts should help in two ways. First, semantic features are more general than words, which can suffer from sparsity. Second, given semantic features, a classifier can directly learn interactions between them, which should be more robust than interactions between individual words.

In this paper, we present lightly supervised classifiers that label words with respect to 10 semantic concepts associated with Human Needs categories: EMOTION, ENTERTAINMENT, EQUIPMENT, FOOD/DRINK, INTERPERSONAL, MEDICAL, MENTAL-PROCESS, MONEY/JOB, PEOPLE, and OTHER. Seed words for each semantic class are used as supervision, and pre-trained embedding vectors are used as word features. We explore three classification models: logistic regression, instance-based learning, and prototypical neural networks (Snell et al., 2017). Finally, the semantic class predictions are used as features for Human Needs event categorization, improving both recall and precision for this task.

2 Related Work

Previous work in NLP on affective events has primarily focused on identifying the affective polarity of events in narrative fables (Goyal et al.,

*Proceedings of the Eighth Joint Conference on Lexical and Computational Semantics (*SEM)*, pages 198–204

Minneapolis, June 6–7, 2019. ©2019 Association for Computational Linguistics

2013), tweets (Li et al., 2014), news (Deng et al., 2013; Deng and Wiebe, 2014), and personal blogs (Ding and Riloff, 2016; Reed et al., 2017; Ding and Riloff, 2018b). Recently, Ding et al. (2018) further characterized affective events in terms of human needs categories: *Physiological*, *Health*, *Leisure*, *Social*, *Financial*, *Cognition*, and *Freedom*, which can explain why an event is positive or negative. Subsequently, Ding and Riloff (2018a) designed supervised learning models and a semi-supervised co-training model to assign affective events to Human Needs categories.

Our work exploits recent advances in distributed word representations and semantic embeddings (e.g., (Mikolov et al., 2013; Pennington et al., 2014; Peters et al., 2018; Devlin et al., 2018)), and is related to domain adaptation of word embeddings (e.g., (Sarma et al., 2018)). But we aim to recognize a specific set of semantic concepts, rather than a specialized domain with domain-specific texts. The LIWC dictionary (Pennebaker et al., 2007) contains word lists for semantic categories that are similar to our targeted semantic concepts, but its coverage is insufficient. Our work is also related to semantic lexicon induction (Thelen and Riloff, 2002; McIntosh and Curran, 2009; Qadir and Riloff, 2012; De Benedictis et al., 2013; Gupta and Manning, 2015), contextual semantic tagging (Huang and Riloff, 2010), and fine-grained entity recognition (Fleischman and Hovy, 2002; Ling and Weld, 2012). Our goal, however, is not to generate a dictionary, or assign semantic meanings in sentence contexts. Instead, our classifier learns to recognize words that belong to a small set of relevant semantic classes based only on their pre-trained embedding vectors.

3 Lightly Supervised Semantic Classification

We hypothesized that Human Needs categorization would benefit from recognizing words that belong to the 10 semantic concepts listed in Table 1, based on our analysis of the Human Needs definitions presented in (Ding et al., 2018). In this section, we present lightly supervised models that learn to assign words to these classes.

3.1 Seeding

The input to our classifiers is a small set of seed words for each targeted semantic class. The affective events data set that we will use for our study

ENTERTAINMENT: play game movie story trip party birthday song music video
INTERPERSONAL: meet visit kiss share lie relationship hug marry agree admit
MENTAL-PROCESS: know remember read guess dream forget understand explain study memory
MEDICAL: die hurt pain kill sick blood hospital dead drug surgery
MONEY/JOB: job pay money deal sell business price sale purchase dollar
EQUIPMENT: car phone computer bike camera chair boat machine desk laptop
FOOD/DRINK: eat water food dinner drink lunch breakfast cake meal chocolate
PEOPLE: people friend guy girl man kid mom someone everyone family
EMOTION: good love nice fun bad happy best better smile enjoy laugh hate kind beautiful wrong amazing awesome funny crazy worry
OTHER: be have do get go time say make think take day come look thing tell start way try last year

Table 1: Semantic Concepts and Seed Words

(Section 5) was generated from the ICWSM 2009 and 2011 blog corpora (Burton et al., 2009, 2011), so we selected seed words from these corpora as well. We used the following procedure to identify commonly used words for each category: we sorted all word lemmas by frequency and selected the k top-ranked words belonging to each semantic concept. We set k=10 for all classes, except we set k=20 for EMOTION and OTHER because they are extremely large categories.[1] Table 1 shows the seeds selected for each semantic class.

3.2 Classification

We created three classification models: logistic regression, instance-based learning, and prototypical neural networks. For all three classifiers, we used the Word2Vec 300D pre-trained embeddings (Mikolov et al., 2013) as features. The seed words served as training examples, along with 500 randomly selected unlabeled words as additional seeds for the OTHER category, since it needs to represent a large and diverse "None-of-the-Above" class.

The first model is a one-vs.-rest logistic regression classifier, built using the scikit-learn toolkit (Pedregosa et al., 2011) with default parameters.

The second model uses instance-based classification. This method first creates a prototype representation for each semantic class as the mean of the word embeddings of its seeds. Given a new

---

[1] The k values were chosen arbitrarily without experimentation, so tuning these values could potentially further improve performance.

word, a probability distribution is computed over the semantic classes as the softmax of the negative Euclidean distance to each class prototype. The class with the highest probability is chosen.

The third model uses prototypical neural networks (Snell et al., 2017), which have performed well on "few-shot" learning tasks with limited labeled training data, because of its simple inductive bias. We created a single layer feed-forward network with ReLU activations as the embedding function f. To learn parameters for f, we use the same training algorithm as Snell et al. (2017) except that we train on all semantic classes in each training episode, and both the support set and query set consist of 5 randomly selected examples per class. During training, we use the following parameters: the dimension of the embedding representation layer is 32, the learning rate is .01, and the weight decay is .0001. We train the model for 20 epochs with 100 episodes for each epoch.

To predict the class label for a new word, the process is the same as the instance-based model, except that the learned embedding is used. First, we create a prototype embedding c_k for each semantic class k using Equation 1, where S_k contains all the labeled seed words for class k.

$$c_k = \frac{1}{|S_k|} \sum_{x_i \in S_k} f(x_i) \qquad (1)$$

Given a new word, a probability distribution over the classes is computed as the softmax of the negative Euclidean distance d to each prototype, as shown in Equation 2.

$$p(y = k|x) = \frac{\exp(-d(f(x), c_k))}{\sum_{k'} \exp(-d(f(x), c_{k'}))} \qquad (2)$$

4 Human Needs Categorization

Our goal is to explore whether semantic classification of terms can improve Human Needs categorization of affective events. Toward this end, we used the Human Needs categorization framework described in Ding and Riloff (2018a) which is a *co-training model* that iteratively trains two models with different views of the data: (1) an *event expression classifier* that uses the words in an event expression as input, and (2) an *event context classifier* that uses the sentence contexts that mention an event as input. An event expression is represented as a tuple consisting of 4 components: (Agent, Predicate, Theme, PP). The event

expression classifier is a logistic regression model that takes the embedding of an event expression as input, which is computed as the average over the embeddings of its individual words. The architecture and models are the same, but in this paper we aim to improve the event expression classifier by incorporating semantic classification.

Given an event expression, we extract two types of semantic features from the head words of its 4 components. For each of the 4 head words, we create 10 real-valued features representing the confidence scores produced by the classifier for each of the 10 semantic classes. In addition, we create 10 binary features (one per semantic class) indicating whether *any* of the head words belongs to each class, based on the classifier's predicted labels. Consequently, for each event expression the semantic classifier generates 50 semantic features.

5 Evaluation

We conducted two sets of experiments to evaluate the impact of our semantic classifiers. First, we show the results of adding semantic features to the event expression classifier for Human Needs categorization. Second, we evaluate the impact of the enhanced event expression classifier in the full co-training model. We used the evaluation data set created by Ding and Riloff (2018a), which contains 542 affective events with manually assigned Human Needs labels. To ensure a fair comparison, we used the same evaluation settings: we perform 3-fold cross-validation on the evaluation data and report the average Precision, Recall, and F1 scores over the folds.

5.1 Human Needs Categorization Results

Table 2 shows the results of experiments with the event expression classifier. The first row, Embed (D&R 2018a), shows the performance of Ding & Riloff's original event expression classifier, which is a logistic regression model with event expression embeddings as features. The next three rows show the performance of a logistic regression model that uses our semantic features instead. We show results for semantic features produced by each of our three models: instance-based classification (Sem:InstBased), logistic regression (Sem:LR), and the prototypical neural network (Sem:ProtoNets). The LR and ProtoNets models

Features	Precision	Recall	F1
Embed (D&R 2018a)	64.2	51.7	54.8
Sem:InstBased	53.7	42.4	45.1
Sem:LR	72.3	46.8	52.0
Sem:ProtoNets	63.1	48.8	52.4
Embed+Sem:InstBased	64.2	55.2	58.1
Embed+Sem:LR	**68.7**	57.3	60.8
Embed+Sem:ProtoNets	67.5	**58.7**	**61.9**

Table 2: Results for Human Needs Categorization with Event Expression Classifiers

achieve an F1 score[2] $\geq$ .52, which is not far below the performance of the D&R model that uses embedding features.

The last three rows of Table 2 show results for the event expression classifier with features for *both* the event expression embedding and the 50 semantic features produced by one of our three semantic classifiers. All of these models outperform the original D&R model. The best model, ProtoNets, substantially improves Human Needs categorization from 54.8% → 61.9%.

Human Need Category	D&R 2018a			Our Results		
	Pr	R	F1	Pr	R	F1
Physio	81	68	74	86.7	68.3	**76.3**
Health	68	50	57	71.6	59.3	**64.8**
Leisure	69	63	66	74.8	64.0	**68.8**
Social	68	79	73	73.9	82.4	**77.9**
Finance	67	44	52	60.5	47.8	**52.9**
Cognition	92	46	58	83.8	54.2	**65.5**
Emotion	64	74	69	65.5	74.2	**69.6**
None	48	52	50	49.0	53.3	**51.1**
AVG	69.7	59.5	62.4	70.7	62.9	**65.9**

Table 3: Results for Human Needs Categorization with Co-Training Models

In the next set of experiments, we evaluated the impact of the new event expression classifier in the co-training model for Human Needs categorization. Table 3 shows the results for the original co-training model reported in our previous work (Ding and Riloff, 2018a) alongside the results for our enhanced co-training model, which is identical except that we replaced the original event expression classifier with our Embed+Sem:ProtoNets model. We used the same experimental settings, running our co-training model for 20 iterations and reporting the best results[3]. Table 3 shows the Precision (Pr), Recall (R), and F1 scores for each

---

Human Needs category and the macro-averaged (AVG) scores. The enhanced co-training model improves performance on every Human Needs category, increasing the average F1 score from 62.4% to 65.9%.

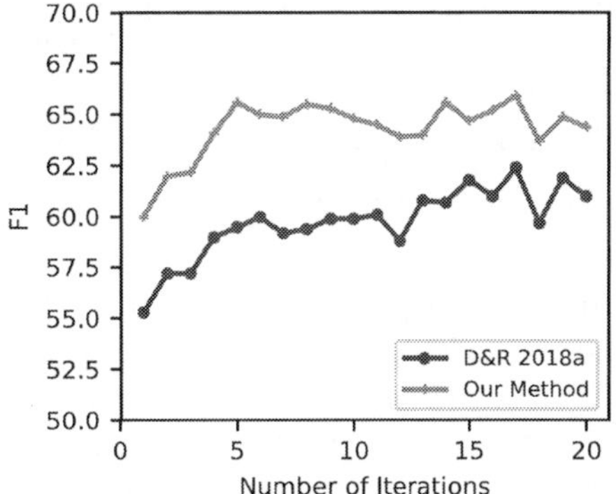

Figure 1: Performance of Co-training Models with Semantic Class Features at Different Iterations

Figure 1 shows the performance of the original co-training method D&R 2018a and our new method with semantic features learned by Embed+Sem:ProtoNets model after each iteration. This result shows that enhancing the event expression classifier with semantic features helps the co-training model improve more rapidly and achieve better performance than the original model for each iteration.

5.2 Analysis of Semantic Classification

We also informally evaluated the quality of the semantic labels assigned by the semantic classifier, to better understand its strengths and weaknesses. One of the authors assigned each word[4] in the evaluation data to one of the 10 semantic classes. Then we compared these human labels to the predicted labels from the semantic classifier.

Table 4 shows the performance for each semantic class. Overall, the classifier achieved a macro-averaged F1 score of 68.8%. Performance across the semantic classes varies, with several classes achieving high precision and high or moderate recall (OTHER, PEOPLE, ENTERTAINMENT, EMOTION, INTERPERSONAL, MENTAL-PROCESS), a few achieving high recall but low to moderate precision (FOOD/DRINK, MONEY/JOB), and a few with moderate recall and precision (EQUIPMENT, MEDICAL). Overall, these results demonstrate

---

[2]Note that this result is the average F1 score over the cross-validation folds, not the F1 score of the average precision and average recall.

[3]Our co-training method achieved the best result after 17 iterations.

[4]Except not pronouns.

Semantic Classes	Precision	Recall	F1
OTHER	79.5	91.0	84.9
PEOPLE	94.2	75.4	83.8
FOOD/DRINK	57.1	92.3	70.6
ENTERTAINMENT	89.1	54.7	67.8
EQUIPMENT	62.5	66.7	64.5
EMOTION	80.0	51.2	62.5
INTERPERSONAL	84.6	47.8	61.1
MENTAL-PROCESS	77.3	48.6	59.6
MEDICAL	64.5	51.3	57.1
MONEY/JOB	37.9	73.3	50.0
AVG	72.7	65.2	68.8

Table 4: Semantic Classification Results

that the semantic classifier produced fairly good predictions for most categories given only light supervision. One could almost certainly further improve these scores with more seed examples or by incorporating readily available external resources for categories such as EMOTION and MEDICAL, which would likely yield further gains for Human Needs categorization. More generally, our lightly supervised approach for training a semantic classifier demonstrates that one can rapidly create a classifier for a specific set of semantic concepts that are important for an application domain.

$\langle$I, gain, pleasure$_{\text{EMOTION}}$, $\rangle$
$\langle$I, be, busy, with my homework$_{\text{MENTAL-PROCESS}}$ $\rangle$
$\langle$we, finish, tour$_{\text{ENTERTAINMENT}}$, $\rangle$
$\langle$our pizza$_{\text{FOOD/DRINK}}$, arrive, , $\rangle$
$\langle$my eye, hurt$_{\text{MEDICAL}}$, bad$_{\text{EMOTION}}$, , $\rangle$
$\langle$I, try to cooperate$_{\text{INTERPERSONAL}}$, , $\rangle$
$\langle$I, dance$_{\text{ENTERTAINMENT}}$, , with my mom$_{\text{PEOPLE}}$ $\rangle$
$\langle$I, dance$_{\text{ENTERTAINMENT}}$, , with my friend$_{\text{PEOPLE}}$ $\rangle$
$\langle$I, not function, , at work$_{\text{MONEY/JOB}}$ $\rangle$
$\langle$day, be, magical$_{\text{EMOTION}}$, $\rangle$
$\langle$people$_{\text{PEOPLE}}$, buy$_{\text{MONEY/JOB}}$, home, $\rangle$
$\langle$we, grow, hungry$_{\text{FOOD/DRINK}}$, $\rangle$
$\langle$I, forget$_{\text{MENTAL-PROCESS}}$, paper, $\rangle$
$\langle$I, not learn$_{\text{MENTAL-PROCESS}}$, something, $\rangle$
$\langle$I, buy$_{\text{MONEY/JOB}}$, film$_{\text{ENTERTAINMENT}}$, $\rangle$
$\langle$house phone$_{\text{EQUIPMENT}}$, not work$_{\text{MONEY/JOB}}$, , $\rangle$
$\langle$epidural$_{\text{MEDICAL}}$, start to work$_{\text{MONEY/JOB}}$, , $\rangle$

Table 5: Examples of Affective Events with Automatically Predicted Semantic Classes

Table 5 presents some examples of affective events and their semantic classes that are assigned by the Prototypical Networks Model. All the unlabeled words in the table were assigned to OTHER class[5]. Besides the words

---

[5]In our experiments, we did not apply the semantic classifier to prepositions and pronouns, but directly assign first person pronouns to OTHER, and assign second and third person pronouns to PEOPLE.

(e.g., "pleasure$_{\text{EMOTION}}$", "pizza$_{\text{FOOD/DRINK}}$", "cooperate$_{\text{INTERPERSONAL}}$") that were classified correctly, some words in events also received incorrect semantic category labels. For example, the "work" in "house phone not work" and "epidural start to work" was incorrectly classified to MONEY/JOB, which suggests that it may be beneficial to further improve the performance of semantic categorization of words in events by considering the contextual meaning of polysemous words. In addition, our set of semantic classes was selected based on our intuition about what concepts are most relevant to the human needs categories, but it might be worthwhile for future work to more thoroughly explore a large set of semantic concepts.

6 Conclusions

We proposed to improve human needs categorization of affective events by adding semantic features that classify terms into related semantic concepts. We designed lightly supervised models that learn to classify words with respect to semantic concepts using only their pre-trained word embedding vectors and seed words as training data. We then showed that representing semantic concepts improves both the precision and recall for Human Needs categorization of events.

Acknowledgements

This material is based in part upon work supported by the National Science Foundation under Grant Number IIS-1619394. Any opinions, findings, and conclusions or recommendations expressed in this material are those of the authors and do not necessarily reflect the views of the National Science Foundation. The authors thank Tianyu Jiang for his feedback and comments on the paper.

References

Kevin Burton, Akshay Java, and Ian Soboroff. 2009. The ICWSM 2009 Spinn3r dataset. In *Third Annual Conference on Weblogs and Social Media*.

Kevin Burton, Niels Kasch, and Ian Soboroff. 2011. The ICWSM 2011 Spinn3r dataset. In *Proceedings of the Annual Conference on Weblogs and Social Media*.

Flavio De Benedictis, Stefano Faralli, and Roberto Navigli. 2013. Glossboot: Bootstrapping multilingual domain glossaries from the web. In *Proceedings of the 51st Annual Meeting of the Association for Computational Linguistics*.

Lingjia Deng, Yoonjung Choi, and Janyce Wiebe. 2013. Benefactive/malefactive event and writer attitude annotation. In *Proceedings of the 51st Annual Meeting of the Association for Computational Linguistics*.

Lingjia Deng and Janyce Wiebe. 2014. Sentiment propagation via implicature constraints. In *Proceedings of the 14th Conference of the European Chapter of the Association for Computational Linguistics*.

Jacob Devlin, Ming-Wei Chang, Kenton Lee, and Kristina Toutanova. 2018. Bert: Pre-training of deep bidirectional transformers for language understanding. *arXiv preprint arXiv:1810.04805*.

Haibo Ding, Tianyu Jiang, and Ellen Riloff. 2018. Why is an event affective? classifying affective events based on human needs. In *the AAAI-18 Workshop on Affective Content Analysis*.

Haibo Ding and Ellen Riloff. 2016. Acquiring knowledge of affective events from blogs using label propagation. In *Proceedings of the AAAI Conference on Artificial Intelligence*.

Haibo Ding and Ellen Riloff. 2018a. Human needs categorization of affective events using labeled and unlabeled data. In *Proceedings of the 2018 Conference of the North American Chapter of the Association for Computational Linguistics: Human Language Technologies (NAACL 2018)*.

Haibo Ding and Ellen Riloff. 2018b. Weakly supervised induction of affective events by optimizing semantic consistency. In *Proceedings of the AAAI Conference on Artificial Intelligence*.

Michael Fleischman and Eduard Hovy. 2002. Fine grained classification of named entities. In *Proceedings of the 19th International Conference on Computational Linguistics*.

A. Goyal, E. Riloff, and H. Daumé III. 2013. A Computational Model for Plot Units. *Computational Intelligence*, 29(3):466–488.

Sonal Gupta and Christopher D Manning. 2015. Distributed representations of words to guide bootstrapped entity classifiers. In *Proceedings of the 2015 Conference of the North American Chapter of the Association for Computational Linguistics: Human Language Technologies*.

Ruihong Huang and Ellen Riloff. 2010. Inducing domain-specific semantic class taggers from (almost) nothing. In *Proceedings of the 48th Annual Meeting of the Association for Computational Linguistics*.

Jiwei Li, Alan Ritter, Claire Cardie, and Eduard Hovy. 2014. Major life event extraction from twitter based on congratulations/condolences speech acts. In *Proceedings of Empirical Methods in Natural Language Processing*.

Xiao Ling and Daniel S Weld. 2012. Fine-grained entity recognition. In *Twenty-Sixth AAAI Conference on Artificial Intelligence*.

Abraham Harold Maslow, Robert Frager, James Fadiman, Cynthia McReynolds, and Ruth Cox. 1970. *Motivation and personality*, volume 2. Harper & Row New York.

Manfred Max-Neef, Antonio Elizalde, and Martin Hopenhayn. 1991. *Human Scale Development: Conception, Application and Further Reflections*. The Apex Press.

T. McIntosh and J. Curran. 2009. Reducing semantic drift with bagging and distributional similarity. In *Proceedings of the 47th Annual Meeting of the Association for Computational Linguistics*.

Tomas Mikolov, Ilya Sutskever, Kai Chen, Greg S Corrado, and Jeff Dean. 2013. Distributed representations of words and phrases and their compositionality. In *Advances in neural information processing systems*.

F. Pedregosa, G. Varoquaux, A. Gramfort, V. Michel, B. Thirion, O. Grisel, M. Blondel, P. Prettenhofer, R. Weiss, V. Dubourg, J. Vanderplas, A. Passos, D. Cournapeau, M. Brucher, M. Perrot, and E. Duchesnay. 2011. Scikit-learn: Machine learning in Python. *Journal of Machine Learning Research*, 12:2825–2830.

James W Pennebaker, Roger J Booth, and Martha E Francis. 2007. Linguistic inquiry and word count: LIWC2007. *Austin, TX: liwc.net*.

Jeffrey Pennington, Richard Socher, and Christopher D Manning. 2014. GloVe: Global vectors for word representation. In *Proceedings of the Conference on Empirical Methods in Natural Language Processing*.

Matthew E. Peters, Mark Neumann, Mohit Iyyer, Matt Gardner, Christopher Clark, Kenton Lee, and Luke Zettlemoyer. 2018. Deep contextualized word representations. In *Proceedings of the 2018 Conference of the North American Chapter of the Association for Computational Linguistics (NAACL 2018)*.

Ashequl Qadir and Ellen Riloff. 2012. Ensemble-based semantic lexicon induction for semantic tagging. In *Proceedings of the First Joint Conference on Lexical and Computational Semantics*. Association for Computational Linguistics.

Lena Reed, JiaQi Wu, Shereen Oraby, Pranav Anand, and Marilyn A. Walker. 2017. Learning lexico-functional patterns for first-person affect. In *Proceedings of the 55th Annual Meeting of the Association for Computational Linguistics*.

P. Sarma, Y. Liang, and W. Sethares. 2018. Domain adapted word embeddings for improved sentiment classification. In *Proceedings of the ACL 2018 Workshop on Deep Learning Approaches for Low-Resource NLP*.

Jake Snell, Kevin Swersky, and Richard Zemel. 2017. Prototypical networks for few-shot learning. In *Advances in Neural Information Processing Systems*.

M. Thelen and E. Riloff. 2002. A bootstrapping method for learning semantic lexicons using extraction pattern contexts. In *Proceedings of the 2002 Conference on Empirical Methods in Natural Language Processing*.

Hoa Trong Vu, Graham Neubig, Sakriani Sakti, Tomoki Toda, and Satoshi Nakamura. 2014. Acquiring a dictionary of emotion-provoking events. In *Proceedings of the 14th Conference of the European Chapter of the Association for Computational Linguistics*.

Word Embeddings (Also) Encode Human Personality Stereotypes

Oshin Agarwal
University of Pennsylvania
oagarwal@seas.upenn.edu

Funda Durupinar
Bilkent University
fundad@cs.bilkent.edu.tr

Norman I. Badler
University of Pennsylvania
badler@seas.upenn.edu

Ani Nenkova
University of Pennsylvania
nenkova@seas.upenn.edu

Abstract

Word representations trained on text reproduce human implicit bias related to gender, race and age. Methods have been developed to remove such bias. Here, we present results that show that human stereotypes exist even for much more nuanced judgments such as personality, for a variety of person identities beyond the typically legally protected attributes and that these are similarly captured in word representations. Specifically, we collected human judgments about a person's Big Five personality traits formed solely from information about the occupation, nationality or a common noun description of a hypothetical person. Analysis of the data reveals a large number of statistically significant stereotypes in people. We then demonstrate the bias captured in lexical representations is statistically significantly correlated with the documented human bias. Our results, showing bias for a large set of person descriptors for such nuanced traits put in doubt the feasibility of broadly and fairly applying debiasing methods and call for the development of new methods for auditing language technology systems and resources.

1 Introduction

Implicit association tests probe biases individuals may harbor, by measuring the reaction times of people when asked to sort word stimuli with clearly positive/negative valance and words associated with racial groups or less morally relevant categories such as insects/flowers and musical instruments/weapons (Greenwald et al., 1998). Recent work has revealed that word representations trained on large text corpora reproduce human bias in preference to flowers and musical instruments, but also disturbingly on gender, race and age-related bias (Caliskan et al., 2017).

These findings pose a dilemma. Having systems learn that flowers/musical instruments are pleasant and insects/weapons unpleasant appears to be useful common sense knowledge that systems can leverage to better interact with people[1]. Having racist, sexist and ageist systems however is highly undesirable, as these are integrated in broader technologies like machine translation, which can reinforce the stereotype[2]. Stereotypes are highly problematic because even simply evoking them can trigger change in behavior (Duguid and Thomas-Hunt, 2015; Spencer et al., 2016).

Guided by these compelling arguments, many researchers have started looking for ways to debias word representations and language technologies. In response to the examples in the supplementary materials in (Caliskan et al., 2017), that Google Translate translates 'doctor' as male and 'nurse' as female, Google has indeed rolled out a new version of their systems for certain language pairs, in which both translation versions are displayed[3]. Similarly, earlier work has zeroed in on the gender bias in word representation and has proposed methods for debiasing, which take in a set of words to be debiased as an argument to the algorithm (Bolukbasi et al., 2016). Work further developing this line of analysis and debiasing has appeared in recent computational linguistics venues (Zhao et al., 2017, 2018; Rudinger et al., 2018). This line of work is in stark contrast with earlier work in the field, which treated human stereotypes encoded in text as common sense knowledge that could be helpful in automating tasks such as named entity tagging and coreference resolution (Bergsma and Lin, 2006; Ji and Lin, 2009).

In this complex context, we set out to study how broad stereotypes are, both in terms of groups

---

[1] Such knowledge will for example make it possible to accurately interpret the pragmatic meaning of a person exclaiming "You have a spider on your shoulder!"

[2] https://bit.ly/2HXkipB

[3] https://bit.ly/2B0nVHZ

*Proceedings of the Eighth Joint Conference on Lexical and Computational Semantics (*SEM)*, pages 205–211
Minneapolis, June 6–7, 2019. ©2019 Association for Computational Linguistics

they may affect and the subtlety of distinction involved in the stereotype. For this purpose, we turn to personality stereotypes evoked by a single descriptor of a person, such as nationality, profession and arbitrary words describing people. We verify that people hold stereotypes about personality and that the human stereotypes can be recovered fairly accurately from word representations. Given the wide variety of descriptors to which stereotypes apply, we argue that an approach different from classic debiasing approaches for dealing with the problem ought to be established. We discuss some of these thoughts and considerations in the concluding section of this paper.

2 Big Five Personality Traits

The Big 5 personality traits, OCEAN, are the most common framework for studying personality in psychology studies (John and Srivastava, 1999). In this framework, personality is described in five dimensions: openness to experience, conscientiousness, extroversion, agreeableness and neuroticism. One of the most compact instruments to assess personality in this scale is the Ten Item Personality Inventory (TIPI) (Gosling et al., 2003). TIPI defines the extreme ends of each personality dimension by two simple descriptions:

O conventional/uncreative $\leftrightarrow$ open to new experiences/complex

C disorganized/careless $\leftrightarrow$ dependable/self-disciplined

E reserved/quiet $\leftrightarrow$ extroverted/enthusiastic

A critical/quarrelsome $\leftrightarrow$ sympathetic/warm

N calm/emotionally stable $\leftrightarrow$ anxious/easily upset

OCEAN personality traits have been used in a number of computational linguistics studies such as developing dialog systems whose generation components can be tuned to project specific personality (Mairesse and Walker, 2007), predicting perceived personality from social media posts (Celli et al., 2013; Kosinski et al., 2013), automatic personality detection from essays (Majumder et al., 2017) and predicting specific traits, such as neuroticism, strongly linked with risk for depression and anxiety (Resnik et al., 2013).

3 Human Stereotype Collection

We collected human personality stereotypes for 98 professions and 135 nationalities, recruiting participants on Amazon Mechanical Turk[4]. The professions were drawn from the list of nouns that are children of the node 'person' in the WordNet Is-A hierarchy. The list is large, with over 2,300 entries overall. From this list, two of the authors selected 98 professions. Similarly, nationalities were drawn for the CIA fact book and narrowed down to 135 by two of the authors. We used the Ten Item Personality Inventory (TIPI) (Gosling et al., 2003) to elicit the participant expectations about the personality of people with given nationalities or professions. Participants were given tasks consisting of ten nationalities/professions, to be judged for a single personality trait. The top of the page displayed the TIPI ends for the personality dimensions presented above. The participants were asked to rate where a person with the given profession/nationality will fall on a 7-point scale. The middle of the scale is interpreted as *'have no expectation/could be either'*, -3 corresponds to the negative end of the dimension defined by the description on the left above and 3 corresponds with the positive end of the dimension defined by the description on the right. The order of the nationalities/professions was randomly assigned in each task. One of the ten professions/ nationalities in the task was a repeat. This was used for quality control. Participants who gave different rating for the repeated nationality/profession were excluded from the study, as were participants who gave the same answer for all ten nationalities/ professions.

Only participants residing in the United States were given access to the task.

4 Analysis of Human Bias

After excluding inconsistent participants, we had 30 judgments for the vast majority of nationalities and 25 judgments for the professions.

We use the Wilcoxon signed-rank test to determine if the mean of the human judgments for each of the five personality traits is different from zero at 95% confidence. We found that 92.5% of the nationalities had at least one statistically significant personality trait; about 40% had numerical values greater than 1 or less than -1 on the seven point scale, indicating a high bias. Similarly, 98% of the professions had at least one statistically significant with personality trait[5]; about 94% had numerical

---

[4]Data available at `https://github.com/oagarwal/personality-bias`

[5]We do not perform any adjustments for multiple com-

	Professions				Nationalities			
	mean > 0	mean < 0	mean > 1	mean < -1	mean > 0	mean < 0	mean > 1	mean < -1
O	33.6	31.6	27.5	18.3	23.7	17.03	18.5	11.8
C	77.5	1	67.3	1	32.5	5.9	16.2	0
E	37.7	18.3	28.5	9.1	19.2	40.7	14.8	5.9
A	41.8	16.3	27.5	9.1	37	9.6	9.6	1.4
N	6.1	31.6	3	12.2	23.7	20	8.1	12.5

Table 1: Percentage of professions and nationalities with statistically significant human bias towards specific personality traits i.e mean different from zero at 95% confidence using Wilcoxon signed rank test.

Num of sig traits	Professions		Nationalities	
	Sig	Sig $\|mean\| > 1$	Sig	Sign $\|mean\| > 1$
0	2.04	6.12	7.40	54.81
1	5.10	18.36	25.18	14.07
2	24.48	47.95	25.92	17.77
3	40.81	21.42	17.77	7.40
4	20.40	5.10	19.25	5.18
5	7.14	1.02	3.70	0.74

Table 2: Column 1 is percentage of professions or nationalities with n out of 5 statistically significant personality traits i.e mean different from zero at 95% confidence using Wilcoxon signed rank test. Column 2 is percentage of professions or nationalities with n out of 5 statistically significant personality traits and absolute value of mean greater than equal to 1 indicating high bias.

values greater than 1 or less than -1. Often people, including the authors, expect bias to be negative but most of the bias we observe is positive: certain groups were perceived to be agreeable, open to experiences, conscientious and not neurotic. These results can be seen in Table 1.

The existence of national stereotypes (from members of the same nation) has been documented, and also shown not to correlate at all with actual self-reported or perceived personalities of the members of the culture (Terracciano et al., 2005). In our study, the nationality stereotypes are from Americans towards other cultures and are likely similarly unfounded. Many of the stereotypes we observe in our study are predictable: Australians and Swedish are ranked at the top positive end for openness; Japanese and Chinese are most conscientious; Americans are extroverts; Canadians and New Zealanders are rated as most agreeable. In professions, priests and accountants are perceived as least open; drug dealers as least conscientious; chemists and mathematicians as introverts; drug dealers and prosecutors as disagreeable; tour guides and pianists as least neurotic.

There were few professions/nationalities for which all five dimensions of personality were statistically significant. Australians, Finnish, New Zealanders, tour guides, designers, house decora-

tors, art dealers have highly positive bias towards them. Judges and senators have also significant bias in all traits, but direction varies across traits for them. Overall statistics are shown in Table 2.

5   Personality Bias Prediction

In this section, we test the extent to which the stereotypes in the human data can be explained by co-occurrence statistics between the nationality/ profession and descriptors related to the personality dimensions. Prior work (Bhatia, 2016) has shown that co-occurrence statistics can be used to predict human bias towards probability of occurrence of real-life events such as terrorist attacks.

In the prominent work on word representations and bias (Caliskan et al., 2017), human stereotypes were reconstructed by substituting human reaction times in sorting words with the cosine similarity between sets of words. In the original psychology studies, the word stimuli are drawn from prior studies which established that people consider certain words to be highly positive or negative. For example, some words with positive connotations used in the study include 'freedom, rainbow, miracle, laughter' and words with negative connotations include 'abuse, sickness, tragedy, ugly'.

We do not do any similar pre-screening of descriptors. The personality descriptors in our study come from a standard instrument developed for personality assessment (see Table 3). Predictions in our final evaluation are performed for a broad

___
parisons. A number of these findings may be spurious but the number of significant finding far exceeds the 5% expected significant results due to statistical chance.

Trait	Positive-end words	Negative-end words
O	intelligent, perceptive, analytical, reflective, curious, imaginative, creative, cultured, refined, sophisticated	unintelligent, imperceptive, unanalytical, unreflective, uninquisitive, unimaginative, uncreative, uncultured, unrefined, unsophisticated
C	organized, responsible, reliable, conscientious, practical, thorough, hardworking, thrifty, cautious, serious	disorganized, irresponsible, undependable, negligent, impractical, careless, lazy, extravagant, rash, frivolous
E	extroverted, energetic, talkative, enthusiastic, bold, active, spontaneous, assertive, adventurous, sociable	introverted, unenergetic, silent, unenthusiastic, timid, inactive, inhibited, unassertive, unadventurous, unsociable
A	warm, kind, cooperative, unselfish, polite, agreeable, trustful, generous, flexible, fair	cold, unkind, uncooperative, selfish, rude, disagreeable, distrustful, stingy, inflexible, unfair
N	angry, tense, nervous, envious, unstable, discontented, insecure, emotional, guilt-ridden, moody	calm, relaxed, at ease, not envious, stable, contended, secure, unemotional, guilt-free, steady

Table 3: Goldberg markers for personality traits

category of person descriptors, demonstrating that a long list of arbitrary person categories may trigger stereotypes in people and that these stereotypes are recoverable from text embeddings.

We use off-the-shelf word representations to measure the (cosine) similarity between a list of personality descriptors and a target nationality or profession. We experimented with GloVe representations (Pennington et al., 2014) trained on Common crawl (6B tokens, 400K vocab, 300d) and symmetric pattern (SP) based representations (Schwartz et al., 2015). We used TIPI to collect human judgments but these descriptors of personality are likely too short for the noisy automatic creation of personality stereotypes. For this reason, we use a larger inventory of personality trait descriptors, Goldbergs Big Five markers (Goldberg, 1992). It has about ten descriptors associated with each of the positive and negative dimensions of a personality trait, all shown in Tables 3.

Different words and phrases are present in the two vector representations in our study. While multi-word expressions such as 'drug dealer' and 'movie star' are present in the SP embeddings, they are missing from the GloVe embeddings. Some other words such as 'guilt-ridden' and 'guilt-free' are present in GloVe embeddings but missing from the SP embeddings. Results for each representation are reported using all markers and person descriptors available in the representation.

Let t denote a target description of a person (eg. doctor), pd be the set of *positive* Goldberg personality markers (eg. energetic, extrovert) for a trait and nd be the set of *negative* Goldberg personality markers (eg. reserved, introvert)) for a trait. We first develop a baseline where the predicted bias score is the difference between the mean of the cosine similarity of target description t with each of the positive markers for the trait, and the mean cosine similarity of t with each of the negative markers for the trait. We build separate models for each of the five personality traits. Each of the models has descriptions of both nationalities and professions and we do not differentiate between the two.

$$score = \frac{\sum_{p \in pd} sim(t,p)}{|pd|} - \frac{\sum_{n \in nd} sim(t,n)}{|nd|}$$

Next, we use linear regression to predict the personality scores using as features the cosine similarity of target description of the person with each of the Goldberg personality markers (eg. energetic, introvert) for the trait.

$$score = \sum_{p \in pd} w_p sim(t,p) + \sum_{n \in nd} w_n sim(t,n)$$

where $w_{n,p}$ are weights learned by regression for each of the Golderberg personality markers.

We do leave-one-out cross validation because we have human judgements for just 233 descriptions of people. Finally, we calculate the Spearman correlation of the scores on the n test points, one from each model in cross validation with the average human scores.

Further, we test the model on new descriptions from WordNet[6]. We randomly selected 140 descriptions and crowdsourced judgments about them in the same manner as the training data. The resulting correlations can shown in Table 4.

On the leave-one-out results on the training data consisting of nationalities and professions, the regression model is clearly superior to the unsupervised baseline. On the test data, the best correlation for Conscientiousness and Agreeableness is achieved by the baseline with SP representations.

---

[6]Specifically 2,638 descriptions, not in the training data, that are hyponyms of 'person' upto depth 4.

	Train				Test			
	Baseline		Linear Regr		Baseline		Linear Regr	
	Glove	SP	Glove	SP	Glove	SP	Glove	SP
O	0.230	0.160	0.519	**0.615**	0.359	0.380	**0.524**	0.365
C	0.439	0.618	0.683	**0.686**	0.459	**0.695**	0.503	0.611
E	0.364	0.274	**0.481**	0.298	0.180	0.174	**0.272**	0.246
A	0.131[*]	0.295	**0.407**	0.396	0.414	**0.538**	0.421	0.451
N	0.092[*]	0.201	0.299	**0.438**	0.244	0.396	**0.449**	0.343

[*] Not significant

Table 4: Spearman correlation between human bias and predicted personality on the leave-one-out predictions for the training set, and on generic noun descriptions for the test set.

Description	Trait	Human bias	Glove	SP
Cook	O	1.59	1.97	0.59
Assistant	C	1.30	2.12	1.55
Herbalist	E	-0.91	-0.46	-0.8
Fugitive	A	-1.14	-0.36	-2.24
Ex-husband	N	1.25	1.11	-

Table 5: Predicted scores on new descriptions.

We also computed the class of bias for each of the predictions—positive bias, negative bias and no bias.[7] The accuracy was 55-60% for each of the cases except neuroticism (42%). Both representations assigned the same bias class for 65%, 80%, 73%, 79% and 93% descriptions for OCEAN traits respectively. There is no clear word representation that works consistently better.

All correlations are statistically significant and hold up well between the training and test data, even though the test data has much more varied descriptions of people. Notably, Openness and Conscientiousness are predicted most accurately and for a number of personality dimensions the results on the heterogeneous test set are higher than for the training set of nationality and professions.

Some examples which stood out, of test descriptions and bias scores are shown in Table 5.[8] People have a significant bias which is being predicted by the classifier based on embeddings as well. The classifier (Glove) predicted high bias i.e score ≥ 1 or ≤ -1 for 21%, 23%, 14.5%, 11% and 2.5% of the 2,638 WordNet person descriptors for the OCEAN traits respectively.

6 Discussion and conclusion

We introduced a corpus of human stereotypes of personality. We showed that the off the shelf vec-

tor space representations can be leveraged to derive personality stereotypes from corpora. We used the model to make predictions on thousands of person descriptors, with larger samples. This list allows us to inspect a much larger scope of possible bias than smaller targeted categories. For example, in much more controversial direction of work, our approach can be used to train a model that predicts sentiment valence, possibly starting with words from prior studies. Then we can, as we did in the work here, predict which other words may have similar bias, potentially recovering many more nuanced groups.

Our findings indicate that debiasing methods *that need explicit set of words to be debiased* are unlikely to be effective in removing all stereotype-like data. Moreover, as has been now revealed, debiasing methods only mask the bias rather than fully remove it from influence on downstream tasks like clustering and gendered prediction (Gonen and Goldberg, 2019).

One of the earliest paper reporting correlation between lexical co-occurrence and human implicit bias association tests has a somewhat more optimist view (Lynott et al.). They provide examples in which people exhibit gender and racial implicit bias but when asked to be thoughtful in performing a task, they make decisions not aligned with that bias. This view aligns with the model of two systems of thinking—fast stereotypes that are highly inaccurate in many cases and slow, deliberate thinking that overrides these stereotypes (Kahneman, 2011). It remains an open problem what the slow processing mechanisms should be for automated systems but clearly developing such systems and the necessary benchmarks to test these would mark an important milestone in the development of language technology.

---

[7]We consider predicted scores between 1 and -1 to mean that there is no bias.

[8]Predictions on all the 2,638 WordNet descriptions are also available at https://github.com/oagarwal/personality-bias

References

Shane Bergsma and Dekang Lin. 2006. Bootstrapping path-based pronoun resolution. In *Proceedings of the 21st International Conference on Computational Linguistics and the 44th Annual Meeting of the Association for Computational Linguistics*, ACL-44, pages 33–40, Stroudsburg, PA, USA. Association for Computational Linguistics.

Sudeep Bhatia. 2016. Vector space semantic models predict subjective probability judgments for real-world events. In *Proceedings of the 38th annual conference of the cognitive science society*, pages 1937–1942.

Tolga Bolukbasi, Kai-Wei Chang, James Y Zou, Venkatesh Saligrama, and Adam T Kalai. 2016. Man is to computer programmer as woman is to homemaker? debiasing word embeddings. In *Advances in neural information processing systems*, pages 4349–4357.

Aylin Caliskan, Joanna J Bryson, and Arvind Narayanan. 2017. Semantics derived automatically from language corpora contain human-like biases. *Science*, 356(6334):183–186.

Fabio Celli, Fabio Pianesi, David Stillwell, and Michal Kosinski. 2013. Workshop on computational personality recognition (shared task). In *Proceedings of the Workshop on Computational Personality Recognition*.

Michelle M Duguid and Melissa C Thomas-Hunt. 2015. Condoning stereotyping? how awareness of stereotyping prevalence impacts expression of stereotypes. *Journal of Applied Psychology*, 100(2):343.

Lewis R Goldberg. 1992. The development of markers for the big-five factor structure. *Psychological assessment*, 4(1):26.

Hila Gonen and Yoav Goldberg. 2019. Lipstick on a pig: Debiasing methods cover up systematic gender biases in word embeddings but do not remove them. *NAACL'19*.

Samuel D Gosling, Peter J Rentfrow, and William B Swann Jr. 2003. A very brief measure of the big-five personality domains. *Journal of Research in personality*, 37(6):504–528.

Anthony G Greenwald, Debbie E McGhee, and Jordan LK Schwartz. 1998. Measuring individual differences in implicit cognition: the implicit association test. *Journal of personality and social psychology*, 74(6):1464.

Heng Ji and Dekang Lin. 2009. Gender and animacy knowledge discovery from web-scale n-grams for unsupervised person mention detection. In *Proceedings of the 23rd Pacific Asia Conference on Language, Information and Computation, PACLIC 23, Hong Kong, China, December 3-5, 2009*, pages 220–229.

Oliver P John and Sanjay Srivastava. 1999. The big five trait taxonomy: History, measurement, and theoretical perspectives. *Handbook of personality: Theory and research*, 2(1999):102–138.

Daniel Kahneman. 2011. *Thinking, fast and slow*, volume 1. Farrar, Straus and Giroux New York.

Michal Kosinski, David Stillwell, and Thore Graepel. 2013. Private traits and attributes are predictable from digital records of human behavior. *Proceedings of the National Academy of Sciences*, page 201218772.

Dermot Lynott, Louise Connell, Kerry S O'Brien, and Himanshu Kansal. Modelling the iat: Implicit association test reflects shallow linguistic environment and not deep personal attitudes.

François Mairesse and Marilyn Walker. 2007. Personage: Personality generation for dialogue. In *Proceedings of the 45th Annual Meeting of the Association of Computational Linguistics*, pages 496–503.

N. Majumder, S. Poria, A. Gelbukh, and E. Cambria. 2017. Deep learning-based document modeling for personality detection from text. *IEEE Intelligent Systems*, 32(2):74–79.

Jeffrey Pennington, Richard Socher, and Christopher Manning. 2014. Glove: Global vectors for word representation. In *Proceedings of the 2014 conference on empirical methods in natural language processing (EMNLP)*, pages 1532–1543.

Philip Resnik, Anderson Garron, and Rebecca Resnik. 2013. Using topic modeling to improve prediction of neuroticism and depression in college students. In *Proceedings of the 2013 conference on empirical methods in natural language processing*, pages 1348–1353.

Rachel Rudinger, Jason Naradowsky, Brian Leonard, and Benjamin Van Durme. 2018. Gender bias in coreference resolution. In *Proceedings of the 2018 Conference of the North American Chapter of the Association for Computational Linguistics: Human Language Technologies, Volume 2 (Short Papers)*, pages 8–14. Association for Computational Linguistics.

Roy Schwartz, Roi Reichart, and Ari Rappoport. 2015. Symmetric pattern based word embeddings for improved word similarity prediction. In *Proceedings of the Nineteenth Conference on Computational Natural Language Learning*, pages 258–267.

Steven J Spencer, Christine Logel, and Paul G Davies. 2016. Stereotype threat. *Annual review of psychology*, 67:415–437.

Antonio Terracciano, Ahmed M Abdel-Khalek, N Adam, Lucia Adamovová, C-k Ahn, H-n Ahn, Bader M Alansari, Lidia Alcalay, Jüri Allik, Alois Angleitner, et al. 2005. National character does not reflect mean personality trait levels in 49 cultures. *Science*, 310(5745):96–100.

Jieyu Zhao, Tianlu Wang, Mark Yatskar, Vicente Ordonez, and Kai-Wei Chang. 2017. Men also like
shopping: Reducing gender bias amplification using corpus-level constraints. In *Proceedings of the
2017 Conference on Empirical Methods in Natural
Language Processing, EMNLP 2017, Copenhagen,
Denmark, September 9-11, 2017*, pages 2979–2989.

Jieyu Zhao, Tianlu Wang, Mark Yatskar, Vicente Ordonez, and Kai-Wei Chang. 2018. Gender bias in
coreference resolution: Evaluation and debiasing
methods. In *Proceedings of the 2018 Conference of
the North American Chapter of the Association for
Computational Linguistics: Human Language Technologies, Volume 2 (Short Papers)*, pages 15–20. Association for Computational Linguistics.

Automatic Accuracy Prediction for AMR Parsing

Juri Opitz and **Anette Frank**
Research Training Group AIPHES
Leibniz ScienceCampus "Empirical Linguistics and Computational Language Modeling"
Department for Computational Linguistics
69120 Heidelberg
{opitz,frank}@cl.uni-heidelberg.de

Abstract

Abstract Meaning Representation (AMR) represents sentences as directed, acyclic and rooted graphs, aiming at capturing their meaning in a machine readable format. AMR *parsing* converts natural language sentences into such graphs. However, evaluating a parser on new data by means of comparison to manually created AMR graphs is very costly. Also, we would like to be able to detect parses of questionable quality, or preferring results of alternative systems by selecting the ones for which we can assess good quality. We propose AMR *accuracy prediction* as the task of predicting several metrics of correctness for an automatically generated AMR parse – in absence of the corresponding gold parse. We develop a neural end-to-end multi-output regression model and perform three case studies: firstly, we evaluate the model's capacity of predicting AMR parse accuracies and test whether it can reliably assign high scores to gold parses. Secondly, we perform parse selection based on predicted parse accuracies of candidate parses from alternative systems, with the aim of improving overall results. Finally, we predict system ranks for submissions from two AMR shared tasks on the basis of their predicted parse accuracy averages. All experiments are carried out across two different domains and show that our method is effective.

1 Introduction

Abstract Meaning Representation (AMR) (Banarescu et al., 2013) represents the semantic structure of a sentence, including concepts, semantic operators and relations, sense-disambiguated predicates and their arguments. As a machine readable representation of the meaning of a sentence, AMR is potentially useful for many NLP tasks. Among other applications it has been used in machine translation (Jones et al., 2012), text

```
(a / asbestos
  :polarity -
  :time (n / now)
  :location (t / thing
    :ARG1-of (p / produce-01
    :ARG0 (w / we))))
```

Figure 1: Humanly produced AMR for: *There is no asbestos in our products now.* Numbered predicates refer to PropBank senses (Palmer et al., 2005).

summarization (Liu et al., 2015; Dohare and Karnick, 2017) and question answering (Mitra and Baral, 2016). Since the introduction of AMR, many approaches to AMR parsing have been proposed: graph-based pipeline systems which rely on an alignment step (Flanigan et al., 2014, 2016) or transition-based parsers relying on dependency annotation (Wang et al., 2015b,a, 2016a). In the following we will denote the former by **JAMR** and the latter by **CAMR**. More recently, end-to-end neural systems have been proposed which produce linearized AMR graphs within character-based (van Noord and Bos, 2017b) or word-based (Konstas et al., 2017) encoding models. Both approaches greatly profit from large amounts of silver training data. The silver data is obtained with self-training (Konstas et al., 2017) or the aid of additional parsers, where only parses with considerable agreement are chosen to extend the training data (van Noord and Bos, 2017b). Lyu and Titov (2018) formulate a neural model that jointly predicts alignments, concepts and relations. Their system – henceforth called **GPLA** (Graph Prediction with Latent Alignments) – defines the current state-of-the-art in AMR parsing.

A system that can perform accuracy prediction for AMR parsing can be used in a variety of ways: (i) *estimating the quality of downstream tasks* that deploy AMR parses. E.g., in a document summarization scenario, we might expect lower qual-

*Proceedings of the Eighth Joint Conference on Lexical and Computational Semantics (*SEM)*, pages 212–223
Minneapolis, June 6–7, 2019. ©2019 Association for Computational Linguistics

ity of a summary if the estimated quality of AMR parses used as a basis for the summary is low; (ii) AMR parsing accuracy estimation can be used to produce *high-quality automatically parsed data*: by filtering the outputs of single parsing systems in self-training, by selecting high-quality outputs from different parsing systems in a tri-parsing setting, or else by predicting overall rankings over alternative parsing systems applied to in- or out-of-domain data; (iii) finally, AMR parse accuracy prediction could be used in the context of a *parser-supported treebank construction* process. E.g., in an active learning scenario, we can select useful targets for manual annotation based on their expected efficiency for parser improvement – the fine-grained evaluation measures predicted by our system can be used for targeted improvements. In the simplest case, we can provide the human annotator with automatic parses where only few flaws have to be mended. Hence, AMR accuracy prediction systems have the potential to tremendously reduce manual annotation cost and time.

Contributions We define AMR accuracy prediction as the task of predicting a rich suite of metrics to assess various subtasks covered by AMR parsing (e.g. negation detection or semantic role labeling). To approach this task, we use the AMR evaluation suite suggested by Damonte et al. (2017) and develop a hierarchical multi-output regression model for automatically performing evaluation of 12 different tasks involved in AMR parsing (Sections §3 and §4; our code is publicly accessible[1]). We perform experiments in three different scenarios on unseen in-domain and out-of-domain data and show that our model (i) is able to predict scores with significant correlation to gold scores and (ii) can be used to rank *parses* on a *sentence-level* or to rank *parsers* on a *corpus-level* (§5).

2   Related Work

Automatic accuracy prediction for syntactic parsing comes closest to what we are doing. Ravi et al. (2008) propose a feature-based SVM regression model with RBF kernel that predicts syntactic parser performance on different domains. Like us, they aim at a cheap and effective means for estimating a parser's performance. However, in contrast to their work, our method is *domain* and *parser* agnostic: we do not take into account characteristics of the domains of interest and do not provide any performance statistics of the competing parsing systems as features to our regressor. Biici (2016) addresses the task without any domain-dependent features, which results in a lower correlation to gold scores – even if additional features from a background language model are incorporated. In contrast to the prior systems that predict a single score, we predict an ensemble of metrics suitable for assessing AMR parse quality with respect to different linguistic aspects. Also, our system does not rely on externally derived features or complex pre-processing. Moreover, an AMR graph differs in important ways from a syntactic tree. Nodes in AMR do not explicitly correspond to words (as in dependency trees) or phrases (as in constituency trees). AMR structure elements can exist without any alignment to words in the sentence. To our knowledge, we are the first to propose an accuracy prediction model for AMR parsing, and offer the first general end-to-end parse accuracy prediction model that predicts an ensemble of scores for different linguistic aspects.

Automatic accuracy prediction has also been researched for PoS-tagging (Van Asch and Daelemans, 2010) and in machine translation. For example, Soricut and Narsale (2012) predict BLEU scores for machine-produced translations. Under the umbrella of *quality estimation* researchers try to predict, i.a., the post-editing time or missing words in an automatic translation (Cai and Knight, 2013; Joshi et al., 2016; Chatterjee et al., 2018; Kim et al., 2017; Specia et al., 2013). The fact that manually creating an AMR graph is significantly more costly than a translation provides another compelling argument for investigating automatic AMR accuracy prediction techniques .[2]

In recent work, Dickinson and Smith (2011, 2017); Jain et al. (2015); Rehbein and Ruppenhofer (2018) detect annotation errors in automatically produced dependency parses. The latter approach uses active learning and ensemble parsing in combination with variational inference. They predict edge labelling and attachment errors and use a back-and-forth encoding mechanism from non-structured to structured tree data in order to provide the variational inference model with the

---

[2]Creating an AMR graph requires trained linguists and takes on average 8 to 13 minutes, cf. Banarescu et al. (2013)

```
(a / asbestos           (a / asbestos
  :time (n / now)         :polarity -
  :polarity -             :location (p / product)
  :location (p / product  :time (n / now))
    :poss (w / we)))

(a / asbesto            metr.(F1)| GP   JA   CA |
  :polarity -           ---------|---------------|
  :ARG1 (w / we         Smatch   | 70 | 30 | 67 |
    :ARG1-of (p / product  SRL   |  0 | 14 |  0 |
      :mod (n / now))))  Concepts | 67 | 44 | 50 |
                         IgnVars  | 55 |  0 | 60 |
```

Figure 2: Three AMR parses for: *There is no asbestos in our products now*, generated by GPLA (top), JAMR (bottom), CAMR (right). Light and severe errors are found in GPLA and JAMR parses; CAMR fails to provide *we*, the manufacturer of the product. Bottom right: F1 for Smatch and three example subtasks from evaluation against the gold parse (given in Figure 1).

needed unstructured data. Their work differs from ours in three important aspects: firstly, they predict errors in specific edges or nodes, while we predict an accuracy score over the complete graph. Moreover, our model does not *need* several candidate parses as input – when several multiple parses are available, our model can be exploited for ranking (cf. Sections §5.2 & §5.3). Finally, our method is independent of live human feedback.

3 Accuracy Metrics for AMR Parsing

Automatic AMR parses are often deficient. Consider the examples in Figure 2. All parsers correctly detect the negation and its scope. The GPLA parse (top) provides a graph structure close to the gold annotation (Figure 1). However, it does not correctly analyze the possessive *our (product)*, which in the gold parse is represented as an object produced by the speaker (*we*). Instead it recognizes a location in the speaker's possession. JAMR (middle) fails to detect the concept in focus (*asbestos*), possibly due to a false-positive stemming mistake. Moreover, it fails to represent that *asbestos* is (not) in the product: it misses the *:location*-edge from *asbestos* to *product*.

AMR accuracy metrics Usually, a predicted AMR graph G is evaluated against a gold graph G' using triple matching based on a maximally scoring variable mapping. For finding the optimal variable mapping, Integer Linear Programming (ILP) can be used in the Smatch metric (Cai and Knight, 2013), which produces precision, recall and F1 score between G and G'. While it is important to obtain a global measure of parse accuracy, we may also be interested in a quality assessment

that focuses on specific subtasks or meaning aspects, such as entity linking, negation detection or word sense disambiguation (WSD). For example, if a parser commits a WSD error this might be less harmful than e.g., failing to capture negation, or missing or wrongly predicting a semantic role. However, the Smatch calculation would treat many of such errors with equal weight – a property which in some cases may be undesirable.

To alleviate this issue, Damonte et al. (2017) proposed an extended AMR evaluation suite which allows parser performance inspection with regard to 11 additional subtasks captured by AMR. In total, 36 metrics can be computed (precision, recall and F1 for 12 tasks). F1 scores for three example metrics are displayed in Figure 2 (bottom, right): *Smatch*, *SRL* (Smatch computed on arg-i roles), *IgnoreVars* (triple overlap after replacing variables with concepts) and *Concepts* (F1 for concept identification).[3] GPLA produces the overall best parse but it is is outperformed by the other systems in *SRL* (JAMR) and *IgnoreVars* (CAMR).

Task definition We adopt the proposed metrics by Damonte et al. (2017) and use them as target metrics for our task of AMR parse accuracy prediction. Given an automatic AMR graph G and a corresponding sentence S, we estimate precision, recall and F1 of the main task (Smatch) *and* of the subtasks, as they would emerge from comparing G with its gold counterpart G'.

One of our hypotheses is that predicting a wide range of accuracy metric scores for individual aspects of AMR structures will aid our model to better predict the global Smatch scores. We will therefore investigate a hierarchical model that builds on predicted subtask measures in order to predict the global smatch score. Being able to predict fine-grained quality aspects of AMR parses will also be useful to assess and exploit differences of alternative system outputs and provides a basis for guiding system development or targeted annotation in an active learning setting.

4 Neural Accuracy Prediction Model

We propose a neural hierarchical multi-output regression model for accuracy prediction of AMR

---

[3]The other subtasks are: *Unlabelled* (Smatch after edge label removal), *No WSD* (Smatch after PropBank sense removal), *NS frames* (PropBank frame identification without sense), *Wikification* (entity linking), *NER* (named entity recognition), *Reentrancy* (Smatch over re-entrant edges).

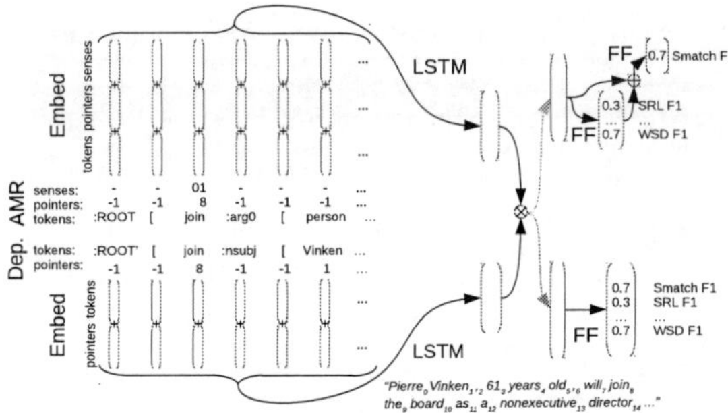

Figure 3: Our model: green: Evaluation metrics computed in a non-hierarchical fashion. orange: Main evaluation metric is computed on top of secondary metrics.

parses. Its architecture is outlined in Figure 3.

Inputs Our model takes the following inputs: (i) a linearized AMR and a linearized dependency graph (implementation details in §5). The motivation for feeding the dependency parse instead of the original sentence is due to the moderate similarity of dependency and AMR structures.[4] We examine drawbacks and benefits of providing automatic dependency parses more closely in our ablation experiments (§5.4). In addition, (ii) we produce alignments between sentence tokens and tokens in the sequential AMR structure, as well as between sentence tokens and the linearized dependency structure, and feed these sequences of pointers to our accuracy prediction model. The intuition of using pointers is to provide the model with richer information via shallow alignment between AMR, dependencies and the sequence of sentence tokens (see Section §5 for implementation details). Finally, (iii) we feed a sequence of PropBank sense indicators for AMR predicates.

Joint encoding of AMR and dependency parses for metric prediction Embedding layers are shared between AMR/dependency pointers and AMR/dependency tokens. We embed the three sequences representing the AMR graph (tokens, pointers and senses) in three matrices and sum them up element-wise (indicated with + in Figure 3). The same procedure is applied to the linearized dependency graph (tokens and pointers). The resulting matrices are processed by two two-layered Bi-LSTMs to yield vectorized representations for (i) the AMR graph and (ii) the dependency tree (i.e., the last states of forward and backward reads are concatenated). Thereafter, we apply element-

---

[4]c.f. Groschwitz et al. (2018); Chen and Palmer (2017).

wise multiplication, subtraction and addition to both vector representations and concatenate the resulting vectors ($\otimes$ in Figure 3). The joint AMR-dependency representation is further processed by a feed forward layer (FF) with sigmoid activation functions in order to predict, in total, 36 different metrics (green, Figure 3).

Hierarchical prediction of multiple metrics The task naturally lends itself to be formulated in a hierarchical multi-task setup (orange, Figure 3). In this strand, we first compute the 33 fine-grained subtask metrics and on their basis we caclulate the Smatch scores (precision, recall, F1) as our primary metrics. In order to accomplish this, we collect the outputs from the subtask metric prediction layer in a vector and concatenate it with the previous layer's representation ($\oplus$ in Figure 3). The resulting vector is fed through a last FF layer to predict the metrics for the task of main interest (Smatch). Our intuition is that the estimated quality of the parse with respect to the subtask metrics informs the model and allows it to better predict the overall quality.

Loss In the non-hierarchical case, we denote our full model with $f_\theta : X \rightarrow [0,1]^d$ with parameters θ, where d describes the dimensionality of the score vector (one dimension represents one metric) and $D = \{(X_i, y_i)\}_{i=1}^N, y_i \in [0,1]^d$ is our training data. In the non-hierarchical model, we minimize the mean squared error:

$$\ell(f_\theta) = \frac{1}{dN} \sum_{i=1}^{N} \sum_{j=1}^{d} (y_{i,j} - f_\theta(X_i)_j)^2 \quad (1)$$

For our hierarchical model, we have two functions, $f_\theta : X \rightarrow [0,1]^{(d-k)}$ which returns the output vector for the $(d-k)$ subtask metrics and $f'_{\theta'} : X \rightarrow [0,1]^k$ which returns the output vector for our k main metrics (in our experiments, $k = 3$ for Smatch recall, precision and F1). Then,

$$\ell'(f_\theta, f'_{\theta'}) = \frac{\lambda_1}{(d-k)N} \sum_{i=1}^{N} \sum_{j=1}^{d-k} (y_{i,j} - f_\theta(X_i)_j)^2$$

$$+ \frac{\lambda_2}{kN} \sum_{i=1}^{N} \sum_{j=d-k+1}^{d} (y_{i,j} - f'_{\theta'}(X_i)_{j-(d-k)})^2$$

defines the total loss over the two entangled metric prediction models. Note that $\theta \subset \theta'$, which means that by optimizing the parameters of f' with gradient descent, we also concurrently optimize all

parser	training		development	
	Smatch (F1)	% def.	Smatch (F1)	% def.
JAMR	0.79	86.7	0.69	91.8
CAMR	0.75	93.6	0.66	95.7
GPLA	0.86	83.4	0.76	90.0

Table 1: Parser output evaluation on training and development partitions of LDC2015E86. Smatch F1: avg. over Smatch F1 per sentence, % def.: percentage of deficient parses (i.e., parses with Smatch F1 < 1).

data set	LDC2015E86	LDC2015R36	BioAMRTest
domain	news	news	medical
nb. sentences	19,572	1,053	500
avg. sent. len.	21	22.35	36.52
nb. auto. parses	58,716	13,689	3,000
used as	train/dev/test	test	test

Table 2: Statistics of data sets used in this work.

parameters of f. By this construction, the hierarchical model instantiates a two-task model with shared parameters. For our experiments, we manually set the loss weights $\lambda_1 = 0.2$, $\lambda_2 = 1$.

5 Experiments

Data Since our goal is to predict the accuracy of an automatic parse, we need a data set containing automatically produced AMR parses and their scores, as they would emerge from comparison to gold parses. Our largest data set, LDC2015E86, comprises 19,572 sentences and comes in a predefined training, development and test split. We parse this data set with three parsers, JAMR (Flanigan et al., 2014, 2016), CAMR (Wang et al., 2015b,a, 2016a) and GPLA (Lyu and Titov, 2018). Since the three parsers have been trained on the training data partition, we naturally obtain more accurate parses for the training partition than for development and test data. Table 1, however, indicates that we still obtain a considerable amount of deficient parses for training. Based on the parser outputs we compute evaluations comparing the automatic parses with the gold parses by using *amr-evaluation-tool-enhanced*[5], a bug-fixed version of the script that computes the metrics of Damonte et al. (2017). This allows us to create full-fledged training, development and test instances for our accuracy prediction task. Each instance consists of a sentence and an AMR parse as input and a vector of metric scores as target.

Our second data set, LDC2015R36, comprises submissions to the SemEval-2016 Task 8 (May, 2016). We have 1053 parses from each of the 11 team submissions (and 2 baseline systems).[6] Our

third dataset, BioAMRTest is used as the test set in the SemEval-2017 Task 9 (May and Priyadarshi, 2017) and consists of 500 parses from each of the 6 teams.[7] The shared task organizers kindly made this data available for our experiments.

Preprocessing For dependency annotation, we parse all sentences with spacyV2.0[8]. For sequentializing the AMR and dependency graph representations we take intuitions from van Noord and Bos (2017b) & Konstas et al. (2017) and output tokens by performing a depth-first-search over the graph. We replace the AMR negation token '-' and strings representing numbers with special tokens. The vocabularies (tokens, senses and pointers) are computed from our training partition of LDC2015E86 and comprise all tokens with a frequency ≥ 5 (tokens with lesser frequency are replaced by an *OOV*-token). PropBank senses of predicates are removed and collected in an extra list that is parallel to the tokens in the linearized AMR sequence. For each linearized AMR and dependency tree we generate a sequence with index pointers to tokens in the original sentence (-1 for tokens which do not explicitly refer to any token in the sentence, e.g. brackets, 'subj' or 'arg0' relations). Extraction of token-pointers from the dependency graph is trivial. For every concept in the linearized AMR we execute a search for the corresponding token in the sentence, looking for exact matches with surface tokens and lemmas.

Training For the optimization of the accuracy prediction model we use only the development and training sections of LDC2015E86 and the corresponding automatic parses together with the gold scores. Details on the training cycle can be found in the *Supplemental Material* §A (the loss is de-

---

[5]https://github.com/ChunchuanLv/amr-evaluation-tool-enhanced

[6]Riga (Barzdins and Gosko, 2016), CMU (equal to JAMR) (Flanigan et al., 2016), Brandeis (Wang et al., 2016b), UofR (Peng and Gildea, 2016), ICL-HD (Brandt et al., 2016), M2L (Puzikov et al., 2016), UMD (Rao et al., 2016), DynamicPower (Butler, 2016), TMF (Bjerva et al., 2016), UCL+Sheffield (Goodman et al., 2016) and CU-NLP (Foland and Martin, 2016).

[7]TMF-1 and TMF-2 (van Noord and Bos, 2017a), DAN-GNT (Nguyen and Nguyen, 2017), Oxford (Buys and Blunsom, 2017), RIGOTRIO (Gruzitis et al., 2017) and JAMR (Flanigan et al., 2016)

[8]https://spacy.io/

	ρ LDC2015E86			ρ BioAMRTest		
	P	R	F1	P	R	F1
Smatch	0.74	0.79	0.78	0.54	0.41	0.47
Concepts	0.56	0.65	0.64	0.67	0.55	0.62
Frames	0.7	0.71	0.72	0.67	0.56	0.63
IgnoreVars	0.76	0.8	0.79	0.33	0.27	0.29
Named Ent.	0.81	0.81	0.81	0.5	0.48	0.5
Negations	0.87	0.87	0.87	0.33	0.32	0.32
No WSD	0.75	0.78	0.78	0.54	0.41	0.46
NS frames	0.76	0.75	0.77	0.72	0.59	0.67
Reentrancies	0.77	0.79	0.8	0.52	0.45	0.48
SRL	0.72	0.74	0.75	0.47	0.43	0.45
Unlabeled	0.71	0.75	0.75	0.6	0.45	0.51
Wikification	0.87	0.85	0.86	0.24	0.23	0.23

Table 3: Pearson correlation coefficient (ρ) over various metrics and across domains. Explanations of the metrics and AMR subtasks are in Section §3 and fn. 3

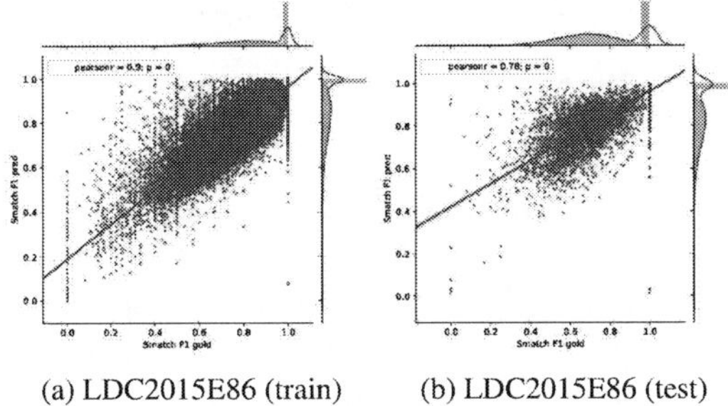

(a) LDC2015E86 (train)   (b) LDC2015E86 (test)

Figure 4: Predicted (y-axis) & gold (x-axis) Smatch F1.

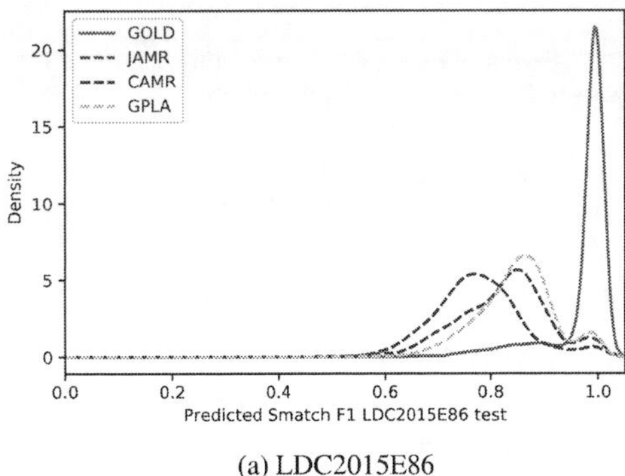

(a) LDC2015E86

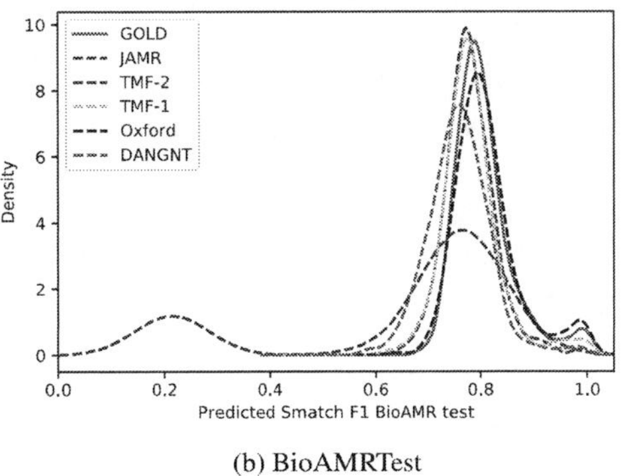

(b) BioAMRTest

Figure 5: Probability density function estimations for predicted F1 Smatch scores using Scott's method (Scott, 2012) with respect to candidate parses from different systems.

scribed in §4). We use the same single (hierarchical) model for all three evaluation studies, proving its applicability across different scenarios (a non-hierarchical model is only instantiated for the ablation experiments in Section §5.4).

5.1 Correlation with Gold Accuracy

The primary goal in our first experiment is to test whether the system is able to differentiate good from bad parses. This capacity is expressed by a high correlation of predicted accuracies with true accuracies on unseen data and by the ability to assign high scores to gold parses. We evaluate on the test partition of LDC2015E86 and BioAMRTest.

Correlation results The results are displayed in Table 3. Over all metrics, in-domain and out-of-domain, we achieve significant correlations with the gold scores ($p < 0.005$ for every metric). While on LDC2015E86 the model has learned to predict the KB linking F1 ($\rho = 0.86$) and negation detection F1 with high correlation to the gold

scores ($\rho = 0.87$), Concept assessment poses the greatest challenge ($\rho = 0.64$). For the out-of-domain data BioAMRTest, these two facts seem almost reversed: here, the assessment of KB linking poses difficulties ($\rho = 0.23$) while the Concept F1 predictions are better ($\rho = 0.62$). The main metrics of interest (Smatch precision, recall and F1) can be predicted with high correlation on in-domain data ($\rho \geq 0.74$, cf. also Figure 4) and solid correlation for out-of-domain data ($\rho \geq 0.41$).

Find the Gold AMR! Now, we want to test our system's capacity to reliably predict high Smatch F1 scores for unseen gold AMR parses. Ideally, the scores should be close or equal to 1. For in-domain data, it appears to work well: a large amount of Smatch predictions for gold AMR graphs are very close to one (Figure 5a).

Evidently, our system also gets the ranking of the parsing systems right: the distribution of the state-of-the-art (GPLA) is shifted right towards

	percentile						
dataset	5	25	75	90	95	97	99
LDC15E86	0.83	0.99	1.0	1.0	1.0	1.0	1.0
BioAMRTest	0.74	0.77	0.83	0.88	0.93	0.98	1.0

Table 4: Various percentiles of Smatch F1 predictions for gold graphs.

higher predicted F1 scores, whereas the distribution of CAMR is shifted left towards lower scores. Also, more than 75% of gold parses have a predicted Smatch score of more than 0.99 (Table 4).

On the other hand, finding gold parses in the BioAMRtest data is much harder: about 75% of Smatch scores get assigned a score of 0.83 or lower and only 1% of gold parses are predicted as perfect (Table 4). The estimated probability density function for gold parses (red solid line in Figure 5b) struggles to discriminate itself from the functions corresponding to the flawed parses of the automatic systems. Nevertheless, the prediction score density for gold parses is situated more on the right hand side than most others. In other words, we find that in the out-of-domain data gold parses tend to be assigned above-average scores.

To sum up, our observations for the out-of-domain data stand in some contrast to what we observe for the in-domain data. However, this outcome can be plausibly explained: assuming that the out-of-domain gold parses have some unfamiliar properties, a system that has never seen such parses cannot judge well whether they are gold or not. In fact, it can be interpreted positively that the system hesitates to assign maximum scores to gold parses from a domain in which the model is completely inexperienced. Additionally, bio-medial texts involve difficult concepts, naming conventions and complicated noun phrases which are hard to understand even for non-expert humans (e.g., *TAK733 led to a decrease in pERK and G1 arrest in most of these melanoma cell lines regardless of their origin, driver oncogenic mutations and in vitro sensitivity to TAK733".*). Taking all this into account, the results for out-of-domain data may be not as bad as they perhaps appear at first glance.

5.2 Application Study: AMR Parse Ranking

Our automatic accuracy prediction method naturally lends itself for ranking parser outputs. For any sentence, provided automatic parses by competing systems can be ranked according to the

	Smatch LDC2015E86			Smatch BioAMRTest		
	P	R	F1	P	R	F1
lower-bound	64.9	57.9	60.5	41.7	31.3	34.3
random	72.4	67.0	69.1	60.3	50.3	54.0
ours	**76.6**	**73.5**	**74.8**	64.9	56.0	59.2
upper-bound	79.3	75.2	76.9	73.2	65.2	68.5
JAMR	71.4	66.5	68.4	48.4	39.7	42.9
CAMR	69.5	60.4	64.0	-	-	-
GPLA	76.3	73.4	74.6	-	-	-
TMF-1	-	-	-	56.0	46.5	49.3
TMF-2	-	-	-	70.0	54.5	60.5
DANGNT	-	-	-	**70.2**	58.6	**63.1**
Oxford	-	-	-	65.8	**59.0**	61.6
RIGOTRIO	-	-	-	65.0	50.8	56.4

Table 5: Results (sentence averages) of different AMR parsing (bottom part) and ranking (top part) systems on two test sets. Upper part: results when selecting from alternative parses: lower-bound (upper-bound): oracle selecting the worst (best) AMR parse; ours: results when selecting the best parse according to our models' accuracy prediction (hierarchical model).

scores predicted by our system. This scenario arises, e.g., when we run several AMR parsers over a large corpus with the aim of selecting the best parse for each sentence in order to collect silver training data.[9] In the worst case, we do not have any prior knowledge about a parser's performance (we may not even know the source of a parse). We use the test partition from LDC2015E86 and BioAMRTest to rank, for each sentence, the automatic candidate parses provided by the different parsers. In LDC2015E86 we assume not to be agnostic about the parsers as their performances on the development data of this data set are known (in terms of their sentence-average F1 Smatch score). Consider that we are given a sentence and three automatic parses. We select the maximum-score parse, where the score is defined by predicted Smatch F1 plus the average Smatch F1 of the parse-producing parser on the development data. As baselines in this scenario we (i) randomly choose a parse from the three options or (ii) always choose the parse of GPLA. On BioAMRTest, however, we have no prior information about the submitted systems. We select from 6 automatic parses for each sentence. Since now we are completely parser agnostic, the baseline is to randomly select a parse from the candidate set.

Results The results are displayed in Table 5. For our in-domain test data, LDC2015E86, selecting

<hr>

[9]In a self-training scenario, we also could set a threshold of minimum predicted accuracy to select confident parses.

	Smatch LDC2015E86		Smatch BioAMRTest	
	$\bar{\rho}$	%pos	$\bar{\rho}$	%pos
lower-bound	-1	0.0	-1	0.0
random	0.00	50.0	0.00	50.0
ours	**0.54**	**77.0**	**0.22**	**70.4**
upper-bound	1.00	100.0	1.00	100.0

Table 6: Results of different parse-ranking systems with respect to sentence-level parse rankings. $\bar{\rho}$: average Pearson-r on a sentence level. %pos: ratio of predicted rankings with positive ρ to gold ranking.

the best parse according to our model's predicted accuracy score improves over *all* individual parser results: the obtained average Smatch F1 per sentence increases (i) slightly by 0.2 pp. compared to always choosing outputs from GPLA and (ii) observably by 5.7 pp. compared to randomly selecting a parse from the competing system outputs. The difference compared to always choosing GPLA seems negligible which perhaps can be explained by the fact that GPLA has been shown to be on par or better than doubly-blind human annotators.[10] The oracle that always selects the best parse (*upper-bound* in Table 5) shows little room for improvement: it achieves 2.1 pp. Smatch F1 increase compared to our model. This margin is small and further success might also be hampered by peculiarities in the manual annotations. On BioAMRTest, no prior information about the systems is available. Using our model's predicted scores to select from the alternative system outputs, we can boost Smatch F1 by 5.2 pp. compared to randomly selecting a parse. Compared to always selecting the parses of the best submitted system (in-hindsight), we lag behind by 3.9 pp.

Since our data comprises outputs from several parsers with varying performance, we can study the performance of our approach in combination with different parsers (Figure 6). When only choosing among CAMR and JAMR outputs, on LDC2015E86, our system boosts the F1 by 2.7 pp. compared to randomly selecting a parse, and by 0.6 pp. compared to always choosing the parse from the better system (determined on dev, here: JAMR). Choosing from CAMR and GPLA or JAMR and GPLA makes little difference: in most cases our system selects the GPLA parse and the difference to only choosing GPLA parses is

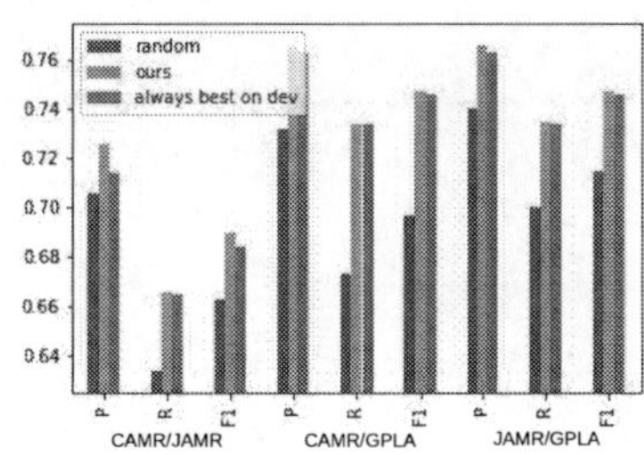

Figure 6: Using our model to predict the best parse out of two candidate parses, each from a different system.

marginal. Moreover, across both test sets, the majority of rankings assigned by our method have positive correlations with the true rankings (Table 6): 77% of all assigned rankings have a positive correlation with the true ranking (70% for biomedical). In sum, we can draw two conclusions from this experiment: given a sentence, ranking AMR parser outputs using our accuracy prediction model, on in-domain and out-of-domain unseen data (i) clearly improves performance when non state-of-the-art parsers are applied or if we are not informed about the parsers' performances and (ii) does not worsen results in other cases.

5.3 Application Study: Predict System Ranks

In our final case study, we use our accuracy prediction model to predict a ranking over systems. We use our model to rank the unseen submitted system parses of the SemEval-2017 Task 9 (evaluated on BioAMRTest) and SemEval-2016 Task 8 (evaluated on LDC2015R36) according to average predicted F1 Smatch scores. Again, we assume a parser-agnostic setting, meaning we have no prior knowledge of the submitted systems (i.e. we just consider their outputs). In this setting, we do not rank individual parses given a sentence, but rank the system outputs, according to estimated average Smatch F1 per sentence. We evaluate against the final team rankings of the two shared tasks.

Results The results are displayed in Table 7. On BioAMRTest we have a good, albeit non statistically significant correlation with the true team ranking. On the in-domain LDC2015R36 test set we see a significant correlation of $\rho = 0.645$ ($p_{1,2} < 0.05$). In this shared task, many teams were competitive and differences between the best teams were marginal. For example, in the true ranking, places 1 to 6 achieved between 0.60 and 0.62 Smatch F1. Notably, the first four teams ac-

---

[10]GPLA (Lyu and Titov, 2018) achieves a high 74.4% corpus-level Smatch F1 (primarily news texts), while a prior annotation study (Banarescu et al., 2013) reported doubly blind annotation corpus-level F1 of 0.71 (for web texts).

	Rank LDC2015R36		Rank BioAMRTest	
	rank r	rank $\hat{r}$	rank r	rank $\hat{r}$
DANGNT	-	-	1	3
Oxford	-	-	2	1
TMF-2	-	-	3	2
RIGOTRIO	-	-	4	5
TMF-1	-	-	5	4
JAMR	7	7	6	6
RIGA	1	4	-	-
Brandeis	2	3	-	-
CU-NLP	3	1	-	-
UCL+Sheffield	4	2	-	-
ICL-HD	5	8	-	-
M2L	6	10	-	-
JAMR-base	8	12	-	-
UofR	9	11	-	-
TMF	10	5	-	-
UMD	11	6	-	-
DynamicPower	12	13	-	-
det. baseline	13	9	-	-
ρ	0.645 ($p_1 = 0.017, p_2 = 0.011$)		0.771 ($p_1 = 0.072, p_2 = 0.051$)	

Table 7: True rank r (given corpus-Smatch) and predicted rank $\hat{r}$ (based on sentence average Smatch computed using our model). p_1: probability of non-correlation. p_2: probability that a randomly produced ranking achieves equal or greater ρ (estimated over 10^6 random rankings). For team names, see fn. 6 & 7.

cording to the true ranking and the first four teams according to our predicted ranking fall into the same group. This shows that our model successfully assigned high ranks to low error submissions.

5.4 Ablation Experiments

We finally perform ablation experiments to evaluate the impact of individual model components. We experiment with five different setups. (i) instead of stacking two Bi-LSTMs, we use only one Bi-LSTM (*one-lstm*, Table 8). (ii) instead of the dependency tree, we feed the words in the order as they occur in the sentence (*no-dep*). (iii) *no-pointers*: we remove the token-pointers from our model. (iv), instead of using the hierarchical setup, we predict all metrics on the same level (green in Figure 3, *no-HL* in Table 8) and (v), *no-HMTL*: we optimize the non-hierarchical model only with respect to Smatch, disregarding the AMR subtasks. Remarkably, the dependency tree greatly helps the model on in-domain data over all measures (-37 total Δ without dependencies) but hurts the model on out-of-domain data (+27 total Δ). A possible explanation is the degradation of the dependency parse quality: bio-medical data not only poses a challenge for our model, but also for the dependency parser. With special regard to the main AMR evaluation measure, Smatch F1, the learned pointer embeddings provide useful input on the in-domain test data (-4 Δ without pointers).

	LDC2015R36						BioAMRTest					
	complete	*one lstm*	*no-dep*	*no-pointers*	*no-HL*	*no-HMTL*	*complete*	*one lstm*	*no-dep*	*no-pointers*	*no-HL*	*no-HMTL*
	ρ			Δ			ρ			Δ		
Smatch	78	-1	-1	-4	-3	-2	47	0	+5	+4	+2	-3
Concepts	64	-1	-4	-3	-4	-	62	0	+3	+2	0	-
Frames	72	0	-5	0	-1	-	63	0	+1	+1	-1	-
IgnoreVars	79	-1	-1	-1	-2	-	29	+5	+6	+5	+4	-
Named Ent.	81	+2	-3	+2	+3	-	50	-18	-9	-7	-9	-
Negations	87	-1	-1	+1	0	-	32	-16	+2	-1	-4	-
No WSD	78	-1	0	-1	-2	-	46	+2	+6	+5	+3	-
NS frames	77	0	-7	0	0	-	67	+1	+1	0	-1	-
Reentrancies	80	0	-9	+1	+2	-	48	0	+2	0	+1	-
SRL	75	-1	-4	0	+1	-	45	-4	+3	0	+2	-
Unlabeled	75	-1	0	-1	-1	-	51	0	+1	+4	+2	-
Wikification	86	0	-2	+1	+2	-	23	+5	+6	+6	+7	-
$\sum_i \Delta_i$	**0**	-5	<u>-37</u>	-5	-5	-2	0	<u>-25</u>	**+27**	+19	+6	-3

Table 8: ρ correlation (F1) differences over different setups (columns), test sets (out-of-domain, in-domain) and subtasks (rows). $\pm x$: plus and minus x pp.ρ.

6 Conclusion

AMR parser evaluation with human gold annotation is very costly. Our main contributions in this work are two-fold: Firstly, we introduced the concept of automatic AMR accuracy prediction. Given only an automatic parse and the sentence, from whence it was derived, the goal is to predict evaluation metrics cheaply and possibly at runtime. Secondly, we framed the task as a multiple-output regression task and developed a hierarchical neural model to predict a rich suite of AMR evaluation metrics. We presented three case studies proving (i) the feasibility of automatic AMR accuracy prediction in general (significant correlation with gold scores on unseen in-domain and out-of-domain data) and (ii) the applicability of our model in two use cases. In the first study, we ranked different automatic candidate parses per sentence, outperforming the random selection baseline by 5.7 pp. average Smatch F1 (in-domain) and 5.2 pp. (out-of-domain). In the second study, we ranked team submissions to two AMR shared tasks and our method was able to reproduce rankings similar to the true rankings.

Acknowledgments

This work has been supported by the German Research Foundation (grant no. GRK 1994/1) and the Leibniz Association (grant no. SAS-2015-IDS-LWC) and the Ministry of Science, Research, and Art of Baden-Württemberg. We are grateful to the NVIDIA corporation for donating the GPU used in this research.

References

Laura Banarescu, Claire Bonial, Shu Cai, Madalina Georgescu, Kira Griffitt, Ulf Hermjakob, Kevin Knight, Philipp Koehn, Martha Palmer, and Nathan Schneider. 2013. Abstract meaning representation for sembanking.

Guntis Barzdins and Didzis Gosko. 2016. Riga at semeval-2016 task 8: Impact of smatch extensions and character-level neural translation on amr parsing accuracy. In *Proceedings of the 10th International Workshop on Semantic Evaluation (SemEval-2016)*, pages 1143–1147. Association for Computational Linguistics.

Ergun Biici. 2016. Predicting the performance of parsing with referential translation machines. *The Prague Bulletin of Mathematical Linguistics*, 106(1):31 – 44.

Johannes Bjerva, Johan Bos, and Hessel Haagsma. 2016. The meaning factory at semeval-2016 task 8: Producing amrs with boxer. In *Proceedings of the 10th International Workshop on Semantic Evaluation (SemEval-2016)*, pages 1179–1184. Association for Computational Linguistics.

Lauritz Brandt, David Grimm, Mengfei Zhou, and Yannick Versley. 2016. Icl-hd at semeval-2016 task 8: Meaning representation parsing - augmenting amr parsing with a preposition semantic role labeling neural network. In *Proceedings of the 10th International Workshop on Semantic Evaluation (SemEval-2016)*, pages 1160–1166. Association for Computational Linguistics.

Alastair Butler. 2016. Dynamicpower at semeval-2016 task 8: Processing syntactic parse trees with a dynamic semantics core. In *Proceedings of the 10th International Workshop on Semantic Evaluation (SemEval-2016)*, pages 1148–1153. Association for Computational Linguistics.

Jan Buys and Phil Blunsom. 2017. Oxford at semeval-2017 task 9: Neural amr parsing with pointer-augmented attention. In *Proceedings of the 11th International Workshop on Semantic Evaluation (SemEval-2017)*, pages 914–919. Association for Computational Linguistics.

Shu Cai and Kevin Knight. 2013. Smatch: an evaluation metric for semantic feature structures. In *ACL (2)*, pages 748–752. The Association for Computer Linguistics.

Rajen Chatterjee, Matteo Negri, Marco Turchi, Frédéric Blain, and Lucia Specia. 2018. Combining quality estimation and automatic post-editing to enhance machine translation output. In *AMTA (1)*, pages 26–38. Association for Machine Translation in the Americas.

Wei-Te Chen and Martha Palmer. 2017. Unsupervised amr-dependency parse alignment. In *Proceedings of the 15th Conference of the European Chapter of the Association for Computational Linguistics: Volume 1, Long Papers*, pages 558–567. Association for Computational Linguistics.

Marco Damonte, Shay B. Cohen, and Giorgio Satta. 2017. An incremental parser for abstract meaning representation. In *Proceedings of the 15th Conference of the European Chapter of the Association for Computational Linguistics: Volume 1, Long Papers*, pages 536–546. Association for Computational Linguistics.

Markus Dickinson and Amber Smith. 2011. Detecting dependency parse errors with minimal resources. In *Proceedings of the 12th International Conference on Parsing Technologies*, pages 241–252. Association for Computational Linguistics.

Markus Dickinson and Amber Smith. 2017. Simulating dependencies to improve parse error detection. In *Proceedings of the 15th International Workshop on Treebanks and Linguistic Theories (TLT15), Bloomington, IN, USA, January 20-21, 2017.*, volume 1779 of *CEUR Workshop Proceedings*, pages 76–88. CEUR-WS.org.

Shibhansh Dohare and Harish Karnick. 2017. Text summarization using abstract meaning representation. *CoRR*, abs/1706.01678.

Jeffrey Flanigan, Chris Dyer, Noah A. Smith, and Jaime G. Carbonell. 2016. CMU at semeval-2016 task 8: Graph-based AMR parsing with infinite ramp loss. In *SemEval@NAACL-HLT*, pages 1202–1206. The Association for Computer Linguistics.

Jeffrey Flanigan, Sam Thomson, Jaime Carbonell, Chris Dyer, and Noah A. Smith. 2014. A discriminative graph-based parser for the abstract meaning representation. In *Proceedings of the 52nd Annual Meeting of the Association for Computational Linguistics (Volume 1: Long Papers)*, pages 1426–1436. Association for Computational Linguistics.

William Foland and James H. Martin. 2016. Cu-nlp at semeval-2016 task 8: Amr parsing using lstm-based recurrent neural networks. In *Proceedings of the 10th International Workshop on Semantic Evaluation (SemEval-2016)*, pages 1197–1201. Association for Computational Linguistics.

Xavier Glorot and Yoshua Bengio. 2010. Understanding the difficulty of training deep feedforward neural networks. In *AISTATS*, volume 9 of *JMLR Proceedings*, pages 249–256. JMLR.org.

James Goodman, Andreas Vlachos, and Jason Naradowsky. 2016. Ucl+sheffield at semeval-2016 task 8: Imitation learning for amr parsing with an alpha-bound. In *Proceedings of the 10th International Workshop on Semantic Evaluation (SemEval-2016)*, pages 1167–1172. Association for Computational Linguistics.

Jonas Groschwitz, Matthias Lindemann, Meaghan Fowlie, Mark Johnson, and Alexander Koller. 2018. AMR dependency parsing with a typed semantic algebra. *CoRR*, abs/1805.11465.

Normunds Gruzitis, Didzis Gosko, and Guntis Barzdins. 2017. Rigotrio at semeval-2017 task 9: Combining machine learning and grammar engineering for amr parsing and generation. In *Proceedings of the 11th International Workshop on Semantic Evaluation (SemEval-2017)*, pages 924–928. Association for Computational Linguistics.

Sambhav Jain, Naman Jain, Bhasha Agrawal, and Rajeev Sangal. 2015. Employing oracle confusion for parse quality estimation. In *Computational Linguistics and Intelligent Text Processing*, pages 213–226, Cham. Springer International Publishing.

Bevan K. Jones, Jacob Andreas, Daniel Bauer, Karl Moritz Hermann, and Kevin Knight. 2012. Semantics-based machine translation with hyperedge replacement grammars. In *COLING*, pages 1359–1376. Indian Institute of Technology Bombay.

Nisheeth Joshi, Iti Mathur, Hemant Darbari, and Ajai Kumar. 2016. Quality estimation of english-hindi machine translation systems. In *Proceedings of the Second International Conference on Information and Communication Technology for Competitive Strategies*, ICTCS '16, pages 53:1–53:5, New York, NY, USA. ACM.

Hyun Kim, Hun-Young Jung, Hongseok Kwon, Jong-Hyeok Lee, and Seung-Hoon Na. 2017. Predictor-estimator: Neural quality estimation based on target word prediction for machine translation. *ACM Trans. Asian Low-Resour. Lang. Inf. Process.*, 17(1):3:1–3:22.

Diederik P. Kingma and Jimmy Ba. 2014. Adam: A method for stochastic optimization. *CoRR*, abs/1412.6980.

Ioannis Konstas, Srinivasan Iyer, Mark Yatskar, Yejin Choi, and Luke Zettlemoyer. 2017. Neural amr: Sequence-to-sequence models for parsing and generation. In *Proceedings of the 55th Annual Meeting of the Association for Computational Linguistics (Volume 1: Long Papers)*, pages 146–157. Association for Computational Linguistics.

Fei Liu, Jeffrey Flanigan, Sam Thomson, Norman Sadeh, and Noah A. Smith. 2015. Toward abstractive summarization using semantic representations. In *Proceedings of the 2015 Conference of the North American Chapter of the Association for Computational Linguistics: Human Language Technologies*, pages 1077–1086. Association for Computational Linguistics.

Chunchuan Lyu and Ivan Titov. 2018. Amr parsing as graph prediction with latent alignment. In *Proceedings of the 56th Annual Meeting of the Association for Computational Linguistics (Volume 1: Long Papers)*, pages 397–407. Association for Computational Linguistics.

Jonathan May. 2016. Semeval-2016 task 8: Meaning representation parsing. In *Proceedings of the 10th International Workshop on Semantic Evaluation (SemEval-2016)*, pages 1063–1073, San Diego, California. Association for Computational Linguistics.

Jonathan May and Jay Priyadarshi. 2017. Semeval-2017 task 9: Abstract meaning representation parsing and generation. In *Proceedings of the 11th International Workshop on Semantic Evaluation (SemEval-2017)*, page 536–545, Vancouver, Canada. Association for Computational Linguistics, Association for Computational Linguistics.

Arindam Mitra and Chitta Baral. 2016. Addressing a question answering challenge by combining statistical methods with inductive rule learning and reasoning. In *Proceedings of the Thirtieth AAAI Conference on Artificial Intelligence, February 12-17, 2016, Phoenix, Arizona, USA.*, pages 2779–2785. AAAI Press.

Khoa Nguyen and Dang Nguyen. 2017. UIT-DANGNT-CLNLP at semeval-2017 task 9: Building scientific concept fixing patterns for improving CAMR. In *Proceedings of the 11th International Workshop on Semantic Evaluation, SemEval@ACL 2017, Vancouver, Canada, August 3-4, 2017*, pages 909–913. Association for Computational Linguistics.

Rik van Noord and Johan Bos. 2017a. The meaning factory at semeval-2017 task 9: Producing amrs with neural semantic parsing. In *Proceedings of the 11th International Workshop on Semantic Evaluation (SemEval-2017)*, pages 929–933. Association for Computational Linguistics.

Rik van Noord and Johan Bos. 2017b. Neural semantic parsing by character-based translation: Experiments with abstract meaning representations. *Computational Linguistics in the Netherlands Journal*, 7:93–108.

Martha Palmer, Daniel Gildea, and Paul Kingsbury. 2005. The proposition bank: An annotated corpus of semantic roles. *Comput. Linguist.*, 31(1):71–106.

Xiaochang Peng and Daniel Gildea. 2016. Uofr at semeval-2016 task 8: Learning synchronous hyperedge replacement grammar for amr parsing. In *Proceedings of the 10th International Workshop on Semantic Evaluation (SemEval-2016)*, pages 1185–1189.

Yevgeniy Puzikov, Daisuke Kawahara, and Sadao Kurohashi. 2016. M2L at semeval-2016 task 8: AMR parsing with neural networks. In *Proceedings of the 10th International Workshop on Semantic Evaluation, SemEval@NAACL-HLT 2016, San Diego, CA, USA, June 16-17, 2016*, pages 1154–1159. The Association for Computer Linguistics.

Sudha Rao, Yogarshi Vyas, Hal Daumé III, and Philip Resnik. 2016. Clip$@$umd at semeval-2016 task 8: Parser for abstract meaning representation using learning to search. In *Proceedings of the 10th International Workshop on Semantic Evaluation (SemEval-2016)*, pages 1190–1196. Association for Computational Linguistics.

Sujith Ravi, Kevin Knight, and Radu Soricut. 2008. Automatic prediction of parser accuracy. In *Proceedings of the Conference on Empirical Methods in Natural Language Processing*, pages 887–896. Association for Computational Linguistics.

Ines Rehbein and Josef Ruppenhofer. 2018. Sprucing up the trees – error detection in treebanks. In *Proceedings of the 27th International Conference on Computational Linguistics*, pages 107–118. Association for Computational Linguistics.

David W Scott. 2012. Multivariate density estimation and visualization. In *Handbook of computational statistics*, pages 549–569. Springer.

Radu Soricut and Sushant Narsale. 2012. Combining quality prediction and system selection for improved automatic translation output. In *Proceedings of the Seventh Workshop on Statistical Machine Translation*, pages 163–170. Association for Computational Linguistics.

Lucia Specia, Kashif Shah, Jose G. C. De Souza, Trevor Cohn, and Fondazione Bruno Kessler. 2013. Quest - a translation quality estimation framework. In *In Proceedings of the 51th Conference of the Association for Computational Linguistics (ACL), Demo Session*.

Vincent Van Asch and Walter Daelemans. 2010. Using domain similarity for performance estimation. In *Proceedings of the 2010 Workshop on Domain Adaptation for Natural Language Processing*, DANLP 2010, pages 31–36, Stroudsburg, PA, USA. Association for Computational Linguistics.

Chuan Wang, Sameer Pradhan, Xiaoman Pan, Heng Ji, and Nianwen Xue. 2016a. Camr at semeval-2016 task 8: An extended transition-based amr parser. In *Proceedings of the 10th International Workshop on Semantic Evaluation (SemEval-2016)*, pages 1173–1178, San Diego, California. Association for Computational Linguistics.

Chuan Wang, Sameer Pradhan, Xiaoman Pan, Heng Ji, and Nianwen Xue. 2016b. Camr at semeval-2016 task 8: An extended transition-based amr parser. In *Proceedings of the 10th International Workshop on Semantic Evaluation (SemEval-2016)*, pages 1173–1178.

Chuan Wang, Nianwen Xue, and Sameer Pradhan. 2015a. Boosting transition-based amr parsing with refined actions and auxiliary analyzers. In *Proceedings of the 53rd Annual Meeting of the Association for Computational Linguistics and the 7th International Joint Conference on Natural Language Processing (Volume 2: Short Papers)*, pages 857–862, Beijing, China. Association for Computational Linguistics.

Chuan Wang, Nianwen Xue, and Sameer Pradhan. 2015b. A transition-based algorithm for amr parsing. In *Proceedings of the 2015 Conference of the North American Chapter of the Association for Computational Linguistics: Human Language Technologies*, pages 366–375, Denver, Colorado. Association for Computational Linguistics.

A Supplemental Material

Hyper parameters and weights initialization
We initialize all parameters of the model randomly. Embedding vectors of dimension 128 are drawn from $U(0.05, 0.05)$ and the LSTM weights (neurons: 128) and weights of the feed forward output layers are sampled from a Glorot uniform distribution (Glorot and Bengio, 2010). For future work, initializing the embedding layer with pre-trained vectors could further increase the performance. In this work, however, we learn all parameters from the given data. We fit our model using Adam (Kingma and Ba, 2014) (learning rate: 0.001) on the training data over 20 epochs with mini batches of size 16. We apply early stopping according to the maximum Pearson's ρ (with regard to Smatch F1) on the development data. $\rho = \frac{\sum_{i=1}^{n}(x_i-\bar{x})(y_i-\bar{y})}{\sqrt{\sum_{i=1}^{n}(x_i-\bar{x})^2}\sqrt{\sum_{i=1}^{n}(y_i-\bar{y})^2}}$ quantifies the linear relationship between predicted scores $(x_1, ..., x_n)$ and true scores $(y_1, ..., y_n)$.

An Argument-Marker Model for Syntax-Agnostic Proto-Role Labeling

Juri Opitz and **Anette Frank**
Research Training Group AIPHES,
Leibniz ScienceCampus "Empirical Linguistics and Computational Language Modeling"
Department for Computational Linguistics
69120 Heidelberg
{opitz, frank}@cl.uni-heidelberg.de

Abstract

Semantic proto-role labeling (SPRL) is an alternative to semantic role labeling (SRL) that moves beyond a categorical definition of roles, following Dowty's feature-based view of *proto-roles*. This theory determines *agenthood* vs. *patienthood* based on a participant's instantiation of more or less typical agent vs. patient properties, such as, for example, *volition* in an event. To perform SPRL, we develop an ensemble of hierarchical models with self-attention and concurrently learned predicate-argument-markers. Our method is competitive with the state-of-the art, overall outperforming previous work in two formulations of the task (multi-label and multi-variate Likert scale prediction). In contrast to previous work, our results do not depend on gold argument heads derived from supplementary gold tree banks.

1 Introduction

Deciding on a linguistically sound, clearly defined and broadly applicable inventory of semantic roles is a long-standing issue in linguistic theory and natural language processing. To alleviate issues found with classical thematic role inventories, Dowty (1991) argued for replacing categorical roles with a feature-based, composite notion of semantic roles, introducing the *theory of semantic proto-roles (SPR)*. At its core, it proposes two prominent, composite role types: *proto-agent* and *proto-patient*. Proto-roles represent multi-faceted, possibly graded notions of *agenthood* or *patienthood*. For example, consider the following sentence from Bram Stoker's *Dracula* (1897):

(1) *He opened it* [the letter] *and read it gravely.*

'Davidsonian' analyses based on SR and SPR of the event *open* are displayed in Figure 1. The SPR analysis provides more detail about the event and the roles of the involved entities. Whether an

$$\text{SR}: \quad \exists e \big[open(e) \wedge agent(e, c^*) \wedge theme(e, l^*) \big]$$
$$\text{SPR}: \quad \exists e \big[open(e) \wedge volition(e, c^*) \wedge aware(e, c^*) \wedge sentient(e, c^*) \wedge manipulated(e, l^*) \wedge changes\text{-}state(e, l^*) \wedge ... \big]$$

Figure 1: Two different 'Davidsionian' event analyses of *open*. c^* and l^* refer to the *count* and *letter* entities.

argument is considered an *agent* or *patient* follows from the proto-typical properties the argument exhibits: e.g., *being manipulated* is proto-typical for patient, while *volition* is proto-typical for an agent. Hence, in both events of (1) the count is determined as agent, and the letter as patient.

Only recently two SPR data sets have been published. Reisinger et al. (2015) developed a property-based proto-role annotation schema with 18 properties. One Amazon Mechanical Turk crowd worker (selected in a pilot annotation) answered questions such as *how likely is it that the argument mentioned with the verb changes location?* on a 5-point Likert or responded *inapplicable*. This dataset (news domain) will henceforth be denoted by **SPR1**. Based on the experiences from the SPR1 annotation process, White et al. (2016) published **SPR2** which follows a similar annotation schema. However, in contrast to SPR1, the new data set contains doubly annotated data from the web domain for 14 refined properties.

Our work makes the following contributions: In Section §2, we provide an overview of previous SPRL work and outline a common weakness: reliance on gold syntax trees or gold argument heads derived from them. To alleviate this issue, we propose a span-based, hierarchical neural model (§3) which learns marker embeddings to highlight the predicate-argument structures of events. Our experiments (§4) show that our model, when combined in a simple voter ensemble, outperforms all previous works. A single model performs only

*Proceedings of the Eighth Joint Conference on Lexical and Computational Semantics (*SEM)*, pages 224–234
Minneapolis, June 6–7, 2019. ©2019 Association for Computational Linguistics

slightly worse, albeit having weaker dependencies than previous methods. In our analysis, we (i) perform ablation experiments to analyze the contributions of different model components. (ii) we observe that the small SPR data size introduces a severe sensitivity to different random initializations of our neural model. We find that combining multiple models in a simple voter ensemble makes SPRL predictions not only slightly better but also significantly more robust. We share our code with the community and make it publicly available.[1]

2 Related Work

SPRL Teichert et al. (2017) formulate the semantic role labeling task as a multi-label problem and develop a conditional random field model (CRF). Given an argument phrase and a corresponding predicate, the model predicts which of the 18 properties hold. Compared with a simple feature-based linear model by Reisinger et al. (2015), the CRF exhibits superior performance by more than 10 pp. macro F1. Incorporating features derived from additional gold syntax improves the CRF performance significantly. For treating the task as a multi-label problem, the Likert classes $\{1, 2, 3\}$ and *inapplicable* are collapsed to $-$ and Likert classes $\{4, 5\}$ are mapped to $+$. Subsequent works, including ours, conform to this setup.

Rudinger et al. (2018) are the first to treat SPRL as a multi-variate Likert scale regression problem. They develop a neural model whose predictions have good correlation with the values in the testing data of both SPR1 and SPR2. In the multi-label setting, their model compares favourably with Teichert et al. (2017) for most proto-role properties and establishes a new state-of-the-art. Pre-training the model in a machine translation setting helps on SPR1 but results in a performance drop on SPR2. The model takes a sentence as input to a Bi-LSTM (Hochreiter and Schmidhuber, 1997) to produce a sequence of hidden states. The prediction is based on the hidden state corresponding to the head of the argument phrase, which is determined by inspection of the gold syntax tree.

Recently, Tenney et al. (2019) have demonstrated the capacities of contextualized word embeddings across a wide variety of tasks, including SPRL. However, for SPRL labeling they proceed similar to Rudinger et al. (2018) in the sense that they extract the gold heads of arguments in their dependency-based SPRL approach. Instead of using an LSTM to convert the input sentence to a sequence of vectors they make use of large language models such as ELMo (Peters et al., 2018) or BERT (Devlin et al., 2018). The contextual vectors corresponding to predicate and the (gold) argument head are processed by a projection layer, self-attention pooling (Lee et al., 2017) and a two-layer feed forward neural network with sigmoid output activation functions. To compare with Rudinger et al. (2018), our basic model uses standard GloVe embeddings. When our model is fed with contextual embeddings a further observable performance gain can be achieved.

To summarize, previous state-of-the-art SPRL systems suffer from a common problem: they are dependency-based and their results rely on gold argument heads. Our approach, in contrast, does not rely on any supplementary information from gold syntax trees. In fact, our marker model for SPRL is agnostic to any syntactic theory and acts solely on the basis of argument spans which we highlight with position markers.

SRL The task of automatically identifying predicate-argument structures and assigning roles to arguments was firstly investigated by Gildea and Jurafsky (2002). Over the past years, SRL has witnessed a large surge in interest. Recently, very competitive end-to-end neural systems have been proposed (He et al., 2018a; Cai et al., 2018; He et al., 2018b). Strubell et al. (2018) show that injection of syntax can help SRL models and Li et al. (2019) bridge the gap between span-based and dependency-based SRL, achieving new state-of-the-art results both on the span based CoNLL data (Carreras and Màrquez, 2005; Pradhan et al., 2013) and the dependency-based CoNLL data (Surdeanu et al., 2008; Hajič et al., 2009). A fully end-to-end S(P)RL system has to solve multiple sub-tasks: identification of predicate-argument structures, sense disambiguation of predicates and as the main and final step, labeling their argument phrases with roles. Up to the present, SPRL works (including ours) focus on the main task and assume the prior steps as complete.

Research into SPRL is still in its infancy, especially in comparison to SRL. One among many reasons may be the fact that, in contrast to semantic roles, semantic proto-roles are multidimensional. This introduces more complexity:

---

[1] https://gitlab.cl.uni-heidelberg.de/opitz/sprl

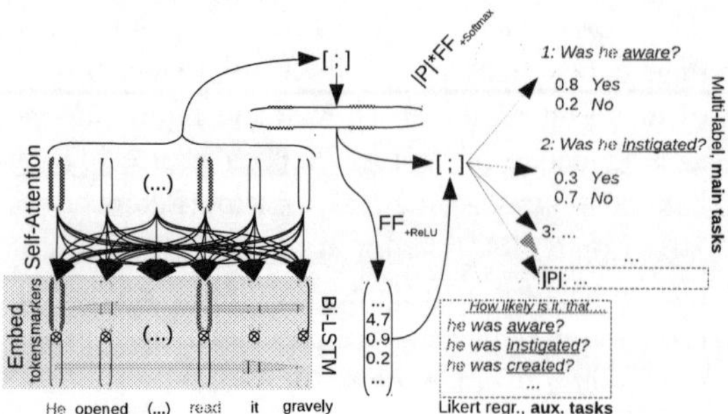

Figure 2: Model outline. *Input*: (i) a sequence of vectors representing the words and (ii) a sequence of vectors which serve to highlight predicate and argument. *Processing*: 1. element-wise multiplication of the two sequences ($\otimes$); 2. generation of hidden states with forward and backward Bi-LSTM reads ($\Longrightarrow$ & $\Longleftarrow$); 3. self-attention mechanism builds a new sequence of hidden states by letting every hidden state attend to every other hidden state; 4. concatenation of the hidden states to generate a vector representation ($[;]$). *Output*: (i) use vector representation to output Likert scale auxiliary predictions (FF_{ReLU}) and (ii) concatenate auxiliary predictions to the vector representation ($[;]$) to finally (iii) compute the multi-label predictions at the top level ($|P| \cdot \text{FF}_{Softmax}$; P: set of proto role properties).

given a predicate and an argument, the task is no more to predict *a single* label (as in SRL), but a *list* of multiple labels or even a multi-variate Likert scale. Another reason may be related to the available resources. The published SPR data sets comprise significantly fewer examples. The design of annotation guidelines and pilot studies with the aim of in-depth proto-role annotations is a hard task. In addition, the SPR data were created, at least to a certain extent, in an experimental manner: one of the goals of corpus creation was to explore possible SPR annotation protocols for humans. We hope that a side-effect of this paper is to spark more interest in SPR and SPRL.

3 Attentive Marker Model

Since the work of Teichert et al. (2017), the SPRL problem has been phrased as follows: given a *(sentence, predicate, argument)* tuple, we need to predict for all possible argument properties from a given property-inventory whether they hold or not (regression: *how likely are they to hold?*).

Following previous work (Rudinger et al., 2018), the backbone of our model is a Bi-LSTM. To ensure further comparability, pretrained 300 dimensional GloVe embeddings (Pennington et al., 2014) are used for building the input sequence

$(e_1, ..., e_T)$. In contrast to Rudinger et al. (2018), we multiply a sequence of *marker embeddings* $(m_1, ..., m_T)$ element-wise with the sequence of word vectors: $(e_1 \cdot m_1, ..., e_T \cdot m_T)$ ($\otimes$, Figure 2). We distinguish three different marker embeddings that indicate the position of the argument in question (red, Figure 2), the predicate ($green$, Figure 2) and remaining parts of the sentence. This is to some extent similar to He et al. (2017) who learn two predicate indicator embeddings which are concatenated to the input vectors and serve the purpose of showing the model whether a token is the predicate or not. However, in SPRL we are also provided with the argument phrase. We will see in the ablation experiments that it is paramount to learn a dedicated embedding. Embedding multiplication instead of concatenation has the advantage of fewer LSTM parameters (smaller input dimension). Besides, it provides the model with the option to learn large coefficients of the word vector dimensions of predicate and argument vectors. This should immediately draw the model's attentiveness to the argument and predicate phrases which now are accentuated.

The sequence of marked embeddings is further processed by a Bi-LSTM in order to obtain a sequence of hidden states $S = (s_1, ..., s_T)$. In Figure 2, forward and backward LSTM reads are indicated by $\Longrightarrow$ and $\Longleftarrow$.

From there, we take intuitions from Zheng et al. (2018) and compute the next sequence of vectors by letting every hidden state attend to every other hidden state, which is expressed by the following formulas:

$$h_{t,t'} = \tanh(QS_t + KS_{t'} + \beta)$$
$$e_{t,t'} = \sigma(v^T h_{t,t'} + \alpha)$$
$$a_t = softmax(e_t)$$
$$z_t = \sum_{t'} a_{t,t'} \cdot s_{t'}$$

Q, K are weight matrices, β is a bias vector, α is a bias scalar and v a weight vector. Letting every hidden state attend to every other hidden state gives the model freedom in computing the argument-predicate composition. This is desirable, since arguments and predicates frequently are in long-distance relationships. For example, in Figure 3 we see that in the SPR1 data predicates and arguments often lie more than 10 words apart and a non-negligible amount of cases consists of distances of more than 20 words.

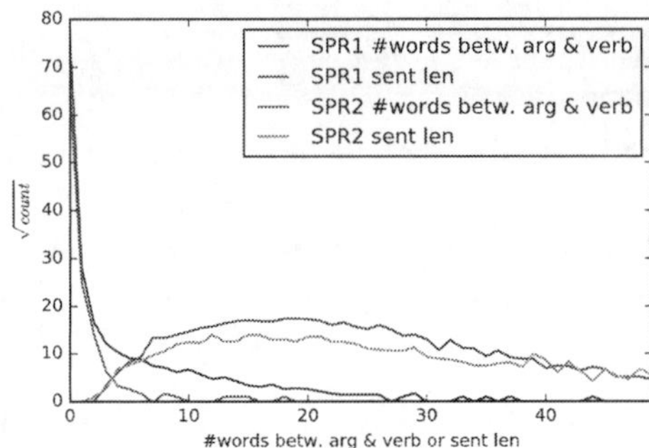

Figure 3: Distribution of the number of words between argument and verb (distance relationship) and sentence lengths in the data sets SPR1 and SPR2.

We proceed by concatenation, $\mathbf{z} = [z_1; ...; z_T]$, and compute intermediate outputs approximating the property-likelihood Likert scales. This is achieved with weight matrix A and $ReLU$ activation functions (FF_{+ReLU}, Figure 2):

$$a = ReLU(A\mathbf{z}). \tag{1}$$

To perform multi-label prediction with $|P|$ possible labels we use $[a; \mathbf{z}]$ for computing the final decisions with $2|P|$ output neurons and $|P|$ separate weight matrices ($|P|^*FF_{+softmax}$, Figure 2), one for each property $p \in P$:

$$o_p = softmax(W^p[a; \mathbf{z}]). \tag{2}$$

For example, given the 18 proto-role properties contained in SPR1, we learn $|P| = 18$ weight matrices and use the Softmax functions to produce 18 vectors of dimension 2 as outputs. The first dimension $o_{p,0}$ represents the predicted probability that property p does *not apply* ($o_{p,1}$: probability for p *applies*). For the regression task, we reduce the number of output neurons from $2|P|$ to $|P|$ and use $ReLU$ activation functions instead. We hypothesize that the hierarchical structure can support the model in making predictions on the top layer. E.g., if the argument is predicted to be most likely *not sentient* and very likely to be *manipulated*, the model may be less tempted to predict an *awareness* label at the top layer. The auxiliary loss for any datum is given as the mean square error over the auxiliary output neurons:

$$\ell' = \frac{\lambda'}{|P|} \sum_{p \in P} (a_p^\star - a_p)^2 \tag{3}$$

In case of the multi-label formulation, our main loss for an example is the average cross entropy loss over every property:

$$\ell = -\frac{\lambda}{|P|} \sum_{p \in P} (o_{p,1}^\star \log o_{p,1} + o_{p,2}^\star \log o_{p,2}), \tag{4}$$

where $o_{p,0}^\star = \mathbf{I}(\neg\mathbf{p})$ and $o_{p,1}^\star = \mathbf{I}(\mathbf{p})$ i.e. the gold label indicator.

4 Experiments

Data We use the same data setup and split as Teichert et al. (2017); Rudinger et al. (2018); Tenney et al. (2019). For determining the gold labels, we also conform to prior works and (i) collapse classes in the multi-label setup from $\{NA, 1, 2, 3\}$ and $\{4, 5\}$ to classes '$-$' and '$+$' and (ii) treat NA as 1 in the Likert regression formulation. For doubly annotated data (SPR2), the Likert scores are averaged; in the multi-label setup we consider values ≥ 4 as '$+$' and map lesser scores to '$-$'. More data and pre-processing details are described in the Supplement §A.1.

Baselines As baselines we present the results from previous systems: the state-of-the-art by Rudinger et al. (2018) is denoted in our tables as **RUD'18**, the linear feature-based classifier by Reisinger et al. (2015) as **REI'15** and the CRF developed by Teichert et al. (2017) as **TEI'17**. Like previous works, we use macro F1 as the global performance metric in the multi-label scenario and macro-averaged Pearson's ρ (arithmetic mean over the correlation coefficients for each property, details can be found in the Supplement A.1) We refer to the system results as reported by Rudinger et al. (2018). The most recent work, which evaluates large language models on a variety of tasks including SPRL, is denoted by **TEN'19** (Tenney et al., 2019). In this case, we present the micro F1 results as reported in their paper.

Model instantiation We introduce four main models: (i) **Marker**: our basic, span-based single-model system. For (ii) **MarkerE**, we fit an ensemble of 50 **Marker**s with different random seeds. Computationally, training 50 neural models in this task is completely feasible since neither SPR1 nor SPR2 contain more than 10,000 training examples (parallelized training took approximately 2 hours). The ensemble predicts unseen testing data by combining the models' decisions in a simple majority vote when performing multi-label prediction

227

or, when in the regression setup, by computing the mean of the output scores (for every property). We also introduce (iii) **MarkerB**, and (iv) **MarkerEB**. These two systems differ in only one aspect from the previously mentioned models: instead of GloVe word vectors, we feed contextual vectors extracted from the BERT model (Devlin et al., 2018). More precisely, we use the transformer model *BERT-base-uncased*[2] and sum the inferred activations over the last four layers. The resulting vectors are concatenated to GloVe vectors and then processed by the Bi-LSTM.

We fit all models with gradient descent and apply early stopping on the development data (maximum average Pearson's ρ for multi-variate Likert regression, maximum macro F1 for the multi-label task). Further hyper parameter choices and details about the training are listed in Appendix §A.2.

4.1 Multi-Label Prediction Results

News texts The results on newspaper data (SPR1) are displayed in Table 1 (left-hand side). Our basic ensemble (**MarkerE**) improves massively in the property *location*[3] (+19.1 pp. F1). A significant loss is experienced in the property *changes possession* (-9.6). Overall, our ensemble method outperforms all prior works (REI'15: +17.7 pp. macro F1; TEI'17: +6.2, RUD'18: +1.0). Our ensemble method provided with additional contextual word embeddings (**MarkerEB**) yields another large performance gain. The old state-of-the-art, RUD'18, is surpassed by more than 6.0 pp. macro F1 (a relative improvement of 8.6%). With regard to some properties, the contextual embeddings provide massive performance gains over our basic **MarkerE**: *stationary* (+9.5 pp. F1), *makes physical contact* (+21.3), *change of location* (+14.1) and *created* (+17.3). The only loss is incurred for the property which asks if an argument is *destroyed* (-12.3). This specific property appears to be difficult to predict for all models. The best score in this property is achieved by **MarkerE** with only 26.6 F1.

Web texts On the web texts (SPR2), due to less previous works, we also use three label selection strategies as baselines: a *majority* label baseline, a *constant* strategy which always selects the positive label and a *random* baseline which samples a pos-

itive target label according to the occurrence ratio in the training data (*maj, constant & ran*, Table 2, left-hand side).

Our basic **MarkerE** method yields massive improvements over both baselines (more than +10 pp. F1) in 4 out of 14 proto-role properties. For *argument changes possession* and *awareness* the improvement over both baselines is more than +25 pp. F1 and for *sentient* more than +40 pp. However, in the *partitive* property, the constant-label baseline remains unbeaten by a large margin (-21.7 pp.). Overall, all Marker models yield large performance increases over the baselines. For example, **MarkerE** yields significant improvements both over *random* (+27.7 pp. macro F1), *constant* (+9.5) and *majority* (+45.0).

Intriguingly – while the contextual embeddings provide a massive performance boost on news texts (SPR1), – they appear not to be useful for our model on the web texts. The macro F1 score of **MarkerEB** is slightly worse (-1 pp.) than that of **MarkerE** and the micro F1 score is only marginally better (+0.9). The same holds true for the single-model instances: **Marker** performs better than **MarkerB** by 2.2 pp. macro F1 albeit marginally worse micro F1 wise by 0.5 pp.

Why exactly the contextual embeddings fail to provide any valuable information when labeling arguments in web texts, we cannot answer with certainty. A plausible cause could be overfitting problems stemming from the increased dimensionality of the input vectors. In fact, the contextual embeddings increase the number of word vector features by more than two times over the dimension of the GloVe embeddings. This inflates the number of parameters in the LSTM's weight matrices. As a consequence, the likelihood of overfitting is increased – an issue which is further aggravated by the fact that SPR2 data are significantly fewer than SPR1 data. SPR2 contains less than five thousand predicate-argument training examples, roughly half the size of SPR1.

Another source of problems may be rooted in the target-label construction process for SPR2. This question does not arise when using SPR1 data since all annotations were performed by a single annotator. The SPR2 data, in contrast, contains for each predicate-argument pair, two annotations. In total, the data was annotated by many crowd workers – some of whom provided many and some provided few annotations. Perhaps, averaging Lik-

---

[2] https://github.com/google-research/bert

[3] *i.e. does the argument describe the location of the event?*

property	multi-label (ML), F1 score							regression (LR), ρ				
	previous works			ours					ours			
	REI'15	TEI'17	RUD'18	MarkerE	Marker	MarkerEB	MarkerB	RUD'18	MarkerE	Marker	MarkerEB	MarkerB
awareness	68.8	87.3	89.9	89.4	88.1	*93.4*	**91.6**	0.897	0.880	0.868	**0.922**	**0.915**
chg location	6.6	35.6	45.7	**50.5**	**53.2**	*64.6*	**57.1**	0.702	**0.768**	**0.744**	**0.835**	**0.814**
chg state	54.6	66.1	71.0	66.6	68.2	*71.5*	66.1	0.604	**0.651**	**0.621**	**0.701**	**0.653**
chg possession	0.0	38.8	58.0	48.4	55.5	**55.7**	*59.5*	0.640	0.609	0.576	*0.652*	0.582
created	0.0	44.4	39.7	34.8	46.5	**52.2**	*56.1*	0.549	**0.593**	0.498	*0.669*	**0.614**
destroyed	17.1	0.0	24.2	*26.6*	19.9	14.3	22.2	0.346	**0.368**	0.220	*0.412*	**0.347**
existed after	82.3	87.5	85.9	87.0	82.9	*88.5*	84.8	0.619	0.612	0.571	*0.695*	0.669
existed before	79.5	84.8	85.1	**87.4**	**85.4**	*90.1*	**85.8**	0.710	0.704	0.668	*0.781*	0.741
existed during	93.1	95.1	95.0	**95.2**	94.3	*95.8*	94.0	0.673	**0.675**	0.626	*0.732*	0.714
exists as physical	64.8	76.4	82.7	**83.7**	80.6	*88.1*	**85.8**	0.834	0.807	0.777	*0.871*	0.856
instigated	76.7	85.6	88.6	86.6	86.4	*88.9*	87.6	0.858	0.856	0.842	*0.879*	0.860
location	0.0	18.5	53.8	**72.9**	**69.8**	*78.9*	**76.1**	0.619	**0.755**	**0.742**	*0.849*	0.820
makes physical contact	21.5	40.7	47.2	45.7	32.3	*67.0*	**61.1**	0.741	0.716	0.671	*0.801*	0.772
manipulated	72.1	86.0	86.8	**86.9**	86.7	*89.6*	86.5	0.737	**0.738**	0.705	*0.774*	0.751
pred changed arg	54.0	67.8	70.7	68.1	67.6	*72.8*	66.1	0.592	**0.621**	0.579	*0.714*	0.664
sentient	42.0	85.6	90.6	89.5	88.3	*95.4*	**92.2**	0.925	0.904	0.887	*0.959*	0.951
stationary	13.3	21.4	47.4	41.0	25.0	**50.5**	*54.5*	0.711	0.666	0.654	*0.771*	0.739
volitional	69.8	86.4	88.1	88.3	86.7	*91.6*	**90.1**	0.882	0.873	0.863	*0.911*	0.903
micro	71.0	81.7	83.3	**83.6**	82.0	*86.8*	83.5	-	-	-	-	-
macro	55.4	65.9	71.1	**72.1**	69.3	*77.5*	**73.8**	0.706	**0.711**	0.673	*0.774*	0.743

Table 1: SPR1 results. **bold**: better than all previous work; ***bold***: overall best.

property	multi-label (ML), F1 score							regression (LR), ρ				
	baselines			ours					ours			
	maj	ran	const	MarkerE	Marker	MarkerEB	MarkerB	RUD'18	MarkerE	Marker	MarkerEB	MarkerB
awareness	0.0	48.9	67.1	**92.7**	**92.3**	*94.0*	**91.1**	0.879	**0.882**	0.868	*0.902*	0.878
chg location	0.0	12.0	21.7	**28.6**	**35.1**	*38.0*	18.2	0.492	**0.517**	0.476	*0.563*	**0.507**
chg possession	0.0	5.5	6.6	**33.3**	**33.3**	35.6	*41.1*	0.488	**0.520**	0.483	*0.549*	**0.509**
chg state	0.0	19.5	31.3	29.7	27.1	**41.4**	*45.2*	0.352	0.351	0.275	*0.444*	**0.369**
chg state continuous	0.0	9.2	21.7	**25.3**	19.8	**26.8**	*30.4*	0.352	**0.396**	0.321	*0.483*	**0.423**
existed after	94.1	86.1	94.1	94.0	92.4	94.0	*94.5*	0.478	0.469	0.403	*0.507*	0.476
existed before	89.5	80.0	89.5	**91.0**	**90.5**	*92.0*	89.8	0.616	**0.645**	0.605	*0.690*	0.664
existed during	98.0	96.2	97.0	98.0	97.8	*98.1*	*98.1*	0.358	*0.374*	0.280	0.354	0.301
instigated	0.0	48.9	70.5	**77.9**	**78.0**	78.9	78.7	0.590	0.582	0.540	*0.603*	**0.599**
partitive	0.0	10.4	*24.2*	2.5	16.5	9.2	2.4	0.359	0.283	0.213	*0.374*	0.330
sentient	0.0	47.6	44.3	**91.9**	**91.6**	*93.7*	92.0	0.880	0.874	0.859	*0.892*	0.872
volitional	0.0	39.1	61.8	**88.1**	**87.2**	*89.7*	88.5	0.841	0.839	0.825	*0.870*	0.854
was for benefit	0.0	31.6	48.8	**61.1**	**59.2**	60.2	*63.4*	0.578	**0.580**	0.525	*0.598*	0.569
was used	79.3	66.1	79.3	77.9	78.0	77.6	*79.9*	0.203	0.173	0.093	*0.288*	0.264
micro	65.0	62.9	61.4	**84.0**	**83.4**	*84.9*	83.9	-	-	-	-	-
macro	25.9	43.2	61.4	**70.9**	69.7	69.9	67.5	0.534	**0.535**	0.483	*0.580*	0.544

Table 2: SPR2 results. **bold**: better than previous work and/or baselines; ***bold***: overall best.

ert scale annotations of two random annotators is not the right way to transform SPR2 to a multi-label task. Future work may investigate new transformation strategies. For example, we can envision a strategy which finds reliable annotators and weighs the choices of those annotators higher than those of less reliable annotators. This should result in an improved SPR2 gold standard for both multi-label and multi-variate Likert scale SPRL systems.

4.2 Likert Scale Regression Results

News texts MarkerE achieves large performance gains for the properties *location* and *change of location* ($\Delta\rho$: +0.136 & $\Delta\rho$: +0.066, Table 1). This is in accordance with the results for these two properties in the multi-label predic-tion setup. Our model is outperformed by RUD'18 in the property *stationary* ($\Delta\rho$: -0.045). All in all, **MarkerE** outperforms RUD'18 (Δ macro ρ: +0.005). When providing additional contextual word embeddings from the large language model, the correlations intensify for almost all role properties. Overall, the contextual embeddings in **MarkerEB** yield an observable improvement of +0.063 Δ macro ρ over **MarkerE** (which solely uses GloVe embeddings).

Web texts Our **MarkerE** model outperforms RUD'18 slightly by +0.001$\Delta\rho$ (Table 2). However, if we compare with RUD'18's model setup which achieved the best score on the SPR1 testing data (pre-training with a supervised MT task, macro regression result SPR2: 0.521ρ), we

	Method	*span* or *dep.*	gold head	STL	ensembling	C-embeddings	SPR1 ML	SPR1 LR	SPR2 ML	SPR2 LR	SPR1 ML	SPR2 ML
					used by system		macro result				micro result	
previous	REI'15	span	no	no	no	no	55.4	-	-	-	71.0	-
	TEI'17	dependency	yes (full parse)	no	no	no	65.9	-	-	-	81.7	-
	RUD'18	dependency	yes	no	no	no	69.3	0.697	-	0.534	82.2	-
	RUD'18$_{(+MT\ pretrain)}$	dependency	yes	yes	no	no	71.1	0.706	-	0.521	83.3	-
	TEN'19	dependency	yes	no	no	yes (BERT concat)	-	-	-	-	84.7	83.0
	TEN'19	dependency	yes	no	no	yes (BERT lin. comb.)	-	-	-	-	86.1†	83.8
ours	Marker	span	no	no	no	no	69.3	0.682	67.9†	0.483	80.8	81.1
	MarkerE	span	no	no	yes	no	<u>72.1</u>	<u>0.711</u>	**<u>70.9</u>**	<u>0.535</u>	<u>83.6</u>	<u>84.0</u>
	MarkerB	span	no	no	no	yes (BERT sum)	73.5†	0.741†	67.5	0.544†	84.9	83.9†
	MarkerEB	span	no	no	yes	yes (BERT sum)	**77.5**	**0.774**	69.9	**0.580**	**86.8**	**84.9**

Table 3: Main results, system properties and requirements of SPRL systems. Overall best system is marked in **bold**, best system using GloVe is <u>underlined</u>, best single-model system is marked by †. STL: supervised transfer-learning (e.g., RUD'18: pre-training on MT task). C-embeddings: contextual word embeddings (BERT-base). ML: multi-label prediction; LR: multi-variate Likert regression. *BERT concat*: last four BERT layers are concatenated. *BERT lin. comb.*: optimized linear combination of last four BERT layers (our BERT based models sum the last four layers). The Table is further discussed in the Section *Discussion* §4.3.

achieve a significantly higher macro-average ($\Delta\rho$: +0.014). Yet again, when our model is provided with contextual word embeddings, a large performance boost is the outcome. In fact, **MarkerEB** outperforms **MarkerE** by +0.045 Δ macro ρ and RUD'18's best performing configuration by +0.046. This stands in contrast to the multi-labeling results on this type of data, where the contextual embeddings did not appear to provide any performance increase. As previously discussed (§4.1), this discrepancy may be rooted in the task generation process of SPR2 which requires transforming two annotations per example to one ground truth (the two annotations per example stem from two out of, in total, 50 workers).

4.3 Discussion

Leaving the contextual word embedding inputs aside, the performance differences of our Marker models to RUD'18 may seem marginal for many properties. Albeit our **MarkerE** yields an observable improvement of 1.0 pp. macro F1 in the multi-label setup, in the regression setup the performance gains are very small ($\Delta\rho$ SPR1: +0.005, $\Delta\rho$ SPR2: +0.001, Table 1 & 3). In addition, our model as a single model instance (**Marker**) is outperformed by RUD'18's approach both in the regression and in the multi-label setup. However, it is important to note that the result of our system has substantially fewer dependencies (Table 3).

Firstly, our model does not rely on supplementary gold syntax – in fact, since it is span-based, our model is completely agnostic to any syntax. Besides our approach, only REI'15 does not depend on supplementary gold syntax for the dis-

played results. However, *all* of our models outperform REI'15's feature-based linear classifier in *every* property (+17 pp. macro F1 in total) except for *destroyed* (where **MarkerEB** performed slighly worse by -2.8 pp. F1). Also, results of SRL systems on semantic role labeling data show that span-based SRL systems often lag behind a few points in accuracy (cf. Li et al. (2019), Table 1). When provided with the syntactic head of the argument phrase, a model may immediately focus on what is important in the argument phrase. When solely fed the argument-span, which is potentially very long, the model has to find the most important parts of the phrase on its own and is more easily distracted. Additionally, identifying the head word of an argument may be more important than getting the boundaries of the span exactly right. In other words, span-based SPRL models may be more robust when confronted with slightly erroneous spans compared to dependency-based models which may be vulnerable to false positive heads. However, this hypothesis has to be confirmed or disproven experimentally in future work.

Further information about differences of various SPRL approaches is displayed in Table 3. In sum, despite having significantly fewer dependencies on external resources, our approach proves to be competitive with all methods from prior works, including neural systems. When combined in a simple ensemble, our model outperforms previous systems. When we feed additional contextual word embeddings, the results can be boosted further by a large margin. In the following section, we show that ensembling SPRL models has

	Ensembling worse		Ensembling better		
Data	$p \in [0.005, 0.05)$	$p < 0.005$	$p \in [0.005, 0.05)$	$p < 0.005$	NS
SPR1	0	1	5	9	3
SPR2	1	1	5	2	5

Table 4: McNemar significance test results of **MarkerEB** against **MarkerB**. Counts of properties for which a significance category applies (NS: #properties with insignificant difference).

another advantage besides predictive performance gains. Namely, it decreases SPRL model sensitivities towards different random initializations. As a result, we find that a simple neural voter committee (ensemble) offers more robust SPRL predictions compared to a randomly selected committee-member (single model).

4.4 Analysis

Ensembling increases accuracy To investigate whether ensembling improves proto-role labeling results significantly, we conduct McNemar significance tests (McNemar, 1947) comparing the predictions of **MarkerB** and **MarkerEB**. The significance test results summarized in Table 4 are unambiguous: for many proto-role properties, ensembling helps to improve performance significantly (SPR1: $\frac{14}{18}$ cases; SPR2: $\frac{7}{14}$ cases; significance level: $p < 0.05$). However, for few cases, ensembling resulted in significantly worse predictions (SPR1: *change of location*; SPR2: *change of location*, *instigated* and *partitive*; significance level: $p < 0.05$). For the rest of the properties, differences in predictions remain insignificant.

Ensembling increases robustness Additionally, we find that ensembling increases the robustness of our neural models. Consider Figure 4, where we display the performance difference of a n-voter ensemble to the same ensemble after one additional voter joined ($n+1$-voter ensemble). The difference fluctuates wildly while the ensemble is still small. This suggests that a different random seed yields significantly different predictions. Hence, our a single neural Marker model is very vulnerable to the quirks of random numbers. However, when more voters join, we see that the predictions become notably more stable. An outcome which holds true for both data sets and two different ensemble model configurations (**MarkerE** and **MarkerEB**). We draw two conclusions from this experiment: (i) a single neural SPRL model is extremely sensitive to different random initial-

		ablated component				
Data	MarkerEB	SelfAtt	mark.	pred-mark.	arg-mark.	hier.
SPR1	77.5	73.1	50.7	76.3	60.1	76.7
SPR2	69.9	67.3	59.3	68.2	63.3	68.9

Table 5: Multi-labeling F1 macro scores for different MarkerEB model configurations over SPR1 and SPR2.

izations. Finally, (ii) a simple voter ensemble has the potential to alleviate this issue. In fact, when we add more voters, the model converges towards stable predictions which are less influenced by the quirks of random numbers.

Model Ablations All ablation experiments are conducted with **MarkerEB** in the multi-label formulation. We proceed by ablating different components in a leave-one-out fashion: (i) the self-attention components of the ensemble model are removed (SelfAtt in Table 5); (ii) we abstain from highlighting (a) the arguments and predicates, (b) only the predicates and (c) only the arguments (mark. pred-mark. and arg-mark. in Table 5); Finally, (iii) we remove the hierachical structure and do not predict auxiliary outputs (hier. in Table 5).

From all ablated components, removing simultaneously both predicate and argument-markers hurts the model the most (SPR1: -26.8 pp. macro F1; SPR2: -10.6). Only ablating the argument-marker also causes a great performance loss (SPR1: -17.4, SPR2: - 6.6). On the other hand, when only the predicate marker is ablated, the performance decreases only slightly (SPR1: - 1.2, SPR2: -1.7). In other words, it appears to be of paramount importance to provide our model with indicators for the argument position in the sentence, but it is of lesser importance to point at the predicate. The self-attention component can boost the model's performance by up to +4.4 pp. F1 on SPR1 and +2.6 on SPR2. The hierarchical structure with intermediate auxiliary Likert scale outputs leads to gains of approximately +1 pp. macro F1 in both data sets. This indicates that indeed the finer Likert scale annotations provide auxiliary information of value when predicting the labels at the top layer, albeit the performance difference appears to be rather small.

5 Conclusion

In our proposed SPRL ensemble model, predicate-argument constructs are highlighted with concurrently learned marker embeddings and self-

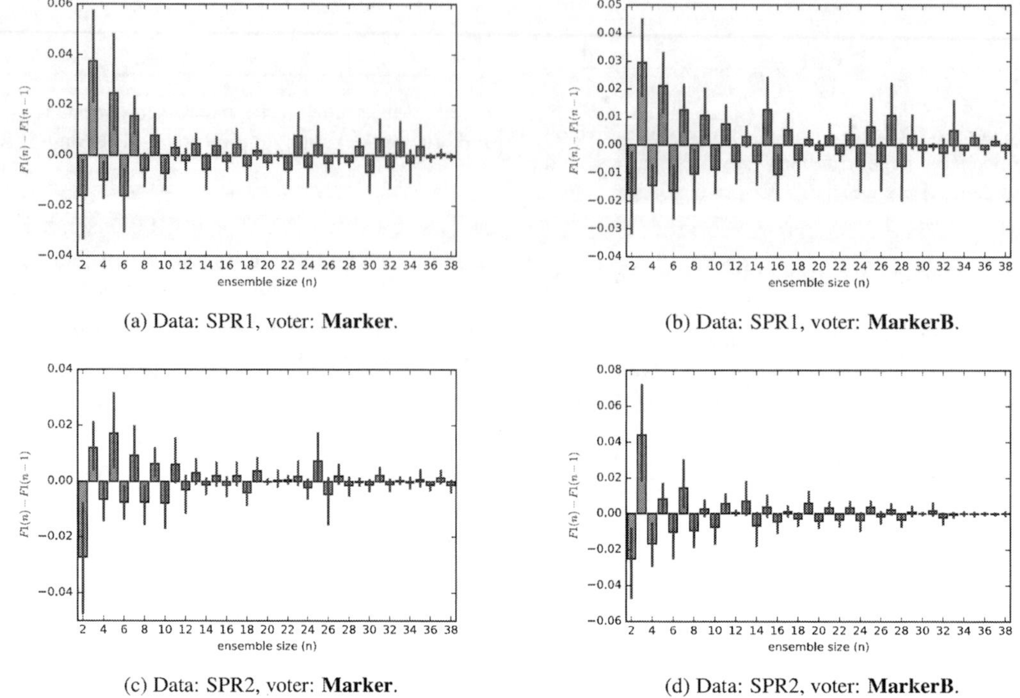

(a) Data: SPR1, voter: Marker.

(b) Data: SPR1, voter: MarkerB.

(c) Data: SPR2, voter: Marker.

(d) Data: SPR2, voter: MarkerB.

Figure 4: Adding more voters leads to convergence in SPRL predictions. x-axis: number of voter models partaking in the ensemble. y-axis: F1 mean difference over all proto-roles from the ensemble with x voters compared to the ensemble with $x - 1$ voters. Thin bars represent standard deviations.

attention enables the model to capture long-distance relationships between arguments and predicates. The span-based method is competitive with the dependency-based state-of-the-art which uses gold heads. When combined in a simple ensemble, the method overall outperforms the state-of-the-art on newspaper texts (multi-label prediction macro F1: +1.0 pp.). When fed with contextual word embeddings extracted from a large language model, the method outperforms the state-of-the-art by 6.4 pp. macro F1. Our method is competitive with the state-of-the-art for Likert regression on texts from the web domain. In the multi-label setting, it outperforms all baselines by a large margin. Furthermore, we have shown that a simple Marker model voter ensemble is very suited for conducting SPRL, for two reasons: (i) results for almost every proto-role property are significantly improved and (ii) considerably more robust SPRL predictions are obtained.

We hope that our work sparks more research into semantic proto-role labeling and corpus creation. Dowty's feature-based view on roles allows us to analyze predicate-argument configurations in great detail – an issue which we think is located in the marrow of computational semantics.

Acknowledgements

This work has been supported by the German Research Foundation as part of the Research Training Group Adaptive Preparation of Information from Heterogeneous Sources (AIPHES) under grant no. GRK 1994/1 and by the Leibniz ScienceCampus "Empirical Linguistics and Computational Language Modeling", supported by the Leibniz Association under grant no. SAS-2015-IDS-LWC and by the Ministry of Science, Research, and Art of Baden-Württemberg.

References

Jiaxun Cai, Shexia He, Zuchao Li, and Hai Zhao. 2018. A full end-to-end semantic role labeler, syntactic-agnostic over syntactic-aware? In *Proceedings of the 27th International Conference on Computational Linguistics*, pages 2753–2765. Association for Computational Linguistics.

Xavier Carreras and Lluís Màrquez. 2005. Introduction to the conll-2005 shared task: Semantic role labeling. In *Proceedings of the ninth conference on computational natural language learning (CoNLL-2005)*, pages 152–164.

Jacob Devlin, Ming-Wei Chang, Kenton Lee, and Kristina Toutanova. 2018. BERT: pre-training of deep bidirectional transformers for language understanding. *CoRR*, abs/1810.04805.

David Dowty. 1991. Thematic proto-roles and argument selection. *Language*, 67:547–619.

Daniel Gildea and Daniel Jurafsky. 2002. Automatic labeling of semantic roles. *Computational linguistics*, 28(3):245–288.

Jan Hajič, Massimiliano Ciaramita, Richard Johansson, Daisuke Kawahara, Maria Antònia Martí, Lluís Màrquez, Adam Meyers, Joakim Nivre, Sebastian Padó, Jan Štěpánek, et al. 2009. The conll-2009 shared task: Syntactic and semantic dependencies in multiple languages. In *Proceedings of the Thirteenth Conference on Computational Natural Language Learning: Shared Task*, pages 1–18. Association for Computational Linguistics.

Luheng He, Kenton Lee, Omer Levy, and Luke Zettlemoyer. 2018a. Jointly predicting predicates and arguments in neural semantic role labeling. In *Proceedings of the 56th Annual Meeting of the Association for Computational Linguistics (Volume 2: Short Papers)*, pages 364–369, Melbourne, Australia. Association for Computational Linguistics.

Luheng He, Kenton Lee, Mike Lewis, and Luke Zettlemoyer. 2017. Deep semantic role labeling: What works and what's next. In *Proceedings of the 55th Annual Meeting of the Association for Computational Linguistics (Volume 1: Long Papers)*, pages 473–483, Vancouver, Canada. Association for Computational Linguistics.

Shexia He, Zuchao Li, Hai Zhao, and Hongxiao Bai. 2018b. Syntax for semantic role labeling, to be, or not to be. In *Proceedings of the 56th Annual Meeting of the Association for Computational Linguistics (Volume 1: Long Papers)*, volume 1, pages 2061–2071.

Sepp Hochreiter and Jürgen Schmidhuber. 1997. Long short-term memory. *Neural computation*, 9(8):1735–1780.

Diederik P. Kingma and Jimmy Ba. 2014. Adam: A method for stochastic optimization. *CoRR*, abs/1412.6980.

Kenton Lee, Luheng He, Mike Lewis, and Luke Zettlemoyer. 2017. End-to-end neural coreference resolution. In *Proceedings of the 2017 Conference on Empirical Methods in Natural Language Processing*, pages 188–197, Copenhagen, Denmark. Association for Computational Linguistics.

Zuchao Li, Shexia He, Hai Zhao, Yiqing Zhang, Zhuosheng Zhang, Xi Zhou, and Xiang Zhou. 2019. Dependency or span, end-to-end uniform semantic role labeling. *CoRR*, abs/1901.05280.

Quinn McNemar. 1947. Note on the sampling error of the difference between correlated proportions or percentages. *Psychometrika*, 12(2):153–157.

Jeffrey Pennington, Richard Socher, and Christopher D. Manning. 2014. Glove: Global vectors for word representation. In *Empirical Methods in Natural Language Processing (EMNLP)*, pages 1532–1543.

Matthew Peters, Mark Neumann, Mohit Iyyer, Matt Gardner, Christopher Clark, Kenton Lee, and Luke Zettlemoyer. 2018. Deep contextualized word representations. In *Proceedings of the 2018 Conference of the North American Chapter of the Association for Computational Linguistics: Human Language Technologies, Volume 1 (Long Papers)*, pages 2227–2237, New Orleans, Louisiana. Association for Computational Linguistics.

Sameer Pradhan, Alessandro Moschitti, Nianwen Xue, Hwee Tou Ng, Anders Björkelund, Olga Uryupina, Yuchen Zhang, and Zhi Zhong. 2013. Towards robust linguistic analysis using ontonotes. In *Proceedings of the Seventeenth Conference on Computational Natural Language Learning*, pages 143–152.

Drew Reisinger, Rachel Rudinger, Francis Ferraro, Craig Harman, Kyle Rawlins, and Benjamin Van Durme. 2015. Semantic proto-roles. *Transactions of the Association for Computational Linguistics*, 3:475–488.

Rachel Rudinger, Adam Teichert, Ryan Culkin, Sheng Zhang, and Benjamin Van Durme. 2018. Neural-davidsonian semantic proto-role labeling. In *Proceedings of the 2018 Conference on Empirical Methods in Natural Language Processing*, pages 944–955. Association for Computational Linguistics.

Emma Strubell, Patrick Verga, Daniel Andor, David Weiss, and Andrew McCallum. 2018. Linguistically-informed self-attention for semantic role labeling. In *Proceedings of the 2018 Conference on Empirical Methods in Natural Language Processing*, pages 5027–5038.

Mihai Surdeanu, Richard Johansson, Adam Meyers, Lluís Màrquez, and Joakim Nivre. 2008. The conll-2008 shared task on joint parsing of syntactic and semantic dependencies. In *Proceedings of the Twelfth Conference on Computational Natural Language Learning*, pages 159–177. Association for Computational Linguistics.

Adam R. Teichert, Adam Poliak, Benjamin Van Durme, and Matthew R. Gormley. 2017. Semantic proto-role labeling. In *AAAI*, pages 4459–4466. AAAI Press.

Ian Tenney, Patrick Xia, Berlin Chen, Alex Wang, Adam Poliak, R Thomas McCoy, Najoung Kim, Benjamin Van Durme, Sam Bowman, Dipanjan Das, and Ellie Pavlick. 2019. What do you learn from context? probing for sentence structure in contextualized word representations. In *International Conference on Learning Representations*.

Aaron Steven White, Drew Reisinger, Keisuke Sakaguchi, Tim Vieira, Sheng Zhang, Rachel Rudinger, Kyle Rawlins, and Benjamin Van Durme. 2016. Universal decompositional semantics on universal dependencies. In *Proceedings of the 2016 Conference on Empirical Methods in Natural Language Processing*, pages 1713–1723.

Guineng Zheng, Subhabrata Mukherjee, Xin Luna Dong, and Feifei Li. 2018. Opentag: Open attribute value extraction from product profiles. In *Proceedings of the 24th ACM SIGKDD International Conference on Knowledge Discovery & Data Mining*, pages 1049–1058. ACM.

A Supplemental Material

A.1 Notes

Calculation of macro F1 The global performance metric for multi-label SPRL is defined as 'macro F1'. To ensure full comparability of results, we use the same formula as prior works (Rudinger et al., 2018):

$$\frac{2 \cdot P_{macro\ avg.} \cdot R_{macro\ avg.}}{P_{macro\ avg.} + R_{macro\ avg.}}, \qquad (5)$$

where P and R are *Precision* and *Recall* and *macro avg.* means the unweighted mean of these quantities computed over all proto-role properties. The above macro F1 metric, though not explicitly displayed in the prior work papers, has been confirmed by the main authors (email).

Calculation of Pearson's ρ Person's ρ quantifies the linear relationship between two random variables X and Y. Computed over a sample $\{(x_i, y_i)\}_1^n$ it is calculated with the following formula:

$$\rho = \frac{\sum_{i=1}^{n}(x_i - \bar{x})(y_i - \bar{y})}{\sqrt{\sum_{i=1}^{n}(x_i - \bar{x})^2}\sqrt{\sum_{i=1}^{n}(y_i - \bar{y})^2}} \qquad (6)$$

Given $|P|$ proto-role properties and corresponding correlation coefficients $\rho_1, ...\rho_{|P|}$, the macro Pearson's ρ is calculated as

$$macro\ \rho = \frac{\sum_{i=1}^{|P|}\rho_i}{|P|}. \qquad (7)$$

hyper-parameter	choice
λ (main loss)	1
λ' (aux. losses)	0.2
optimizer	Adam (Kingma and Ba, 2014)
optimizer param.	$\beta_1 = 0.9, \beta_2 = 0.999, \epsilon = 1e^{-07}$
learning rate	0.001
Bi-LSTM units	$2 \cdot 64$
max. seq length	30
padding	pre
Marker embeddings,init	$U(-0.05, +0.05)$
Fixed embeddings, init	GloVe 300d (Pennington et al., 2014)

Table 6: Hyper parameter configuration.

Data split of SPR1 (Teichert et al., 2017) reframed the SPRL task as a multi-label problem. Previously the task was to answer, given a predicate and an argument, one specific proto-role question (binary label or single output regression). Now we need to predict all proto-role questions at once (multi-label or multi-ouput regression). In order to allow this formulation of the task, the authors needed to redefine the original train-dev-test split of SPR1 (recent works, including ours, all use the re-defined split).

Reported Numbers In the EMNLP publication of Rudinger et al. (2018) we found a few minor transcription errors in the result tables (confirmed by email communication with the main authors, who plan to upload an errata section). In the case of transcription errors, we took the error-corrected numbers which were sent to us via email.

A.2 Hyperparameters & Preprocessing

The hyper parameter configuration of our model are displayed in Table 6. *Sequence pruning*: Consider that $I = \{i\}$ is the index of the predicate and $J = \{j, ..., k\}$ are the indices corresponding to the argument. As long as the input sequence length is longer than maximum length (30, cf. Table 6), we clip left tokens so that the index of the token $m < \min I \cup J$, then we proceed to clip tokens to the right so that $m > \max I \cup J$, for the very rare cases that this was not sufficient we proceed to clip tokens with $m \notin I \cup J$ (the marker sequences are adjusted accordingly). The clipping strategy ensures that predicate and argument tokens are present in every input sequence. Sequences which are shorter than 30 words are *pre-padded* with zero vectors.

Probing What Different NLP Tasks Teach Machines about Function Word Comprehension

Najoung Kim[†,*], **Roma Patel**[φ], **Adam Poliak**[†], **Alex Wang**[∂],
Patrick Xia[†], **R. Thomas McCoy**[†], **Ian Tenney**[△], **Alexis Ross**[◇],
Tal Linzen[†], **Benjamin Van Durme**[†], **Samuel R. Bowman**[∂], **Ellie Pavlick**[φ,*]
[†]Johns Hopkins University [φ]Brown University
[∂]New York University [△]Google AI Language [◇]Harvard University

Abstract

We introduce a set of nine challenge tasks that test for the understanding of function words. These tasks are created by structurally mutating sentences from existing datasets to target the comprehension of specific types of function words (e.g., prepositions, *wh*-words). Using these probing tasks, we explore the effects of various pretraining objectives for sentence encoders (e.g., language modeling, CCG supertagging and natural language inference (NLI)) on the learned representations. Our results show that pretraining on CCG—our most syntactic objective—performs the best on average across our probing tasks, suggesting that syntactic knowledge helps function word comprehension. Language modeling also shows strong performance, supporting its widespread use for pretraining state-of-the-art NLP models. Overall, no pretraining objective dominates across the board, and our function word probing tasks highlight several intuitive differences between pretraining objectives, e.g., that NLI helps the comprehension of negation.

1 Introduction

Many recent advances in NLP have been driven by new approaches to representation learning—i.e., the design of models whose primary aim is to yield representations of words or sentences that useful for a range of downstream applications (Bowman et al., 2017). Approaches to representation learning typically differ in either the architecture of the model used to learn the representations, the objective used to train that network, or both. Varying these factors can significantly impact performance on a broad range of NLP tasks (McCann et al., 2017; Peters et al., 2018; Devlin et al., 2019).

This paper investigates the role of pretraining objectives of sentence encoders, with respect to their capacity to understand function words (e.g., prepositions, conjunctions). Although the importance of finding an effective pretraining objective for learning better (or more generalizable) representations is well acknowledged, relatively few studies offer a controlled comparison of diverse pretraining objectives, holding model architecture constant.

We ask whether the linguistic properties implicitly captured by pretraining objectives measurably affect the types of linguistic information encoded in the learned representations. To this end, we explore whether qualitatively different objectives lead to demonstrably different sentence representations. We focus our analysis on function words because they play a key role in compositional meaning—e.g., introducing and identifying discourse referents or representing relationships between entities or ideas—and are not yet considered to be well-modeled by distributional semantics (Bernardi et al., 2015). Our results suggest that different pretraining objectives give rise to differences in function word comprehension; for instance, we see that natural language inference helps understanding negation, and grounded language helps understanding spatial descriptors. However, overall, we find that the observed differences are not always straightforwardly interpretable, and further investigation is needed to determine what specific aspects of pretraining tasks, yield good representations of function words.

The analyses we present contribute new results in an ongoing line of research aimed at providing a finer-grained understanding of what neural networks capture about linguistic structure (Conneau et al., 2018; Poliak et al., 2018b; Linzen et al., 2018; Tenney et al., 2019, *i.a.*). Our contributions are:

---

*Corresponding authors: Najoung Kim (n.kim@jhu.edu),
Ellie Pavlick (ellie_pavlick@brown.edu)

*Proceedings of the Eighth Joint Conference on Lexical and Computational Semantics (*SEM)*, pages 235–249
Minneapolis, June 6–7, 2019. ©2019 Association for Computational Linguistics

Acceptability		
wh-word	**why** are you so chippy about posh people?	✓
	...a Mr. Nice Guy like Melcher, **what** is now 46	X
Def.	... **the** case is remarkable for **the** cooperation ...	✓
	... **a** case is remarkable for **a** cooperation ...	X
Coord.	I have also tried monthly data **and** the results are the same.	✓
	Rooms very clean **but** smelled very fresh.	X
EOS	the forehead is gathered in a frown **//** the mouth is slightly parted to reveal the teeth	✓
	the forehead is gathered in a frown the mouth **//** is slightly parted to reveal the teeth	X

NLI				
Prep.	**With** a single jerk the man's head tore free.	→	The man's head tore free **from** a single jerk.	✓
	With a single jerk the man's head tore free.	→	The man's head tore free **without** a single jerk.	X
Negation	This is a common problem.	→	This is **not** an **uncommon** issue we are facing.	✓
	This is **not** a common problem.	→	This is **not** an **uncommon** issue we are facing.	X
Spatial	To reach ... turn **left** up a small alleyway	→	do not turn **right** up the alleyway ...	✓
	To reach ... turn **left** up a small alleyway	→	Turn **right** up the alleyway ...	X
Quant.	**all** taken up yeah	→	There are not still **some** left	✓
	all taken up yeah	→	There are still **some** left	X
Comp.	Today there are **more** than 300,000.	→	Today there are not **less** than 300,000.	✓
	Today there are **more** than 300,000.	→	Today there are **less** than 300,000.	X

Table 1: Examples of sentences and sentence pairs corresponding to each of our probing datasets. The highlighted words are those that are relevant to the phenomena targeted by each set.

- We provide an in-depth exploration into how different pretraining objectives for sentence encoders affect the information encoded by the output representations. We isolate the effects of different pretraining objectives by holding the model architecture constant.

- We study function words, which have been under-studied in previous works on representation learning, but are critical to language understanding.

- We release nine new datasets,[1] quality-controlled by both linguists and non-linguist annotators, to facilitate ongoing work and follow-up analysis.

2 Function Word Probing Tasks

2.1 Approach

We introduce nine new probing tasks aimed at evaluating models' understanding of function words. We focus on function words because although they are key building blocks of composi-

tional meaning and are highly frequent, they have received relatively little attention in the probing literature and in the distributional semantics literature. Each task targets the understanding of a specific type of function word; illustrative examples are given in Table 1. Our expectation is that different pretraining objectives (see Section 3.2) will yield sentence representations which measurably differ in their performance on these probing tasks.

We use two different formats for our probing tasks: acceptability judgment and natural language inference (NLI). The former uses a binary classification approach (acceptable/unacceptable) for probing a single sentence vector, in line with works such as Conneau et al. (2018) and Adi et al. (2017). The latter uses an entailment-based approach similar to White et al. (2017) and Poliak et al. (2018b), which is a ternary classification task (*entailment, contradiction, neutral*) over sentence pairs. The format is selected based on the suitability to the particular function word type in question.

To generate our probing datasets, we make structural modifications to sentences drawn from existing corpora, targeting a particular type of function word. We heuristically apply modifica-

<hr>

[1] The datasets are released as part of the Diverse Natural Language Inference Collection (DNC, Poliak et al., 2018b), available at `http://decomp.io`.

tions which we believe are likely to produce a specific label, and then recruit human annotators in order to produce the final labels used in our evaluations. The result is a publicly available suite of nine task datasets (four acceptability tasks and five NLI tasks) consisting of 3,710 annotated examples. Appendix C lists the sizes of each dataset.

2.2 Acceptability Judgment-Based Tasks

We cast acceptability as a binary classification task following the format of such judgments commonly used in linguistics, in a similar manner to Warstadt et al. (2018). All tasks follow a common protocol of first identifying sentences that contain the construction that we are interested in, and then mutating half of the identified sentences to generate infelicitous versions of the original sentences. Unless stated otherwise, the original sentences are drawn from the test set of the Billion Word Benchmark (BWB, Chelba et al., 2013).

Wh-Words Understanding *wh*-words (i.e., *who, what, where, when, why, how*) depends on understanding the context and correctly identifying the antecedent, which may not be overtly present in the sentence. For instance, recognizing the infelicity of *I talked about who I live* requires knowing that the (unstated) antecedent must be a place and not a person. Our dataset consists of sentences that contain one of the six *wh*-words listed above. Half of these sentences are mutated versions of the original which are generated by replacing the original *wh*-word with a different *wh*-word randomly selected from the remaining five options.

Definite-Indefinite Articles The definiteness task probes the understanding of definiteness that arises by the use of the definite article (*the*) versus indefinite articles (*a* and *an*). We find sentences containing multiple occurrences of *the* or multiple occurrences of *a*, and, for half of them, swap all such occurrences (i.e., replacing *the* with a^2 or vice-versa). This gives us four types of sentences: unchanged sentences with multiple definite articles, unchanged sentences with multiple indefinite articles, sentences with all definite articles replaced by the indefinite article, and sentences with all indefinite articles replaced by the definite article. Our intent is that the former two types will be judged felicitous while the latter two will be infelicitous despite the fact that the sentence would be

syntactically well-formed. We only focus on the cases with multiple occurrences of the same article, because replacing a single article most of the time did not significantly affect the acceptability (although it often did affect the actual meaning).

Coordinating Conjunctions Correct understanding of coordinating conjunctions (*and, but, or*) requires contextual comprehension of the two conjoined linguistic units, since different coordinating conjunctions express different logical relations, meaning their use is often restricted by the meanings of the conjoined items. We take sentences that contain coordinating conjunctions, and replace half of them with a version that contains a different conjunction. For example, the sentence *Room's very clean **but** smelled very fresh* is infelicitous despite being syntactically well-formed; *but* is unnatural here because the conjoined clauses do not form a clear contrast. Judging this sentence to be infelicitous requires a proper understanding of the ideas expressed in the clauses and how they relate to each other.

End-of-Sentence The end-of-sentence (EOS) task tests a model's ability to identify semantically coherent chunks (i.e., sentences) in running text. In written text this is often indicated by punctuation marks such as periods, but humans are able to easily identify sentences even without overt markers. Thus, we take pairs of sentences from the same paragraph of the WikiText-103 (Merity et al., 2017) test set and remove all punctuation marks and capitalization, and concatenate each sentence pair to create a line of running text.[3] Half of the dataset consists of a pair of valid sentences, and the other half consists of a pair of potentially invalid sentences generated from an incorrect segmentation of the running text, where the incorrect segmentation index is obtained by sampling from a Gaussian distribution centered around the correct index ($\sigma = 2$) and rounding to the nearest integer.

2.3 NLI-Based Tasks

Our NLI-based probing tasks ask whether the choice of function word affects the inferences licensed by a sentence. These tasks consist of a pair of sentences—a premise p and a hypothesis h—and ask whether or not p entails h. We exploit the label changes induced by a targeted mutation of

---

[2]When we replace *the* with *a*, we choose *a/an* as necessary based on the word it precedes.

[3]We use WikiText instead of BWB because adjacent sentences in BWB are not logically contiguous and therefore may not be from the same discourse context.

the sentence pairs taken from the Multi-genre Natural Language Inference dataset (MNLI, Williams et al., 2018). The rationale is that, if a change to a single function word in the premise changes the entailment label, that function word must play a significant role in the semantics of the sentence.

Prepositions We manually curate a list of prepositions (see Appendix D) that are likely to be swapped with each other without affecting the grammaticality of the sentence. We generate mutated NLI pairs by finding occurrences of the prepositions in our list and randomly replacing them with other prepositions in the list. Our list consists of a set of locatives[4] and several other manually-selected prepositions that are not strictly locatives but are likely to be substitutable (*about, for, to, with, without*).

Comparatives Comparatives express qualitative or quantitative differences between entities. For instance, a sentence that states *A is more than B* and another that states *B is more than A* lead to different inferences. We select a list of common comparatives (e.g., *more/less, bigger/smaller*) and select pairs from MNLI that contain a comparative phrase in both the premise and the hypothesis. We apply several mutations to the sentences, including negating the premise and/or hypothesis, and swapping comparatives (e.g., replacing *bigger* with *smaller*).[5]

Quantification The quantification task tests the understanding of natural language expressions of quantities, including common quantifiers (*all, some*), number words (*two, twenty*), and proportion (*half, one-third, quarter*). We select NLI pairs that contain at least one quantifier in both the premise and the hypothesis, and apply mutations of negating sentences and/or replacing quantifiers with syntactically appropriate substitutes.

Spatial Expressions The spatial expressions task probes the understanding of words that denote spatial relations between entities. Changing the spatial configuration often leads to different inferences; for instance, *A is to the left of B* implies that *B is to the right of A*, but not that *A is to the right of B*. We select a set of words that

describe spatial configurations which are not necessarily prepositions (e.g., *left, right, close, far*). Again, we find MNLI pairs containing these words and negate/substitute to generate mutated pairs.

Negation This task probes whether models are able to understand negations, in particular explicit negation using the word *not*, lexical negation using antonyms, and the interaction between them. We first identify premise-hypothesis pairs from the MNLI dataset that contain antonym pairs (e.g., *dirty* appears in p and *clean* in h) and generate all possible patterns of negation with the two mutation strategies: swapping antonyms and adding explicit negation. That is, we use each of lexical negation, explicit negation, and their combination to mutate the premise and/or the hypothesis. We generate all 16 possible patterns of negation for a given premise-hypothesis (p, h) pair. For each of p and h we can either apply or not apply each of four possible mutations: lexical negation, explicit negation, both, and none.

2.4 Annotation

We recruit human annotators on Amazon Mechanical Turk to produce the final labels for the heuristically-generated datasets described above. We collect three labels per sentence (or per pair of sentences for EOS and NLI probing sets). We use the majority label in our final dataset, and discard examples on which there is no majority consensus. For more details about our annotation protocol, including compensation, refer to Appendix C.

Acceptability Tasks Human annotators are presented with a single (mutated or unmutated) sentence and are given the options {*natural, unnatural, neither*}. We discard sentences in which the majority label does not agree with our expected label. That is, we only include mutated sentences with a majority label of *unnatural* and unmutated sentences with a majority label of *natural*. We collect around 500 annotated examples with balanced label ratio for each probing set. We release our sentences in small batches until we have approximately 250 *unnatural* examples per task. To create the final dataset, we pool all answers from all batches and take a subset of the *natural* sentences so that the label ratio is balanced, prioritizing examples with perfect inter-annotator agreement.

Natural Language Inference Tasks For the NLI tasks, we collect common-sense entailment

---

[4]Locative prepositions are those that denote place or position: e.g., *in, on, near*, etc.

[5]We note that Dasgupta et al. (2018) also focus on comparatives, but they exclusively look at artificial sentences containing *more/less*.

judgments from annotators on a 5-point Likert scale on which 1 denotes 'definitely contradiction' and 5 denotes 'definitely entailment', following Zhang et al. (2017). This finer-grained scale is intended to avoid confounds arising from borderline cases. Except for the use of scaled judgments, our instructions follow the MNLI guidelines. Specifically, our instructions said to assume that the sentences co-refer and that the first sentence (p) states a true fact, describes a scenario, or expresses an opinion, and to then indicate how likely it is that the second sentence (h) is also true, describes the same scenario, or expresses the same opinion.

Annotators could also select an option indicating that one or both of the sentences did not make sense; we discarded (p, h) pairs for which at least one annotator chose this option. We map judgments of 5 and 4 to *entailment*, 3 to *neutral*, and 2 and 1 to *contradiction*, and treat the majority label as the correct label after this mapping.

Agreement and Quality Control In constructing our final evaluation sets, we removed examples on which there was no majority consensus. For the binary acceptability tasks, we manually prefiltered sentences that were felicitous even after the heuristic modification. For the NLI tasks, we removed pairs that contained ungrammatical sentences that were not flagged by annotators via manual postfiltering. See Appendix C for more details.

3 Experimental Design

3.1 Pretraining Architecture

Since our focus is on comparing differences in pretraining objectives, we fix the architecture for all sentence encoders. We use the pretrained character-level convolutional neural network (CNN) from ELMo (Peters et al., 2018) that replaces word embeddings (see Bowman et al. (2018) or Tenney et al. (2019) for similar usages of the CNN layer). This acts as a base input layer that uses no information beyond the word, and allows us to avoid potentially difficult issues surrounding unknown word handling in transfer learning.

We feed the word representations to a 2-layer 1024d bidirectional LSTM (Hochreiter and Schmidhuber, 1997). A downstream task-specific model sees both the top-layer hidden states of this model and, through a skip connection, the original representation of each word. We train a version of this model on each task in Section 3.2. Ad-

ditional experimental details are in given in Appendix A. Our codebase is open-source[6] and built using AllenNLP (Gardner et al., 2017) and PyTorch (Paszke et al., 2017).

Classification Tasks For classification pretraining tasks (NLI, DisSent), we use an attention mechanism inspired by BiDAF (Seo et al., 2017). Given the sequence of output states of the core BiLSTM for both sentences in an example, we compute dot-product based attention between all pairs of words between the sentences to form a sequence of attention-contextualized word representations. We use an additional BiLSTM followed by max-pooling to obtain an attention-contextualized vector representation of each sentence h_1 and h_2. We use the *heuristic matching* feature vector $[h_1; h_2; h_1 \cdot h_2; |h_1 - h_2|]$ (Mou et al., 2016) as input to an MLP.

Sequence-to-Sequence Tasks For sequence-to-sequence pretraining tasks (machine translation and skip-thought), we use a single-layer 1024d LSTM as the decoder, initialized with the max-pooled output of the encoder. We use a linear projection bottleneck layer to reduce the dimension of the output of the decoder by half before the output softmax layer.

3.2 Pretraining Tasks

Our main experiments compare seven pretraining tasks which we believe capture different aspects of linguistic meaning and which yield reasonable performance when used on a benchmark task such as MNLI.[7] For our purposes, a *task* is a dataset-training objective pair. We attempt to select a set of tasks diverse enough to highlight performance differences due to pretraining objectives. We additionally report results using BERT (Devlin et al., 2019) (base, uncased) to demonstrate that our probing sets prove challenging even for state-of-the-art models.

Language Modeling We train a left-to-right word-level language model on BWB, which was successfully used by Peters et al. (2018) for pretraining sentence encoders. Because language modeling is trivial for a bidirectional LSTM, we follow Peters et al. (2018) by training separate forward and backward two-layer 1024d language

---

[6]`https://github.com/`
`jsalt18-sentence-repl/jiant`

[7]Around 70% development set accuracy; see Appendix B.

models and concatenate their hidden states as token representations.

Skip-Thought　Drawing from Kiros et al. (2015) and Tang et al. (2017), we train a sequence-to-sequence model on skip-thought, which is a task of generating the next sentence in the discourse given the previous sentence. We use the learned encoder as our sentence encoder. Since this objective requires running text, we use sentences from WikiText-103 as training data.

CCG Supertagging　We train a model to predict the Combinatory Categorial Grammar (CCG) supertag for each word, with sentences from CCG-Bank (Hockenmaier and Steedman, 2007). Supertags are similar to part-of-speech tags but capture more syntactic context ("almost-parsing"; Bangalore and Joshi, 1999).

Discourse (DisSent)　We train a model on DisSent (Jernite et al., 2017; Nie et al., 2017), which is an unsupervised task of predicting the discourse marker (e.g., *and*, *because*, or *so*) that connects two clauses. We train our model on a dataset created from WikiText-103 following Nie et al. (2017)'s protocol, which involves extracting pairs of clauses with a specific dependency relation.

Natural Language Inference　Inspired by Conneau et al. (2017), we use the MNLI dataset for NLI pretraining. The task is to predict the entailment label for premise-hypothesis pairs; the possible labels are *entailment, contradiction, neutral*.

Machine Translation　We train a sequence-to-sequence machine translation model with attention on WMT14 English-German (Bojar et al., 2014) and take the encoder as our sentence encoder. McCann et al. (2017) previously showed that pretraining an encoder on translation led to good performance on downstream NLP tasks.

Image-Caption Matching　We train a model on the task of grounding sentences to the images they describe. We use image-caption pairs from the MSCOCO dataset (Lin et al., 2014) with an objective that minimizes the cosine distance between sentence representations and corresponding image features, as described in Kiela et al. (2018).

3.3　Classifiers for Probing Tasks

To probe the sentence encoders pretrained on the different objectives, we freeze the weights of the encoder after pretraining and train an additional model using the outputs of the fixed encoder as inputs. We describe the implementation details for the NLI and acceptability probing sets below.

NLI Tasks　For NLI-type probing, we train an NLI model on top of the representations produced by the pretrained sentence encoder that uses an attention mechanism inspired by Seo et al. (2017) that computes attention between all pairs of words in the two sentences (described in more detail in Section 3.1). We train this component on MNLI and evaluate directly on our NLI probing datasets with no further dataset-specific training.

Acceptability Classification Tasks　For all acceptability tasks except the EOS task, we take the sequence of hidden state outputs from the pretrained encoder as the sentence representation. We aggregate this sequence into a single vector via max-pooling and train a 512d MLP on top of the resulting vector. For the EOS task, we also use max-pooling on each sentence in the pair. We then concatenate the resulting vectors and train an MLP on top of the joint representation.[8] Each task has around 400 training examples (see Appendix C). Due to their small size, we use 10-fold cross validation where each fold is used as the test set exactly once, and report the average test set accuracy.

BERT　For NLI-type probing tasks, we use the fine-tuned MNLI classifier from (Devlin et al., 2019)[9]. For the acceptability classification tasks, we fine-tune the model by adding a sequence-level classifier on top of the pretrained BERT model. The sequence-level classifier is a linear layer that takes in as input the final hidden vector corresponding to the first input token as aggregate representation in the input sequence, and then classifies to the required number of classes for the task, where the label probabilities are computed with a standard softmax. The BERT fine-tuning setup allows a classification output to be indicated with a CLS token. Pairs of sequences are indicated with a SEP token between the pairs. All parameters are fine-tuned jointly to maximize the log-probability

---

[8]We tried training a general acceptability model using CoLA and evaluating directly on our acceptability tasks, as an analogous evaluation setup to the NLI tasks, but all models performed around chance under this setup. This is likely due to the intrinsic difficulty of CoLA for our base model, as suggested by low performance from similar models ("GLUE Baselines") on `https://gluebenchmark.com`.

[9]`https://github.com/google-research/bert`

of the correct label while the hyperparameters are the same as in pretraining.

3.4 Variation from Random Restarts

In order to calibrate the degree of variation that can be expected due to random restarts, we run each of our probing tasks on five different random initializations of the sentence encoder weights. These sentence encoders were not pretrained, and we trained MLPs for each probing task on top of the randomly initialized sentence encoders. The expectation is that if pretraining has measurable effects on the probing results, the variance across different pretrained models would be greater than the variance across random restart models. Across five random restarts, the average standard deviation across our probing set was around 1 percentage point. The mean and 95% confidence interval for each probing task are reported in Appendix E.

4 Results

4.1 Overall Performance

Figure 1 shows the performances of models trained on each pretraining task on our probing datasets. We also provide comparison with a randomly initialized encoder with no pretraining, which is known to be a strong baseline (Bowman et al., 2018). We observe that different pretraining tasks have different strengths and weaknesses; there is no single pretraining task that achieves the best (or worst) performance across the board. This implies that even the best encoders, such as BERT, are unable to capture function word semantics fully, and suggests further research into combining advantages of different tasks. Furthermore, most models are far from human performance, with only a few exceptions (e.g., BERT on conjunctions). This demonstrates that our probing datasets serve as useful challenge sets, in addition to permitting fine-grained analysis.

Looking into each probing set in more detail, we see several intuitive patterns on how pretraining might affect probing performance. Among the pretrained models (not including BERT), the NLI model did best on the negation[10] and conjunction tasks, both of which involve words that play central roles in inferential reasoning. The CCG model

yields the best result for EOS, which could be attributed to the task's emphasis on structure; it is the only task that where the target labels directly represent compositional structure.

Surprisingly, we find that pretraining can sometimes hurt performance. For instance, pretraining uniformly hurts performance on comparatives with the exception of skip-thought, which is still within random variation range. In fact, for many probing sets, the choice of pretraining task affects whether it helps or hurts performance; for instance, pretraining on NLI helps with negation, whereas pretraining on image-caption matching and CCG lowers performance. This suggests that pretraining can be helpful, but *only* helpful if we pretrain on a task that provides useful information in solving the probing set. For instance, in Section 4.3 we discuss how the image-caption matching objective may bias models to discard information about certain preposition senses. Overall, we observe that language modeling is a useful pretraining task, which aligns with its effectiveness for pretraining models that achieve state-of-the-art NLP results. However, the most beneficial task on average (in terms of both raw accuracy and gains over random baseline) is CCG, our most syntactic task, which suggests that syntactic knowledge is important for function word comprehension. We also note that CCG achieves this result with the smallest number of training examples out of all pretraining tasks compared.

We furthermore see that our probing sets are challenging even for BERT—although BERT substantially improves performance on many probing sets, and obtains superhuman performance on conjunctions and EOS,[11] it also shows clear weaknesses in several probing sets (e.g., *wh*-words and prepositions) where it is outperformed even by a randomly initialized baseline with no pretraining.

4.2 Correlations between Pretaining Tasks

To further investigate whether our probing sets differentiate between pretraining objectives, we look into correlations between the model predictions; given two pretraining tasks i and j, how often does a model trained on i make the exact same prediction as a model trained on j? Figure 2 shows the correlations across all probing sets in aggregate, and for the *wh*-words and prepositions sets specif-

---

[10] We additionally find that this improvement is specifically due to the NLI model's capacity to understand explicit negation using *not*, rather than lexical negation with antonymy. See Appendix F for differences between negation subtypes.

[11] We speculate that this might be an effect of the next-sentence classification task that BERT is pretrained on.

	majority	rand	ccg 38K	dis 151K	nli 393K	img 592K	skip 4M	mt 3.4M	lm 30.3M	bert	human
whwords	0.50	0.51	0.63	0.53	0.55	0.52	0.54	0.55	0.67	0.50	0.86
spatial	0.46	0.29	0.35	0.25	0.23	0.37	0.38	0.29	0.29	0.47	0.85
quant	0.48	0.19	0.22	0.19	0.18	0.21	0.25	0.19	0.22	0.48	0.87
prep	0.38	0.46	0.45	0.47	0.50	0.41	0.42	0.47	0.45	0.34	0.77
neg	0.40	0.55	0.49	0.56	0.59	0.49	0.50	0.54	0.52	0.64	0.80
eos	0.50	0.51	0.82	0.59	0.62	0.70	0.61	0.68	0.71	0.90	0.82
def	0.50	0.59	0.66	0.60	0.61	0.62	0.59	0.61	0.72	0.52	0.86
conj	0.50	0.53	0.61	0.63	0.68	0.55	0.57	0.59	0.63	0.97	0.86
comp	0.49	0.34	0.32	0.28	0.30	0.28	0.35	0.29	0.28	0.49	0.84
all	0.47	0.44	0.51	0.46	0.47	0.46	0.47	0.47	0.50	0.59	0.84

Figure 1: Accuracy for each pretraining task on each probing set. The leftmost column shows the majority-class baseline, and the rightmost column shows individual annotator accuracy on the final probing set. Blue denotes performance improvement over randomly initialized encoder baseline and orange denotes performance decrease.

Overall

	rand	dis	lm	mt	nli	ccg	skip	img
rand	1.00	0.79	0.73	0.74	0.73	0.69	0.66	0.66
dis	0.79	1.00	0.76	0.75	0.75	0.72	0.67	0.65
lm	0.73	0.76	1.00	0.75	0.71	0.75	0.69	0.66
mt	0.74	0.75	0.75	1.00	0.73	0.71	0.66	0.66
nli	0.73	0.75	0.71	0.73	1.00	0.68	0.62	0.62
ccg	0.69	0.72	0.75	0.71	0.68	1.00	0.69	0.69
skip	0.66	0.67	0.69	0.66	0.62	0.69	1.00	0.66
img	0.66	0.65	0.66	0.66	0.62	0.69	0.66	1.00

Prepositions

	rand	dis	lm	mt	nli	ccg	skip	img
rand	1.00	0.82	0.74	0.80	0.79	0.74	0.74	0.50
dis	0.82	1.00	0.74	0.79	0.78	0.71	0.74	0.48
lm	0.74	0.74	1.00	0.76	0.74	0.74	0.70	0.49
mt	0.80	0.79	0.76	1.00	0.76	0.74	0.71	0.50
nli	0.79	0.78	0.74	0.76	1.00	0.69	0.67	0.43
ccg	0.74	0.71	0.74	0.74	0.69	1.00	0.71	0.52
skip	0.74	0.74	0.70	0.71	0.67	0.71	1.00	0.48
img	0.50	0.48	0.49	0.50	0.43	0.52	0.48	1.00

Wh-Words

	rand	dis	lm	mt	nli	ccg	skip	img
rand	1.00	0.74	0.59	0.65	0.75	0.62	0.60	0.66
dis	0.74	1.00	0.64	0.66	0.76	0.64	0.58	0.65
lm	0.59	0.64	1.00	0.63	0.64	0.68	0.57	0.57
mt	0.65	0.66	0.63	1.00	0.66	0.62	0.57	0.61
nli	0.75	0.76	0.64	0.66	1.00	0.63	0.61	0.67
ccg	0.62	0.64	0.68	0.62	0.63	1.00	0.56	0.59
skip	0.60	0.58	0.57	0.57	0.61	0.56	1.00	0.62
img	0.66	0.65	0.57	0.61	0.67	0.59	0.62	1.00

Figure 2: Prediction overlap on the probing tasks for models trained on different pretraining tasks (i.e., how often models make identical predictions on a particular probing set).

ically (see Appendix G for all sets).

We observe that models pretrained on different tasks do make different predictions overall, with image-caption matching and skip-thought being the tasks that make predictions that deviate the most from others (left). NLI and image-caption matching are the least correlated pair of tasks among all. The difference between image-captioning and other tasks is the most prominent in the preposition probing set; it makes predictions that are only weakly correlated with others (middle). We hypothesize that this is due to the duality of preposition semantics; most prepositions have both concrete and abstract senses, and the image model is biased to focus on the former.

To illustrate, consider the preposition *below*, which can denote a spatial configuration (e.g., *the boots end below the knee*) or an abstract relation (numeric or qualitative comparison; e.g., *her score is below sixty*). In the preposition dataset, *below* occurs 17 times, 11 of which are spatial and 6 abstract. For the spatial usage, both MNLI and image-caption models have 64% accuracy (7/11). The NLI model shows 50% accuracy for pairs containing abstract uses (3/6), but the image-captioning model answers none of them correctly (0/6). Here is an example of a numeric usage of *below* that the NLI model answered correctly but the image model answered incorrectly:

P: *Only those whose incomes do not exceed 125 percent of the federal poverty level qualify . . .*

H: *Those whose incomes are **below** 125 percent qualify . . .* (P→H)

The image model's bias towards the spatial usage is intuitive, since the numeric usage of *below* (i.e., as a counterpart to *exceed*) is difficult to learn from visual clues only. This concrete-abstract duality, which is not specific to *below* but common to most other prepositions (Schneider et al., 2018), may partially explain why the image-caption model behaves so differently from all other models, which are not trained on a multimodal objective.

4.3 Data Size and Genre Effects

As can be seen from the varying sizes of the pretraining dataset reported in Figure 1, seeing more data at pretrain time does not imply better performance on probing tasks. Also, as noted before, the fact that pretraining can hurt probing performance suggests that if the task is not the "right" task, adding more datapoints at pretrain time is not necessarily beneficial for probing performance.

Another potential confound is vocabulary overlap between pretraining and probing task datasets. Since all pretraining task datasets have different sets of vocabulary, the variance in the results could be attributed to the amount of words in the probing set already seen at pretrain time. To investigate this possibility, we compute the ratio of overlapping words between the pretraining and probing datasets. A regression analysis shows that vocabulary overlap overall does not predict better performance on the probing set ($p > .05$). No single probing set performance was significantly affected by vocabulary overlap either (all $p > .05$ after Bonferroni correction for multiple comparisons).

5 Related Work

An active line of work focuses on "probing" neural representations of language. Ettinger et al. (2016, 2017); Zhu et al. (2018), *i.a.,* use a task-based approach similar to ours, where tasks that require a specific subset of linguistic knowledge are used to perform qualitative evaluation. Gulordava et al. (2018), Giulianelli et al. (2018), Rønning et al. (2018), and Jumelet and Hupkes (2018) make a focused contribution towards a particular linguistic phenomenon (agreement, ellipsis, negative polarity). Using recast NLI, Poliak et al. (2018a) probe for semantic phenomena in neural machine translation encoders. Staliūnaite and Bonfil (2017); Mahler et al. (2017); Ribeiro et al. (2018) use similar strategies to our structural mutation method, although their primary goal was to break existing systems by adversarial modifications rather than to compare different models. Ribeiro et al. (2018) and our work both test for proper comprehension of the modified expressions, but our modifications are designed to induce semantic changes whereas their modifications are intended to preserve the original meaning. Our strategy is close to that of Naik et al. (2018), but our modifications are more constrained and lexically targeted.

The design of our NLI-style probing tasks follows the recent line of work which advocates for NLI as a general-purpose format for diagnostic tasks (White et al., 2017; Poliak et al., 2018b). This idea is similar in spirit to McCann et al. (2018), which advocates for question answering as a general-purpose format, to edge probing (Tenney et al., 2019) which probes for syntactic and semantic structures via a common labeling format, and to GLUE (Wang et al., 2018) which aggregates a variety of tasks that share a common sentence-classification format. The primary difference in our work is that we focus specifically on the understanding of function words in context. We also present a suite of several tasks, but each one focuses on a particular structure, whereas tasks proposed in the works above generally aggregate multiple phenomena. Each of our tasks isolates each function word type and employ a targeted modification strategy that gives us a more narrowly-focused, informative scope of analysis.

6 Conclusion

We propose a new challenge set of nine tasks that focus on probing function word comprehension. Although we use our challenge set to compare the effects of pretraining, the probing sets themselves are architecture- and evaluation setup-agnostic. The results show that models pretrained with different objectives do generate different predictions (e.g., image models have a bias towards concrete preposition senses), and that no single objective leads to models that perform best or worst across all probing tasks. This suggests that there are 'gaps' in the linguistic knowledge learned from a single pretraining objective that could be complemented by other objectives, and this calls for further research into how different pretraining objectives could be productively combined. On average, CCG supertagging—our most syntactic task—is the most beneficial pretraining task for function word comprehension, even more so than language modeling which has achieved state-of-the-art results in recent advances in NLP. In addition to contributing to the discussion of finding effective pretraining tasks, we hope that our exploratory study initiates further discussions about modeling function words and their contribution to compositional meaning.

Acknowledgments

The work was conducted at the 2018 Frederick Jelinek Memorial Summer Workshop on Speech and Language Technologies, and supported by Johns Hopkins University with unrestricted gifts from Amazon, Facebook, Google, Microsoft and Mitsubishi Electric Research Laboratories.

References

Yossi Adi, Einat Kermany, Yonatan Belinkov, Ofer Lavi, and Yoav Goldberg. 2017. Fine-grained analysis of sentence embeddings using auxiliary prediction tasks. In *International Conference on Learning Representations*.

Srinivas Bangalore and Aravind K Joshi. 1999. Supertagging: An approach to almost parsing. *Computational Linguistics*, 25(2):237–265.

Raffaella Bernardi, Gemma Boleda, Raquel Fernandez, and Denis Paperno. 2015. Distributional semantics in use. In *Proceedings of the First Workshop on Linking Computational Models of Lexical, Sentential and Discourse-level Semantics*, pages 95–101, Lisbon, Portugal. Association for Computational Linguistics.

Ondrej Bojar, Christian Buck, Christian Federmann, Barry Haddow, Philipp Koehn, Johannes Leveling, Christof Monz, Pavel Pecina, Matt Post, Herve Saint-Amand, Radu Soricut, Lucia Specia, and Aleš Tamchyna. 2014. Findings of the 2014 workshop on statistical machine translation. In *Proceedings of the Ninth Workshop on Statistical Machine Translation*, pages 12–58, Baltimore, Maryland, USA. Association for Computational Linguistics.

Samuel Bowman, Yoav Goldberg, Felix Hill, Angeliki Lazaridou, Omer Levy, Roi Reichart, and Anders Sgaard, editors. 2017. *Proceedings of the 2nd Workshop on Evaluating Vector Space Representations for NLP*. Association for Computational Linguistics, Copenhagen, Denmark.

Samuel R. Bowman, Ellie Pavlick, Edouard Grave, Benjamin Van Durme, Alex Wang, Jan Hula, Patrick Xia, Raghavendra Pappagari, R. Thomas McCoy, Roma Patel, Najoung Kim, Ian Tenney, Yinghui Huang, Katherin Yu, Shuning Jin, and Berlin Chen. 2018. Looking for ELMo's friends: Sentence-level pretraining beyond language modeling. *CoRR*, abs/1812.10860.

Ciprian Chelba, Tomas Mikolov, Mike Schuster, Qi Ge, Thorsten Brants, Phillipp Koehn, and Tony Robinson. 2013. One billion word benchmark for measuring progress in statistical language modeling. *arXiv:1312.3005*.

Alexis Conneau, Douwe Kiela, Holger Schwenk, Loïc Barrault, and Antoine Bordes. 2017. Supervised learning of universal sentence representations from natural language inference data. In *Proceedings of the 2017 Conference on Empirical Methods in Natural Language Processing*, pages 670–680.

Alexis Conneau, Germán Kruszewski, Guillaume Lample, Loïc Barrault, and Marco Baroni. 2018. What you can cram into a single $&!#* vector: Probing sentence embeddings for linguistic properties. In *Proceedings of the 56th Annual Meeting of the Association for Computational Linguistics (Volume 1: Long Papers)*, pages 2126–2136. Association for Computational Linguistics.

Ishita Dasgupta, Demi Guo, Andreas Stuhlmüller, Samuel J Gershman, and Noah D Goodman. 2018. Evaluating compositionality in sentence embeddings. *arXiv:1802.04302*.

Jacob Devlin, Ming-Wei Chang, Kenton Lee, and Kristina Toutanova. 2019. BERT: Pre-training of deep bidirectional transformers for language understanding. In *Proceedings of the 2019 Conference of the North American Chapter of the Association for Computational Linguistics: Human Language Technologies, Volume 1 (Long Papers)*.

Allyson Ettinger, Ahmed Elgohary, and Philip Resnik. 2016. Probing for semantic evidence of composition by means of simple classification tasks. In *Proceedings of the 1st Workshop on Evaluating Vector-Space Representations for NLP*, pages 134–139. Association for Computational Linguistics.

Allyson Ettinger, Sudha Rao, Hal Daumé III, and Emily M. Bender. 2017. Towards linguistically generalizable NLP systems: A workshop and shared task. In *Proceedings of the First Workshop on Building Linguistically Generalizable NLP Systems*, pages 1–10, Copenhagen, Denmark. Association for Computational Linguistics.

Matt Gardner, Joel Grus, Mark Neumann, Oyvind Tafjord, Pradeep Dasigi, Nelson F. Liu, Matthew Peters, Michael Schmitz, and Luke S. Zettlemoyer. 2017. AllenNLP: A deep semantic natural language processing platform.

Mario Giulianelli, Jack Harding, Florian Mohnert, Dieuwke Hupkes, and Willem Zuidema. 2018. Under the hood: Using diagnostic classifiers to investigate and improve how language models track agreement information. In *Proceedings of the 2018 EMNLP Workshop BlackboxNLP: Analyzing and Interpreting Neural Networks for NLP*, pages 240–248, Brussels, Belgium. Association for Computational Linguistics.

Kristina Gulordava, Piotr Bojanowski, Edouard Grave, Tal Linzen, and Marco Baroni. 2018. Colorless green recurrent networks dream hierarchically. In *Proceedings of the 2018 Conference of the North American Chapter of the Association for Computational Linguistics: Human Language Technologies, Volume 1 (Long Papers)*, pages 1195–1205, New Orleans, Louisiana. Association for Computational Linguistics.

Kaiming He, Xiangyu Zhang, Shaoqing Ren, and Jian Sun. 2016. Deep residual learning for image recognition. In *Proceedings of the IEEE conference on Computer Vision and Pattern Recognition*, pages 770–778.

Sepp Hochreiter and Jürgen Schmidhuber. 1997. Long short-term memory. *Neural Computation*, 9(8):1735–1780.

Julia Hockenmaier and Mark Steedman. 2007. Ccg-bank: A corpus of ccg derivations and dependency structures extracted from the penn treebank. *Computational Linguistics*, 33(3).

Yacine Jernite, Samuel R. Bowman, and David Sontag. 2017. Discourse-based objectives for fast unsupervised sentence representation learning. *arXiv:1705.00557*.

Jaap Jumelet and Dieuwke Hupkes. 2018. Do language models understand anything? O n the ability of lstms to understand negative polarity items. In *Proceedings of the 2018 EMNLP Workshop BlackboxNLP: Analyzing and Interpreting Neural Networks for NLP*, pages 222–231, Brussels, Belgium. Association for Computational Linguistics.

Douwe Kiela, Alexis Conneau, Allan Jabri, and Maximilian Nickel. 2018. Learning visually grounded sentence representations. In *Proceedings of the 2018 Conference of the North American Chapter of the Association for Computational Linguistics: Human Language Technologies, Volume 1 (Long Papers)*, pages 408–418, New Orleans, Louisiana. Association for Computational Linguistics.

Ryan Kiros, Yukun Zhu, Ruslan R Salakhutdinov, Richard Zemel, Raquel Urtasun, Antonio Torralba, and Sanja Fidler. 2015. Skip-thought vectors. In *Advances in Neural Information Processing Systems*, pages 3294–3302.

Tsung-Yi Lin, Michael Maire, Serge Belongie, James Hays, Pietro Perona, Deva Ramanan, Piotr Dollár, and C Lawrence Zitnick. 2014. Microsoft coco: Common objects in context. In *European Conference on Computer Vision*, pages 740–755. Springer.

Tal Linzen, Grzegorz Chrupala, and Afra Alishahi, editors. 2018. *Proceedings of the First Workshop on Analyzing and Interpreting Neural Networks for NLP (BlackboxNLP)*. Association for Computational Linguistics, Brussels, Belgium.

Taylor Mahler, Willy Cheung, Micha Elsner, David King, Marie-Catherine de Marneffe, Cory Shain, Symon Stevens-Guille, and Michael White. 2017. Breaking NLP: Using morphosyntax, semantics, pragmatics and world knowledge to fool sentiment analysis systems. In *Proceedings of the First Workshop on Building Linguistically Generalizable NLP Systems*, pages 33–39. Association for Computational Linguistics.

Bryan McCann, James Bradbury, Caiming Xiong, and Richard Socher. 2017. Learned in translation: Contextualized word vectors. In *Advances in Neural Information Processing Systems*, pages 6297–6308.

Bryan McCann, Nitish Shirish Keskar, Caiming Xiong, and Richard Socher. 2018. The natural language decathlon: Multitask learning as question answering. *arXiv:1806.08730*.

Stephen Merity, Caiming Xiong, James Bradbury, and Richard Socher. 2017. Pointer sentinel mixture models. In *International Conference on Learning Representations*.

Lili Mou, Rui Men, Ge Li, Yan Xu, Lu Zhang, Rui Yan, and Zhi Jin. 2016. Natural language inference by tree-based convolution and heuristic matching. In *Proceedings of the 54th Annual Meeting of the Association for Computational Linguistics (Volume 2: Short Papers)*, pages 130–136, Berlin, Germany. Association for Computational Linguistics.

Aakanksha Naik, Abhilasha Ravichander, Norman Sadeh, Carolyn Rose, and Graham Neubig. 2018. Stress test evaluation for natural language inference. In *Proceedings of the 27th International Conference on Computational Linguistics*, pages 2340–2353.

Allen Nie, Erin D. Bennett, and Noah D. Goodman. 2017. DisSent: Sentence representation learning from explicit discourse relations. *arXiv:1710.04334*.

Adam Paszke, Sam Gross, Soumith Chintala, Gregory Chanan, Edward Yang, Zachary DeVito, Zeming Lin, Alban Desmaison, Luca Antiga, and Adam Lerer. 2017. Automatic differentiation in pytorch. *NIPS 2017 Autodiff Workshop*.

Matthew Peters, Mark Neumann, Mohit Iyyer, Matt Gardner, Christopher Clark, Kenton Lee, and Luke Zettlemoyer. 2018. Deep contextualized word representations. In *Proceedings of the 2018 Conference of the North American Chapter of the Association for Computational Linguistics: Human Language Technologies, Volume 1 (Long Papers)*, pages 2227–2237. Association for Computational Linguistics.

Adam Poliak, Yonatan Belinkov, James Glass, and Benjamin Van Durme. 2018a. On the evaluation of semantic phenomena in neural machine translation using natural language inference. In *Proceedings of the 2018 Conference of the North American Chapter of the Association for Computational Linguistics: Human Language Technologies, Volume 2 (Short Papers)*, pages 513–523, New Orleans, Louisiana. Association for Computational Linguistics.

Adam Poliak, Aparajita Haldar, Rachel Rudinger, J. Edward Hu, Ellie Pavlick, Aaron Steven White, and Benjamin Van Durme. 2018b. Collecting diverse natural language inference problems for sentence representation evaluation. In *Proceedings of the 2018 Conference on Empirical Methods in Natural Language Processing*, pages 67–81. Association for Computational Linguistics.

Sashank J. Reddi, Satyen Kale, and Sanjiv Kumar. 2018. On the convergence of Adam and beyond. In *International Conference on Learning Representations*.

Marco Tulio Ribeiro, Sameer Singh, and Carlos Guestrin. 2018. Semantically equivalent adversarial rules for debugging nlp models. In *Proceedings of the 56th Annual Meeting of the Association for Computational Linguistics (Volume 1: Long Papers)*, pages 856–865. Association for Computational Linguistics.

Ola Rønning, Daniel Hardt, and Anders Søgaard. 2018. Linguistic representations in multi-task neural networks for ellipsis resolution. In *Proceedings of the 2018 EMNLP Workshop BlackboxNLP: Analyzing and Interpreting Neural Networks for NLP*, pages 66–73. Association for Computational Linguistics.

Nathan Schneider, Jena D. Hwang, Vivek Srikumar, Jakob Prange, Austin Blodgett, Sarah R. Moeller, Aviram Stern, Adi Bitan, and Omri Abend. 2018. Comprehensive supersense disambiguation of english prepositions and possessives. In *Proceedings of the 56th Annual Meeting of the Association for Computational Linguistics (Volume 1: Long Papers)*, pages 185–196. Association for Computational Linguistics.

Min Joon Seo, Aniruddha Kembhavi, Ali Farhadi, and Hannaneh Hajishirzi. 2017. Bidirectional attention flow for machine comprehension. *International Conference on Learning Representations*.

Ieva Staliūnaite and Ben Bonfil. 2017. Breaking sentiment analysis of movie reviews. In *Proceedings of the First Workshop on Building Linguistically Generalizable NLP Systems*, pages 61–64. Association for Computational Linguistics.

Shuai Tang, Hailin Jin, Chen Fang, Zhaowen Wang, and Virginia de Sa. 2017. Rethinking skip-thought: A neighborhood based approach. In *Proceedings of the 2nd Workshop on Representation Learning for NLP*, pages 211–218. Association for Computational Linguistics.

Ian Tenney, Patrick Xia, Berlin Chen, Alex Wang, Adam Poliak, R Thomas McCoy, Najoung Kim, Benjamin Van Durme, Sam Bowman, Dipanjan Das, and Ellie Pavlick. 2019. What do you learn from context? probing for sentence structure in contextualized word representations. In *International Conference on Learning Representations*.

Alex Wang, Amapreet Singh, Julian Michael, Felix Hill, Omer Levy, and Samuel R Bowman. 2018. GLUE: A multi-task benchmark and analysis platform for natural language understanding. *arXiv:1804.07461*.

Alex Warstadt, Amanpreet Singh, and Samuel R Bowman. 2018. Neural network acceptability judgments. *arXiv:1805.12471*.

Aaron Steven White, Pushpendre Rastogi, Kevin Duh, and Benjamin Van Durme. 2017. Inference is everything: Recasting semantic resources into a unified evaluation framework. In *Proceedings of the*

Eighth International Joint Conference on Natural Language Processing (Volume 1: Long Papers), pages 996–1005. Asian Federation of Natural Language Processing.

Adina Williams, Nikita Nangia, and Samuel Bowman. 2018. A broad-coverage challenge corpus for sentence understanding through inference. In *Proceedings of the 2018 Conference of the North American Chapter of the Association for Computational Linguistics: Human Language Technologies, Volume 1 (Long Papers)*, pages 1112–1122. Association for Computational Linguistics.

Sheng Zhang, Rachel Rudinger, Kevin Duh, and Benjamin Van Durme. 2017. Ordinal common-sense inference. *Transactions of the Association of Computational Linguistics*, 5(1):379–395.

Xunjie Zhu, Tingfeng Li, and Gerard de Melo. 2018. Exploring semantic properties of sentence embeddings. In *Proceedings of the 56th Annual Meeting of the Association for Computational Linguistics (Volume 2: Short Papers)*, pages 632–637, Melbourne, Australia. Association for Computational Linguistics.

Appendix

A Experimental Details

Image-Caption Matching We train on image-caption pairs from the MSCOCO dataset (Lin et al., 2014) to minimize the cosine distance between representations of the sentence and corresponding image. Specifically, we encode the sentence with the BiLSTM encoder. We use a Resnet-101 (He et al., 2016), a CNN pretrained on ImageNet to obtain a 1024-dimensional feature representation for the image. We linearly transform the encoder output of the sentence to the size of the image representation and use a cosine embedding loss against the two vectors, i.e., minimize the cosine distance between two representations to allow mapping sentences to their corresponding images.

Regularization We regularize with dropout with $p = 0.2$. Dropout is placed after the input layer, each LSTM layer, and each MLP layer in the task-specific classifier.

Preprocessing We use Moses tokenizer with a maximum sequence length of 40 tokens. Because we used a character-based word encoder, we have no word-level vocabulary, except for sequence-to-sequence tasks, where we use an output vocabulary of 20,000 tokens. For translation, we use BPE tokenization; for skip-thought we use the Moses tokenizer.

Training Details We optimize using AMSGrad (Reddi et al., 2018) with a learning rate of 1e-3 for text generation tasks and 1e-4 otherwise. We evaluate on the validation set every 1,000 iterations and stop training if we fail to get a best result after 20 evaluations. We multiply the learning rate by 0.5 whenever validation performance fails to improve for more than 4 validation checks. We also stop training if the learning rate falls below 1e-6. At the end of training, we load the best checkpoint.

Acceptability task evaluation For the acceptability tasks, we use a 10-fold cross-validation evaluation setup because we are training task-specific classifiers for each probing task and the datasets are small. We split each dataset into 10 folds with balanced label ratio within each fold, and test on each fold using the other 9 as train and development sets (8 folds train, 1 fold dev). The accuracy reported in the paper for the acceptability tasks is test accuracy averaged across all folds.

B MNLI Development Set Accuracy for Pretrained Models

	MNLI (dev)
Random	73.8
CCG	69.6
DisSent	73.6
MNLI	75.6
IMG	62.6
Skip	67.4
MT	72.0
LM	72.6

Table 2: MNLI development set accuracy for each pretrained model.

C Annotation Protocol

We recruited three annotators per sentence or sentence pair on Amazon Mechanical Turk to control the quality of the labels for our heuristically generated datasets. For the acceptability judgment task sentences, individual sentence or sentence pair example was presented to the annotators and they were asked to choose between the options *natural, unnatural, neither*, after reading the given example. The examples were presented in sets of five sentences (individual sentence tasks) or three sentence pairs (sentence pair tasks) in random order,

with the option to stop at any point during the process. The annotators were compensated with $.1 per five sentences (or three sentence pairs). For NLI task sentences, the annotators were presented with six sentence pairs, for which they were asked to provide judgment on a five-point scale about the inferrability of the second sentence from the first. The annotators were compensated with $.1 per six sentence pairs. See Table 3 for inter-annotator agreement and the final size of the dataset.

	Agree	Unan.	Accuracy	Size
Negation	60.3	40.5	80.2	598
Spatial	70.0	43.4	85.0	180
Quant.	73.8	48.8	86.9	448
Comp.	68.7	40.7	84.3	100
Prep	54.7	33.1	77.4	358
wh-words	72.5	58.7	86.2	584
Def.	72.0	58.1	86.0	508
Coord.	75.3	62.9	87.6	456
EOS	64.9	47.3	82.4	478

Table 3: Pairwise inter-annotator agreement ($n = 3$), % of examples with unanimous agreement, and individual annotator accuracy according to the expected label for each task in the final probing dataset.

D List of Prepositions Used for the NLI Probing Set

about, above, across, after, against, ahead of, all over, along, among, around, at, before, behind, below, beneath, beside, by, for, from, in, in front of, inside, inside of, into, near, nearby, next to, on, on top of, out of, outside, outside of, over, past, through, to, under, up, within, with, without

E Random Initialization Variance

	$\mu (\pm\sigma)$
Prep	46.14 ($\pm$0.78)
Negation	53.66 ($\pm$0.74)
Spatial	25.34 ($\pm$1.87)
Quant.	19.38 ($\pm$0.86)
Comp.	31.8 ($\pm$1.51)
wh-words	51.37 ($\pm$0.36)
def/indef articles	57.77 ($\pm$0.97)
coord.	54.39 ($\pm$0.96)
EOS	52.74 ($\pm$1.30)

Table 4: Mean and 95% CI of probing task performance across five different random initializations.

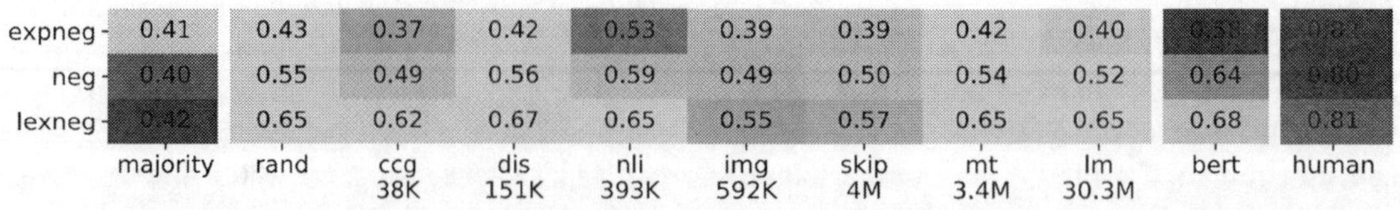

	majority	rand	ccg 38K	dis 151K	nli 393K	img 592K	skip 4M	mt 3.4M	lm 30.3M	bert	human
expneg	0.41	0.43	0.37	0.42	0.53	0.39	0.39	0.42	0.40	0.51	[illegible]
neg	0.40	0.55	0.49	0.56	0.59	0.49	0.50	0.54	0.52	0.64	[illegible]
lexneg	0.42	0.65	0.62	0.67	0.65	0.55	0.57	0.65	0.65	0.68	0.81

Figure 3: Accuracy of each pretrained model on subsets of the negation probing set. *neg* is the accuracy for the whole negation probing set. *lexneg* shows accuracy for the subset of sentence pairs negated using antonyms and *expneg* sentences explicitly negated using *not*. The leftmost column shows the majority-class baseline, and the rightmost column shows individual annotator accuracy on the final evaluation set. Blue denotes performance improvement over randomly initialized encoder baseline and orange denotes performance decrease.

F   Subset Accuracy for the Negation Probing Set

In Figure 3, we see that the NLI model's improvement on the negation probing set mostly derives from its improvement on explicit negation rather than lexical negation.

G   Prediction Overlap between Models

We show prediction overlap heatmaps for all probing tasks in Figure 4.

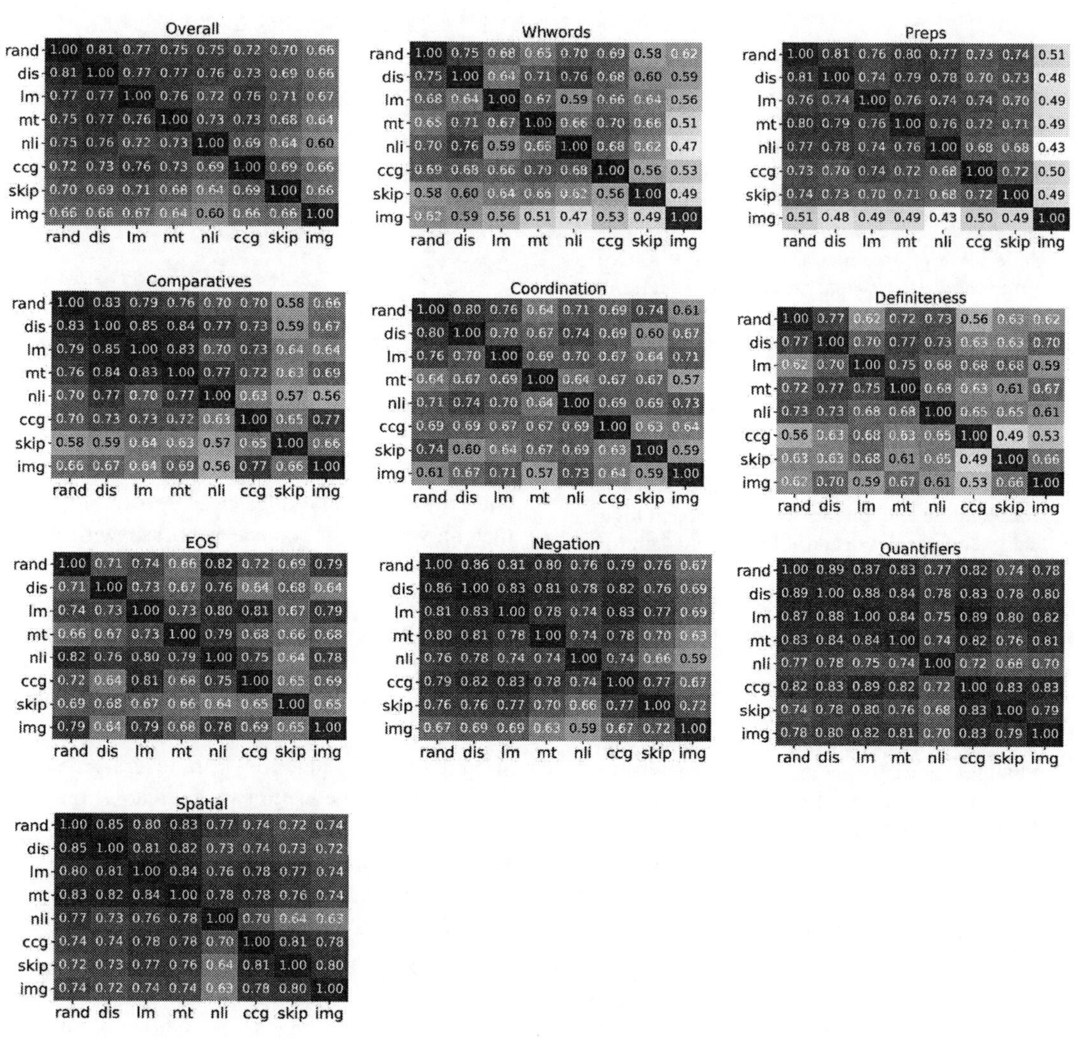

Figure 4: Heatmaps of prediction overlap for all probing tasks, between models pretrained with different objectives.

HELP: A Dataset for Identifying Shortcomings of Neural Models in Monotonicity Reasoning

Hitomi Yanaka[1,2], Koji Mineshima[2], Daisuke Bekki[2],
Kentaro Inui[1,3], Satoshi Sekine[1], Lasha Abzianidze[4], and Johan Bos[4]
[1]RIKEN, [2]Ochanomizu University, [3]Tohoku University, Japan
[4]University of Groningen, Netherlands
{hitomi.yanaka, satoshi.sekine}@riken.jp,
mineshima.koji@ocha.ac.jp, bekki@is.ocha.ac.jp,
inui@ecei.tohoku.ac.jp, {l.abzianidze, johan.bos}@rug.nl

Abstract

Large crowdsourced datasets are widely used for training and evaluating neural models on natural language inference (NLI). Despite these efforts, neural models have a hard time capturing logical inferences, including those licensed by phrase replacements, so-called monotonicity reasoning. Since no large dataset has been developed for monotonicity reasoning, it is still unclear whether the main obstacle is the size of datasets or the model architectures themselves. To investigate this issue, we introduce a new dataset, called HELP, for handling entailments with lexical and logical phenomena. We add it to training data for the state-of-the-art neural models and evaluate them on test sets for monotonicity phenomena. The results showed that our data augmentation improved the overall accuracy. We also find that the improvement is better on monotonicity inferences with lexical replacements than on downward inferences with disjunction and modification. This suggests that some types of inferences can be improved by our data augmentation while others are immune to it.

1 Introduction

Natural language inference (NLI) has been proposed as a benchmark task for natural language understanding. This task is to determine whether a given statement (premise) semantically entails another statement (hypothesis) (Dagan et al., 2013). Large crowdsourced datasets such as SNLI (Bowman et al., 2015a) and MultiNLI (Williams et al., 2018) have been created from naturally-occurring texts for training and testing neural models on NLI. Recent reports showed that these crowdsourced datasets contain undesired biases that allow prediction of entailment labels only from hypothesis sentences (Gururangan et al., 2018; Poliak et al., 2018b; Tsuchiya, 2018). Moreover, these standard datasets come with the so-called

Upward	*Some **changes in personal values** are simply part of growing older*
(MultiNLI)	⇒ *Some **changes in values** are a part of growing older*
Downward	*At most ten **commissioners** spend time at home*
(FraCaS)	⇒ *At most ten **female commissioners** spend time at home*

Table 1: Upward and downward inferences.

upward monotonicity inferences (see Table 1), i.e., inferences from subsets to supersets (*changes in personal values* $\sqsubseteq$ *changes in values*), but they rarely come with **downward** monotonicity inferences, i.e., inferences from supersets to subsets (*commissioners* $\sqsupseteq$ *female commissioners*). Downward monotonicity inferences are interesting in that they allow to replace a phrase with a more specific one and thus the resulting sentence can become longer, yet the inference is valid.

FraCaS (Cooper et al., 1994) contains such logically challenging problems as downward inferences. However, it is small in size (only 346 examples) for training neural models, and it covers only simple syntactic patterns with severely restricted vocabularies. The lack of such a dataset on a large scale is due to at least two factors: it is hard to instruct crowd workers without deep knowledge of natural language syntax and semantics, and it is also unfeasible to employ experts to obtain a large number of logically challenging inferences.

Bowman et al. (2015b) proposed an artificial dataset for logical reasoning, whose premise and hypothesis are automatically generated from a simple English-like grammar. Following this line of work, Geiger et al. (2018) presented a method to construct a complex dataset for multiple quantifiers (e.g., *Every dwarf licks no rifle* ⇒ *No ugly dwarf licks some rifle*). These datasets contain downward inferences, but they are designed not to require lexical knowledge. There are also NLI datasets which expand lexical knowledge by replacing words using lexical rules (Monz and de Rijke, 2001; Glockner et al., 2018; Naik et al., 2018;

*Proceedings of the Eighth Joint Conference on Lexical and Computational Semantics (*SEM), pages 250–255*
Minneapolis, June 6–7, 2019. ©2019 Association for Computational Linguistics

Poliak et al., 2018a). In these works, however, little attention has been paid to downward inferences.

The GLUE leaderboard (Wang et al., 2019) reported that neural models did not perform well on downward inferences, and this leaves us guessing whether the lack of large datasets for such kind of inferences that involve the interaction between lexical and logical inferences is an obstacle of understanding inferences for neural models.

To shed light on this problem, this paper makes the following three contributions: (a) providing a method to create a large NLI dataset[1] that embodies the combination of lexical and logical inferences focusing on monotonicity (i.e., phrase replacement-based reasoning) (Section 3), (b) measuring to what extent the new dataset helps neural models to learn monotonicity inferences, and (c) by analyzing the results, revealing which types of logical inferences are solved with our training data augmentation and which ones are immune to it (Section 4.2).

2   Monotonicity Reasoning

Monotonicity reasoning is a sort of reasoning based on word replacement. Based on the monotonicity properties of words, it determines whether a certain word replacement results in a sentence entailed from the original one (van Benthem, 1983; Icard and Moss, 2014). A polarity is a characteristic of a word position imposed by monotone operators. Replacements with more general (or specific) phrases in ↑ (or ↓) polarity positions license entailment. Polarities are determined by a function which is always upward monotone ($+$) (i.e., an order preserving function that licenses entailment from specific to general phrases), always downward monotone ($-$) (i.e., an order reversing function) or neither, non-monotone.

Determiners are modeled as binary operators, taking noun and verb phrases as the first and second arguments, respectively, and they entail sentences with their arguments narrowed or broadened according to their monotonicity properties. For example, the determiner *some* is upward monotone both in its first and second arguments, and the concepts can be broadened by replacing its hypernym (*people* ⊒ *boy*), removing modifiers (*dancing* ⊒ *happily dancing*), or adding

disjunction. The concepts can be narrowed by replacing its hyponym (*schoolboy* ⊑ *boy*), adding modifiers, or adding conjunction.

(1)   *Some* [NP *boys*↑]$^{+}$ [VP *are happily dancing*↑]$^{+}$
⇒   *Some* [NP *people*] [VP *are dancing*]
⇏   *Some* [NP *schoolboys*] [VP *are dancing and singing*]

If a sentence contains negation, the polarity of words over the scope of negation is reversed:

(2)   *No* [NP *boys*↓]$^{-}$ [VP *are happily dancing*↓]$^{-}$
⇒   *No* [NP *one*] [VP *is dancing*]
⇏   *No* [NP *schoolboys*] [VP *are dancing and singing*]

If the propositional object is embedded in another negative or conditional context, the polarity of words over its scope can be reversed again:

(3)   *If* [*there are no* [NP *boys*↑]$^{-}$ [VP *dancing happily*↑]$^{-}$]$^{-}$, [*the party might be canceled*]$^{+}$
⇒   *If* [*there is no* [NP *one*] [VP *dancing*]], [*the party might be canceled*]

In this way, the polarity of words is determined by monotonicity operators and syntactic structures.

3   Data Creation

We address three issues when creating the inference problems: (a) Detect the monotone operators and their arguments; (b) Based on the syntactic structure, induce the polarity of the argument positions; (c) Using lexical knowledge or logical connectives, narrow or broaden the arguments.

3.1   Source corpus

We use sentences from the Parallel Meaning Bank (PMB, Abzianidze et al., 2017) as a source while creating the inference dataset. The reason behind choosing the PMB is threefold. First, the fine-grained annotations in the PMB facilitate our automatic monotonicity-driven construction of inference problems. In particular, semantic tokenization and WordNet (Fellbaum, 1998) senses make narrow and broad concept substitutions easy while the syntactic analyses in Combinatory Categorial Grammar (CCG, Steedman, 2000) format and semantic tags (Abzianidze and Bos, 2017) contribute to monotonicity and polarity detection. Second, the PMB contains lexically and syntactically diverse texts from a wide range of genres. Third, the gold (silver) documents are fully (partially) manually verified, which control noise in the automated generated dataset. To prevent easy inferences, we use the sentences with more than five tokens from 5K gold and 5K silver portions of the PMB.

---

[1] Our dataset and its generation code will be made publicly available at https://github.com/verypluming/HELP.

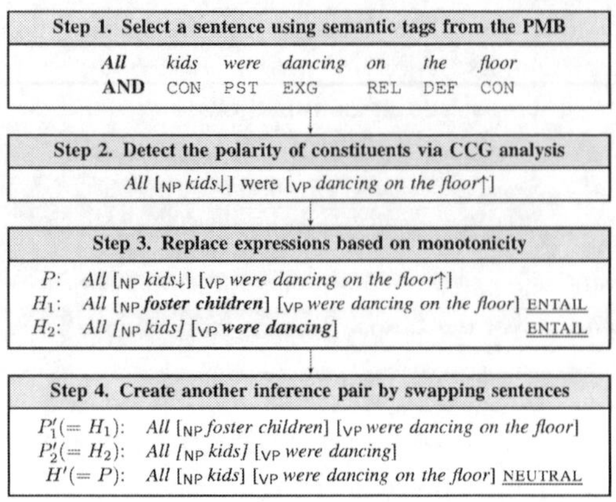

Step 1. Select a sentence using semantic tags from the PMB

All	*kids*	*were*	*dancing*	*on*	*the*	*floor*
AND	CON	PST	EXG	REL	DEF	CON

Step 2. Detect the polarity of constituents via CCG analysis

All [NP *kids↓*] *were* [VP *dancing on the floor↑*]

Step 3. Replace expressions based on monotonicity

P: *All* [NP *kids↓*] [VP *were dancing on the floor↑*]
H_1:   *All* [NP ***foster children***] [VP *were dancing on the floor*]   ENTAIL
H_2:   *All* [NP *kids*] [VP ***were dancing***]   ENTAIL

Step 4. Create another inference pair by swapping sentences

$P'_1(= H_1)$:   *All* [NP *foster children*] [VP *were dancing on the floor*]
$P'_2(= H_2)$:   *All* [NP *kids*] [VP *were dancing*]
$H'(= P)$:   *All* [NP *kids*] [VP *were dancing on the floor*]   NEUTRAL

Figure 1: Illustration for creating the HELP dataset.

3.2 Methodology

Figure 1 illustrates the method of creating the HELP dataset. We use declarative sentences from the PMB containing monotone operators, conjunction, or disjunction as a source (Step 1). These target words can be identified by their semantic tags: AND (*all, every, each, and*), DIS (*some, several, or*), NEG (*no, not, neither, without*), DEF (*both*), QUV (*many, few*), and IMP (*if, when, unless*). In Step 2, after locating the first (NP) and the second (VP) arguments of the monotone operator via a CCG derivation, we detect their polarities with the possibility of reversing a polarity if an argument appears in a downward environment.

In Step 3, to broaden or narrow the first and the second arguments, we consider two types of operations: (i) lexical replacement, i.e., substituting the argument with its hypernym/hyponym (e.g., H_1) and (ii) syntactic elimination, i.e., dropping a modifier or a conjunction/disjunction phrase in the argument (e.g., H_2). Given the polarity of the argument position ($\uparrow$ or $\downarrow$) and the type of replacement (with more general or specific phrases), the gold label (*entailment* or *neutral*) of a premise-hypothesis pair is automatically determined; e.g., both (P, H_1) and (P, H_2) in Step 3 are assigned *entailment*. For lexical replacements, we use WordNet senses from the PMB and their ISA relations with the same part-of-speech to control naturalness of the obtained sentence. To compensate missing word senses from the silver documents, we use the Lesk algorithm (Lesk, 1986). In Step 4, by swapping the premise and the hypothesis, we create another inference pair and assign its gold label; e.g., (P'_1, H') and (P'_2, H') are created and assigned *neutral*. By swapping a sentence pair created by syntactic elimination, we can create a pair

Section	Size	Example
Up	7784	*Tom bought some **Mexican sunflowers** for Mary* ⇒*Tom bought some **flowers** for Mary*****
Down	21192	*If there's no **water**, there's no whisky****** ⇒*If there's no **facility**, there's no whisky*
Non	1105	*Shakespeare wrote both **tragedy and comedy**** ⇒*Shakespeare wrote both **tragedy and drama***
Conj	6076	*Tom removed his glasses* ⇒*Tom removed his glasses **and rubbed his eyes****
Disj	438	*The trees are barren* ⇒*The trees are barren **or bear only small fruit****

Table 2: Examples in HELP. The sentence with an asterisk is the original sentence from the PMB.

such as (P'_2, H') in which the hypothesis is more specific than the premise.

3.3 The HELP dataset

The resulting dataset has 36K inference pairs consisting of upward monotone, downward monotone, non-monotone, conjunction, and disjunction. Table 2 shows some examples. The number of vocabulary items is 15K. We manually checked the naturalness of randomly sampled 500 sentence pairs, of which 146 pairs were unnatural. As mentioned in previous work (Glockner et al., 2018), there are some cases where WordNet for substitution leads to unnatural sentences due to the context mismatch; e.g., an example such as P: *You have no driving happening* ⇒ H: *You have no driving experience*, where P is obtained from H by replacing *experience* by its hypernym *happening*. Since our intention is to explore possible ways to augment training data for monotonicity reasoning, we include these cases in the training dataset.

4 Experiments

We use HELP as additional training material for three neural models for NLI and evaluate them on test sets dealing with monotonicity reasoning.

4.1 Experimental settings

Models   We used three models: BERT (Devlin et al., 2019), BiLSTM+ELMo+Attn (Wang et al., 2019), and ESIM (Chen et al., 2017).

Training data   We used three different training sets and compared their performance; MultiNLI (392K), MultiNLI+MQ (the dataset for multiple quantifiers introduced in Section 1; Geiger et al., 2018) (892K), and MultiNLI+HELP (429K).

Test data   We used four test sets: (i) the GLUE diagnostic dataset (Wang et al., 2019) (upward monotone, downward monotone, non-monotone,

Model	Train Data	Up (30)	$\triangle$	Down (30)	$\triangle$	Non (22)	$\triangle$	Conj (32)	$\triangle$	Disj (38)	$\triangle$	Total (152)	$\triangle$	FraCaS (80)	$\triangle$	SICK (4927)	$\triangle$	MNLI match (10000)	$\triangle$	MNLI mismatch (10000)	$\triangle$
BERT	MNLI	50.4		-67.5		23.1		52.5		-6.1		17.8		65.0		55.4		**84.6**		**83.4**	
	+MQ	59.6	+9.2	-49.3	+18.2	14.0	-9.1	62.1	+9.6	-18.8	-12.7	26.3	+8.5	**68.8**	+3.8	58.2	+2.8	78.4	-6.2	78.6	-4.8
	+HELP	**67.0**	+16.6	**29.8**	+97.3	**47.9**	+24.8	**72.1**	+19.6	**-4.1**	+2.0	**51.2**	+33.4	**68.8**	+3.8	**60.0**	+4.6	84.4	-0.2	83.1	-0.3
BiLSTM	MNLI	22.2		-9.4		-2.7		42.4		-9.9		-3.5		68.9		53.8		**76.4**		**76.1**	
+ELMo	+MQ	22.2	0.0	8.1	+17.5	-5.7	-3.0	42.4	0.0	**-9.8**	+0.1	5.7	+9.2	65.9	-3.0	**54.0**	+0.2	71.4	-5.0	70.7	-5.4
+Attn	+HELP	**32.4**	+10.2	**22.9**	+32.3	**3.7**	+6.4	**45.6**	+3.2	-9.9	0.0	**17.0**	+20.5	**71.3**	+2.4	**54.0**	+0.2	75.2	-1.2	74.1	-2.0
ESIM	MNLI	14.9		-14.0		6.0		29.8		-3.6		1.1		47.5		43.9		**71.3**		**70.7**	
	+MQ	27.2	+12.3	-7.8	+6.2	3.4	-2.6	5.2	-24.6	-13.0	-9.4	6.8	+5.7	43.7	-3.8	53.1	+9.2	68.6	-3.7	68.2	-2.5
	+HELP	**31.4**	+16.5	**24.7**	+38.7	**8.0**	+2.0	**32.6**	+2.8	**7.1**	+10.7	**27.0**	+25.9	**48.8**	+1.3	**56.6**	+12.7	71.1	-0.2	70.1	-0.6

Table 3: Evaluation results on the GLUE diagnostic dataset, FraCaS, SICK, and MultiNLI (MNLI). The number in parentheses is the number of problems in each test set. $\triangle$ is the difference from the model trained on MNLI.

conjunction, and disjunction sections), (ii) FraCaS (the generalized quantifier section), (iii) the SICK (Marelli et al., 2014) test set, and (iv) MultiNLI matched/mismatched test set. We used the Matthews correlation coefficient (ranging $[-1, 1]$) as the evaluation metric for GLUE. Regarding other datasets, we used accuracy as the metric. We also check if our data augmentation does not decrease the performance on MultiNLI.

4.2 Results and discussion

Table 3 shows that adding HELP to MultiNLI improved the accuracy of all models on GLUE, FraCaS, and SICK. Regarding MultiNLI, note that adding data for downward inference can be harmful for performing upward inference, because lexical replacements work in an opposite way in downward environments. However, our data augmentation minimized the decrease in performance on MultiNLI. This suggests that models managed to learn the relationships between downward operators and their arguments from HELP.

The improvement in accuracy is better with HELP than that with MQ despite the fact that the size of HELP is much smaller than MQ. MQ does not deal with lexical replacements, and thus the improvement is not stable. This indicates that the improvement comes from carefully controlling the target reasoning of the training set rather than from its size. ESIM showed a greater improvement in accuracy compared with the other models when we added HELP. This result arguably supports the finding in Bowman et al. (2015b) that a tree architecture is better for learning some logical inferences. Regarding the evaluation on SICK, Talman and Chatzikyriakidis (2018) reported a drop in accuracy of 40-50% when BiLSTM and ESIM were trained on MultiNLI because SICK is out of the domain of MultiNLI. Indeed, the accuracy of each model, including BERT, was low at 40-60%.

When compared among linguistic phenomena,

the improvement by adding HELP was better for upward and downward monotone. In particular, all models except models trained with HELP failed to answer 68 problems for monotonicity inferences with lexical replacements. This indicates that such inferences can be improved by adding HELP.

The improvement for disjunction was smaller than other phenomena. To investigate this, we conducted error analysis on 68 problems of GLUE and FraCaS, which all the models misclassified. 44 problems are neutral problems in which all words in the hypothesis occur in the premise (e.g., *He is either in London or in Paris $\nRightarrow$ He is in London*). 13 problems are entailment problems in which the hypothesis contains a word or a phrase not occurring in the premise (e.g., *I don't want to have to keep entertaining people $\Rightarrow$ I don't want to have to keep entertaining people who don't value my time*). These problems contain disjunction or modifiers in downward environments where either (i) the premise P contains all words in the hypothesis H yet the inference is invalid or (ii) H contains more words than those in P yet the inference is valid.[2] Although HELP contains 21K such problems, the models nevertheless misclassified them. This indicates that the difficulty in learning these non-lexical downward inferences might not come from the lack of training datasets.

5 Conclusion and Future Work

We introduced a monotonicity-driven NLI data augmentation method. The experiments showed that neural models trained on HELP obtained the higher overall accuracy. However, the improvement tended to be small on downward monotone inferences with disjunction and modification, which suggests that some types of inferences can

---

[2]Interestingly, certain logical inferences including disjunction and downward monotonicity are difficult also for humans to get (Geurts and van der Slik, 2005).

be improved by adding data while others might require different kind of *help*.

For future work, our data augmentation can be used for multilingual corpora. Since the PMB annotations sufficed for creating HELP, applying our method to the non-English PMB documents seems straightforward. Additionally, it is interesting to verify the quality and contribution of a dataset which will be created by using our method on an automatically annotated and parsed corpus.

Acknowledgement

We thank our three anonymous reviewers for helpful suggestions.

References

Lasha Abzianidze, Johannes Bjerva, Kilian Evang, Hessel Haagsma, Rik van Noord, Pierre Ludmann, Duc-Duy Nguyen, and Johan Bos. 2017. The Parallel Meaning Bank: Towards a multilingual corpus of translations annotated with compositional meaning representations. In *Proceedings of the 15th Conference of the European Chapter of the Association for Computational Linguistics*, pages 242–247.

Lasha Abzianidze and Johan Bos. 2017. Towards universal semantic tagging. In *Proceedings of the 12th International Conference on Computational Semantics (IWCS 2017)*, pages 1–6.

Johan van Benthem. 1983. Determiners and logic. *Linguistics and Philosophy*, 6(4):447–478.

Samuel R. Bowman, Gabor Angeli, Christopher Potts, and Christopher D. Manning. 2015a. A large annotated corpus for learning natural language inference. In *Proceedings of the 2015 Conference on Empirical Methods in Natural Language Processing*, pages 632–642.

Samuel R. Bowman, Christopher Potts, and Christopher D. Manning. 2015b. Recursive neural networks can learn logical semantics. In *Proceedings of the 3rd Workshop on Continuous Vector Space Models and their Compositionality*, pages 12–21.

Qian Chen, Xiaodan Zhu, Zhen-Hua Ling, Si Wei, Hui Jiang, and Diana Inkpen. 2017. Enhanced lstm for natural language inference. In *Proceedings of the 55th Annual Meeting of the Association for Computational Linguistics*, pages 1657–1668.

Robin Cooper, Richard Crouch, Jan van Eijck, Chris Fox, Josef van Genabith, Jan Jaspers, Hans Kamp, Manfred Pinkal, Massimo Poesio, Stephen Pulman, et al. 1994. FraCaS–a framework for computational semantics. *Deliverable*, D6.

Ido Dagan, Dan Roth, Mark Sammons, and Fabio Massimo Zanzotto. 2013. *Recognizing Textual Entailment: Models and Applications*. Synthesis Lectures on Human Language Technologies. Morgan & Claypool Publishers.

Jacob Devlin, Ming-Wei Chang, Kenton Lee, and Kristina Toutanova. 2019. BERT: Pre-training of deep bidirectional transformers for language understanding. In *Proceedings of the 2019 Conference of the North American Chapter of the Association for Computational Linguistics: Human Language Technologies*.

Christiane Fellbaum. 1998. *WordNet: An Electronic Lexical Database*. Language, Speech, and Communication. MIT Press.

Atticus Geiger, Ignacio Cases, Lauri Karttunen, and Christopher Potts. 2018. Stress-testing neural models of natural language inference with multiply-quantified sentences. *CoRR*, abs/1810.13033.

Bart Geurts and Frans van der Slik. 2005. Monotonicity and processing load. *Journal of Semantics*, 22(1):97–117.

Max Glockner, Vered Shwartz, and Yoav Goldberg. 2018. Breaking NLI systems with sentences that require simple lexical inferences. In *Proceedings of the 56th Annual Meeting of the Association for Computational Linguistics*, pages 650–655.

Suchin Gururangan, Swabha Swayamdipta, Omer Levy, Roy Schwartz, Samuel Bowman, and Noah A. Smith. 2018. Annotation artifacts in natural language inference data. In *Proceedings of the 2018 Conference of the North American Chapter of the Association for Computational Linguistics: Human Language Technologies*, pages 107–112.

Thomas Icard and Lawrence Moss. 2014. Recent progress in monotonicity. *LILT*, 9(7):167–194.

Michael Lesk. 1986. Automatic sense disambiguation using machine readable dictionaries: How to tell a pine cone from an ice cream cone. In *Proceedings of the 5th Annual International Conference on Systems Documentation*, pages 24–26.

Marco Marelli, Stefano Menini, Marco Baroni, Luisa Bentivogli, Raffaella Bernardi, and Roberto Zamparelli. 2014. A SICK cure for the evaluation of compositional distributional semantic models. In *Proceedings of the 9th International Conference on Language Resources and Evaluation*, pages 216–223.

Christof Monz and Maarten de Rijke. 2001. Lightweight entailment checking for computational semantics. In *Proceedings of the 3rd International Workshop on Inference in Computational Semantics*, pages 1–15.

Aakanksha Naik, Abhilasha Ravichander, Norman Sadeh, Carolyn Rose, and Graham Neubig. 2018. Stress test evaluation for natural language inference. In *Proceedings of the 27th International Conference on Computational Linguistics*, pages 2340–2353.

Adam Poliak, Aparajita Haldar, Rachel Rudinger, J. Edward Hu, Ellie Pavlick, Aaron Steven White, and Benjamin Van Durme. 2018a. Collecting diverse natural language inference problems for sentence representation evaluation. In *Proceedings of the 2018 EMNLP Workshop BlackboxNLP: Analyzing and Interpreting Neural Networks for NLP*, pages 337–340.

Adam Poliak, Jason Naradowsky, Aparajita Haldar, Rachel Rudinger, and Benjamin Van Durme. 2018b. Hypothesis only baselines in natural language inference. In *Proceedings of the Seventh Joint Conference on Lexical and Computational Semantics*, pages 180–191.

Mark Steedman. 2000. *The Syntactic Process*. MIT Press.

Aarne Talman and Stergios Chatzikyriakidis. 2018. Testing the generalization power of neural network models across NLI benchmarks. *CoRR*, abs/1810.09774.

Masatoshi Tsuchiya. 2018. Performance impact caused by hidden bias of training data for recognizing textual entailment. In *Proceedings of the 11th International Conference on Language Resources and Evaluation*.

Alex Wang, Amanpreet Singh, Julian Michael, Felix Hill, Omer Levy, and Samuel R. Bowman. 2019. GLUE: A multi-task benchmark and analysis platform for natural language understanding. In *International Conference on Learning Representations*.

Adina Williams, Nikita Nangia, and Samuel Bowman. 2018. A broad-coverage challenge corpus for sentence understanding through inference. In *Proceedings of the 2018 Conference of the North American Chapter of the Association for Computational Linguistics: Human Language Technologies*, pages 1112–1122.

On Adversarial Removal of Hypothesis-only Bias in Natural Language Inference

Yonatan Belinkov[13*]   **Adam Poliak**[2*]
Stuart M. Shieber[1]   **Benjamin Van Durme**[2]   **Alexander Rush**[1]
[1]Harvard University   [2]Johns Hopkins University   [3]Massachusetts Institute of Technology
{belinkov,shieber,srush}@seas.harvard.edu
{azpoliak,vandurme}@cs.jhu.edu

Abstract

Popular Natural Language Inference (NLI) datasets have been shown to be tainted by hypothesis-only biases. Adversarial learning may help models ignore sensitive biases and spurious correlations in data. We evaluate whether adversarial learning can be used in NLI to encourage models to learn representations free of hypothesis-only biases. Our analyses indicate that the representations learned via adversarial learning may be less biased, with only small drops in NLI accuracy.

1 Introduction

Popular datasets for Natural Language Inference (NLI) - the task of determining whether one sentence (premise) likely entails another (hypothesis) - contain hypothesis-only biases that allow models to perform the task surprisingly well by only considering hypotheses while ignoring the corresponding premises. For instance, such a method correctly predicted the examples in Table 1 as contradictions. As datasets may always contain biases, it is important to analyze whether, and to what extent, models are immune to or rely on known biases. Furthermore, it is important to build models that can overcome these biases.

Recent work in NLP aims to build more robust systems using adversarial methods (Alzantot et al., 2018; Chen & Cardie, 2018; Belinkov & Bisk, 2018, *i.a.*). In particular, Elazar & Goldberg (2018) attempted to use adversarial training to remove demographic attributes from text data, with limited success. Inspired by this line of work, we use adversarial learning to add small components to an existing and popular NLI system that has been used to learn general sentence representations (Conneau et al., 2017). The adversarial

---

| A dog runs through the woods near a cottage |
| ▶ The dog is *sleeping* on the ground |

| A person writing something on a newspaper |
| ▶ A person is *driving* a fire truck |

| A man is doing tricks on a skateboard |
| ▶ *Nobody* is doing tricks |

Table 1: Examples from SNLI's development set that Poliak et al. (2018)'s hypothesis-only model correctly predicted as contradictions. The first line in each section is a premise and lines with ▶ are corresponding hypotheses. The italicized words are correlated with the "contradiction" label in SNLI

techniques include (1) using an external adversarial classifier conditioned on hypotheses alone, and (2) creating noisy, perturbed training examples. In our analyses we ask whether hidden, hypothesis-only biases are no longer present in the resulting sentence representations after adversarial learning. The goal is to build models with less bias, ideally while limiting the inevitable degradation in task performance. Our results suggest that progress on this goal may depend on which adversarial learning techniques are used.

Although recent work has applied adversarial learning to NLI (Minervini & Riedel, 2018; Kang et al., 2018), this is the first work to our knowledge that explicitly studies NLI models designed to ignore hypothesis-only biases.

2 Methods

We consider two types of adversarial methods. In the first method, we incorporate an external classifier to force the hypothesis-encoder to ignore hypothesis-only biases. In the second method, we randomly swap premises in the training set to create noisy examples.

---

* Equal contribution

*Proceedings of the Eighth Joint Conference on Lexical and Computational Semantics (*SEM)*, pages 256–262
Minneapolis, June 6–7, 2019. ©2019 Association for Computational Linguistics

2.1 General NLI Model

Let (P, H) denote a premise-hypothesis pair, g denote an encoder that maps a sentence S to a vector representation v, and c a classifier that maps v to an output label y. A general NLI framework contains the following components:

- A **premise encoder** g_P that maps the premise P to a vector representation p.

- A **hypothesis encoder** g_H that maps the hypothesis H to a vector representation h.

- A **classifier** c_{NLI} that combines and maps p and h to an output y.

In this model, the premise and hypothesis are each encoded with separate encoders. The NLI classifier is usually trained to minimize the objective:

$$L_{\mathrm{NLI}} = L(c_{\mathrm{NLI}}([g_P(P); g_H(H)], y)) \quad (1)$$

where $L(\tilde{y}, y)$ is the cross-entropy loss. If g_P is not used, a model should not be able to successfully perform NLI. However, models without g_P may achieve non-trivial results, indicating the existence of biases in hypotheses (Gururangan et al., 2018; Poliak et al., 2018; Tsuchiya, 2018).

2.2 AdvCls: Adversarial Classifier

Our first approach, referred to as AdvCls, follows the common adversarial training method (Goodfellow et al., 2015; Ganin & Lempitsky, 2015; Xie et al., 2017; Zhang et al., 2018) by adding an additional adversarial classifier c_{Hypoth} to our model. c_{Hypoth} maps the hypothesis representation h to an output y. In domain adversarial learning, the classifier is typically used to predict unwanted features, e.g., protected attributes like race, age, or gender (Elazar & Goldberg, 2018). Here, we do not have explicit protected attributes but rather *latent* hypothesis-only biases. Therefore, we use c_{Hypoth} to predict the NLI label given only the hypothesis. To successfully perform this prediction, c_{Hypoth} needs to exploit latent biases in h.

We modify the objective function (1) as

$$\begin{aligned} L &= L_{\mathrm{NLI}} + \lambda_{\mathrm{Loss}} L_{\mathrm{Adv}} \\ L_{\mathrm{Adv}} &= L(c_{\mathrm{Hypoth}}(\lambda_{\mathrm{Enc}} \mathrm{GRL}_\lambda(g_H(H)), y)) \end{aligned}$$

To control the interplay between c_{NLI} and c_{Hypoth} we set two hyper-parameters: λ_{Loss}, the importance of the adversarial loss function, and λ_{Enc}, a scaling factor that multiplies the gradients after reversing them. This is implemented by the scaled gradient reversal layer, GRL_λ (Ganin & Lempitsky, 2015). The goal here is modify the representation $g_H(H)$ so that it is maximally informative for NLI while simultaneously minimizes the ability of c_{Hypoth} to accurately predict the NLI label.

2.3 AdvDat: Adversarial Training Data

For our second approach, which we call AdvDat, we use an unchanged general model, but train it with perturbed training data. For a fraction of example (P, H) pairs in the training data, we replace P with P', a premise from another training example, chosen uniformly at random. For these instances, during back-propagation, we similarly reverse the gradient but only back-propagate through g_H. The adversarial loss function L_{RandAdv} is defined as:

$$L(c_{\mathrm{NLI}}([\mathrm{GRL}_0(g_P(P')); \lambda_{\mathrm{Enc}} \mathrm{GRL}_\lambda(g_H(H))], y))$$

where GRL_0 implements gradient blocking on g_P by using the identity function in the forward step and a zero gradient during the backward step. At the same time, GRL_λ reverses the gradient going into g_H and scales it by λ_{Enc}, as before.

We set a hyper-parameter $\lambda_{\mathrm{Rand}} \in [0, 1]$ that controls what fraction P's are swapped at random. In turn, the final loss function combines the two losses based on λ_{Rand} as

$$L = (1 - \lambda_{\mathrm{Rand}})L_{\mathrm{NLI}} + \lambda_{\mathrm{Rand}} L_{\mathrm{RandAdv}}$$

In essence, this method penalizes the model for correctly predicting y in perturbed examples where the premise is uninformative. This implicitly assumes that the label for (P, H) should be different than the label for (P', H), which in practice does not always hold true.[1]

3 Experiments & Results

Experimental setup Out of 10 NLI datasets, Poliak et al. (2018) found that the Stanford Natural Language Inference dataset (SNLI; Bowman et al., 2015) contained the most (or worst) hypothesis-only biases—their hypothesis-only model outperformed the majority baseline by roughly 100% (going from roughly 34% to 69%). Because of the large magnitude of these biases, confirmed

---

[1] As pointed out by a reviewer, a pair labeled as neutral might end up remaining neutral after randomly sampling the premise, so adversarially training in this case might weaken the model. Instead, one could limit adversarial training to cases of entailment or contradiction.

by Tsuchiya (2018) and Gururangan et al. (2018), we focus on SNLI. We use the standard SNLI split and report validation and test results. We also test on SNLI-hard, a subset of SNLI that Gururangan et al. (2018) filtered such that it may not contain unwanted artifacts.

We apply both adversarial techniques to InferSent (Conneau et al., 2017), which serves as our general NLI architecture.[2] Following the standard training details used in InferSent, we encode premises and hypotheses separately using bi-directional long short-term memory (BiLSTM) networks (Hochreiter & Schmidhuber, 1997). Premises and hypotheses are initially mapped (token-by-token) to Glove (Pennington et al., 2014) representations. We use max-pooling over the BiLSTM states to extract premise and hypothesis representations and, following Mou et al. (2016), combine the representations by concatenating their vectors, their difference, and their multiplication (element-wise).

We use the default training hyper-parameters in the released InferSent codebase.[3] These include setting the initial learning rate to 0.1 and the decay rate to 0.99, using SGD optimization and dividing the learning rate by 5 at every epoch when the accuracy deceases on the validation set. The default settings also include stopping training either when the learning rate drops below 10^{-5} or after 20 epochs. In both adversarial settings, the hyper-parameters are swept through $\{0.05, 0.1, 0.2, 0.4, 0.8, 1.0\}$.

Results   Table 2 reports the results on SNLI, with the configurations that performed best on the validation set for each of the adversarial methods.

Model	Val	Test	Hard
Baseline	84.25	84.22	68.02
AdvCls	84.58	83.56	66.27
AdvDat	78.45	78.30	55.60

Table 2: Accuracies for the approaches. Baseline refers to the unmodified, non-adversarial InferSent.

As expected, both training methods perform worse than our unmodified, non-adversarial InferSent baseline on SNLI's test set, since they remove biases that may be useful for performing this

[2]Code developed is available at https://github.com/azpoliak/robust-nli.
[3]https://github.com/facebookresearch/InferSent

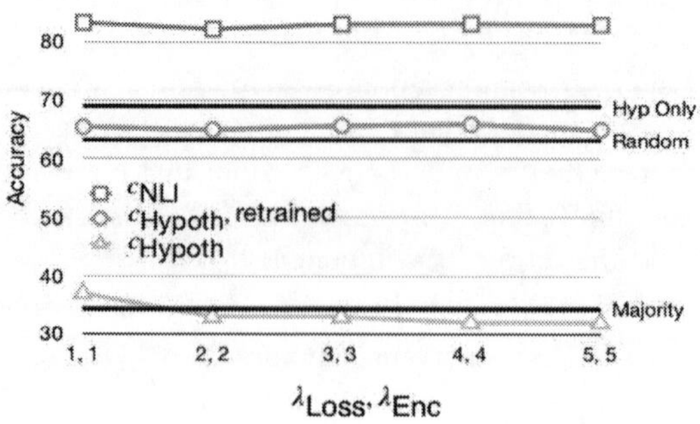

(a) Hidden biases remaining from AdvCls

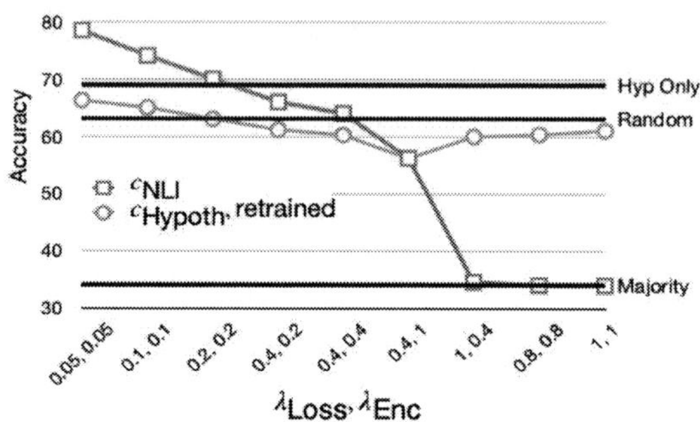

(b) Hidden biases remaining from AdvDat

Figure 1: Validation results when retraining a classifier on a frozen hypothesis encoder (c_{Hypoth}, retrained) compared to our methods (c_{NLI}), the adversarial hypothesis-only classifier (c_{Hypoth}, in AdvCls), majority baseline, a random frozen encoder, and a hypothesis-only model.

task. The difference for AdvCls is minimal, and it even slightly outperforms InferSent on the validation set. While AdvDat's results are noticeably lower than the non-adversarial InferSent, the drops are still less than 6% points.[4]

4   Analysis

Our goal is to determine whether adversarial learning can help build NLI models without hypothesis-only biases. We first ask whether the models' learned sentence representations can be used by a hypothesis-only classifier to perform well. We then explore the effects of increasing the adversarial strength, and end with a discussion of indicator words associated with hypothesis-only biases.

4.1   Hidden Biases

Do the learned sentence representations eliminate hypothesis-only biases after adversarial training?

[4]This drop may indicate that SNLI-hard may still have biases, but, as pointed out by a reviewer, an alternative explanation is a general loss of information in the encoded hypothesis. However, Subsection 4.3 suggests that the loss of information is more focused on biases.

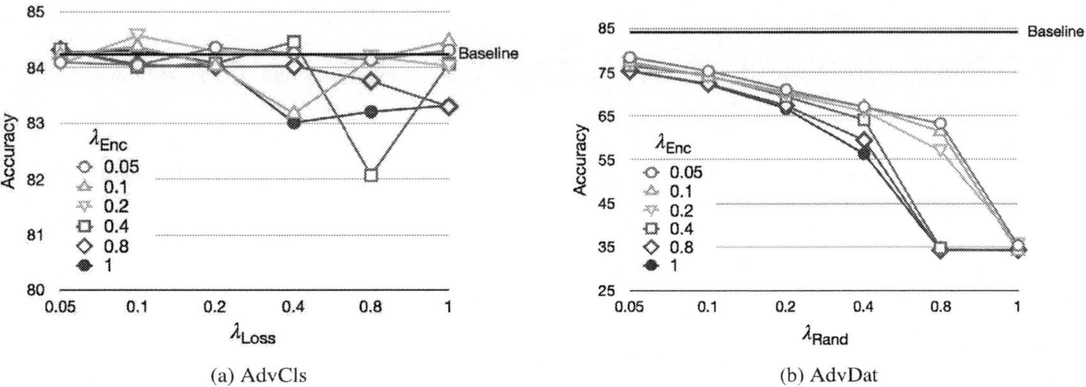

(a) AdvCls   (b) AdvDat

Figure 2: Results on the validation set with different configurations of the adversarial methods.

We freeze sentence encoders trained with the studied methods, and retrain a new classifier that only accesses representations from the frozen hypothesis encoder. This helps us determine whether the (frozen) representations have hidden biases.

A few trends can be noticed. First, we confirm that with AdvCls (Figure 1a), the hypothesis-only classifier (c_{hypoth}) is indeed trained to perform poorly on the task, while the normal NLI classifier (c_{NLI}) performs much better. However, retraining a classifier on frozen hypothesis representations (c_{Hypoth}, retrained) boosts performance. In fact, the retrained classifier performs close to the fully trained hypothesis-only baseline, indicating the hypothesis representations still contain biases. Consistent with this finding, Elazar & Goldberg (2018) found that adversarially-trained text classifiers preserve demographic attributes in hidden representations despite efforts to remove them.

Interestingly, we found that even a frozen random encoder captures biases in the hypothesis, as a classifier trained on it performs fairly well (63.26%), and far above the majority class baseline (34.28%). One reason might be that the word embeddings (which are pre-trained) alone contain significant information that propagates even through a random encoder. Others have also found that random encodings contain non-trivial information (Conneau et al., 2018; Zhang & Bowman, 2018). The fact that the word embeddings were not updated during (adversarial) training could account for the ability to recover performance at the level of the classifier trained on a random encoder. This may indicate that future adversarial efforts should be applied to the word embeddings as well.

Turning to AdvDat, (Figure 1b), as the hyper-parameters increase, the models exhibit fewer bi-

ases. Performance even drops below the random encoder results, indicating it may be better at ignoring biases in the hypothesis. However, this comes at the cost of reduced NLI performance.

4.2 Adversarial Strength

Is there a correlation between adversarial strength and drops in SNLI performance? Does increasing adversarial hyper-parameters affect the decrease in results on SNLI?

Figure 2 shows the validation results with various configurations of adversarial hyper-parameters. The AdvCls method is fairly stable across configurations, although combinations of large λ_{Loss} and λ_{Enc} hurt the performance on SNLI a bit more (Figure 2a). Nevertheless, all the drops are moderate. Increasing the hyper-parameters further (up to values of 5), did not lead to substantial drops, although the results are slightly less stable across configurations (Appendix A). On the other hand, the AdvDat method is very sensitive to large hyper-parameters (Figure 2b). For every value of λ_{Enc}, increasing λ_{Rand} leads to significant performance drops. These drops happen sooner for larger λ_{Enc} values. Therefore, the effect of stronger hyper-parameters on SNLI performance seems to be specific to each adversarial method.

4.3 Indicator Words

Certain words in SNLI are more correlated with specific entailment labels than others, e.g., negation words ("not", "nobody", "no") correlated with CONTRADICTION (Gururangan et al., 2018; Poliak et al., 2018). These words have been referred to as "give-away" words (Poliak et al., 2018). Do the adversarial methods encourage models to make predictions that are less affected by these biased indicator words?

259

		Score		Percentage decrease from baseline		
Word	Count	$\hat{p}(l|w)$	Baseline	AdvCls (1,1)	AdvDat (0.4,1)	AdvDat (1,1)
sleeping	108	0.88	0.24	15.63	53.13	-81.25
driving	53	0.81	0.32	-8.33	50	-66.67
Nobody	52	1	0.42	14.29	42.86	14.29
alone	50	0.9	0.32	0	83.33	0
cat	49	0.84	0.31	7.14	57.14	-85.71
asleep	43	0.91	0.39	-18.75	50	12.5
no	31	0.84	0.36	0	52.94	-52.94
empty	28	0.93	0.3	-16.67	83.33	-16.67
eats	24	0.83	0.3	37.5	87.5	-25
naked	20	0.95	0.46	0	83.33	-33.33

Table 3: Indicator words and how correlated they are with CONTRADICTION predictions. The parentheses indicate hyper-parameter values: $(\lambda_{\text{Loss}}, \lambda_{\text{Enc}})$ for AdvCls and $(\lambda_{\text{Rand}}, \lambda_{\text{Enc}})$ for AdvDat. Baseline refers to the unmodified InferSent.

For each of the most biased words in SNLI associated with the CONTRADICTION label, we computed the probability that a model predicts an example as a contradiction, given that the hypothesis contains the word. Table 3 shows the top 10 examples in the training set. For each word w, we give its frequency in SNLI, its empirical correlation with the label and with InferSent's prediction, and the percentage decrease in correlations with CONTRADICTION predictions by three configurations of our methods. Generally, the baseline correlations are more uniform than the empirical ones ($\hat{p}(l|w)$), suggesting that indicator words in SNLI might not greatly affect a NLI model, a possibility that both Poliak et al. (2018) and Gururangan et al. (2018) do concede. For example, Gururangan et al. (2018) explicitly mention that "it is important to note that even the most discriminative words are not very frequent."

However, we still observed small skews towards CONTRADICTION. Thus, we investigate whether our methods reduce the probability of predicting CONTRADICTION when a hypothesis contains an indicator word. The model trained with AdvDat (where $\lambda_{\text{Rand}} = 0.4$, $\lambda_{\text{Enc}} = 1$) predicts contradiction much less frequently than InferSent on examples with these words. This configuration was the strongest AdvDat model that still performed reasonably well on SNLI (Figure 2b). Here, AdvDat appears to remove some of the biases learned by the baseline, unmodified InferSent. We also provide two other configurations that do not show such an effect, illustrating that this behavior highly depends on the hyper-parameters.

5 Conclusion

We employed two adversarial learning techniques to a general NLI model by adding an external adversarial hypothesis-only classifier and perturbing training examples. Our experiments and analyses suggest that these techniques may help models exhibit fewer hypothesis-only biases. We hope this work will encourage the development and analysis of models that include components that ignore hypothesis-only biases, as well as similar biases discovered in other natural language understanding tasks (Schwartz et al., 2017), including visual question answering, where recent work has considered similar adversarial techniques for removing language biases (Ramakrishnan et al., 2018; Grand & Belinkov, 2019).

6 Acknowledgements

This work was supported by JHU-HLTCOE, DARPA LORELEI, and the Harvard Mind, Brain, and Behavior Initiative. We thank the anonymous reviewers for their comments. Views and conclusions contained in this publication are those of the authors and should not be interpreted as representing official policies or endorsements of DARPA or the U.S. Government.

References

Moustafa Alzantot, Yash Sharma, Ahmed Elgohary, Bo-Jhang Ho, Mani Srivastava, and Kai-Wei Chang. Generating Natural Language Adversarial Examples. In *Proceedings of the 2018 Conference on*

Empirical Methods in Natural Language Processing, pp. 2890–2896, 2018.

Yonatan Belinkov and Yonatan Bisk. Synthetic and Natural Noise Both Break Neural Machine Translation. In *International Conference on Learning Representations*, 2018. URL `https://openreview.net/forum?id=BJ8vJebC-`.

Samuel R. Bowman, Gabor Angeli, Christopher Potts, and Christopher D. Manning. A large annotated corpus for learning natural language inference. In *Proceedings of the 2015 Conference on Empirical Methods in Natural Language Processing (EMNLP)*. Association for Computational Linguistics, 2015.

Xilun Chen and Claire Cardie. Multinomial adversarial networks for multi-domain text classification. In *Proceedings of the 2018 Conference of the North American Chapter of the Association for Computational Linguistics: Human Language Technologies, Volume 1 (Long Papers)*, pp. 1226–1240. Association for Computational Linguistics, 2018. URL `http://aclweb.org/anthology/N18-1111`.

Alexis Conneau, Douwe Kiela, Holger Schwenk, Loïc Barrault, and Antoine Bordes. Supervised Learning of Universal Sentence Representations from Natural Language Inference Data. In *Proceedings of the 2017 Conference on Empirical Methods in Natural Language Processing*, pp. 670–680. Association for Computational Linguistics, 2017. URL `http://aclweb.org/anthology/D17-1070`.

Alexis Conneau, Germán Kruszewski, Guillaume Lample, Loïc Barrault, and Marco Baroni. What you can cram into a single \$&!#* vector: Probing sentence embeddings for linguistic properties. In *Proceedings of the 56th Annual Meeting of the Association for Computational Linguistics (Volume 1: Long Papers)*, pp. 2126–2136. Association for Computational Linguistics, 2018. URL `http://aclweb.org/anthology/P18-1198`.

Yanai Elazar and Yoav Goldberg. Adversarial Removal of Demographic Attributes from Text Data. In *Proceedings of the 2018 Conference on Empirical Methods in Natural Language Processing*, pp. 11–21. Association for Computational Linguistics, 2018. URL `http://aclweb.org/anthology/D18-1002`.

Yaroslav Ganin and Victor Lempitsky. Unsupervised Domain Adaptation by Backpropagation. In *International Conference on Machine Learning*, pp. 1180–1189, 2015.

Ian J Goodfellow, Jonathon Shlens, and Christian Szegedy. Explaining and Harnessing Adversarial Examples. In *International Conference on Learning Representations (ICLR)*, 2015.

Gabriel Grand and Yonatan Belinkov. Adversarial Regularization for Visual Question Answering: Strengths, Shortcomings, and Side Effects. In *Proceedings of the 2nd Workshop on Shortcomings in Vision and Language (SiVL) at NAACL-HLT*, June 2019.

Suchin Gururangan, Swabha Swayamdipta, Omer Levy, Roy Schwartz, Samuel Bowman, and Noah A. Smith. Annotation Artifacts in Natural Language Inference Data. In *Proceedings of the 2018 Conference of the North American Chapter of the Association for Computational Linguistics: Human Language Technologies, Volume 2 (Short Papers)*, pp. 107–112, New Orleans, Louisiana, June 2018. Association for Computational Linguistics. URL `http://www.aclweb.org/anthology/N18-2017`.

Sepp Hochreiter and Jürgen Schmidhuber. Long short-term memory. *Neural computation*, 9(8):1735–1780, 1997.

Dongyeop Kang, Tushar Khot, Ashish Sabharwal, and Eduard Hovy. AdvEntuRe: Adversarial Training for Textual Entailment with Knowledge-Guided Examples. In *Proceedings of the 56th Annual Meeting of the Association for Computational Linguistics (Volume 1: Long Papers)*, pp. 2418–2428, Melbourne, Australia, July 2018. Association for Computational Linguistics. URL `http://www.aclweb.org/anthology/P18-1225`.

Pasquale Minervini and Sebastian Riedel. Adversarially Regularising Neural NLI Models to Integrate Logical Background Knowledge. In *Proceedings of the 22nd Conference on Computational Natural Language Learning (CoNLL 2018)*. Association for Computational Linguistics, 2018.

Lili Mou, Rui Men, Ge Li, Yan Xu, Lu Zhang, Rui Yan, and Zhi Jin. Natural Language Inference by Tree-Based Convolution and Heuristic Matching. In *Proceedings of the 54th Annual Meeting of the Association for Computational Linguistics (Volume 2: Short Papers)*, pp. 130–136, Berlin, Germany, August 2016. Association for Computational Linguistics. URL `http://anthology.aclweb.org/P16-2022`.

Jeffrey Pennington, Richard Socher, and Christopher Manning. Glove: Global vectors for word representation. In *Proceedings of the 2014 conference on empirical methods in natural language processing (EMNLP)*, pp. 1532–1543, 2014.

Adam Poliak, Jason Naradowsky, Aparajita Haldar, Rachel Rudinger, and Benjamin Van Durme. Hypothesis Only Baselines in Natural Language Inference. In *Proceedings of the Seventh Joint Conference on Lexical and Computational Semantics*, pp. 180–191, New Orleans, Louisiana, June 2018. Association for Computational Linguistics. URL `http://www.aclweb.org/anthology/S18-2023`.

Sainandan Ramakrishnan, Aishwarya Agrawal, and Stefan Lee. Overcoming Language Priors in Visual Question Answering with Adversarial Regularization. In *NIPS*, pp. 1548–1558, 2018.

Roy Schwartz, Maarten Sap, Ioannis Konstas, Leila Zilles, Yejin Choi, and Noah A. Smith. Story Cloze Task: UW NLP System. In *Proceedings of LSDSem*, 2017.

Masatoshi Tsuchiya. Performance Impact Caused by Hidden Bias of Training Data for Recognizing Textual Entailment. In *11th International Conference on Language Resources and Evaluation (LREC2018)*, 2018.

Qizhe Xie, Zihang Dai, Yulun Du, Eduard Hovy, and Graham Neubig. Controllable invariance through adversarial feature learning. In *Advances in Neural Information Processing Systems*, pp. 585–596, 2017.

Brian Hu Zhang, Blake Lemoine, and Margaret Mitchell. Mitigating unwanted biases with adversarial learning. In *Proceedings of the 2018 AAAI/ACM Conference on AI, Ethics, and Society*, pp. 335–340. ACM, 2018.

Kelly Zhang and Samuel Bowman. Language Modeling Teaches You More than Translation Does: Lessons Learned Through Auxiliary Task Analysis. In *Proceedings of the 2018 EMNLP Workshop BlackboxNLP: Analyzing and Interpreting Neural Networks for NLP*, pp. 359–361, Brussels, Belgium, November 2018. Association for Computational Linguistics. URL `http://www.aclweb.org/anthology/W18-5448`.

A Stronger hyper-parameters for AdvCls

Figure 3 provides validation results using AdvCls with stronger hyper-parameters to complement the discussion in §4.2. While it is difficult to notice trends, all configurations perform similarly and slightly below the baseline. These models seem to be less stable compared to using smaller hyper-parameters, as discussed in §4.2.

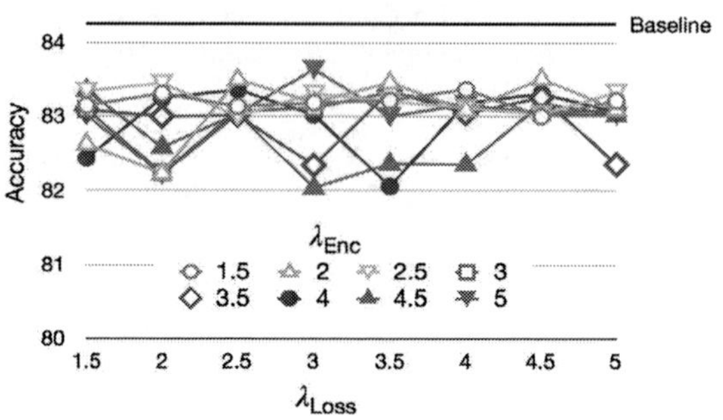

Figure 3: Validation results using AdvCls with stronger hyper-parameters.

Bayesian Inference Semantics: A Modelling System and A Test Suite

Jean-Philippe Bernardy   **Rasmus Blanck**   **Stergios Chatzikyriakidis**
Shalom Lappin   **Aleksandre Maskharashvili**
University of Gothenburg
`firstname.lastname@gu.se`

Abstract

We present BIS, a Bayesian Inference Semantics, for probabilistic reasoning in natural language. The current system is based on the framework of Bernardy et al. (2018), but departs from it in important respects. BIS makes use of Bayesian learning for inferring a hypothesis from premises. This involves estimating the probability of the hypothesis, given the data supplied by the premises of an argument. It uses a syntactic parser to generate typed syntactic structures that serve as input to a model generation system. Sentences are interpreted compositionally to probabilistic programs, and the corresponding truth values are estimated using sampling methods. BIS successfully deals with various probabilistic semantic phenomena, including frequency adverbs, generalised quantifiers, generics, and vague predicates. It performs well on a number of interesting probabilistic reasoning tasks. It also sustains most classically valid inferences (instantiation, de Morgan's laws, etc.). To test BIS we have built an experimental test suite with examples of a range of probabilistic and classical inference patterns.

1 Introduction

On a traditional view of inference, the entailment relation between the premises of an argument and its conclusion holds *iff* the argument is logically valid in a proof or model theory. More recently, computational approaches to entailment in natural text, such as Recognising Textual Entailment (RTE, Dagan et al. (2009)) have attempted to capture inferences that depend on lexical meaning and real world knowledge, as well as logical structure. In the latter sorts of inference, the conclusions often follow from the premises within a certain range of probability values.

In this paper we present Bayesian Inference Semantics (BIS), a probabilistic semantics for natural language that assigns probability values, rather than Boolean truth-values, to sentences. The probability of a sentence is the likelihood that an idealised speaker, as represented by our model, would accept the assertion that it expresses. Our framework builds on the approach proposed by Bernardy et al. (2018). It is Bayesian in that it constructs models in which asserted constraints provide Bayesian evidence that models use to determine whether objects satisfy particular properties.

Objects are represented as vectors in a model space S, and properties are subspaces in S. Satisfaction of a property is expressed as membership in the corresponding subspace of S. The probability density over the space of possible situations corresponds to the *a priori* density of objects in these subspaces, and is specified through Bayesian priors. The system leverages the probabilistic functional programming language WebPPL (Goodman and Stuhlmüller, 2014) to evaluate Bayesian posteriors. English sentences are parsed using Ranta's Grammatical Framework (GF, `http://www.grammaticalframework.org/`, 2004), and the parses are compositionally mapped into interpretations within BIS's probabilistic models.

We apply BIS to inferences, most of which are probabilistic in nature, and so closely related to RTE concerns. We have constructed a test suite of 78 inferences on which we have developed and tested BIS. The premises in each argument provide Bayesian evidence for the models in which the inference is interpreted, and its conclusion is assigned a (posterior) probability value.[1]

In Section 2 we describe BIS. We explain the syntax-model interface that our GF parses provide, and we characterise how our models are constructed. The models employ Monte Carlo

---

[1] Our test set, and the code for BIS are available at `https://github.com/GU-CLASP/bbclm2019`.

*Proceedings of the Eighth Joint Conference on Lexical and Computational Semantics (*SEM)*, pages 263–272
Minneapolis, June 6–7, 2019. ©2019 Association for Computational Linguistics

Markov Chain (MCMC) sampling[2] on objects to estimate membership in the property classes that correspond to the predicates identified in GF parses of our input sentences.

Section 3 presents our inference system and our test set. BIS currently handles a range of generalised quantifiers, sentential and VP negation, modal and temporal adverbs, measure and comparative adjectives, common nouns, and a variety of logical connectives. It treats VPs and common nouns as monadic predicates. We show how BIS handles both probabilistic and logically valid inferences over a series of examples from the test set. We specify the coverage that the system currently achieves for this set. We have designed BIS to capture inferences involving gradable predicates like *tall*, where the application of the predicate is clear for upper and lower bound cases, but increasingly indeterminate for intermediate instances between these points. BIS handles arguments in which neither a predicate nor its contrary apply. It also covers both wide and narrow scope readings of certain quantifiers.

We discuss other approaches to probabilistic semantic inference in Section 4. Finally, in Section 5 we identify the issues that we plan to take up in future work, and state our conclusions.

2 System Description

2.1 Overview

Our system for probabilistic semantics is comprised of three phases: (i) parsing, using the GF tool, (ii) compositional Montegovian Semantics, written in Haskell, and (iii) computation of entailment probability.

Our syntax is encoded in the Grammatical Framework (GF) formalism. GF converts a syntactically well-formed sentence into an abstract syntax tree, which is mapped to semantics. The adequacy of the mapping is guaranteed by using the same types in the GF abstract syntax as in the Haskell semantics. The main constructions are described below.

Our semantics blends aspects of Montague semantics, vector space models, and Bayesian inference. It adopts the main ideas of Bernardy et al. (2018), which we summarise here.

A sentence is interpreted as a probabilistic program returning a Boolean value. Individuals are

represented as (probabilistic) vectors. Other syntactic categories are mapped to functional types, following the Montague Grammar paradigm. BIS evaluates the validity of an inference as follows. It expresses the priors as a distribution over individuals and predicates. The premises of the inference impose conditions on the model that correspond to Bayesian observations. We then compute the truth-value of the conclusion using posterior distributions for input variables, yielding a Bernouilli distribution. Its expected value (a real number between 0 and 1) corresponds to a probabilistic measure of entailment. Fig. 1 gives a schematic view of BIS's architecture.

This value can be computed symbolically, for example by using the precise semantics for probabilistic programming of Borgström et al. (2013). However symbolic expressions may contain intractable integrals. Therefore we resort to approximating the result by using MCMC sampling, as described by Goodman et al. (2008), and implemented in their WebPPL tool.

2.2 Basics

Consider the sentence "John is a musician". Our GF grammar parses this sentence as:
CltoS Pos (S1 John (Bare (IsA Musician))).
We briefly review the combinators used above. *CltoS* is of type $Pol \rightarrow Cl \rightarrow S$: it produces a declarative sentence from a polarity (positive or negative) and a declarative clause. *S1* is of type $NP \rightarrow AVP \rightarrow Cl$, taking a noun phrase and a (possibly modified) verb phrase to return a declarative clause. Here, AVP is understood as VP phrase that might have been modified by a modal adverb. There is no modifier in this example, which is signaled by the combinator *Bare*, of type $VP \rightarrow AVP$. The types of the remaining constants are $IsA : CN \rightarrow VP$, $John : NP$, and $Musician : CN$.

Because the types are the same in Haskell and in GF, any abstract syntax tree given by GF will be a well-typed Haskell expression. To obtain a complete semantics, our model treats *John* and *Musician* as random representatives of their respective classes, and they are sampled accordingly. Then the truth value of the sentence is evaluated (there is no premise in this case).

```
modelJohnMusician = do
  john ← newInd
  musician ← newPred
  return (cltoS pos (s1 john (bare (isA musician))))
```

[2]For detailed discussion of MCMC see Brooks (1998); Roberts and Rosenthal (2004).

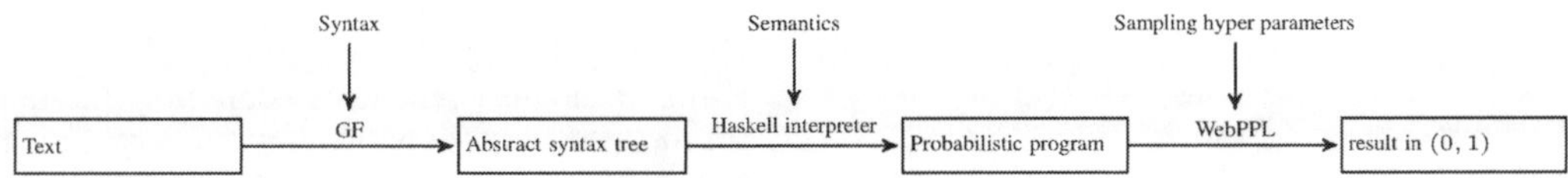

Figure 1: Phases in our system

Running the model, with our implementation, gives the following result:

```
false : 0.67      true : 0.33
```

In the absence of further information, an arbitrary predicate has a chance of (around) 0.33 to hold of an arbitrary individual. This number follows from the way that we model predicates, as described in Section 2.3.

To record assumptions about individuals and predicates, we use the *observe* primitive of Borgström et al. (2013), which ensures that a given proposition holds, and so influences the posteriors. In the MCMC implementation, if the argument to an *observe* call is false, then the corresponding choice of parameters is not retained in the final computation of posteriors. So, for instance, assume that we add the premise that "Most people are musicians" to the earlier example. The premise is parsed as *CltoS Pos (S1 (QNP Most Person) (Bare (IsA Musician)))*, where *QNP*: *Quant* → *CN* → *NP* and *Most* : *Quant*. The semantics is:

$$modelJohnMusicianMost = \mathbf{do}$$
$$john \leftarrow newInd$$
$$musician \leftarrow newPred$$
$$observe\ (cltoS\ pos\ (s1\ (qNP\ most\ person)$$
$$\qquad\qquad (bare\ (isA\ musician))))$$
$$return\ (cltoS\ pos\ (s1\ john\ (bare\ (isA\ musician))))$$

The premise raises the estimated probability value of the conclusion to

```
true : 0.834     false : 0.166
```

2.3 Predicates and their negation

Our basic assumption is that (in the absence of other information) individuals are drawn from a multi-variate normal distribution of dimension k, with a zero mean vector and a unit covariance matrix, where k is a hyperparameter of the system. Any *logical* predicate is represented as a subspace of all individuals. We make the additional simplifying assumption that every atomic lexical predicate p is represented by three components: (1) A vector v_p. The projection of any individual x onto this direction ($x \cdot v_p$) corresponds to the degree to which x exhibits the characteristics corresponding

to p. (2) A threshold θ_p^+, such that if $x \cdot v_p > \theta_p^+$ then x is (probabilistically) considered to satisfy p. (3) Another threshold θ_p^-, such that if $x \cdot v_p < \theta_p^-$, then the contrary of the predicate (expressed as VP negation) applies. This procedure allows BIS to express the indeterminacy attached to both measure and non-measure predicates in cases at the border of a classifier, in a fully uniform way.

The vectors v_p are sampled from the same multi-variate normal distribution as individuals, but unlike individuals, these vectors are normalised. Both thresholds are sampled in a standard normal distribution. At all times, we maintain a positive gap between these thresholds: $\theta_p^- < \theta_p^+$. Hence, in our system, the law of the excluded middle does not hold at the linguistic level, since for a given individual x and a predicate p we may well have $\theta_p^- < x \cdot v_p < \theta_p^+$. For example, it is possible that neither "John is a musician" nor "John isn't a musician" apply. Notice that this is not a case of epistemic uncertainty. Rather, in this example, John does not clearly satisfy the property of being a musician and, at the same time, he cannot be regarded as a non-musician. This state of affairs is illustrated in Fig. 2.

2.4 Adjectives and Measure Predicates

Adjectives behave like other predicates. They come with a direction and two thresholds, allowing for the proposition "It is not the case that John is tall, and it is not the case that John isn't tall" to hold in some models.

BIS supports reasoning with units of measures, as in "John is 6 feet tall". We can also express height in various units of measures ("John is 180 cm tall"). To capture the scaling needed for *any* metric we introduce an additional layer of interpretation, which corresponds to units of measure. Each unit of measure u is represented by a pair of a factor f_u and a bias b_u, both drawn from normal distributions. This yields a transformation $t_u(x) = f_u x + b_u$. The numbers provided in the input ("6", "180") are then compared with the transformed measure predicates corresponding to the adjective. (In our example $t_{feet}(john \cdot v_{tall}) = 6$.)

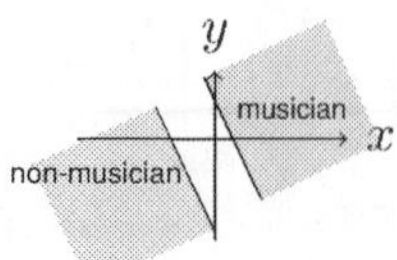

Figure 2: A representation of the predicate "musician" and its negation. The blue and red areas indicate the corresponding subspaces.

This allows BIS to simultaneously infer posterior distributions for individuals, predicates and units of measures.

2.5 Quantifiers

BIS uses the same mechanism for handling quantifiers as Bernardy et al. (2018) do. To interpret a sentence such as "Most musicians are tall", it runs an inner instance of an inference corresponding to "If x is a musician, then x is tall". Then, it imposes, as a posterior of the outer model, the condition that the probabilistic evaluation of the inner inference is higher than a given threshold θ_{most}.

We allow a sentence to contain several generalised quantifiers, such as in "Most bass players are taller than most guitarists", and there are two possibilities to consider when implementing support for this. The first is to nest one application of the above procedure within another. This gives an inner model "If x is a bass player, then x is taller than most guitarists", and an inner-inner inference problem "If y is a guitarist, then x is taller than y". The other is to use a single inner model, with simultaneous quantification over all variables: "If x is a bass players and y is a guitarist, then x is taller than y". The first interpretation is inefficient. Each inner model demands a separate MCMC sampling. When running two-levels of sampling the speed is inversely propositional to the square of samples used. But the second interpretation is not quite correct. The threshold that is being used can only commutatively compound the thresholds of both quantifiers that are used. Therefore, the model would not distinguish between the sentences "Every bass player is taller than most guitarists" and "Most bass players are taller than every guitarist", although their semantics are distinct. For this reason, we opt for the inefficient but precise first procedure, even while we recognise that the second option is a viable way of doing rough grained estimated reasoning.

Finally, we note that it is very inefficient to use the inner-instance sampling method to ensure that a model satisfies sentences containing the universal quantifier, such as "Every musician is a logician". The priors must be set in a particular way to ensure that the subspace of "musicians" is included in that of "logicians". The defining vectors must be exactly parallel. Therefore sampling converges slowly. To deal with this problem we instead impose on the model the requirement that the cosine similarity between the vectors corresponding to "musician" and "logician" is greater than 0.99, and that the threshold $\theta^+_{musician}$ is greater than $\theta^+_{logician}$. These conditions produce a near-perfect containment of "musician" in "logician".

3 Test Suite

In order to illustrate BIS's coverage we have constructed a test suite. We construct a test suite rather than use any of the existing test suites for inference because all of the latter (e.g. the FraCaS test suite (Cooper et al., 1996), RTE (Dagan et al., 2006), and SNLI (Bowman et al., 2015)) are not designed to assess probabilistic inference, but categorical entailment. They are annotated for three-way (YES, NO, UNK), or binary (YES, NO) values for entailment. In the latter case, the categories NO and UNK of the three-way task are collapsed into a single category. By contrast, we are interested in capturing the full distribution of probability over an inference. Our suite includes 78 examples, each with one or more premises followed by a conclusion. The examples are annotated with respect to the semantic phenomena that figure in the inference. Here is the first example from our test suite:

(T1) P1. Every violinist is a musician.
P2. Musicians generally read music.
H.   If John is a violinist, then John reads music.
Label: QUANTIFIER, MODAL ADVERB

Below, we describe several phenomena that an adequate natural language inference system ought to capture. These are particularly important for semantic frameworks designed to handle probabilistic reasoning. While most examples in the current version of the test suite involve probabilistic reasoning, others are classically valid entailments.

We briefly comment on the current state of the art of our system with respect to each of the examples that we present. It is important to note that none of the inferences in our test suite turn on real world knowledge, beyond the information contained in the premises. This is due to the fact that our models estimate the likelihood of an inference as the conditional probability of the conclusion, given the premises. The premises serve as priors on the models generated to evaluate the conclusion. The models sample the possible relations among the individuals and properties that interpret the NPs and predicates in the conclusion, given only the restrictions imposed by the relations among the individuals and the properties that interpret the statements in the premises.

All the phenomena presented in this section (as seen in examples under the label (Tn), where n is a number of an example in the test suite) are supported by our system.

3.1 Relation to classical logic

Although our main goal is not to embed a particular logic into our system, it is useful to know the relation between our system and a specified logic. This allows us to evaluate whether our system can be used in situations where precise reasoning is required.

BIS nearly supports full classical propositional logic, using the sentential connectives "and", "or", "if ... then ...", together with "it is not the case that". To see that it goes beyond intuitionistic propositional logic we check that it validates the law of the excluded middle, de Morgan's laws, and Peirce's formula. However, BIS does not sustain *reductio ad absurdum* as a rule of inference. The system evaluates an inference by constructing a model for the premises of the inference and evaluating the hypothesis in that model. This means that in arguments where the premises are inconsistent (as would be the case in an attempt to use *reductio*) the system fails to construct such a model. It would not evaluate the hypothesis in that model, yielding no result at all. Therefore the consequence relation is not monotone, as the addition of an extra inconsistent premise makes the computation diverge. By contrast, the system assigns probability 1 to $\models A \wedge \neg A \to B$ for any choice of A and B.

VP-level negation does not interact with sentential negation in the way that one might expect. GF only provides binary clausal polarity, whereas our implementation of predicates requires a many-valued logic. Therefore, VP negation in examples such as "John isn't a guitarist" rules out both that John is a guitarist, and that John is in the

undecided area between $\theta^-_{guitarist}$ and $\theta^+_{guitarist}$. Hence, "John isn't a guitarist" implies "It is not the case that John is a guitarist", but the converse implication does not hold. As a consequence of our treatment of VP negation, the universal quantifier ("all") and the existential quantifier ("some") are not interdefinable, as they are in classical logic. So, for example, "All musicians read music" implies "It is not the case that some musicians don't read music", but not the other way around.

Instantiation: Instantiation, one of the main inference rules in the Aristotelian syllogism, is supported in our system. The following test suite example is evaluated as *true* with probability 1.

(T31) P1. All intermediate logic students are Stones fans.
       P2. John is an intermediate logic student.
       H.   John is a Stones fan.
       Label: INSTANTIATION

Chains of universal affirmatives: The system does not perform very well on examples that chain universal quantifiers together to form valid FOL inferences. Consider the following:

(T76) P1. All violinists are musicians.
       P2. All musicians read music.
       H.   All violinists read music.
       Label: QUANTIFIERS, FOL VALIDITY

Here, we would expect a probability of 1 for the conclusion, but the actual result is slightly lower. The reason for this is that our system evaluates the universal quantifier by measuring the cosine similarity between the corresponding vectors (> 0.99) as well as comparing the thresholds θ^+_p for the two predicates. Even if the cosine similarity between the vectors corresponding to "violinist" and "musician" is close to 1, and the one between "musician" and "read music" is also, this does not imply that the cosine similarity between "violinist" and "read music" is 1.

By contrast, the following example is assigned a probability close to 1, because the percentage determiner is treated as a generalised quantifier, triggering an inner-model inference.

(T77) P1. All violinists are musicians.
       P2. All musicians read music.
       H.   99 percent of violinists read music.
       Label: QUANTIFIERS, PERCENTAGE DETERMINER

Higher-order case: Universally quantified sentences connected via implications Consider an example with more complex cases of conditionals of the form "if X then Y", where X and Y are quantified assertions.

(T78) P1. Every guitarist is a logician.
      P2. If every guitarist is a logician, then every musician reads music.
      P3. John is a musician.
      H. John reads music.
      Label: IMPLICATION, QUANTIFIER, PROPER NAME

BIS performs well for (T78), assigning the inference a probability close to 1. To test that it works as expected for P2 of (T78), we substitute "Few musicians read music" for "Every musician reads music". BIS assigns the conclusion false with a high probability to H of (T78), which is a reasonable estimated value for this variant of the argument pattern.

3.2 Generalised quantifiers and generics

In addition to examples with universal quantification, our test suite includes cases with other generalised quantifiers (few, most, etc.), and generics expressed as bare plurals.

(T54) P1. Few people are basketball players.
      P2. Basketball players are taller than most non basketball players.
      P3. John is a basketball player.
      H. John is taller than most people.
      Label: COMPARATIVE ADJECTIVE, MODAL ADVERB

3.3 Gradation, Adjectives, and Comparatives

We test our system on gradation, adjectival modification, and comparatives against the sorts of examples discussed in the linguistic semantics literature, e.g. by Klein (1980).

In English, a (positive) adjective such as "tall" can be turned into the comparative "taller", which has the property of transitivity (if $X\,taller\,Y$ and $Y\,taller\,Z$, then $X\,taller\,Z$). Moreover, the adjective and the comparative derived from it are related in meaning, as the example (T15) illustrates (H holds given that P1 and P2 hold). If $X\,taller\,Y$ and $tall(Y)$, then $tall(X)$.

BIS does well on tasks where an inference involves transitivity of a relation expressed as a comparative adjective. The system computes a probability of 1 for (T15).

(T15) P1. Mary is tall.
      P2. John is taller than Mary.
      H. John is tall.
      Label: COMPARATIVE ADJECTIVE, TRANSITIVITY

3.4 Modal Adverbs

BIS handles modal adverbs, such as "usually", "always", "rarely" (sometimes called adverbs of frequency), which can be used to turn categorical judgments into probabilistic ones. Examples where both adverbs of frequency and quantifiers (including generics and generalised quantifiers) interact are particularly interesting. They are not only complex from a computational modelling perspective. They are also semantically difficult. Their interpretations are not straightforward.

As we are interested in probabilistic judgments, we test our model against similar examples that contain probabilistic modifiers, as in (T17) below. The main difference between (T15) and (T17), is that (T17) contains the modal frequency adverbs "usually" and "always" that interact with a comparative. They trigger frequency based semantic relations that condition probabilistic inferences.

(T17) P1. John is always as punctual as Mary.
      P2. Sam is usually more punctual than John.
      H. Sam is more punctual than Mary.
      Label: QUANTIFIER, MODAL/TEMPORAL ADVERB

BIS computes a value of 0.7 for this example.

3.5 Vagueness

Finally, we take up measure predicates that involve vagueness.

(T38) P1. Mary is 190 centimeters tall. Mary is tall.
      P2. Molly is 184 centimeters tall. Molly is tall.
      P3. Ruth is 180 centimeters tall. Ruth is tall.
      P4. Helen is 178 centimeters tall. Helen is tall.
      P5. Athena is 166 centimeters tall. Athena isn't tall.
      P6. Artemis is 157 centimeters tall. Artemis isn't tall.
      P7. Joanna is 160 centimeters tall. Joanna isn't tall.
      P8. Kate is 162 centimeters tall. Kate isn't tall.
      P9. Christine is x centimeters tall.
      H. Chistine isn't tall
      Label: QUANTIFIER, MODAL ADVERB

We perform 15 runs for 18 values of x uniformly distributed in the range 145cm to 201cm. BIS generates encouraging results for this case. The conclusion is always true with high probability where x is lower than 166, the highest measurement judged to be not tall. There is a slight deviation when x is 166, where 3 cases return false with probabilities from 0.5 to 0.85. In the intermediate cases, for which we expect the vagueness effect, we see a near incremental increase of false judgments values with higher probabilities. From 174 cm and upwards, the system returns false consistently. After the lowest judgment of tallness (178), the system returns false with very high probability (many cases are 1).

BIS offers a gradient treatment of measure predicates (through tweaking of priors), expressing vagueness, but it is not yet fully incremental or stable. We seem to be on the right track in our treatment of measure predicates. Improving this aspect of BIS is one of our priorities for future work.

4 Related and Future Work

We do not have any baseline to compare our system to. The only implemented approach similar to ours is the one proposed by Goodman and Lassiter (2015); Lassiter and Goodman (2017). This system is not tested against a test suite. Furthermore, it is not designed to deal with the range of syntactic structures or complex inference patterns that BIS handles. Adapting the Goodman-Lassiter model to allow for such testing would require changes that undermine a comparison with BIS.

Goodman and Lassiter (2015); Lassiter and Goodman (2017) implement a probabilistic semantics in WebPPL. They regard the probability of a declarative sentence as the most highly valued interpretation that a hearer assigns to the utterance of a speaker in a specified context. On this approach, speakers express unambiguous meanings in specified contexts through their utterances, and hearers estimate the likelihood of distinct interpretations as corresponding to those that the speaker intends to convey. Their account requires the existence of a univocal, non-vague speakers meaning that hearers seek to identify by distributing probability among alternative readings. Goodman and Lassiter posit a boundary point parameter for graded modifiers, where the value of this parameter is determined in context. They adopt a classical Montagovian treatment of generalised quantifiers, and their framework has limited coverage of syntactic and semantic structures.

We take the probability value of a sentence to be the likelihood that a competent speaker would endorse an assertion, given specified premises. Predication is intrinsically vague, and we do not as-

sume a sharply delimited reading for a predication that hearers attempt to converge on by estimating the probability of alternative readings. All predication consists in applying a classifier to new instances, on the basis of supervised training. BIS does not posit a contextually dependent cut off boundary for graded predicates or non-graded predicates. Instead, we adopt an integrated approach to both types of classifier on which a property term allows for vague borders. BIS applies a probabilistic treatment of generalised quantifiers, and it covers higher-order quantifiers like *most*.

The design of BIS is inspired by the Bayesian compositional semantic framework proposed by Bernardy et al. (2018). But BIS differs from this framework in a number of important respects. First, it has a comprehensive syntax-semantics interface through GF parsing. Second, it is intended to cover inference in a systematic way, including logically valid, as well as probabilistic arguments. Third, BIS has considerably wider coverage than the framework of Bernardy et al. (2018), and it is constructed in such a way as to permit straightforward extension to new types of sentence structure and inference patterns.

van Eijck and Lappin (2012) distribute probability values for natural language sentences over the set of possible worlds. The probability of a sentence is the sum of the probability values of the worlds in which it is true. If these worlds are understood as maximal consistent sets of propositions, as in classical theories of formal semantics, then it is unclear how they can be represented in a computationally tractable way.[3] Our system avoids these problems by sampling only the individuals and properties (vector dimensions) required to estimate the probability of a given set of statements.

Cooper et al. (2015) propose a compositional semantics within a probabilistic type theory (ProbTTR). They take the probability of a sentence to be a judgment on the likelihood that a given situation is of a particular type, specified in terms of ProbTTR. They do not offer an explicit treatment of vagueness or probabilistic inference. It is also not clear to what extent their type theory is required to achieve a viable compositional probabilistic semantics.

Emerson and Copestake (2017a,b) provide a

---

[3]Lappin (2015) discusses the complexity problems posed by the representation of complete worlds.

probabilistic model in order to identify 'features' of objects in terms of the properties that apply to those objects. They build their model as a graphical probabilistic model. They also interpret universal and existential quantifiers from a probabilistic perspective. "As are Bs" is represented as a conditional probability of B given A, for all elements of the space, which is equal to the sum (integral) over all elements. To compute it, they make use of the variational inference for graphical probabilistic models.

Pfeifer and colleagues (Pfeifer and Sanfilippo, 2018; Pfeifer, 2013; Gilio et al., 2015) study inference in a probabilistic setting by estimating the probability of the conclusion given the probabilities of the premises. They employ p-validity by Adams (1998). To be p-valid the uncertainty of a conclusion in an inference should not increase the cumulative uncertainties of its premises. Their approach differs from ours in several ways. The main one is that we build a model (using Bayesian updating of priors) where the premises hold, and then we observe how probable the hypothesis is in this model. By contrast, they provide an analytic estimation of the conclusion, given its premises. They require that certain properties on conditional probabilities hold. Conditional probabilities are primitives for modelling an implication ("if A then B"). This allows them to avoid problems when estimating $A \rightarrow B$ when A is false. In the current work, we take "if...then..." statements to be cases of material implication ($A \rightarrow B = \neg A \vee B$) instead of conditional probability.

In future work we will explore the interpretation of the "if...then..." construction as a conditional probability, and we may incorporate Pfeifer and colleagues' insights into our semantics.

We plan to extend the current test suite to examples that contain phenomena which are not yet represented there. This will allow us to increase both BIS' coverage and its power. We intend to organise the test suite in a more structured way, by introducing a more systematic and fine-grained classification of example types, and example complexity. To illustrate what we have in mind, imagine that BIS gives the correct result for test suite example n_1, but fails on n_2, where the two cases are labelled as of the same type, but n_2 is simpler than n_1. Given such a typology and complexity hierarchy over examples, it becomes easier to detect the source of peculiar behaviour in the system.

We will also take into account that some examples might not make sense in a probabilistic setting. As Suppes (1966) remarks, statistical syllogisms require a specific formulation in order to be well posed as probabilistic problems. Building such a structured test suite is a challenging task.

In our model, we have sentence-level and predicate-level negation, which we refer to as *weak* and *strong* negation, respectively. In this way, we obtain a logic which deviates from both classical first-order and intuitionistic logic. We will explore the formal properties of this alternative logic, and we will consider the most efficient way of encoding it in BIS.

We observed in the previous section that chained transitive inferences become problematic for BIS in proportion to the length of the chain. This is due to errors that originate in Monte Carlo Methods of approximating integrals, which BIS uses to generate its models. We will experiment with an alternative approach that calculates the required integrals symbolically. On this strategy BIS would invoke Monte Carlo Methods only as a last resort, when symbolic computation is not feasible.

5 Conclusion

This paper describes BIS, an implemented Bayesian system for probabilistic inference. We have tested BIS on a test suite for probabilistic and classically valid arguments, which we have constructed for this task. While the test suite is still under development, it is, to our knowledge, unique in that its examples make probabilistic judgments based purely on the knowledge contained in the premises. The arguments do not require additional world knowledge beyond the information contributed by the premises to support their conclusions. We will reorganise and extend this suite to achieve a fine-grained, labelled typology for its examples.

While BIS follows the approach outlined by Bernardy et al. (2018) in many respects, it handles a wider and richer range of phenomena. In addition to providing a systematic Bayesian inference system, it offers a unique treatment of vagueness through a distinction between two types of negation, and an alternative procedure for computing interpretations for quantifiers.

We have also noted some of the limitations of the current system. Most of these are due to the fact that BIS does not yet encode certain linguistic phenomena. Other problems arise because of BIS's current method for sampling and computing (numerical) approximations. We will address these issues in future work. BIS's current level of performance suggests that it can be scaled up to a wide coverage semantic system for probabilistic natural language inference.

In extending our test suite our primary objective is to provide a better platform for evaluating probabilistic semantic approaches. One way of obtaining more reliable gradient judgments of entailment is to submit inferences to crowd source assessment on a four or five point scale, and to map this scale into probability values (or ranges of values). The mean judgments of such an annotated suite would provide a gold standard for evaluating the performance of a probabilistic inference system. We are also interested in testing BIS on a standard dataset for logical inference, like the FraCaS test suite, that is annotated for categorical inference judgments. Success would consist in assigning high probability to yes cases, low probability to no cases, and intermediate values to unk instances. We could also crowd source the FraCas set, and use the mean judgments that we obtain as the target values for our system.

Acknowledgements

The research reported in this paper was supported by grant 2014-39 from the Swedish Research Council, which funds the Centre for Linguistic Theory and Studies in Probability (CLASP) in the Department of Philosophy, Linguistics, and Theory of Science at the University of Gothenburg. We are grateful to our colleagues in CLASP for helpful discussion of some of the ideas presented here. We also thank three anonymous reviewers for their useful comments on an earlier draft of the paper.

References

Ernest Adams. 1998. *A Primer of Probability Logic*. Stanford: CSLI Publications.

Jean-Philippe Bernardy, Rasmus Blanck, Stergios Chatzikyriakidis, and Shalom Lappin. 2018. A compositional Bayesian semantics for natural language. In *Proceedings of the International Workshop on Language, Cognition and Computational Models, COLING 2018, Santa Fe, New Mexico*, pages 1–11.

Johannes Borgström, Andrew D. Gordon, Michael Greenberg, James Margetson, and Jurgen Van Gael. 2013. Measure transformer semantics for Bayesian machine learning. *Logical Methods in Computer Science*, 9:1–39.

Samuel R Bowman, Gabor Angeli, Christopher Potts, and Christopher D Manning. 2015. A large annotated corpus for learning natural language inference. In *Proceedings of EMNLP*, pages 632–642.

Stephen P. Brooks. 1998. Markov chain monte carlo method and its application. *Journal of the Royal Statistical Society. Series D (The Statistician)*, 47(1):69–100.

R. Cooper, D. Crouch, J. van Eijck, C. Fox, J. van Genabith, J. Jaspars, H. Kamp, D. Milward, M. Pinkal, M. Poesio, and S. Pulman. 1996. Using the framework. Technical report LRE 62-051r, The FraCaS consortium.

R. Cooper, S. Dobnik, S. Lappin, and S. Larsson. 2015. Probabilistic type theory and natural language semantics. *Linguistic Issues in Language Technology*, 10:1–43.

Ido Dagan, Bill Dolan, Bernado Magnini, and Dan Roth. 2009. Recognizing textual entailment: Rational, evaluation and approaches. *Natural Language Engineering*, 15:1–17.

Ido Dagan, Oren Glickman, and Bernardo Magnini. 2006. The PASCAL recognising textual entailment challenge. In *Machine learning challenges. Evaluating predictive uncertainty, visual object classification, and recognising tectual entailment*, pages 177–190. Springer.

Guy Emerson and Ann Copestake. 2017a. Semantic composition via probabilistic model theory. In *IWCS 2017 - 12th International Conference on Computational Semantics - Long papers*.

Guy Emerson and Ann Copestake. 2017b. Variational inference for logical inference. *CoRR*, abs/1709.00224.

Angelo Gilio, Niki Pfeifer, and Giuseppe Sanfilippo. 2015. Transitive reasoning with imprecise probabilities. In *Symbolic and Quantitative Approaches to Reasoning with Uncertainty*, pages 95–105, Cham. Springer International Publishing.

N. Goodman and D. Lassiter. 2015. Probabilistic semantics and pragmatics: Uncertainty in language and thought. In S. Lappin and C. Fox, editors, *The Handbook of Contemporary Semantic Theory, Second Edition*, pages 655–686. Wiley-Blackwell, Malden, Oxford.

N. Goodman, V. K. Mansinghka, D. Roy, K. Bonawitz, and J. Tenenbaum. 2008. Church: a language for generative models. In *Proceedings of the 24th Conference Uncertainty in Artificial Intelligence (UAI)*, pages 220–229.

Noah D Goodman and Andreas Stuhlmüller. 2014. The Design and Implementation of Probabilistic Programming Languages. http://dippl.org. Accessed: 2018-12-10.

Ewan Klein. 1980. A semantics for positive and comparative adjectives. *Linguistics and Philosophy*, 4(1):1–45.

Shalom Lappin. 2015. Curry typing, polymorphism, and fine-grained intensionality. In Shalom Lappin and Chris Fox, editors, *The Handbook of Contemporary Semantic Theory, Second Edition*, pages 408–428. Wiley-Blackwell, Malden, MA and Oxford.

Daniel Lassiter and Noah Goodman. 2017. Adjectival vagueness in a Bayesian model of interpretation. *Synthese*, 194:3801–3836.

Niki Pfeifer. 2013. The new psychology of reasoning: A mental probability logical perspective. *Thinking & Reasoning*, 19(3-4):329–345.

Niki Pfeifer and Giuseppe Sanfilippo. 2018. Probabilistic semantics for categorical syllogisms of figure II. In *Scalable Uncertainty Management*, pages 196–211. Springer International Publishing.

Aarne Ranta. 2004. Grammatical framework. *Journal of Functional Programming*, 14(2):145–189.

Gareth O. Roberts and Jeffrey S. Rosenthal. 2004. General state space markov chains and mcmc algorithms. *Probab. Surveys*, 1:20–71.

Patrick Suppes. 1966. Probabilistic inference and the concept of total evidence. In Jaakko Hintikka and Patrick Suppes, editors, *Aspects of Inductive Logic*, volume 43 of *Studies in Logic and the Foundations of Mathematics*, pages 49–65. Elsevier.

J. van Eijck and S. Lappin. 2012. Probabilistic semantics for natural language. In Z. Christoff, P. Galeazzi, N. Gierasimszuk, A. Marcoci, and S. Smets, editors, *Logic and Interactive Rationality (LIRA), Volume 2*. ILLC, University of Amsterdam.

Target Based Speech Act Classification in Political Campaign Text

Shivashankar Subramanian   **Trevor Cohn**   **Timothy Baldwin**
School of Computing and Information Systems
The University of Melbourne
shivashankar@student.unimelb.edu.au   {t.cohn, tbaldwin}@unimelb.edu.au

Abstract

We study pragmatics in political campaign text, through analysis of speech acts and the target of each utterance. We propose a new annotation schema incorporating domain-specific speech acts, such as *commissive-action*, and present a novel annotated corpus of media releases and speech transcripts from the 2016 Australian election cycle. We show how speech acts and target referents can be modeled as sequential classification, and evaluate several techniques, exploiting contextualized word representations, semi-supervised learning, task dependencies and speaker meta-data.

1   Introduction

Election campaign text is a core artifact in political analysis. Campaign communication can influence a party's reputation, credibility, and competence, which are primary factors in voter decision making (Fernandez-Vazquez, 2014). Also, modeling the discourse is key to measuring the role of party in *constructive democracy* — to engage in constructive discussion with other parties in a democracy (Gibbons et al., 2017).

Speech act theory (Austin, 1962; Searle, 1976) can be used to study such pragmatics in political campaign text. Traditional speech act classes have been studied to analyze how people engage with elected members (Hemphill and Roback, 2014), and how elected members engage in discussions (Shapiro et al., 2018), with a particular focus on pledges (Artés, 2011; Naurin, 2011, 2014; Gibbons et al., 2017). Also, election manifestos have been analyzed for prospective and retrospective messages (Müller, 2018). In this work, we combine traditional speech acts with those proposed by political scientists to study political discourse, such as *specific pledges*, which can also help to verify the pledges' fulfilment after an election (Thomson et al., 2010).

In addition to speech acts, it is important to identify the target of each utterance — that is, the political party referred to in the text — in order to determine the discourse structure. Here, we study the effect of jointly modeling the speech act and target referent of each utterance, in order to exploit the task dependencies. That is, this paper is an application of discourse analysis to the pragmatics-rich domain of political science, to determine the intent of every utterance made by politicians, and in part, automatically extract pledges at varying levels of specificity from campaign speeches and press releases.

We assume that each utterance is associated with a unique speech act (similar to Zhao and Kawahara (2017)) and target party,[1] meaning that a sentence with multiple speech acts and/or targets must be segmented into component utterances. Take the following example, from the Labor Party:

(1)   Labor will contribute \$43 million towards the Roe Highway project <u>and we call on the WA Government to contribute funds to get the project underway.</u>

The example is made up of two utterances (with and without an underline), belonging to speech act types *commissive-action-specific* and *directive*, referring to different parties (LABOR and LIBERAL), resp. In our initial experiments, we perform target based speech act classification (i.e. joint speech act classification and determination of the target of the utterance) over gold-standard utterance data (Section 6), but return to perform automatic utterance segmentation along with target based speech act classification (Section 7).

While speech act classification has been applied to a wide range of domains, its application to polit-

---

[1]Zhao and Kawahara (2017) do not address the target referent classification task in their work.

*Proceedings of the Eighth Joint Conference on Lexical and Computational Semantics (*SEM)*, pages 273–282
Minneapolis, June 6–7, 2019. ©2019 Association for Computational Linguistics

Utterance	Speech act	Target party	Speaker
Tourism directly and indirectly supports around 38000 jobs in TAS.	*assertive*	NONE	LABOR
We will invest $25.4 million to increase forensics and intelligence assets for the Australian Federal Police	*commissive-action-specific*	LIBERAL	LIBERAL
Labor will prioritise the Metro West project if elected to government.	*commissive-action-vague*	LABOR	LABOR
A Shorten Labor Government will create 2000 jobs in Adelaide.	*commissive-outcome*	LABOR	LABOR
Federal Labor today calls on the State Government to commit the final $75 million to make this project happen.	*directive*	LIBERAL	LABOR
Good morning everybody.	*expressive*	NONE	LABOR
The Coalition has already delivered a $2.5 billion boost to our law enforcement and security agencies.	*past-action*	LIBERAL	LIBERAL
Malcolm Turnbull's health cuts will rip up to $1.4 billion out of Australians' pockets every year	*verdictive*	LIBERAL	LABOR

Table 1: Examples with speech act and target party classes. "Speaker" denotes the party making the utterance.

ical text is relatively new. Most speech act analyses in the political domain have relied exclusively on manual annotation, and no labeled data has been made available for training classifiers. As it is expensive to obtain large-scale annotations, in addition to developing a novel annotated dataset, we also experiment with a semi-supervised approach by utilizing unlabeled text, which is easy to obtain.

The contributions of this paper are as follows: (1) we introduce the novel task of target based speech act classification to the analysis of political discourse; (2) we develop and release a dataset (can be found here `https://github.com/shivashankarrs/Speech-Acts`) based on political speeches and press releases, from the two major parties — Labor and Liberal — in the 2016 Australian federal election cycle; and (3) we propose a semi-supervised learning approach to the problem by augmenting the training data with in-domain unlabeled text.

2 Related Work

The recent adoption of NLP methods has led to significant advances in the field of computational social science (Lazer et al., 2009), including political science (Grimmer and Stewart, 2013). With the increasing availability of datasets and computational resources, large-scale comparative political text analysis has gained the attention of political scientists (Lucas et al., 2015). One task of particular importance is the analysis of the functional intent of utterances in political text. Though it has received notable attention from many political scientists (see Section 1), the primary focus of almost all work has been to derive insights from manual annotations, and not to study computational approaches to automate the task.

Another related task in the political communication domain is reputation defense, in terms of party credibility. Recently, Duthie and Budzynska (2018) proposed an approach to mine ethos support/attack statements from UK parliamentary debates, while Naderi and Hirst (2018) focused on classifying sentences from Question Time in the Canadian parliament as defensive or not. In this work, our source data is speeches and press releases in the lead-up to a federal election, where we expect there to be rich discourse and interplay between political parties.

Speech act theory is fundamental to study such discourse and pragmatics (Austin, 1962; Searle, 1976). A speech act is an illocutionary act of conversation and reflects shallow discourse structures of language. Due to its predominantly small-data setting, speech act classification approaches have generally relied on bag-of-words models (Qadir and Riloff, 2011; Vosoughi and Roy, 2016), although recent approaches have used deep-learning models through data augmentation (Joty and Hoque, 2016) and learning word representations for the target domain (Joty and Mohiuddin, 2018), outperforming traditional bag-of-words approaches.

Another technique that has been applied to compensate for the sparsity of labeled data is semi-supervised learning, making use of auxiliary unlabeled data, as done previously for speech act classification in e-mail and forum text (Jeong et al., 2009). Zhang et al. (2012) also used semi-supervised methods for speech act classification over Twitter data. They used transductive SVM and graph-based label propagation approaches to annotate unlabeled data using a small seed training set. Joty and Mohiuddin (2018) leveraged out-of-domain labeled data based on a domain adversarial learning approach. In this work, we focus on target based speech act analysis (with a custom class-set) for political campaign text and use a deep-learning approach by incorporating contextualized word representations (Peters et al., 2018) and a cross-view training framework (Clark et al., 2018) to leverage in-domain unlabeled text.

3 Problem Statement

Target based speech act classification requires the segmentation of sentences into utterances, and labelling of those utterances according to speech act and target party. In this work we focus primarily on speech act and target party classification.

Our speech act coding schema is comprised of: *assertive, commissive, directive, expressive, past-action*, and *verdictive*. An *assertive* commits the speaker to something being the case. With a *commissive*, the speaker commits to a future course of action. Following the work of Artés (2011) and Naurin (2011), we distinguish between *action* and *outcome* commissives. Action commissives (*commissive-action*) are those in which an action is to be taken, while outcome commissives (*commissive-outcome*) can be defined as a description of reality or goals. Secondly, similar to Naurin (2014) we also classify action commissives into vague (*commissive-action-vague*) and specific (*commissive-action-specific*), according to their specificity. This distinction is also related to text specificity analysis work addressed in the news (Louis and Nenkova, 2011) and classroom discussion (Lugini and Litman, 2017) domains. A *directive* occurs when the speaker expects the listener to take action in response. In an *expressive*, the speaker expresses their psychological state, while a *past-action* denotes a retrospective action of the target party, and a *verdictive* refers to an assessment on prospective or retrospective actions.

Examples of the eight speech act classes are

# Doc	# Sent	# Utt	Avg Utterance Length
258	6609	7641	19.3

Table 2: Dataset Statistics: number of documents, number of sentences, number of utterances, and average utterance length

given in Table 1, along with the target party (LABOR, LIBERAL, or NONE), indicating which party the speech act is directed towards, and the "speaker" party making the utterance (information which is provided for every utterance).

3.1 Utterance Segmentation

Sentences are segmented both in the context of speech act and target party — when a sentence has utterances belonging to more than one speech act or/and more than one target. For example, the following sentence conveys a pledge (*commissive-outcome*) followed by the party's belief (*assertive*), with the utterance boundary indicated by $|$:

(2) We will save Medicare $|$ because Medicare is more than just a standard of health.

Further, the following (from the Labor party) has segments comparing LABOR and LIBERAL:

(3) Our party is united – $|$ the Liberals are not united.

4 Election Campaign Dataset

We collected media releases and speeches from the two major Australia political parties — Labor and Liberal — from the 2016 Australian federal election campaign. A statistical breakdown of the dataset is given in Table 2. We compute agreement over 15 documents, annotated by two independent annotators, with disagreements resolved by a third annotator. The remaining documents are annotated by the two main annotators without redundancy. Agreement between the two annotators for utterance segmentation based on exact boundary match using Krippendorff's alpha (α) (Krippendorff, 2011) is 0.84. Agreement statistics for the classification tasks (Cohen, 1960; Carletta, 1996) are given in Tables 3 and 4.

Speech act	%	Kappa (κ)
assertive	40.8	0.85
commissive-action-specific	12.4	0.84
commissive-action-vague	6.6	0.73
commissive-outcome	4.9	0.72
directive	1.7	0.92
expressive	1.9	0.88
past-action	6.3	0.76
verdictive	25.4	0.82

Table 3: Speech act agreement statistics

Target party	%	Kappa (κ)
LABOR	45.9	0.92
LIBERAL	39.1	0.90
NONE	15.0	0.86

Table 4: Target party agreement statistics

5 Proposed Approach

Our approach to labeling utterances for speech act and target party classification is as follows. Utterances are first represented as a sequence of word embeddings, and then using a bidirectional Gated Recurrent Unit ("biGRU": Cho et al. (2014)). The representation of each utterance is set to the concatenation of the last hidden state of both the forward and backward GRUs, $\mathbf{h}_i = \left[\overrightarrow{\mathbf{h}}_i, \overleftarrow{\mathbf{h}}_i \right]$. After this, the model has a softmax output layer. This network is trained for both the speech act (eight class) and target party (three class) classification tasks, minimizing cross-entropy loss, denoted as $\mathcal{L}_S$ and $\mathcal{L}_T$ respectively.

Our approach has the following components:

ELMo word embeddings ("biGRU$_{\text{ELMo}}$"): As word embeddings we use a 1024d learned linear combination of the internal states of a bidirectional language model (Peters et al., 2018).

Semi-supervised Learning: We employ a cross-view training approach (Clark et al., 2018) to leverage a larger volume of unlabeled text. Cross-view training is a kind of teacher–student method, whereby the model "teaches" another "student" model to classify unlabelled data. The student sees only a limited form of the data, e.g., through application of noise (Sajjadi et al., 2016; Wei et al., 2018), or a different view of the input, as used herein. This procedure regularises the learning of the teacher to be more robust, as well as increasing the exposure to unlabeled text.

We augment our dataset with over 36k sentences from Australian Prime Minister candidates' election speeches.[2] On these unlabeled examples, the model's probability distribution over targets $p_\theta(y|s)$ is used to fit auxiliary model(s), $p_\omega(y|s)$, by minimising the Kullback-Leibler (KL) divergence, $\text{KL}(p_\theta(y|s), p_\omega(y|s))$. This consensus loss component, denoted $\mathcal{L}_{\text{unsup}}$, is added to the supervised training objective ($\mathcal{L}_S$ or $\mathcal{L}_T$).

We evaluate the following auxiliary models:[3]

- a forward GRU ("biGRU$_{\text{CVT}_{\text{fwd}}}$");
- separate forward and backward GRUs ("biGRU$_{\text{CVT}_{\text{fwdbwd}}}$"); and
- a biGRU with word-level dropout ("biGRU$_{\text{CVT}_{\text{worddrop}}}$").

The intuition is that the student models only have access to restricted views of the data on which the teacher network is trained, and therefore this acts as a regularization factor over the unlabeled data when learning the teacher model.

Multi-task Learning ("biGRU$_{\text{Multi}}$"): For speech act classification, target party classification is considered as an auxiliary task, and vice versa. Accordingly, a separate model is built for each task, with the other task as an auxiliary task, in each case using a linearly weighted objective $\mathcal{L}_S + \alpha \mathcal{L}_T$, where $\alpha \geq 0$ is tuned separately in each application. The intuition here is to capture the dependencies between the tasks, e.g., *commissive* is relevant to the Speaker party only.

Meta-data (biGRU$_{\text{Meta}}$): We concatenate a binary flag encoding the speaker party ($\mathbf{m}_i$) alongside the utterance embedding $\mathbf{h}_i$, i.e., $[\mathbf{h}_i, \mathbf{m}_i]$. This representation is passed through a hidden layer with ReLU-activation, then projected onto a output layer with softmax activation for both the classification tasks.

6 Evaluation

We compare the models presented in Section 5 with the following baseline approaches:

- Support Vector Machine ("SVM$_{\text{BoW}}$") with with unigram term-frequency representation.

- Multi-layer perceptron ("MLP$_{\text{BoW}}$") with unigram term-frequency representation.

---

[2] https://primeministers.moadoph.gov.au/collections/election-speeches

[3] Note that auxliary models share parameters with the corresponding components of main (teacher) model, with the exception of their output layers.

ID	Approach	Speech act		Target party	
		Accuracy	Macro-F1	Accuracy	Macro-F1
1	Meta$_{naive}$	—	—	0.55	0.43
2	SVM$_{BoW}$	0.56	0.41	0.60*[1]	0.56*[1]
3	MLP$_{BoW}$	0.60*[2]	0.47*[2]	0.61*[1]	0.57*[1]
4	DAN$_{GloVe}$	0.53	0.30	0.59	0.54
5	GRU$_{GloVe}$	0.56	0.46	0.58	0.55
6	biGRU$_{GloVe}$	0.57	0.48	0.59	0.56
7	MLP$_{ELMo}$	0.62*[3]	0.53*[3]	0.58	0.57
8	biGRU$_{ELMo}$	**0.68***[7]	**0.57***[7]	0.63*[2,3,7]	0.60*[2,3,7]
9	biGRU$_{ELMo + CVT_{fwd}}$	0.66	0.55	0.63	0.58
10	biGRU$_{ELMo + CVT_{fwdbwd}}$	**0.68**	0.54	0.61	0.56
11	biGRU$_{ELMo + CVT_{worddrop}}$	**0.69**	**0.57**	0.66*[8]	0.60
12	biGRU$_{ELMo + CVT_{worddrop} + Multi}$	**0.69**	**0.58**	0.65	0.60
13	biGRU$_{ELMo + CVT_{worddrop} + Meta}$	**0.68**	**0.58**	**0.71***[11]	**0.66***[8,11]

Table 5: Classification results showing average performance based on 10 runs. * indicates results significantly better than the indicated approaches (based on ID in the table) according to a paired t-test ($p < 0.05$). Boldface shows the overall best results and results insignificantly different from the best. Meta$_{naive}$ is not applicable for speech act classification. Note that all approaches use gold-standard segmentation for evaluation.

Speech act	MLP$_{ELMo}$	Our approach
assertive	0.77	0.80
commissive-action-specific	0.65	0.69
commissive-action-vague	0.45	0.48
commissive-outcome	0.28	0.39
directive	0.58	0.59
expressive	0.55	0.58
past-action	0.45	0.48
verdictive	0.48	0.61

Table 6: Speech act class-wise F1 score.

Target party	biGRU$_{ELMo}$	Our approach
LABOR	0.68	0.74
LIBERAL	0.65	0.75
NONE	0.46	0.48

Table 7: Target party class-wise F1 score.

- Deep Averaging Networks ("DAN$_{GloVe}$") (Iyyer et al., 2015), GRU ("GRU$_{GloVe}$"), and biGRU ("biGRU$_{GloVe}$") with pre-trained 300d GloVe embeddings (Pennington et al., 2014).

- MLP with average-pooling over pre-trained ELMo word embeddings ("MLP$_{ELMo}$").

- Using speaker party as the predicted target party ("Meta$_{naive}$").

We average results across 10 runs with 90%/10% training/test random splits. Hyperparameters are tuned over a 10% validation set randomly sampled and held out from the training set. We evaluate using accuracy and macro-averaged F-score, to account for class-imbalance. We compare the baseline approaches against our proposed approach (different components given in Section 5). We evaluate the effect of each component by adding them to the base model (biGRU$_{ELMo}$), e.g., biGRU model with ELMo embeddings and word-level dropout based semi-supervised approach is given as biGRU$_{ELMo + CVT_{worddrop}}$. Results for speech act and target party classification are given in Table 5. The corresponding class-wise performance for both speech act and target party tasks with our approach (biGRU$_{ELMo + CVT_{worddrop} + Meta}$) compared against the competitive approach from Table 5 is given in Table 6 and Table 7 respectively (and also discussed further in Section 8). All the approaches are evaluated with the gold-standard segmentation. Utterance segmentation is discussed in Section 7.

From the results in Table 5, we observe that the biGRU[4] performs better than the other approaches, and that ELMo contextual embeddings (biGRU$_{ELMo}$) boosts the performance appreciably. Apart from ELMo, the semi-supervised learning methods (biGRU$_{ELMo + CVT_{worddrop}}$) provide a boost in performance for the target party

---

[4]The biGRU model uses ReLU activations, a 128d hidden layer for speech act classification and 64d hidden layer for target party classification, and dropout rate of 0.1.

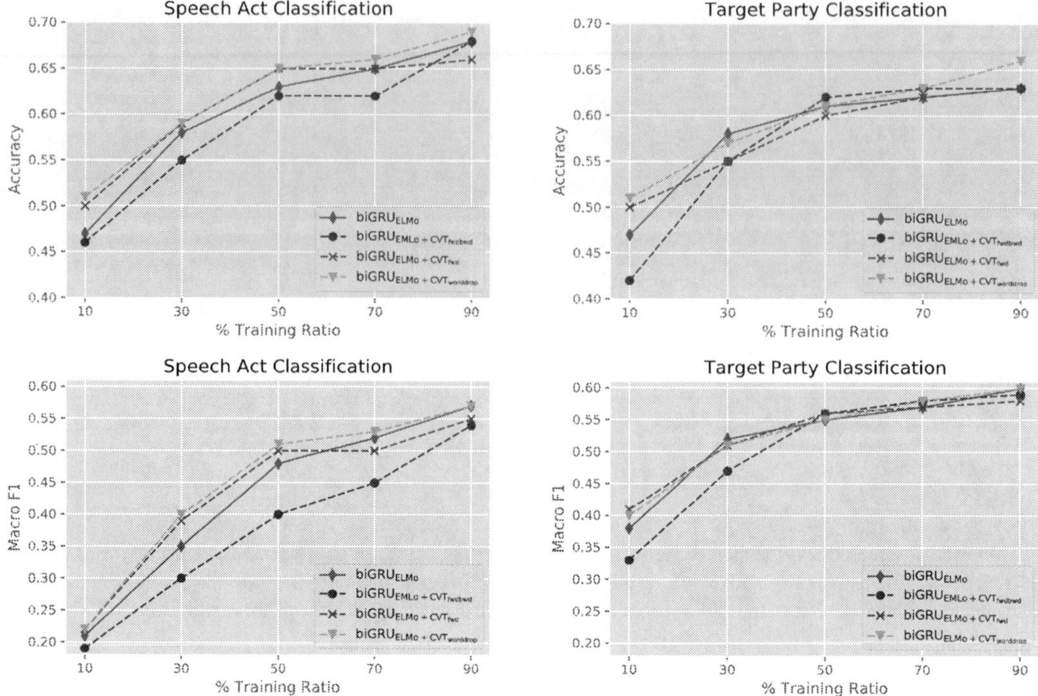

Figure 1: Classification performance across different training ratios. Note that 90% is using all the training data, as 10% is used for validation.

task (wrt accuracy) using all the training data. $\text{biGRU}_{\text{ELMo + CVT}_{\text{worddrop}}}$ and $\text{biGRU}_{\text{ELMo + CVT}_{\text{fwd}}}$ provide gains in performance for the speech act task, especially with fewer training examples ($\leq 50\%$ of training data, see Figure 1). Performance of semi-supervised learning models with cross-view training (which leverages in-domain unlabeled text) is compared against $\text{biGRU}_{\text{ELMo}}$, which is a supervised approach. Results across different training ratio settings are given in Figure 1. From this, we can see that $\text{biGRU}_{\text{ELMo + CVT}_{\text{worddrop}}}$ and $\text{biGRU}_{\text{ELMo + CVT}_{\text{fwd}}}$ performs better than $\text{biGRU}_{\text{ELMo + CVT}_{\text{fwdbwd}}}$ in almost all cases. With a training ratio $\leq 50\%$, $\text{biGRU}_{\text{ELMo + CVT}_{\text{worddrop}}}$ achieves a comparable performance to $\text{biGRU}_{\text{ELMo + CVT}_{\text{fwd}}}$.

Multi-task learning ($\text{biGRU}_{\text{ELMo + CVT}_{\text{worddrop}} + \text{Multi}}$) provides only small improvements for the speech act task. Further, when we add speaker party meta-data ($\text{biGRU}_{\text{ELMo + CVT}_{\text{worddrop}} + \text{Meta}}$), it provides large gains in performance for the target party task. Overall, the proposed approach ($\text{biGRU}_{\text{ELMo + CVT}_{\text{worddrop}} + \text{Meta}}$) provides the best performance for the target party task. Its performance is better than the $\text{biGRU}_{\text{ELMo + Meta}}$

model, which does not leverage the additional unlabeled text using semi-supervised learning, where it achieves 0.70 accuracy and 0.65 Macro F1. Also, ELMo and semi-supervised methods ($\text{biGRU}_{\text{ELMo + CVT}_{\text{worddrop}}}$ and $\text{biGRU}_{\text{ELMo + CVT}_{\text{fwd}}}$) provide significant improvements for the speech act task, especially under sparse supervision scenarios (see Figure 1, for training ratio $\leq 50\%$).

7 Segmentation Results

In the previous experiments, we used gold-standard utterance data, but next we experiment with automatic segmentation. We use sentences as input, based on the NLTK sentence tokenizer (Bird et al., 2009), and automatically segment sentences into utterances based on token-level segmentation, in the form of a `BI` binary sequence classification task using a CRF model (Hernault et al., 2010).[5] We use the following set of features for each word: token, word shape (capitalization, punctuation, digits), Penn POS tags based on SpaCy, ClearNLP dependency labels (Choi and Palmer, 2012), relative position in the sentence, and features for the

---

[5]We also experimented with a neural CRF model, but found it to be less accurate.

Utterance	Target party	Speaker
Our new Tourism Infrastructure Fund will bring more visitor dollars and more hospitality jobs to Cairns, Townsville and the regions.	LABOR	LABOR
Just as he sold out 35,000 owner-drivers in his deal with the TWU to bring back the "Road Safety Remuneration Tribunal".	LABOR	LIBERAL
Then in 2022, we will start construction of the first of 12 regionally superior submarines, the single biggest investment in our military history.	LIBERAL	LIBERAL

Table 8: Scenarios where "Speaker" meta-data benefits the target party classification task.

adjacent words (based on this same feature representation). We compute segmentation accuracy (SA: Zimmermann et al. (2006)), which measures the percentage of segments that are correctly segmented, i.e. both the left and right boundary match the reference boundaries. SA for the CRF model is 0.87. Secondly, to evaluate the effect of segmentation on classification, we compute joint accuracy (JA). It is similar to SA but also requires correctness of the speech act and target party. In cascaded style, JA using the CRF model for segmentation and $\mathrm{biGRU}_{\mathrm{ELMo + CVT_{worddrop} + Meta}}$ for speech act and target party classification is 0.60 and 0.64 respectively. Here, segmentation errors lead to a small drop in performance.

8 Error Analysis

We analyze the class-wise performance and confusion matrix for our best performing approach ($\mathrm{biGRU}_{\mathrm{ELMo + CVT_{worddrop} + Meta}}$). Speech act and target party class-wise performance is given in Tables 6 and 7 respectively. We can see that the proposed approach provides improvement across all classes, while achieving comparable performance for *directive*. Recognizing *commissive-outcome* can be seen to be tougher than other classes. In addition, we analyze the results to identify cases where having "Speaker" party information is beneficial for predicting the target party of sentences. Some of those scenarios are given in Table 8, where the meta-data enables predicting the target party correctly even when there is no explicit reference to the party or leaders.

Confusion matrices for the speech act and target party classification tasks are given in Figure 2. Some observations from the confusion matrices are: (a) *assertive* and *verdictive* are often misclassified as each other; (b) *commissive-action-vague* utterances are often misclassified as *commissive-action-specific*; and (c) LABOR and LIBERAL classes are often misclassified as each

other for the target party classification task.

9 Qualitative Analysis

Here we provide the policy-wise speech act distribution for both parties, which indicates the difference in their predilection for the indicated six policy areas (Figure 3). We provide results for the six most frequent policy categories, for each of which, the campaign text is first classified into one of the policy-areas that are relevant to Australian politics, by building a Logistic Regression classifier with data obtained from ABC Fact Check.[6] Some observations (based on Figure 3) are as follows:

- The incumbent government (LIBERAL) uses more *directive*, *expressive*, *verdictive*, and *past-action* utterances than the opposition (LABOR).
- LIBERAL's text has relatively more pledges (*commissive-action-vague*, *commissive-action-specific* and *commissive-outcome*) on **economy** compared to LABOR, whereas LABOR has more pledges on **social services** and **education**. This is as expected for right- and left-wing parties respectively. Other policy-areas have a comparable number of pledges from both parties. Overall, party-wise salience towards these policy areas correlates highly with the relative breakdowns in the Comparative Manifesto Project (Volkens et al., 2017): where the relative share of sentences from the LABOR and LIBERAL manifestos[7] for **welfare state (health and social services)** is 22:7, **education** is 9:6, **economy** is 11:23, and **technology & infrastructure (communication, infrastructure)** is 17:19.
- Across policy-areas, *specific* pledges are

---

[6]`https://www.abc.net.au/news/factcheck`
[7]`https://manifesto-project.wzb.eu/down/data/2018b/datasets/MPDataset_MPDS2018b.csv`

Figure 2: Confusion matrix for speech act and target party classification tasks.

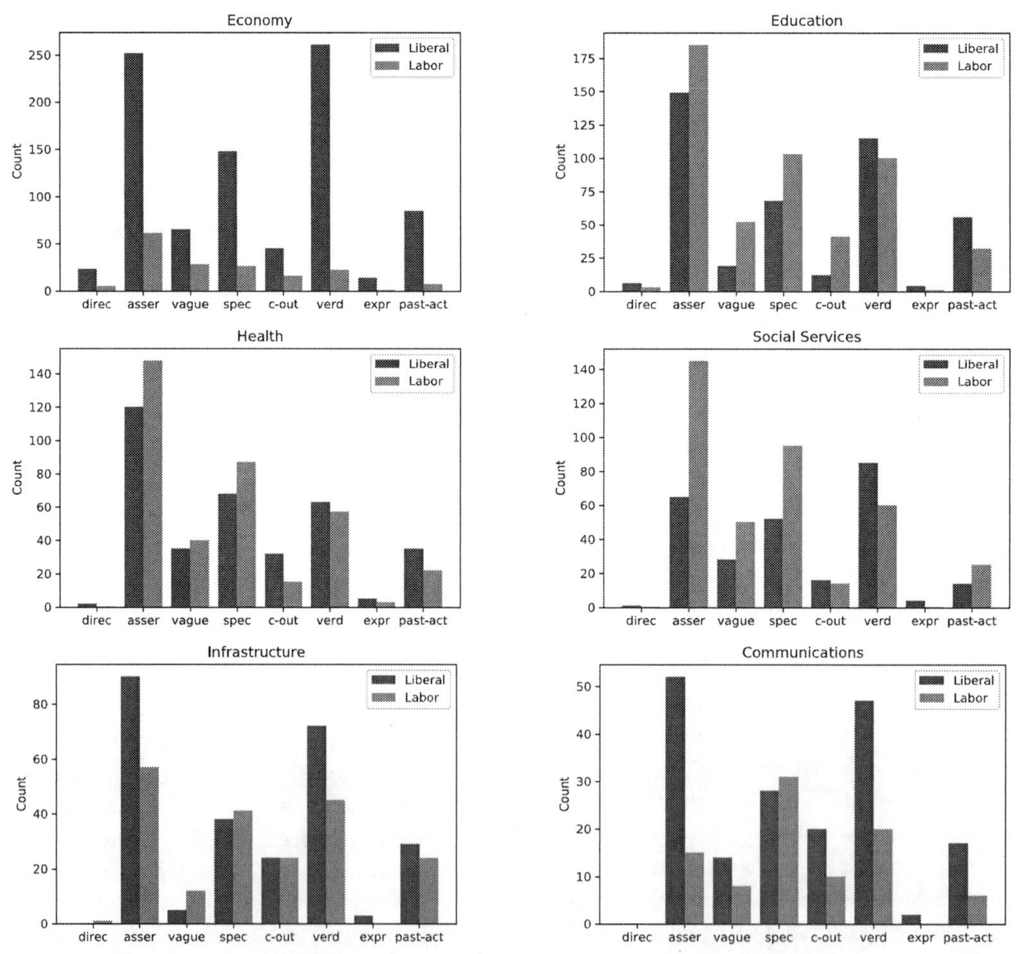

Figure 3: Policy-wise speech act analysis. Classes include: *directive* ("direc"), *assertive* ("asser"), *commissive-action-vague* ("vague"), *commissive-action-specific* ("spec"), *commissive-outcome* ("c-out"), *verdictive* ("verd"), *expressive* ("expr"), and *past-action* ("past-act")

more frequent than *vague* ones. This aligns with previous studies done by Naurin (2014) and Gibbons et al. (2017).

10 Conclusion and Future Work

In this work we present a new dataset of election campaign texts, based on a class schema of speech acts specific to the political science domain. We study the associated problems of identifying the referent political party, and segmentation. We showed that this task is feasible to annotate, and present several models for automating the task. We use a pre-trained language model and also leverage auxiliary unlabeled text with semi-supervised learning approach for the target based speech act classification task. Our results are promising, with the best method being a semi-supervised biGRU with ELMo embeddings for the speech act task, and the model additionally incorporating speaker meta-data for the target party task. We provided qualitative analysis of speech acts across major policy areas, and in future work aim to expand this analysis further with fine-grained policies and ideology-related analysis.

Acknowledgements

We thank the anonymous reviewers for their insightful comments and valuable suggestions. This work was funded in part by the Australian Government Research Training Program Scholarship, and the Australian Research Council.

References

J. Artés. 2011. Do Spanish politicians keep their election promises? *Party Politics*, 19(1):143–158.

J. L. Austin. 1962. *How to do things with words.* Clarendon Press, Oxford.

Steven Bird, Ewan Klein, and Edward Loper. 2009. *Natural Language Processing with Python: Analyzing Text with the Natural Language Toolkit.* O'Reilly Media, Inc.

Jean Carletta. 1996. Assessing agreement on classification tasks: the kappa statistic. *Computational Linguistics*, 22(2):249–254.

Kyunghyun Cho, Bart van Merriënboer, Caglar Gulcehre, Dzmitry Bahdanau, Fethi Bougares, Holger Schwenk, and Yoshua Bengio. 2014. Learning phrase representations using RNN encoder–decoder for statistical machine translation. In *Proceedings of the 2014 Conference on Empirical Methods in Natural Language Processing*, pages 1724–1734.

Jinho D Choi and Martha Palmer. 2012. Guidelines for the clear style constituent to dependency conversion. *Technical Report 01–12: Institute of Cognitive Science, University of Colorado Boulder.*

Kevin Clark, Minh-Thang Luong, Christopher D Manning, and Quoc V Le. 2018. Semi-supervised sequence modeling with cross-view training. In *Proceedings of the 2018 Conference on Empirical Methods in Natural Language Processing*, pages 1914–1925.

Jacob Cohen. 1960. A coefficient of agreement for nominal scales. *Educational and Psychological Measurement*, 20(1):37–46.

Rory Duthie and Katarzyna Budzynska. 2018. A deep modular RNN approach for ethos mining. In *Proceedings of the 27th International Joint Conference on Artificial Intelligence*, pages 4041–4047.

Pablo Fernandez-Vazquez. 2014. And yet it moves: The effect of election platforms on party policy images. *Comparative Political Studies*, 47(14):1919–1944.

Andrew Gibbons, Aaron Martin, and Andrea Carson. 2017. Do parties keep their election promises?: A study of the 43rd Australian Parliament (2010-2013). *Australian Political Studies Association.*

Justin Grimmer and Brandon M Stewart. 2013. Text as data: The promise and pitfalls of automatic content analysis methods for political texts. *Political analysis*, 21(3):267–297.

Libby Hemphill and Andrew J Roback. 2014. Tweet Acts: How Constituents Lobby Congress via Twitter. In *Proceedings of the 17th ACM Conference on Computer Supported Cooperative Work & Social Computing*, pages 1200–1210.

Hugo Hernault, Danushka Bollegala, and Mitsuru Ishizuka. 2010. A sequential model for discourse segmentation. In *Proceedings of the International Conference on Intelligent Text Processing and Computational Linguistics*, pages 315–326.

Mohit Iyyer, Varun Manjunatha, Jordan Boyd-Graber, and Hal Daumé III. 2015. Deep unordered composition rivals syntactic methods for text classification. In *Proceedings of the 53rd Annual Meeting of the Association for Computational Linguistics and the 7th International Joint Conference on Natural Language Processing*, pages 1681–1691.

Minwoo Jeong, Chin-Yew Lin, and Gary Geunbae Lee. 2009. Semi-supervised speech act recognition in emails and forums. In *Proceedings of the 2009 Conference on Empirical Methods in Natural Language Processing*, pages 1250–1259.

Shafiq Joty and Enamul Hoque. 2016. Speech act modeling of written asynchronous conversations with task-specific embeddings and conditional structured models. In *Proceedings of the 54th Annual Meeting of the Association for Computational Linguistics*, pages 1746–1756.

Shafiq Joty and Tasnim Mohiuddin. 2018. Modeling speech acts in asynchronous conversations: A neural-CRF approach. *Computational Linguistics*, pages 1–36.

Klaus Krippendorff. 2011. Computing krippendorff's alpha-reliability. *Technical Report, University of Pennsylvania.*

David Lazer, Alex Sandy Pentland, Lada Adamic, Sinan Aral, Albert Laszlo Barabasi, Devon Brewer, Nicholas Christakis, Noshir Contractor, James Fowler, Myron Gutmann, et al. 2009. Life in the network: The coming age of computational social science. *Science*, 323(5915):721.

Annie Louis and Ani Nenkova. 2011. Automatic identification of general and specific sentences by leveraging discourse annotations. In *Proceedings of 5th International Joint Conference on Natural Language Processing*, pages 605–613.

Christopher Lucas, Richard A Nielsen, Margaret E Roberts, Brandon M Stewart, Alex Storer, and Dustin Tingley. 2015. Computer-assisted text analysis for comparative politics. *Political Analysis*, 23(2):254–277.

Luca Lugini and Diane Litman. 2017. Predicting specificity in classroom discussion. In *Proceedings of the 12th Workshop on Innovative Use of NLP for Building Educational Applications*, pages 52–61.

Stefan Müller. 2018. Prospective and retrospective rhetoric: A new dimension of party competition and campaign strategies. In *Manifesto Corpus Conference.*

Nona Naderi and Graeme Hirst. 2018. Using context to identify the language of face-saving. In *Proceedings of the 5th Workshop on Argument Mining*, pages 111–120.

E. Naurin. 2011. *Election Promises, Party Behaviour and Voter Perception.* Palgrave Macmillan.

E. Naurin. 2014. Is a promise a promise? Election pledge fulfillment in comparative perspective using Sweden as an example. *West European Politics.*

Jeffrey Pennington, Richard Socher, and Christopher Manning. 2014. GloVe: Global vectors for word representation. In *Proceedings of the 2014 Conference on Empirical Methods in Natural Language Processing*, pages 1532–1543.

Matthew Peters, Mark Neumann, Mohit Iyyer, Matt Gardner, Christopher Clark, Kenton Lee, and Luke Zettlemoyer. 2018. Deep contextualized word representations. In *Proceedings of the 2018 Conference of the North American Chapter of the Association for Computational Linguistics: Human Language Technologies*, pages 2227–2237.

Ashequl Qadir and Ellen Riloff. 2011. Classifying sentences as speech acts in message board posts. In *Proceedings of the Conference on Empirical Methods in Natural Language Processing*, pages 748–758.

Mehdi Sajjadi, Mehran Javanmardi, and Tolga Tasdizen. 2016. Regularization with stochastic transformations and perturbations for deep semi-supervised learning. In *Proceedings of the Advances in Neural Information Processing Systems*, pages 1163–1171.

J. R. Searle. 1976. *A Taxonomy of Illocutionary Acts.* Linguistic Agency University of Trier.

Matthew A. Shapiro, Libby Hemphill, and Jahna Otterbacher. 2018. Updates to congressional speech acts on Twitter. In *Proceedings of the American Political Science Association Annual Meeting.*

Robert Thomson, Terry Royed, and Elin Naurin. 2010. The Program-to-Policy Linkage: A Comparative Study of Election Pledges and Government Policies in the United States, the United Kingdom, the Netherlands and Ireland. In *Proceedings of the American Political Science Association Annual Meeting.*

Andrea Volkens, Pola Lehmann, Theres Matthieß, Nicolas Merz, Sven Regel, and Bernhard Weßels. 2017. *The Manifesto Data Collection. Manifesto Project (MRG/CMP/MARPOR). Version 2017b.* Wissenschaftszentrum Berlin für Sozialforschung.

Soroush Vosoughi and Deb Roy. 2016. Tweet acts: A speech act classifier for Twitter. In *Proceedings of the Tenth International AAAI Conference On Web And Social Media*, pages 711–715.

Xiang Wei, Boqing Gong, Zixia Liu, Wei Lu, and Liqiang Wang. 2018. Improving the improved training of Wasserstein GANs: A consistency term and its dual effect. In *Proceedings of the International Conference on Learning Representations.*

Renxian Zhang, Dehong Gao, and Wenjie Li. 2012. Towards scalable speech act recognition in Twitter: tackling insufficient training data. In *Proceedings of the Workshop on Semantic Analysis in Social Media*, pages 18–27.

Tianyu Zhao and Tatsuya Kawahara. 2017. Joint learning of dialog act segmentation and recognition in spoken dialog using neural networks. In *Proceedings of the Eighth International Joint Conference on Natural Language Processing*, pages 704–712.

M Zimmermann, A Stolcke, and E Shriberg. 2006. Joint segmentation and classification of dialog acts in multiparty meetings. In *Proceedings of the 2006 IEEE International Conference on Acoustics, Speech and Signal Processing*, pages 581–584.

Incivility Detection in Online Comments

Farig Sadeque
School of Information
University of Arizona
Tucson, AZ 85721
farig@email.arizona.edu

Stephen Rains
Dept. of Communication
University of Arizona
Tucson, AZ 85721
srains@email.arizona.edu

Yotam Shmargad
School of Govt. and Public Policy
University of Arizona
Tucson, AZ 85721
yotam@email.arizona.edu

Kate Kenski
Dept. of Communication
University of Arizona
Tucson, AZ 85721
kkenski@email.arizona.edu

Kevin Coe
Dept. of Communication
University of Utah
Salt Lake City, UT 84112
kevin.coe@utah.edu

Steven Bethard
School of Information
University of Arizona
Tucson, AZ 85721
bethard@email.arizona.edu

Abstract

Incivility in public discourse has been a major concern in recent times as it can affect the quality and tenacity of the discourse negatively. In this paper, we present neural models that can learn to detect name-calling and vulgarity from a newspaper comment section. We show that in contrast to prior work on detecting toxic language, fine-grained incivilities like name-calling cannot be accurately detected by simple models like logistic regression. We apply the models trained on the newspaper comments data to detect uncivil comments in a Russian troll dataset, and find that despite the change of domain, the model makes accurate predictions.

1 Introduction

Online harassment, colloquially known as cyberbullying or cyber harassment, has been rampant since the introduction of the Internet to the general population. It has been a major cause of concern since the mid- and late-90's, and is a thoroughly researched topic in the fields of social science, behavioral science, network science and computer security. Cyberbullying is a form of harassment that is carried out using electronic modes of communication like computer, phone, and in almost all the cases in recent years, the Internet. Cyberbullying is defined as a "willful and repeated harm inflicted through the medium of electronic text" by Patchin and Hinduja (2006)- but this phenomenon goes far beyond the scope of just electronic text. A more comprehensive definition of cyberbullying can be found in one of their later works, where they defined cyberbullying as "a form of harassment using electronic mode of communication" (Hinduja and Patchin, 2008). Fauman (2008) described cyberbullying as "bullying through the use of technology such as the Internet and cellular phones".

The spectrum of online harassment is vast; hence, we focus on one segment of this phenomenon: online incivility. Incivility has been rampant in American society for quite some time. Incivility is described as *features of discussion that convey an unnecessarily disrespectful tone toward the discussion forum, its participants, or its topics* (Coe et al., 2014). While it is often said that incivility is "very much in the eye of the beholder" and what is civil to someone may be uncivil to another (Kenski et al., 2017), some are universal nevertheless. One study has suggested that 69% of Americans believe that incivility in public discourse has become a rampant problem, and only 6% do not identify it as a problem (Shandwick, 2018). The average number of incivility encounters per week has also risen drastically in both the physical world and cyberspace. Social media encounters are especially alarming: a person who encountered any form of incivility anywhere, had on average 5.4 uncivil encounters per week in online social media platforms in 2018, which is almost double the amount from late 2016.

In this paper, we present machine learning models that can identify two prominent forms of incivility, name-calling and vulgarity, based on user-generated contents from public discourse platforms. We focused trained recurrent neural network models on an annotated newspaper comment section and showed that our model outperforms several baselines, including a state-of-the-art model based

*Proceedings of the Eighth Joint Conference on Lexical and Computational Semantics (*SEM)*, pages 283–291
Minneapolis, June 6–7, 2019. ©2019 Association for Computational Linguistics

on pre-trained contextual embeddings. We applied our newspaper-comments-trained model to a datsaets of Russian troll tweets to observe how the model generalizes from one platform to another.

2 Related Works

Kenski et al. (2017) divided incivility into several different forms, including name-calling, vulgarity, lying accusation, pejorative, and aspersion. They took comments posted by regulars in a newspaper website, and annotated these for the various forms of incivility. Their research focused mostly on the demographics and other individual attributes of readers of these comments and how they perceived incivility in these comments.

Rains et al. (2017) focused more on the perpetrators of incivility rather than the readers. They researched a handful of news articles published in the Arizona Daily Star newspaper website and the comments posted about these articles, then manually annotated these comments and their posters for their incivility and political orientation. The authors found that conservatives were significantly less likely to be uncivil in these public discussions compared to liberals, and the likelihood of liberals being uncivil increased with the presence of conservatives in the same discussion. Liberals were also found to be more repercussive compared to the conservatives.

Recent work has focused on particular forms of incivility, as described in the following sections.

2.1 Generic incivility

Reynolds et al. (2011) developed machine learning models that can detect cyberbullying by identifying curse and insult words in social media posts. They have collected a small set of posts from a website named *formspring.me* and used various non-sequential learning algorithms on this dataset to build a binary classifier for cyberbullying detection.

2.2 Vulgarity

Cachola et al. (2018) used a vulgarity score for better sentiment prediction from a collection of 6800 tweets. They found that vulgarity interacts with key demographic variables like gender, age, religiosity, etc. Other research has also identified demographic keys closely associated with vulgarity: Wang et al. (2014) presented a quantitative analysis on the frequency of curse word usage in Twitter and their variation with certain demographics, and Gauthier et al. (2015) analyzed the usage of swear words based on Tweeter users' age and gender. As none of these papers present any machine learning model that can be used for vulgarity detection, Holgate et al. (2018) claim their work to be the first in vulgarity prediction. They classified functionality of vulgarity in five different cohorts: aggression, emotion expression, emphasis, auxiliary and signalling group identity; and used binary logistic regression classifiers to identify vulgar texts. They also showed the correlation among demographic variables and vulgarity and found that age, faith, and political ideology have significant correlation with vulgarity usage.

2.3 Racism/sexism

Waseem and Hovy (2016) has presented machine learning models that can be used to detect racism and sexism in social media. They have collected and annotated a set of almost 17000 tweets, and used them to build character based n-gram models for offensive tweet detection. They have provided an extensive list of criteria that identify a tweet as racially and sexually offensive, and showed that demographic information does not add much performance to a character-level model.

2.4 Personal attacks

Wulczyn et al. (2017) introduced a methodology to generate annotations for personal attacks. They have used crowdsourcing to identify a set of Wikipedia comments, and used a machine learning model to imitate this annotation on a much larger scale. Agrawal and Awekar (2018) have developed deep neural models that can detect cyberbullying (Reynolds et al., 2011), racism/sexism (Waseem and Hovy, 2016), and personal attacks (Wulczyn et al., 2017) in multiple social media platforms. They claim that theirs is the first work to systematically analyze cyberbullying in social media towards building deep prediction models. They have shown that hand-crafted features using lexicons is not a good idea as abusive word vocabularies vary a lot from one social media platform to another, and swear words are not always considered to be uncivil in social media.

2.5 Name-calling

Habernal et al. (2018) analyzed ad hominem attacks in *Change My View*, a "good faith" argumentation platform that is hosted on Reddit.

They identified posts that Reddit moderators had marked as violating the forum's rules against ad hominem atacks. To identify such posts, they used stacked bidirectional Long-Short Term Memory networks (LSTMs) and Convolutional Neural Networks (CNNs), and achieved 78% and 81% accuracy, respectively. One of their most interesting findings was that in 48.6% of the cases, ad hominem attacks are in the last comment of the thread, which shows that personal attacks and name-callings can affect user participation in public discourses.

Works that closely resemble what we are trying to do have one major issue with the datasets that have been used- they are often annotated by mechanical turks (Wulczyn et al., 2017; Reynolds et al., 2011). Incivility is based on the perception of the person in the receiving end, and this perception varies wildly from person to person. Using turkers that we know almost nothing about is not ideal- as difference in perception may introduce unintended bias in the dataset. Hence, we need a dataset that is annotated by experts who have extensive knowledge on incivility detection. Coe et al. (2014) presents one such dataset, and we plan to use this for our incivility detection task (more on this in Section 4).

3 Incivility Classification and Definitions

For our work, we will use the incivility classification presented by Coe et al. (2014): name-calling, vulgarity, aspersion, lying accusations and pejorative for speech. We focus on the two most prevalent forms of these in Coe et al. (2014)'s data: name-calling and vulgarity.

name-calling Ad hominem attacks. Although ad hominem attacks are often used to derail a conversation by using derogatory terms towards another person, the authors have included every instances of derogatory remarks, irrespective of target and intention. For example, *At least the morons in the state capital no longer have control of this process!* is identified as a name-calling comment as it has the word *moron* in it (Kenski et al., 2017).

vulgarity Contents that include any sort of curse words, including minor ones such as *damn* (Kenski et al., 2017). For example, *I hope the voters will kick that politician out on his pompous ass next election.* is marked as vulgar, as it contains the word *ass* in it.

4 Data

Coe et al. (2014) graciously shared with us the data that they collected from the comment section of the *Arizona Daily Star* newspaper. They collected articles and comments between 17 October 2011 and 6 November 2011 from eight news sections: Business, Entertainment, Lifestyles, Local News, Nation and World, Opinion, Sports, and State News. All their data was downloaded and saved manually by one research assistant one day after the articles were posted to provide enough time for the article to garner comments, yet not long enough for the article to be deleted. At the end of the data collection period, a total of 706 articles and 6535 comments were collected, out of which they coded 6444 for further analysis.

They used three teams of 3-5 research assistants to code articles and comments for incivility. The teams had extensive training on the coding procedures (Coe et al., 2014). The coding process took approximately six weeks, and chance-corrected intercoder reliability was established prior to the coding, which ranged between 0.61 to 1.0 Krippendorff's alpha score for different codes. In addition to coding the incivilities present in the comments, they also coded a variety of other metadata, e.g., the author's name, reactions received for other readers (thumbs up or thumbs down), word counts, etc. All the results of the coding procedure were saved in a metadata file created using Microsoft Excel. Comments were saved in separate PDF files named based on the news sections, articles and dates.

5 Challenges in Identifying incivilities from User Contents

As we have mentioned before that incivility is in the eye of the beholder, it is sometimes challenging to identify what can be unequivocally considered as uncivil interaction. Informed by the Coe et al. (2014) data, the following sections discuss some of these challenges.

5.1 Frequency

Although researchers have identified incivilities being rampant in public discourse (Shandwick, 2018), it is still minuscule compared to regular civil discourses in any social platform. As most of our identification and prediction techniques are data-driven, it is difficult to create a model that can identify incivilities from this small number of examples.

5.2 Linguistic Variations and Creativity

Oftentimes people refrain from using an exact version of an uncivil phrase and use an abbreviation or spelling variation of that phrase instead. For example, in *All BS, just like the politicians – the same crap*, the term BS is clearly an abbreviation of the word *bullshit*. However, there are also instances in the data where BS is used to abbreviate a person's name, which clearly is not an example of uncivil comment. Also, people often like to write uncivil words in spellings that are a derivative form. For example, people often use *sh!t* instead of *shit*, which clearly are the same thing in a public discourse. Hundreds of these variations may exist, making for a challenging identification problem.

Another challenge in identifying incivilities is that people can be really creative when they try to attack someone. This often happens when someone tries to indulge in ad hominem attacks with plausible deniability. For example, we have observed people using the word *DemocRat* instead of *Democrat* to identify someone with a democratic political orientation. Although these two words look similar, and sound exactly the same, *DemocRat* indicates that the target democrat is also a *rat*, a colloquial word for a spy, or a dishonest person. There are many other examples of this kind of variation, e.g. *democraps*. This phenomenon is sometimes referred as *Obscenity Obfuscation*, and researchers have found that it is becoming increasingly common in user generated contents in all sorts of social media platforms (Rojas-Galeano, 2017).

5.3 Difficulty in Comprehension

It is sometimes difficult to understand whether a word or a phase is used in an uncivil manner without understanding the context. For example, the word *lazy* can be used to describe the state of something that is actually slow or ineffective (e.g., *lazy algorithms*), or it can be used as an ad hominem attack on someone (e.g., *the lazy politicians have ruined this country*). As understanding the context of a content in a public discourse is difficult, separating these cases based on their contexts is challenging.

6 Incivility Prediction

In this section, we focus on our attempt to create a machine learning model that can be used as an incivility filter for moderators in social media plat-

forms. Our model will exclusively use features obtained from the contents and reciprocations in the platform, while avoiding the demographic information that was used heavily by prior work. This will allow our models to be used on the large portion of online discourse where such demographic information is unavailable, e.g., where users are anonymous.

6.1 Data preparation

We will train our incivility prediction models on the Coe et al. (2014) data discussed in section 4. However, that data were designed for use in social science research, not natural language processing research, and thus there were several challenges in working with the data as they were collected, including:

- The comments were saved in PDFs, and the metadata referenced each comment by a number that was drawn (not typed) into the PDF beside the comment.

- The naming conventions for the files were inconsistent (spelling variations, variable length identifiers, etc.)

- Dates were saved using multiple formats (ddmmyy, dd-mm-yy, etc.)

- There were no specific markers in the text that identified the start and end of a comment.

- Many comments contained quotations from other comments, also with no consistent markers of where quotes began or ended.

We solved these problems using a combination of regular expressions (e.g., for normalizing dates), brute-force techniques (e.g., quotations were identified by comparing against all previous comments), and manual revision (e.g., renaming the files whose names were too inconsistent to be resolved automatically).

The resulting set of annotated comments were saved in JSON format for further computational analysis. We ended up with 6175 comments from the original set of 6444 comments after the extraction and cleaning process.

6.2 Prediction Task

Our main focus was to build a prediction model that can work as a filter for incivility in public discourse. We were also interested in how a model trained on public discourse data would work on a social media platform. We first divided our dataset into three smaller sets: train, development and test sets. Comments are randomly assigned to sets, and we ended up with 3950 comments in the training set, 989 comments in the validation set and 1236 comments in the test set. We set the the test set aside for our final evaluation, and worked only on the training and validation dataset to find the best model that can fit the problem.

6.3 Baselines

We found a similar task in Kaggle[1] (Wulczyn et al., 2017) that tries to identify toxicity of comments in the discourse section of Wikipedia. In that task, the best performing model was a recurrent neural network model with gated recurrent units (GRUs; Cho et al., 2014), but some simple non-sequential models (logistic regressions and support vector machines) also performed almost as well as the sequential model on that task.

For our baseline, we used two non-sequential machine learning techniques: logistic regression and support vector machines, using TF-IDF vectors obtained over words in the comments. We also considered a state-of-the-art out-of-the-box text classification model as a baseline, the Flair text classification model (Akbik et al., 2018), which uses GloVe word embeddings (Pennington et al., 2014) and pre-trained contextual word embeddings derived from two character-level language models. Flair achieved state-of-the-art performance in part-of-speech tagging and named-entity recognition tasks, and we thought that the character-based nature of the Flair model might be helpful in the face of the linguistic variation and creativity challenges we discussed earlier.

6.4 Model

Our model was inspired by the top performing systems in the Kaggle competition, and started with FastText embeddings (Joulin et al., 2016) for each of the words in a comment. These word vectors were fed to a recurrent layer consisting of bidirectional GRUs. The outputs of the GRUs were fed to an average pooling layer and a max pooling layer, which were then concatenated[2]. The output of the pooling was then fed through a sigmoid layer to

produce the outputs. To avoid overfitting, we used a dropout layer (Srivastava et al., 2014) with 0.2 probability in between the input and hidden layer. We set the maximum length of input to 500 words for each comment, as this garnered the best validation performance in our preliminary analysis. We set class weights based on the frequency of name-calling and vulgarity: non-name-calling comments are 7 times more common than the name-calling ones, and non-vulgar comments are 35 times more common than vulgar ones, so we used a weighting scheme of 1:7 for name-calling and 1:35 for vulgarity. The model was trained with the Adam optimizer (Kingma and Ba, 2015) on mini-batches of size 32, with other hyperparameters set to their defaults. We trained each instance of this model for at most 500 epochs, with the option of early stopping if the validation accuracy did not improve for 10 consecutive epochs. A general structure of this model is shown in figure 1.

To further improve our model, we wanted to incorporate any metadata that were available to use. Coe et al. (2014) found that the thumbs up and thumbs downs received by a comment, the section of the article, and the author of the article all had some significance regarding incivility in the forum. So we introduced these metadata as features in our model. We created normalized feature vectors built on these attributes, and introduced them as auxiliary features right before the sigmoid layer, by concatenating them with the output of the pooling layers.

We also explored external resources that could improve our model. We created a pretrained model on the Kaggle dataset discussed earlier, as it had a large amount of annotated comments (over 160 thousand comments obtained from Wikipedia contributor's community). We used the same RNN model to train on the Kaggle data until it reached convergence, then retrained the model using our *Arizona Daily Star* data. The only portion of the model that was not shared between the pre-training (on Kaggle) and the training (on Arizona Daily Star) was the output sigmoid layers.

6.5 Experimental Results

The performance of the different models can be seen in table 1. Flair outperformed both of the other two baselines (36.55 vs. 23.35 and 18.46 F_1 in name-calling. Logistic regression and support vector machine models failed to detect single

---

[1] https://www.kaggle.com/c/jigsaw-toxic-comment-classification-challenge

[2] This type of pooling worked well for Demidov (2018), and also performed well in our preliminary analysis.

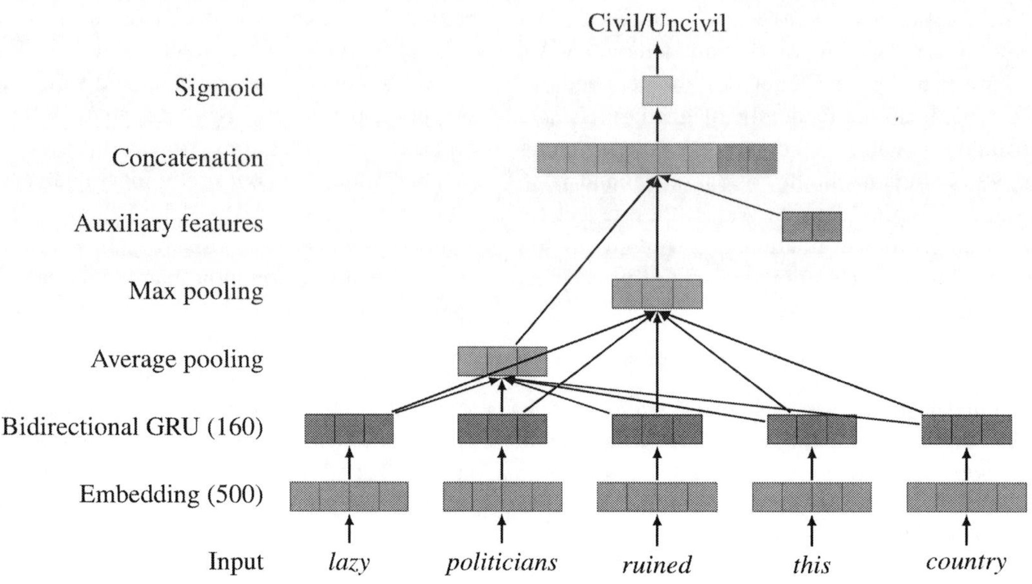

Figure 1: General structure of the RNN model. Auxiliary features are optional.

| | Validation | | | | | |
| | Name-calling | | | Vulgarity | | |
	Prec	Rec	F_1	Prec	Rec	F_1
Logistic regression	56.13	11.05	18.46	-	0.00	0.00
Support vector machine	54.10	14.89	23.35	-	0.00	0.00
Flair	52.17	28.12	36.55	25.00	7.41	11.43
GRU	43.65	61.72	51.13	37.50	66.67	48.00
GRU with auxiliary features	44.38	59.85	50.96	37.50	66.67	48.00
GRU with pretraining	69.44	19.53	29.79	50.00	11.11	18.03

| | Test | | | | | |
| | Name-calling | | | Vulgarity | | |
	Prec	Rec	F_1	Prec	Rec	F_1
GRU	45.76	50.63	48.07	48.72	57.57	52.77

Table 1: Performance of the models in terms of Precision (Prec), Recall (Rec), and F-measure (F_1).

instances of vulgarity in the development dataset, hence, Flair automatically outperformed these two. But our GRU-based model easily outperformed the Flair model (51.13 vs. 36.55 F_1 in name-calling, and 48.00 vs. 11.43 F_1 in vulgarity). These results stand in contrast to the Kaggle competition on toxicity detection, where such baselines performed nearly as well as the best (GRU-based) model, and all models achieved high levels of performance (>0.98 area under receiver operating characteristic curve). This suggests that the finer-grained incivility detection formulated by Coe et al. (2014) is more challenging than simple toxicity detection.

Adding the auxiliary features (upvotes, etc.) to the GRU-based model had virtually zero effect, with slight improvement on the model's precision but a slight drop in recall for name-calling, and absolutely no change for vulgarity. Using the Kaggle dataset to pre-train our GRU-based model before training on the *Arizona Daily Star* data yielded very high precisions, but at the cost of very low recalls. This suggests that while there is some overlap between the two tasks (toxicity detection and incivility detection), the differences between the tasks make it difficult to directly leverage the data from one task in the other.

name-calling		Vulgarity	
Tweet text	Score	Tweet text	Score
RT Jason_toronto: immigrant4trump Delusional Waters, Head Clown Schumer, Joke Perez, Senile Pelosi, Sleazy Schiff	0.997	Damn #BillCosby !! Damn damn damnnnn	0.996
#IHateItWhen incompetent idiots try to teach us how to live	0.997	I'm just going to say it. This is the stupidest tweet I've seen today. This BS bullying is not	0.973
@dapsixer GOP POTUS GOPChairwoman Primary these GOP candidates	0.979	"White Nationalism" WTH came up with this moniker? democrats?	0.985
#alis Dobbs obliterates Mitch McConnell and his pathetic excuses	0.989	Hell hath no fury like a bureaucrat scorned	0.969

Table 2: Examples of the GRU-based model predictions on the Russian troll Twitter data.

Since the GRU model with no auxiliary features or pre-training performed best on the development set, we evaluated the performance of this model on the test set. It achieved 48.07 F-measure for name-calling and 52.77 for vulgarity, scores roughly similar to what we had seen on the development data.

7 Incivility Prediction in Twitter

Though we built our models to detect incivilities in newspaper comments, we were interested in how well they would perform in other domains of social media. Karan and Šnajder (2018) has showed that cross-domain adaptation for detecting abusive language is possible- hence we would like to observe how well our model performs on a set of tweets.

In June 2018, The United States House Intelligence Committee released a list of 3841 Twitter account names that were human-operated troll accounts associated with Russia's Internet Research Agency. Darren Linvill and Patrick Warren from Clemson University collected all the tweets published since June 2015 from these accounts, cleaned them, and published a set of almost 3 million tweets (Linvill and Warren, 2018). These tweets are publicly available in FiveThirtyEight's Github page[3].

As prior research suggest that trolls are a big source of incivility in social media platforms (Fauman, 2008; Hinduja and Patchin, 2008), we took this opportunity to observe how our model performs on this dataset. We downloaded all the tweet texts and ran our GRU-based model on these texts. Results of this experiment can be found in the author's GitHub repository[4].

7.1 Observations

Our model identified 13% of all tweets as name-calling and 1.7% as vulgarity. These are roughly similar to the Arizona Daily Star training data, which had 14% name-calling and and 2.8% vulgarity. Though we do not have access to the expert annotators used by Coe et al. (2014), but we can nonetheless get an approximate measure of our model's performance by sampling predictions from our model and estimating the true label following the Coe et al. (2014) annotation guidelines.

To measure our model's precision, we took the 250 tweets that our model was most certain contained name-calling, and the 250 tweets that our model was most certain contained vulgarity. We manually reviewed each of these 500 tweets, and found only 7 instances of mistakenly tagged name-calling and 5 instances of mistakenly tagged vulgarity. To get a rough sense of our model's recall, we looked at the other end of the model's prediction spectrum. Based on a manual review of the model's prediction, the model almost never makes a mistake when the prediction score is below 10%; we found only one instance of mistaken name-calling, and no instance of mistaken vulgarity in the bottom 250 tweets that we manually annotated.

Table 2 shows some example tweets and the prediction scores from our model. The bottom two examples under name-calling and the bottom one example under vulgarity represent mistakes. In the first name-calling error, the model is confident (probability 0.979) that there is a name-calling,

[3]https://github.com/fivethirtyeight/russian-troll-tweets

[4]anonymized

perhaps because the terms GOP and POTUS frequently appear with name-calling in our training data. In the second name-calling error, the model is confident (probability 0.989) that there is a name-calling, likely because of the presence of the word *pathetic*, which is an aspersion, attacking an idea, not a name-calling, attacking a person. In the vulgarity error, *hell* has not been used to reference the religious concept of hell, but the word strongly associated with vulgarity in the training data. The table also shows some examples of reasonable successes of the model, for example, handling vulgar abbreviations like BS (short for *bullshit*) and WTH (short for *Who the hell*).

8   Future Works and Conclusion

Our work here aims towards keeping a civil environment in public discourse forums and social media platforms. Our goal was to build a filtering system that could work alongside human moderators to reduce their workload, be objective and independent of user reporting, and perform well on previously unseen social media streams. There is much work to do in this area: annotation of a large random sample of the troll tweets can give a more thorough estimate of model performance, and various forms of domain adaptation like self-training might be applied to improve the performance of the model. We have used word n-grams for features in our baseline models, which can be improved by using features obtained from domain-specific lexicons. There are lexicons of abusive words (Wiegand et al., 2018)- which can be used to create non-sequential models with smaller feature sets. Whether these simpler models are better is yet to be proven - as Agrawal and Awekar (2018) has shown that vocabulary of words used for cyberbullying varies significantly from one social media platform to another. They have also showed that swear words are not necessary to be uncivil in online social media- hence these types of detection techniques should not rely on such hand-crafted features.

One research question that follows this work is to observe whether incivility affects user engagement in social media. Prior research has observed that receiving replies can have effects in a user's engagement (Joyce and Kraut, 2006; Sadeque et al., 2015), and the language of these replies can also have consequences (Arguello et al., 2006). Habernal et al. (2018) has showed that 48% of comments that included ad hominem attacks ended the argument – which is indicative of lower engagement by the entire community. Hence, we believe that incivility has a significant influence on user engagement, and in turn may contribute to a community's sustainability. This is yet to be proven, and more work needs to be performed to prove or disprove this hypothesis.

In this paper, we have presented a recurrent neural that can identify incivilities in public discourse. Though trained on a corpus of newspaper comments, we have initial evidence that it also performs well in detecting incivilities in Twitter. We believe our model will be able to serve as a wide-range incivility filter in other social media platforms.

References

Sweta Agrawal and Amit Awekar. 2018. Deep learning for detecting cyberbullying across multiple social media platforms. *CoRR*, abs/1801.06482.

Alan Akbik, Duncan Blythe, and Roland Vollgraf. 2018. Contextual string embeddings for sequence labeling. In *COLING 2018, 27th International Conference on Computational Linguistics*, pages 1638–1649.

Jaime Arguello, Brian S. Butler, Elisabeth Joyce, Robert Kraut, Kimberly S. Ling, Carolyn Rosé, and Xiaoqing Wang. 2006. Talk to me: Foundations for successful individual-group interactions in online communities. In *Proceedings of the SIGCHI Conference on Human Factors in Computing Systems*, CHI '06, pages 959–968, New York, NY, USA. ACM.

Isabel Cachola, Eric Holgate, Daniel Preoţiuc-Pietro, and Junyi Jessy Li. 2018. Expressively vulgar: The socio-dynamics of vulgarity and its effects on sentiment analysis in social media. In *Proceedings of the 27th International Conference on Computational Linguistics*, pages 2927–2938.

Kyunghyun Cho, Bart van Merrienboer, Dzmitry Bahdanau, and Yoshua Bengio. 2014. On the properties of neural machine translation: Encoder-decoder approaches. In *Eighth Workshop on Syntax, Semantics and Structure in Statistical Translation (SSST-8)*.

Kevin Coe, Kate Kenski, and Stephen A. Rains. 2014. Online and uncivil? patterns and determinants of incivility in newspaper website comments. *Journal of Communication*, 64(4):658–679.

Vladimir Demidov. 2018. Kernel submission for kaggle toxic classification challenge. `https://www.kaggle.com/yekenot/pooled-gru-fasttext`? Last Accessed: 2018-12-02.

Michael A. Fauman. 2008. Cyber bullying: Bullying in the digital age. *American Journal of Psychiatry*, 165(6):780–781.

Michael Gauthier, Adrien Guille, Fabien Rico, and Anthony Deseille. 2015. Text mining and twitter to analyze british swearing habits. In *Handbook of Twitter for Research*.

Ivan Habernal, Henning Wachsmuth, Iryna Gurevych, and Benno Stein. 2018. Before name-calling: Dynamics and triggers of ad hominem fallacies in web argumentation. *arXiv preprint arXiv:1802.06613*.

Sameer Hinduja and Justin W. Patchin. 2008. Cyberbullying: An exploratory analysis of factors related to offending and victimization. *Deviant Behavior*, 29(2):129–156.

Eric Holgate, Isabel Cachola, Daniel Preoţiuc-Pietro, and Junyi Jessy Li. 2018. Why swear? analyzing and inferring the intentions of vulgar expressions. In *Proceedings of the 2018 Conference on Empirical Methods in Natural Language Processing*, pages 4405–4414.

Armand Joulin, Edouard Grave, Piotr Bojanowski, and Tomas Mikolov. 2016. Bag of tricks for efficient text classification. *CoRR*, abs/1607.01759.

Elisabeth Joyce and Robert E. Kraut. 2006. Predicting continued participation in newsgroups. *Journal of Computer-Mediated Communication*, 11(3):723–747.

Mladen Karan and Jan Šnajder. 2018. Cross-domain detection of abusive language online. In *Proceedings of the 2nd Workshop on Abusive Language Online (ALW2)*, pages 132–137, Brussels, Belgium. Association for Computational Linguistics.

Kate Kenski, Kevin Coe, and Stephen A. Rains. 2017. Perceptions of uncivil discourse online: An examination of types and predictors. *Communication Research*, 0(0):0093650217699933.

Diederik Kingma and Jimmy Ba. 2015. Adam: A method for stochastic optimization. International Conference on Learning Representation.

Darren L. Linvill and Patrcik L. Warren. 2018. Troll factories: The internet research agency and state-sponsored agenda building. `https://www.rcmediafreedom.eu/Publications/Academic-sources/Troll-Factories-The-Internet-\Research-Agency-and-State-Sponsored\-Agenda-Building`.

Justin W. Patchin and Sameer Hinduja. 2006. Bullies move beyond the schoolyard: A preliminary look at cyberbullying. *Youth Violence and Juvenile Justice*, 4(2):148–169.

Jeffrey Pennington, Richard Socher, and Christopher D. Manning. 2014. Glove: Global vectors for word representation. In *Empirical Methods in Natural Language Processing (EMNLP)*, pages 1532–1543.

Stephen A. Rains, Kate Kenski, Kevin Coe, and Jake Harwood. 2017. Incivility and political identity on the internet: Intergroup factors as predictors of incivility in discussions of news online. *Journal of Computer-Mediated Communication*, 22(4):163–178.

Kelly Reynolds, April Kontostathis, and Lynne Edwards. 2011. Using machine learning to detect cyberbullying. In *2011 10th International Conference on Machine learning and applications and workshops*, volume 2, pages 241–244. IEEE.

Sergio Rojas-Galeano. 2017. On obstructing obscenity obfuscation. *ACM Trans. Web*, 11(2):12:1–12:24.

Farig Sadeque, Thamar Solorio, Ted Pedersen, Prasha Shrestha, and Steven Bethard. 2015. Predicting continued participation in online health forums. In *SIXTH INTERNATIONAL WORKSHOP ON HEALTH TEXT MINING AND INFORMATION ANALYSIS (LOUHI)*, page 12.

Weber Shandwick. 2018. Civility in america 2018: Civility at work and in our public squares. `https://www.webershandwick.com/wp-content/uploads/2018/06/Civility-in-America-VII-FINAL.pdf`. Last Accessed: 2018-06-11.

Nitish Srivastava, Geoffrey E Hinton, Alex Krizhevsky, Ilya Sutskever, and Ruslan Salakhutdinov. 2014. Dropout: a simple way to prevent neural networks from overfitting. *Journal of Machine Learning Research*, 15(1):1929–1958.

Wenbo Wang, Lu Chen, Krishnaprasad Thirunarayan, and Amit P. Sheth. 2014. Cursing in english on twitter. In *Proceedings of the 17th ACM Conference on Computer Supported Cooperative Work & Social Computing*, CSCW '14, pages 415–425, New York, NY, USA. ACM.

Zeerak Waseem and Dirk Hovy. 2016. Hateful symbols or hateful people? predictive features for hate speech detection on twitter. In *Proceedings of the NAACL Student Research Workshop*, pages 88–93, San Diego, California. Association for Computational Linguistics.

Michael Wiegand, Josef Ruppenhofer, Anna Schmidt, and Clayton Greenberg. 2018. Inducing a lexicon of abusive words – a feature-based approach. In *Proceedings of the 2018 Conference of the North American Chapter of the Association for Computational Linguistics: Human Language Technologies, Volume 1 (Long Papers)*, pages 1046–1056, New Orleans, Louisiana. Association for Computational Linguistics.

Ellery Wulczyn, Nithum Thain, and Lucas Dixon. 2017. Ex machina: Personal attacks seen at scale. In *Proceedings of the 26th International Conference on World Wide Web*, pages 1391–1399. International World Wide Web Conferences Steering Committee.

Generating Animations from Screenplays

Yeyao Zhang[1,3]**, Eleftheria Tsipidi**[1] **,**
Sasha Schriber[1]**, Mubbasir Kapadia**[1,2]**, Markus Gross**[1,3]**, Ashutosh Modi**[1]
[1]Disney Research, [2]Rutgers University, [3]ETH Zurich
yezhang@inf.ethz.ch
{etsipidi,sasha.schriber}@disneyresearch.com
mubbasir.kapadia@rutgers.edu
{gross,ashutosh.modi}@disneyresearch.com

Abstract

Automatically generating animation from natural language text finds application in a number of areas e.g. movie script writing, instructional videos, and public safety. However, translating natural language text into animation is a challenging task. Existing text-to-animation systems can handle only very simple sentences, which limits their applications. In this paper, we develop a text-to-animation system which is capable of handling complex sentences. We achieve this by introducing a text simplification step into the process. Building on an existing animation generation system for screenwriting, we create a robust NLP pipeline to extract information from screenplays and map them to the system's knowledge base. We develop a set of linguistic transformation rules that simplify complex sentences. Information extracted from the simplified sentences is used to generate a rough storyboard and video depicting the text. Our sentence simplification module outperforms existing systems in terms of BLEU and SARI metrics.We further evaluated our system via a user study: 68 % participants believe that our system generates reasonable animation from input screenplays.

1. Introduction

Generating animation from texts can be useful in many contexts e.g. movie script writing (Ma and Kevitt, 2006; Liu and Leung, 2006; Hanser et al., 2010), instructional videos (Lu and Zhang, 2002), and public safety (Johansson et al., 2004). Text-to-animation systems can be particularly valuable for screenwriting by enabling faster iteration, prototyping and proof of concept for content creators.

In this paper, we propose a text-to-animation generation system. Given an input text describing a certain activity, the system generates a rough animation of the text. We are addressing a practical setting, where we do not have any annotated data for training a supervised end-to-end system. The aim is not to generate a polished, final animation, but a *pre-visualization* of the input text. The purpose of the system is not to replace writers and artists, but to make their work more efficient and less tedious. We are aiming for a system which is robust and could be deployed in a production environment.

Existing text-to-animation systems for screenwriting (§2) visualize stories by using a pipeline of Natural Language Processing (NLP) techniques for extracting information from texts and mapping them to appropriate action units in the animation engine. The NLP modules in these systems translate the input text into predefined intermediate action representations and the animation generation engine produces simple animation from these representations.

Although these systems can generate animation from carefully handcrafted simple sentences, translating real screenplays into coherent animation still remains a challenge. This can be attributed to the limitations of the NLP modules used with regard to handling complex sentences. In this paper, we try to address the limitations of the current text-to-animation systems. Main contributions of this paper are:

- We propose a screenplay parsing architecture which generalizes well on different screenplay formats (§3.1).
- We develop a rich set of linguistic rules to reduce complex sentences into simpler ones to facilitate information extraction (§3.2).
- We develop a new NLP pipeline to generate animation from actual screenplays (§3).

The potential applications of our contributions are not restricted to just animating screenplays. The techniques we develop are fairly general and can be used in other applications as well e.g. in-

*Proceedings of the Eighth Joint Conference on Lexical and Computational Semantics (*SEM), pages 292–307*
Minneapolis, June 6–7, 2019. ©2019 Association for Computational Linguistics

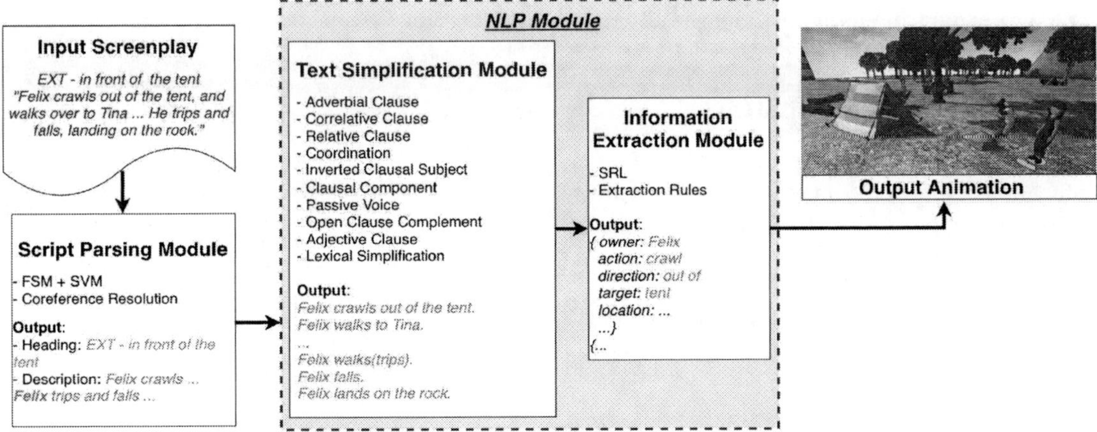

Figure 1: System Architecture: Screenplays are first segmented into different functional blocks. Then, the descriptive action sentences are simplified. Simplified sentences are used to generate animation.

formation extraction tasks.

2. Related Work

Translating texts into animation is not a trivial task, given that neither the input sentences nor the output animations have a fixed structure. Prior work addresses this problem from different perspectives (Hassani and Lee, 2016).

CONFUCIUS (Ma and Kevitt, 2006) is a system that converts natural language to animation using the FDG parser (Tapanainen and Järvinen, 1997) and WordNet (Miller, 1995). ScriptViz (Liu and Leung, 2006) is another similar system, created for screenwriting. It uses the Apple Pie parser (Sekine, 1998) to parse input text and then recognizes objects via an object-specific reasoner. It is limited to sentences having conjunction between two verbs. SceneMaker (Hanser et al., 2010) adopts the same NLP techniques as proposed in CONFUCIUS (Ma and Kevitt, 2006) followed by a context reasoning module. Similar to previously proposed systems, we also use dependency parsing followed by linguistic reduction (§3.2).

Recent advances in deep learning have pushed the state of the art results on different NLP tasks (Honnibal and Johnson, 2015; Wolf et al., 2018; He et al., 2017). We use pre-trained models for dependency parsing, coreference resolution and SRL to build a complete NLP pipeline to create intermediate action representations. For the action representation (§3.4), we use a key-value pair structure inspired by the PAR architecture (Badler et al., 2000), which is a knowledge base of representations for actions performed by virtual agents.

Our work comes close to the work done in the area of Open Information Extraction (IE) (Niklaus et al., 2018). In particular, to extract information, Clause-Based Open IE systems (Del Corro and Gemulla, 2013; Angeli et al., 2015; Schmidek and Barbosa, 2014) reduce a complex sentence into simpler sentences using linguistic patterns. However, the techniques developed for these systems do not generalize well to screenplay texts, as these systems have been developed using well-formed and factual texts like Wikipedia, Penn TreeBank, etc. An initial investigation with the popular Open IE system OLLIE (Open Language Learning for Information Extraction) (Mausam et al., 2012) did not yield good results on our corpus.

Previous work related to information extraction for narrative technologies includes the CARDINAL system (Marti et al., 2018; Sanghrajka et al., 2018), as well as the conversational agent PICA (Falk et al., 2018). They focus on querying knowledge from stories. The CARDINAL system also generates animations from input texts. However, neither of the tools can handle complex sentences. We build on the CARDINAL system. We develop a new NLP module to support complex sentences and leverage the animation engine of CARDINAL.

Recently, a number of end-to-end image generation systems have been proposed (Mansimov et al., 2015; Reed et al., 2016). But these systems do not synthesize satisfactory images yet, and are not suitable for our application. It is hoped that the techniques proposed in this paper could be used for automatically generating labelled data (e.g. (text,video) pairs) for training end-to-end text-to-animation systems.

3. Text-to-Animation System

We adopt a modular approach for generating animations from screenplays. The general overview of our approach is presented in Figure 1. The system is divided into three modules:

- **Script Parsing Module:** Given an input screenplay text, this module automatically extracts the relevant text for generating the animation (§3.1).
- **NLP Module:** It processes the extracted text to get relevant information. This has two submodules:
  - **Text Simplification Module:** It simplifies complex sentences using a set of linguistic rules (§3.2).
  - **Information Extraction Module:** It extracts information from the simplified sentences into pre-defined action representations (§3.4).
- **Animation Generation Module:** It generates animation based on action representations (§3.5).

3.1. Script Parsing Module

Typically, *screenplays* or *movie scripts* or *scripts* (we use the terms interchangeably), are made of several scenes, each of which corresponds to a series of consecutive motion shots. Each scene contains several functional components[1]: *Headings* (time and location), *Descriptions* (scene description, character actions), *Character Cues* (character name before dialog), *Dialogs* (conversation content), *Slug Lines* (actions inserted into continuous dialog) and *Transitions* (camera movement). In many scripts, these components are easily identifiable by indentation, capitalization and keywords. We call these scripts *well-formatted*, and the remaining ones *ill-formatted*. We want to segment the screenplays into components and are mainly interested in the Descriptions component for animation generation.

Well-formatted Scripts: We initially tried ScreenPy (Winer and Young, 2017) to annotate the well-formatted scripts with the component labels. However, ScreenPy did not perform well on our data. We developed our own model, based on Finite State Machines (FSM), for parsing

---

Algorithm 1 Syntactic Simplification Procedure

```
1:  procedure SYNTACTIC SIMPLIFICATION(sent, temp)
2:      Q ← empty queue
3:      HS ← empty integer hash set
4:      RES ← empty list
5:      Q.push(sent)                       ▷ push input sentence to queue
6:      while Q ≠ Empty do
7:          str ← Q.pop()
8:          if hash(str) ∈ HS then
9:              RES.append(str)            ▷ have seen this sentence
10:             continue
11:         HS.add(str)              ▷ mark current sentence as already seen
12:         transform ← False
13:         for a in analyzers do
14:             if !transform & a.identify(str) then
15:                 transform ← True
16:                 simplified = a.transform(str)
17:                 correct_verb_tense(simplified)
18:                 Q.push(simplified)
19:         if transform ≠ True then
20:             RES.append(str)
21:     return RES
```

---

scripts (for details refer to Appendix A). Due to space limitations, we do not describe the FSM model; the key idea is that the model uses hand-crafted transition rules to segment the input screenplay and generates (paragraph, component name) pairs.

Ill-formatted Scripts: Taking all the (paragraph, component name) pairs generated by the FSM as ground truth, an SVM model is trained to segment ill-formatted screenplays with inconsistent indentations. For extracting features, each paragraph is encoded into a fix-sized vector using a pre-trained Universal Sentence Encoder. The SVM is trained and tested on a 9:1 train-test data split. The result shows an accuracy of 92.72 % on the test set, which is good for our purposes, as we are interested mainly in the Descriptions component.

Coreference Resolution: Screenplays contain a number of ambiguous entity mentions (e.g. pronouns). In order to link mentions of an entity, an accurate coreference resolution system is required. The extracted Descriptions components are processed with the NeuralCoref[2] system. Given the text, it resolves mentions (typically pronouns) to the entity they refer to in the text. To facilitate entity resolution, we prepend each Description component with the Character Cues component which appears before it in the screenplay (e.g. [character]MARTHA: [dialog]"I knew it!" [description]She then jumps triumphantly → MARTHA. She then jumps triumphantly).

3.2. Text Simplification Module

In a typical text-to-animation system, one of the main tasks is to process the input text to extract

---

Syntactic Structure	*Identify* procedure	*Transform* procedure
Coordination	search if *cc* and *conj* in dependency tree	cut *cc* and *conj* link. If *conj* is verb, mark it as new root; else replace it with its sibling node.
Pre-Correlative Conjugation	locates position of keywords: "either", "both","neither"	removed the located word from dependency tree
Appositive Clause	find *appos* token and its head (none)	glue appositive noun phrase with "to be"
Relative Clause	find *relcl* token and its head	cut *appos* link, then traverse from root. Then, if no "wh" word present, put head part after anchor part; else, we divide them into 5 subcases (Table 2)
Adverbial Clause Modifier	find *advcl* token and its head. Also conjuncts of head token	cut *advcl* edge. If *advcl* token does not have subject, add subject of root as *advcl*'s most-left child and remove *prep* and *mark* token. Then traverse from both root and *advcl* token
Inverted Clausal Subject	*attr* token has to be the child of head of *csubj* token	change position of actual verb and subject
Clausal Complement	find *ccomp* token in dependency tree	cut *ccomp* link, add subject to subordinate clause if necessary
Passive Voice	check presence of *nsubjpass* or *csubjpass* optionally for *auxpass* and *agent*	cut *auxpass* link if any. Cut *nsubjpass* or *csubjpass* link. Prepend subject token to verb token's right children. Finally append suitable subject.
Open Clause Complement	find *xcomp* verb token adn actual verb token	if *aux* token presents, cut *aux* link, then replace xcomp-verb in subject's children with actual-verb, traverse from actual-verb; else, cut *xcomp* link, traverse from xcomp-verb
Adjective Clause	find *acl* verb token and its head	cut *acl* link. Link subject node with it. Traverser from *acl* node

Table 1: Linguistic rules for text simplification module

the relevant information about actions (typically verbs) and participants (typically subject/object of the verb), which is subsequently used for generating animation. This works well for simple sentences having a single verb with one subject and one (optional) object. However, the sentences in a screenplay are complicated and sometimes informal. In this work, a sentence is said to be complicated if it deviates from easily extractable and simple subject-verb-object (and its permutations) syntactic structures and possibly has multiple actions mentioned within the same sentence with syntactic interactions between them. By syntactic structure we refer to the dependency graph of the sentence.

In the case of screenplays, the challenge is to process such complicated texts. We take the text simplification approach, i.e. the system first simplifies a complicated sentence and then extracts the relevant information. Simplification reduces a complicated sentence into multiple simpler sentences, each having a single action along with its participants, making it straightforward to extract necessary information.

Recently, end-to-end Neural Text Simplification (NTS) systems (Nisioi et al., 2017; Saggion, 2017) have shown reasonable accuracy. However, these systems have been trained on factual data such as Wikipedia and do not generalize well to screenplay texts. Our experiments with such a pretrained neural text simplification system did not yield good results (§5.1). Moreover, in the context of text-to-animation, there is no standard labeled corpus to train an end-to-end system.

There has been work on text simplification using linguistic rules-based approaches. For example, (Siddharthan, 2011) propose a set of rules to manipulate sentence structure to output simplified sentences using syntactic dependency parsing. Similarly, the YATS system (Ferrés et al., 2016) implements a set of rules in the JAPE language (Cunningham et al., 2000) to address six syntactic structures: **Passive Constructions, Appositive Phrases, Relative Clauses, Coordinated Clauses, Correlated Clauses** and **Adverbial Clauses**. Most of the rules focus on case and tense correction, with only 1-2 rules for sentence splitting. We take inspiration from the YATS system, and our system incorporates modules to identify and transform sentence structures into simpler ones using a broader set of rules.

In our system, each syntactic structure is handled by an *Analyzer*, which contains two processes: *Identify* and *Transform*. The *Identify* process takes in a sentence and determines if it contains a particular syntactic structure. Subsequently, the *Transform* process focuses on the first occurrence of the identified syntactic structure and then splits and assembles the sentence into simpler sentences. Both *Identify* and *Transform* use Part-of-Speech (POS) tagging and dependency parsing (Honnibal and Montani, 2017) modules implemented in spaCy 2.0[3]

The simplification algorithm (Algorithm 1) starts with an input sentence and recursively processes it until no further simplification is possible. It uses a queue to manage intermediate simplified sentences, and runs in a loop until the queue is empty. For each sentence, the system applies each syntactic analyzer to *Identify* the correspon-

---

[3]https://spacy.io

Type	Example Input Sentence	System Output Sentence 1	System Output Sentence 2
Coordination	She LAUGHS, and[**cc**] gives[**conj**] Kevin a kiss.	She laughs.	She gives Kevin a kiss.
Pre-Correlative	It's followed by another squad car, both[**preconj**] with sirens blaring.	It's followed by another squad car, with sirens blaring.	–
Appositive	Kevin is reading a book the Bible[**appos**]	Kevin reads a book	The book is the Bible.
Relative-dobj	She pulls out a letter *which*[**dobj**] she hands[**relcl**] to Keven	Shee pulls out a letter	She hands a lettre to Kevin.
Relative-pobj	A reef encloses the cove *where*[**pobj**] he came[**relcl**] from.	A reef encloses the cove	he comes from the cove.
Relative-nsubj	Frank gestures to the SALESMAN, *who*[**nsubj**]'s waiting[**relcl**] on a woman	the SALESMAN waits on a woman.	Frank gestures to the SALESMAN.
Relative-advmod	Chuck is in the stage of exposure *where*[**advmod**] the personality splits[**relcl**]	Chuck is in the stage of exposure	the personality splits at exposure.
Relative-poss	The girl, *whose*[**poss**] name is[**relcl**] Helga, cowers.	The girl cowers	The girl 's name is Helga
Relative-omit	Kim is the sexpot Peter saw[**relcl**] in Washington Square Park	Peter sees Kim in Washington Square Park.	Kim is the sexpot.
Adverbial	Jim panics as[**advcl**] his mom reacts, shocked.	Jim panics, shocked.	Jim's mom reacts.
Adverbial-remove	Suddenly there's a KNOCK at the door, immediately after[**prep**] which JIM'S MOM enters[**advcl**].	Suddenly there 's a KNOCK at the door.	Immediately JIM 'S MOM enters.
Inverted Cl. Subject	Running[**csubj**] towards Oz is Steve Stifler	Steve Stifler runs towards Oz.	–
Clausal Component	The thing is, it actually sounds[**ccomp**] really good.	The thing is.(will be eliminated by the filter)	It actually sounds really good.
Passive Voice	They[**nsubjpass**] are suddenly illuminated by the glare of headlights.	Suddenly the glare of headlights illuminateds them.	–
Open Clausal	The sophomore comes running[**xcomp**] through the kitchen.	The sophomore runs through the kitchen.	The sophomore comes.
Adjective	Stifler has a toothbrush hanging[**acl**] from his mouth.	A toothbrush hangs from Stifler's mouth.	Stifler has a toothbrush.

Table 2: Syntactic simplification rules applied on example sentences.

ding syntactic structure in the sentence (line 14). If the result is positive, the sentence is processed by the *Transform* function to convert it to simple sentences (line 16). Each of the output sentences is pushed by the controller into the queue (line 19). The process is repeated with each of the *Identify* analyzers (line 13). If none of the analyzers can be applied, the sentence is assumed to be simple and it is pushed into the result list (line 21). We summarize linguistic rules in Table 1 and examples are given in Table 2. Next, we describe the coordination linguistic rules. For details regarding other rules, please refer to Appendix B.

Coordination: Coordination is used for entities having the same syntactic relation with the head and serving the same functional role (e.g. subj, obj, etc.). It is the most important component in our simplification system. The parser tags word units such as "and" and "as well as" with the dependency label *cc*, and the conjugated words as *conj*. Our system deals with coordination based on the dependency tag of the conjugated word.

In the case of coordination, the *Identify* function simply returns whether *cc* or *conj* is in the dependency graph of the input sentence. The *Transform* function manipulates the graph structure based on the dependency tags of the conjugated words as shown in Figure 2. If the conjugated word is a verb, then we mark it as another root of the sentence. Cutting *cc* and *conj* edges in the graph and

traversing from this new root results in a new sentence parallel to the original one. In other cases, such as the conjugation between nouns, we simply replace the noun phrases with their siblings and traverse from root again.

3.3. Lexical Simplification

In order to generate animation, actions and participants extracted from simplified sentences are mapped to existing actions and objects in the animation engine. Due to practical reasons, it is not possible to create a library of animations for all possible actions in the world. We limit our library to a predefined list of 52 actions/animations, expanded to 92 by a dictionary of synonyms (§3.5). We also have a small library of pre-uploaded objects (such as "campfire", "truck" and others).

To animate unseen actions not in our list, we use a word2vec-based *similarity* function to find the nearest action in the list. Moreover, we use WordNet (Miller, 1995) to exclude antonyms. This helps to map non-list actions (such as "squint at") to the similar action in the list (e.g. "look"). If we fail to find a match, we check for a mapping while including the verb's preposition or syntactic object. We also use WordNet to obtain hypernyms for further checks, when the *similarity* function fails to find a close-enough animation. Correspondingly, for objects, we use the same *similarity* function and WordNet's holonyms.

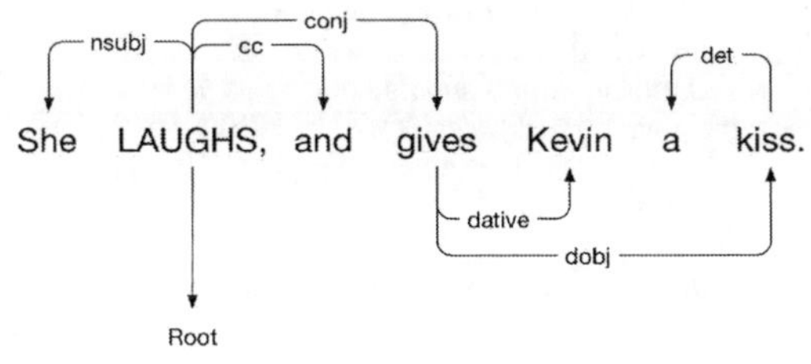

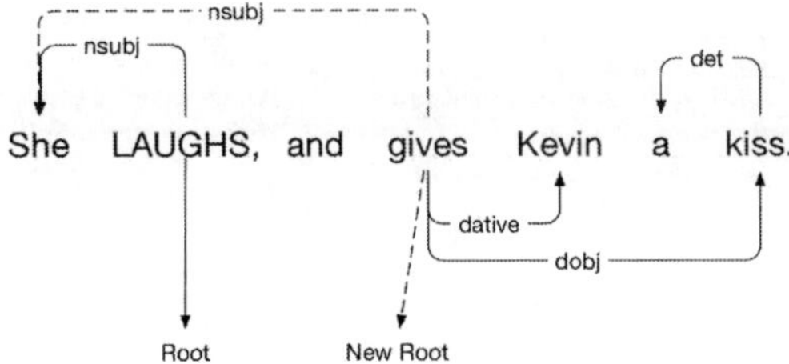

(a) original dependency graph   (b) dependency graph after *Transform*

Figure 2: *Transform* in an example coordination sentence. Firstly the dependency links of *cc* and *conj* are cut. Then we look for a noun in the left direct children of the original root *LAUGHS* and link the new root *gives* with it. In-order traverse from the original root and the new root will result in simplified sentences as shown in Table 2.

Our list of actions and objects is not exhaustive. Currently, we do not cover actions which may not be visual. For out of list actions, we give the user a warning that the action cannot be animated. Nevertheless, this is a work in progress and we are working on including more animations for actions and objects in our knowledge base.

3.4. Action Representation Field (ARF): Information Extraction

For each of the simplified sentences, information is extracted and populated into a predefined key-value pair structure. We will refer to the keys of this structure as *Action Representation Fields (ARFs)*. These are similar to entities and relations in Knowledge Bases. ARFs include: *owner, target, prop, action, origin_action, manner, modifier_location, modifier_direction, start-time, duration, speed, translation, rotation, emotion, partial_start_time* (for more details see Appendix C). This structure is inspired by the PAR (Badler et al., 2000) architecture, but adapted to our needs.

To extract the ARFs from the simplified sentences, we use a Semantic Role Labelling (SRL) model in combination with some heuristics, for example creating word lists for *duration, speed, translation, rotation, emotion*. We use a pretrained Semantic Role Labelling model[4] based on a Bi-directional LSTM network (He et al., 2017) with pre-trained ELMo embeddings (Peters et al., 2018). We map information from each sentence to the knowledge base of animations and objects.

3.5. Animation Generation

We use the animation pipeline of the CARDINAL system. We plug in our NLP module in CARDINAL to generate animation. CARDINAL creates pre-visualizations of the text, both in storyboard form and animation. A storyboard is a series of pictures that demonstrates the sequence of scenes from a script. The animation is a 3-D animated video that approximately depicts the script. CARDINAL uses the Unreal game engine (Games, 2007) for generating pre-visualizations. It has a knowledge base of pre-baked animations (52 animations, plus a dictionary of synonyms, resulting in 92) and pre-uploaded objects (e.g. "campfire", "tent"). It also has 3-D models which can be used to create characters.

4. Text-to-Animation Corpus

We initially used a corpus of Descriptions components from ScreenPy (Winer and Young, 2017), in order to study linguistic patterns in the movie script domain. Specifically, we used the "heading" and "transition" fields from ScreenPy's published JSON output on 1068 movie scripts scraped from IMSDb. We also scraped screenplays from SimplyScripts and ScriptORama[5]. After separating screenplays into well-formatted and ill-formatted, Descriptions components were extracted using our model (§3.1). This gave a corpus of Descriptions blocks from 996 screenplays.

The corpus contains a total of 525,708 Descriptions components. The Descriptions components contain a total of 1,402,864 sentences. Out of all the Descriptions components, 49.45 % (259,973) contain at least one verb which is in the animation list (henceforth called "action verbs"). Descriptions components having at least one action verb have in total 920,817 sentences. Out of the-

---

[4]AllenNLP SRL model: `https://github.com/allenai/allennlp`

[5]`http://www.simplyscripts.com` and `http://www.script-o-rama.com`

297

Carl touches Ellie's shoulder as the doctor explains. Ellie drops her head in her hands.			
System output	Annotator I	Annotator II	$BLEU_2(\%)$
Carl touches Ellie 's shoulder	carl touches ellie's shoulder	carl touches ellie's shoulder.	38.73
the doctor explains	the doctor explains	the doctor is talking.	100
Ellie drops Ellie head in Ellie hands	ellie drops her head in her hands	ellie drops her head in her hands.	48.79

Table 3: Differences between system output and annotator responses

	$BLEU$	$SARI$
NTS-w2v	61.45	36.04
YATS	58.83	48.75
Our System	**67.68**	**50.65**

Table 4: Results on syntactic simplification

se, 42.2 % (388,597) of the sentences contain action verbs. In the corpus, the average length of a sentence is 12 words.

5. Evaluation and Analysis

There are no standard corpora for text-to-animation generation. It is also not clear how should such systems be evaluated and what should be the most appropriate evaluation metric. Nevertheless, it is important to assess how our system is performing. We evaluate our system using two types of evaluation: Intrinsic and Extrinsic. Intrinsic evaluation is for evaluating the NLP pipeline of our system using the BLEU metric. Extrinsic evaluation is an end-to-end qualitative evaluation of our text-to-animation generation system, done via a user study.

5.1. Intrinsic Evaluation

To evaluate the performance of our proposed NLP pipeline, 500 Descriptions components from the test set were randomly selected. Three annotators manually translated these 500 Descriptions components into simplified sentences and extracted all the necessary ARFs from the simplified sentences. This is a time intensive process and took around two months. 30 % of the Descriptions blocks contain verbs not in the list of 92 animation verbs. There are approximately 1000 sentences in the test set, with average length of 12 words. Each Descriptions component is also annotated by the three annotators for the ARFs.

Taking inspiration from the text simplification community (Nisioi et al., 2017; Saggion, 2017), we use the BLEU score (Papineni et al., 2002) for evaluating our simplification and information extraction modules. For each simplified sentence s_i

we have 3 corresponding references r_i^1, r_i^2 and r_i^3. We also evaluate using the SARI (Xu et al., 2016) score to evaluate our text simplification module.

5.1.1. Sentence Simplification

Each action block a is reduced to a set of simple sentences $S_a = \{s_1, s_2, ...s_{n_a}\}$. And for the same action block a, each annotator t, $t \in \{1, 2, 3\}$ produces a set of simplified sentences $R_a^t = \{r_1^t, r_2^t, ...r_{m_a^t}^t\}$. Since the simplification rules in our system may not maintain the original ordering of verbs, we do not have sentence level alignment between elements in S_a and R_a^t. For example, action block $a = He$ *laughs after he jumps into the water* is reduced by our system into two simplified sentences $S_a = \{s_1 = He\ jumps\ into\ the\ water, s_2 = He\ laughs\}$ by the temporal heuristics, while $annotator_3$ gives us $R_a^3 = \{r_1^3 = He\ laughs, r_2^3 = He\ jumps\ into\ the\ water\}$. In such cases, sequentially matching s_i to r_j will result in a wrong (hypothesis, reference) alignment which is (s_1, r_1^3) and (s_2, r_2^3).

To address this problem, for each hypothesis $s_i \in S_a$, we take the corresponding reference $r_i^t \in R_a^t$ as the one with the least Levenshtein Distance (Navarro, 2001) to s_i, i.e,

$$r_i^t = \arg\min_{r_j^t} lev\_dist(s_i, r_j^t), \forall j \in \{1, ..., m_a^t\}$$

As per this alignment, in the above example, we will have correct alignments (s_1, r_2^3) and (s_2, r_1^3). Thus, for each simplified sentence s_i we have 3 corresponding references r_i^1, r_i^2 and r_i^3. The aligned sentences are used to calculate corpus level BLEU score[6] and SARI score[7].

The evaluation results for text simplification are summarized in Table 4. We compare against YATS (Ferrés et al., 2016) and neural end-to-end text simplification system NTS-w2v (Nisioi et al.,

---

[6]We used NLTK's API with default parameters: `http://www.nltk.org/api/nltk.translate.html#nltk.translate.bleu_score.corpus_bleu`

[7]Implementation available at `https://github.com/cocoxu/simplification/`

Field	$BLEU_1$	Field	$BLEU_1$
owner	56.16	**org_action**	80.92
target	41.85	**manner**	84.84
prop	28.98	**location**	71.89
action	70.46	**direction**	70.83
emotion	57.89		

Table 5: Results on textual ARFs (%)

Field	P	R	$F1$
s_time	86.49	68.63	76.53
rot.	82.04	81.16	81.60
duration	94.72	73.92	83.04
transl.	75.49	86.47	80.61
speed	94.41	79.50	86.32

Table 6: Result on Non-textual ARFs(%)

2017). YATS is also a rule-based text simplification system. As shown in Table 4, our system performs better than YATS on both the metrics, indicative of the limitations of the YATS system. A manual examination of the results also showed the same trend. However, the key point to note is that we are not aiming for text simplification in the conventional sense. Existing text simplification systems tend to summarize text and discard some of the information. Our aim is to break a complex sentence into simpler ones while preserving the information.

An example of a Descriptions component with $BLEU_2$ scores is given in Table 3. In the first simplified sentence, the space between *Ellie* and *'s* causes the drop in the score. But it gives exactly the same answer as both annotators. In the second sentence, the system output is the same as the annotator I's answer, so the $BLEU_2$ score is 1. In the last case, the score is low, as annotators possibly failed to replace *her* with the actual Character Cue *Ellie*. Qualitative examination reveals, in general, that our system gives a reasonable result for the syntactic simplification module. As exemplified, BLEU is not the perfect metric to evaluate our system, and therefore in the future we plan to explore other metrics.

5.1.2. ARF Evaluation

We also evaluate the system's output for action representation fields against gold annotations. In our case, some of the fields can have multiple (2 or 3) words such as *owner, target, prop, action, origin_action, manner, location* and *direction*. We use $BLEU_1$ as the evaluation metric to measure the BOW similarity between system output and ground truth references. The results are shown in Table 5.

In identifying *owner, target* and *prop*, the system tends to use a fixed long mention, while annotators prefer short mentions for the same character/object. The score of *prop* is relatively lower than all other fields, which is caused by a systematic SRL mapping error. The relatively high accu-

racy on the *action* field indicates the consistency between system output and annotator answers.

Annotation on the *emotion* ARF is rather subjective. Responses on the this field are biased and noisy. The $BLEU_1$ score on this is relatively low. For the other non-textual ARFs, we use precision and recall to measure the system's behavior. Results are shown in Table 6. These fields are subjective: annotators tend to give different responses for the same input sentence.

rotation and *translation* have Boolean values. Annotators agree on these two fields in most of the sentences. The system, on the other hand, fails to identify actions involving *rotation*. For example, in the sentence *"Carl closes CARL 's door sharply"* all four annotators think that this sentence involves rotation, which is not found by the system. This is due to the specificity of rules on identifying these two fields.

speed, duration and *start_time* have high precision and low recall. This indicates the inconsistency in annotators' answers. For example, in the sentence *"Woody runs around to the back of the pizza truck"*, two annotators give 2 seconds and another gives 1 second in *duration*. These fields are subjective and need the opinion of the script author or the director. In the future, we plan to involve script editors in the evaluation process.

5.2. Extrinsic Evaluation

We conducted a user study to evaluate the performance of the system qualitatively. The focus of the study was to evaluate (from the end user's perspective) the performance of the NLP component w.r.t. generating reasonable animations.

We developed a questionnaire consisting of 20 sentence-animation video pairs. The animations were generated by our system. The questionnaire was filled by 22 participants. On an average it took around 25 minutes for a user to complete the study.

We asked users to evaluate, on a five-point *Likert scale* (Likert, 1932), if the video shown was a reasonable animation for the text, how much of

	Strongly Disagree	Disagree	Neutral	Agree	Strongly Agree
The animation shown in the video is a reasonable visualization of the text.	13.64 %	18.18 %	22.95 %	28.64 %	16.59 %
All the actions mentioned in the text are shown in the video.	15.68 %	20 %	22.96 %	20.68 %	20.68 %
All the actions shown in the video are mentioned in the text.	12.96 %	11.14 %	16.36 %	23.18 %	36.36 %

Table 7: User Study Results

the text information was depicted in the video and how much of the information in the video was present in the text (Table 7). The 68.18 % of the participants rated the overall pre-visualization as neutral or above. The rating was 64.32 % (neutral or above) for the conservation of textual information in the video, which is reasonable, given limitations of the system that are not related to the NLP component. For the last question, 75.90 % (neutral or above) agreed that the video did not have extra information. In general, there seemed to be reasonable consensus in the responses. Besides the limitations of our system, disagreement can be attributed to the ambiguity and subjectivity of the task.

We also asked the participants to describe qualitatively what textual information, if any, was missing from the videos. Most of the missing information was due to limitations of the overall system rather than the NLP component: facial expression information was not depicted because the character 3-D models are deliberately designed without faces, so that animators can draw on them. Information was also missing in the videos if it referred to objects or actions that do not have a close enough match in the object list or animations list. Furthermore, the animation component only supports animations referring to a character or object as a whole, not parts, (e.g. "Ben raises his head" is not supported).

However, there were some cases where the NLP component can be improved. For example, lexical simplification failed to map the verb "watches" to the similar animation "look". In one case, syntactic simplification created only two simplified sentences for a verb which had three subjects in the original sentence. In a few cases, lexical simplification successfully mapped to the most similar animation (e.g."argue" to "talk") but the participants were not satisfied - they were expecting a more exact animation. We plan to address these shortcomings in future work.

6. Conclusion and Future Work

In this paper, we proposed a new text-to-animation system. The system uses linguistic text simplification techniques to map screenplay text to animation. Evaluating such systems is a challenge. Nevertheless, intrinsic and extrinsic evaluations show reasonable performance of the system. The proposed system is not perfect, for example, the current system does not take into account the discourse information that links the actions implied in the text, as currently the system only processes sentences independently. In the future, we would like to leverage discourse information by considering the sequence of actions which are described in the text (Modi and Titov, 2014; Modi, 2016). This would also help to resolve ambiguity in text with regard to actions (Modi et al., 2017; Modi, 2017). Moreover, our system can be used for generating training data which could be used for training an end-to-end neural system.

Acknowledgments

We would like to thank anonymous reviewers for their insightful comments. We would also like to thank Daniel Inversini, Isabel Simó Aynés, Carolina Ferrari, Roberto Comella and Max Grosse for their help and support in developing the Cardinal system. Mubbasir Kapadia has been funded in part by NSF IIS-1703883 and NSF S&AS-1723869.

References

Gabor Angeli, Melvin Jose Johnson Premkumar, and Christopher D Manning. 2015. Leveraging linguistic structure for open domain information extraction. In *Proceedings of the 53rd Annual Meeting of the Association for Computational Linguistics and the 7th International Joint Conference on Natural Language Processing (Volume 1: Long Papers)*, volume 1, pages 344–354.

Norman I. Badler, Rama Bindiganavale, Jan Allbeck, William Schuler, Liwei Zhao, and Martha Palmer.

2000. Embodied conversational agents. chapter Parameterized Action Representation for Virtual Human Agents, pages 256–284. MIT Press, Cambridge, MA, USA.

Hamish Cunningham, Diana Maynard, and Valentin Tablan. 2000. Jape: a java annotation patterns engine.

Luciano Del Corro and Rainer Gemulla. 2013. Clausie: clause-based open information extraction. In *Proceedings of the 22nd international conference on World Wide Web*, pages 355–366. ACM.

Jessica Falk, Steven Poulakos, Mubbasir Kapadia, and Robert W Sumner. 2018. Pica: Proactive intelligent conversational agent for interactive narratives. In *Proceedings of the 18th International Conference on Intelligent Virtual Agents*, pages 141–146. ACM.

Daniel Ferrés, Montserrat Marimon, Horacio Saggion, and Ahmed AbuRa'ed. 2016. Yats: Yet another text simplifier. In *Natural Language Processing and Information Systems*, pages 335–342, Cham. Springer International Publishing.

Epic Games. 2007. Unreal engine. *Online: https://www. unrealengine. com*.

Eva Hanser, Paul Mc Kevitt, Tom Lunney, and Joan Condell. 2010. Scenemaker: Intelligent multimodal visualization of natural language scripts. In *Proceedings of the 20th Irish Conference on Artificial Intelligence and Cognitive Science*, AICS'09, pages 144–153, Berlin, Heidelberg. Springer-Verlag.

Kaveh Hassani and Won-Sook Lee. 2016. Visualizing natural language descriptions: A survey. *ACM Comput. Surv.*, 49(1):17:1–17:34.

Luheng He, Kenton Lee, Mike Lewis, and Luke Zettlemoyer. 2017. Deep semantic role labeling: What works and what's next. In *Proceedings of the 55th Annual Meeting of the Association for Computational Linguistics (Volume 1: Long Papers)*, volume 1, pages 473–483.

Matthew Honnibal and Mark Johnson. 2015. An improved non-monotonic transition system for dependency parsing. In *Proceedings of the 2015 Conference on Empirical Methods in Natural Language Processing*, pages 1373–1378, Lisbon, Portugal. Association for Computational Linguistics.

Matthew Honnibal and Ines Montani. 2017. spacy 2: Natural language understanding with bloom embeddings, convolutional neural networks and incremental parsing. *To appear*.

Richard Johansson, David Williams, Anders Berglund, and Pierre Nugues. 2004. Carsim: a system to visualize written road accident reports as animated 3d scenes. In *Proceedings of the 2nd Workshop on Text Meaning and Interpretation*, pages 57–64. Association for Computational Linguistics.

R. Likert. 1932. A technique for the measurement of attitudes. *Archives of Psychology*, 22(140):1–55.

Zhi-Qiang Liu and Ka-Ming Leung. 2006. Script visualization (scriptviz): a smart system that makes writing fun. *Soft Computing*, 10(1):34–40.

Ruqian Lu and Songmao Zhang. 2002. *Automatic generation of computeranimation: using AI for movie animation*. Springer-Verlag.

Minhua Ma and Paul Kevitt. 2006. Virtual human animation in natural language visualisation. *Artif. Intell. Rev.*, 25(1-2):37–53.

Elman Mansimov, Emilio Parisotto, Jimmy Lei Ba, and Ruslan Salakhutdinov. 2015. Generating images from captions with attention. *arXiv preprint arXiv:1511.02793*.

Marcel Marti, Jodok Vieli, Wojciech Witoń, Rushit Sanghrajka, Daniel Inversini, Diana Wotruba, Isabel Simo, Sasha Schriber, Mubbasir Kapadia, and Markus Gross. 2018. Cardinal: Computer assisted authoring of movie scripts. In *23rd International Conference on Intelligent User Interfaces*, pages 509–519. ACM.

Mausam, Michael Schmitz, Robert Bart, Stephen Soderland, and Oren Etzioni. 2012. Open language learning for information extraction. In *Proceedings of the 2012 Joint Conference on Empirical Methods in Natural Language Processing and Computational Natural Language Learning*, pages 523–534. Association for Computational Linguistics.

George A. Miller. 1995. Wordnet: A lexical database for english. *COMMUNICATIONS OF THE ACM*, 38:39–41.

Ashutosh Modi. 2016. Event embeddings for semantic script modeling. In *Proceedings of The 20th SIGNLL Conference on Computational Natural Language Learning*.

Ashutosh Modi. 2017. *Modeling common sense knowledge via scripts*. Ph.D. thesis, Universität des Saarlandes.

Ashutosh Modi and Ivan Titov. 2014. Inducing neural models of script knowledge. In *Conference on Computational Natural Language Learning (CoNLL)*.

Ashutosh Modi, Ivan Titov, Vera Demberg, Asad Sayeed, and Manfred Pinkal. 2017. Modelling semantic expectation: Using script knowledge for referent prediction. *Transactions of the Association for Computational Linguistics*, 5:31–44.

Gonzalo Navarro. 2001. A guided tour to approximate string matching. *ACM computing surveys (CSUR)*, 33(1):31–88.

Thomas Wolf, James Ravenscroft, Julien Chaumond, and Maxwell Rebo. 2018. Neuralcoref: Coreference resolution in spacy with neural networks. Available online at https://github.com/huggingface/neuralcoref.

Wei Xu, Courtney Napoles, Ellie Pavlick, Quanze Chen, and Chris Callison-Burch. 2016. Optimizing statistical machine translation for text simplification. *Transactions of the Association for Computational Linguistics*, 4:401–415.

Appendix A

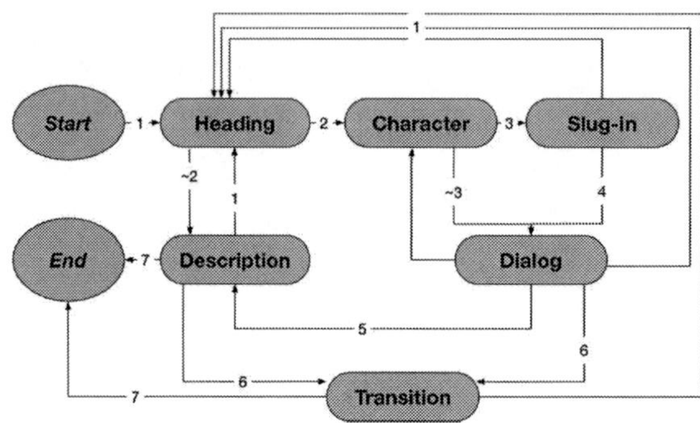

Figure 3: FSM of Well-formatted Screenplay Parser. Numbers of link are Rules and $\sim$ means logical NOT

ID	Rule Summary
1	If input is uppercase and contains heading words such as 'INT', 'EXT'. etc, return True, otherwise False
2	If input is uppercase and contains character words such as 'CONT.', '(O.S)', or if #indentation > most frequent #indentation, return True. Otherwise False
3	If input starts with '(' , return True, otherwise False
4	If input ends with ')', return True, otherwise False
5	If $|\#lastindents - \#currentindents| < 3$, return True, otherwise False
6	If the input is uppercase and contains transition words such as 'DISSOLVE', 'CUT TO'. etc, return True, otherwise False
7	If the input equals to 'THE END', return True. Otherwise False.

Table 8: FSM Transition Rules

COMPLEX: Another parent , Mike Munson , sits on the bench with a tablet and uses an app to track and analyze the team 's shots.
NSELSTM-B: Another parent, Mike Munson, sits on the bench with a tablet and uses an app to track.
YATS: Another parent sits on the bench with a tablet and uses an app to track and examines the team' s shots. This parent is Mike Munson.
OURS: Another parent is Mike Munson. Another parent sits on the bench with a tablet. Another parent uses an app.
COMPLEX: Stowell believes that even documents about Lincoln's death will give people a better understanding of the man who was assassinated 150 years ago this April.
NSELSTM-B: Stowell believes that the discovery about Lincoln's death will give people a better understanding of the man.
YATS: Stowell believes that even documents about Lincoln' s death will give people a better reason of the man. This man was assassinated 150 years ago this April.
OURS: Stowell believes. Even documents about Lincoln 's death give people a better understanding of the man. Somebody assassinates the man 150 years ago this April.

Table 9: Example Model Outputs

Appendix B: Algorithms

Algorithm 2 Identify Adverbial Clause

```
1: procedure ADVERBIAL CLAUSE IDENTIFY PROCEDURE(sent)                                    ▷ The input sentence
2:     find tokens in sents with dependency tag ROOT and ADVCL (we call it advcl)
3:     if no ADVCL token in sents then
4:         return False
5:     find father token of advcl as father
6:     if father is not a VERB then
7:         we make it as a VERB                                                            ▷ We correct POS error here
8:     find conjunction tokens of father as conjuncts
9:     if NOUN in advcl's left subtree then
10:         subject ← this NOUN
11:     else
12:         subject ← NOUN in father's left subtree
13:     return True
```

Algorithm 3 Transform Adverbial Clause

```
1: procedure ADVERBIAL CLAUSE TRANSFORM PROCEDURE(sent)                                   ▷ The input sentence
2:     cut edge between root and advcl token                             ▷ remove advcl token from root's children
3:     if advcl verb does not have its own subject then
4:         add subject as advcl's most left direct child
5:     remove PREP and MARK token in advcl's children, modify temporal id accordingly
6:     str1 ← traverse_a_string(root)
7:     str2 ← correct_tense(traverse_a_string(advcl))
8:     return [str1, str2]
```

Algorithm 4 Identify() in Relative Clause Analyzer

```
1: procedure RELATIVE CLAUSE IDENTIFY PROCEDURE(sent)                                      ▷ The input sentence.
2:     if no RELCL token in sent then
3:         return False
4:     anchor ← RELCL token
5:     head ← anchor's head token
6:     wg ← NULL
7:     for token t in anchor's children do
8:         if t.tag ∈ [WDT, WP, WP$, WRB] then
9:             wh ← t
10:     return True
```

Algorithm 5 Transform() in Relative Clause Analyzer

```
1: procedure RELATIVE CLAUSE TRANSFORM PROCEDURE(root, anchor, head, wh)   ▷ Root of dependency tree, the recl anchor token, its head, and
                                                                            wh-word
2:     cut relcl edge between head and anchor
3:     str1 ← traverse_a_string(root)
4:     if wh = NULL then                                                   ▷ No Wh-word in the sentence, concatenate
5:         str2 ←traverse_a_string(anchor) + traverse_a_string(head)
6:     else
7:         wh-dep ← dependency tag of wh
8:         wh-head ← head of wh
9:         remove wh in anchor's children
10:         if wh-dep= DOBJ then                                                                  ▷ wh is verb
11:             str2← traverse_a_string(wh-head) + traverse_a_string(anchor)
12:         else if wh-dep= POBJ then                                                     ▷ wh-head is preposition
13:             put head after wh-head in anchor's children
14:             str2 ← traverse_a_string(anchor)
15:         else if wh-dep∈ [NSUBJ, NSUBJPASS] then                                             ▷ wh is subject
16:             str2 ← traverse_a_string(wh-head) + traverse_a_string(anchor)
17:         else if wh-dep= ADVMOD then                                                   ▷ wh is time or location
18:             prep ← 'at'
19:             str2 ← traverse_a_string(anchor) + prep+ traverse_a_string(wh-head)
20:         else if wh-dep= POSS then                                                          ▷ wh = whose
21:             str2 ← traverse_a_string(wh-head) + be verb+ traverse_a_string(anchor)
22:     correct verb tense in str1 and str2
23:     return [str1, str2]
```

Algorithm 6 Transform() in Coordination Analyzer

```
1: procedure COORDINATION TRANSFORM PROCEDURE(sents)          ▷ Input sentence
2:     results ← empty list
3:     find root of dependency tree of sents
4:     find first cc(if any) and conj token in denpendency tree and their head token main
5:     embed all conjugate words of main in a list conjus
6:     cut conj edge between main and cc and conj
7:     if no object for main then
8:         try find object in conj's right children
9:     str1 ← traverse_a_string(root)
10:    results.append(str1)
11:    for conj in conjs do
12:        type ← get_conj_type(main, conj)
13:        if type=VERB&VERB then
14:            correct part-of-speech tag if necessary              ▷ spaCy tends to tag verb as noun
15:            if conj has its own subject then
16:                new-root ← conj
17:            else
18:                if main=root then
19:                    new-root ← conj
20:                else
21:                    replace main with conj in root's children
22:                    new-root ← root
23:        else                                          ▷ Other cases such as NOUN&NOUN, AD*&AD*, apply same rule
24:            main-head ← head of main
25:            replace main with conj in main-head's children
26:            new-root ← root
27:        str2 ← traverse_a_string(new-root)
28:        results.append(str2)
29:    return results
```

Algorithm 7 Identify() in Passive Analyzer

```
1: procedure PASSIVE VOICE IDENTIFY PROCEDURE(sents)          ▷ Input sentence
2:     is-passive ← False
3:     for token t in sents do
4:         if t.dep ∈ [CSUBJPASS, NSUBJPASS] then
5:             subj-token ← t
6:             verb-token ← t.head
7:             is-passive ← True
8:         if t.dep ∈ [AUXPASS] and t.head = verb-token then
9:             auxpass-token ← t
10:        if t.dep ∈ [AGENT] and t.text = 'by' then
11:            by-token ← t
12:    return is-passive
```

Algorithm 8 Transform() in Passive Analyzer

```
1: procedure PASSIVE VOICE TRANSFORM PROCEDURE(sents)          ▷ Input sentence
2:     if auxpass-token ≠ NULL then
3:         cut auxpass edge
4:     cut nsubjpass or csubj edge
5:     prepend subject-token to verb-token's right children
6:     if by-token ≠ NULL then
7:         cut by-agent edge
8:         add by-token's right children to verb-token's left children
9:     else
10:        add 'Somebody' to verb-token's left children
11:    correct verb tense for verb-token
12:    return traverse_a_string(root-token)
```

Algorithm 9 Transform() in Appositive Clause Analyzer

```
1: procedure APPOSITIVE CLAUSE TRANSFORM PROCEDURE(anchor, head)   ▷ The APPOS token and its head token.
2:     cut edge between anchor and head token                     ▷ remove anchor from head's right children
3:     str1 ← traverse_a_string(root token of input sentence)
4:     str2 ← traverse_a_string(head) + be_verb + traverse_a_string(anchor)
5:     correct verb tense in str1 and str2
6:     return [str1, str2]
```

Algorithm 10 Identify() in Inverted Clausal Subject Analyzer

```
1: procedure INVERTED CLAUSAL SUBJECT IDENTIFY PROCEDURE(sents)          ▷ Input sentence
2:     for Token t in sents do
3:         if t.dep = CSUBJ and t.tag ∈ [VBN, VBG] and t.head.lemma='be' then
4:             attr ← token with dependency label attr in t.head's right children
5:             if attr = NULL then                               ▷ attr is the actual subject of the sentence
6:                 return False                                  ▷ Make sure this is an inverted sentence
7:             actual-verb ← t
8:             be-verb ← t.head
9:             return True
10:    return False
```

Algorithm 11 Transform() in Inverted Clausal Subject Analyzer

1: **procedure** INVERTED CLAUSAL SUBJECT TRANSFORM PROCEDURE(*sents*) ▷ Input sentence
2:     get access to actual-verb, be-verb and attr in identify procedure 10
3:     change position of actual-verb and attr in be-verb's children
4:     **return** [traverse_a_string(be-verb)]

Algorithm 12 Transform() in CCOMP Analyzer

1: **procedure** CLAUSE COMPONENT TRANSFORM PROCEDURE(*sents*) ▷ Input sentence
2:     cut CCOMP link in dependency tree
3:     subject ← find ccomp verb's subject
4:     **if** subject $\neq$ NULL and subject $\neq$ DET(e.g. 'that') **then**
5:         **if** original verb do not have object **then**
6:             make subject as original verb's object
7:     **else if** subject = DET (e.g. 'that') **then**
8:         find root verb's object, substitute 'that'
9:     str1 ← traverse_a_string(ccomp verb)
10:    str2 ← traverse_a_string(original verb)
11:    **return** [str1, str2]

Algorithm 13 Transform() in XCOMP Analyzer

1: **procedure** OPEN CLAUSAL COMPONENT TRANSFORM PROCEDURE(*sents*) ▷ Input sentence
2:     subject-token ← find_subject(xcomp-verb-token) ▷ find subject of the actual verb
3:     results ← empty list
4:     **if** AUX $\notin$ *sents* **then** ▷ for some cases two verbs needs to be output
5:         cut xcomp link
6:         results.add(traverse_a_string(xcomp-verb-token))
7:     remove AUX token in the dependency tree
8:     replace xcomp-verb-token in subject's children with actual-verb-token
9:     results.add(traverse_a_string(actual-verb-token))
10:    **return** results

Algorithm 14 Transform() in ACL Analyzer

1: **procedure** ADJECTIVE CLAUSE TRANSFORM PROCEDURE(*sents*) ▷ Input Sentence
2:     cut acl edge in dependency tree
3:     str1 ← traverse_a_string(root-token)
4:     mid-fix ← empty string
5:     **if** acl-token.tag = VBN and by-token in acl-token's right children **then**
6:         mid-fix ← 'be'
7:     update acl-verb-token's left children with [acl-noun, mid-fix, [t $\in$ acl-verb-token.lefts where t.dep $\notin$ [AUX]]
8:     correct acl-verb-tense
9:     str2 ← traverse_a_string(acl-verb-token)
10:    **return** [str1, str2]

Algorithm 15 Get-Temporal Function at Line 5 in Algorithm 3

1: **procedure** ADVERBIAL CLAUSE TEMPORAL INFO EXTRACTION PROCEDURE($prep-or-mark, cur-temp$)▷ The PREP or MARK token in input sentence
2:     flag ← False ▷ whether we change the temp
3:     **if** prep-or-mark.type = PREP **then**
4:         sign ← -1
5:     **else**
6:         sign ← 1
7:     text ← prep-or-mark.text.lower()
8:     **if** text = *as* **then**
9:         flag ← True
10:    **else if** text $\in$ [*until, till*] **then**
11:        flag ← True
12:        cur-temp ← cur-temp + sign
13:    **else if** text = *after* **then**
14:        flag ← True
15:        cur-temp ← cur-temp - sign
16:    **else if** text = *before* **then**
17:        flag ← True
18:        cur-temp ← cur-temp + sign
19:    **return** [flag, cur-temp]

Appendix C: Action Representation Fields

Action Representation Fields (ARFs) in the demo sentence *James gently throws a red ball to Alice in the restaurant from back*, extracted with SRL:

- **owner**: James
- **target**: a red ball
- **prop**: to Alice
- **action**: throw
- **origin_action**: throws
- **manner**: gently
- **modifier_location**: in the restaurant
- **modifier_direction**: from back

In this case, our output for the *prop* and *target* is not correct; they should be swapped. This is one example where this module can introduce errors.

Additional ARFs, extracted heuristically:

- **startTime**: Calculated by current scene time

- **duration**: We have a pre-defined list of words that when appearing in the sentence, they will indicate a short duration (e.g "run" or "fast") and therefore the *duration* will be set to 1 second; in contrast, for words like "slowly" we assign a duration of 4 seconds; otherwise, the duration is 2 seconds.

- **speed**: Similarly to *duration*, we have pre-defined lists of words that would affect the speed of the pre-baked animation: "angrily" would result in faster movement, but "carefully" in slower movement. We have 3 scales: 0.5, 1, 2 which corresponds to *slow, normal* and *fast*.

- **translation**: We have a list of *actions* which would entail a movement in from one place to another, e.g. "go". If the value of the *action* exists in this list, it is set to True, otherwise False.

- **rotation**: If the *action* exists in our list of verbs that entail rotation, this field is True, otherwise False. Rotation refers to movement in place e.g. "turn" or "sit".

- **emotion**: We find the closet neighbor of each word in the sentence in list of words that indicate emotion, using word vector similarity. If the similarity exceeds an empirically tested threshold, then we take the corresponding emotion word as the *emotion* field of this action.

- **partial_start_time**: an important field, since it controls the sequence order of each action. It determines which actions happen in parallel and which happen sequentially. This is still an open question. We solve this problem when doing sentence simplification. Together with the input sentence, current time is also fed into each *Analyzer*. There are several rules in some of the *Analyzers* to obtain temporal information. For example, in Line 5 of the *Adverbial Clause Analyzer* (c.f.3), we assign different temporal sequences for simplified actions. The algorithm is shown in Algorithm 15. The *sign* together with specific prepositions determines the change direction of current temporal id. In the *Coordination Analyzer*, the current temporal id changes when it encounters two verbs sharing same subject. Then the later action will get a bigger temporal id.

Author Index

Association for Computational Linguistics
209 N. Eighth Street
Stroudsburg, Pennsylvania 18360

ISBN 978-1-5108-8759-6